The Right to Political Participation

I0882234

This book provides a comparative analysis of how judgments from the European Court of Human Rights (ECtHR) and the Inter-American Court of Human Rights (IACtHR) affect political participation and electoral justice at the national level.

Looking at specific countries, the work analyses the legal impact the implementation of the ECtHR and the IACtHR judgments has, with a specific focus on cases in which the regional court concerned uses the "democratic argument," that is, an argument related to democracy and political rights. The reasoning is that, although democracy is a much wider concept, judgments concerning violations of political rights and electoral justice provide reliable indicators to assess the status and sustainability of democracy in a State. Moreover, the analysis of the violations of political rights and electoral justice allows an in-depth comparison between the two regional human rights systems. Mindful of the broader scope of the fall-out generated by the non-implementation of judgments, including in socio-economic terms, the book includes a section exploring how judgments issued by the ECtHR and the IACtHR affect voters' participation in the countries under their jurisdiction. To this end, an original dataset including the 47 Member States of the Council of Europe and the 20 countries which recognised the adjudicatory jurisdiction of the IACtHR is built.

Multidisciplinary in aim and scope of analysis, the book will be an invaluable resource for researchers, academics, and policy-makers working in the areas of constitutional law, international human rights law, and political economy.

Gabriella Citroni is Researcher in International Law and Adjunct Professor of International Human Rights Law at the University of Milano-Bicocca (Milan, Italy). She is in charge of the course on "Enforced Disappearances in International Law" at the LL.M. in International Humanitarian Law and Human Rights organised by the Geneva Academy of International Humanitarian Law and Human Rights. She acts as senior legal advisor of the NGO TRIAL International. She has published extensively in the field of international human rights law.

Irene Spigno is General Director of the Inter-American Academy of Human Rights of the Autonomous University of Coahuila (Mexico) and Director of its Centre for Comparative Constitutional Studies. She holds a Ph.D. in Comparative Constitutional Law from the University of Siena in Italy and is full professor of Comparative Constitutional Law at the Autonomous University of Coahuila (Mexico). Her research interests include freedom of expression, and in particular hate speech, constitutional justice, multiculturalism in comparative perspective, and gender studies.

Palmina Tanzarella is Researcher in Constitutional Law at University of Milano-Bicocca (Milan, Italy). She teaches Italian and European Constitutional Law and State Building. She published on the European and Inter-American protection of Human Rights. At present, her research includes hate speech as limitation of freedom of expression in the European framework. She collaborates as advisor with the International Center for Transitional Justice (ICTJ).

Comparative Constitutional Change

Comparative Constitutional Change has developed into a distinct field of constitutional law. It encompasses the study of constitutions through the way they change and covers a wide scope of topics and methodologies. Books in this series include work on developments in the functions of the constitution, the organisation of powers and the protection of rights, as well as research that focuses on formal amendment rules and the relation between constituent and constituted power. The series includes comparative approaches along with books that focus on single jurisdictions, and brings together research monographs and edited collections which allow the expression of different schools of thought. While the focus is primarily on law, where relevant the series may also include political science, historical, philosophical, and empirical approaches that explore constitutional change.

Also in the series:

Icelandic Constitutional Reform
People, Processes, Politics
Edited by Ágúst Þór Árnason and Catherine Dupré

Dynamic Federalism
A New Theory for Cohesion and Regional Autonomy
Patricia Popelier

Peace, Discontent and Constitutional Law
Challenges to Constitutional Order and Democracy
Edited by Martin Belov

For more information about this series, please visit: www.routledge.com/Comparative-Constitutional-Change/book-series/COMPCONST

The Right to Political Participation

A Study of the Judgments of the European and Inter-American Courts of Human Rights

Edited by Gabriella Citroni, Irene Spigno, and Palmina Tanzarella

Routledge
Taylor & Francis Group
LONDON AND NEW YORK

First published 2022
by Routledge
2 Park Square, Milton Park, Abingdon, Oxon OX14 4RN

and by Routledge
605 Third Avenue, New York, NY 10158

Routledge is an imprint of the Taylor & Francis Group, an informa business

British Library Cataloguing-in-Publication Data
A catalogue record for this book is available from the British Library

Library of Congress Cataloging-in-Publication Data
Names: Citroni, Gabriella, editor. | Spigno, Irene, 1980- editor. | Tanzarella, Palmina, editor.
Title: The right to political participation: a study of the judgments of the European and Inter-American Courts of Human Rights/edited by Gabriella Citroni, Irene Spigno, and Palmina Tanzarella.
Description: Abingdon, Oxon [UK]; New York, NY: Routledge, 2021. | Series: Comparative constitutional change |
Includes bibliographical references and index.
Identifiers: LCCN 2021034714 (print) | LCCN 2021034715 (ebook) | ISBN 9781032134444 (hardback) | ISBN 9781032134475 (paperback) | ISBN 9781003229247 (ebook)
Subjects: LCSH: European Court of Human Rights. | Inter-American Court of Human Rights. | International human rights courts–Europe. | International human rights courts–America. | Judgments–Europe. | Judgments–America. | Judicial process–Europe. | Judicial process–America. | Political rights. | Political participation. | Democracy.
Classification: LCC K3240.5 .R54 2021 (print) | LCC K3240.5 (ebook) | DDC 341.4/834–dc23
LC record available at https://lccn.loc.gov/2021034714
LC ebook record available at https://lccn.loc.gov/2021034715

ISBN: 978-1-032-13444-4 (hbk)
ISBN: 978-1-032-13447-5 (pbk)
ISBN: 978-1-003-22924-7 (ebk)

DOI: 10.4324/9781003229247

Typeset in Galliard
by Deanta Global Publishing Services, Chennai, India

Contents

List of contributors

Laura Cappuccio is Professor of Constitutional Law at the University of Naples Federico II (Italy).

Gabriella Citroni is Researcher in International Law and Adjunct Professor of International Human Rights Law at the University of Milano-Bicocca (Milan, Italy).

Yessica Esquivel Alonso is Director of the Center for Political Rights of the Inter-American Academy of Human Rights of the Autonomous University of Coahuila (Mexico).

José Antonio Estrada Marún is Senior Researcher and Professor at the Center of Comparative Constitutional Studies of the Inter-American Academy of Human Rights of the Autonomous University of Coahuila (Mexico).

Simone Gianello is Researcher in Comparative Public Law at University of Milano-Bicocca (Milan, Italy).

Diana Vanessa Gutiérrez Espinoza is Research Assistant at the Center for Economic, Social, Cultural, and Environmental Rights of the Inter-American Academy of Human Rights of the Autonomous University of Coahuila (Mexico).

Francesca Mussi is Research Fellow in International Law, School of Law of the University of Trento (Italy).

Alessandra Osti is Research Fellow in Comparative Public Law – University of Milan (Italy).

Simone Pellegrino is Associate Professor of Public Economics at the University of Torino (Italy).

Simone Penasa is Assistant Professor in Comparative Public Law at the Faculty of Law of the University of Trento (Italia).

Francesca Pirola is a Ph.D. student of the International Joint Doctorate Programme of the University of Milano-Bicocca (Milan, Italy) and the University of Nice Cote d'Azur (France).

Luis Efrén Ríos Vega is Senior Researcher and Professor at the Inter-American Academy of Human Rights of the Autonomous University of Coahuila and judge of the Superior Tribunal of Justice of the State of Coahuila (Mexico).

Magda Yadira Robles Garza is the University Human Rights Ombudsperson of the Autonomous University of Coahuila (Mexico).

Fernando Gustavo Ruz Dueñas is Researcher at the Center for Comparative Constitutional Studies of the Inter-American Academy of Human Rights of the Autonomous University of Coahuila (Mexico).

Lillian Sánchez Calderoni is Researcher at the Center for Economic, Social, Cultural, and Environmental Rights of the Inter-American Academy of Human Rights of the Autonomous University of Coahuila (Mexico).

Valentina Rita Scotti is Associate Professor in Comparative Public Law at the European Law and Governance School of the European Public Law Organization (EPLO).

Irene Spigno is the General Director and Full Professor of the Inter-American Academy of Human Rights of the Autonomous University of Coahuila (Mexico).

Palmina Tanzarella is Researcher in Constitutional Law at University of Milano-Bicocca (Milan, Italy).

Gilberto Turati is Professor of Public Finance at the Department of Economics and Finance, School of Economics, of the Università Cattolica del Sacro Cuore, Rome (Italy).

Irene Valotti is Child Protection Specialist at S.O.S Il Telefono Azzurro ONLUS and at time of writing she was Research Fellow at University Milano-Bicocca (Italy).

Paolo Zicchittu is Assistant Professor in Constitutional Law at the University of Milano-Bicocca (Milan, Italy).

Foreword

The Right of Rights

We are living in the age of constitutional rights. For many years now, constitutions have codified increasingly more and more rights, beginning long before Noberto Bobbio and Louis Henkin theorised the origins and implications of the proliferation of rights around the world.[1] We can trace the rise of constitutional rights to end of the Second World War. New constitutions emerged in the aftermath of destruction as part of a coordinated project to rebuild the global order on a foundation of rights protection. In the first year of post-war peace, the median constitution in the world codified 20 rights; today that number has more than doubled to 41.[2]

Of course, all rights are not created equal. Constitutional interpretation inevitably generates a constitutional hierarchy when codified rights collide.[3] And sometimes constitutional designers will even specify that a given right is more important than others. In Germany, for example, constitutional designers left no doubt about what sits at the top of the constitutional pyramid: no right stands above the right to human dignity, codified as unamendable in the Basic Law and interpreted by the Federal Constitutional Court as the country's "highest constitutional principle."[4]

Writing roughly 200 years ago, William Cobbett offered his own perspective on which right stands above all others, and he also explained why. There was no doubt in his mind:

> Our rights in society are numerous; the right of enjoying life and property; the right of exerting our mental and physical power in an innocent manner;

1 See Bobbio N., *L'età dei diritto*, Giulio Einaudi, Turin, 1990; Henkin L., *The Age of* Rights, Columbia University Press, New York, 1990.

2 Chilton A., Versteeg M., *How Constitutional Rights Matter*, Oxford University Press, Oxford, 2020, pp. 83–84.

3 See, e.g., Beatty D.M., *The Ultimate Rule of Law*, Oxford University Press, New York, 2004; Fallon, R.H. Jr., *Strict Judicial Scrutiny*, in UCLA L. Rev., 54, 2007, 1267.

4 Eppler Case (1980), 54 BVerfGE 148, in Kommers D.P., Miller R.A. (eds), *The Constitutional Jurisprudence of the Federal Republic of Germany*, 3d ed. Duke University Press, Durham, 2012, at 406–407.

> but the great right of all, and without which, there is in fact no right, *is the right of taking part in the making of the laws by which we are governed.* This right is founded on that law of nature already spoken of; it springs out of the very principle of civil society, for what compact, what agreement, what common assent, can possibly be imagined, by which men would give up all the rights of nature, all the free enjoyment of their bodies and their minds, in order to subject themselves to rules and laws, in the making of which they should have nothing to say, and which should be enforced upon them without their assent. The great right, therefore, of every man, the right of rights, is the right of having a share in the making of the laws, to which the good of the whole makes it his duty to submit.[5]

For Cobbett, then, the most important right – what he called "the right of rights" – is the right to political participation. As Cobbett acknowledged, there would be no other right without it. For Cobbett, it is the condition precedent for all rights because it inheres in the basic nature of civil society. At once an individual right and a group right, the right of political participation is a vehicle for persons to voice their preferences and then to aggregate them as members of a community.

Cobbett was not writing on a blank slate. He was drawing from an older tradition of thought and practice, memorialised in higher law as early as 1789 when the National Assembly of France approved *La déclaration des droits de l'homme et du citoyen.* Known as the Declaration of the Rights of Man and the Citizen, this pivotal text in modern constitutionalism made clear that "law is the expression of the general will" and moreover that "every citizen has a right to participate personally, or through his representative, in its foundation."[6] This right of rights – the right to political participation – has a long intellectual lineage with noteworthy constitutional origins.

At its core, the right to political participation is the right to democracy. This umbrella right includes the right to vote, the right to run for office, the right to form a political party, the right free and fair elections, and other key rights that help democracy take root and ultimately thrive.

Scholars have taught us a great deal about democracy in the world – how it emerges, how it develops, and how to protect it.[7] Yet most existing studies have

5 R. Huish (ed.), *Memoirs of the Late William Cobbett, Esq.*, John Saunders, London, 1836, Vol. I, at 305 (italics in original).

6 *La déclaration des droits de l'homme et du citoyen*, art. 6 (1789), *translated by* The Avalon Project at the Yale Law School, Lillian Goldman Law Library: https://avalon.law.yale.edu/18th_century/rightsof.asp.

7 See, e.g., A. Applebaum, *Twilight of Democracy*, Doubleday, New York, 2020; L. Diamond, *Developing Democracy: Toward* Consolidation, The Johns Hopkins University Press, Baltimore, 1999; T. Ginsburg, A.Z. Huq, *How to Save a Constitutional Democracy*, The University of Chicago Press, Chicago, 2018; S.P. Huntington, *The Third Wave: Democratization in the Late Twentieth* Century, University of Oklahoma Press, Norman, 1991; S. Levitsky, D.

focused on countries grappling internally to consolidate their democracy. Much less attention has been given to the state of national democracies within multi-level jurisdictional contexts, particularly where supranational actors, namely supranational courts, oversee the conduct of domestic actors. We have considerably more to learn on that front, especially as supranational courts continue to grow in age, prestige, and power.

Today, as democracy fights for its survival in all regions of the world, many have looked to supranational courts as an embankment against the rising tide of authoritarianism. Supranational courts indeed do seem like a strong shield to protect the essential features of democracy and its subsidiary rights. But whether supranational courts can in reality live up to this high expectation is a question still without a concrete answer. The question must therefore be asked, considered, and debated intently until it can be answered with reliable empirical evidence: how well do supranational courts defend democracy?

This new book on *The Right to Political Participation: A Study of the Judgments of the European and Inter-American Courts of Human Rights* arrives at just the right time to help answer this crucial question for democratic resilience in the world. Edited by a trio of excellent scholars of public law – each with complementary and overlapping expertise on European, constitutional, comparative, and international law – this volume evaluates how well the European Court of Human Rights and its counterpart, the Inter-American Court of Human Rights, protect the right to political participation. What results from the 15 superb jurisdictional studies in this book is a deep dive into the promise and performance of these two supranational courts, specifically in how they respond to attacks on the right to political participation in its different forms of expression. The chapters take readers on a learning expedition from Chile to Italy, from Hungary to Venezuela, and across the countries of the former Yugoslavia, stopping along the way both at jurisdictions that are well-known to scholars of comparative constitutional law and also at other countries whose constitutional politics are profoundly fascinating but not nearly as well-known to the world.

The Right to Political Participation is a winner on three fronts that yield excellence and impact in scholarship on comparative constitutionalism: timing, substantive content, and jurisdictional coverage. In the last half-century, there has never been more concern than now about whether democracy is sustainable. Gabriella Citroni, Irene Spigno, and Palmina Tanzarella have brought together an outstanding roster of scholars at a time when the world is searching for solutions to the most pressing public law challenge of our time. This book reveals whether and how supranational courts are meeting the moment, and it draws from a rich set of diverse countries that, together, remind us that we can learn a great deal about the right of rights not only from familiar American and European jurisdictions but also equally from some of the understudied ones. For all these

ZIBLATT, *How Democracies* Die, Broadway Books, New York, 2018; A. LIJPHART, *Patterns of Democracy*, Yale University Press, New Haven, 1999.

reasons and more, *The Right to Political Participation* is an invaluable resource for scholars interested in the future of democracy and in the capacity of supranational courts to defend it.

Richard Albert
Professor of World Constitutions and
Director of Constitutional Studies
The University of Texas at Austin

Acknowledgements

The book is the result of a three-year multidisciplinary research project funded by the School of Law of the University of Milano-Bicocca (Milano, Italy), conducted jointly with the *Academia Interamericana de Derechos Humanos* (Saltillo, Mexico). The authors wish to thank the institutions concerned for the support received.

The authors are greatly indebted to Mr. Chris Callan for his dedication and the thorough linguistic revision of the contributions.

List of acronyms and abbreviations

ACHR	American Convention on Human Rights
CoE	Council of Europe
CM	Committee of Ministers
ECHR	European Convention for the Protection of Human Rights and Fundamental Freedoms
ECtHR	European Court of Human Rights
EU	European Union
HRCttee	Human Rights Committee
IACHR	Inter-American Commission on Human Rights
IACtHR	Inter-American Court of Human Rights
ICCPR	International Covenant on Civil and Political Rights
OAS	Organization of the American States
Protocol 1	Protocol No. 1 to the Convention for the Protection of Human Rights and Fundamental Freedoms
TEU	Treaty on European Union
UK	United Kingdom of Great Britain

The Role of International Human Rights Courts in ensuring the right to political participation and promoting sustainable democracy and the methodology behind the research

Gabriella Citroni, Irene Spigno, and Palmina Tanzarella

Regional Courts and human rights

The approval of the Universal Declaration of Human Rights in 1948 brought about a radical change in the paradigm of human rights protection. Subsequently, a number of relevant documents were drafted and institutional bodies were set up at the universal as well as regional levels to interpret and implement them.

Within this framework, the European and the Inter-American systems of protection of fundamental human rights have played a significant role. In both cases, States have ratified specific human rights treaties – the European Convention on Human Rights and the American Convention on Human Rights (hereinafter ECHR and ACHR) respectively – whose implementation is monitored by the European Court of Human Rights and by the Inter-American Court of Human Rights (hereinafter the ECtHR and the IACtHR respectively). It is noteworthy that the African Court of Human and Peoples' Rights is also playing an increasingly significant role, especially with regard to electoral justice and political rights. However, mostly due to space constraints, the present book will not analyse the latter's case law and will instead be limited to the European and Inter-American contexts.

Points of convergence between the two Courts' adjudicative and interpretative activities have established a unique language of rights and circulating standards, models, and general principles, in the definition and implementation of fundamental human rights.

This "circulation" does not mean that there is a simple vertical imposition of jurisprudence or a direct and clear repercussion from one regional Court to the other and the corresponding States parties. The adjudicative and interpretative phase demonstrates a more complex dynamic in which each regional Court draws from the common constitutional heritage of States parties, and, conversely, the latter – throughout the different national branches – draw from the principles established by the regional Courts. The outcome is the creation of a common heritage of rights. As many authoritative scholars have warned and

DOI: 10.4324/9781003229247-1

supported by a consolidated judicial trend, the two regional Courts no longer operate only from a subsidiary point of view; instead, they behave as though "almost constitutional" Courts.

Moreover, in the face of gross and repetitive violations of fundamental human rights – which do not only affect the individual sphere of the victim, but also undermine the very basis of the democratic system – regional Courts declare States internationally responsible, and order the adoption of measures to remedy the violations perpetrated and to overcome structural and legislative deficiencies. In addition to imposing individual remedies, if they detect structural problems at the domestic level, the ECtHR and the IACtHR also order the adoption of general measures of reparation.

Usually, the international responsibility for breaches of the European and the American Convention by States can be summarised as follows: States have an obligation to: a) bring an end to the breach; b) provide an adequate remedy to the injured party to eliminate the consequences of the act contrary to what the respective treaty establishes; c) offer appropriate guarantees of non-repetition. For these reasons, when these Courts hold the respondent State accountable for breaches of the respective Convention, their rulings require institutional reforms and the amendment of domestic legislation, including constitutional provisions, based on what the Courts deem appropriate.

However, the judgments adopted by these two Courts do not formally possess the character of "direct effect"; they acquire it in an interpretative context, prompting the national legislator or judges to take action to comply with the measures concerned. Mention should also be made of the compliance with the principles enshrined in the judgments of the two Courts by States that are not directly involved in the case. In general, the Courts' judgments certainly have the value of "*res iudicata*." In some cases, they produce *erga omnes* effects: this is the case for those States that, at the constitutional level, provide the compulsory respect for the judgments of the respective regional Court, or because judges and any administrative authorities are forced to consider the Convention as a parameter on the basis of the control of conventionality doctrine (for the Court of San José), or of the parameters interposed (for the Court of Strasbourg). In both cases, States do not always appear to promptly react or demonstrate a willingness to follow up on the remedial measures imposed by the two Courts. Implementation (or lack thereof) of their judgments at the national level can today be considered the main indicator for measuring the degree of internationalisation of constitutional law or, at least, of the constitutionalisation of international law, with significant socio-economic consequences on States parties.

The sustainability of democracy: The need for a comparative analysis

Judgments issued by the ECtHR and the IACtHR generate significant legal and economic consequences on national landscapes. Their implementation at the national level is among the main indicators of the status of the protection of human rights and, ultimately, of the health of the rule of law and democracy in each State party, as well as in the region. However, it is no surprise that, on both continents, certain States seek to escape the scrutiny of the competent regional Court. This trend is indisputably related to recent social and political changes (although with significant differences between Europe and the Americas). The ECtHR and IACtHR case law on measures of reparation has been strongly criticised by some States as being unduly intrusive and the relevant judgments have thus remained unimplemented. An in-depth analysis of the jurisprudence of both Courts and its consequences at the domestic level seems in order.

The aim of the book is to analyse the legal impact of the implementation of the ECtHR and IACtHR judgments at the national level, with a specific focus on cases in which the regional court concerned uses the "democratic argument" (arguments related to democracy, political rights and electoral justice – Art. 3 of the Protocol 1 to the ECHR or Art. 23 of the ACHR). The choice is due to the fact that, although democracy is a much wider concept, judgments concerning violations of political rights and electoral justice – and especially the analysis of the status of the implementation of the corresponding measures of reparation identified – provide reliable indicators to assess the status and sustainability of democracy in a State. Moreover, an analysis of the violations of political rights and electoral justice allows an in-depth comparison between the two regional human rights systems.

Mindful of the broader scope of the fall-out generated by the non-implementation of judgments, including in socio-economic terms, this book includes a section exploring how judgments issued by the ECtHR and the IACtHR affect the participation of voters in the countries under their jurisdiction. To this end, an original dataset including the 47 Member States of the Council of Europe and the 20 States which have recognised the adjudicatory jurisdiction of the IACtHR (also including the 5 States that have ratified the ACHR, without recognising the adjudicatory competence of the IACtHR) has been built. Data on the most relevant explanatory variables which are able to help provide an understanding of the criteria followed by people to vote and their voting behaviour have been collected from the Voter Turnout Database provided by the International Institute for Democracy and Electoral Assistance (International IDEA). The time span covers the period 1994–2019 for European countries (from the adoption of Protocol 11 to the ECHR until 2019), whilst it covers 1979–2019 for American countries (from the entry into force of the ACHR until 2019). In particular, the following types of data are taken into account: type of electoral system (presidential, parliamentary, or assembly-elected president); election type (presidential or parliamentary); year of election; voter turnout; number of parties/candidates; closeness of the election; GDP per capita; share of urban population. Moreover, the date and type of judgment by the two Courts are considered. This variable relates to judgments in which the ECtHR has found violations of Art. 3 of Protocol 1 to the ECHR and those in which the IACtHR has declared violations of Art. 23 of the ACHR. This section of the book has been realised through empirical research, based on multivariate regression models with a pooled time-series cross-sectional design, considering voter turnout as the dependent variable and the whole set of institutional and socio-economic information as covariates, together with the main variable of interest, i.e., a dummy picking up whether the court concerned has identified a violation of voting rights before an election takes place.

This book is multidisciplinary in aim and scope of analysis, in that it looks at the subject-matter through the lenses of constitutional law, international human rights law, as well as political economy.

The methodology

This book contains 15 national case studies (10 from the European system and 5 from the Inter-American one) focusing on the analysis carried out by the ECtHR and IACtHR in judgments in which a violation of Art. 3 of Protocol 1 to the ECHR and Art. 23 of the ACHR respectively has been found.

Furthermore, this book contains one stand-alone section which seeks to assess the sustainability of democracy in a comprehensive manner, the issue being measured on the basis of an empirical analysis founded on political economy considerations.

This book provides an insight into the legal consequences which the implementation (or lack thereof) of the ECtHR and IACtHR judgments has at the national level, with a specific focus on cases where the regional court concerned uses the "democratic argument" (arguments related to democracy, political rights, and electoral justice – Art. 3 of the Protocol 1 to the ECtHR or Art. 23 of the IACtHR) on a "national report/approach" basis.

The first two chapters – respectively dedicated to the European and the Inter-American system of human rights – have the following structure: an introduction and context section, in which each author concisely contextualises the institutional relationship between the constitutional structure and the corresponding regional system of protection of human rights, especially as far as the reception of regional case law is concerned. This part underlines how this relationship has developed since the ratification of the corresponding regional treaty and the acceptance of the relevant jurisdiction. This part also illustrates – with general references – the "presence" of each State under consideration in the regional system; i.e. the number of judgments in which the State's international responsibility has been declared, and the general status of the implementation of regional judgments at the national level, among others. Each national report also provides general references to the democratic status of the country analysed.

Moreover, in each national report the selected judgments in which the violation of Art. 3 of the Protocol 1 to the ECHR and Art. 23 of the ACHR respectively has been found will be analysed. This analysis will take into account the summary of the case, the reasoning developed by the regional court with a specific focus on the "democratic argument." Finally, each contribution deals with the measures of reparation (individual and general) ordered by the regional court as far as the violation of Art. 3 of the Protocol 1 to the ECHR or Art. 23 of the ACHR is concerned.

The third and final section of each national report focuses on the assessment of the legal and economic impact of the implementation (or lack thereof) of ECtHR and IACtHR judgments at the national level.

As mentioned, this book also includes a stand-alone final chapter providing an empirical analysis of a relevant dataset from a political economy point of view.

All the national reports included in the present book are up to date as of September 2020.

At the end of this book, some general conclusions are offered with the aim of assessing the consequences – both legal and economic – of the implementation (or lack thereof) of the judgments rendered by regional human rights Courts on cases concerning the right to vote and electoral justice have in terms of the status and sustainability of democracy in a given State.

Part I

The European Court of Human Rights

1 The (lack of) impact of the European Court of Human Rights' judgement on the protection of political rights in Azerbaijan

Palmina Tanzarella *

Introduction and context

Among those Council of Europe Member States that are part of the European Convention of Human Rights (hereinafter ECHR), Azerbaijan is the State which has been most frequently held responsible for the violation of the right to vote (Art. 3 of Protocol 1 ECHR).

The country faces significant challenges with respect to the exercise of fundamental freedoms – such as the freedom of assembly and association and the freedom of expression – pointing to systematic harassment and criminal prosecution of those who express views that are critical towards the government, and to a practice of intimidation and harassment of voters.

Since the entry into force of the Convention in 2002, the Court has made 170 judgments, of which 169 represent at least 1 violation of the ECHR. In particular, 25 judgments exclusively relate to the violation of the right to vote.

This quantity may not stand out if read in conjunction with the total violations registered about the Freedom of Assembly and Association (34 out of 169), the Freedom of Expression (6 out of 169) and the Right to a Fair Trial (66 out of 169),[1] but it clearly shows that the issue of sustainability of the democratic rules in Azerbaijan is rather problematic and far from being fulfilled.[2]

In this regard, the European Court of Human Rights (hereinafter ECtHR) does everything in its power. It is not a coincidence that the first infringement procedure *ex* Art. 46, para, 4 under the Convention was stated against Azerbaijan, seeking to ensure the execution of its previous judgments. According to this

* Researcher in Constitutional Law, University of Milano-Bicocca. The author wishes to express her gratitude to Dr. Irene Valotti for preparing the materials about the electoral turnout and the separation of power in Azerbaijan, which have proven very useful for the drafting of the present paper.

1 For a pretty complete analysis about the violation of the Right to a Fair Trial and the Freedom of Association, see Hajiyev K., "The directions of influence of the case law of the European Court of Human Rights in Azerbaijan," in Motoc I., Ziemele I. (eds.), *The impact of the ECHR on democratic change in Central and Eastern Europe. Judicial Perspectives*, Cambridge University Press, Cambridge, 2016, 57–79, at 64–73.

2 See the Official Statistics published on the European Court of Human Rights website. www.echr.coe.int/Pages/home.aspx?p=reports&c=. Last access 10 September 2020.

DOI: 10.4324/9781003229247-3

article, the Committee of Ministers – by decision adopted by a majority vote of two-thirds of the representatives entitled to sit in the Committee – have the possibility to refer to the Court the question as to whether a State party has failed to abide by the final judgment of the Court.

In this respect, since Azerbaijan disregarded the Committee of Ministers' measures, the Grand Chamber ordered that Azerbaijan release Ilgar Mammadov – an opposition candidate for the presidential election of 2013 – who was illegitimately placed in pre-trial detention, as the Court itself stated in its judgment of May 2014.[3]

Why does Azerbaijan try to ignore its European obligations? Legally the Azerbaijan constitutional system appears to be in line with the international standard of the democratic rules. Indeed, after the collapse of the former Soviet Union and having obtained independence in 1991, with the approval of the Democratic Constitution of 1995 Azerbaijan was on the road to reforms. The Constitution itself includes clauses that, at least formally, are typical of a pluralistic and egalitarian regime. It assures fundamental rights (both individual and social ones), the separation of powers, and embraces a secular perspective. In order to be more in line with the Western tradition in 2002, the country ratified the European Convention, thereby accepting the Strasbourg jurisdiction. As a matter of fact, even before the ratification, the ECHR and its jurisprudence were seen almost as a lighthouse by the national judges, providing them with assistance in interpreting some difficult cases during the transition period towards democracy. Moreover, during the preparation of the new civil, criminal, and procedural reforms, adopted before the ratification of the Convention, the European specialists helped the local authorities with the preparation of those texts, in particular the Venice Commission.[4]

Even more impressive is the position that the Convention and the wider international clauses occupy in the source of law system. The General Principles of the Constitution clearly establish that in terms of foreign policy the Azerbaijan Republic is limited by provisions resulting from international agreements, wherein the Azerbaijan Republic is one of the parties.[5] Subsequently, in the part covering the sources of law of the entire legislative system, it is explicitly proclaimed that the international conventions, to which Azerbaijan is party, are an integral part of

3 See ECtHR, *Mammadov v. Azerbaijan*, 22 May 2014. Regarding the Infringement procedure, see Grand Chamber, Proceedings under Art. 46 § 4 in the Case of *Ilgar Mammadov v. Azerbaijan*, 29 May 2019. In the literature, Çali B., *No Going Nuclear in Strasbourg. The Infringement Decision in Ilgar Mammadov v. Azerbaijan by the European Court of Human Rights*, in Verfassungblog, May 30 2019; Dzehtsiarou K., *How many judgments does one need to enforce a judgment? The first ever infringement proceedings at the European Court of Human Rights*, in Strasbourg Observer Blog, 4 June 2019; Buyse A., *First Infringement Proceedings Judgment of the European Court: Ilgar Mammadov v Azerbaijan*, in ECHR Blog, 31 May 2019; Tanzarella P., *Mammadov c. Azerbaijan: la prima procedura d'infrazione. Un'occasione mancata?*, in Quaderni costituzionali, 3, 2019, 713–715.

4 For a complete list of the Venice Commission' opinions, see www.venice.coe.int/webforms/documents/default.aspx?country=41&year=all&other=true.

5 See Art. 7 of the Azerbaijan Constitution.

the Azerbaijani legislation.[6] Moreover, Art. 151 of the Constitution stipulates that in case of contradictions between the normative acts of the country's legislative system – with the exception of the Constitution – and the acts adopted by a referendum and international documents to which Azerbaijan is party, the international document shall prevail.[7]

The juridical landscape just described shows how the country under scrutiny is well equipped to guarantee the protection of freedoms, additionally thanks to the course plotted by the ECtHR jurisprudence. In relation to the human rights defence, specifically, the Constitution seems to grant to the ECHR and to the ECtHR a sort of constitutional authority.[8] Nevertheless, as discussed below, Azerbaijan gives off a strong sign of resistance.

Undoubtedly, there are historical and political explanations behind this. In the past, it had never experienced the democratic categories, as it had always been dominated by the Soviet Union, except for a short period of independence (1918–1920). The population seems to underestimate the culture of rights and liberties, preferring to put more attention on economic wealth.

Consequently, Azerbaijan is ranked 146 out of 167 in the Democracy Index of 2019, which shows that the levels of political participation, the political culture, and the electoral process are seriously insufficient.[9]

Let us now consider the ECtHR judgments, condemning Azerbaijan for the violation of the right to vote, *ex* Art. 3 of Prot. 1, and the level of the implementation of the judgments. In the final part, we will draw some general conclusions on the role that the European Court of Strasbourg plays in the building of democracy in the country.

The violations of electoral rights in the ECtHR judgments

A general overview about electoral rights in Azerbaijan

Before examining a selection of the ECtHR cases law regarding electoral rights, it is important to provide a preliminary outline about the electoral context that will help to shed light on some systemic challenges.

6 See Art. 148 of the Azerbaijan Constitution.

7 Abdullahzade, C., *The status of international treaties in the legal system of Azerbaijan*, in Review of Central and East European Law, 32, 2, 2007, 233–256.

8 In this regard, see Art. 71, according to which the "Rights and liberties of a human being and citizen may be partially and temporarily restricted [only] on announcement of war, martial law and state of emergency, and also mobilization, taking into consideration international obligations of the Azerbaijan Republic. Population of the Republic shall be notified in advance about restrictions as regards their rights and liberties"; see also Art. 12, according to which the "Rights and liberties of a person and citizen listed in the present Constitution are implemented in accordance with international treaties wherein the Azerbaijan Republic is one of the parties." In the literature, see Martin C.H., *Comparative human rights jurisprudence in Azerbaijan: Theory, practice and prospects*, in Journal of Transnational Law & Policy, 14, 2, 2005, 215–252.

9 The Democracy index is available at www.eiu.com/public/topical_report.aspx?campaignid=democracyindex2019.

Azerbaijan has a strong presidential system, with wide powers vested in the Presidency.

The President – the head of the executive power – appoints and chairs the Cabinet of Ministers and appoints all executive authorities at the central and regional level; moreover, he/she is responsible for nominating the judges of the Constitutional Court, Supreme Court, Economic Court, and other courts, as well as the General Prosecutor, who are formally appointed by the Parliament. A 2016 constitutional amendment – a source of concern for several international human rights bodies[10] – granted the President the power to call for early presidential elections without defining specific conditions, and extended the presidential term from five to seven years.

The executive branch exercises broad authority relative to the *Milli Majilis* (Parliament). The unicameral Parliament is composed of 125 deputies, serving for a 5-year term, who are elected under a majoritarian system from 125 single-member constituencies.[11]

About the right to vote, all citizens over 18 years of age are able to exercise it, except those recognised as incapable by a Court decision.[12] Voter registration is passive, and voter lists are extracted from a permanent voter register which is maintained by the Central Election Commission. Voters are registered according to their place of permanent residence, provided that they have been resident for at least 6 of the last 12 months prior to the election being announced. However, there are some vulnerable groups. Members of national minorities making up around 10% of the population of Azerbaijan face challenges in filling in ballots and accessing results, due to their native language being written in a different alphabet; there being no legal requirement to produce ballots or other election material in minority languages. More than half of the polling stations (54%) visited by OSCE observers were assessed as being not accessible for voters with disabilities. Women are heavily underrepresented in politics and there are no specific measures to promote the participation of women in political and public life.

Meanwhile, the right to stand for parliament is granted to eligible voters who are at least 25 years of age, who do not hold dual citizenship or obligations to other States, and who do not have a prior conviction for a serious crime. The Election Code lists categories of officials who must resign from their position prior to registering as a candidate and includes professional military personnel,

10 See Venice Commission "*Opinion on the Draft Modifications to the Constitution Submitted to the Referendum of 26 September 2016*," 18 October 2016. Moreover, the UN Human Rights Committee (HRC) in its "*Concluding observations on the fourth periodic report of Azerbaijan*" (16 November 2016), CCPR/C/AZE/CO/4, para. 43, calls on the State party to "bring its electoral regulations and practices into compliance with the Covenant [...] including by ensuring fully transparent elections and a genuine pluralistic political debate."

11 A 2002 constitutional amendment eliminated the proportional list component of parliamentary elections. All 125 members of Parliament are now elected in single seat constituencies, in a single round of voting.

12 See para. 2 of Art. 56 of the Azerbaijan Constitution.

judges, government officials, and religious officials. Candidates may be self-nominated or nominated by a registered political party,[13] a coalition of parties, or a group of voters. Candidates are required to support their candidature with signatures from 450 registered voters.

Under the Constitution, the right to stand for President is granted to any voter who is at least 35 years of age, who does not hold dual citizenship or obligations to other States, who does not have a previous conviction for a serious crime, who has permanently resided in Azerbaijan for at least 10 years, and has a university degree.[14] A candidate can be self-nominated or nominated by a registered political party, a coalition of registered parties, or an initiative group of at least 100 voters. All nominated candidates have to submit at least 40,000 signatures from registered voters in support with a minimum of 50 signatures from at least 60 constituencies, and to disclose their financial assets.

The President is elected by popular vote, by an absolute majority of votes cast; if no candidate receives more than half of the votes, a second round is held between the two candidates who obtained the highest number of votes.[15] Constitutional amendments in 2009, confirmed by a national referendum, removed the limitation on the two consecutive terms that a person may serve as President.[16]

Elections are administered by a three-tiered structure comprising the Central Election Commission (CEC), the Constituency Election Commissions, and the Precinct Election Commissions: for all these commissions, one-third of the members should each represent the parliamentary majority, minority, and independent deputies, and the commissions' chairpersons are also nominees of the parliamentary majority. As we will see, this formula, in practice, gives pro-government forces control of all commissions, undermining trust in the impartiality of election administration.

13 According to the Ministry of Justice, more than 50 political parties are currently registered.

14 Some of these requirements, especially the educational and residential requirements, may be seen as unreasonable restrictions and thus contrary to international standards. UN Human Rights Committee (HRC), General Comment 25 (1996), para. 15: "any restrictions on the right to stand for election [...] must be justifiable on objective and reasonable criteria. Persons who are otherwise eligible to stand for election should not be excluded by unreasonable or discriminatory requirements such as education, residence or descent, or by political affiliation." See also, Venice Commission, *Code of Good Practices in Electoral Matters* (2002), Section 1.1(c).

15 Presidential elections are primarily regulated by the 1995 Constitution (last amended in 2016) and the 2003 Election Code (amended in 2013 and 2017).

16 In the opinion of the Council of Europe's Commission for Democracy through Law (Venice Commission), the elimination of the abovementioned limitation constitutes a serious set-back on Azerbaijan's road to a consolidated democracy. OSCE, *Republic of Azerbaijan, Presidential Election 15 October 2008: OSCE/ODIHR Election Observation Mission Final Report*, 15 December 2008, 5.

OSCE, *Republic of Azerbaijan, Presidential Election 9 October 2013: OSCE/ODIHR Election Observation Mission Final Report*, 24 December 2013, pp. 4–5.

OSCE, *Republic of Azerbaijan, Early Presidential Election 11 April 2018: ODIHR Election Observation Mission Final Report*, 18 July 2018, 4–7.

Equipped with this knowledge, the following paragraph will turn to the analysis of the ECtHR cases law, which points out matters of concern, some of them already mentioned above.

The right to stand for elections

The 25 ECtHR judgments concerning violations of Art. 3 of the Protocol 1 all focus on the protection of the right to stand for election. Even though there are several aspects raising concerns in respect of the right to vote, to date, applications to the European Court of Strasbourg have only concerned the passive side of electoral rights. Generally, while election days have been calm and peaceful, domestic and international observers have reported significant occurrences of serious irregularities and procedural violations, including ballot-box stuffing.[17]

In particular, there are two specific areas of electoral irregularities that have been drawn to the European Court's attention, namely the issue of registration on the electoral roll and the invalidation of electoral results.

Before undertaking a careful analysis of the argumentation of the Court as regards these two groups of cases law, let us look at the general principle of free elections that the Court itself has established towards Azerbaijan in the leading case *Namat Aliyev v. Azerbaijan*.[18]

The applicant complained about a series of irregularities in parliamentary elections, including unlawful interference, undue influence, ballot-box stuffing, the harassment of observers, inaccuracies in the electoral rolls and discrepancies in electoral protocols. At the domestic level, he first applied to the Constituency Electoral Commission, which rejected the complaints as being unsubstantiated, without offering further elaboration. Meanwhile the Central Electoral Commission did not even reply to the applicant. Subsequently, the Court of Appeal and then the Supreme Court dismissed his claims; the latter on the ground that he had failed to formally lodge a claim with the Central Electoral Commission.

The Court has established that the rights guaranteed by Art. 3 of Protocol 1 do not only cover the process of the organisation and management of the voting process, but also the method through which the outcome of elections should be reviewed, as well as how to deal with disputes concerning the counting of votes

17 See the Final Report of the OSCE/ODIHR, Election Observation Mission concerning the elections of 6 November 2005; Among the ECtHR jurisprudence, *Shukurov v. Azerbaijan*, 27 October 2016: a case concerning electoral irregularities in the parliamentary elections of November 2010; *Gahramanli and Others v. Azerbaijan*, 8 October 2015: complaints brought by the applicants, candidates of various opposition political parties, about electoral fraud and irregularities during the 2010 parliamentary elections; ECtHR, *Karimov v. Azerbaijan*, 25 September 2014: allegations by an opposition candidate about irregularities in the 2005 parliamentary elections.

18 ECtHR, *Namat Aliyev v. Azerbaijan*, 8 April 2010.

and the validation of election results.[19] At stake is not the applicant's right to win the election, but his right to stand freely and effectively in it. The fact that there is a wide difference in votes between candidates does not matter when it comes to independently examining the extent of the irregularities, before determining their effects on the overall result of the election.[20] In the words of the Court:

> Article 3 of Protocol 1 requires the Court not to ascertain merely that the election outcome as such was not prejudiced, but to verify that the applicant's individual right to stand for election was not deprived of its effectiveness and that its essence had not been impaired.[21]

Therefore, effectiveness is the first ingredient for an appropriately functioning electoral system. That means that the State must assure both that everyone who wishes to run for elections is able to do so, and that there is an effective examination of individual complaints and appeals on matters concerning electoral rights. This is because, as with many other articles of the ECHR, Art. 3 of Protocol 1 contains positive obligations with a procedural character that help to maintain general confidence in the State's management of the electoral process.[22]

In actual fact, in its previous and consolidated jurisprudence the Court has always specified that a mere mistake or irregularity in the electoral process would not in and of itself signify the unfairness of the elections per se. What is crucial is compliance with the general principles of equality, transparency, impartiality, and the independence of the electoral administration. In particular, the concept of free elections would be at risk only if there is evidence of procedural breaches that would be capable of thwarting the free expression of the opinion of the people, for instance through gross distortion of the voters' intent; and where such complaints do not receive effective examination at domestic level.[23] Thus, in order to attract the scrutiny of the Court in relation to the manner in which election-related complaints have been dealt with at the domestic level, the applicant must demonstrate that those complaints were both "serious and arguable."[24]

Consequently, the second ingredient for achieving an appropriately functioning electoral system is the absence of arbitrariness in the judicial verdicts.

According to the electoral rules, in Azerbaijan complaints and appeals can be filed by a broad range of electoral stakeholders via election commissions

19 *Ibidem*, para. 81. See also ECtHR, *Kovach v. Ukraine*, 7 February 2008, para. 55; *Kerimova v. Azerbaijan*, 30 September 2010, para. 54; *Davydov and Others v. Russia*, 30 May 2017; *Mugemangango v. Belgium* [GC], 10 July 2020.

20 *Namat v. Azerbaijan*, cited above, para. 75.

21 *Ibidem*.

22 *Ibidem*, para. 81.

23 See *Davydov and Others v. Russia*, cited above, para. 287; *Mugemangango v. Belgium*, cited above, para. 72.

24 *Namat Aliyev v. Azerbaijan*, cited above, para. 78. See also *Gahramanli and Others v. Azerbaijan*, 8 October 2015, para. 73.

and the courts. Complaints and appeals should be decided within 2 days if filed within 30 days of election day, and immediately if submitted on election day. Nevertheless, a number of civil society and opposition parties expressed a lack of confidence in the independence of electoral dispute resolution bodies. These events have often been mirrored in the ECtHR judgments, starting with the leading case under scrutiny in this section. Indeed, in the *Namat Alyev* case (such as in other repetitive cases), the Court carefully scrutinises whether the conclusions reached by the domestic courts in examining the applicant's claims are devoid of arbitrariness. In doing so, the Court, recalling the Venice Commission's Code of Good Practices in Electoral Matters,[25] is careful in also examining the excessively formalistic reasons given by the domestic courts.[26]

In sum, the Courts condemned Azerbaijan because the applicant's complaints had not been effectively addressed at the domestic level and had been dismissed in an arbitrary manner. The same reasons are provided in the following cases concerning irregularities in elections.[27]

Registration

Among the many irregularities which have been noted in the election procedure, there are serious concerns about the candidate registration process, particularly in terms of the verification of signatures.[28] Again, the European Court focuses its

25 See the Code of Good Practice in Electoral Matters (Guidelines and Explanatory Report) (CDL-AD (2002) 23 rev), adopted by the European Commission for Democracy Through Law ("the Venice Commission") at its 51st and 52nd sessions (5–6 July and 18–19 October 2002).

26 *Namat Alyev v. Azerbaijan*, cited above paras. 85–86.

27 *Karimov v. Azerbaijan*, 25 September 2014, where an opposition candidate denounced irregularities during the 2005 parliamentary elections, namely the use of special polling stations for the military in circumstances not permitted under the Azerbaijan Electoral Code. *Gahramanli and Others v. Azerbaijan*, cited above, where the applicants (candidates for various opposition political parties) accused the Electoral Commission members of interfering with the election process by, undue influence on voter choice, obstruction of observers, ballot-box stuffing during the 2010 parliamentary elections. *Shukurov v. Azerbaijan*, 27 October 2016 and *Aslan Ismayilov and Others v. Azerbaijan*, 13 April 2017, *Samadbayli and Others v. Azerbaijan*, 13 April 2017, where the applicants complained that, the domestic authorities, including the electoral commissions and courts, had failed to properly examine his complaints and to investigate his allegations concerning certain irregularities and breaches of electoral law. In particular, the examination of his appeal by the Supreme Court had been deprived of all effectiveness because the election results had already been approved by the Constitutional Court.

28 See *Abil v. Azerbaijan (no.2)*, 5 December 2019: case concerning the applicant being disqualified from running in parliamentary elections. *Abdalov and Others v. Azerbaijan*, 11 July 2019: case concerning the applicants' complaint about facing such long delays in registering as candidates for 2010 parliamentary elections that they had no time to campaign and compete effectively. *Seyidzade v. Azerbaijan*, 3 December 2009: arbitrary refusal to register the applicant (a former clergy member) as a candidate for parliamentary elections despite his having resigned from all positions that could be seen as involving "professional religious activity."

scrutiny on the existence of arbitrariness, in particular in relation to the refusal and to the delay of the registration of candidates on the electoral list.

Regarding the group of 11 judgments concerning the refusal of the candidate registration due to the invalidation of supporting signatories, the *Tahirov* case[29] neatly summarises the shortcomings and inefficiencies of Azerbaijan's system.

As a general principle, the ECtHR has always stated that the number of signatures required for the presentation of a list of candidates does not constitute an impediment to the expression of the opinion of the people.[30] However, such measures must pursue the legitimate aim of a reasonable selection of the candidates in order to ensure their representative character and at the same time avoid improper candidatures being put forward, as the whole process must be proportionate to that aim.[31]

Similarly, a requirement for such signatures has to be accompanied by certificates showing that the signatories were registered on the electoral rolls and therefore pursue the legitimate aim of ensuring that the signatories have voting rights and that each of them is supporting only one candidature.[32] Yet, the imposition of a minimum number of signatures and their verification must comply with the rule of law and protect the integrity of the elections.

It is precisely on this subject that it was found by the Court in the *Tahirov* case[33] that the safeguards provided by the Electoral Board were not sufficient for the Court. Indeed, the Electoral Board rejected the applicant's candidature, on the basis of experts who assess the validity of the signatures. In addition, the applicant was not able to attend the Board's meetings or to submit his arguments, none of which had even been examined by the Board. The rejection of the applicant's candidature on account of the alleged invalidity of the signatures he had provided was thus arbitrary. Supported by the OSCE,[34] the Court noted the systemic nature of these shortcomings and a number of candidatures which were arbitrarily rejected on those grounds in other judgments. Thus, it declared a violation of Art. 3, Protocol 1 in the present case and in all other similar cases.

Article 3 also impacts the way that election campaigns are conducted, since the rights it guarantees do not remain confined to the candidature itself. Thus, in the *Abdalov and Others* case,[35] the Court declared a violation of the right to

29 ECtHR, *Tahirov v. Azerbaijan*, 11 June 2015.

30 *Asensio Serqueda v. Spain*, Commission decision, 9 May 1994; *Federación nacionalista Canaria v. Spain* (dec.), 7 June 2001; *Brito Da Silva Guerra and Sousa Magno v. Portugal* (dec.), 17 June 2008; *Mihaela Mihai Neagu v. Romania* (dec.), 6 March 1994, para. 31.

31 Thus, a threshold of 100,000 signatures, representing 0.55% of all citizens registered on the electoral roll, was found to be compliant with Art. 3 of Protocol 1 (*Mihaela Mihai Neagu v. Romania*, cited above).

32 Accordingly, the Court found that it was not therefore disproportionate to reject a candidature which did not satisfy the formalities in question (*Brito Da Silva Guerra and Sousa Magno v. Portugal*, cited above).

33 ECtHR, *Tahirov v. Azerbaijan*, cited above

34 OCSE, Final Report on the Parliamentary Elections of 7 November 2010, 25 January 2011.

35 ECtHR, *Abdalov and Others v. Azerbaijan*, 11 July 2019.

stand for election for the fact that the applicants were registered late for the 2010 parliamentary elections. The reasons for the findings were the lack of safeguards against arbitrariness in the candidate registration procedures and the delays in the examination of their appeals attributable to the electoral authorities and the courts. As a consequence, the applicant had no or very little time to campaign.

Invalidation of the election results

Transparency and the absence of arbitrariness are still the two main guiding criteria for the evaluation of cases in which the decision-making process concerning the ineligibility or the invalidation of election results are involved.[36] This is why the Court insists on the necessity to entrust such important tasks to an impartial body, which enjoys a very circumscribed discretion, as well as the need to respect a strict procedure that can guarantee a fair, objective, and sufficiently reasonable decision and prevent any abuse of power on the relevant authority.[37]

It is settled case law that the Court, where it engages in such an examination, confines itself to ascertaining whether the decision rendered by the domestic body is arbitrary or manifestly unreasonable in nature.[38] In the Azerbaijan jurisprudence, it is quite straightforward for the Court to demonstrate a high level of that irrationality.

In this regard, the *Kerimova* case is emblematic. The Central Election Commission invalidated the election results of the applicant (which initially was declared the winner of the parliamentary election of 2005) because two officials were convicted of having falsified the election results. The high number of votes obtained by the applicant was still sufficient in order to declare her the winner. Nevertheless, the election authorities failed to provide any reasons to explain why the alleged breaches had altered the outcome of the elections. Nor did they even consider the possibility of recounting the votes. Furthermore, neither the electoral authorities, nor the domestic courts attempted to determine in whose favour the alleged irregularities had worked. Consequently, the Court found that the national authorities had, nevertheless, invalidated the results in breach of domestic electoral law, and without taking into account the limited impact of the effects of the tampering of the two officials. By doing so, the domestic decision not only arbitrarily infringed the applicant's electoral rights by depriving her of the benefit of being elected to Parliament, but also essentially helped the officials to obstruct the election.

36 See the leading case *Davydov and Others v. Russia*, cited above, para. 288.

37 ECtHR, *Podkolzina v. Latvia*, 9 April 2002, para. 35; *Kovach v. Ukraine*, 7 February 2008, paras. 54–55; *Kerimova v. Azerbaijan*, cited above, paras. 44–45; *Riza and Others v. Bulgaria*, 13 October 2015, para. 144.

38 ECtHR, *Kerimli and Alibeyli v. Azerbaijan*, 10 January 2012, paras. 38–42.

The European Court reached similar conclusions even when the domestic judge, who had invalidated the election results, was part of the Constitutional Court. Generally, this is because of a lack of factual basis in its decisions, especially where the Constitutional Court's decision contained no indication as to what specific documents had been examined, what specific requirements of the Electoral Code had been missing, and what specific shortcomings were found in the Constituency Electoral Commission records.[39]

The legal and economic impact of the ECtHR judgments

Ten years on from the declaration of the first violation of Art. 3, Protocol 1, not one of the twenty-five judgments of the European Court has yet been implemented.

When analysing the records of the Committee of Ministers (hereinafter CM) it immediately emerges how reluctant Azerbaijan is to honour the commitments of the Convention. In actual fact, as we will see below, the requests of the CM are very detailed, in some circumstances without leaving much discretion to the State on the choice of measures.

Normally, the CM tries to reach an agreement with the domestic authorities on how to remedy the violations. Theoretically, the State has the right to decide on how it approaches the execution of the ECtHR judgments. Considering that the ECtHR judgments are declaratory in nature, most of the time it is sufficient to pay whatever damages the Court imposes in the sentence, according to para. 2 of Art. 41 of ECHR. Nevertheless, when the CM or the Court itself realises that individual and structural reforms need to be adopted, both of them insist on specific remedies. A typical individual measure that the European authorities have prescribed is the release of applicants who are illegitimately detained. With respect to the structural remedies, especially from the introduction of the pilot judgments custom,[40] the Court requires some specific legislative or judicial actions in order to solve problems that affect the entire system which generate a sequence of the same violations.

When it comes to violations of electoral rights in Azerbaijan, the European Court does not specify individual or structural measures to adopt in its judgments, underlining only the reasons why the State was considered responsible for the harm caused. Only in the *Gahramanli and Others* case did the Court indicate that the respondent State should be encouraged to envision a reform of the structural composition of the electoral commissions, with the aim of improving the effectiveness of the examination of the individual election-related complaints.

On the contrary, since December 2013 the CM, which has continued to monitor the State executions of the Namat Aliyev Group, has ever specifically stated the necessity of adopting general measures to implement new electoral law

39 *Ibidem*.
40 Leading case *Broniosky v. Poland*, 22 June 2004.

to ensure the independence, transparency, and legal quality of the procedure in front of the electoral commissions. In addition, the CM has required action to be taken in the sense of improving the system of supervision of the proper conduct of the elections to prevent arbitrariness and, in particular, to:

Co-operate with the Venice Commission and make full use of the additional possibilities offered by the Action Plan of the Council of Europe for Azerbaijan.

Make sure that a clear message is sent to the electoral commissions by the highest competent authorities stating that no illegal or arbitrary action will be tolerated.

In this context, the Committee has even underlined the crucial importance of targeted practical guidance from the Supreme Court, based on the European Court's judgments, complemented, if necessary, by appropriate instructions to electoral commissions.

The CM also highlighted the importance of ensuring that the proceedings in front of the Constitutional Court provide the guarantees required by the Convention, in particular with regard to the right to appear in person before it and with regard to transparency (a violation that occurred in the *Kerimli and Alibeyli* case).[41]

Instead, in respect of individual measures, the only action that has been requested is the payment of damages calculated by the Court. As the CM stated in its first meeting, individual measures in respect of the applicants' rights to participate in free elections are closely linked to the question of general measures. In fact, as the Committee noted, it is not possible to eliminate the effects of the violations, other than by the just satisfaction awarded and the adoption of structural measures.[42]

In any case, Azerbaijan has not taken the measures suggested so far. It has simply organised training and awareness-raising activities for members of the electoral commissions. But, according to the CM, these actions alone do not respond to the findings of the Court, in particular the Court's conclusions that the procedures before the electoral commissions and the national courts did not afford safeguards against arbitrariness. Moreover, to date the domestic authorities do not provide an assessment regarding the impact of them.[43]

On the contrary, the just satisfaction awarded by the Court was fully paid in all cases except four, where payment was partially made.[44] It would appear that making the required payment is less problematic than the adoption of structural measures, perhaps because the total amount is not too demanding. As the table below shows, the pecuniary damages, non-pecuniary damages and the costs and

41 *Kerimli and Alibeyli v. Azerbaijan*, cited above.

42 CM, 1179th meeting (September 2013).

43 A detailed summary of the situation regarding general measures can be found in the Notes for the 1265th meeting (September 2016) (DH) (CM/Notes/1265/H46-4).

44 *Aslan Ismayilov and others*, cited above; *Samadbayli and others*, cited above; *Abil (no.2)* cited above; *Abdalov and others*, cited above.

expenses that, in accordance with Art. 41 ECHR, the Court calculated for each of the 21 sentences executed, amounts to €282,000.

Cases	*Pecuniary damages*	*Non-pecuniary damages*	*Cost and expenses*	*Total*
Namat Aliyev	–	€7,500	€1,600	€9,100
Abil	–	€7,500	€1,600	€9,100
Atakishi	–	€7,500	€1,385	€8,885
Hajili	–	€7,500	€1,600	€9,100
Kerimli and Alibeyli	–	€5,000	€3,600	€8,600
Kerimova	€50,000	€7,500	€1,600	€59,100
Orujov	–	€7,500	–	€7,500
Khanhuseyn Aliyev	–	€7,500	–	€7,500
Mammadov no. 2	–	€7,500	€1,600	€9,100
Karimov	–	€7,500	€2,544	€10,044
Tahirov	–	€7,500	€2,150	€9,650
Bagirov and Others	Not specified	Not specified	–	€18,000
Gasimli and Others	–	€10,000	€5,000	€15,000
Vugar Aliyev and Others	–	€10,000	€4,000	€14,000
Annagi Hajibeyli	–	€10,000	€2,600	€12,600
Gahramanli and Others	–	€10,000	€850	€10,850
Seyidzade	–	€7,500	€1,000	€8,500
Gaya Aliyev	–	€10,000	€6,000	€16,000
Mammadli and Others	–	€10,000	€4000	€14,000
Soltanov and Others	–	€10,000	€4,100	€14,100
Shukurov	–	€1,000	€1,000	€10,000

It is clear that the sums awarded are not so substantial as to consider the European condemnation a valid deterrent to violating the Convention. Even accounting for the costs expended in organising the training and the awareness-raising activities for structural reforms, it is clear that, from an economic point of view, the impact of European jurisprudence on Azerbaijan is insignificant.

Some concluding remarks

The above analysis has shown how far Azerbaijan is from becoming a democratic State. Anyone who lives in a consolidated democratic country would agree with the European Court's findings on violations concerning the right to stand for elections. The principles enunciated in the cases above mentioned appear intuitive and obvious for juridical systems that elaborate democratic values over centuries of history. It bears repeating that the ECtHR has asked Azerbaijan to provide equal, transparent, and impartial procedural rules in order to ensure regular elections. On the contrary, the electoral bodies in charge of ensuring that there is respect for the procedures in Azerbaijan indisputably act with a high degree of arbitrariness.

What is the possible reason for the non-implementation of European judgments? It may have something to do with the fact that Azerbaijan still does not have the proper tools to adequately face the transitional state building process. Or is it that the country is not willing to change its democratic assets? On closer inspection, the electoral reforms that the CM has asked to be adopted are not especially challenging, as they only require a minimal effort at a legislative and/or judicial level. However, neither the Parliament – which can freely approve new laws in line with requests by European institutions – nor the Constitutional Court and the Supreme Court – which can both interpret domestic law as much as they can to ensure conformity with the European Convention principles – take the European "diktat" seriously, as shown by their open refusal to fulfil their international obligations.

This is even more evident if we consider the general level of the protection of human rights in Azerbaijan. As mentioned in the introductory paragraph, Azerbaijan is in a very serious condition: the guarantees of all the fundamental rights, especially those related to democratic standards, such as the freedom of expression, the right to assembly, and the right to association are precarious. As well as those found in electoral law, the European Courts have also found violations of the Convention in other areas, but again Azerbaijan has sought to delay executing the final judgment.[45]

Evidently, the political majority of Azerbaijan refuses to take steps that concretely convert the system to embrace a democratic perspective,[46] receiving strong support from the domestic courts in spite of the principle of the independence of the judiciary. Indeed, despite the fact that in several areas the Constitutional Court has shown a collaborative attitude towards the European Court,[47] as described above, in the field of the right to stand for elections and of the freedom

45 According to some scholars, the weak execution of judgments of the European Court in Central and Eastern Europe is a sign of an authoritarian judicial culture and of a lack of self-criticism of judicial structures. See Cernic J., *Glass Half Empty Execution of Judgments of the European Court of Human Rights in Central and Eastern Europe*, in Baltic Yearbook of International Law, 15, 2015, 285–302.

46 Remezaite R., *The impact of the European Court of Human Rights on democratisation in Azerbaijan: Securing freedom of the press*, in Nordic Journal of Human Rights, 31, 4, 2013, 532–551.

47 Some cases are described in Martin, C.H., *Comparative Human Rights jurisprudence in Azerbaijan*, cited above, at 230–247.

Meaningful are the words of the former Chairman of the Azerbaijani Constitutional Court, who wrote "The interpretation of conventional norms on citizens and human rights and freedoms by [the] European Court of Human Rights is binding for all who ratified the European Convention on Human Rights and Fundamental Freedoms. For the time being, a lot of domestic statutes contradict [...] the principles enshrined in the European Convention and are interpreted by European Court of Human Rights. In this situation the Constitutional Courts of CIS countries should play the role of mechanism that ensures the harmonization of European and domestic constitutional law within the process of interpretation of constitutional provisions." Hajiyev K., *The interpretation of the provisions of Constitution and law by Constitutional Courts*, in Hajiyev K., Guliyev R. (eds.), 2002, *Ibidem*, at 171–172.

of expression, it does not show any real effort to interpret the cases in the light of the principles of the Convention and its jurisprudence.

At the same time, there are many political dissenters, who have tried to stand for elections and who represent a significant part of the population, who have appealed to the European Court to speak out against the abuses of an authoritarian regime disguised as a democratic one.[48] As a matter of fact, the integration into the European supranational system is vital for minorities, as they alone do not have enough political strength to enforce the democratic principles. Things may be different from the past, and instead of seeing bloody revolutions, it is not unexpected to see the state building democratic process going on, largely as a result of diplomatic and international agreements, nonetheless the entire process suffers from a certain slowness.[49] This is particularly true with regard to Azerbaijan, whose 2010 written Constitution is included among the democratic charters.[50] Nonetheless, as already stated, this is far from being enforced.

Consequently, the role of the European Court of Human Rights is crucial in assisting minorities to consolidate democracy,[51] especially in contexts – such as the one of Azerbaijan – where the supranational institutions are described in the public discourse as enemies by the majority, in particular by their Presidents.[52]

Generally speaking, the problem is that the contribution of the European Court looks weak, at least in the short term.[53] The power exercised in the execution of the judgments is too limited, being subject to the precarious balance between the organs of the Committee of Ministers and the domestic institutions. In the face of the juridical value of the decisions of the Committee of Ministers,

48 Herron E.S., *Measuring Dissent in Electoral Authoritarian Societies Lessons From Azerbaijans 2008 Presidential Election and 2009 Referendum*, in Comparative Political Studies, 44, 11, 2011, 1557–1583.

49 See Grodeland A.B., *Public and Elite Perceptions of Supranational Courts: The European Perspective*, Review of Central and East European Law, 39, 1, 2014, 41–94.

50 As already noted in the introductory section, the Constitution of Azerbaijan is shaped as a democratic Constitution might be, in terms of the protection of human rights, and the separation of power. In addition, it is very respectful of international obligations, indicating that international conventions shall prevail over the domestic legislation (see. Art. 151 of the Constitution).

51 See Kosař D., Lixinski L., *Domestic Judicial Design by International Human Rights Court*, in American Journal of International Law, 109, 4, 2015, 713–760; Sweeney J.A., *Restorative Justice and Transitional Justice at the ECHR*, in International Criminal Law Review, 12 , 2012, 313–337; Balak A, Koch A., Bruch N., *The Legitimacy of Human Rights Courts: A Grounded Interpretivist Analysis of the European Court of Human Rights*, in Human Rights Quarterly, 35, 2013, 955–984.

52 See Terzyan A., *Sustaining Power through External Threats: The Power of Enemy Images in Russia and Azerbaijan*, in Journal of Liberty and International Affairs, 6, 2, 2020, 45–56.

53 It has been stated that "crucial to the success of international standards and institutions [...] is the degree to which national courts respect decisions of the international human rights tribunals and incorporate their jurisprudence into national decisions." Jarmul H.D., "Effects of Decisions of Regional Human Rights Tribunals on National Courts," in Franck T.M., Fox G.H. (eds.), *International law decisions in national courts*, Brill-Nijhoff, Leiden, 1996, 247 ff.

the margin of discretion left to the State in deciding the measures to be taken has the effect of undermining the authority of the European organs. Indeed, the latter are not in a position to force the country into accepting what is appropriate in order to fulfil the Court's judgments. They can only seek to convince them to adopt the measures which they think are suitable. Therefore, the Committee acts only on the ground of political persuasion and not on the ground of juridical obligations, thus allowing domestic authorities to take their time or water down the remedies suggested.

This is particularly true for the execution of the Court's judgments that implicitly require structural adjustments. Since the European Court's jurisprudence has the characteristic of being focused on a specific case – that is to say focused on the peculiarities and the circumstances of the situation – the principal task of the Court is to ensure the protection of the specific fundamental right claimed by the applicant. In short, the Strasbourg Court does not have the judicial obligation to censure the systematic holes in the entire domestic judicial system, despite the latter's effects on the general level of human rights protection. Even when the Court has to establish a justified restriction of human rights claimed in the appeal, it adopts a self-restrained approach, with an awareness that the domestic authorities are in a better position to evaluate the correct balance between the rights, taking into account the specific context. As is well known, from a subsidiarity perspective, the Court has developed the so-called "margin of appreciation doctrine," specifically in order to ensure that it takes on only those cases in which the core meaning of a fundamental right is at stake. In this respect, the Court has more and more often declared a violation of Art. 18 of the Convention, according to which "the restrictions permitted under [the] Convention to the said rights and freedoms shall not be applied for any purpose other than those for which they have been prescribed."[54] Otherwise, the European Court leaves to national institutions the possibility to consider on the one hand the legitimate aim of the restriction; and on the other hand, the presence of a particular social pressure, which prevents a completely full protection of human rights under scrutiny.[55]

54 See Tan F., *The Dawn of Article 18 ECHR: Safeguard Against European Rule of Law Backsliding?*, in Goettingen Journal of International Law, 9, 1, 2018, 109–142; Cali B., *Coping with Crisis: Whither the Variable Geometry in the Jurisprudence of the European Court of Human Rights*, in Wisconsin International Law Journal, 35, 2, 2018, 237–276.

55 Mac Donald R.St., "The Margin of Appreciation in the European System for the Protection of Human Rights," in Mac Donald R.St. et al. (eds.), *The European System for the Protection of Human Rights*, Dordrecht/Boston, MA/London, Kluwer Law International, 1993, 83–124; Yourow H.C., *The margin of appreciation doctrine in the dynamics of European Human Rights Jurisprudence*, Martinus Nijhoff, The Hague/Boston, MA/London, 1996; Hutchinson M.R., *The Margin of Appreciation Doctrine in the European Court of Human Rights*, in International & Comparative Law Quarterly, 48, 3, 1999, 638–650; Sweeney J.A, *Margins of Appreciation: Cultural Relativity and the European Court of Human Rights in the Post-Cold War Era*, in ICLQ, 54, 2, 2005, 459–474; Brems E., "The margin of appreciation doctrine of the European Court of Human Rights, accommodating diversity within Europe," in Forsythe D.P. and McMahon, P.C. (eds.), *Human Rights and Diver-*

For all the reasons just mentioned, it is clear that the European Court does not have the typical power of a Constitutional Court, even though some scholars have defined it as a "quasi" Constitutional Court.[56] In short, the entire system is a hybrid supranational organisation, which simply does not have sufficient juridical strength.

Hence, how can we get through this impasse? Are there other judicial ways to move forward if the political path proves to be ineffective?

We might offer two suggestions. One concerns the relationship between the internal organs of the Council of Europe in charge of the fulfilment of the ECHR. The other involves the Council of Europe's organs together with the domestic judiciary.

Regarding the first proposal, much has been done so far,[57] firstly in giving the possibility of opening infringement proceedings *ex* Art. 46 ECHR, despite the fact that its first application did not meet the expectations of the jurists in terms of solving the endemic and systematic violation of basic human rights.[58] Nevertheless, we will see what happens in the long term, when the same European Court finally finds a way to enforce this new procedural technique.

---

sity: Area Studies Revisited, Lincoln, Nebraska, 2003; Spielmann D., *Allowing the Right Margin: The European Court of Human Rights and The National Margin of Appreciation Doctrine: Waiver or Subsidiarity of European Review? (2011–2012)*, in Cambridge Yearbook of European Legal Studies, 14, 2012, 381–418; Dzehtsiarow K., *European Consensus and the Legitimacy of the European Court of Human Rights*, Cambridge University Press, Cambridge, 2015.

56 Arai-Takahashi Y., *The Margin of Appreciation Doctrine and the Principle of Proportionality in the Jurisprudence of the ECHR*, Cambridge University Press, Cambridge, 2002; Bates E., *The Evolution of the European Convention on Human Rights: From Its Inception to the Creation of a Permanent Court of Human Rights*, Oxford University Press, Oxford, 2010, at 25, 399–400, 441–443, 461–467, 479, 497–498; Hennette-Vauchez S., "Constitutional v. International? When unified reformatory rationales mismatch the plural paths of legitimacy of ECHR law," in Christoffersen J., Rask Madsen M. (eds.), *The European Court of Human Rights Between Law and Politics*, Oxford University Press, Oxford, 2011, 144 ss., at 150–151; Kosař D., *Policing Separation of Powers: A New Role for the European Court of Human Rights?*, in European Constitutional Law Review, 8, 2012, 33–62, at 60–61; Grabenwarter C., *The European Convention on Human Rights: Inherent Constitutional Tendencies and the Role of the European Court of Human Rights*, in ELTE Law Journal, 1, 2014, 101–116; Van der Sloot, B., *The Quality of Law: How the European Court of Human Rights Gradually Became European Constitutional Court for Privacy Cases*, in Journal of Intellectual Property, Information Technology and Electronic Commerce Law, 11, 2, 2020, 160–185.

57 Sicilianos, L., *The Involvement of the European Court of Human Rights in the Implementation of its Judgments: Recent Developments under Article 46 ECHR*, in Netherlands Quarterly of Human Rights, 32, 3, 2014, 235–262; Leach P. et al., *Responding to systemic human rights violations: an analysis of "pilot judgments" of the European Court of Human Rights and their impact at national level*, Cambridge University Press, Cambridge, 2010. More in general, Donald A. and Speck A., *The European Court of Human Rights' Remedial Practice and its Impact on the Execution of Judgments*, in Human Rights Law Review, 19, 2019, 83–117.

58 De Londras F., Dzehtsiarou K., *Mission Impossible: Addressing Non-Execution through Infringement Proceedings in the European Court of Human Rights*, in International and Comparative Law Quarterly, 66, 2, 2017, 467–490.

In any case, the proposal put forward by those who think that much stronger involvement by the Parliamentary Assembly is necessary in order to help the Court and the Committee to supervise Strasbourg judgments deserves attention.[59] This is because the Assembly is particularly well placed to facilitate the implementation of the Court's judgments.[60]

Gradually the Assembly has become more closely involved in this task, at first thanks to the work of the Assembly's Committee on Legal Affairs and Human Rights,[61] created in 1993, whose role is to report to the Assembly "when problems arise [...] on the compliance with judgments by the ECtHR."[62] Later, thanks to the adoption of Resolution 1226 (2000), by virtue of which the Assembly undertook to play a larger role itself in supervising judgments of the Court, for example, by allowing rapporteurs to visit countries with major structural problems and where the delays in the execution of judgments are unacceptable. The aim is to discuss the reasons for the failure to execute the judgments with members of national parliaments and government representatives, hoping to find the right solution together. Consequently, over the years, some States have decided to open dedicated national legislative offices that oversee the implementation of the Strasbourg Court judgments.[63]

Briefly, despite the continuing existence of a number of major structural deficiencies within the State parties, such as with Azerbaijan, the growing role of the Assembly in proposing solutions can be strategic in terms of the fulfilment of the Court judgments, especially in light of its privileged relationship with national parliamentary representatives. In this respect, the Assembly shall find a way to communicate with the legislative branch of Azerbaijan.

Regarding the second proposal, aimed at reinforcing collaboration with the domestic judiciary, this can be achieved if the CoE's organs at least find a way to have a dialogue with the Supreme Court and the Constitutional Court.[64] As stated by the current President of the European Court, "the overarching theme of the decade-long Convention reform process has been that of shared responsibility" which can be realistic with "strong, independent and impartial domestic

59 See Drzemczewski A., *The Parliamentary Assembly's Involvement in the Supervision of the Judgments of the Strasbourg Court*, in Netherlands Quarterly of Human Rights, 28, 2, 2010, 164–178.

60 See Leach, P., *The effectiveness of the Committee of Ministers in supervising the enforcement of judgments of the European Court of Human Rights*, in Public Law, 3, 2006,443–456; Id., *Opinion. On Reform of the European Court of Human Rights*, in European Human Rights Law Review, 6, 2009, 725–736.

61 See http://assembly.coe.int/Mainf.asp?link=/Committee/JUR/roleE.htm.

62 Order No. 485 (1993) on the general policy of the Council of Europe, para. 2.

63 For an overview see Drzemczewski A., *The Parliamentary Assembly's Involvement in the Supervision of the Judgments*, cited above, 175–176.

64 The importance of engaging in a strong dialogue between the CoE's and State's actor is underlined by Abdelgawad E., *Dialogue and the Implementation of the European Court of Human Rights' Judgments*, in Netherlands Quarterly of Human Rights, 34, 4, 2016, 340–363.

courts, which function within a national system that is governed by the rule of law."[65]

For Azerbaijan, this means that the Constitutional Court, in evaluating electoral laws, and laws more generally which are inconsistent with the ECHR and its jurisprudence, has the duty to declare their unconstitutionality, in accordance with what that same Constitution provides. This is especially the case where there are no problems of incompatibility between the Constitution disposals and the European Convention, such as in the cases law about the right to stand for elections.

There is much to do so, at either the political or juridical level, in a State where the state building process is far from complete. For the European Court this is a bet still to be won.

Bibliography

ABDELGAWAD E., *Dialogue and the Implementation of the European Court of Human Rights' Judgments*, in Netherlands Quarterly of Human Rights, 34, 4, 2016, 340–363.

ABDULLAHZADE C., *The Status of International Treaties in the Legal System of Azerbaijan*, in Review of Central and East European Law, 32, 2, 2007, 233–256.

ARAI-TAKAHASHI Y., *The Margin of Appreciation Doctrine and the Principle of Proportionality in the Jurisprudence of the ECHR*, Cambridge University Press, Cambridge, 2002.

BALAK A, KOCH A., BRUCH N., *The Legitimacy of Human Rights Courts: A Grounded Interpretivist Analysis of the European Court of Human Rights*, in Human Rights Quarterly, 35, 2013, 955–984.

BATES E., *The Evolution of the European Convention on Human Rights: From Its Inception to the Creation of a Permanent Court of Human Rights*, Oxford University Press, Oxford, 2010.

BREMS E., "The Margin of Appreciation Doctrine of the European Court of Human Rights, Accommodating Diversity within Europe", in FORSYTHE D.P., MCMAHON, P.C. (eds.), *Human Rights and Diversity: Area Studies Revisited*, University of Nebraska Press, Lincoln, Nebraska, 2003.

BUYSE A., *First Infringement Proceedings Judgment of the European Court: Ilgar Mammadov v Azerbaijan*, in ECHR Blog, 31 May 2019.

CALI B., *Coping with Crisis: Whither the Variable Geometry in the Jurisprudence of the European Court of Human Rights*, in Wisconsin International Law Journal, 35, 2, 2018, 237–276.

CERNIC J., *Glass Half Empty Execution of Judgments of the European Court of Human Rights in Central and Eastern Europe*, in Baltic Yearbook of International Law, 15, 2015, 285–302.

65 See the discourse of the present Chairman of the Strasbourg Court Róbert Spanó, on the occasion of the 70th anniversary of the European Court.

De Londras F., Dzehtsiarou K., *Mission Impossible: Addressing Non-Execution through Infringement Proceedings in the European Court of Human Rights*, in International and Comparative Law Quarterly, 66, 2, 2017, 467–490.

Donald A., Speck A., *The European Court of Human Rights' Remedial Practice and its Impact on the Execution of Judgments*, in Human Rights Law Review, 19, 2019, 83–117.

Drzemczewski A., *The Parliamentary Assembly's Involvement in the Supervision of the Judgments of the Strasbourg Court*, in Netherlands Quarterly of Human Rights, 28, 2, 2010, 164–178.

Dzehtsiarow K., *European Consensus and the Legitimacy of the European Court of Human Rights*, Cambridge University Press, Cambridge, 2015.

Dzehtsiarou K., *How Many Judgments Does One Need to Enforce a Judgment? The First Ever Infringement Proceedings at the European Court of Human Rights*, in Strasbourg Observer Blog, 4 June 2019.

Grabenwarter C., *The European Convention on Human Rights: Inherent Constitutional Tendencies and the Role of the European Court of Human Rights*, in ELTE Law Journal, 1, 2014, 101–116.

Grodeland A.B., *Public and Elite Perceptions of Supranational Courts: The European Perspective*, in Review of Central and East European Law, 39, 1, 2014, 41–94.

Hajiyev K., "The Directions of Influence of the Case Law of the European Court of Human Rights in Azerbaijan", in Motoc I., Ziemele I. (eds.), *The Impact of the ECHR on Democratic Change in Central and Eastern Europe. Judicial Perspectives*, Cambridge University Press, Cambridge, 2016, 57–79.

Hennette-Vauchez S., "Constitutional v. International? When Unified Reformatory Rationales Mismatch the Plural Paths of Legitimacy of ECHR Law", in Christoffersen J., Rask Madsen M. (eds.), *The European Court of Human Rights Between Law and Politics*, Oxford University Press, Oxford, 2011.

Herron E.S., *Measuring Dissent in Electoral Authoritarian Societies Lessons From Azerbaijans 2008 Presidential Election and 2009 Referendum*, in Comparative Political Studies, 44, 11, 2011, 1557–1583.

Hutchinson M.R., *The Margin of Appreciation Doctrine in the European Court of Human Rights*, in International & Comparative Law Quarterly, 48, 3, 1999, 638–650.

Jarmul H.D., "Effects of Decisions of Regional Human Rights Tribunals on National Courts", in Franck T.M., Fox G.H. (eds.), *International Law Decisions in National Courts*, Brill-Nijhoff, Leiden, 1996.

Kosař D., *Policing Separation of Powers: A New Role for the European Court of Human Rights?*, in European Constitutional Law Review, 8, 2012, 33–62.

Kosař D., Lixinski L., *Domestic Judicial Design by International Human Rights Court*, in American Journal of International Law, 109, 4, 2015, 713–760.

Leach P., *The Effectiveness of the Committee of Ministers in Supervising the Enforcement of Judgments of the European Court of Human Rights*, in Public Law, 3, 2006,443–456.

Leach P., *Opinion. On Reform of the European Court of Human Rights*, in European Human Rights Law Review, 6, 2009, 725–736.

Leach P. et al., *Responding to Systemic Human Rights Violations: An Analysis of 'Pilot Judgments' of the European Court of Human Rights and Their Impact at National Level*, Cambridge University Press, Cambridge, 2010.

Mac Donald R.St., "The Margin of Appreciation in the European System for the Protection of Human Rights", in Mac Donald R.St. et al. (eds), *The European*

System for the Protection of Human Rights, Kluwer Law International, Dordrecht/Boston, MA/London, 1993, 83–124.

MARTIN C.H., *Comparative Human Rights Jurisprudence in Azerbaijan: Theory, Practice and Prospects*, in Journal of Transnational Law & Policy, 14, 2, 2005, 215–252.

REMEZAITE R., *The Impact of the European Court of Human Rights on Democratisation in Azerbaijan: Securing Freedom of the Press*, in Nordic Journal of Human Rights, 31, 4, 2013, 532–551.

SICILIANOS L., *The Involvement of the European Court of Human Rights in the Implementation of Its Judgments: Recent Developments under Article 46 ECHR*, in Netherlands Quarterly of Human Rights, 32, 3, 2014, 235–262.

SPIELMANN D., *Allowing the Right Margin: The European Court of Human Rights and The National Margin of Appreciation Doctrine: Waiver or Subsidiarity of European Review? (2011–2012)*, in Cambridge Yearbook of European Legal Studies, 14, 2012, 381–418.

SWEENEY J.A, *Margins of Appreciation: Cultural Relativity and the European Court of Human Rights in the Post-Cold War Era*, in ICLQ, 54, 2, 2005, 459–474.

SWEENEY J.A., *Restorative Justice and Transitional Justice at the ECHR*, in International Criminal Law Review, 12, 2012, 313–337.

TAN F., *The Dawn of Article 18 ECHR: Safeguard Against European Rule of Law Backsliding?*, in Goettingen Journal of International Law, 9, 1, 2018, 109–142.

TANZARELLA P., *Mammadov c. Azerbaijan: la prima procedura d'infrazione. Un'occasione mancata?*, in Quaderni costituzionali, 3, 2019, 713–715.

TERZYAN A., *Sustaining Power Through External Threats: The Power of Enemy Images in Russia and Azerbaijan*, in Journal of Liberty and International Affairs, 6, 2, 2020, 45–56.

YOUROW H.C., *The Margin of Appreciation Doctrine in the Dynamics of European Human Rights Jurisprudence*, Martinus Nijhoff, The Hague/Boston, MA/London, 1996.

VAN DER SLOOT B., *The Quality of Law: How the European Court of Human Rights Gradually Became European Constitutional Court for Privacy Cases*, in Journal of Intellectual Property, Information Technology and Electronic Commerce Law, 11, 2, 2020, 160–185.

2 Crackdown on dissent

The Court of Strasbourg and the right to vote in Bulgaria

Paolo Zicchittu

Setting the framework: Post-Communism, human rights standards, and the constitution

Over the last three decades, Post-Communist countries in Central and Eastern Europe have struggled to achieve democracy and social stability by transforming their economies, political systems, and statehood. Their main aspiration has been to make these progressions irreversible through the adoption of the European Convention of Human Rights (ECHR) and the accession to the EU.[1] From the Bulgarian perspective, this picture appears even more puzzling in light of the great efforts made to fulfil the requirements of transition towards fundamental freedoms.[2] The major factor leading to a stable liberal society was the adoption of the 1991 Constitution. The new Bulgarian Fundamental Law ensured institutional stability and the integrity of electoral processes, serving as a pillar for any further development in terms of liberal democracy and human rights safeguards.[3]

To this end, the Constitution proclaims its supremacy and contains an extensive chapter devoted to fundamental freedoms being directly applicable, irrevocable, and enforceable before national Courts. The standards of constitutional provisions on human rights are sufficiently high. The Fundamental Law encompasses most individual, civil, political, social, economic, and cultural rights, and it

1 See Dryzek J., Holmes L., *Post-Communist Democratization*, Cambridge University Press, Cambridge, 2001, 21–24; Linz J., Stepan A., *Problems of Democratic Transition and Consolidation: Southern Europe, South America and Post-Communist Europe*, JHUP, Baltimore and London, 1996, 342–345; and *passim* Mayhew A., *Recreating Europe: The European Union's Policy Towards Central and Eastern Europe*, Cambridge University Press, Cambridge, 1999.

2 Kramer H., *The European Community's Response to the "New Eastern Europe,"* in Journal of Common Market Studies, 31, 1993, 213–244.; Dimitrova A., Dragneva R., *Bulgaria's Road to the European Union: Progress, Problems and Perspectives*, in Perspectives on European Politics and Society, 2, 2006, 79–104; Elster J., Offe C., Preuss U., *Institutional Design in Post-Communist Societies*, Cambridge University Press, Cambridge, 1998, 46–53.

3 Cf. Kornezov A., "Bulgaria," in Laffranque J. (ed.), *The Protection of Fundamental Rights Post-Lisbon*, Tallinn, 2012, 259–283.; Ganev V., *Bulgaria's Symphony of Hope*, in Journal of Democracy, 8, 1997, 125–140; Schwartz H., *The Struggle for Constitutional Justice in Post-Communist Europe*, London, 2000, 57–63.

DOI: 10.4324/9781003229247-4

is usually interpreted to implicitly include all classic general principles of modern legal orders, such as the rule of law, non-retroactivity, proportionality, protection of legitimate expectations, and the due process clause.[4] According to Art. 57, para. 1, of the Bulgarian Constitution, human rights are irrevocable. The rigidity of this declaration is, however, more political than legal because the Fundamental Law does not contain any eternity clause or unamendable provisions. Therefore, the article at issue can be modified or even abolished by the Grand National Assembly, albeit this would be very unlikely from both a political and practical point of view.[5]

The constitutional norms on human rights were inspired and complemented by international standards. The most important sources are the ECHR, the International Covenant on Civil and Political Rights, the Universal Declaration of Human Rights, and the International Covenant on Social, Economic and Cultural Rights.[6] Hence, the Council of Europe and the Court of Strasbourg could be considered as strategic international actors entitled to influence human rights definitions in Bulgaria and to develop extensive criteria, not only when the Constitution was drafted, but also during its implementation over the years.[7]

Actually, the Fundamental Law makes no explicit reference to the ECHR and expressly proclaims the supremacy as well as the direct effect of the Constitution over any supranational provision.[8] Nonetheless, Art. 5, para. 4, stipulates that

> international Treaties, which have been ratified in accordance with the constitutional procedure, promulgated and having come into force with respect to the Republic of Bulgaria, shall be part of the legislation of the State. They shall have primacy over any conflicting provision of the domestic legislation.

4 Tanchev E., Belov M., *Constitutional Gradualism: Adapting to EU Membership and Improving the Judiciary in the Bulgarian Constitution*, in European Public Law, 14, 2008, 3–19. More generally, see Ludwikowski R., *Fundamental Constitutional Rights in the New Constitutions of Central and Eastern Europe*, in Cardozo Journal of International and Comparative Law, 73, 1995, 73–162.

5 Tanchev E., *Introduction to Constitutional Law*, Sofia, 2003.

6 See Hughes J., Sasse G., Gordon C., *Conditionality and Compliance in the EU's Eastward Enlargement: Regional Policy and the Reform of Sub-National Government*, in Journal of Common Market Studies, 42, 2004, 523–551; Vachudova M., *Europe Undivided: Democracy, Leverage and Integration after Communism*, Oxford, 2005, 87–92.

7 In this respect, Epstein R., Sedelmeier U., *Beyond Conditionality: International Institutions in Post-Communist Europe after Enlargement*, in Journal of European Public Policy, 15, 2008, 795–805; Börzel T.A., *Member State Responses to Europeanization*, in Journal of Common Market Studies, 40, 2002, 194–214; Iancu D., *Local Reforms by Political Conditionality: Trials and Errors in Central and Eastern Europe*, in Theoretical and Applied Economics, 24, 2019, 73–86.

8 Art. 5, paras. 1 and 2, of the Bulgarian Constitution states that: "The Constitution shall be the supreme law, and no other law shall contravene it. The provisions of the Constitution shall apply directly." Cf. in addition Belov M., *Constitutional Law in Bulgaria*, Amsterdam, 2019, 32–37.

As a result, the international agreements – including the ECHR – ratified, published, and entered into force occupy a hierarchical position immediately below the Constitution and the interpretative decisions of the domestic Constitutional Court.[9] This is due to the fact that the Bulgarian system adopts a monist regime for the introduction of international treaties into its national legal order. The ratification act is a formal one: it does not have normative content, as it is simply a tool to invest an international treaty with internal legal validity.[10]

The ECHR thus forms part and parcel of domestic law, is directly applicable and prevails over contravening sub-constitutional provisions of internal statutes. The idea of the Constituent was for the Fundamental Law as the "core of national sovereignty" to overcome international treaties. Yet, no institutions of the constituted power – that is to say, neither the Parliament nor the Government, the judiciary, nor the President – can violate Bulgaria's international obligations, since any act in this sense would automatically be invalid due to the primacy of international law. Art. 149 adds that

> the Constitutional Court rules on requests for declaring the unconstitutionality of a statute or the incompatibility of a statute with the generally recognised principles of the international law or with an international agreement to which Bulgaria is a contracting party.

Therefore, questions regarding the application of the ECHR in a judicial or administrative process may only arise when there are doubts concerning its constitutionality.[11] The Fundamental Law in fact provides for a preliminary control on the international treaties legitimacy before their ratification. This obligation has been extensively interpreted as attributing to the Constitutional Court also a right of judicial review over the conformity of the European Court of Human Rights (ECtHR) decisions with the Bulgarian Constitution.[12] Nevertheless, this control is not compulsory because it can be performed only following an initiative by one-fifth of the MPs, the President of the Republic, the Council of Ministers, the State Prosecutor General, the Supreme Court of Cassation, or the Supreme Administrative Court.[13]

9 See Tanchev E., "The Primacy or Supremacy of International and EU Law in the Context of Contemporary Constitutional Pluralism," in Birmontiene T. (ed.), *Modern Tendencies of Constitutional Justice: The Relation between National and International Law*, Vilnius, 2014, 69–75.

10 *Passim* Tashev R., *General Theory of Law*, Sofia, 2004.

11 Tanchev E., Belov M., "The Bulgarian Constitutional Order. Supranational Constitutionalism and European Governance," in Albi A., Bardutzki S. (eds.), *National Constitutions in European and Global Governance: Democracy, Rights, the Rule of Law*, The Hague, 2019, 1132 ff.

12 Constitutional Court of Bulgaria, Decision no. 9 of 1999.

13 See, e.g., Dimitrov H., *The Bulgarian Constitutional Court and Its Interpretive Jurisdiction*, in Columbia Journal of Transnational Justice, 38, 1999, 459–505; Schwartz H., "The New East European Constitutional Courts," in Dick-Howard A. (ed.), *Constitution-Making in Eastern Europe*, Baltimore, 1993, 163–207.

Since the entry into force of the ECHR in Bulgaria on 7 May 1992, the total number of cases transmitted for supervision amounts to 721; 545 cases have been successfully closed following the reaching of a final resolution. In 2019, the Court of Strasbourg dealt with 766 applications, 746 of which were declared inadmissible or struck out. The ECtHR delivered 19 judgments, concerning 20 applications, and in 13 of them it found at least 1 violation of the Convention.[14] The most relevant infringements concern prohibition of torture and inhuman or degrading treatment having regard to the excessive delays in criminal proceedings and the lack of investigation into certain aspects of the offences.[15] The Committee of Ministers observed that, in over 45 judgments against Bulgaria, it had already found the authorities failed to comply with their obligation to carry out an effective investigation, and it deemed that these recurrent shortcomings disclosed the existence of a systemic problem. Approximately 40 applications on detention conditions in Bulgaria are currently pending. They highlight another structural problem within the national prison system and justified a pilot-judgment procedure because of the serious and persistent nature of the difficulties identified.[16]

In general terms, however, thanks to its membership in the Convention's legal system, Bulgaria has made some progress in strengthening democracy and human rights protection. Since 1993, elections have been regular, free, and fair, while the rule of law and the separation of powers have been maintained with the significant contribution of the Constitutional Court. The latter has not only been able to guarantee the principles enshrined in the Fundamental Law but has also prevented direct attacks on the independence of the judiciary.[17] Similarly, Bulgaria has represented a diplomatic alternative to the ethnic unrest and violent conflict elsewhere in the Balkans, by promoting the peaceful resolution of minority rights post-1989. No significant ethnic conflicts occurred immediately upon the fall of Communism, and national problems were mainly resolved by debating in the political arena. This was greatly facilitated by the fact that the Turkish population had representation in Parliament through the "Movement of Rights and Freedoms" (DPS), which has gathered about 8% of the votes in most elections to date.[18]

14 European Court of Human Rights Annual Report 2019.

15 *Ibidem*.

16 *Ibidem*.

17 See Melone A.P., *Creating Parliamentary Government: The Transition to Democracy in Bulgaria*, Columbus, 1998, 74–77; Bozhilova D., *Measuring Successes and Failure of EU-Europeanization in the Eastern Enlargement: Judicial Reform in Bulgaria*, in European Journal of Law Reform, 11, 2007, 285–318; Bell J.D., "Democratization and Political Participation in "Post-Communist" Bulgaria," in Dawisha K., Parrott B. (eds.), *Politics, Power and the Struggle for Democracy in South-East Europe*, Cambridge University Press, Cambridge, 1997, 367–375.

18 Bechev D., *From Policy-Takers to Policy-Makers? Observations on Bulgarian and Romanian Foreign Policy Before and After EU Accession*, in Perspectives on European Politics and Society, 10, 2009, 210–224.; Nikova E., "Bulgaria in the Balkans," in Bell J.D. (ed.), *Bulgaria*

The democratic balance reached by Bulgaria during the last 20 years remains, however, slow and fragile, with particular regard to the rights of persons placed in institutions, the human rights of migrants, and media freedom.[19] In fact, corruption and the gradual ascent of populist claims risk to overshadow the advancements made so far.[20] Despite achieving both internal stability and reliable external relations with its neighbours, Bulgaria is still seen by Western Countries as a State unable to receive credit for its transition and capacity to permanently implement the rule of law in terms of strict adherence to a set of liberal-democratic canons at every level of society by promoting a culture of law-abiding citizenship.[21] With a number of weak spots, Bulgaria falls into the bottom ranks as regards the quality of its democracy. Reports by Transparency International under the "Corruption Perceptions Index" show that Bulgaria is the EU's most corrupt Member State. In 2018, the European Commission found that national Government had done almost nothing to stem the tide of corruption and organised crime, in addition to the untrustworthy functioning public institutions the Country suffers from.[22] Anti-corruption laws are ignored, and people frequently face situations of bribery, rely on basic services being undermined by funds misappropriation, and face indifference when seeking redress from authorities.[23]

Another serious criticism relates to the insufficient reform of the judiciary. The Government not only interferes with the Courts' independence, by attempting to

in Transition: Politics, Economics, Society and Culture after Communism, Boulder, 1998, 294 ff.

19 See Börzel T.A., Risse T., *When Europe Hits Home: Europeanization and Domestic Change*, in European Integration Online Papers, 4, 2000, 1 ff.; Iancu D., *Local Reforms by Political Conditionality*, cited above; Zankina E., *Populism, Voters and Cleavages in Bulgarian Politics*, in Czech Journal of Political Science, 24, 2017, 56–71.

20 Cf. Krasteva A., "The Post-Communist Rise of National Populism: Bulgarian Paradoxes," in Lazaridis G., Campani G., Benveniste A. (eds.), *The Rise of the Far Right in Europe*, London, 2016, 161–200; Chalova B., De Waele J.M., *Bulgaria: A Fertile Ground for Populism?*, in Slovak Journal of Political Sciences, 11, 2011, 25–54; Raycheva L., Peicheva D., *Populism in Bulgaria Between Politicization of Media and Mediatization of Politics*, in Mediatization Studies, 1, 2017, 69–80.

21 Pavlovska-Hilaiel S., *The EU's Losing Battle against Corruption in Bulgaria*, in Hague Journal on the Rule of Law, 7, 2015, 199–217; Endre S., "The bad, the worse, and the worst: guesstimating the level of corruption," in Kotkin S., Sajo A.(eds.), *Political Corruption in Transition: A Sceptic's Handbook*, Budapest, 2002, 91–113.

22 Cf. *ex plurimis*, Wolf S., *Assessing Eastern Europe's Anti-Corruption Performance: Views from the Council of Europe, OECD and Transparency International*, in Global Crime, 11, 2010, 99 ff.; Hristova-Kurzydlowski D., *Programming EU Funds in Bulgaria: Challenges, Opportunities and the Role of Civil Society*, in Studies of Transition States and Societies, 5, 2013, 22–40.

23 Smilov D., *Anticorruption Agencies: Expressive, Constructivist and Strategic Uses*, in Crime, Law and Social Change, 53, 2009, 67–77; Stoyanov A., *Administrative and Political Corruption in Bulgaria: Status and Dynamics (1998-2006)*, in Romanian Journal of Political Science, 37, 2008, 6–23; Tanasoiu C., Racovita M., *Post-Accession (Anti-)Corruption Record in Romania and Bulgaria*, in L'Europe en Formation, 96, 2012, 243–263.

influence their composition, but also restricts their budget and use of premises.[24] Most changes were limited to judges appointments and touched upon the institutional rearrangement required by the Constitution. Furthermore, the adoption of procedural laws underpinning the comprehensive functioning of judicial power was postponed until 2014, with problems in terms of administration, recruitment, and material support.[25] Likewise, Bulgaria has made insufficient strides in administrative reform. The causes for delay in adopting a basic legal structure for a professional and depoliticised administration lie in political *elites* and external advisers.[26] Several Bulgarian Governments have replaced considerable numbers of top- and mid-level officials. This was often the result of politically motivated decisions taken in the absence of clear dismissal criteria. On the other hand, external advice on reform did not focus on the role of administration until 2005. The last few years marked a new commitment to introducing the principles of professionalism and independence with the adoption of the "Administration Act," the "Local Self-Rule Act," and the "Civil Service Act." Explicit standards for discharging civil servants' functions were set up, underpinned by a system of disciplinary measures, and oversight by the "State Administrative Commission."[27]

In this scenario, the Bulgarian party system remains competitive and quite volatile, featuring both long-term players and cycles in which new parties emerge while others decline. There were multiple peaceful transfers of power between rival political groups since the end of the Communist regime in 1990.[28] Bulgarian

24 See Nozharov S., *Economic Growth and the Reform of the Judicial System of Bulgaria in the Period 2000–2015*, in IDEAS Working Paper Series from Federal Reserve Bank of St Louis, 96, 2016, 1–12; Frison-Roche F., Sodev S., *The Issues Involved in the Reform of the Bulgarian Judicial System*, in International Review of Administrative Sciences, 86, 2005, 593–606; Noutcheva G., Bechev D., *The Successful Laggards: Bulgaria and Romania on the Road to EU Membership*, in East European Politics and Societies, 22, 2008, 114–144.

25 Cf. Roudik P., *Bulgaria: Constitutional Amendment Provides for Judicial Reform*, Sofia, 2015. Similarly, Anastasakis O., Bechev D., *EU Conditionality in South-East Europe: Bringing Commitment to the Process*, in European Balkan Observer, 1, 2003, 4–20; Racovita M., *Europeanization and Effective Democracy in Romania and Bulgaria*, in Romanian Journal of Political Science, 11, 2011, 28–50.

26 Zankina E., *Public Administration Reform in Bulgaria: Top-Down and Externally Driven Approach*, in Central European Public Administration Review, 18, 2020, 90–120; Katsamunska P., *Good Governance and Reform of Public Administration in Bulgaria*, in Economic Alternatives, 1, 2010, 51–60; Baker R., Democracy versus Bureaucracy: Transforming the Nature of the Civil Service in Bulgaria, in Id. (ed.), *Comparative Public Management*, Westport, 1994, 53–65.

27 See *ex multis* Ellison B., *Public Administration Reform in Eastern Europe: A Research. Note and a Look at Bulgaria*, in Administration and Society, 39, 2007, 221–232; Borissova O., "Public Administration Reform in Bulgaria," in von Breska E., Brusis M. (eds.), *Central and Eastern Europe on the Way Into the EU: Reforms of the Regional Administration in Bulgaria, the Czech Republic, Estonia, Hungary, Poland and Slovakia*, Munich, 1999, 1–13; Zankina E., "Public Administration Characteristics and Performance in EU28: Bulgaria," in Palaric E., Thijs N., Hammerschmid G. (eds.), *A Comparative Overview of Public Administration Characteristics and Performance in EU28*, 2018, 66–94.

28 From this of point of view, Kanev D., Hristova-Valtcheva K., "Bulgaria," in Viola D. (ed.), *Routledge Handbook of European Elections*, London-New York, 2016, 633–653; Prot-

citizens are generally free to make independent political choices, even if economic oligarchs dominate the major parties and influence their platforms. This problem is exacerbated by a lack of transparency in campaign finance law and by the absence of limits for private donations to political organisations.[29] Especially in smaller municipalities, voters' control marginalises ethnical and social minority groups, since the law dictates that electoral campaigns must be conducted in the national language, which hinders outreach efforts to non-Bulgarian speaking communities. Along with the Turkish minority, the most disadvantaged are the Roma, who suffer socio-political exclusion, poverty, and acts of police brutality.[30]

The right to vote in Bulgaria before the European Court of Human Rights

In this context, the ECtHR dealt only with three cases concerning the protection of electoral rights in Bulgaria on the basis of Art. 3, Protocol 1, of the Convention: *Ekoglasnost*,[31] *Riza*,[32] and *Kulinski and Sabev*.[33]

The case of *Ekoglasnost v. Bulgaria* regards the inability of a party to submit two documents required by the electoral law, in order to present candidates.[34] Ekoglasnost is an independent political movement established in 1989 focusing its activities on major environmental and social issues.[35] The party rapidly gained public support to become the leading opposition group to the Communist regime. Between 1990 and 2001, it presented candidates in all parliamentary

---

SYK O., SACHARIEW K., *Recruitment and Representation of Ethnic Minorities under Proportional Representation: Evidence from Bulgaria*, in East European Politics and Societies, 26, 2010, 1–26; SWIANIEWICZ P., *The Political Budget Cycle in Earmarked Taxes for Local Public Services: A Comparison of Poland and Bulgaria*, in Journal of Comparative Policy Analysis: Research and Practice, 21, 2019, 463–480.

29 Cf. *passim* ANDREEV S., *Types of Populist Parties and the Future of Democracy in Bulgaria*, in Political Studies, 4, 2007, 3–30; KANEV D., *The 2014 Elections in Bulgaria: Political Instability Without End*, in Journal for Labour and Social Affairs in Eastern Europe. Engagement and Political Change: Walls Reconstructed? 17, 2014, 175–192; MAVRODIEVA I., *Manifestations of Populism in Post-Communist Democracy in Bulgaria*, in French Journal for Media Research, 14, 2020.

30 More generally, read BOGDANOV L. ANGELOV G., *Roma Integration in Bulgaria: Necessary Reforms and Economic Effects*, Sofia, 2007, 56–62; DOBREVA A., *Access to Electoral Rights in Bulgaria*, in EUDO Citizenship Observatory, 23, 2013, 4–15; VASSILEV R., *The Roma of Bulgaria: A Pariah Minority*, in The Global Review of Ethnopolitics, 3, 2004, 40–51.

31 ECtHR, *Ekoglasnost v. Bulgaria*, Application no. 30386/05, 6 November 2012.

32 ECtHR, *Riza and Others v. Bulgaria*, Applications nos. 48555/10 and 48377/10, 13 October 2015.

33 ECtHR, *Kulinski and Sabev v. Bulgaria*, Application no. 63849/09, 21 July 2016.

34 See, e.g., BAUMGARTL B., "Environmental Protest as a Vehicle for Transition: The Case of Ekoglasnost in Bulgaria," in VÁRI A., TAMÁS P. (eds), *Environment in Democratic Transition: Politics and Policy in Central and Eastern Europe*, New York, 157–175; GIATZIDIS E., *An Introduction to Post-communist Bulgaria: Political, Economic, and Social Transformation*. New York, 2002.

35 Cf. LUDZHEV D., *The Revolution in Bulgaria, 1989–1991*, Sofia, 2008.

elections and obtained a good number of seats in the National Assembly.[36] In 2005, Ekoglasnost requested to be registered as a participant in the forthcoming political elections. After examining the application, the Central Electoral Commission found that 3 documents were missing – namely the payment of an electoral deposit, a certificate from the Court of Audit showing the submission of the annual financial reports for the past 3 years, and the signatures of at least 5,000 voters supporting the participation in the elections – and gave the party 3 days to file them. After this deadline expired unsuccessfully, the CEC denied the registration.[37]

Ekoglasnost then appealed, arguing that the relevant provisions of the electoral law were simply unconstitutional. They contended, in particular, that the deposit was far too high, the requirement to submit their last 3 annual reports had been belatedly introduced in April 2005, and the presentation of a list of 5,000 signatures carried the risk of exposing the party's supporters to pressure from the governing political forces. The Administrative Court dismissed Ekoglasnost's appeal, finding that the disputed provisions were not declared incompatible with the Constitution: political parties have to satisfy the conditions laid down by the electoral law in order to run for parliamentary elections. On the grounds that one or more of the above conditions had not been fulfilled, ten parties were denied the right to participate in the voting on 25 June 2005.[38]

Relying on Art. 3, Protocol 1, Ekoglasnost appealed to the ECtHR, complaining that the three new conditions for the presentation of candidates introduced shortly before the poll had prevented it from taking part in the elections. The Court preliminarily reiterates that the subjective rights to vote and stand for election are implicit in Art. 3, in addition to the obligation for each Country to hold elections within the legislature. It also restates that member States have a broad margin of appreciation as to the application of these requirements.[39] In this respect, the judges observe that the three new conditions at issue had been provided by domestic law with reference to all parties wishing to take part in parliamentary elections. The purpose of such measures was to ensure the participation

36 Czekalski T., *Ekoglasnost and Eco-Transformation. Bulgarian Environmental Movement in the First Years of the Political Transformation*, in Balcanica Posnaniensia, 26, 2019, 232–245.

37 In this sense, O'Brien T., *A Long, Brown Shadow? The Impact of Non-democratic Legacies on the Environment in Portugal and Bulgaria*, in Perspectives on European Politics and Society, 10, 2009, 308–325; Spirova M., *Political Parties in Post-Communist Systems: Formation, Persistence and Change*, New York, 2007, 74–80 and Kalotay K., *FDI in Bulgaria and Romania in the Wake of EU Accession*, in Journal of East-West Business, 14, 2008, 5–40.

38 Among the scholars Kolarova R., Spirova M., *Bulgaria 2016*, in European Journal of Political Research, 56, 2017, 36–43; Krastanova R., *The Green Movement and the Green Parties in Bulgaria: Between System Integration and System Change*, in Friedrich Ebert Foundation Policy Papers, 27, 2012, 2–40; Spirova M., Sharenkova-Toshkova R., "Bulgaria since 1989," in Ramet S., Hassenstab C. (eds.), *Central and Southeast European Politics since 1989*, Cambridge University Press, Cambridge, 2019, 449–476.

39 ECtHR, *Ekoglasnost v. Bulgaria*, cited above, paras. 57–59. Cf. furthermore *Mathieu-Mohin and Clerfayt v. Belgium*, *Podkolzina v. Latvia*.

of political groups being sufficiently representative and complying with rules on the transparency of political financing. The conditions established for the elections had thus pursued a legitimate aim.[40]

The obligation for political parties to submit annual financial reports to the Court of Audit had existed since 2001. Nonetheless, until April 2005 the failure to comply with it had not made it impossible for parties to participate in the elections: they would simply have lost their grant from the State. The statutory obligation to obtain a certificate from the Court of Audit as to the validity of the annual accounts came into force in 2005. However, the draft of the new law on political parties providing for this measure had been tabled in Parliament in 2003 and the National Assembly had publicly debated it throughout 2004. Hence, the Court considered that the adoption of this measure had been foreseeable, and the Ekoglasnost leaders could have expected its introduction well before 2005, taking the necessary measures to ensure that the party's situation was validated by the domestic Court.[41] On the contrary, the judges of Strasbourg found that the bill providing for the electoral deposit and the 5,000 signatures had been tabled in Parliament only on 1 February 2005, and the related public discussions on these measures had taken place between 23 March and 7 April. Following those debates, the two new conditions had been considerably amended. The party leaders were consequently unaware of these further requirements until their final enactment by Parliament on 7 April 2005. As the elections had been scheduled on 25 June 2005, and political movements were obliged to present their candidates no later than 46 days before the election date, Ekoglasnost had barely 1 month to obtain the signatures and pay the deposit. The party did not manage to fulfil such prerequisites and was hence prevented from standing for election.[42]

In settling the dispute, the ECtHR recalls *ad adiuvandum* the "Code of Good Practice" of the Venice Commission, which strongly emphasises the importance of the electoral law stability, and submits that any changes in the fundamental elements of the electoral system made less than one year before an election would seem to be dictated by immediate political interests. In legal systems imposing specific conditions for participating in the elections, the introduction of new requirements shortly before the date of the vote could mean the automatic disqualification of coalitions enjoying significant popular support or opposition parties, therefore benefitting political formations currently in power. Such a practice is clearly incompatible with the democratic order and undermines citizens' trust in their Executive.[43] In the present case, the minimum one-year period advocated by the Venice Commission for introducing substantial amendments to the electoral law was not observed. The disputed revisions were enacted two months

40 *Ibidem*, paras. 62–64. See *ad adiuvandum Asensio Serqueda v. Spain*, *Soukhovetski v. Ukraine*, and *X and Others v. Austria*.

41 *Ibidem*, paras. 65–66.

42 *Ibidem*, para. 67.

43 *Ibidem*, paras. 68–69. Cf. also *Georgian Labour Party v. Georgia*, and *Tănase v. Moldova*.

before the election date and one month before the deadline for the presentation of parties' candidates. The Court accepts that, by introducing an election deposit and a requirement of 5,000 signatures, the Bulgarian legislature had been seeking to solve the problem raised by the numerous organisations that did not have real political legitimacy. But at the same time, the judges hold that a bill providing for these same restrictive measures could have been scheduled, debated, enacted, and published earlier. By introducing at such a late stage the election deposit and the requirement of 5,000 signatures, Bulgarian authorities failed to strike a fair balance between the legitimate interests of society as a whole and the right of Ekoglasnost to be fairly represented in political elections.[44]

The case of "*Riza and others v. Bulgaria*" instead concerns the right to stand for election and the right to vote. The applicants are a Bulgarian citizen, the "Movement for rights and freedoms," and 101 Bulgarian residents of Turkish origin and Muslim faith, who exercised their right to vote in 17 polling stations located in Turkey, where the results of the general elections were subsequently declared null and void.

On 5 July 2009, parliamentary elections were held. Bulgarian citizens living abroad were entitled to vote. When the results were counted, six parties and coalitions exceeded the threshold of 4% of votes cast and were included in the proportional distribution of seats in the National Assembly: the DPS obtained 14.45% of the valid votes, which made it the third political party in the whole Country. The movement was the clear winner in 17 polling stations opened in Turkey.[45] In accordance with the proportional representation system, the electoral board assigned 33 seats to the DPS. This attribution was partly amended following an appeal to the Constitutional Court by another political group for the annulment of the election of seven DPS deputies on account of a number of anomalies that occurred at the Turkish polling stations.[46] On 16 February 2010, the Court gave its judgment, rejecting the request for the annulment of the election of the 7 MPs, but decided to deduct from the results obtained by each political party all those votes which had been obtained in 23 electoral districts in Turkey. The Bulgarian Court declared that the votes in question were valid, nevertheless they had to be deducted from the election results on account of anomalies in the electoral rolls as well as in the ballot reports.[47] Mr Riza and the DPS alleged that

44 *Ibidem*, paras.70–72.

45 Rechel B., *Ethnic Diversity in Bulgaria: Institutional Arrangements and Domestic Discourse*, in The Journal of Nationalism and Ethnicity, 36, 2008, 331–350; Bakalova M., *The Bulgarian Turkish Names: Conflict and Democratic Transition*, in Innovation, 19, 2006, 233–246; Pamporov A., *Social Distances and Ethnic Stereotypes to Ethnic Minorities in Bulgaria*, Sofia, 2009.

46 From a wider perspective, see Green E., Zografova Y., *Interethnic Relations in Bulgaria*, Sofia, 2014.

47 Kănev K., "Muslim Minorities, and the Democratisation Process in Bulgaria," in Hac Isalihoğlu M., Asku F.(eds.), *Proceedings of the International Conference on Minority Issues in the Balkans and the EU*, İstanbul, 2007, 79–89.

the annulment of the ballots had unjustifiably interfered with their right to stand for election, while other applicants assumed that such an annulment constituted a violation of their active electoral rights.

In this respect, the ECtHR reiterates that every Member State, as the ultimate guarantor of pluralism, shall organise democratic elections "under conditions which will ensure the free expression of the opinion of the people in the choice of the legislature."[48] Contracting States have a wide margin of appreciation in that sphere. Electoral systems seek to fulfil objectives, which are sometimes scarcely compatible with each other, to accurately reflect the opinions of the people and to channel currents of thought so as to promote the emergence of a sufficiently clear and coherent political will. In these circumstances, electoral procedures imply the equal treatment of all citizens in the exercise of their right to vote and their right to stand for election.[49] This does not mean, however, that all votes must necessarily have identical weight as regards the outcome of the election, nor that all candidates must have the same chances of victory. No electoral system can eliminate wasted votes and the elections cannot be conducted under any form of pressure in the choice of one or more candidates. Once the wishes of the people have been freely expressed, no subsequent amendment to the organisation of the electoral system may call that choice into question, except in the presence of compelling grounds for the democratic order.[50] The Court considers that the active aspect of the rights guaranteed by Art. 3 of Protocol no. 1 does not provide for the adoption of measures allowing expatriates to exercise their right to vote from their place of residence. Yet, since the presumption in a democratic State must be in favour of inclusion, such measures were deemed consonant with that provision.[51]

As regards the passive aspect of electoral rights, the judges of Strasbourg believe that it is not restricted to the mere possibility of standing for election: once elected, the person concerned is also entitled to sit as a member of Parliament.[52] The ECtHR must then ensure that the decision-making process on ineligibility or contestation of election results is accompanied by criteria framed to prevent arbitrary decisions. Such a finding must be reached, above all, by a body providing minimum guarantees of impartiality. Similarly, the discretion enjoyed by the organ concerned must not be exorbitantly wide and must be circumscribed with precision by domestic law. Lastly, the procedure for declaring a candidate ineligi-

48 *Riza and Others v. Bulgaria*, para. 136.

49 *Ibidem*, para. 137. Among the scholars, cf. Dayioğlu A., *Changing Aspects of Minority Policy in Bulgaria after 1989: The Case of the Muslim-Turkish Minority*, in Hacisalihoğlu M., Aksu F. (eds.), Proceedings of the International Conference on Minority Issues in the Balkans and the EU, İstanbul, 2007, 89–109.

50 Cf. *Riza and Others v. Bulgaria*, para. 138. See also *Yumak and Sadak v. Turkey, and Lykourezos v. Greece.*

51 *Ibidem*, para. 139.

52 *Ibidem*, para. 140. Cf. *Sadak and Others v. Turkey* (no. 2), *Sitaropoulos* and *Giakoumopoulos v. Greece, and Namat Aliyev v. Azerbaijan.*

ble must be such as to ensure a fair and objective decision, avoiding any abuse of power on the part of the relevant authority.[53] The European judges also restate that, under the subsidiarity principle in the context of electoral disputes, they are not called upon to determine whether the irregularities in the voting procedure complained of amounted to violations of the relevant domestic legislation. The ECtHR frames its role in assessing an unjustified interference in the freedom to choose the legislature as confined to establishing whether the domestic Court's decision was arbitrary or manifestly unreasonable.[54]

Those considerations led the Court of Strasbourg to note that the challenged judgment of the Bulgarian Court had a direct impact on the applicants' right to vote, by excluding their preferences from the election results. In addition, the domestic decision affected the right to stand for general elections both of Mr Riza, who lost his mandate as a deputy in the National Assembly, as well as of the DPS, which had 18,140 votes deducted from its total score.[55] The ECtHR therefore concludes that the Bulgarian Constitutional Court annulled the election in 22 polling stations abroad on purely administrative grounds affecting the electorate's choice and distorting the results. Moreover, the Electoral Law in force at the time was not clear and foreseeable enough, and thus it infringed the recommendations of the "Code of Good Conduct" of the Venice Commission, especially by failing to provide for the possibility of organising elections in the event of the voting being annulled.[56] The ECtHR bears in mind that organising elections in the territory of another Country is subject to the risk of major operational obstacles and additional costs.[57] However, it considers that the holding of new elections in constituencies with evidence of irregularities by electoral commissions in the voting procedure would have reconciled the legitimate aim of annulling the election results, i.e., protecting the lawfulness of the electoral procedure, with the subjective rights of voters and candidates in the general elections.[58] On those grounds, the annulment by the national Court of the election results in the polling sta-

53 *Ibidem*, paras. 141–143. Additionally, *Podkolzina v. Latvia, Kovach v. Ukraine, and Kerimova v. Azerbaijan.*

54 *Ibidem*, paras. 145–156. See also *Babenko v. Ukraine, Partija "Jaunie Demokrati" and Partija "Musu Zeme" v. Latvia, and Kerimli and Alibeyli v. Azerbaijan.*

55 *Ibidem*, paras. 157–159. Cf. *passim* EMINOV A., *Turkish and Other Muslim Minorities in Bulgaria*, London, 1997, 88 ff; DEMIRTAŞ-COŞKUN B., *An Anatomy of Turkish-Bulgarian Relations (1990–2009): Opportunities, Challenges, and Prospects*, in TÜRKEŞ M. (ed.), Turkish-Bulgarian Relations: Past and Present, İstanbul, 2010, 115–132.

56 *Ibidem*, paras. 160–164.

57 *Ibidem*, paras. 165–170. ZOGRAFOVA Y., ANDREEV B., *Opportunities for Development of Tolerant Intergroup Representations and Relationships*, in NAYDENOVA P., SHTERIONOV S., BORISOVA-MARINOVA K. (eds.), The Demographic Situation and the Development of Bulgaria, Sofia, 2014, 315—324.

58 *Ibidem*, paras. 171–175. Accordingly, NITZOVA P., *Bulgaria: Minorities, Democratization, and National Sentiments*, in 25 Nationalities Papers, 1997, 729–739 and KOLAROVA R., *Tacit Agreements in the Bulgarian Transition to Democracy: Minority Rights and Constitutionalism*, in 15 The University of Chicago Law School Roundtable, 1993, 23–51.

tions, the cancellation of Mr Riza's parliamentary mandate, and the DPS' loss of a National Assembly seat assigned under the proportional system amounted to an interference in the exercise of both their active and passive electoral rights.[59]

Finally, the case of "*Kulinski and Sabev v. Bulgaria*" involves the constitutional ban on prisoners' voting rights. The applicants, two nationals sentenced respectively for hooliganism, robbery, and murder, complained that, in accordance with the Bulgarian legislation, they were not allowed as convicted prisoners to vote in the elections for the European Parliament and the Grand National Assembly. They alleged that this prohibition violated their right to vote, considering that such a general, automatic, and indiscriminate restriction is disproportionate to any legitimate aim pursued.[60]

In that regard, the ECtHR recognises the Government's argument that the ban on voting for convicted prisoners is aimed at promoting the rule of law principles and enhancing civic responsibility. However, the Court decides that the restriction is unjustified.[61] As a matter of fact, prisoners continue to enjoy all fundamental rights and freedoms guaranteed under the Convention, except for the right to liberty, where lawfully imposed detention expressly falls within the scope of Art. 5 ECHR. Any restrictions on the other rights must be justified.[62] There is no question, therefore, that a prisoner should forfeit his rights merely because of his *status* as a person detained; nor is there any room under the Convention – where broadmindedness and tolerance are the acknowledged hallmarks of democratic society – for pure disenfranchisement based automatically on what might offend public opinion.[63] This standard of tolerance does not prevent a democratic society from taking steps to protect itself against activities intended to destroy the rights or freedoms set forth in the ECHR. Art. 3 of Protocol 1 enshrines the individual's capacity to influence the composition of the law-making power, and it does not exclude that restrictions on electoral rights could be imposed on an individual who has, for example, seriously abused a public position, or whose conduct threatened to undermine the rule of law. Nonetheless, this measure must

59 *Ibidem*, paras. 176–179.

60 For a general framework, read Dhami M., Cruise P., *Prisoner Disenfranchisement: Prisoner and Public Views of an Invisible Punishment*, in 13 Analyses of Social Issues and Public Policy, 2013, 211–227; Easton S., *Prisoners' Rights: Principles and Practice*, London-New York, 2011; Fredman S., *From Dialogue to Deliberation: Human Rights Adjudication and Prisoners' Rights to Vote*, in Hunt M., Hooper H., Yowell P. (eds.), Parliaments and Human Rights Redressing the Democratic Deficit, Oxford, 2015, 447–468.

61 In that regard, *Kulinski and Sabev v. Bulgaria*, paras. 33–35.

62 *Kulinski and Sabev v. Bulgaria*, paras. 36–38. See *Hirst v. UK* (no. 2). From a comparative perspective, Murray C., *A Perfect Storm: Parliament and Prisoner Disenfranchisement*, in 66 Parliamentary Affairs, 2013, 511–539; Bates E., *Analysing the Prison Voting Saga and the British Challenge to Strasbourg*, in 14 Human Rights Law Review, 2014, 503–540; Hervieu N., *Prisoner Voting Rights: Never Ending Story for a Decisive Issue (ECtHR, Grand Chambre, Scoppola v. Italy, no. 3)*, in 94 Revue Trimestrielle des Droits de l'Homme, 2013, 348–376.

63 *Ibidem*, para. 39. Similarly, *Brânduşe v. Romania* (no. 2).

not be applied lightly, and the principle of proportionality requires a discernible link between sanction and conduct.[64]

In reaching this conclusion, the ECtHR observes that the applicants had been deprived of the right to vote as a result of a blanket ban on polling, which applied to all convicted persons being in detention. This kind of prohibition is categorical: it stems from the Constitution and is reproduced in several ordinary laws. All prisoners' right to vote is restricted under the Bulgarian legislation, providing no decision-making room for authorities to decide differently on the basis of the circumstances of the case, the severity of the criminal act, or the behaviour of the person convicted.[65] While States have a certain margin of appreciation in this respect, an automatic and indiscriminate restriction of the right protected under Art. 3 of Protocol 1 is not acceptable. By depriving convicted individuals of the right to vote, a key tool of civic participation is taken away from those in prison. In that sense, detainees are to a certain extent moved outside the realm of citizenship in order to enhance civic responsibility.[66] Slowly but surely, convicts are in this way distanced from other citizens, and the question remains whether the disenfranchisement resulting from the application of such an interference is desirable and legitimate. Consequently, the Court holds that voting is an essential element of the democratic process, which should not be casually removed, as there is no room in the Convention for the old idea of "civic death" that lies behind the ban on convicted prisoners' voting. Of course, in some instances, removing the right to vote could be justified, but such interferences should not be applied too easily, for they pertain to the core of citizenship, and may have severe implications for the ability of an individual to participate in a democratic society.[67]

Fundamental civil and political freedoms, such as the right to vote, are universal and do not depend on the moral character of the rights holder.[68] The act of voting is an important element of social participation, which reinforces awareness of one's civic duties and obligations. Restoring the vote affirms that individuals are entitled to equal concern and respect, regardless of their past deeds. Even if the public do not always fully value their own voting rights, in so far as they often will not turn out to vote, this does not detract from the symbolic importance of

64 *Ibidem*, para. 40. See in addition Mauer M., *Voting Behind Bars: An Argument for Voting by Prisoners*, in 54 Howard Law Journal, 2011, 549–557; Ramsay P., *Voters should not be in Prison! The Rights of Prisoners in a Democracy*, in 16 Critical Review of International Social and Political Philosophy, 2013, 421–438.

65 *Ibidem*, para. 40.

66 With reference to the entire ECtHR case law on prisoners' right to vote Celiksoy E., *Execution of the Judgments of the European Court of Human Rights in Prisoners' Right to Vote Cases*, in 20 Human Rights Law Review, 2020, 555–581.

67 *Ibidem*, para. 41.

68 In this respect, the applicants' situation was comparable to that examined by the ECtHR in the case of Anchugov and *Gladkov v. Russia*. Correspondingly, unlike in the case of *Scoppola v. Italy* (no. 3), the Court had underlined that the removal of the right to vote – not by a decision of a judge but in law – did not, in itself, give rise to a violation of art. 3 of Protocol no. 1.

suffrage.[69] In conclusion, the Court notes that, albeit detainees regained their right to vote upon their release, this specific circumstance does not change the fact that under the law in force at the election time all convicted prisoners in Bulgaria, including the applicants, regardless of their conduct and the gravity of the offences committed, were deprived of a fundamental right.[70]

A truly soft impact

Prima facie, the Strasbourg decisions concerning the enjoyment of electoral rights sparked a considerable reform process within the Bulgarian legal system. Such activism reflects a more general trend by national authorities to act upon the requests made by the Council of Europe and to pursue dialogue with the Committee of Ministers in order to adapt the domestic legal order to the standards encompassed in the ECtHR's decisions.[71]

More precisely, considering the *Ekoglasnost* case, the Government submitted an action plan on 14 April 2015 and the Execution Department sent a comment to all authorities involved on 29 January 2016. Most recently, on 24 February 2020, a revised action – currently under assessment – was presented to prevent new disproportionate infringement of the applicant's passive electoral rights and comply with Bulgaria's obligation under Art. 46, para. 1, ECHR.[72]

With reference to individual measures, national authorities recalled that the applicant had not submitted a just satisfaction claim and expressed the view that no specific individual measures were necessary.[73]

The situation is different with regard to general measures. The Government indeed noted that the judgment revolves around basic principles of electoral law, and it considered that the most efficient manner of ensuring these requirements would be to carry out an extensive dissemination of the decision to all bodies concerned. For this purpose, domestic authorities prepared a detailed legal analysis of the decision and explained the main conclusions reached therein in a circular letter; special attention was drawn to the Venice Commission's opinion regarding the stability of the electoral law, and the timing for the adoption of amendments to the voting legislation.[74] The target of such awareness-raising measures was, firstly, the Bulgarian Parliament and the administrative bodies involved in the amendment process of the electoral law, namely the Ministries, the Electoral Commission, and its regional offices.

69 *Ibidem*, para. 42.

70 More generally, Dhami M., *Prisoner Disenfranchisement Policy: A Threat to Democracy?* in Analyses of Social Issues and Public Policy, 5, 2015, 235–247.

71 See *amplius* Human Rights in Bulgaria, Annual Report 2019, 3–18, Bulgaria Press Country Profile 2020, European Court of Human Rights, and Bulgaria Country Factsheet 2019, Department for the Execution of Judgments.

72 Cf. *Ekoglasnost v. Bulgaria*, Status of Execution.

73 *Ibidem.*

74 Action Plan Communication 2013, *Case Ekoglasnost v. Bulgaria*.

Moreover, the Government considered crucial to involve the Constitutional Court, as under the Fundamental Law, the Court has jurisdiction to rule on disputes concerning the lawfulness of parliamentary elections and annul election results in cases of serious violations. The constitutional judges can impose sanctions on late amendments to the electoral legislation if they are viewed as posing the risk of seriously altering electoral results or if they have critically affected the electoral process.[75] For these reasons, the Government raised awareness about the judgment also among individuals and bodies enumerated exhaustively in the Constitution – such as 1/5 of the 240 MPs, the President of the Republic, the Council of Ministers, the Court of Cassation, the Supreme Administrative Court, the Prosecutor-General, the Ombudsman, and the Supreme Bar Council – being entitled to challenge the constitutionality of statutes, which violate citizens' rights and freedoms. Usually, a political party, a coalition or individual candidates, whose passive electoral rights may have been affected by late amendments to the electoral law do not have direct access to the Constitutional Court. Nonetheless, the "internal rules" of the body confer on that judge the discretionary power to determine the parties involved in proceedings before it.[76]

The Department for the Execution of Judgments sent comments to the domestic authorities on 14 September 2020, in relation to the draft bill for the amendment of the Electoral Code, adopted on a first reading by the Parliament on 3 September 2020. The outline proposes amendments to fundamental electoral rules, also changing the system for elections of the Grand National Assembly (half of the Deputies are to be designated by proportional representation and half by majority voting). It drew the authorities' attention to the fact that "according to the Ekoglasnost judgment, if provisions modifying fundamental electoral rules are applied in the elections less than one year after their adoption this would be contrary to the principle of the stability of the electoral law."[77]

Having regard to the case of *Riza*, an action plan was submitted on 27 July 2016. In addition, comments from the Department for the Execution of Judgments of the ECtHR were most recently sent on 27 June 2018 and 1 March 2019.[78]

As to the individual measures, the Court affirmed that the finding of an infringement constitutes just satisfaction for the violation of Mr Riza's right to stand for election and for the violation of the other applicants' right to vote. The European judges awarded just satisfaction also in respect of costs and expenses, considering that no specific individual measure was possible. To this end the Republic of

75 Action Plan Communication 2019, *Case Ekoglasnost v. Bulgaria*. In the event that an amendment to the electoral law is declared unconstitutional, the version prior to the modification regains its effect.

76 Cf. Tanchev E., *Introduction to Constitutional Law*, cited above.

77 The Sofia News, 3 September 2020 in www.novinite.com/archives/2020-9-3.

78 Cf. *Riza and Others v. Bulgaria*, Status of Execution.

Bulgaria is in the process of making payment, converting into Bulgarian levies the sum of 6,000 EUR for legal costs. [79]

As concerns the general measures, national authorities disseminated the judgment, by translating the decision into Bulgarian and publishing it on the Ministry of Justice website. The Government testified that the violation of Art. 3, Protocol 1 stemmed from the fact that, under the 2001 electoral law, it was impossible to provide for new elections to be held in the case of the annulment of the ballot in one or more polling stations. New elections would have made it possible to reconcile the legitimate aim of preserving the electoral processes with the applicants' subjective rights. But, given the impossibility of organising new consultations, the annulment of the election results caused an unjustified interference with the right to vote.[80]

The 2001 electoral law was repealed in 2011. Art. 306, paras 4 and 5, of the 2014 "Election Code" provided for the holding of new parliamentary elections only in the event of the annulment of the results in their entirety. The assessment of the Bulgarian authorities is awaited as to whether it is necessary to amend the new provisions in order to give the possibility of holding new parliamentary elections only for the districts affected by the invalidation, in the event of the annulment of voting in one or more polling stations. As regards the polling stations abroad, the Government is also providing information on the formal requirements concerning the different types of voters' lists.[81]

Regarding finally the case of *Kulinski and Sabev*, and the indiscriminate ban on prisoners' voting rights enshrined in the Constitution, national authorities provided an action plan on 3 April 2017, and comments of the ECtHR's Department for the Execution were sent on 22 December, while a revised action plan is still awaited.[82]

With reference to the individual measures, the ECtHR did not award any compensation for moral damages but granted only indemnification for costs and expenses duly paid by the authorities. Having regard to the circumstances of the case, the Court considered that the finding of a violation constituted sufficient just satisfaction for any non-pecuniary damage sustained by the applicants. In fact, while Mr Sabev is serving his life prison sentence, Mr Kulinski was released on 30 December 2009: therefore, at the time of delivering the judgment, his electoral rights were not restricted, and he was not suffering the consequences of this specific violation. In connection with the expenses incurred before the Court, the judges considered reasonable to award the sum of 2,727 EUR.[83]

Examining the general measures adopted, the judgment has been translated into Bulgarian, published, and disseminated. The Government recalled, however,

79 *Ibidem.*

80 Action Plan Communication 2016, *Riza and others v. Bulgaria.*

81 *Ibidem.*

82 See *Kulinski and Sabev v. Bulgaria*, Status of Execution.

83 Action Plan Communication 2017, *Kulinski and Sabev v. Bulgaria.*

that the provision restricting the voting rights of detainees is expressly established in Art. 42, para. 1 of the Constitution, under which "every citizen above the age of 18, with the exception of those placed under judicial interdiction or serving a prison sentence, shall be free to elect state and local authorities and vote in referendums." The ban is also reproduced in articles 243 and 350 of the "Election Code." To this end, the Government affirmed that concrete steps for preventing future similar violations need to be examined by domestic authorities, choosing the most effective means to discharge the obligations under Art. 46 ECHR.[84] Nonetheless, assuming that the prohibition on prisoners' voting rights is established by the Fundamental Law, it is not sufficient for Parliament simply to modify electoral legislation, but rather it is also necessary to revise the Constitution. To comply with the Convention, the National Assembly must adopt a draft bill for constitutional amendment in three readings held on three different days with a three-quarters majority of all deputies. The revision can be initiated by the President, or by one-quarter of MPs, if the adjustment is to be adopted by the Parliament, or by one-half of the MPs in the case of amendment by the Grand National Assembly. A very high degree of political *consensus* is thus required both for taking a decision to summon the Grand National Assembly and for the adoption of the constitutional amendments. It is not by chance that, since 1990, no Grand National Assembly has been summoned, even though such a suggestion has been made from time to time by politicians and scholars.[85]

In light of these considerations, the impact of the ECtHR case law at national level is rather limited. Some legislative reforms, which have begun to adapt the Bulgarian legal system to the standards defined by the Court of Strasbourg, are certainly underway, although they have not been definitively approved yet. The provisional nature of the statutory measures adopted does not allow to appreciate their systemic effects so far. For the same reason, even the economic impact arising from the implementation of the ECtHR's decisions regarding Art. 3, Protocol 1, cannot be fully assessed. At the moment, indeed, the only costs concern the administrative expenses for translating, publishing, and disseminating the judgments, and the ones related to the just satisfaction afforded to the injured party.

Some concluding remarks: Political rights' protection between national sovereignty and the principle *pacta sunt servanda*

In sum, within the Bulgarian legal system, the Strasbourg judgments have not significantly affected the exercise of electoral rights. It is certainly true that the cases related to Bulgaria are relatively limited, but the application of the Convention

84 *Ibidem.*

85 See for example Constitutional Court of Bulgaria, Decision no. 3 of 2003 and Constitutional Court of Bulgaria, Decision no. 3 of 2004. Cf. also Dimitrov H., *The Bulgarian Constitutional Court and Its Interpretive Jurisdiction*, cited above.

concerned structural issues, such as the exercise of prisoners' right to vote or, more extensively, the use of electoral legislation as a mechanism to crackdown on political dissent of minorities. These are unquestionably fundamental aspects of any democratic system that must be corrected in order to guarantee Bulgaria's full adhesion to the Convention. The reasons why national authorities have not yet been adequately reformed to facilitate the right to political participation are both regulatory and structural.

As to the regulatory aspects, we noted that in the Bulgarian legal system the Convention occupies a hierarchical position immediately below the Constitution. Then, the Fundamental Law should overcome the ECHR, because it represents the "durable core" of national sovereignty.[86] Consistent with this provision, the Constitutional Court could rule on the legitimacy of the Convention, as interpreted by the European judges, even going so far as to declare its incompatibility with the Fundamental Law.[87] This approach could in the long run undermine the appropriate compliance with international obligations and reinterpret the meaning of the democratic principles. Such practices consist indeed in refusing to carry out ECtHR judgments that could jeopardise the domestic system, and in reaffirming the supremacy of national sovereignty over fundamental rights protection.[88]

Within this framework, the activity of the constitutional Court may cause unpredictability in international relations, by transforming the principle *pacta sunt servanda* from a rigid and clear obligation of observing international agreements into a vague and ambiguous duty of general compliance with broad standards. This could also undermine the legitimate expectations of the member States and their citizens as well as the rule of law, changing the initial scope of the ECHR in a way that cannot be predicted in advance and bearing on legal certainty and legitimate expectations of the contracting State.[89] In this respect, the judicial "mastering of the meaning" of Treaty provisions may have a curved trajectory and lead to far-reaching shifts in the obligations the States initially undertook.

86 Vorhaus J., *On Degradation. Article 3, Protocol No. 1, of the European Convention on Human Rights*, in 1 Common Law World Review, 2002, 374–399; Dawson-Edwards C., *Enfranchisement Convicted Felons: Current Research on Opinions towards Felon Voting Rights*, in Journal of Offender Rehabilitation, 46, 2008, 13–29; Beckman L., "Global Diffusion and the Role of Courts in Shaping the Human Right to Vote," in Brysk A. (ed.), *Globalization of Law and Human Rights: From Norms to Fulfilment*, London, 63–82.

87 Hyland R., *Pacta Sunt Servanda: A Meditation*, in Virginia Journal of International Law, 34, 1994, 405–435; Lekkas S., Tzanakopoulos A., Pacta Sunt Servanda versus Flexibility in the Suspension and Termination of Treaties, in Tams C.J., Tzanakopoulos A., Zimmermann A. (eds.), *Research Handbook on the Law of Treaties*, Northampton, 2014, 312–340.

88 See Behan C., *Citizen Convicts: Prisoners, Politics, and the Vote*, Manchester, 2014; Foster S., *Prisoners' Voting Rights, and the ECHR: Still Hazy after All These Years*, in Coventry Law Journal, 15, 2012, 75–83.

89 See for instance, Davison-Vecchione D., *Beyond the Forms of Faith: Pacta Sunt Servanda and Loyalty*, in German Law Journal, 16, 2015, 1163–1190; Lukashuk I., *The Principle Pacta Sunt Servanda and the Nature of Obligation under International Law*, in The American Journal of International Law, 83, 1989, 513–518.

This notwithstanding, the Constitutional Court has so far avoided undermining the ECHR in practice, by taking a pro-integration role that carefully took into account the jurisprudence of the Court of Strasbourg, and interpreted domestic legislation in conformity with the Convention, establishing a successful dialogue with the ECtHR.[90] In other words, basic constitutional provisions, and key decisions of the Constitutional Court, which proclaim the unconstitutionality of conventional legal standards, or declare that such values endanger basic domestic law principles, are manifestations of national sovereignty vis-à-vis international obligations.[91] Consequently, the biased jurisprudence of the Court of Strasbourg may in the end produce a sort of "judicial ping-pong," which would barely be reconcilable with the principle of representative democracy and would be detrimental to the observance of legal certainty and the rule of law.[92]

An eloquent example of this friction between national identity and international human rights protection is provided by the case of *Kulinski and Sabev*, given that the ban on voting for detainees serving prison sentences is established by the Fundamental Law. Recognising the hierarchical primacy of the Constitution over all sources of law, the Bulgarian legal system emphasises the possibility of reinterpreting the Convention in order not to give effect to the ECtHR's judgments as conflicting obligations under domestic legislation or because that interpretation exceeds its duties as understood and confirmed by Bulgaria when it became party to the Convention.[93] It is quite clear that, in these circumstances, the decision could be fully implemented only as a result of a constitutional amendment creating all the conditions necessary to change the domestic legislation, which reproduces the ban on voting for convicted prisoners. In this way, however, Bulgaria will be forced to face a harsh alternative: respecting its Constitution, while denying the protection of a human right, or applying the Convention, but abdicating its sovereignty.[94] Those

90 In that regard, Tanchev E., "Constitution and the Rule of Law," in Bell J.D. (ed.), *Bulgaria in Transition: Politics, Economics, Society and Culture after Communism, Boulder*, 1998, 65–93; Drumeva E., "Primacy of the EU law in the National Constitutional Space: Reflections," in Pernice I., Tanchev E. (eds.), *Ceci nest pas une Constitution. Constitutionalization without a Constitution*, Baden-Baden, 2009, 100–104.

91 Cf. Binder C., "The Pacta Sunt Servanda Rule in the Vienna Convention on the Law of Treaties: A Pillar and its Safeguards," in Buffard I., Crawford J., Pellet A., Wittich S. (eds.), *International Law between Universalism and Fragmentation*, Leiden, 2008, 317–322; Lachs M., "Pacta Sunt Servanda," in Bernhardt R. (ed.), *Encyclopedia of Public International Law*, Amsterdam, 1997, 364–430.

92 Cf. Gormley W.P., *The Codification of Pacta Sunt Servanda by the International Law Commission: The Preservation of Classical Norms of Moral Force and Good Faith*, in St. Louis University Law Journal, 367–429; Aust A., *Pacta Sunt Servanda*, in Wolfrum R. (ed.), Max Planck Encyclopedia of Public International Law, Oxford, 2007, 43–63.

93 See *amplius* Verhoeven J., "The Law of Responsibility, and the Law of Treaties," in Crawford J., Pellet A., Olleson S. (eds.), *The Law of International Responsibility*, Oxford University Press, Oxford, 2010, 109–130.

94 Cf. Ganev V., *Prisoners' Rights, Public Services, and Institutional Collapse in Bulgaria*, in 4 East European Constitutional Review, 1995, 76–83. From a broader comparative perspective see Smirnova M., *Russian Constitutional Court Affirms Russian Constitution's Suprem-*

growing concerns about the unduly broad interpretations of the Convention must be regarded in terms of constitutional and political recognition of international law, as the acceptance of treaty obligations is based on free consensus and considers the relevant national interests.[95] The dialogue between national and international justice systems in this field could be resolved only in the spirit of a genuine cooperation. Ultimately, the implementation of the *Kulinski and Sabev* decision implies a political assessment of two different issues, both deserving legal protection.[96]

With reference to the structural level of the right to vote, it is strictly linked to the historical and political background of Bulgaria. In that regard, it should first be noted that the re-establishment of free elections in 1990 was greeted with active interest and very high turnout. However, as time passed, enthusiasm waned while public perception of elections became predominantly associated with questionable practices or even outright fraud.[97] Greater ruling party control over voting registration and polling station protocols, paying citizens in return for their vote for a certain candidate, and the so-called "electoral tourism" – i.e., Bulgarian nationals living abroad being transported to polling stations in an organised manner to support a specific political party – decreased trust in the electoral process, focusing the debate on manipulation of voting.[98]

Despite this public attention, the issue of voting rights and procedures, with special reference to voters who do not clearly fall within the category of resident citizens, is recurrently used to stifle dissent or to harass political, religious, or ethnic minorities, especially when those groups enjoy the opportunity to actively participate in elections, as in the case of the Bulgarian Turks.[99] Such malpractice

acy over ECtHR Decisions, in *UK Constituzional Law Blog*, 17 July 2015; KUCHER A.N., GORLENKO A.A., STAKHEEV D.S., *Ruling of the Constitutional Court of the Russian Federation on Enforcement of ECHR Judgments*, in www.debevoise.com, 17 August 2015.

95 BINDER C., *Stability and Change in Times of Fragmentation. The Limits of Pacta Sunt Servanda Revisited*, in Leiden Journal of International Law, 25, 2012, 909–934; BERNHARDT R., *Evolutive Treaty Interpretation, Especially of the European Convention on Human Rights*, in German Yearbook of International Law, 42, 1999, 11–25; TREVES T., "Aspects of Legitimacy of Decisions of International Courts and Tribunals," in WOLFRUM R., RÖBEN *v.* (eds.), *Legitimacy of International Law*, Berlin, 2008, 170–188.

96 WEHBERG H., *Pacta Sunt Servanda*, in American Journal of International Law, 53, 1959, 775–786; SIMMA B., "Human Rights and State Responsibility", in REINISCH A., KRIEBAUM U. (eds.), *The Law of International Relations*, Utrecht, 2007, 359–383; BOS M., *Theory and Practice of Treaty Interpretation*, in Netherlands International Law Review, 32, 1980, 3–38.

97 TODOROV A., *Citizens, Parties, Elections: Bulgaria 1879–2009*, Sofia, 2010; CHALOVA B., DE WAELE J.M., *Bulgaria*, cited above; VAN BIEZEN I., *Political Parties in New Democracies: Party Organization in Southern and East-Central Europe*, Basingstoke, 2003.

98 See HARPER M., *The 2001 Parliamentary and Presidential Elections in Bulgaria*, in 22 Electoral Studies, 2003, 335–344; SPIROVA M., *Political Parties in Post-Communist Systems*, cited above; KOLEV K., *Bulgaria: Electoral Volatility, Polarization and Financial Deficits Lead to Reduction in Clientelism*, in KITSCHELT H. (ed.), Research and Dialogue on Programmatic Parties and Party Systems, Stockholm, 2013, 40–62.

99 Cf. KRASTEVA A., TODOROV A., *Ethnic Minorities and Political Representation: The Case of Bulgaria*, in South-Eastern Europe, 35, 2011, 8–31; TZENOVA R., *The Electoral System and the Fragmentation of the Party System in Bulgaria 1991–2001*, Sofia, 2003.

has featured in every election campaign for the last 15 years or more, and it has very rarely been discussed in the frame of civil rights, pluralistic social inclusion, and intensified involvement of political groups. Overwhelmingly, the disenfranchisement of citizens abroad, resident non-citizens, and citizens who are serving a prison sentence, while having different justifications, were used to manipulate election results in order to favour the government majority parties.[100] The political reasoning for marginalising specific groups is rooted in their real or potential electoral relevance. People from the Bulgarian-Turkish diaspora, migrators on economic grounds, and ethnic nationals who historically lived beyond the borders of the current State of Bulgaria compose indeed an electoral constituency potentially capable of seriously opposing the governing party "Citizens for European Development of Bulgaria" (GERB) and its leader, Boyko Borisov.[101]

In particular, the Bulgarian-Turkish diaspora has a clear representation in domestic political life with the "Movement for Rights and Freedoms." This party has a vast ethnic electoral base and rhetoric.[102] Nevertheless, its leadership has moved towards opening up to other voters including those within the Roma minority and Bulgarian Christians. DPS got 14.45% of popular support in the 2009 elections and 14.84% in 2014, obtaining in both cases 36 seats in Parliament. In the 2009 elections, 98.6% of all votes cast at polling stations in Turkey were in favour of the Movement.[103] The DPS' intensified political activity historically had even more impact over local elections, due to the concentration of Bulgarian-Turkish votes in certain municipalities, meaning that just a few hundred voters could substantially influence the overall political result by actively participating in the decision-making process.[104] DPS has hence gradually

100 Ganev V., *History, Politics, and the Constitution: Ethnic Conflict and Constitutional Adjudication in Post-Communist Bulgaria*, in Slavic Review, 63, 2004, 66–89; Karasimeonov G., *Past and New Cleavages in Post-Communist Bulgaria*, in Karasimeonov G., Lawson K., Rommele A. (eds.), Cleavages, Parties, and Voters: Studies from Bulgaria, the Czech Republic, Hungary, Poland, and Romania, 1999, 109–123; Spirova M., *A Tradition We don't Mess with: Party Patronage in Bulgaria*, in Kopecký P., Mair P., Spirova M. (eds.), Party Patronage and Party Government in European Democracies, Oxford, 2012, 54–72.

101 See Vassilev R., *Post-Communist Bulgaria's Ethnopolitics*, in Global Review of Ethnopolitics, 1, 2001, 37–53; Zankina E., *New Cleavages and Populist Mobilization in Bulgaria*, Warsaw, 2015; Stoychev S.P., *The Controlled Voting in Bulgaria*, Sofia, 2016, 49–60.

102 Read Kanev D., *Muslim Minorities, and the Democratisation Process in Bulgaria*, in Hacısalihoğlu M., Aksu F. (eds.), Proceedings of the International Conference on Minority Issues in the Balkans and the EU, İstanbul, 2007, 79–88; Lewis S., *Islam in Bulgaria*, in Aramco World, 45, 1994, 20–29; Bogoev P., *The Bulgarian Constitution and Minority Rights in 1989–1999. Ten Years Later. Lessons Learned for the Future*, Sofia, 2000.

103 Cf. Nitzova P., *Bulgaria: Minorities, Democratization, and National Sentiments*, cited above; Dayıoğlu A., *Changing Aspects of Minority Policy in Bulgaria after 1989*, cited above; Demirtaş-Coşkun B., *An Anatomy of Turkish-Bulgarian Relations (1990–2009)*, cited above.

104 Flores-Juberias C., *Post-Communist Electoral Systems and National Minorities: A Dilemma in Five Paradigms*, in Stein J.P., Sharpe M.E. (eds.), The Politics of National Minority Participation in Post-Communist Europe, New York, 2019, 31–65; Eminov A., *The Turks in*

secured a pivotal role in the party system dynamics, shifting alliances and positions, but always remaining of crucial significance for the making and breaking of governments in the Country. These developments over the past 30 years have made a clear statement about the position the party – and the Turkish minority – could occupy in Bulgarian politics, creating a strong backlash among the majority, driven by dissatisfaction with the questionable practices of the party *elites*.[105]

Correspondingly, Ekoglasnost represented the first chance to express political discontent in Bulgaria, since it was one of the primary national parties opposing the Communist regime.[106] It started as a protest group seeking to improve the environmental situation, playing a prominent part in the demonstrations that led to the collapse of socialism and to the democratic transition, but it continued its political action as a solid and well-structured party, which developed into a key factor in the subsequent parliamentary elections, especially as it promoted a broader conception of human rights and freedoms.[107] As a result, Ekoglasnost became a central component of political opposition at different levels of government. The movement held two ministerial posts – for Finance and for the Environment – and expressed the President and the Vice-President of the Union of Democratic Forces (UDF).[108] In Bulgaria, where dialogue between Government and social partners remains underdeveloped, Ekoglasnost has been able to establish an effective working relationship with the civil society exercising significant pressure for reforms and increasing public participation.[109]

Going back to the original discussion, the logic behind the approach followed by the Bulgarian legal system towards the right to vote is essentially borrowed

Bulgaria: Post-1989 Developments, in 27 Nationalities Papers, 1999, 31–55; Bernd R., *The Bulgarian Ethnic Model: Reality or Ideology*, in Europe-Asia Studies, 59, 2007, 1201–1215 and *passim* Crampton R., *Bulgaria*, Oxford, 2007.

105 Naxidou E., *Nationalism versus Multiculturalism: The Minority Issue in Twenty-first Century Bulgaria*, in Nationalities Papers, 40, 2012, 85–105; Bernd R., *State Control of Minorities in Bulgaria*, in Journal of Communist Studies and Transition Politics, 23, 2007, 352–370; Warhola J., Boteva O., *The Turkish Minority in Contemporary Bulgaria*, in Nationalities Papers, 31, 2003, 260–264.

106 For the early history of Ekoglasnost, see Carter F.W., "Bulgaria", in Carter F.W., Turnock D. (eds.), *Environmental Problems in Eastern Europe*, London, 1993, 38–62; Baumgartl B., *Transition and Sustainability: Interest and Actors in Eastern European Environmental Policy*, The Hague, 1997, 63–82; Boyadzhiev V., *Critical Analysis on the Bulgarian Parliamentary Electoral System*, in Geographica Timisiensis, 19, 2010, 155–162.

107 Bell J.D., *Bulgaria*, in White S., Bart J., Lewis P.G. (eds.), Developments in Eastern European Politics, Basingstoke, 1993, 83–97.

108 See Jancar-Webster B., *Environmental Movement and Social Change in the Transition Countries*, in Environmental Politics, 7, 1998, 69–90; Glenn J.K., *Contentious Politics and Democratization: Comparing the Impact of Social Movements on the Fall of Communism in Eastern Europe*, in Political Studies, 2003, 103–120; Russell J., *Environmental Issues in Eastern Europe: Setting and Agenda*, London, 1991, 18–29.

109 Cf. Carmin J., Fagan A., *Environmental Mobilisation and Organisations in Post socialist Europe and the Former Soviet Union*, in 19 Environmental Politics, 2015, 689–707; Letki N., *Socialization for Participation? Trust, Membership and Democratization in East-Central Europe*, in Political Research Quarterly, 57, 2004, 665–679.

from consociationalism. Electoral rules are interpreted and applied in order to negatively influence the chances of oppositions parties, small dissident movements, and ethnic minorities gaining representation in the legislature, which would in turn lead to a government alternative.[110] The Europeanisation of electoral rights thus represents a cultural as well as a legal change of perspective, since in Bulgaria the safeguard of political and ethnic minorities has been often minimised by security concerns. In that regard, the Court of Strasbourg and the Council of Ministers can effectively enhance electoral rights, by helping to determine the shape of minority discussions in the domestic legal order and encouraging all the minorities to raise State's violations of their rights before the ECtHR. The Convention's framework then takes on a symbolic meaning and provides a unique space for democratisation, as it gives a different approach to political participation.[111]

Bibliography

Anastasakis O., Bechev D., *EU Conditionality in South-East Europe: Bringing Commitment to the Process*, in 1 European Balkan Observer, 2003, 4–20.

Andreev S., *Types of Populist Parties, and the Future of Democracy in Bulgaria*, in 4 Political Studies, 2007, 3–30.

Aust A., *Pacta Sunt Servanda*, in Wolfrum R. (ed.), Max Planck Encyclopedia of Public International Law, Oxford University Press, Oxford, 2007, 43–63.

Bakalova M., *The Bulgarian Turkish Names: Conflict and Democratic Transition*, in 19 Innovation, 2006, 233–246.

Baker R., *Democracy versus Bureaucracy: Transforming the Nature of the Civil Service in Bulgaria*, in Baker R. (ed.), Comparative Public Management, Westport, 1994, 53–65.

Bates E., *Analysing the Prison Voting Saga, and the British Challenge to Strasbourg*, in 14 Human Rights Law Review, 2014, 503–540.

Baumgartl B., *Environmental Protest as a Vehicle for Transition: The Case of Ekoglasnost in Bulgaria*, in Vári A., Tamás P. (eds), Environment in Democratic Transition: Politics and Policy in Central and Eastern Europe, New York, 2013, 157–175.

Baumgartl B., *Transition and Sustainability: Interest and Actors in Eastern European Environmental Policy*, The Hague, 1997, 63–82.

110 In this sense, Rusev M., Vladimirova P., *Electoral Geography of Bulgaria*, Sofia, 2010; Kostadinova T., *Voter Turnout Dynamics in Post-Communist Europe*, in European Journal of Political Science Research, 42, 2003, 741–759.

111 On the backspin effect of Europeanisation cf. Toneva-Metodieva L., *Prospects for a Democratic Transformation of Post-Communist Society: The Case of Bulgaria*, in Region: Regional Studies of Russia, Eastern Europe, and Central Asia, 44, 2018, 35–50; Mitropolitski S., *EU Integration: An Enforcement of or an Impediment to National Identity in Bulgaria and Macedonia*, in Region: Regional Studies of Russia, Eastern Europe, and Central Asia, 40, 2014, 309–326.

BECHEV D., *From Policy-Takers to Policy-Makers? Observations on Bulgarian and Romanian Foreign Policy Before and After EU Accession*, in Perspectives on European Politics and Society, 2009, 210–224.

BECKMAN L., *Global Diffusion, and the Role of Courts in Shaping the Human Right to Vote*, in BRYSK A. (ed.), Globalization of Law and Human Rights: From Norms to Fulfilment, London, 63–82.

BEHAN C., *Citizen Convicts: Prisoners, Politics, and the Vote*, Manchester, 2014.

BELL J.D., *Bulgaria*, in WHITE S., BART J. and LEWIS P.G. (eds.), Developments in Eastern European Politics, Basingstoke, Macmillan, 1993, 83–97.

BELL J.D., *Democratization and Political Participation in "Post-Communist" Bulgaria*, in DAWISHA K., PARROTT B. (eds.), Politics, Power and the Struggle for Democracy in South-East Europe, Cambridge, 1997, 367–375.

BELOV M., *Constitutional Law in Bulgaria*, Amsterdam, 2019, 32–37.

BERND R., *State Control of Minorities in Bulgaria*, in 23 Journal of Communist Studies and Transition Politics, 2007, 352–370.

BERND R., *The Bulgarian Ethnic Model: Reality or Ideology*, in 59 Europe-Asia Studies, 2007, 1201–1215.

BERNHARDT R., *Evolutive Treaty Interpretation, Especially of the European Convention on Human Rights*, in 42 German Yearbook of International Law, 1999, 11–25.

BINDER C., *Stability and Change in Times of Fragmentation. The Limits of Pacta Sunt Servanda Revisited*, in 25 Leiden Journal of International Law, 2012, 909–934.

BINDER C., *The Pacta Sunt Servanda Rule in the Vienna Convention on the Law of Treaties: A Pillar and its Safeguards*, in BUFFARD I., CRAWFORD J., PELLET A., WITTICH S. (eds.), International Law between Universalism and Fragmentation, Leiden, 2008, 317–322.

BOGDANOV L. ANGELOV G., *Roma Integration in Bulgaria: Necessary Reforms and Economic Effects*, Sofia, 2007, 56–62.

BOGOEV P., *The Bulgarian Constitution and Minority Rights in 1989–1999. Ten Years Later.* Lessons Learned for the Future, Sofia, 2000.

BORISSOVA O., *Public Administration Reform in Bulgaria*, in VON BRESKA E., BRUSIS M. (eds.), Central and Eastern Europe on the Way Into the EU: Reforms of the Regional Administration in Bulgaria, the Czech Republic, Estonia, Hungary, Poland and Slovakia, Munich, 1999, 1–13.

BÖRZEL T.A., *Member State Responses to Europeanization*, in 40 Journal of Common Market Studies, 2002, 194–214.

BÖRZEL T.A., RISSE T., *When Europe Hits Home: Europeanization and Domestic Change*, in 4 European Integration Online Papers, 2000, 1.

BOS M., *Theory and Practice of Treaty Interpretation*, in 32 Netherlands International Law Review, 1980, 3–38.

BOYADZHIEV V., *Critical Analysis on the Bulgarian Parliamentary Electoral System*, in 19 Geographica Timisiensis, 2010, 155–162.

BOZHILOVA D., *Measuring Successes and Failure of EU-Europeanization in the Eastern Enlargement: Judicial Reform in Bulgaria*, in 11 European Journal of Law Reform, 2007, 285–318.

CARMIN J., FAGAN A., *Environmental Mobilisation and Organisations in Post socialist Europe and the Former Soviet Union*, in 19 Environmental Politics, 2015, 689–707.

CARTER F.W., *Bulgaria*, in CARTER F.W., TURNOCK D. (eds.), Environmental Problems in Eastern Europe, London, 1993, 38–62.

CELIKSOY E., *Execution of the Judgments of the European Court of Human Rights in Prisoners' Right to Vote Cases*, in 3 Human Rights Law Review, 2020, 555–581.

CHAKRABARTI S., RABB D., *Should Prisoners Have the Right to Vote?*, in Prospect Magazine, 2014.

CHALOVA B., DE WAELE J.M., *Bulgaria: A Fertile Ground for Populism?*, in 11 Slovak Journal of Political Sciences, 2011, 25–54.

CRAMPTON R., Bulgaria, Oxford University Press, Oxford, 2007.

CZEKALSKI T., *Ekoglasnost and Eco-Transformation. Bulgarian Environmental Movement in the First Years of the Political Transformation*, in 26 Balcanica Posnaniensia, 2019, 232–245.

DAVISON-VECCHIONE D., *Beyond the Forms of Faith: Pacta Sunt Servanda and Loyalty*, in 16 German Law Journal, 2015, 1163–1190.

DAWSON-EDWARDS C., *Enfranchisement Convicted Felons: Current Research on Opinions towards Felon Voting Rights*, in 46 Journal of Offender Rehabilitation, 2008, 13–29.

DAYIOĞLU A., *Changing Aspects of Minority Policy in Bulgaria after 1989: The Case of the Muslim-Turkish Minority*, in HACISALIHOĞLU M., AKSU F. (eds.), Proceedings of the International Conference on Minority Issues in the Balkans and the EU, İstanbul, 2007, 89–109.

DEMIRTAŞ-COŞKUN B., *An Anatomy of Turkish-Bulgarian Relations (1990–2009): Opportunities, Challenges, and Prospects*, in TÜRKEŞ M. (ed.), Turkish-Bulgarian Relations: Past and Present, İstanbul, 2010, 115–132.

DHAMI M., *Prisoner Disenfranchisement Policy: A Threat to Democracy?*, in 5 Analyses of Social Issues and Public Policy, 2015, 235–247.

DHAMI M., CRUISE P., *Prisoner Disenfranchisement: Prisoner and Public Views of an Invisible Punishment*, in 13 Analyses of Social Issues and Public Policy, 2013, 211–227.

DIMITROV H., *The Bulgarian Constitutional Court and Its Interpretive Jurisdiction*, in 38 Columbia Journal of Transnational Justice, 1999, 459–505.

DIMITROVA A., DRAGNEVA R., *Bulgaria's Road to the European Union: Progress, Problems and Perspectives*, in 2 Perspectives on European Politics and Society, 2006, 79–104.

DOBREVA A., *Access to Electoral Rights in Bulgaria*, in 23 EUDO Citizenship Observatory, 2013, 4–15.

DRUMEVA E., *Primacy of the EU Law in the National Constitutional Space: Reflections*, in PERNICE I., TANCHEV E. (eds.), Ceci nest pas une Constitution. Constitutionalization without a Constitution, Baden-Baden, 2009, 100–104.

DRYZEK J., HOLMES L., *Post-Communist Democratization*, Cambridge, 2001, 21–24.

EASTON S., *Prisoners' Rights: Principles and Practice*, London-New York, 2011.

ELLISON B., *Public Administration Reform in Eastern Europe: A Research. Note and a Look at Bulgaria*, in 39 Administration and Society, 2007, 221–232.

ELSTER J., OFFE C., PREUSS U., *Institutional Design in Post-Communist Societies*, Cambridge, 1998, 46–53.

EMINOV A., *The Turks in Bulgaria: Post-1989 Developments*, in 27 Nationalities Papers, 1999, 31–55.

EMINOV A., *Turkish and Other Muslim Minorities in Bulgaria*, London, 1997.

ENDRE S., *The Bad, the Worse, and the Worst: Guesstimating the Level of Corruption*, in KOTKIN S., SAJO A. (eds.), Political Corruption in Transition: A Sceptic's Handbook, Budapest, 2002, 91–113.

Epstein R., Sedelmeier U., *Beyond Conditionality: Intemational Institutions in Post-Communist Europe after Enlargement*, in 15 Journal of European Public Policy, 2008, 795–805.

Flores-Juberias C., *Post-Communist Electoral Systems and National Minorities: A Dilemma in Five Paradigms*, in Stein J.P., Sharpe M.E. (eds.), The Politics of National Minority Participation in Post-Communist Europe, New York, 2019, 31–65.

Foster S., *Prisoners' Voting Rights and the ECHR: Still Hazy after All These Years*, in 15 Coventry Law Journal, 2012, 75–83.

Fredman S., *From Dialogue to Deliberation: Human Rights Adjudication and Prisoners' Rights to Vote*, in Hunt M. Hooper H.J. and Yowell P. (eds.) Parliaments and Human Rights Redressing the Democratic Deficit, Hart Publishing, Oxford and Portland, Oregon, 2015, 447–468.

Frison-Roche F., Sodev S., *The Issues Involved in the Reform of the Bulgarian Judicial System*, in 86 International Review of Administrative Sciences, 2005, 593–606.

Ganev V., *History, Politics, and the Constitution: Ethnic Conflict and Constitutional Adjudication in Post-Communist Bulgaria*, in 63 Slavic Review, 2004, 66–89.

Ganev V., *Bulgaria's Symphony of Hope*, in 8 Journal of Democracy, 1997, 125–140.

Ganev V., *Prisoners' Rights, Public Services, and Institutional Collapse in Bulgaria*, in 4 East European Constitutional Review, 1995, 76–83.

Georgieva K., *Environmental Policy in South-Eastern Europe: Green Desires, Gray Realities*, in 3 Environmental Impact Assessment Review, 1992, 239–244.

Giatzidis E., *An Introduction to Post-communist Bulgaria: Political, Economic, and Social Transformation*. New York, 2002.

Glenn J.K., *Contentious Politics and Democratization: Comparing the Impact of Social Movements on the Fall of Communism in Eastern Europe*, in 51 Political Studies, 2003, 103–120.

Gormley W.P., *The Codification of Pacta Sunt Servanda by the International Law Commission: The Preservation of Classical Norms of Moral Force and Good Faith*, in 14 St. Louis University Law Journal, 1969–1970, 367–429.

Green E., Zografova Y., *Interethnic Relations in Bulgaria*, Sofia, 2014.

Harper M., *The 2001 Parliamentary and Presidential Elections in Bulgaria*, in 22 Electoral Studies, 2003, 335–344.

Hervieu N., *Prisoner Voting Rights: Never Ending Story for a Decisive Issue (ECtHR, Grand Chambre, Scoppola v. Italy, no. 3)*, in 94 Revue Trimestrielle des Droits de l'Homme, 2013, 348–376.

Hristova-Kurzydlowski D., *Programming EU Funds in Bulgaria: Challenges, Opportunities, and the Role of Civil Society*, in 5 Studies of Transition States and Societies, 2013, 22–40.

Hughes J., Sasse G., Gordon C., *Conditionality and Compliance in the EU's Eastward Enlargement: Regional Policy and the Reform of Sub-National Government*, in 42 Journal of Common Market Studies, 2004, 523–551.

Hyland R., *Pacta Sunt Servanda: A Meditation*, in 34 Virginia Journal of International Law, 1994, 405–435.

Iancu D., *Local Reforms by Political Conditionality: Trials and Errors in Central and Eastern Europe*, in 24 Theoretical and Applied Economics, 2019, 73–86.

Jancar-Webster B., *Environmental Movement and Social Change in the Transition Countries*, in 7 Environmental Politics, 1998, 69–90.

Kalotay K., *FDI in Bulgaria and Romania in the Wake of EU Accession*, in 14 Journal of East-West Business, 2008, 5–40.

Kanev D., Hristova-Valtcheva K., *Bulgaria*, in Viola D. (ed.), Routledge Handbook of European Elections, London-New York, 2016, 633–653.

Kanev D., The 2014 Elections in Bulgaria: Political Instability Without End, in 17 Journal for Labour and Social Affairs in Eastern Europe Engagement and Political Change: Walls Reconstructed? 2014, 175–192.

Kanev D., *Muslim Minorities, and the Democratisation Process in Bulgaria*, in Hac Isalihoğlu M., Asku F. (eds.), Proceedings of the International Conference on Minority Issues in the Balkans and the EU, İstanbul, 2007, 79–89.

Karasimeonov G., *Past and New Cleavages in Post-Communist Bulgaria*, in Karasimeonov G., Lawson K., Rommele A. (eds.), Cleavages, Parties, and Voters: Studies from Bulgaria, the Czech Republic, Hungary, Poland, and Romania, Praeger, London, 1999, 109–123.

Katsamunska P., *Good Governance and Reform of Public Administration in Bulgaria*, in 1 Economic Alternatives, 2010, 51–60.

Kitschelt H. (ed.), Research and Dialogue on Programmatic Parties and Party Systems, Stockholm, 2013, 40–62.

Kolarova R., Spirova M., *Bulgaria 2016*, in 56 European Journal of Political Research, 2017, 36–43.

Kolarova R., *Tacit Agreements in the Bulgarian Transition to Democracy: Minority Rights and Constitutionalism*, in 1 The University of Chicago Law School Roundtable, 1993, 23–51.

Kolev K., Bulgaria: Electoral Volatility, Polarization and Financial Deficits Lead to Reduction in Clientelism, 2012, .40–62.

Kornezov A., *Bulgaria*. in Laffranque J. (ed.), The Protection of Fundamental Rights Post-Lisbon, Tallinn, 2012, 259–283.

Kostadinova T., *Voter Turnout Dynamics in Post-Communist Europe*, in 42 European Journal of Political Science Research, 2003, 741–759.

Kramer H., *The European Community's Response to the "New Eastern Europe"*, in 31 Journal of Common Market Studies, 1993, 213–244.

Krastanova R., *The Green Movement and the Green Parties in Bulgaria: Between System Integration and System Change*, in 27 Friedrich Ebert Foundation Policy Papers, 2012, 2–40.

Krasteva A., Todorov A., *Ethnic Minorities and Political Representation: The Case of Bulgaria*, in 35 South-Eastern Europe, 2011, 8–38.

Krasteva A., *The Post-Communist Rise of National Populism: Bulgarian Paradoxes*, in Lazaridis G., Campani G., Benveniste A. (eds.), The Rise of the Far Right in Europe, London, 2016, 161–200.

Kucher A.N., Gorlenko A.A., Stakheev D.S., *Ruling of the Constitutional Court of the Russian Federation on Enforcement of ECHR Judgments*, in www.debevoise .com, 17 Aug 2015.

Lachs M., *Pacta Sunt Servanda*, in Bernhardt R. (ed.), Encyclopedia of Public International Law, Amsterdam, 1997, 364–430.

Lekkas S., Tzanakopoulos A., *Pacta Sunt Servanda versus Flexibility in the Suspension and Termination of Treaties*, in Tams C.J., Tzanakopoulos A., Zimmermann A. (eds.), Research Handbook on the Law of Treaties, Northampton, 2014, 312–340.

Letki N., *Socialization for Participation? Trust, Membership and Democratization in East-Central Europe*, in 57 Political Research Quarterly, 2004, 665–679.

Linz J., Stepan A., *Problems of Democratic Transition and Consolidation: Southern Europe, South America and Post-Communist Europe*, Baltimore and London, 1996, 342–345.

Ludwikowski R., *Fundamental Constitutional Rights in the New Constitutions of Central and Eastern Europe*, in 73 Cardozo Journal of International and Comparative Law, 1995, 73–162.

Ludzhev D., *The Revolution in Bulgaria, 1989–1991*, Sofia, 2008.

Lukashuk I., *The Principle Pacta Sunt Servanda and the Nature of Obligation under International Law*, in 83 The American Journal of International Law, 1989, 513–518.

Mauer M., *Voting Behind Bars: An Argument for Voting by Prisoners*, in 54 Howard Law Journal, 2011, 549–557.

Mavrodieva I., *Manifestations of Populism in Post-Communist Democracy in Bulgaria*, in 14 French Journal for Media Research, 2020, 1–7.

Mayhew A., *Recreating Europe: The European Union's Policy Towards Central and Eastern Europe*, Cambridge, 1999.

Melone A.P., *Creating Parliamentary Government: The Transition to Democracy in Bulgaria*, Columbus, 1998, 74–77.

Mitropolitski S., *EU Integration: An Enforcement of or an Impediment to National Identity in Bulgaria and Macedonia*, in 3 Region: Regional Studies of Russia, Eastern Europe, and Central Asia, 2014, 309–326.

Murray C., *A Perfect Storm: Parliament and Prisoner Disenfranchisement*, in 66 Parliamentary Affairs, 2013, 511–539.

Naxidou E., *Nationalism versus Multiculturalism: The Minority Issue in Twenty-first Century Bulgaria*, in 40 Nationalities Papers, 2012, 85–105.

Nikova E., *Bulgaria in the Balkans*, in Bell J.D. (ed.), Bulgaria in Transition: Politics, Economics, Society and Culture after Communism, Boulder, 1998, 294.

Nitzova P., *Bulgaria: Minorities, Democratization, and National Sentiments*, in 25 Nationalities Papers, 1997, 729–739.

Noutcheva G., Bechev D., *The Successful Laggards: Bulgaria and Romania on the Road to EU Membership*, in 22 East European Politics and Societies, 2008, 114–144.

Nozharov S., *Economic Growth and the Reform of the Judicial System of Bulgaria in the Period 2000–2015*, in 96 IDEAS Working Paper Series from Federal Reserve Bank of St Louis, 2016, 1–12.

O'Brien T., *A Long, Brown Shadow? The Impact of Non-democratic Legacies on the Environment in Portugal and Bulgaria*, in 10 Perspectives on European Politics and Society, 2009, 308–325.

Pamporov A., *Social Distances and Ethnic Stereotypes to Ethnic Minorities in Bulgaria*, Sofia, 2009.

Pavlovska-Hilaiel S., *The EU's Losing Battle Against Corruption in Bulgaria*, in 7 The Hague Journal on the Rule of Law, 2015, 199–217.

Protsyk O., Sachariew K., *Recruitment and Representation of Ethnic Minorities under Proportional Representation: Evidence from Bulgaria*, in 26 East European Politics and Societies, 2010, 1–26.

Racovita M., *Europeanization and Effective Democracy in Romania and Bulgaria*, in 11 Romanian Journal of Political Science, 2011, 28–50.

RAMSAY P., *Voters should not be in Prison! The Rights of Prisoners in a Democracy*, in 16 Critical Review of International Social and Political Philosophy, 2013, 421–438.

RAYCHEVA L., PEICHEVA D., *Populism in Bulgaria Between Politicization of Media and Mediatization of Politics*, in 1 Mediatization Studies, 2017, 69–80.

RECHEL B., *Ethnic Diversity in Bulgaria: Institutional Arrangements and Domestic Discourse*, in 36 The Journal of Nationalism and Ethnicity, 2008, 331–350.

ROUDIK P., *Bulgaria: Constitutional Amendment Provides for Judicial Reform*, Sofia, 2015.

RUSEV M., VLADIMIROVA P., *Electoral Geography of Bulgaria*, Sofia, 2010.

RUSSEL J., *Environmental Issues in Eastern Europe: Setting and Agenda*, London, Royal Institute of International Affairs, 1991, 18–29.

SCHWARTZ H., *The Struggle for Constitutional Justice in Post-Communist Europe*, London, 2000, 57–63.

SCHWARTZ H., *The New East European Constitutional Courts*, in DICK-HOWARD A. (ed.), Constitution-Making in Eastern Europe, Baltimore, 1993, 163–207.

SIMMA B., *Human Rights and State Responsibility*, in REINISCH A., KRIEBAUM U. (eds.), The Law of International Relations, Utrecht, 2007, 359–383.

SMILOV D., *Anticorruption Agencies: Expressive, Constructivist and Strategic Uses*, in 53 Crime, Law and Social Change, 2009, 67–77.

SMIRNOVA M., *Russian Constitutional Court Affirms Russian Constitution's Supremacy over ECtHR Decisions*, in UK Constituzional Law Blog, 17 Jul 2015.

SPIROVA M., SHARENKOVA-TOSHKOVA R., *Bulgaria since 1989*, in RAMET S., HASSENSTAB C. (eds.), Central and Southeast European Politics Since 1989, Cambridge, 2019, pp. 449–476

SPIROVA M., *A Tradition We Don't Mess with: Party Patronage in Bulgaria*, in KOPECKÝ P., MAIR P., SPIROVA M. (eds.), Party Patronage and Party Government in European Democracies, Oxford, 2012, 54–72.

SPIROVA M., *Political Parties in Post-Communist Systems: Formation, Persistence and Change*, New York, 2007, 74–76.

STOYANOV A., *Administrative and Political Corruption in Bulgaria: Status and Dynamics (1998–2006)*, in 37 Romanian Journal of Political Science, 2008, 6–23.

STOYCHEV S.P., *The Controlled Voting in Bulgaria*, Sofia, 2016, 49–60.

SWIANIEWICZ P., *The Political Budget Cycle in Earmarked Taxes for Local Public Services: A Comparison of Poland and Bulgaria*, in 21 Journal of Comparative Policy Analysis: Research and Practice, 2019, 463–480.

TANASOIU C., RACOVITA M., *Post-Accession (Anti-)Corruption Record in Romania and Bulgaria*, in 96 L'Europe en Formation, 2012, 243–263.

TANCHEV E., BELOV M., *The Bulgarian Constitutional Order. Supranational Constitutionalism and European Governance*, in ALBI A., BARDUTZK S. (eds.), National Constitutions in European and Global Governance: Democracy, Rights, the Rule of Law, The Hague, 2019, 1132.

TANCHEV E., BELOV M., *Constitutional Gradualism: Adapting to EU Membership and Improving the Judiciary in the Bulgarian Constitution*, in 14 European Public Law, 2008, 3–19.

TANCHEV E., *The Primacy or Supremacy of International and EU Law in the Context of Contemporary Constitutional Pluralism*, in BIRMONTIENE T. (ed.), Modern Tendencies of Constitutional Justice: The Relation Between National and International Law, Vilnius, 2014, 69–75.

TANCHEV E., *Introduction to Constitutional Law*, Sofia, 2003.

TANCHEV E., *Constitution, and the Rule of Law*, in BELL J.D. (ed.), Bulgaria in Transition: Politics, Economics, Society and Culture after Communism, Boulder, 1998, 65–93.

TASHEV R., *General Theory of Law*, Sofia, 2004.

TODOROV A., *Citizens, Parties, Elections: Bulgaria 1879–2009*, Sofia, 2010.

TONEVA-METODIEVA L., *Prospects for a Democratic Transformation of Post-Communist Society: The Case of Bulgaria*, in 44 Region: Regional Studies of Russia, Eastern Europe, and Central Asia, 2018, 35–50.

TREVES T., *Aspects of Legitimacy of Decisions of International Courts and Tribunals*, in WOLFRUM R., RÖBEN V. (eds.), Legitimacy of International Law, Berlin, 2008, 170–188.

TZENOVA R., *The Electoral System and the Fragmentation of the Party System in Bulgaria 1991–2001*, Sofia.

VACHUDOVA M., *Europe Undivided: Democracy, Leverage and Integration after Communism*, Oxford, 2005, 87–92.

VAN BIEZEN I., *Political Parties in New Democracies: Party Organization in Southern and East-Central Europe*, Basingstoke, 2003.

VASSILEV R., *The Roma of Bulgaria: A Pariah Minority*, in 3 The Global Review of Ethnopolitics, 2004, 40–51.

VASSILEV R., *Post-Communist Bulgaria's Ethnopolitics*, in 1 Global Review of Ethnopolitics, 2001, 37–53.

VERHOEVEN J., *The Law of Responsibility, and the Law of Treaties*, in CRAWFORD J., PELLET A., OLLESON S. (eds.), The Law of International Responsibility, Oxford, 2010, 109–130.

VORHAUS J., *On Degradation. Article 3, Protocol No. 1, of the European Convention on Human Rights*, in 1 Common Law World Review, 2002, 374–399.

WARHOLA J., BOTEVA O., *The Turkish Minority in Contemporary Bulgaria*, in 31 Nationalities Papers, 2003, 260–264.

WEHBERG H., *Pacta Sunt Servanda*, in 53 American Journal of International Law, 1959, 775–786.

WOLF S., *Assessing Eastern Europe's Anti-Corruption Performance: Views from the Council of Europe, OECD and Transparency International*, in 11 *Global Crime*, 2010, 99.

ZANKINA E., *New Cleavages and Populist Mobilization in Bulgaria*, Warsaw, 2015.

ZANKINA E., *Populism, Voters and Cleavages in Bulgarian Politics*, in 24 Czech Journal of Political Science, 2017, 56–71.

ZANKINA E., *Public Administration Characteristics and Performance in EU28: Bulgaria*, in PALARIC E., THIJS N., HAMMERSCHMID G. (eds.), A Comparative Overview of Public Administration Characteristics and Performance in EU28, 2018, 66–94.

ZANKINA E., *Public Administration Reform in Bulgaria: Top-Down and Externally Driven Approach*, in 18 Central European Public Administration Review, 2020, 90–120.

ZOGRAFOVA Y., ANDREEV B., *Opportunities for Development of Tolerant Intergroup Representations and Relationships*, in NAYDENOVA P., SHTERIONOV S., BORISOVA-MARINOVA K. (eds.), The Demographic Situation and the Development of Bulgaria, Sofia, 2014, 315–324.

3 The role of the European Court of Human Rights in Cyprus

Irene Valotti

Introduction and context

Cyprus is an island nation located in the Eastern Mediterranean which, as a result of its strategic position, has served as the frequent object of dispute between the great empires of ancient times. Over time, the island has come under the control of a range of different peoples[1] and the corresponding range of diverse cultures has given rise to a multi-ethnic society made up of various ethnic groups – Greek Cypriots (80%), Turkish Cypriots (18%) and Marionites, Armenians, and Latins (2%) – which have coexisted for centuries in spite of their different religion, customs, language and political aspirations.[2] Indeed, the Turkish Cypriot community – which speaks Turkish and practises Muslim religion – has never lost its ties with Turkey, claiming the split of the island according to the ethnic principle. On the other side, the Greek Cypriot majority – speaking Greek and practising Orthodox Christianity – has consistently voiced its wish over many years to be united with Greece, considering the island to be an extension of the Greek motherland.[3]

During British rule (1878–1960),[4] the colonisers monitored and suppressed inter-ethnic tensions between Greek Cypriots and Turkish Cypriots in order to retain control of the island. Following its independence from the United Kingdom in 1960, Cyprus became an independent Republic with a Greek Cypriot President and a Turkish Cypriot Vice-President, as established in its Constitution.

Unfortunately (but not surprisingly), independence did not ensure peace and the forced marriage between the two communities did not last long: between 1960 and 1974, bloody inter-ethnic conflicts spread across the country, resulting in the complete separation of the two rival communities.[5] Nearly one-third of

1 *Inter alia* Egyptians, Byzantines, Arabs, Ottoman Empire, Great Britain.

2 Encyclopaedia britannica, *Cyprus: People, Ethnic Groups and Languages*, www.britannica.com/place/Cyprus/People accessed 16 September 2020.

3 Urea T., *Cyprus Dispute,* in Revue des Sciences Politiques, 64, 2019, 87–96.

4 Cyprus was placed under the British Empire's administration in 1878 and was formally annexed in 1914.

5 Kyriacou A.P., *An Ethnically Based Federal and Bicameral System: The Case of Cyprus* in International Review of Law and Economics, 20, 2, 2000, 251–268, at 251–252.

DOI: 10.4324/9781003229247-5

each community, forced to leave their homes and displaced by the conflict, were relocated to the side of the island under its respective control. Turkish Cypriots fled from mixed areas to enclaves in the north, and over 2,000 ethnic Greeks moved to Southern Cyprus. Both Turkey and Greece intervened in the conflict to support the affiliated Cypriot community and the escalation of violence in the country forced the United Nations to send peacekeeping forces.[6]

After long years of stalemate in the negotiations seeking a political solution, Turkish Cypriots – under the auspices of Ankara – self-proclaimed a federal state in the north of Cyprus, and in 1983 they declared independence. However, the Turkish Republic of Northern Cyprus has never been recognised by the international community[7] and its existence remains totally dependent on the economy and military presence of Turkey, which exercises effective control over the area.[8]

Over the past 30 years, there have been numerous unsuccessful attempts to bring the conflict to an end and to reach a federal solution to the "Cyprus dispute," which have been mainly sponsored by the United Nations[9] and the European Union.[10]

As of September 2020, Cyprus remains divided, with a buffer zone maintained by the United Nations Peacekeeping Forces separating the two sides (namely the government-controlled area and the Turkish Republic of Northern Cyprus) and the free movement of persons is impeded. As a result, Cypriot society, which for centuries had lived in ethnically mixed cities and villages, is now geographically and politically divided, with the majority of Turkish Cypriots residing in

6 Benvenisti E., *The International Law of Occupation*, Princeton University Press, Princeton, NJ, 2004, 191–194.

7 The UN Security Council declared the declaration of independence of the Turkish Republic of Northern Cyprus legally invalid [UN Security Council Resolution 541 (1983) and Resolution 550 (1984)], and the UN General Assembly has adopted several resolutions condemning Turkish occupation and demanding its withdrawal [*inter alia* UN General Assembly Resolution 3212 (XXIX) of November 20, 1974; Resolution 3395 (XXX) of November 20, 1975; Resolution 33/15 of November 9, 1978; Resolution 34/30 of November 20, 1979; Resolution 37/253 of May 13, 1983 etc.].

8 According to international humanitarian law, the Turkish Republic of Northern Cyprus is a Turkish-occupied territory of the Republic of Cyprus (military occupation of Cyprus by Turkey).

Geneva Academy of International Humanitarian Law and Human Rights, *Rule of Law in Armed Conflict (RULAC): Cyprus*, www.rulac.org/browse/countries/cyprus accessed 22 May 2020.

9 The full text of the Annan Plan is available at www.hri.org/docs/annan/.

Theodoulou M., *The Peace Process: 2004 Annan Plan*, Cyprus Mail, 29 December 2016, https://cyprus-mail.com/2016/12/29/peace-plans-2004-annan-plan/ accessed 15 September 2020.

International Crisis Group, *Cyprus: Three Advantages of the Annan Peace Plan*, 19 April 2004, www.crisisgroup.org/europe-central-asia/western-europemediterranean/cyprus/cyprus-three-advantages-annan-peace-plan accessed 15 September 2020.

10 European Commission, *The EU's Role in the Cyprus Settlement Process: Questions and Answers*, 12 January 2017, https://ec.europa.eu/commission/presscorner/detail/en/MEMO_17_52 accessed 15 September 2020.

the Turkish Republic of Northern Cyprus and the majority of Greek Cypriots living in the south of the island, controlled by the Republic of Cyprus. As at 31 December 2016, it was estimated that there were 272,000 internally displaced persons in Cyprus;[11] an estimated 228,000 persons remain displaced today.[12]

Constitutional framework

The Constitution of Cyprus, composed of 199 Articles grouped into 13 Parts,[13] is a detailed document, which regulates every aspect of the government and administration of the country. It represents the supreme law of the island and no law, rule, regulation, act, or decision by any organ or authority of the State may be contrary to or inconsistent with the constitutional text.[14] The Cypriot constitutional system is based on the principle of legality, the division of authority (executive, legislative, and judicial power)[15] and the impartiality of the judiciary.

Part I (General Provisions) outlines the pillars at the base of the Republic. Art. 1, establishes that Cyprus is an independent and sovereign presidential Republic with a Greek President elected by the Greek Cypriot community and a Turkish Vice-President elected by the Turkish Cypriot community.[16] For the purposes of the Constitution, as outlined in Art. 2, the Greek community comprises all citizens of Greek origin and Greek language, or those who share the Greek cultural traditions or belong to the Greek-Orthodox Church; the Turkish community, on the other hand, comprises all citizens of Turkish origin and Turkish language, or those who share the Turkish cultural traditions or profess to follow the Muslim religion.[17] The official languages of the Republic are Greek and Turkish and all

11 Internal Displacement Monitoring Centre & Norwegian Refugee Council, *Global Report on Internal Displacement 2017*, May 2017, www.internal-displacement.org/publications/2017-global-report-on-internal-displacement accessed 1 September 2020, 114–119.

12 Internal Displacement Monitoring Centre & Norwegian Refugee Council, *Global Report on Internal Displacement 2019*, May 2019, www.internal-displacement.org/sites/default/files/publications/documents/2019-IDMC-GRID.pdf accessed 1 September 2020, 128.

13 Part I, General Provisions; Part II, Fundamental Rights and Liberties; Part III, The President of the Republic, The Vice-President of the Republic and The Council of Ministers; Part IV, The House of Representatives; Part V, The Communal Chambers; Part VI, The Independent Officers of the Republic; Part VII, General; Part VIII, The Forces of the Republic; Part IX, The Supreme Constitutional Court; Part X, The High Court and Subordinate Courts; Part XI, Financial Provisions; Part XII, Miscellaneous Provisions; Part XIII, Final Provisions.

14 As established in Art. 179 of the Constitution.

15 The competence, authority and jurisdiction of the powers of the State are defined in different Parts of Constitution: Part III (executive power), Part IV (legislative power), Parts IX and X (judicial power).

16 Art. 1 of the Constitution: "*The State of Cyprus is an independent and sovereign Republic with a presidential regime, the President being Greek and the Vice-President being Turkish elected by the Greek and the Turkish Communities of Cyprus respectively as hereinafter in this Constitution provided.*"

17 Art. 2 of the Constitution.

the legislative, executive, and administrative acts and documents shall be drawn up in both languages.[18]

The Constitution – as is clear from the beginning – is based on the notion of power sharing due to the ethnic division of the country, and thus requires all Cypriots (including those minority group members who are neither Greek nor Turkish)[19] to declare themselves as Greek or Turkish to be beneficiaries of certain rights, despite the constitutional enunciation of the principle of non-discrimination.[20] According to G. Pikis, a distinguished Cypriot judge,[21] "the acknowledgment of human rights to persons by reference to factors extraneous to human identity is an antinomy to the very concept and object of human rights."[22]

More specifically, 30% of the positions within the executive, legislature, public service and security forces (police and gendarmerie), and 40% of posts in the army are reserved for members of the Turkish community, with the remaining posts and offices allocated to the Greek community.[23]

For instance, as regards executive power, Art. 46 of the Constitution provides that the Council of Ministers shall be composed of seven Greek Ministers and three Turkish Ministers,[24] respectively appointed by the Greek President and the Turkish Vice-President.[25]

As for the legislative power, which is exercised by the House of Representatives, Art. 62 of the Constitution establishes that the number of members of parliament is 50,[26] with 70% (35 seats) elected by the Greek community and 30% (15 seats) by the Turkish community.[27] Three constitutionally recognised religious groups (Armenians, Latins, and Maronites) have each been allocated one seat in parliament, though these representatives do not have voting rights and are only allowed to present their views on issues concerning their religious groups.[28]

The President of the House of Representatives shall be a Greek elected by the representatives elected by the Greek community, and the Vice-President shall be elected by the representatives elected by the Turkish community.[29]

18 Art. 3 of the Constitution.
19 Art. 2(3) of the Constitution.
20 Art. 6 of the Constitution.
21 Georghios M. Pikis is a former member of the International Criminal Court.
22 Pikis G.M., *Constitutionalism – Human Rights – Separation of Powers: The Cyprus Precedent*, Martinus Nijhoff Publishers 2006, 8.
23 Kyriacou, cited above, 252.
24 Art. 46 of the Constitution.
25 Arts. 48 and 49 of the Constitution.
26 In 1985, the number of seats was increased by Parliament to 80, with 56 seats allocated to the Greek Community.
27 Art. 62 of the Constitution.
28 Office For Democratic Institutions and Human Rights (OSCE), *Republic of Cyprus, Parliamentary Elections, 22 May 2016, OSCE/ODIHR Needs Assessment Mission Report*, 30 March 2016, www.osce.org/files/f/documents/2/b/230496.pdf accessed 4 August 2020, 3–4.
29 Art. 72(1) of the Constitution.

However, since 1964, when the Turkish Cypriot community withdrew from cross-community institutions (such as the presidency, government, parliament, and judiciary) their seats have remained vacant, meaning that from that time on, the relevant Articles of the Constitution providing for the quotas to be adhered to by the two communities became impossible to implement in practice, thus excluding the Turkish community from participating in the political life of the country.[30]

Part II of the Constitution (Fundamental Rights and Liberties) is modelled on Section I of the ECHR and provides an extensive charter of human rights,[31] which are central both in terms of provisions and protection. In 2016, an explicit reference to the ECHR was added to the preamble of the Constitution, noting the abolition of the death penalty[32] and the introduction of an additional exception to the right to privacy, referencing Art. 8(2) ECHR.[33]

This Part guarantees all fundamental civil and political rights such as the principle of non-discrimination,[34] the right to life,[35] the prohibition of torture,[36] the prohibition of slavery and forced labour,[37] the right to liberty and security,[38] freedom of movement,[39] no punishment without law,[40] the right to respect for private and family life,[41] freedom of thought, conscience and religion,[42] freedom of speech and expression,[43] freedom of assembly and association,[44] the right to marry,[45] the right of property,[46] the right to an effective remedy,[47] and the right to vote.[48] Moreover, it enshrines several socio-economic rights[49] (such as the right

30 OSCE, cit., 3.
31 From Art. 6 to Art. 35 of the Constitution.
32 The Cypriot Constitution was revised in 2016 by the Law on the Fifteenth Amendment of the Constitution No. 93(I) of 2016. As a result, there is no longer a reference to the death penalty, which had already been abolished in 1999 following the ratification of Protocols 6 and 13 of the ECHR by Cyprus.
33 European Union Agency for Fundamental Rights (FRA), *The EU Charter of Fundamental Rights in Cyprus (Charter Country-Sheet)*, https://fra.europa.eu/sites/default/files/fra_uploads/fra-2019-eu-charter-in-cyprus_en.pdf accessed 26 May 2020.
34 Art. 6 of the Constitution.
35 Art. 7 of the Constitution.
36 Art. 8 of the Constitution.
37 Art. 10 of the Constitution.
38 Art. 11 of the Constitution.
39 Art. 13 of the Constitution.
40 Art. 12 of the Constitution.
41 Art. 15 of the Constitution.
42 Art. 18 of the Constitution.
43 Art. 19 of the Constitution.
44 Art. 21 of the Constitution.
45 Art. 22 of the Constitution.
46 Art. 23 of the Constitution.
47 Art. 30 of the Constitution.
48 Art. 31 of the Constitution.
49 To be exercised within the framework of public interest and common good.

to a decent existence and social security,[50] the right to work[51] and the right to strike),[52] and, in this respect, it goes further in protection than the ECHR.

The judiciary has been extremely active in ensuring the full protection of the rights and liberties enshrined in the Constitution and the content of such judicial protection has been developed in connection with the ECHR system, which Cyprus has actively participated in since its first steps.[53] Indeed, the ECHR has proven to be the yardstick by which the judiciary has sought to establish the appropriate level of protection to put in place. It has also been used to help solve ambiguities in the constitutional text. In several instances, the Cypriot Supreme Court has even exceeded the parameters established by the ECtHR, making direct reference to the need to adopt a higher standard of protection.[54]

Cyprus and the European Human Rights System

As a member of the CoE, Cyprus ratified the ECHR in 1962 and became subject to the jurisdiction of the ECtHR. Cyprus has also ratified the European Social Charter and authorised the European Committee of Social Rights to adjudicate collective complaints against it. In addition, Cyprus is party to other regional human rights treaties *inter alia* the CoE Convention on Action against Trafficking in Human Beings, the CoE Convention on Preventing and Combating Violence against Women and Domestic Violence, the European Convention for the Prevention of Torture and Inhuman or Degrading Treatment or Punishment and the Framework Convention for the Protection of National Minorities. Its human rights policies and practices are additionally monitored by the Commissioner for Human Rights of the CoE, who has visited Cyprus in both 2008 and 2015[55] and, on repeated occasions, has expressed concerns about the grave shortcomings of the national asylum system and the systematic violations of the rights of refugees.[56]

50 Art.9 of the Constitution.

51 Art. 25 of the Constitution.

52 Art. 27 of the Constitution.

53 Kombos C., Laulhé Shaelou S., "The Cypriot Constitution Under the Impact of EU Law: An Asymmetrical Formation," in Albi A., Bardutzky S. (eds.), *National Constitutions in European and Global Governance: Democracy, Rights, the Rule of Law: National Reports*, Asser Press, The Hague, 2019, at 1390.

54 *Ibidem*, The Cypriot Supreme Court has exceeded the parameters established by the ECtHR in *Charalambous and Others* v. *Republic*, Joined Cases 1480/2011, 11 June 2014; *Police* v. *Ekdotiki Eteria* [1982] 2 CLR 63; *David Scattergood* v. *Attorney General* [2005] 1 CLR 142.

55 Commissioner for Human Rights, *Report by Thomas Hammarberg, Commissioner for Human Rights of the Council of Europe, following his visit to the Republic of Cyprus (7–10 July 2008)*, CommDH(2008)36/12, December 2008; COMMISSIONER FOR HUMAN RIGHTS, *Report by Nils Muiznieks, Commissioner for Human Rights of the Council of Europe, following his visit to Cyprus from 7 to 11 December 2015*, CommDH(2016)16/, 31 March 2016.

56 Commissioner for Human Rights, *Letter from the Council of Europe Commissioner for Human Rights, Nils Muiznieks, to Mr Costas Clerides, Attorney General of Cyprus, on the protection of human rights of unaccompanied migrant children*, CommDH (2016) 38.

In a country deeply divided along ethnic lines, which has just emerged from a painful conflict and still remains under partial occupation, it is no surprise that human rights violations are likely to occur.

As highlighted in several reports by the Office of the United Nations High Commissioner for Human Rights, the persistent division of Cyprus affects human rights throughout the island, including the right to life and the question of missing persons, non-discrimination, freedom of movement, property rights, freedom of religion or belief and cultural rights, freedom of opinion and expression, and the right to education.[57]

Given the socio-political context, it is thus not surprising that the ECtHR has been heavily involved not only with cases related to the Turkish presence on the island,[58] but also with violations which have occurred in the government-controlled areas.

Since the entry into force of the Convention, the ECtHR has delivered 84 judgments (out of which there have been 5 by its Grand Chamber, 78 by the Chamber, and 1 by the Committee) and declarations have been made about the State's international responsibility in 60 cases. The ECHR provision which has been violated the most is Art. 6 (right to fair trial); the next most frequent violations are those under Art. 13 (right to an effective remedy), Art. 3 (prohibition of torture), Art. 5 (right to liberty and security), and Art. 8 (right to respect for private and family life). The Court has also given rulings on various issues such as the right to life, voting rights, the principle of non-discrimination, and freedom of expression.[59]

Generally speaking, Cyprus has a good record of making compensation payments within the deadlines set by the Strasbourg Court and has made genuine attempts to comply with most of the ECtHR's judgments relating to individual and general measures.

As emerges from a report by the Department for the Execution of Judgments of the ECtHR on Cyprus, the total number of cases which have been transmitted for supervision since the entry into force of the Convention is 70, the total number of cases closed following a final resolution is 62, and 8 cases were still pending in 2019.[60] As evidenced from this data, the relationship between Cyprus

57 Office of the United Nations High Commissioner for Human Rights, *Question of Human Rights in Cyprus*, 6 February 2019, A/HRC/40/22; Office of the united nations high commissioner for human rights, *Question of Human Rights in Cyprus*, 9 February 2018, A/HRC/37/22; Office of the united nations high commissioner for human rights, *Question of Human Rights in Cyprus*, 23 January 2015, A/HRC/28/20.

58 *Inter alia Loizidou* v. *Turkey*, 25 July 1998; *Cyprus. Turkey* [GC],10 May 2001; *Michaelidou Developments Ltd. and Tymvios* v. *Turkey*, 31 July 2003; *Demades* v. *Turkey*, 31 October 2003; *Xenides-Arestis* v. *Turkey*, 22 December 2005; *Demopoulos and Others* v. *Turkey* [GC], 1 March 2010.

59 Hudoc European Court of Human Rights, *Cyprus*, https://hudoc.echr.coe.int/eng#{" languageisocode":["ENG"],"respondent":["CYP"],"documentcollectionid2":["JUDGME NTS"]} , accessed 26 September 2020.

60 Department for the Execution of Judgments of the European Court of Human Rights,

and the ECtHR may be characterised as an example of harmonious and fruitful coexistence.

This contribution has the purpose of examining the legal and economic impact of the ECtHR on the Cypriot national landscape, with a specific focus on political rights.

Having provided an overview of the Constitution, the democratic status of the country and its presence in the European Human Rights System – crucial issues for understanding the peculiarity of the Republic of Cyprus – let us now focus on the analysis of the *Aziz* case, a landmark judgment where the ECtHR dealt with the issue of Turkish Cypriots' voting rights. The legal and economic impact of the *Aziz* case on the national landscape will be dealt with in the last section of the chapter.

Voting rights of Turkish Cypriots: The *Aziz* case

Mr Ibrahim Aziz ("the applicant") was a Turkish Cypriot national who was refused the right to be registered on the electoral roll by the Ministry of the Interior, therefore preventing him from exercising his voting rights in the 2001 parliamentary elections. As a result, Mr Aziz, lodged an application against the Republic of Cyprus complaining under Art. 3 of Protocol 1 (right to free elections), taken alone or in conjunction with Art. 14 of the ECHR (prohibition of discrimination), that he was prevented from exercising his electoral rights on the grounds of national origin and/or association with a national minority.[61]

Facts

The applicant was born and lived in Nicosia, the capital and the seat of the government of Cyprus, and is one of the few Turkish Cypriots residing in that part of the country under the control of the Republic of Cyprus.

In January 2001, Mr Aziz made a request to the Ministry of the Interior to be registered on the electoral roll in order to vote in the parliamentary elections of 27 May 2001. The Ministry, however, refused to enrol the applicant on the basis of Art. 63 of the Constitution, according to which members of the Turkish community are not allowed to be registered on the Greek Cypriot electoral roll (and vice versa).

Following the rejection of his application, Mr Aziz submitted a complaint to the Supreme Court against the decision of the Ministry of the Interior – relying on Art. 3 of Protocol 1 – and claimed that, following the dissolution of the Communal Chambers and the breakdown of the bi-constitutional setup, the government did not establish two electoral lists (one for Greek Cypriots and

Country Factsheet: Cyprus, 17 December 2019, https://rm.coe.int/1680709743 accessed 27 May 2020.

61 *Aziz* v. *Cyprus*, 22 June 2004.

the other for Turkish Cypriots), thus failing to protect the right to vote of the Turkish minority.

The Supreme Court dismissed Mr Aziz's application drawing on two main arguments.

First of all, the Court highlighted that Art. 5 of the Election of Members of the House of Representatives Law[62] (providing for the right to elect) makes the right to vote conditional on the provisions of Art. 63 of the Constitution, which requires the compilation of two separate electoral lists in which the members of each community are included.

Art. 63(1), indeed, provides that all citizens of the Republic – who are at least 21 years old and who are resident in Cyprus for a period of 6 months before becoming eligible to vote – have the right to be registered as electors in either the Greek or the Turkish electoral list; moreover, it firmly states that members of the Greek community shall only be registered in the Greek electoral list, whereas members of the Turkish community shall only be registered in the Turkish electoral list.[63] Even though the applicant suggested that the abovementioned provisions had to be interpreted in the light of the current situation in Cyprus, which renders impossible in practice the compilation of an electoral list for Turkish Cypriots, the Supreme Court concluded that the right to vote had to be placed under the reservations of Art. 63: therefore, Art. 5 excluded the inclusion in the electoral list of any person other than members of the Greek community.

Moreover, the Supreme Court dismissed the second ground relied upon by the applicant, namely the law of necessity. According to Mr Aziz, the impossibility of there being compiled an electoral list of members of the Turkish community led to the necessity of his inclusion in the Greek electoral list; inclusion which was additionally justified by the applicant's claim to have the same rights and obligations as every other Greek citizen, due to the fact that he was residing in the government-controlled area. However, the Supreme Court rejected this argument, too, claiming that any assessment of necessity is a duty falling upon the legislature and is not a matter for the judiciary, as this would be contrary to the principle of the separation of powers.

62 Art. 5 of 1979 Election of Members of the House of Representatives Law (Law 72/79): *"The right to elect belongs to those who have the qualifications provided for under Art. 63 of the Constitution, that is to say citizens of the Republic who have attained the age of twenty-one and have had their ordinary residence in Cyprus for a period of six months immediately before the date fixed by the Minister, by publication in the Official Gazette of the Republic, as the date of acquisition of the electoral qualifications."*

63 Art. 63(1) of the Constitution: *"Subject to paragraph 2 of this Article every citizen of the Republic who has attained the age of twenty-one years, and has such residential qualifications as may be prescribed in the Electoral Law, shall have the right to be registered as an elector in either the Greek or the Turkish electoral list: provided that the members of the Greek community shall only be registered in the Greek electoral list and the members of the Turkish community shall only be registered in the Turkish electoral list."*

Alleged violations of Art. 3 of Protocol 1

The applicant – once the Supreme Court had dismissed his claim and having exhausted all domestic remedies – addressed a claim to the ECtHR, complaining that he had been prevented from exercising his voting rights in the 2001 parliamentary elections, contrary to Art. 3 of Protocol 1.[64]

Mr Aziz, in his application, reminded the Court that Art. 31 of the Constitution[65] guarantees every citizen the right to vote, while stressing that the Turkish Communal Chamber had ceased to operate in 1963 and that the Greek Communal Chamber had been abolished in 1965.

He further claimed that the Supreme Court had treated him as a member of the Turkish community despite the fact that such a community no longer existed in the government-controlled areas; indeed, according to the applicant, in that part of the country there were only Cypriot citizens with different ethnic origins and there was no point in still talking about two diverse communities. Mr Aziz, therefore, challenged the decision of the Supreme Court, claiming that it should have ruled that the provisions of the Election of Members of the House of Representatives Law were unconstitutional and prevented him from exercising his right to vote. In addition, the applicant claimed that the Supreme Court had erroneously refused to apply the law of necessity in his case (as it had already done in several other cases) and had interpreted the relevant provisions in a restrictive manner, disregarding the very essence of the Constitution.

Finally, Mr Aziz stressed that his case was clearly distinguishable from the case of *Mathieu-Mohin and Clerfayt v. Belgium*,[66] on the basis that, in that case, there was a mechanism in place allowing every citizen to exercise voting rights and that the contended measure was only temporary. On the contrary, the applicant emphasised that, in his specific situation, he only had a theoretical right to vote under the Constitution and, therefore, he has been prevented from participating in the political life of Cyprus.

The government, on the other side, started its defence by noting that Art. 3 of Protocol 1 does not oblige Contracting States to introduce a specific system for appointing the legislature and thus leaves a wide margin of appreciation in this respect.

Under Art. 2 of the Constitution, citizens of the Republic of Cyprus had to belong to either the Greek or the Turkish community. It followed that, according to the government, the spirit of the Constitution – including the electoral system – was that each community participated in the political life of the State through

64 Art. 3 of Protocol 1 provides as follows: *"The High Contracting Parties undertake to hold free elections at reasonable intervals by secret ballot, under conditions which will ensure the free expression of the opinion of the people in the choice of the legislature."*

65 According to Art. 31 of the Constitution *"every citizen has, subject to the provisions of this Constitution and any electoral law of the Republic or of the relevant Communal Chamber made thereunder, the right to vote in any election held under this Constitution or any such law."*

66 *Mathieu-Mohin and Clerfayt* v. *Belgium*, 2 March 1987.

its own representatives respectively elected by their members, according to the percentage and/or numbers allotted to each community by the Constitution.

Integrating new observations into its reasoning, the government emphasised that under Art. 62 of the Constitution members of the Turkish community are not allowed to vote for members of the Greek community and vice versa: members of each community, indeed, "had to vote and elect representatives from their own community in their capacity as members of that community."[67]

According to the government, it followed from the above reasons that Art. 63(1) of the Constitution requires voters to be registered either on the Greek or the Turkish electoral roll, on the basis of the community they belonged to.

The government, moreover, stressed the fact that the Turkish community had withdrawn from the constitutional organs of the State and that, due to the absence of one of the two communities, the House of Representatives and the government were not in practice bi-communally composed; therefore, it alleged that

> it had not been the electoral system as such that had prevented the applicant from voting for the legislature, but rather the absence of the majority of the Turkish community that had prevented him from voting, in his capacity as a member of the Turkish community, for candidates who were members of that community.[68]

Continuing the reasoning, the government affirmed that any action enabling members of the Turkish community residing in the government-controlled area to participate in elections would have constituted a departure from the constitutional system.

In support of its arguments, the government also relied on the *Mathieu-Mohin and Clerfayt v. Belgium* case, where the ECtHR stated that any electoral system shall be assessed in the light of the political evolution of the State and bearing in mind the general context. In this respect, the government considered the electoral arrangements contested by the applicant – if assessed in the context of the whole constitutional framework – to be proportionate and pursuing a legitimate aim.

Finally, the government argued that the applicant, due to the deliberate withdrawal of his membership community, could not have voted for the House of Representatives, having regard to its composition. Otherwise, "a notably insignificant part of the whole population (less than 2%) would have controlled 30% of the House, a fact that would have been intolerably undemocratic."[69]

The ECtHR started its assessment by recalling the general principles of Art. 3 of Protocol 1. Despite recognising that the Article mainly obliges States to hold elections which ensure the free expression of the opinion of the people, the Court emphasised that it has been firmly established in its case-law that this Article also

67 *Aziz v. Cyprus*, cit., para 20.
68 *Ibidem*, para 21.
69 *Ibidem*, para 24.

guarantees individual rights, *inter alia* the right to vote and the right to stand for election, which are not absolute and thus potentially subject to limitations. It is true that States enjoy a wide margin of appreciation in this respect; however, the Court recalled that it is its task to assess, as a last resort, whether the requirements of Art. 3 of Protocol 1 have been complied with. More specifically, the limitations imposed by the State shall not restrict the rights in question to such an extent as to impair their essence and deprive them of effectiveness; moreover, such limitations shall be proportionate and justified by a legitimate aim.[70]

Having analysed the main features of Art. 3 of Protocol 1, the ECtHR moved forward and applied them to the specific case of Mr Aziz.

Firstly, the Court observed that the Constitution of the Republic of Cyprus – which provides for two separate electoral lists, one for each community – came into force in 1960 and that, following the dissolution of the Communal Chambers and the breakdown of the bi-constitutional setup (a situation which began in 1963), the constitutional provisions providing for the parliamentary representation of the Turkish community became impossible to implement in practice.

Secondly, the ECtHR noted that the Cypriot Supreme Court, in deciding the applicant's case, had stated that both Art. 63 of the Constitution and Art. 5 of the Election of Members of the House of Representatives Law do not guarantee the right to vote to Turkish Cypriots residing in the government-controlled area but, nonetheless, refrained from intervening on the basis of the law of necessity to fill such a legislative gap.

Thirdly, although the Strasbourg Court confirmed that States enjoy a considerable margin of appreciation in shaping the system for appointing the parliament and defining its composition, it firmly stressed that these provisions shall not exclude some persons and/or categories of persons from participating in the political life of the country and, in particular, in the choice of the legislature.

Fourthly, it observed the manifest lack of legislation aimed at solving the anomalous situation of the Turkish community, which lead to the fact that the applicant had been completely deprived of his right to vote.

In the light of the above reasons, the ECtHR concluded that the very essence of the right to vote was impaired and found a violation of Art. 3 of Protocol 1.

Alleged violation of Art. 14 of the ECHR

Mr Aziz complained that he was prevented from exercising his right to vote on the grounds of national origin and/or association with a national minority, contrary to Art. 14 of the ECHR.[71]

70 European Court of Human Rights, *Guide on Article 3 of Protocol No. 1 to the European Convention on Human Rights*, 30 April 2019, www.echr.coe.int/Documents/Guide_Art._3_Protocol_1_ENG.pdf accessed on 27 August 2020.

71 According to Art. 14 of the ECHR: "The enjoyment of the rights and freedoms set forth in [the] Convention shall be secured without discrimination on any ground such as sex, race,

The applicant argued that, following the constitutional breakdown, the government has adopted no provision safeguarding the rights of the Turkish community and, on the contrary, has only passed laws tailored to fit the needs of Greek Cypriots. As a consequence, the Turkish minority residing in the government-controlled area has been prevented from exercising its fundamental right to vote and stand in elections since 1964. Moreover, the applicant claimed that the Supreme Court had not applied the law of necessity in his specific case due to his membership of the Turkish community.

The government submitted that no issue arose under Art. 14 of the ECHR because the situation of the applicant was not comparable to the situation of Greek voters, who voted for Greek candidates by virtue of being members of the Greek community.

The ECtHR started its assessment by recalling the general principles enshrined in Art. 14 of the ECHR, which are as follows: firstly, a different treatment is discriminatory if it does not pursue a legitimate aim or if it is disproportionate; secondly, States enjoy a certain latitude in assessing whether and to what extent differences in otherwise similar situations justify a diverse treatment. The Court further noted the ancillary nature of Art. 14, meaning that the provision does not prohibit discrimination as such, but only discrimination in the enjoyment of the rights and freedoms enshrined in the Convention.

Having analysed the main features of Art. 14 of the ECHR, the ECtHR moved forward and applied them to the specific case of Mr Aziz.

First of all, the Court established that the complaint under Art. 14 was not a mere restatement of the objection raised by the applicant under Art. 3 of Protocol 1: indeed, the difference in treatment of Mr Aziz resulted directly from his Turkish origin and from the constitutional provisions regulating the voting rights of the two communities, which became impossible to implement in practice.

According to the Strasbourg Court, such different treatment – which has impeded Turkish Cypriots from voting at any parliamentary elections since 1964 – was not justifiable on reasonable and objective grounds. Therefore, the Court held that the clear inequality in the enjoyment of the right to vote was a fundamental aspect of the case and that there had therefore been a violation of Art. 14 of the Convention taken in conjunction with Art. 3 of Protocol 1.

Application of Art. 41 of the ECHR: Damage, costs, and expenses

The applicant claimed that the impossibility of his ability to vote and stand as a candidate in parliamentary elections solely on the ground that he was a Turkish Cypriot had adversely affected his social status and standing in the community. Moreover, Mr Aziz pointed out that over the years he had been a victim of defamation campaigns in the media and the target of threats from agents of the

colour, language, religion, political or other opinion, national or social origin, association with a national minority, property, birth or other status."

Turkish Republic of Northern Cyprus, owing to the fact that he resided in the government-controlled area of Cyprus despite being of Turkish origin. For these reasons, the applicant claimed 50,000 Cypriot pounds as compensation for the distress, hardship, and psychological damage suffered due to the long-standing denial of his right to vote. The claim was calculated as to include every parliamentary election since 1964.

The government, on its side, contended that the applicant's complaints before both the Supreme Court and the ECtHR were merely focused on his right to vote in the 2001 parliamentary elections, and not on his right to stand as a candidate in that election or in any other election held previous to that.

Furthermore, the government submitted that there was no point in claiming that the mere existence of the contended provisions in the Constitution and in the Electoral Law – without any reference to their actual effect – had caused distress, hardship, and psychological harm to the applicant in every parliamentary election since 1964. Indeed, according to the government, Mr Aziz had found out about the impossibility of his being able to participate in the 2001 parliamentary election only at the moment when his application to the Ministry of the Interior was rejected, and, therefore, his claim as regards the hardship and distress suffered over a period of years had to be considered as unsubstantiated.

Finally, the government noted that any finding of a violation by the ECtHR, with the obligations arising from the judgment, would constitute in itself just satisfaction for the applicant.

The ECtHR, noting that Cyprus had to implement "all the measures as they consider appropriate to fulfil their obligations to secure the right to vote in compliance with this judgment,"[72] concluded that the reform of the electoral system combined with the findings of the judgment constitute sufficient just satisfaction.

The applicant claimed a total of 4,097.30 Cypriot pounds[73] as reimbursement for the costs and expenses incurred before the Supreme Court and the ECtHR, whereas the government left this matter to the discretion of the Court.

The Court acknowledged the costs and expenses incurred by the applicant in the preparation of his case and, making its assessment on an equitable basis as required by Art. 41 of the ECHR, considered it reasonable to make an award of EUR 3,500.[74]

Findings

To summarise, the ECtHR held that there had been a violation of Art. 3 of Protocol 1 and of Art. 14 of the Convention taken in conjunction with Art. 3 of Protocol 1; that the findings of the judgment constituted sufficient just

72 *Aziz v. Cyprus*, cit., para 43.

73 Inclusive of value-added tax.

74 EUR 3,500 to be converted into Cypriot pounds at the date of settlement.

satisfaction for the non-pecuniary damage incurred by the applicant; and that Cyprus must pay the applicant EUR 3,500 in respect of costs and expenses.

The judgment, given by a Chamber composed of 7 judges,[75] became final on 22 September 2004.

The impact of the *Aziz* case at the national level

On September 2004 the ECtHR delivered a landmark judgment in which it found Cyprus responsible for having violated the voting rights of Turkish Cypriots residing in the government-controlled areas, as shown in the section above.

Under Art. 46 of the ECHR, Contracting States undertake to abide by the final judgment of the Court in any case to which they are parties. So, what has been done by the Cypriot Government to solve the electoral discrimination perpetrated against the Turkish community and to advance their political participation?

This section will provide an analysis of the impact of the *Aziz* case at the national level, with the aim of assessing the role played by the Strasbourg Court in advancing democracy in a conflict-affected and ethnically divided country.

The Government of Cyprus, following the ECtHR's judgment in the *Aziz v. Cyprus* case, adopted several measures to fully remedy the consequences for the applicant of the violations found in the case and to prevent similar violations occurring in the future, thus complying with its obligations under Art. 46(1) of the ECHR. The CM, which supervises the execution of final judgments of the ECtHR,[76] having examined and been satisfied by the measures taken by Cyprus, closed its examination of the case.[77]

With regard to just satisfaction, the Cypriot authorities paid 3,500 EUR in respect of cost and expenses, as established by the ECtHR, on 21 October 2004 (a month after the judgment).

As regards individual measures, the applicant's enjoyment of the right to vote was considered as dependent on the general measures which are illustrated below. According to the Strasbourg Court, the legislative reform which Cyprus was to implement to execute the judgment and the findings of the judgment constituted sufficient just satisfaction for Mr Aziz.

With regard to the general measures, two years after the ECtHR's judgment, the Cypriot authorities passed Law 2(I)/2006 [The Exercise of the Right to Vote and be Elected by Members of the Turkish Community with Ordinary Residence in the Free Areas of the Republic (Temporary Provisions) Law] on the exercise of the right to vote and stand for election of members of the Turkish

75 Jean-Paul Costa (French), President, Andris Baka (Hungarian), Loukis Loucaides (Cypriot), Corneliu Birsan (Romanian), Karel Jungwiert (Czech), Mindia Ugrekhelidze (Georgian), Antonella Mularoni (San Marinese).

76 Under the terms of Art. 46(2) ECHR.

77 Committee of Ministers, *Execution of the Judgment of the European Court of Human Rights Aziz against Cyprus*, Resolution CM/ResDH(2007)77.

Cypriot community, who had habitual residence in the government-controlled area, which gave effect to the right of Turkish Cypriots to vote.

The level of expenditure that this legislative reform required is difficult to quantify. Nonetheless, it is conceivable that, due to the enlargement of the number of those entitled to vote and of those to be voted for, it has certainly led to an increase in spending in respect of the ordinary costs of elections, *inter alia* the cost of permanent employees, temporary or part-time employees, field technicians, voter education and outreach, official and provisional ballots, polling place costs, poll workers and related costs (recruiting, training, compensation), absentee voters, ballot counting, preparation of press releases, preparation of legal notices, preparation of candidate guides and forms, processing candidates, meetings, and coordination work with the Ministry of the Interior and other stakeholders, printing and supplies, technology costs, voting and election management systems, translation costs, etc.

Law 2(I)/2006, which entered into force on 10 February 2006, applies to the citizens of the Republic of Cyprus who are members of the Turkish community and have their habitual residence in the government-controlled areas. The Law enables them to exercise their right to vote and to be elected in parliamentary, municipal, and community elections; moreover, it grants them the right to vote in presidential elections, but not the right to stand for President.[78] The Office for Democratic Institutions and Human Rights (OSCE) has criticised the fact that only citizens belonging to the Greek community are able to stand for President, a constitutional restriction based on ethnicity which is considered to be contrary to international standards and thus should be removed.[79]

The Law further provides that Cypriot nationals of Turkish origin are to be registered in a supplementary electoral list which is then incorporated into the main electoral list in accordance with the Civil Registry Law.[80] Moreover, in respect of the right to vote, the requirement is that of habitual residence for a term of six months immediately before the date that electoral qualifications are acquired. In other words, Law 2(I)/2006 does not apply to Cypriot citizens who are members of the Turkish community and reside in the government-controlled area occasionally, from time to time or temporarily; nor can Turkish Cypriots living outside the government-controlled areas claim the right to vote and stand for election.

Following the entry into force of Law 2(I)/2006, members of the Turkish community with their habitual residence in the government-controlled areas were able to participate in the parliamentary elections of 21 May 2006. From the

78 As explained in section 1.2, the Constitution establishes that Greek Cypriots vote for the President and Turkish Cypriots vote for the Vice-President.

79 Office for Democratic Institutions and Human Rights (OSCE), *Republic of Cyprus, Presidential Election, 28 January and February 2018, ODIHR Election Assessment Mission Final Report*, 2 May 2018, www.osce.org/files/f/documents/9/8/379225.pdf accessed 10 September 2020, 6–7.

80 Law 141(I) 2002, as amended.

information given by Cyprus to the CM about the measures it took to comply with the Court's judgment in the case of *Aziz v. Cyprus*, 270 Turkish Cypriots cast their vote in those elections, while one Turkish Cypriot stood as a candidate for member of parliament.[81]

The provisions of Law 2(I)/2006, nonetheless, were challenged by two Turkish Cypriots – Ali Erel and Mustafa Damdelen – living in the part of Nicosia under the control of the Turkish Republic of Northern Cyprus, who claimed that the residence requirements laid down in Law 2(I)2006 were contrary to the Constitution and to the ECHR. Following the dismissal of their complaint by the Cypriot Supreme Court, the applicants addressed the ECtHR claiming a violation of Art. 3 of Protocol 1 (right to free elections), Art. 14 of the ECHR (prohibition of discrimination) and Art. 1 of Protocol 12 (general prohibition of discrimination). The Strasbourg Court – noting the fact that establishing a residence requirement to exercise the right to vote is, as such, compatible with Art. 3 of Protocol 1, and considering that the applicants were not directly affected by the provision[82] – did not find any violation either of voting rights or of the principle of non-discrimination, and thus rejected the application as inadmissible on the ground that it was manifestly ill-founded.[83]

The *Aziz* judgment, promptly translated and published on the website of the Cyprus Bar[84] as well as in the Cyprus Law Tribune,[85] was directly applied by the Cypriot Supreme Court in the case of *Arif Moustafa v. the Ministry of the Interior*,[86] a case concerning the protection of the right to property of a Cypriot citizen of Turkish origin. The case originated from the anomalous situation created following the 1974 Turkish intervention, which led to the displacement of a huge number of Cypriots. In attempting to fulfil the need to rehouse those displaced, the government had assigned the use of the properties of Turkish Cypriots (who had moved to the north) to Greek Cypriots (who had fled from the north to the government-controlled areas) through the enactment of Law 139/1991 [Turkish Cypriot Properties (Administration and Other Matters) Law 1991].[87]

81 Committee of Ministers, *Information about the measures to comply with the judgment in the case of Aziz against Cyprus*, Appendix to Resolution CM/ResDH(2007)77.

82 In fact, the applicants were living voluntarily in an area which was not under the control of the government.

83 *Ali Erel and Mustafa Damdelen v. Cyprus*, 14 December 2010.

84 Cyprus Bar Association, www.cyprusbarassociation.org/.

85 Cyprus Law Tribune, 2005, issue No. 2, 66 ff.

86 *Arif Moustafa v. The Ministry of the Interior* Case No 125/2004 (Supreme Court of Cyprus, 24 September 2004). See also GREEK NEWS, *Court Orders Return of T/C Property to Owner*, 27 September 2004, www.greeknewsonline.com/court-orders-return-of-t-c-property-to-owner/ accessed 27 September 2020.

87 Further amended by Laws No 99(I)/1992, 35(I)/1994, 7(I)/1996, 33(I)/1998, 59(I)/2003.

Trimikliniotis N., Demetriou C., *Displacement in Cyprus, Consequences of Civil and Military Strife: Report 3, Legal Framework in the Republic of Cyprus*, Peace Research Institute Oslo 2012, www.prio.org/utility/DownloadFile.ashx?id=451&type=publicationfile, accessed 27 September 2020, 30–34.

Despite this practice being established by the State, the Supreme Court held that the applicant, a Turkish Cypriot citizen of the Republic, had the right to have his property – which had been used by two Greeks – returned to him, since he had moved from the occupied area of Cyprus to the government-controlled areas in 2012 and was now permanently resident in the latter area. In holding this ground-breaking decision, the Supreme Court directly referred to the principles established in the *Aziz v. Cyprus* case, which has been quoted by the Cypriot judiciary as a guiding light for establishing the proper level of protection.[88]

Despite the legislative reform put in place by Cypriot authorities under Law 2(I)/2006 to protect and implement the political rights of Turkish Cypriots in the government-controlled areas, as required by the ECtHR in the *Aziz* judgment, several international human rights mechanisms have expressed concerns about the effectiveness of the voting rights of this community.

The HRCtee, for instance, in its concluding observations on Cyprus of 31 March 2015,[89] criticised the fact that the amendments to the Electoral Law requiring Turkish Cypriots to register for elections by filling in a form with the Ministry of the Interior – specifying, *inter alia* their residential address – had not been disseminated and translated into the Turkish language. Moreover, the Committee voiced its concern about allegations that a significant number of Turkish Cypriots were impeded from voting during the 2014 European Parliament elections because their residential addresses had not been correctly entered into the government's database.

The HRCtee thus recommended that Cyprus

> should take immediate steps to ensure that Turkish Cypriots had the same rights and obligations as all other Cypriot citizens, both in law and in fact, to vote and stand for elections" and "ensure that all future amendments and laws concerning participation in elections were disseminated and published in both official languages.[90]

88 *Kazali and Others v. Cyprus*, 6 March 2012, para 62 (quoting the Supreme Court of Cyprus in *Arif Moustafa v. the Ministry of Interior*): *"This approach also arises from the jurisprudence of the ECHR as regards the validity of the principle of proportionality, as an objective and reasonable criterion, concerning the restrictions which may be placed on the basis of discrimination in violation of Article 14 of the Convention (which is reflected in Article 28 of the Constitution). It is sufficient for me to refer to a very recent decision in the case of Aziz* v. *Cyprus, 69949/01, 22.6.2004."*

89 Cyprus has signed the ICCPR on 16 December 1966 and ratified the Covenant on 02 April 1969.

To check the ratification status of Cyprus with respect to UN Conventions, see https://tbinternet.ohchr.org/_layouts/15/TreatyBodyExternal/Treaty.aspx?CountryID=45&Lang=EN.

90 UN Human Rights Committee, *Concluding Observations on the Fourth Periodic Report of Cyprus*, 30 April 2015, CCPR/C/CYP/CO/4, paras. 5, 7, Para 22.

In addition, Cyprus was recently under the scrutiny of the Advisory Committee on the Framework Convention for the Protection of National Minorities,[91] which adopted its Fifth Opinion on Cyprus on 7 November 2019.[92]

The term "national minorities," within the meaning of the Framework Convention, is understood to refer only to citizens of the Republic of Cyprus who belong to the Armenian, Marionite, and Latin groups. Nonetheless, the Committee, in analysing the right to self-identification (enshrined in Art. 3 of the Framework Convention)[93] of the abovementioned minorities, whose implementation is hindered by the strict constitutional division of Cypriot society into two communities, pointed out that the right to vote at elections continues to be applied differently. Indeed, as reported by the Advisory Committee, Turkish Cypriots have to register on the electoral roll, whilst Greek Cypriots are automatically registered. According to interlocutors of the Committee, in the 2019 European elections, many Turkish Cypriots were unable to vote due to insufficient information about the procedure required in respect of prior registration on the electoral roll.[94]

The concerns raised by these distinguished human rights mechanisms confront us with the awareness there is still much to do to guarantee the effective implementation of the right to vote of Cypriot citizens of Turkish origin. However, the impact of the *Aziz* case is not to be underestimated as it represents a major turning point in the advancement of democracy in Cyprus.

Conclusion

The continued division of Cyprus – both in law and in practice – has affected and still affects human rights throughout the island, including the right to life and the question of missing persons, non-discrimination, freedom of movement, property rights, and freedom of opinion and expression.

The right to vote and to stand for election cannot fail to be involved in this anomalous situation, marked by the coexistence (more or less peaceful, according

91 The Advisory Committee is composed of 18 independent experts. It monitors the status of implementation of the Framework Convention for the Protection of National Minorities in State parties, and advices the CM of the EU.

92 Advisory Committee on the Framework Convention for the Protection of National Minorities (ACFC), *Fifth Opinion on Cyprus*, 7 November 2019, https://rm.coe.int/5th-op-cyprus-en/16809f932e accessed 26 September 2020.

93 Art. 3 of the Framework Convention for the Protection of National Minorities provides as follows: *"Every person belonging to a national minority shall have the right freely to choose to be treated or not to be treated as such and no disadvantage shall result from this choice or from the exercise of the rights which are connected to that choice. Persons belonging to national minorities may exercise the rights and enjoy the freedoms flowing from the principles enshrined in the present framework Convention individually as well as in community with others."*

94 Advisory Committee, cit., 7–8.

to the times) of two distinct and opposing communities, namely the Greek Cypriot majority and the Turkish Cypriot minority.

Turkish Cypriots, indeed, have been completely deprived of the possibility to participate in the political life of the country and, in particular, in the choice of the legislature since 1964, following the dissolution of the Communal Chambers and the breakdown of the bi-constitutional setup. The Cypriot Government, having failed to set up two electoral lists (one for each community) and to adopt the appropriate legislation to resolve the issue, was found to be in breach of its obligations under Art. 3 of Protocol 1 and of Art. 14 of the ECHR taken in conjunction with Art. 3 of Protocol 1 by the ECtHR in the *Aziz* case. Accordingly, the Strasbourg Court ordered Cyprus to implement all the measures needed to fulfil its obligation to secure the right of Turkish Cypriots living in the government-controlled areas to vote.

Two years after the *Aziz* judgment, the Cypriot authorities passed Law 2(I)/2006 on the exercise of the right to vote and stand for election of members of the Turkish Cypriot community with habitual residence in the government-controlled areas. The Law has on the one hand led to an increase in the cost of elections but has on the other hand given effect to the right of political participation of the Turkish community. The *Aziz v. Cyprus* case has therefore had an impact on the national landscape, both economically and legally. Considering that the benefits in terms of rights outweigh the economic costs of the electoral reform itself, we may conclude that the ECtHR, through its *Aziz* judgment, has played a crucial role in the advancement of democracy and political participation in the ethnically divided Republic of Cyprus.

Bibliography

Advisory Committee on the Framework Convention for the Protection Of National Minorities (ACFC), *Fifth Opinion on Cyprus*, 7 November 2019. Available at https://rm.coe.int/5th-op-cyprus-en/16809f932e.

Benvenisti E., *The International Law of Occupation*, Princeton University Press, Princeton, NJ, 2004.

Commission on Human Rights, *Questions of the Violation of Human Rights and Fundamental Freedoms in Any Part of the World, Including the Question of Human Rights in Cyprus*, 21 March 2003, E/CN.4/2003/31.

Commission on Human Rights, *Questions of the Violation of Human Rights and Fundamental Freedoms in Any Part of the World, Including the Question of Human Rights in Cyprus*, 9 March 2005, E/CN.4/2005/30.

Commissioner for Human Rights, *Report by Thomas Hammarberg, Commissioner for Human Rights of the Council of Europe, following his visit to the Republic of Cyprus (7–10 July 2008)*, CommDH(2008)36/12 December 2008.

Commissioner for Human Rights, *Letter from the Council of Europe Commissioner for Human Rights, Nils Muiznieks, to Mr Costas Clerides, Attorney General of Cyprus, on the protection of human rights of unaccompanied migrant children*, 2016, CommDH (2016) 38.

Commissioner for Human Rights, *Report by Nils Muiznieks, Commissioner for Human Rights of the Council of Europe, following his visit to Cyprus from 7 to 11 December 2015*, CommDH(2016)16/31 March 2016.

Committee of Ministers, *Execution of the Judgment of the European Court of Human Rights Aziz against Cyprus*, 2007, Resolution CM/ResDH (2007)77.

Council of Europe, *Country Factsheet: Cyprus*, 5 June 2020. Available at https://rm.coe.int/1680709743.

Department for the Execution of Judgments of the European Court of Human Rights, *Country Factsheet, Cyprus*, 17 December 2019. Available at https://rm.coe.int/1680709743.

Emilianides A., *Constitutional Law in Cyprus*, 2nd ed., Wolters Kluwer, The Netherlands, 2019.

Encyclopaedia Britannica, *Cyprus: People, Ethnic Groups and Languages*. Available at https://www.britannica.com/place/Cyprus/People accessed 16 September 2020.

European Commission, *The EU's Role in the Cyprus Settlement Process: Questions and Answers*, 12 January 2017. Available at https://ec.europa.eu/commission/presscorner/detail/en/MEMO_17_52.

European Court of Human Rights, *Guide on Article 3 of Protocol No. 1 to the European Convention on Human Rights*, 30 April 2019. Available at https://www.echr.coe.int/Documents/Guide_Art_3_Protocol_1_ENG.pdf.

European Union Agency for Fundamental Rights, *The Eu Charter of Fundamental Rights in Cyprus (Charter Country-Sheet)*. Available at https://fra.europa.eu/sites/default/files/fra_uploads/fra-2019-eu-charter-in-cyprus_en.pdf.

Geneva Academy of International Humanitarian Law and Human Rights, *Rule of Law in Armed Conflict (RULAC): Cyprus*. Available at http://www.rulac.org/browse/countries/cyprus.

Greek News, *Court Orders Return of T/C Property to Owner*, 27 September 2004. Available at https://www.greeknewsonline.com/court-orders-return-of-t-c-property-to-owner/.

European Court Of Human Rights, *Cyprus*. Available at https://hudoc.echr.coe.int/eng#{"languageisocode":["ENG"],"respondent":["CYP"],"documentcollectionid2":["JUDGMENTS"]}.

Human Rights Committee, *Concluding Observations on the Fourth Periodic Report of Cyprus*, 30 April 2015, CCPR/C/CYP/CO/4.

International Crisis Group, *Cyprus: Three Advantages of the Annan Peace Plan*, 19 April 2004. Available at https://www.crisisgroup.org/europe-central-asia/western-europemediterranean/cyprus/cyprus-three-advantages-annan-peace-plan.

Internal Displacement Monitoring Centre & Norwegian Refugee Council, *Global Report on Internal Displacement 2017*, May 2017. Available at https://www.internal-displacement.org/publications/2017-global-report-on-internal-displacement.

Internal Displacement Monitoring Centre & Norwegian Refugee Council, *Global Report on Internal Displacement 2019*, May 2019. Available at https://www.internal-displacement.org/sites/default/files/publications/documents/2019-IDMC-GRID.pdf.

Kedourie E., *The Cyprus Problem and its Solution*, in Middle Eastern Studies 41, 5, 2005, 649–660.

Kliot N., Mansfield Y., *The Political Landscape of Partition: The Case of Cyprus*, in Political Geography, 16, 6, 1997, 495–521.

KOMBOS C., SHAELOU S., "The Cypriot Constitution Under the Impact of EU Law: An Asymmetrical Formation," in ALBI A., BARDUTZKY S. (eds.), *National Constitutions in European and Global Governance: Democracy, Rights, the Rule of Law: National Reports*, Asser Press, The Hague, 2019.

KYRIACOU A., *An ethnically based federal and bicameral system: The Case of Cyprus*, in International Review of Law and Economics, 20, 2, 2000, 251–268.

LOUCAIDES L., *The Judgment of the European Court of Human Rights in the Case of* Cyprus *v.* Turkey, in Leiden Journal of International Law, 15, 1, 2002, 225–236.

MELAKOPIDES C., *The EU's Role in the Cyprus Question*, in Cyprus Review, 21, 2, 2009, 91–113.

Office of the United Nations High Commissioner for Human Rights, *Question of Human Rights in Cyprus*, 23 January 2015, A/HRC/28/20.

Office of the United Nations High Commissioner for Human Rights, *Question of Human Rights in Cyprus*, 9 February 2018, A/HRC/37/22.

Office of the United Nations High Commissioner for Human Rights, *Question of Human Rights in Cyprus*, 6 February 2019, A/HRC/40/22.

Office for Democratic Institutions and Human Rights (OSCE), Republic of Cyprus, Parliamentary Elections, *22 May 2016, OSCE/ODIHR Needs Assessment Mission Report*, 30 March 2016. Available at https://www.osce.org/files/f/documents/2/b/230496.pdf.

Office for Democratic Institutions and Human Rights (OSCE), Republic of Cyprus, Presidential Election*, 28 January and February 2018, ODIHR Election Assessment Mission Final Report*, 2 May 2018, https://www.osce.org/files/f/documents/9/8/379225.pdf accessed 10 September 2020.

ÖZERSAY K., GÜREL A., *Property and Human Rights in Cyprus: The European Court of Human Rights as a Platform of Political Struggle*, in Middle Eastern Studies, 44, 2, 2008, 291–321.

THEODOULOU M., *The Peace Process: 2004 Annan Plan*, Cyprus Mail, 29 December 2016. Available at https://cyprus-mail.com/2016/12/29/peace-plans-2004-annan-plan/.

TRIMIKLINIOTIS N., DEMETRIOU C., *Displacement in Cyprus, Consequences of Civil and Military Strife*: Report 3, *Legal Framework in the Republic of Cyprus*, Peace Research Institute, Oslo 2012. Available at https://www.prio.org/utility/DownloadFile.ashx?id=451&type=publicationfile.

TÜRKMEN F., ÖKTEM E., *Major Rulings of the European Court of Human Rights on Cyprus: The Impact of Politics*, in Mediterranean Politics, 22, 2, 2017, 278–300.

UREA T., *Cyprus Dispute*, in Revue des Sciences Politiques, 64, 2019, 87–96.

ZELEPOS I., *The Historical Background of the Cyprus Problem – Just a Conflict or Ethnic Nationalism?*, in Austrian Review of International and European Law, 19, 2014, 13–27.

4 The right to vote of persons with mental disabilities in Hungary under Art. 3 of Protocol 1 to the European Convention on Human Rights

Simone Gianello

Introduction: The institutional relations between Hungary and the ECHR

The relationship between Hungary and the ECHR can be divided into two phases marked by different degrees of deference towards the obligations deriving from its accession. The first coincides with the coming into force of the Constitution of 1949, as amended in 1989, following the end of the socialist experience. The second started with the adoption of the Fundamental Law in January 2012. An observable difference from a political point of view, rather than from a normative-institutional one, that reveals a deeper change in the way of conceiving the relationship between the national system and the supranational one.

The transition to liberal democracy was also symbolically characterised by the fact that Hungary became the first post-communist country to join the CoE, signing the ECHR in 1990.[1] The post-socialist Constitution followed a dualist approach in dealing with international law.[2] Pursuant to Art. 7 Section 1 "the legal system of the Republic of Hungary accepts the generally recognized principles of international law and shall harmonize the country's domestic law with the obligations assumed under international law." The ECHR had, therefore,

1 As written by Kovacs K., *Cooperative Decision-Making: The Relation between Hungary and Strasbourg*, in ICL Journal, 5, 2, 2011, 188–199, at 189 "it was also a result of the political transformation in 1989, that Hungary became a member State of the Council of Europe and signed the Convention and its additional protocols in 1990. Following a long and careful screening process the convention was ratified in 1992 and Hungary recognized the competence of the Convention's supervisory organs to receive complaints made by individuals."

2 Kovacs K., *Cooperative Decision-Making*, cited above, 195. According to Bárd K., "The Legal Order of Hungary and the European Convention on Human Rights," in Motoc I., Ziemele I. (eds.), *The Impact of the ECHR on Democratic Change in Central and Eastern Europe: Judicial Perspectives*, Cambridge University Press, Cambridge, 2016, 180 from a formal point of view the Convention "promulgated by an Act of Parliament has the same rank as many other acts and in case of conflict the lex posterioris prevails. However, in the [Constitutional Court's] interpretation the act transforming an international treaty is superior to other acts and in the case of conflict the latter have to be annulled."

DOI: 10.4324/9781003229247-6

an infra-constitutional rank in the hierarchy of sources, subject to compliance with the Constitution, but prevailing over parliamentary acts. This has fostered a progressive and systematic harmonisation of national legislation with the ECHR,[3] also supported by jurisprudence of the Constitutional Court, which considered the level of protection provided by the Convention to be a minimum standard for the domestic legislation.[4] Even the national courts, by virtue of the Act L of 2005, Section 13 (1) *on the procedure regarding international treaties* were bound to directly enforce the Convention and ECtHR judgments.

During this period

> the Strasbourg case law has undoubtedly had a remarkable impact on the protection of human rights in Hungary and an influence in shaping the attitude to human right issue. Especially in its early years the HCC observed supranational standards very closely. Since in the beginning of its operation the HCC had no developed interpretative history, the HCC in most of its decisions affecting human rights explicitly referred to the *acquis* of the Convention.[5]

In doing so, the ECtHR has also contributed to strengthening democracy and political pluralism in Hungary through judgments concerning, among other things, the right to vote, to have access to information,[6] and the freedom of assembly.[7]

The entry into force of the new Fundamental Law, at first, did not seem to have affected this balance. Despite the fact that its conservative and nationalist attitude, identifiable since the Preamble (the *National Avowal*), had attracted the critical attention of the institutions of the CoE, above all of the Venice Commission,[8] the Constitution confirmed the dualistic relationship with international law[9] and the Constitutional Court also maintained its traditional approach.

3 As established by the Hungarian Constitutional Court, "the legislation should – if it is necessary by amendment of the constitution – harmonise with the obligation assumed under international law." HCC dec. no. 4/1997.

4 *Ex plurimis* HCC dec. no 61/2011. (VII. 13.) AB. See also Kovacs P., "International Law in the Recent Jurisprudence of the Hungarian Constitutional court opening a new tendency?", in Mezzetti L.(ed.), *International Constitutional Law*, Giappichelli, Torino, 2014, 464 ss.

5 Kovacs K., *Cooperative Decision-Making*, cited above, 193.

6 ECtHR, *Társaság a Szabadságjogokért v. Hungary*, Application no. 37374/05, 15 April 2009.

7 ECtHR, *Bukta and others v. Hungary*, Application no. 25691/04, 17 July 2007.

8 CLD-AD (2011)001, *Opinion on three legal questions arising in the process of drafting the New Constitution of Hungary* – Adopted by the Venice Commission at its 86th Plenary Session (Venice 25–26 March 2011) and CLD-AD (2011)016, *Opinion on the New Constitution of Hungary* – Adopted by the Venice Commission at its 87th Plenary Session (17–18 June 2011).

9 According to art. Q) FL, "in order to create and maintain peace and security, and to achieve the sustainable development of humanity, Hungary shall strive for cooperation with every nation and country of the world (1). Hungary shall ensure harmony between international law and Hungarian law in order to fulfil its obligations under international law (2). Hungary shall accept the generally recognised rules of international law. Other sources of international law shall become part of the Hungarian legal system by publication in the form of legislation (3)".

Even if the decisions of the Court of Strasbourg do not directly impact on the national system since they only produced declaratory effects, nevertheless

> in practice it could help with the interpretation of constitutional rights – secured in the Fundamental law and international convention – as well as with the definition of their content and their field of application. The content of the rights secured in the European convention on human rights is embodied in judgments delivered in individual cases, thus promoting the common perception of the interpretation of human rights. The observance of the Convention and the practice of the ECHR cannot lead to the limitation of the protection of fundamental rights secured by the Fundamental law and to the definition of a lower level of protection of fundamental rights that all contracting parties have to assure, but the national law may establish a different and namely a higher order of requirements in order to promote human rights.[10]

This happened in decision no. 1/2013 (I. 7.) AB whereby the Constitutional Court found unlawful the articles of the new electoral law which imposed the requirement of mandatory registration in order to vote, on the basis that they established a restriction that did not pursue any legitimate purpose.[11] In doing so, the Court expressly referred to the Venice Commission *Code of good practices in electoral matters*, in addition to the ECtHR case law on Protocol 1 Art. 3 ECHR.[12]

Furthermore, for the Constitutional Court, an ECtHR judgment could represent a new factor relevant to the constitutionality verdict. This was the case of Art. 269/B of the Criminal Code which punished the public use of the five-pointed red star, as a symbol of communist totalitarianism. At first, the Court held that the provision was justified by the need to safeguard fundamental values such as democracy and the rule of law.[13] However, after the judgments in *Vajnai v. Hungary*[14] and *Frantonoló v. Hungary*[15] in which the ECtHR declared the aforementioned provision in violation of Art. 10 ECHR, the Constitutional Court has also overturned its jurisprudence by making use of the interpretative principles of the Strasbourg case law.[16]

10 HCC dec. no. 4/2013. (II. 21.) AB, 19.
11 Kelemen K., *Hungary: voter registration declared unconstitutional*, in Dir. Comp., 5 February 2013.
12 HCC, dec. no. 1/2013. (I. 7.) AB, 3.5. See also dec. no. 22 del 2005. (VI. 17.) AB.
13 HCC dec. no. 14/2000. (V. 12.) AB.
14 ECtHR case of *Vajnai v. Hungary*, Application no. 33629/06, 8 July 2008.
15 ECtHR case of *Frantonoló v. Hungary*, Application no. 29459/10, 3 November 2011.
16 HCC dec. no. 4/2013. (II. 21.) AB, p.to 61. It should be remembered that the decision was issued after the Hungarian Parliament had explicitly declared – through Resolution 58/2012 (VII.10) – its refusal to modify the Criminal Code inasmuch as the provision had been issued for the purpose of protecting the democratic social order, with a view to the country's historical past.

Nevertheless, the progressive constitutional retrogression that in a few years has led Hungary to become one of the most striking examples of illiberal democracy has inevitably also affected the relationship between the national and international legal systems, as well as the ECHR. The reform actions of the populist Fidesz-KDNP coalition have been aimed at weakening institutional counterpowers and undermining individual freedoms. A succession of legislative measures – from the functioning of the Constitutional court and electoral systems; to the protection of freedom of expression; the freedom of association; and the protection of religious and minority rights – has often been subjected to censorship by the Venice Commission and even by the EU institutions.[17]

More than anything else, however, the future application of the ECHR was undermined by the approval of the VII Amendment to the FL on 20 June 2018 which added in the *National Avowal*[18] the fundamental obligation for Hungarian institutions to protect the constitutional identity rooted in the historical Constitution. Previously, the Constitutional Court – among those institutions subjected to the *capture* process led by the government majority – had sent signals of moving away from the past. With decision no. 22/2016 (XII. 5.) AB, above all, the judges established that the implementation of supranational obligations depends on their compliance with national sovereignty and constitutional identity.[19] Although the ruling referred to the joint exercise of jurisdiction within the EU and was used to avoid the implementation of the Council decision on the transfer of 1,294 asylum seekers from the territories of Italy and Greece, its effects also involve relationships with the ECHR. The ambiguity of both the aforementioned concepts and the IV amendment to the FL, which substantially nullified the case law of the Constitutional Court prior to 2011 and incorporated into the Basic Law provisions which had been found unconstitutional by its previous judgments,[20]

17 See European Parliament – P8_TA(2018)0340 – *Resolution of 12 September 2018 on a proposal calling on the Council to determine, pursuant to Article 7(1) of the Treaty on European Union, the existence of a clear risk of a serious breach by Hungary of the values on which the Union is founded* (2017/2131(INL)).

18 It must be emphasised that pursuant to art. R), para. 3 and 4 FL its Preamble is not just a mere programmatic declaration, but instead a binding parameter of constitutional interpretation.

19 The Constitutional court established "that the constitutional self-identity of Hungary is a fundamental value not created by the Fundamental Law – it is merely acknowledged by the Fundamental Law. Consequently, constitutional identity cannot be waived by way of an international treaty – Hungary can only be deprived of its constitutional identity through the final termination of its sovereignty, its independent statehood. Therefore, the protection of constitutional identity shall remain the duty of the Constitutional court as long as Hungary is a sovereign State." HCC dec. no. 22/2016. (XII. 5.) AB, 67.

20 Halmai G., *The Fundamental Law of Hungary and the European Constitutional Values*, in DPCE online, 2, 2019, 1503–1524, at 1508 and Chronowski N., Varju M., *Two Eras of Hungarian Constitutionalism: From the Rule of Law to Rule by Law*, in The Hague Journal on the Rule of Law, 8, 2016, 271–289, at 281. On the IV amendment to the FL see also CLD-AD (2013)012, *Opinion on the Fourth Amendment to the Fundamental Law of Hungary* – Adopted by the Venice Commission at its 95th Plenary Session (Venice 14–15 June 2013).

have widened the margin of discretion of public authorities in the regulation of fundamental rights. As a result, this has "renewed serious doubts about the state of liberal constitutionalism in Hungary and Hungary's compliance with its international commitments under the Treaties of the European Union and the European convention on Human Rights."[21]

Alajos Kiss v. Hungary: The right to vote of persons with mental disabilities

One of the common traits of illiberal democracies is the systematic limitation, *rectius* manipulation, of electoral rights in ways aimed at the preservation of power by the political forces leading the country. These methods can affect the regulation of election campaigns, the lack of transparency, public funding, the casting of votes and the control of the results, the electoral formula, and conformation of the constituencies. Each of them is able to influence the expression and the free expression of the vote. Since in such systems the maintenance of an apparent democracy is consubstantial with the legitimacy of power, there is rarely a generalised and blatant violation of electoral rights. *Ex adverso*, as highlighted by the OSCE report on the parliamentary elections of 8 April 2018, we are witnessing free but not fair electoral rounds, where the exercise of electoral rights is only formally guaranteed.[22]

This (perhaps) helps to understand why Hungary in recent years, despite the process of democratic backsliding, has not been condemned under Protocol 1 Art. 3 ECHR. The only exceptions concerned the automatic and indiscriminate disfranchisement of people placed under total or partial guardianship as a consequence of their mental disability. The seminal case was *Alajos Kiss v. Hungary*,[23] followed by *Gajcsi v. Hungary*,[24] and *Harmaty v. Hungary*.[25] In these two proceedings, however, the Strasbourg judges, considering their virtual identity with the latter, confirmed its content, finding no reasons to reach a different conclusion.

Alajos Kiss was a man diagnosed with manic depression and, as a result of his mental health conditions, was placed under partial guardianship. During 2006, shortly

21 Halmai G., *Dismantling Constitutional Review in Hungary*, in Rivista Diritti Comparati, 1, 2019, 31–47, at 36.

22 The parliamentary election, in other words, was "characterized by a pervasive overlap between state and ruling party resources, undermining contestants' ability to compete on an equal basis. Voters had a wide range of political options but intimidating and xenophobic rhetoric, media bias and opaque campaign financing constricted the space for genuine political debate, hindering voter's ability to make a fully informed choice [...] fundamental rights and freedom were respected overall, but exercised in an adverse climate." OSCE Office for Democratic Institution and Human Rights, *Hungary, Parliamentary election 8 April 2018: Final report*, 27 June 2018, 1.

23 ECtHR, *Alajos Kiss v. Hungary*, Application no. 38832/06, 20 May 2008.

24 ECtHR, *Gajcsi v. Hungary*, Application no. 62924/10, 23 September 2014.

25 ECtHR, *Harmaty v. Hungary*, Application no. 63012/10, 21 October 2014.

before the parliamentary elections, he realised he had been omitted from the electoral register. The omission was the consequence of Art. 70 Section 5 of the previous Constitution according to which those who were placed under total or partial guardianship could not participate in the elections. The applicant therefore appealed to the Strasbourg Court, complaining that the disenfranchisement constituted an unjustified deprivation of his right to vote, which was not susceptible to any remedy since it was prescribed by the Constitution, and which was discriminatory in nature. He relied on Art. 3 of Protocol No. 1, read alone or in conjunction with Arts. 13 and 14 of the Convention. He did not dispute the possibility that the restriction could pursue a legitimate aim, as also suggested by the Hungarian government. However, he argued that the deprivation of the right to vote should be subject to a narrow margin of appreciation by the State authorities.

Protocol 1 Art. 3 ECHR establishes a subjective right of crucial importance for democracy and the rule of law.[26] It was initially conceived as an institutional right that imposed on High Contracting Parties the obligation to hold free elections.[27] More recently the Court's jurisprudence has evolved to consider it an individual right to vote and run for office. However, it is not an absolute right and therefore admits the existence of a margin of appreciation for national legislatures.[28] It is for the Court to determine whether the national provisions pursue a legitimate aim in a proportionate manner, considering that the right concerned is not a privilege, and that in democratic states there is a presumption in favour of inclusion.[29]

Regarding the first question, according to the Court, the limitation of the right to vote is lawful if it is aimed at ensuring participation in public affairs only for people who are able to make well-considered and informed choices.[30] The same cannot be said about the proportionality test. Although a wide margin of appreciation is recognised in this area, it is not unlimited. It is the duty of the legislator to choose the most suitable procedure to verify the eligibility to vote of mentally disabled people. Nonetheless, there is no evidence that the Hungarian legislator attempted to weigh up competing interests or assessed the proportionality of the restriction.[31]

In the Court's opinion

> an absolute bar on voting by any person under partial guardianship, irrespective of his or her actual faculties [cannot] falls within an acceptable margin

26 ECtHR, *Aziz v. Cyprus*, Application no. 69949/01, 22 June 2004, para. 25.

27 ECtHR, *Mathieu-Mohin and Clerfayt v. Belgium*, Application no. 38832/06, 2 March 1987, para. 51. See also O'Connell R., *Realising political equality: The European Court of Human Rights and Positive Obligations in a Democracy*, in The Northern Ireland Legal Quarterly, 61, 2010, 263–279, at 264.

28 ECtHR, *Labita v. Italy*, Application no. 26772/95, 6 April 2000, para. 201.

29 ECtHR, *Hirst v. The United Kingdom (no. 2)*, Application no. 74025/01, 6 October 2005, para. 59.

30 ECtHR, *Alajos Kiss v. Hungary*, cited above, para. 38.

31 *Ibid.*, para. 41.

> of appreciation. Indeed, while the Court reiterates that this margin of appreciation is wide, it is not all-embracing [...]. In addition, if a restriction on fundamental rights applies to a particularly vulnerable group in society, who have suffered considerable discrimination in the past, such as the mentally disabled, then the State's margin of appreciation is substantially narrower and it must have very weighty reasons for the restrictions in question.[32]

The reason for this approach

> which questions certain classifications per se, is that such groups were historically subject to prejudice with lasting consequences, resulting in their social exclusion. Such prejudice may entail legislative stereotyping which prohibits the individualised evaluation of their capacities and needs.[33]

On the contrary,

> an indiscriminate removal of voting rights, without an individualised judicial evaluation and solely based on a mental disability necessitating partial guardianship, cannot be considered compatible with the legitimate grounds for restricting the right to vote.[34]

The judgment deserves to be analysed from different points of view. First of all, it should be noted that, from this moment, the ECtHR changed the legal approach to the electoral rights of person without legal capacity,[35] showing an increased degree of interest of certain vulnerable groups.[36] At the same time, it pointed out

32 *Ibid.*, para. 42.

33 *Ibid.*

34 *Ibid.*, para. 44.

35 BODNAR A., *Wahlrechtsausschluss für Entmündigte: Auf Polen kommt Ärger zu*, in VerfBlog, 9 March 2014.

36 Among others, ZIMMERMANN N., *Legislating for the Vulnerable Special Duties under the European Convention on Human Rights*, in Swiss Review of International and European Law, 25, 2015, 539–562, at 540. For an overview of the vulnerability issue, CELIK E., *An Introduction to the Concept of Vulnerability through Human Right and the Visibility of the Concept in European Court of Human Rights Case Law*, in Dokuz Eylul Universitesi Hukuk Fakultesi Dergisi, 22, 2020, 57 ff.; DICIOTTI E., *La vulnerabilità nelle sentenze della Corte europea dei diritti dell'uomo*, in Ars Interpretandi, 2, 2018, 13–34; CHENAL R., *La definizione della nozione di vulnerabilità e la tutela dei diritti fondamentali*, in Ars Interpretandi, 2, 2018, 35–55; L. CORSO, *Vulnerabilità, giudizio di costituzionalità e sentimentalismo*, in Ars Interpretandi, 2, 2018, 57–75; KOPEL C., *Suffrage for People with Intellectual Disabilities and Mental Illness: Observations on a Civic Controversy*, in The Yale Journal of Health Policy, Law, and Ethics, 17, 2017, 209–250; MOROCHOVIC T., *The Weight of Vulnerability: A Comparative Analysis of the Significance of Particular Vulnerability Attributes under ECtHR Jurisprudence in Situations of Extreme Vulnerability concerning Migrants*, in Exeter Law Review, 44, 2017, 85–105; DA LOMBA S., *Vulnerability, Irregular Migrants Health-Related Rights and the European Court on Human Rights*, in European Journal of Health Law, 21, 4, 2014, 339–364.

a new approach to inequality, no longer according to a mainly abstract scheme, linked to the formal dimension, but instead to a social one, connected to a substantive definition of it. Albeit the decision concerned *prima facie* the application of Protocol 1 Art. 3 ECHR, it is closely related to the issue of discrimination provided for by Art. 14 ECHR.[37]

Although the Convention does not refer expressly to the concept of vulnerable group, this terminology had already emerged in the Strasbourg jurisprudence regarding other issues such as race,[38] sexual orientation,[39] and gender.[40] *Mutatis mutandis*, in each of these cases the Court has highlighted the need to ensure special forms of protection for these social groups, identifying from time to time the reasons underlying their vulnerability. In *D.H. and Others v. Czech Republic*, for example, the judges stated that "as a result of their turbulent history and constant uprooting the Roma have become a specific type of disadvantaged and vulnerable minority."[41] However, only in *Alajos Kiss* has the Court developed an organic and relational conceptualisation of vulnerability that transcends the individual dimension to take a collective one.[42] No longer is a determination linked to the specific conditions of the individual, but to the group to which the individual belongs. This vulnerability is caused by cultural constructions through social structures, with no ontological characteristics.[43] In other words, the subjects belonging to the various vulnerable categories are not, in fact, intrinsically vulnerable, but they can become so due to their historical exposure to social discrimination and exclusion. The vulnerability, therefore, should not be presumed but, according to the Strasbourg judges, it must be ascertained case by case. [44]

The ECtHR renounces the Aristotelian argument according to which discrimination is the result of the binary comparison of reasonableness, under which analogous situations must correspond to the same treatment which could legitimately differ if they do not coincide.[45] In its place, the Court uses *a substantive conception of equality*. The focus is placed on the concrete effects

37 Bossuyt M., *Categorical Rights and Vulnerable Groups: Moving away from the Universal Human Being*, in The George Washington International Law Review, 48, 2016, 717–742, at 729–730.

38 ECtHR, *Chapman v. United Kingdom*, Application no. 27238/95, 18 January 2001.

39 ECtHR, *E.B. v. France*, Application no. 43546/02, 22 January 2008.

40 ECtHR, *Abdulaziz, Cabales and Balkandali v. The United Kingdom*, Applications nos. 9214/80; 9473/81; 9474/81, 28 May 1985.

41 ECtHR, *D.H. and Others v. Czech Republic*, Application no. 57325/00, 13 November 2007, para. 182.

42 Mjoll Arnardottir O., *Vulnerability under Article 14 of the European Convention on Human Rights*, in Oslo Law Review, 4, 2017, 150–171, at 158.

43 Bernardini M. G., *Vulnerabilità e disabilità a Strasburgo: il* vulnerable groups approach *in pratica*, in Ars Interpretandi, 2, 2018, 77–93, at 83 and Mjoll Arnardottir O., *Vulnerability under Article 14*, cited above, at 164.

44 Bernardini M. G., *Vulnerabilità e disabilità a Strasburgo*, cited above, at 83.

45 O'Connell R., *Cinderella Comes to the Ball: Art 14 and the Right to Non-Discrimination in the ECHR*, in Legal Studies, 29, 2009, 211–229, at 212.

produced by a legislative provision in respect of a person or group and not on its content.[46] In this way, the abstract idea of the neutrality of a legislative provision is overcome and it is accepted the possibility that under certain conditions (social, cultural, political, etc.) even a formally non-discriminatory provision may substantially become so. In other words, a discriminatory intent "is not a pre-condition for a finding of discrimination: discrimination can arise from a de facto situation."[47] What makes a particularly vulnerable group, therefore, is the weight of social stigmatisation that generates different treatment and exclusion from public life.[48]

Alajos Kiss confirms the above, as the first time the Court extended the notion of a vulnerable group to the mentally disabled.[49] The same was true for *Kiyutin v. Russia* where the judges, using the same arguments, recognised the particular vulnerability also of HIV/AIDS patients as a result of the considerable discrimination they have historically suffered.[50]

The ECHR does not expressly establish specific rights for the protection of people with disabilities; disability is not even mentioned in Art. 14 ECHR on discrimination. Even the Venice Commission *Code of Good Practice in Electoral Matters* (Opinion no. 190/2002) does not refer to disability. At the most,

46 According to Timmer A., *Toward an Anti-Stereotyping Approach for the European Court of Human Rights*, in Human Rights Law Review, 11, 4, 2011, 707–738, at 711 this approach, "also called de facto equality, takes as its starting point the reality of a rule or practice as it is experienced by a disadvantaged group." O'Connell R., *Cinderella Comes to the Ball*, cited above 213. According to the Author "a substantive conception of equality therefore is more concerned with the effects of the law in reality, rather than questions of whether the law on paper makes distinctions. The central question is not whether the law makes distinctions, but whether the effect of the law is to perpetuate disadvantage, discrimination, exclusion or oppression."

47 Timmer A., *Toward an Anti-Stereotyping Approach*, cited above, at 712.

48 Blaker Strand V., Ikdahl I., *Responding to Disadvantage and Inequality through Law*, in Oslo Law Review, 4, 2017, 124 ff., at 126. See also Timmer A., "A quiet revolution: vulnerability in the European Court of Human Rights," in Fineman M., Grear A. (eds), *Vulnerability: reflections on a new ethical foundation for law and politics*, Routledge, Ashgate, 2013, at 160. Widely, on minorities issue, Bowring B., *Case-Law of the European Court of Human Rights Concerning the Protection of Minorities, July 2012 to August 2014*, in European Yearbook of Minority Issues, 12, 2013, 201 ff.

49 Peroni L., Timmer A., *Vulnerable groups: The promise of an emerging concept in European Human Rights Convention Law*, in I-CONS, 11, 4, 2013, 1056–1085, at 1066.

50 ECtHR, *Kiyutin v. Russia*, Application no. 2700/10, 10 March 2011, para. 64 where it says that "since the onset of the epidemic in the 1980s, people living with HIV/Aids have suffered from widespread stigma and exclusion, including within the Council of Europe region [...] in the early years of the epidemic when HIV/Aids diagnosis was nearly always a lethal condition and very little was known about the risk of transmission, people were scared of those infected due to fear of contagion. Ignorance about how the disease spreads has bred prejudice which, in turn, has stigmatised or marginalised those who carry the virus." Bossuyt M., *Categorical Rights and Vulnerable Groups*, cited above 729 and Levitan S., *Kiyutin: Protecting the Human Rights of Persons Living with HIV/AIDS Beyond Immigration*, in Boston College International and Comparative Law Review, 35, 3, Electronic Supplement, 2013, 49–61.

mental incapacity was foreseen as a condition for the deprivation of electoral rights, as long as the limitation was proportional, provided by a law, and imposed by the decision of a court.[51] Nevertheless, as repeatedly stressed by the Court of Strasbourg, the Convention is a living instrument and the list of grounds of discrimination set out therein is not exhaustive.

The ECtHR's renewed attention on disability is relatively recent[52] and, among other aspects, coincides with the entry into force of the UN Convention on the Right of Persons with Disabilities (hereinafter CRPD), ratified by Hungary on 20 July 2007.[53] In *Alajos Kiss* this played a decisive role, as it was the first time the Court of Strasbourg has referred specifically to the UN Convention in its arguments.[54] Pursuant to Art. 29 CRPD the States parties have a duty to ensure

> that persons with disabilities can effectively and fully participate in political and public life on an equal basis with others, directly or through freely chosen representatives, including the right and opportunity for persons with disabilities to vote and be elected,[55]

inter alia "ensuring that voting procedures, facilities and materials are appropriate, accessible and easy to understand and use"[56] and actively promoting "an environment in which persons with disabilities can effectively and fully participate in the conduct of public affairs, without discrimination and on an equal basis with others, and encourage their participation in public affairs." [57]

However, there is a perceptible difference between the CRPD and ECtHR judgment in *Alajos Kiss*. The UN Convention, in fact, is more radical. *In primis* because it excludes *in nuce* that disability – including mental disability – may be the reason for disenfranchisement. Secondly, because it imposes positive obligations on States parties aimed at creating an inclusive environment in which disabled people can effectively take part in public life. A duty to foster equality by taking "all appropriate steps to ensure that reasonable accommodation is provided."[58]

51 Venice Commission, Opinion no. 190/2002, Art. 1.1, Section *d*).

52 ECtHR, *Glor v. Switzerland*, Application no.13444/04, 30 April 2009.

53 Chainoglou K., *The Framework for Protecting the Rights of Persons with Mental Disabilities in Europe Improved Protection for a Growing Yet Marginalized Group*, in Cyprus Human Rights Law Review, 1, 2012, 157–183, at 164 and Broderick A., *A Reflection on Substantive Equality Jurisprudence: The Standard of Scrutiny at the ECtHR for Differential Treatment of Roma and Persons with Disabilities*, in International Journal of Discrimination and the Law, 15, 1–2, 2015, 101–122, at 109.

54 *Alajos Kiss v. Hungary*, para. 44. Among scholars, see Timmer A., *A Strasbourg Victory for the Mentally Disabled*, in Strasbourg Observer, 21 May 2010.

55 Art. 29, Section *a*) CRPD.

56 Art. 29, Section *a*) para. *i* CRPD.

57 Art. 29, Section *b*) CRPD.

58 Art. 5, Section 3 CRPD. See also J. Clifford, *The UN Disability Convention and its Impact on European Equality Law*, in The Equal Rights Review, VI, 2011, 11–25, at 12.

The Strasbourg Court, on the other hand, seems to follow a partially different path – mainly procedural – focused on a qualitative analysis of the Hungarian decision-making system.[59] The Court sounds "to have based its finding primarily on the absolute nature of the ban in question, rather than on a consideration of the wider systemic disadvantage faced by disabled applicants in participating in the political process."[60] As in *Hirst v. The United Kingdom*, the breach of Protocol 1 Art. 3 ECHR by the Hungarian legislation depends on the presence of an "automatic blanket ban" for a whole category of people.[61] Even if the restriction of the right to vote of mentally disabled people may be lawful if it pursues a legitimate purpose, an outright ban on voting for any person subject to partial guardianship is not proportionate. Both *Hirst* and *Alajos Kiss* relate to negative government obligations.[62] In the latter, in particular, the Court does not refer to any positive "tailor-made"[63] duty of the Member State to promote the inclusion of people subjected to partial guardianship in public life. Furthermore, the special vulnerability of their social group, rather than the backbone of the decision, is used by the Court as an additional factor ***ad adiuvandum*** to explain the substantial narrowing of the margin of appreciation and the need for particularly weighty reasons for the restriction in question.[64] This is because "where a particularly important facet of an individual's existence or identity is at stake, the margin of appreciation provided to the State will normally be restricted."[65] Although the ECtHR shows a suspicious *a priori* attitude towards certain classifications *per se*, the particular vulnerability of such a group does not necessarily

59 On this point Kleinlein T., *The Procedural Approach of the European Court of Human Rights: Between Subsidiarity and Dynamic Evolution*, in ICQL, 68, 2019, 91–110.

60 Broderick A., *A Reflection on Substantive Equality Jurisprudence*, cited above 112.

61 ECtHR, *Hirst v. The United Kingdom (no. 2)*, cited above, para. 76.

62 O'Connell R., *Realising Political Equality: The European Court of Human Rights and Positive Obligations in a Democracy*, cited above, at 268.

63 Chainoglou K., *The Framework for Protecting the Rights*, cited above 165.

64 According to Mjoll Arnardottir O., *Vulnerability under Article 14*, cited above, at 163.

65 McGoldrick D., *A Defence of the Margin of Appreciation and an Argument for Its Application by the Human Rights Committee*, in International & Comparative Law Quarterly, 65, 2016, 21–60, at 24. See also Aldao M., *Between Deference and Indifference: Margin of Appreciation, Democracy and Vulnerability Situations in the Caselaw of the European Courts of Human Rights*, in Rev. Derecho del Estado, 44, 2019, 31 and Mjoll Arnardottir O., *The Differences That Make a Difference: Recent Developments on the Discrimination Grounds and the Margin of Appreciation under Article 14 of the European Convention on Human Rights*, in Human Rights Law Review, 14, 4, 2014, 647–670. On the margin of appreciation doctrine, among others, A. Wisniewski, *On the Theory of the Margin of Appreciation Doctrine*, in The Polish Review of International and European Law, 2012, 63 ff.; Gerards J., *Pluralism, Deference and the Margin of Appreciation Doctrine*, in European Law Journal, 17, 2011, 80–120; Tanzarella M., "Il margine di apprezzamento," in Cartabia M. (eds*), I diritti in azione. Universalità e pluralismo dei diritti fondamentali nelle Corti europee*, Il Mulino, Bologna, 2007, 145–181; Benvenisti E., *Margin of Appreciation, Consensus, and Universal Standards*, in New York University Journal of International Law and Politics, 31, 1999, 843 ff. and Feingold C.S., *Doctrine of Margin of Appreciation and the European Convention on Human Rights*, in Notre Dame Law Review, 53, 1977, 90–106.

lead to the prohibition of *ad hoc* legislation, but only a closer scrutiny and the reduction of the state margin of appreciation in balancing the opposing interests. Consequently, despite the discretion generally accorded to Member States to provide for any restrictions on voting rights, the specific vulnerability of the mentally disabled, in the light of the discrimination and social confinement they have historically affected, leaves public authorities less room to intervene and imposes greater attention on individual cases.

On the other hand, analysis of the parliamentary debate has shown an absolute lack of interest on the issue at stake, since there is no evidence of the search for a fair balance that takes into account the rights of people under guardianship. An appropriate internal procedure, "notably a thorough parliamentary and judicial review of the necessity of a measure, can indicate a significantly more lenient proportionality review by the Court and a wider margin of appreciation for Convention State."[66] Indeed, the subsidiarity principle presupposes that national authorities are placed in a better position than the Strasbourg Court to weigh up conflicting rights. Especially when it is a particularly important right such as voting concerning the core of democracy. However, an automatic blanket ban on a vulnerable minority demonstrates a lack of attention on their needs. Moreover, the automatic deprivation of voting rights, being regulated directly by the Constitution, did not allow the national judges to identify more specific solutions.[67]

In conclusion, therefore, the violation of Protocol 1 Art. 3 ECHR does not depend on the disenfranchisement of persons subject to partial guardianship, which under certain conditions can pursue legitimate purposes, but on the lack of proportionality of the domestic provisions which didn't allow any type of *tailor-made* accommodation – for example provided by national courts – which takes into account the individual circumstances.

The implementation of the judgment at the national level

The *Alajos Kiss v. Hungary* judgment has been of paramount importance in terms of the right to free elections[68] both in Hungary and within the CoE. With regard to the latter, it should be noted that after the publication of the judgment, the Council for Democratic Elections and the Venice Commission adopted specific *Interpretative Declarations to the Code of Good Practice in Electoral Matters* on the participation of persons with disabilities in elections. For example, on the principle of universal suffrage, specifying at first that

66 Kleinlein T., *The Procedural Approach of the European Court of Human Rights*, cited above, 94 and McGoldrick D., *A Defence of the Margin of Appreciation*, cited above, at 35. See ECtHR case of *Animal Defenders International v. The United Kingdom*, Application no.48876/08, 22 April 2013, para. 116.

67 ECtHR case of *Shtukaturov v. Russia*, Application no.44009/05, 27 March 2008, para. 95.

68 Bárd K., *The Legal Order of Hungary*, cited above 194.

> no person with disability can be excluded from the right to vote or to stand for election on the basis of her/his physical and/or mental disability unless the deprivation of the right to vote and to be elected is imposed by an individual decision of a court of law because of proven mental disability.[69]

Then, going further, it stated that

> Universal suffrage is a fundamental principle of the European electoral Heritage. People with disabilities may not be discriminated against in this regard, in conformity with Article 29 of the Convention of the United Nations on the Rights of Persons with Disabilities and the case law of the European Court of Human Rights.[70]

On the Hungarian side, the decision also had remarkable consequences. Despite the potentially systemic impact on the disenfranchisement of a whole category, in *Alajos Kiss* and both in *Gajcsi* and *Harmaty*, the Court ordered the Hungarian government to pay an economic penalty, without imposing any requirement of the adoption of structural reforms. In the first case, the Court ruled that the respondent State had to pay the applicant 3,000 Euros for non-pecuniary damages and 5,000 Euros for costs and expenses within 3 months from the date on which the decision became final pursuant to Art. 44 Section 2 ECHR. In the other 2 cases the Court established the payment of 2,700 Euros for non-pecuniary damages and 1,000 Euros for costs and expenses. From this point of view, Hungary has correctly complied with the sentences. As can be seen from the most recent *Action report* by the Hungarian authorities directed to the *Secretariat of the Committee of Ministers*,[71] the government has given just satisfaction to the

69 CLD-AD (2011)036, *Interpretative declaration to the Code of Good Practice in Electoral Matters on the participation of people with disabilities in Elections* – Adopted by the Council for Democratic elections at its 34th meeting (Venice 14 October 2010) and by the Venice Commission at its 84th Plenary Session (Venice 15–16 October 2010), Section II (1.2).

70 CLD-AD (2010)045, *Revised interpretative declaration to the Code of Good Practice in Electoral Matters on the participation of people with disabilities in Elections* – Adopted by the Council for Democratic elections at its 39th meeting (Venice 15 December 2011) and by the Venice Commission at its 89th Plenary Session (Venice 16–17 December 2011), Section II (1.2).

71 DH-DD (2019)1131, *Communication from Hungary concerning the Alajos Kiss group of cases v. Hungary (Application no. 38832/06)*, 1362th meeting (December 2019). On monitoring the implementation of the judgments, see also DH-DD (2019)50, *Communication from Hungary concerning the Alajos Kiss group of cases v. Hungary (Application no. 38832/06)*, 1340th meeting (March 2019); DH-DD(2019)5, *Communication from Hungary concerning the Alajos Kiss group of cases v. Hungary (Application no. 38832/06)*, 1340th meeting (March 2019); DH-DD(2015)9, *Communication from Hungary concerning the case of Alajos Kiss against Hungary (Application no. 38832/06)*, 1222th meeting (10–12 March 2015); DH-DD(2012)1156, *Communication from Hungary concerning the case of Alajos Kiss against Hungary (Application no. 38832/06)*, 11642th meeting (5–7 March 2013).

applicants' claims by paying in full and within the timeframe as follows: Alajos Kiss was paid on 22nd September 2010, Gajcsi on 16th December 2014 and Harmati on 23rd December 2014.

In addition to pecuniary compensation, with the entry into force of the Fundamental Law, the Hungarian Parliament also amended the legal framework for people with mental disabilities. According to the above report, after *Alajos Kiss* the Ministry of Public Administration and Justice sent the judgment to the drafters of the new Constitutional charter to ask for it to be taken it into account. Currently, the right to vote is settled by Art. XVIII FL, which generally establishes that every adult Hungarian citizen "shall have the right to vote and to be voted for in elections of Members of the National Assembly, of local government representatives and mayors and of Members of the European Parliament" (Section 1). The following Section 6 provides that those disenfranchised by a court for a criminal offence or limited mental capacity shall not have the right to vote and to be voted for. Citizens of another Member State of the European Union with domicile in Hungary shall not have the right to be voted for if they have been excluded from the exercise of this right in their country pursuant to the law, a court decision or an authority decision of their State of citizenship. Therefore, by virtue of the Fundamental Law, the disenfranchisement of people with mental illness is no longer automatic as provided for by Art. 70 Section 5 of the old post-communist Constitution but must be adjudicated upon by a court ruling based on an individualised assessment.

However, the new constitutional provisions established *pro-futuro* effects. The problem remained for those who had been deprived of the right to vote as a result of being subjected to total or partial guardianship under the provisions of the old Constitution. Art. 26 Section 2 of the *Transitional Provisions to the Fundamental Law* had foreseen *medio tempore* that

> a person who has been put under guardianship which restricts or excludes his or her disposing capacity by a final judgment at the time of the coming into force of the Fundamental Law shall not have suffrage until such guardianship is terminated or until a court establishes the existence of his or her suffrage.

To avoid the risk of a double standard, some legislative measures have been introduced. According to the *Act CLXXVII of 2013 on Temporary and Enforcement Provisions related to the enactment of Act V of 2013 on the Civil Code*, the national authorities have the obligation to examine *ex officio* the situation of those who found themselves in the same position of the applicants within 5 years of the Civil code's entry into force.[72] The procedure could be initiated at any time by the applicants themselves or by other persons specified by law.[73] By virtue of

72 Act V of 2013 on the Civil Code was enacted on 26 February 2013.

73 Pursuant to Section 2:30 (para 2.) of the Civil Code [*Termination and revision of conservatorship or guardianship*], termination of guardianship or conservatorship may be requested

the legislative changes, on 7 September 2015 the Füzesabony District Court upheld Alajos Kiss' partial guardianship with no preclusion on his right to vote. On 24 November 2011 it abolished the Gajcsi partial guardianship. However, the applicant died on 28 September 2015. Finally, Harmati's case is still pending before the Government Office of Pest County, at the District Office of Érd.

With the entry into force of *Act V of 2013 on the Civil Code*, the rules concerning legal capacity now contained in Title V entitled *Limiting the legal capacity of persons of legal age* have also been amended. Pursuant to Section 2:29 (para. 2) [*Mandatory review of placement under guardianship or conservatorship*] the court ruling on restricting, upholding, or modifying the legal competency of a person shall specify the date by which to initiate the statutory review of conservatorship, where this date: *a*) must be fixed within five years from the date when the ruling becomes legally operative in the case of conservatorship; *b*) must be fixed within ten years from the date when the ruling becomes legally operative in the case of guardianship. By virtue of the *Act CXXX of 2016 on the Code of Civil Procedure*, Section 445 (para. *c*) [*Judgment on placement under custodianship*], if the defendant is placed under custodianship by the court, even in the absence of a corresponding claim, the latter shall decide on the issue of his deprivation of the right to vote. Finally, according to the provisions of the *Act XXXVI of 2013 on Electoral Procedure* Section 13/A (para. 1) [*Exclusion from suffrage*] domestic courts shall decide on exclusion from suffrage in decisions ordering placement under conservatorship limiting competency, decisions ordering placement under conservatorship precluding competency, and decisions issued in the course of proceedings aimed at reviewing conservatorship.[74]

As a consequence, in light of the current legislation, disenfranchisement is no longer the automatic result of the judicial decision to place a person under total or partial guardianship.[75] Guardianship procedures involve a separate assessment of the ability of persons with disabilities to exercise the right to vote and to be

by: *a*) the person in custody; *b*) the spouse, domestic partner, relative in direct line, or sibling living with the person in custody; *c*) the conservator; *d*) the guardian authority or *e*) the public prosecutor.

74 According to Section 13/A (para. 2) Courts shall exclude persons of legal adult age from suffrage whose capacity for reasoning necessary for exercising suffrage only if: *a*) is greatly reduced permanently or recurrently owing to their mental state, unsound mind or pathological addiction or *b*) is permanently and completely lost owing to their mental state or unsound mind. Finally, according to para. 3, if the court does not exclude a legal adult placed under conservatorship from suffrage, "then he or she shall exercise electoral rights personally and shall have the power to make valid legal statements alone in the context of these rights."

75 The same procedure is followed in Conservatorship cases where legal capacity is more broadly limited. Even in these proceedings the loss of electoral rights is not automatic but is decided by the judge called to place a person under guardianship. Pursuant to *Act. V of 2013 on the Civil Code*, Section 2:19 (para. 4–5) [*Conservatorship*] capacity to act may not be limited, not even partially, if protecting the rights of the person concerned can be ensured by other means not affecting his capacity to act. Persons having partially limited capacity to act shall be able to make valid juridical acts independently in all affairs which do not belong to those categories of affairs in which the court has limited their capacity to act.

elected. In each case, it is the duty of the judge to hear the defendant before deciding, in order to weigh his effective legal capacity, unless his mental condition does not allow it.[76] In deciding a case of guardianship, the judges must consider the protection of the best interest of the person at issue and deprive him of the right to vote only in specifically justified cases. To guarantee this standard, medical and psychiatric experts must also be consulted during the trial and they have the task of issuing their own non-binding scientific opinion which the judge is called upon to take into due consideration.

In agreement with the Hungarian authorities, the new legal framework is in accordance with the decision of the ECtHR in *Alajos Kiss*, mainly with the proportionality test provided by the Court's case law. By subjecting the deprivation of the right to vote of people under guardianship to both strict legal conditions and an individualised decision provided by a national court, persons with disabilities are no longer treated as a homogeneous group.[77]

A dissemination action was also carried out to raise awareness among national judges and to contribute to the unification of jurisprudence. The three judgments were translated and published on the government website. During the *National Symposium for Heads of Civil Law division of the domestic courts* held on 21–23 March 2014, memorandum was issued which clarified the scope of the legislative changes. Among other things, it was specified that the courts would have *motu proprio* determined whether the person under guardianship could or could not exercise his or her right to vote. The guidelines for unifying the jurisprudence of the courts on the issue, in turn, were published on the Curia website.

If, therefore, Hungarian legislation and jurisprudential practice seem to have substantially adapted to the obligations of the ECHR and the jurisprudence of the ECtHR, the same cannot be said for those deriving from the CRPD. It has already noted that the Strasbourg Court has expressly referred to the UN Convention in *Alajos Kiss.* Nevertheless, it is clear that there remain different standards adopted with respect to voting rights of people with mental disabilities. In *Zsolt Bujdosó and five others v. Hungary*, the *Committee on the Rights of Persons with Disabilities* condemned Hungary for failing to fulfil its obligations under Art. 29, read alone and in conjunction with Art. 12 of the UN Convention.[78]

76 In compliance with the *Act CXXX of 2016 on the Code of Civil Procedure*, Section 442 (para. 2) [*Preparatory stage*] the party shall mandatorily appear at the preparatory hearing in person. The court shall interview each party to the action in person, unless the whereabouts of the party is unknown or his interview is prevented by an unavertable obstacle.

77 DH-DD (2019)1131, *Communication from Hungary concerning the Alajos Kiss group* (71) 12–14. The report also points out that the case law of national courts has complied with the new legal framework on the right to vote of persons subject to partial or total guardianship. For example, in the leading case no. BH2016.167 (published June 2018) the Curia has expressly decided that "limited legal capacity does not inevitably go hand in hand with an impairment of the requisite mental faculty necessary for the exercise of electoral rights; therefore this latter aspect should always be examined separately."

78 CRPD Communication No. 4/2011, *Zsolt Bujdosó and five others v. Hungary*, 20 settembre 2013.

Also, in this case the authors of the complaint had been deprived of their right to vote as an automatic consequence of being subjected to total or partial guardianship pursuant to Art. 70 of the old Constitution. They complained about the lack of effective remedies available to them as the only chance to restore their voting rights presupposed the complete reset of their legal capacity. This was neither possible nor desirable for the authors, who recognised their intellectual disability and acknowledged that they needed support in managing their business in certain areas of their life.[79] Although the Hungarian government had in the meantime communicated the adoption of the new legislative provisions in compliance – from its point of view – with Protocol 1 Art. ECHR and in line with the ECtHR ruling in *Alajos Kiss*, for the authors these measures were not enough. All people under guardianship are people with disabilities. Their disfranchisement was based specifically on their intellectual disability and was therefore discriminatory. The only possible solution involved a conceptual inversion. The Hungarian authorities should have declared that all persons currently deprived of the right to vote due to their mental disability would regain their right until it was revoked by the decision of a national court.

For the Committee, contrary to the new Hungarian legislation,

> article 29 of the Convention requires States parties to ensure that persons with disabilities can effectively and fully participate in political and public life on an equal basis with others, including by guaranteeing their right to vote. Article 29 does not foresee any reasonable restriction, nor does it allow any exception for any group of persons with disabilities. Therefore, an exclusion of the right to vote on the basis of a perceived, or actual psychosocial or intellectual disability, including a restriction pursuant to an individualised assessment, constitutes discrimination on the basis of disability.[80]

Furthermore, Art. 12 Section 2 CRPD imposes on States parties the duty to recognise and ensure the legal capacity of persons with disabilities on an equal basis with others in all aspects of their life, including political life, which encompasses the right to vote. Under the subsequent Art. 12 Section 3 CRPD they also have a positive obligation to take the necessary steps to ensure that persons with disabilities fully exercise their legal capacity. Conversely, having found the assessment of individuals capacity to be discriminatory in nature, the Committee held that this measure could not be purported to be legitimate. Nor was it proportional to the objective to preserve the integrity of the State party's political system. The Committee recalled that, under Art. 29 of the Convention, the State

79 For the Authors "Hungarian law only provides for one legal measure, guardianship (plenary and partial), for persons with disabilities requiring assistance. While challenging their guardianship under the Civil Code was the only available remedy, it was not an effective remedy for the authors, as courts do not have the power to consider and restore a person's right to vote." CRPD Communication No. 4/2011, para. 3.2.

80 CRPD Communication No. 4/2011, para. 9.4.

party is required to adapt its voting procedures, by ensuring that they are appropriate, accessible, and easy to understand and use, and allowing, where necessary, assistance in voting upon the request of the person with the disability. It is by so doing that the State party will ensure that persons with an intellectual disability cast a competent vote, on an equal basis with others, while guaranteeing the secrecy of the vote.[81]

For the Committee, in conclusion, among the other measures to be taken to comply with the UN Convention obligations, national legislator must consider the repeal of Art. XXIII, Section 6 FL and the enactment of laws that recognise the right to vote of people with disabilities without any assessment of their ability and to provide adequate assistance and make reasonable accommodations in order for them to be able to exercise their political rights.[82]

In spite of the changes introduced in the Hungarian legal system, empirically the statistical data shows the persistence of the national authorities' paternalistic attitude, reluctant to extend the right to vote to people subject to protection. According to the information available from the Hungarian government, in the first years after the entry into force of the Fundamental Law and the new legislative measures, in almost a quarter of the cases judges did not disfranchise the person placed under guardianship. In total guardianship proceedings, however, even if not necessarily automatically, judges very often continued to strip the person in question of their electoral rights, with the exception being where that person was active in the context of public life. This situation, however, was considered not enough by the *Committee on the Rights of Persons with Disabilities.* In a recent report, the Committee highlighted that the mandatory review of the guardianship every five or ten years in cases of partial or full restriction confirmed in almost all cases the previous decision, and also that the number of individuals subject to protection who were deprived of the right to vote tends to decrease with percentages that are still too low.[83]

Conclusions

In sum, *Alajos Kiss v. Hungary* certainly represents a cornerstone for the electoral rights of people with mental disabilities. Not only within the Hungarian borders but, more generally, among the CoE countries. As noted above, the Strasbourg ruling signalled a new approach towards vulnerable groups who have suffered stigmatisation and segregation for their specific circumstances. The ECtHR has marked the path for inclusion in decision-making processes and in public life, even in spite of the differences that can legitimately justify, within certain limits, a differentiated treatment. From this point of view, it is interesting to note how

81 CRPD Communication No. 4/2011, para. 9.6.

82 CRPD Communication No. 4/2011, para. 9.7.

83 CRPD, *Inquiry concerning Hungary carried out by the Committee under article 6 of the Optional Protocol to the Convention*, 13 September 2019, para. 35.

the Court indissolubly links the right to vote to the very existence of a democracy governed by the rule of law. Even if Protocol 1 Art. 3 does not identify an absolute right, the national margin of appreciation is not unlimited. On the contrary, the existence of a particularly vulnerable group justifies a strict scrutiny; therefore, since the guarantee of the right to vote is the backbone of democracy, it is not possible to indiscriminately exclude a whole category of people from its exercise.

Alongside these positive elements, the decision in question nevertheless reveals even more negative ones. Above all, the main limitation can be identified in the absence of positive requirements imposed on domestic authorities to face the situation of vulnerability. On the one hand, judges have elaborated an advanced theory, connected to the substantive idea of equality. No longer hinged on its formal vision, but more "transformative,"[84] which faces discrimination starting from the consideration of the real conditions of each group. As a substantive model of equality is concerned

> with groups that are systematically subject to discrimination, it departs from the assumption of symmetry inherent in formal equality. This means that a substantive model of equality will not adopt a colour blind or gender-neutral approach to distinctions; rather it will look more favourably on measures which promote substantive equality for previously disadvantaged groups.[85]

Given the general approach of the decision, it is more difficult to understand why the Court found Hungary to be in violation as a consequence of the absolute and automatic ban, without providing for any measures to support a positive integration into public life of people placed under total or partial guardianship.

This is the main difference between the *Alajos Kiss* group of cases and the Communication of the CRPD in *Zsolt Bujdosó* where the State party regulatory provisions, even following the entry into force of the Fundamental Law, were still considered unsuitable for guaranteeing the exercise of the right to vote of disabled people on an equal basis with others. The differences between the ECHR and CRPD are known. However, in other cases the Strasbourg Court went so far as to request positive action from the Member States involved to redress forms of unjustified discrimination. In *Horváth and Kiss v. Hungary*, for example, in light of the perpetuation of practices that over-represented Roma children with mild learning difficulties in special schools for children with mental disabilities, the Court ruled that "in such circumstances – and in light of the recognised bias in past placement procedures [...] the State has specific positive obligations to avoid

84 TIMMER A., *Toward an Anti-Stereotyping Approach*, cited above 712. On the matter see also S. FREDMAN, "Beyond the Dichotomy of Formal and Substantive Equality: Towards a New Definition of Equal Rights," in BOEREFIJN I. *et al.* (eds), *Temporary special measures. Accelerating De Facto Equality of Women under Article 4(1) UN Convention on the Elimination of All Forms of Discrimination Against Women*, Intersentia, Antwerp, 2003, 111–115.

85 O'CONNELL R., *Cinderella Comes to the Ball*, cited above 213.

the perpetuation of past discrimination or discriminative practices disguised in allegedly neutral tests."[86] In *Alajos Kiss*, on the other hand, there isn't any indication of the need to adopt positive accommodations that foster the integration of people with mental illnesses into the country's political life.[87]

This seeming *vulnus* can probably be explained by the ECHR's desire to avoid – in accordance with the principle of subsidiarity – excessive interference with national institutions.[88] Doing so, however, risks weakening the real effects of the judgment. Considering the necessary safeguarding of vulnerable groups, the Court continued along a track already trodden in the past: the one outlined in *Hirst* according to which it is the generalised ban of voting rights that violates Protocol 1 Art. 3 ECHR. However, the Court doesn't seem to be aware of the different premises underlying the two judgments. While in the latter case the main issue stemmed from a negative limitation imposed by national legislation, in *Alajos Kiss* there was also the positive factor to be considered, namely, the need to ensure the effective exercise of the right once the ban was removed. On several occasions the Strasbourg Court has already specified that "the Convention is intended to guarantee not rights that are theoretical or illusory but rights that are practical and effective."[89] If the primary purpose of most conventional rights is essentially to protect individuals (or groups) against arbitrary interference from public authorities, then "there are positive obligations inherent in an effective respect of the right in question, requiring states to take measures to actively protect and fulfil Convention rights."[90] Merely establishing the dismissal of the automatic disfranchisement of persons under guardianship doesn't guarantee them the ability to regain the right to vote, even following an individual assessment of a court. As observed above, from the data provided by the *Committee on the Rights of Persons with Disabilities*, even after the ECtHR ruling, there are very few cases

86 ECtHR, *Horváth and Kiss v. Hungary*, Application no. 11146/11, 29 January 2013, para. 116. The case concerned discrimination against applicants of Roma origin, on account of their placement in a special school for children with mental disabilities during their primary education. This placement was based on the result of specific tests aimed at assessing the scholastic aptitude and mental abilities of pupils. According to the Court, these tests did not provide the necessary guarantees to avoid misdiagnosis and misplacement of Roma pupils with presumed mild mental disability or learning difficulties without considering, moreover, their special needs as a community disadvantaged. The relevant legislation, as applied in practice, did not offer adequate guarantees and led to the over-representation and segregation of Roma children in special schools due to the systematic misdiagnosis of mental disability (violation of Protocol 1 Art. 2 read in in conjunction with Article 14 ECHR).

87 According to A. Broderick, *A Reflection on Substantive Equality Jurisprudence*, cited above 112 the Court "seemed to endorse, [...] the participation dimension of substantive equality by recognizing that the exclusion of persons with disabilities from political participation must be subject to scrutiny as to whether it complies with international law. However, the Court did not go further [...] to endorse equality by recognizing that persons with disabilities may need to be accommodated to enable them to participate in society."

88 Kleinlein T., *The Procedural Approach of the European Court of Human Rights*, cited above, 101.

89 ECtHR, *Airey v. Ireland*, Application no. 6289/73, 9 October 1979, para. 24.

90 Zimmermann N., *Legislating for the Vulnerable Special Duties*, cited above 548.

of people subject to protection who have been guaranteed the enjoyment of suffrage. Given the importance of the rights established by Protocol 1 Art. 3 ECHR for the safeguard of democracy and to prevent abuses against the most vulnerable people, a reminder of the further positive duties of national institutions would have been appropriate. For example, through the imposition of special individualised procedures aimed at overcoming the psychological limitations of people with mental disabilities in order to promote their political participation and reduce on the opposite side where it is possible for them to be judicially deprived of the right to vote.

In any case, *Alajos Kiss* represents a positive example of integration and collaboration between Hungary and the European Court on Human Rights, as well as between the latter and other sources of international law such as the UN Convention on the Right of Persons with Disabilities. The Hungarian public authorities have shown a fairly high degree of deference to the ECtHR by aligning the domestic law with the rulings. It would be a mistake, however, to say that the case at stake embodies the rule in the relationship between Hungary and the ECtHR. Several supervisory procedures are currently open before the *Committee of Ministers*. A wide range of systematic offences involving inhuman and degrading treatment, violations of the right to life by police officers and/or lack of adequate investigations,[91] as well as inhuman and degrading conditions of detention,[92] the excessive length of civil and criminal trials and the absence of effective remedies,[93] the issue of irreducible life sentences without eligibility for parole in combination with the lack of an adequate review mechanism of such sentences,[94] and the discrimination of Roma people.[95] Not to mention the well-known premature termination of the mandate of the President and Vice-President of the Supreme Court, still awaiting a definitive solution.[96]

Unfortunately, this is only a partial list, but it highlights the reluctance of the Hungarian government to promptly and unconditionally fulfil the ECtHR's judgments; a trend running the risk of worsening in the current situation of constitutional retrogression, in consideration of the repeated attacks against institutional counterpowers and supranational courts such as the Court of Justice of the European Union and the European Court on Human Rights. As usual, making predictions turns out to be a futile exercise, useful only to be subsequently denied. All that remains is hope for a change in the behaviour of the Hungarian institutions that in this case can see an example to follow and not a model to avoid.

91 ECtHR, *Gubasci v. Hungary*, Application no. 44686/07, 29 June 2011.

92 ECtHR, *Varga and Others v. Hungary*, Applications nos. 14087/12, 45135/12, 73712/12, 34001/12, 44055/13 and 64586/13, 10 March 2015.

93 ECtHR, *Gazsó v. Hungary*, Application no. 48322/12, 16 July 2015.

94 ECtHR, *László Magyar v. Hungary*, Application no. 73593/10, 20 May 2014.

95 *Horváth and Kiss v. Hungary*, cited above, para. 89.

96 ECtHR, *Baka v. Hungary*, Application no. 20261/12, 23 June 2016 and ECtHR, *Erményi v. Hungary*, Application no. 22254/14, 22 November 2016.

Bibliography

ALDAO M., *Between Deference and Indifference: Margin of Appreciation, Democracy and Vulnerability Situations in the Caselaw of the European Courts of Human Rights*, in Rev. Derecho del Estado, 44, 2019, 31.

BÁRD K., "The Legal Order of Hungary and the European Convention on Human Rights", in MOTOC I., ZIEMELE I. (eds.), *The Impact of the ECHR on Democratic Change in Central and Eastern Europe: Judicial Perspectives*, Cambridge University Press, Cambridge, 2016, 176–200.

BENVENISTI E., *Margin of Appreciation, Consensus, and Universal Standards*, in New York University Journal of International Law and Politics, 31, 1999, 843.

BERNARDINI M.G., *Vulnerabilità e disabilità a Strasburgo: il vulnerable groups approach in pratica*, in Ars Interpretandi, 2, 2018, 77–93.

BLAKER STRAND V., IKDAHL I., *Responding to Disadvantage and Inequality through Law*, in Oslo Law Review, 4, 2017, 124.

BODNAR A., *Wahlrechtsausschluss für Entmündigte: Auf Polen kommt Ärger zu*, in VerfBlog, 9 March 2014.

BOSSUYT M., *Categorical Rights and Vulnerable Groups: Moving away from the Universal Human Being*, in The George Washington International Law Review, 48, 2016, 717–742.

BOWRING B., *Case-Law of the European Court of Human Rights Concerning the Protection of Minorities, July 2012 to August 2014*, in European Yearbook of Minority Issues, 12, 2013, 201.

BRODERICK A., *A Reflection on Substantive Equality Jurisprudence: The Standard of Scrutiny at the ECtHR for Differential Treatment of Roma and Persons with Disabilities*, in International Journal of Discrimination and the Law, 15, 1–2, 2015, 101–122.

CELIK E., *An Introduction to the Concept of Vulnerability through Human Right and the Visibility of the Concept in European Court of Human Rights Case Law*, in Dokuz Eylul Universitesi Hukuk Fakultesi Dergisi, 22, 2020, 57.

CHAINOGLOU K., *The Framework for Protecting the Rights of Persons with Mental Disabilities in Europe Improved Protection for a Growing Yet Marginalized Group*, in Cyprus Human Rights Law Review, 1, 2012, 157–183.

CHENAL R., *La definizione della nozione di vulnerabilità e la tutela dei diritti fondamentali*, in Ars Interpretandi, 2, 2018, 35–55.

CHRONOWSKI N., VARJU M., *Two Eras of Hungarian Constitutionalism: From the Rule of Law to Rule by Law*, in The Hague Journal on the Rule of Law, 8, 2016, 271–289.

CLIFFORD J., *The UN Disability Convention and its Impact on European Equality Law*, in The Equal Rights Review, VI, 2011, 11–25.

CORSO L., *Vulnerabilità, giudizio di costituzionalità e sentimentalismo*, in Ars Interpretandi, 2, 2018, 57–75.

DA LOMBA S., *Vulnerability, Irregular Migrants Health-Related Rights and the European Court on Human Rights*, in European Journal of Health Law, 21, 4, 2014, 339–364.

DICIOTTI E., *La vulnerabilità nelle sentenze della Corte europea dei diritti dell'uomo*, in Ars Interpretandi, 2, 2018, 13–34.

FEINGOLD C.S., *Doctrine of Margin of Appreciation and the European Convention on Human Rights*, in Notre Dame Law Review, 53, 1977, 90–106.

Fredman S., "Beyond the Dichotomy of Formal and Substantive Equality: Towards a New Definition of Equal Rights", in Boerefijn I. et al. (eds.), *Temporary Special Measures. Accelerating De Facto Equality of Women under Article 4*(1) UN Convention on the Elimination of All Forms of Discrimination Against Women, Intersentia, Antwerp, 2003, 111–115.

Gerards J., *Pluralism, Deference and the Margin of Appreciation Doctrine*, in European Law Journal, 17, 2011, 80–120.

Halmai G., *Dismantling Constitutional Review in Hungary*, in Rivista Diritti Comparati, 1, 2019, 31–47.

Halmai G., *The Fundamental Law of Hungary and the European Constitutional Values*, in DPCE online, 2, 2019, 1503–1524.

Kelemen K., *Hungary: Voter Registration Declared Unconstitutional*, in Dir. Comp., 5 February 2013.

Kleinlein T., *The Procedural Approach of the European Court of Human Rights: Be-tween Subsidiarity and dynamic Evolution*, in ICQL, 68, 2019, 91–110.

Kopel C., *Suffrage for People with Intellectual Disabilities and Mental Illness: Observations on a Civic Controversy*, in The Yale Journal of Health Policy, Law, and Ethics, 17, 2017, 209–250.

Kovacs K., *Cooperative Decision-Making: The Relation between Hungary and Strasbourg*, in ICL Journal, 5, 2, 2011, 188–199.

Kovacs P., "International Law in the Recent Jurisprudence of the Hungarian Constitutional court opening a new tendency?", in Mezzetti L. (ed), *International Constitutional Law*, Giappichelli, Torino, 2014, 459–470.

Levitan S., *Kiyutin: Protecting the Human Rights of Persons Living with HIV/AIDS Beyond Immigration*, in Boston College International and Comparative Law Review, 35, 3, 2013, 49–61.

McGoldrick D., *A Defence of the Margin of Appreciation and an Argument for Its Application by the Human Rights Committee*, in International & Comparative Law Quarterly, 65, 2016, 21–60.

Mjoll Arnardottir O., *The Differences That Make a Difference: Recent Developments on the Discrimination Grounds and the Margin of Appreciation under Article 14 of the European Convention on Human Rights*, in Human Rights Law Review, 14, 4, 2014, 647–670.

Mjoll Arnardottir O., *Vulnerability under Article 14 of the European Convention on Human Rights*, in Oslo Law Review, 4, 2017, 150–171.

Morochovic T., *The Weight of Vulnerability: A Comparative Analysis of the Significance of Particular Vulnerability Attributes under ECtHR Jurisprudence in Situations of Extreme Vulnerability concerning Migrants*, in Exeter Law Review, 44, 2017, 85–105.

O'Connell R., *Cinderella Comes to the Ball: Art 14 and the Right to Non-Discrimination in the ECHR*, in Legal Studies, 29, 2009, 211–229.

O'Connell R., *Realising political equality: The European Court of Human Rights and Positive Obligations in a Democracy*, in The Northern Ireland Legal Quarterly, 61, 2010, 263–279.

Peroni L., Timmer A., *Vulnerable groups: The promise of an emerging concept in European Human Rights Convention Law*, in I-CONS, 11, 4, 2013, 1056–1085.

Tanzarella M., "Il margine di apprezzamento", in Cartabia M. (eds.), *I diritti in azione. Universalità e pluralismo dei diritti fondamentali nelle Corti europee*, Il Mulino, Bologna, 2007, 145–181.

TIMMER A., *Toward an Anti-Stereotyping Approach for the European Court of Human Rights*, in Human Rights Law Review, 11, 4, 2011, 707–738.

TIMMER A., "A Quiet Revolution: Vulnerability in the European Court of Human Rights", in FINEMAN M., GREAR A. (eds.), *Vulnerability: Reflections on a New Ethical Foundation for Law and Politics*, Routledge, Ashgate, 2013, 147–170.

WISNIEWSKI A., *On the Theory of the Margin of Appreciation Doctrine*, in The Polish Review of International and European Law, 2012, 63.

ZIMMERMANN N., *Legislating for the Vulnerable Special Duties under the European Convention on Human Rights*, in Swiss Review of International and European Law, 25, 2015, 539–562.

5 Italian Democracy in Strasbourg and the compliance with European Court's judgments on political rights

A light in a dark panorama

Irene Spigno

Introduction: Italy and the European system of protection of human rights

Italy is one of the "Founding Fathers" of the European system of protection of fundamental rights. Together with Belgium, Denmark, France, Ireland, Luxembourg, Norway, the Netherlands, the United Kingdom, and Sweden, Italy was one of creators of the Council of Europe, signing the Treaty of London on 5 May 1949. Likewise, it signed the European Convention (Convention for the Protection of Human Rights and Fundamental Freedoms, hereinafter ECHR) on 4 November 1950, and later ratified it through Law no. 848 of 1955.

In Italy, the legal status of international treaties – and its position in the systems of legal sources – is determined by the normative instrument through which it is ratified. Thus, the ECHR provisions have the level of an "intermediate" norm, between the Constitution and the law. This result was achieved in 2007, thanks to the Constitutional Court's "twin judgments," decisions no. 348 and 349.[1] This means that, in the case of a conflict between the ECHR provisions and

1 The ECHR was ratified through an ordinary law as provided for in Art. 70 of the Constitution, and thereby it has "force of law" within the Italian legal order. This position implies that the Convention is subject to the Constitution and constitutional laws; it occupies the same hierarchical position as ordinary laws (and acts with the force of law provided for in Arts. 76 and 77 of the Italian Constitution, as well as regional laws), and can be the object – active and passive – of repeal by a law or act with the force of law. This position has long been confirmed by the Constitutional Court and the Court of Cassation. Both courts excluded the constitutionalisation of the Convention's provisions and their direct applicability in the domestic legal system. This position assumed the exclusion of the possibility that its provisions were subject to a constitutional legitimacy trial in the event of being violated. See further Spigno I., "La ejecución de las decisiones del Tribunal Europeo de Derechos Humanos en Italia," in von Bogdandy, A. et al. (eds.), *Cumplimiento e impacto de las sentencias de la Corte Interamericana y el Tribunal Europeo de Derechos Humanos. Transformando realidades*, Instituto Max Planck de Derecho Público Comparado y Derecho Internacional Público, Instituto de Estudios Constitucionales del Estado de Querétaro, Instituto de Investigaciones Jurídicas, Universidad Nacional Autónoma de México, 2019, 265–316, spec. 268 ff.; Randazzo B., *Giudici*

DOI: 10.4324/9781003229247-7

of national dispositions, if the ECHR does not conflict with any other constitutional norms, the former integrates the parameters of constitutionality provided for in the first paragraph of Art. 117 of the Italian Constitution. Thus, the conflict between the ECHR and the internal provisions become an issue of the constitutional review of legislation.[2] Furthermore, the provisions of the ECHR, as interpreted by the European Court of Human Rights (hereinafter the ECtHR), bind the legislator if they do not conflict with the Italian Constitution's provisions. Therefore, national norms, in contrast to the ECHR, can no longer be subject to disapplication but are subject to a constitutional review of legislation, thus guaranteeing the primacy of the Constitution and, at the same time, a perspective of mutual complementarity between the Convention and the Constitution.[3]

Despite being one of the "Founding Fathers" of the European system of protection of human rights and a State with a reliable democratic constitutional system, Italy turns out to be one of the countries with the highest "presence" in Strasbourg, due to the high number of decisions in which it has been held to have international responsibility for violating one or more of the rights and freedoms recognised in the ECHR.[4] Within this framework, we might wonder: how sustainable is Italian democracy? If we want to find an answer to this question by looking at the Italian presence in Strasbourg as far as the violation of Art. 3, Protocol 1 is concerned[5] we will find a light within a dark panorama. In fact, Italy has rarely been "condemned" by the ECtHR for violating the disposition on "free elections." Among these decisions, we can identify, on the one hand, the cases related to the limitations on the right to vote – before the legislative reform issued in 2006 – of people declared bankrupt and, on the other hand, of those related to the incorrect application of the prevention measure of public security special surveillance. In the following pages, first of all I will concentrate on the right to vote in the Italian constitutional systems (para. 2) and later on, I will analyse the ECtHR judgments in which Italy has been declared to have international responsibility for violating Art. 3 Protocol 1 (para. 3), with a special focus on the reparation measures required and the level of compliance by Italy (para. 4). Finally, few concluding remarks will be developed (para. 5).

---

comuni e Corte europea dei diritti, in Rivista di Diritto Pubblico Comunitario, 2, 2002, 357 ff.; ID., *Giustizia costituzionale sovranazionale. La Corte europea dei diritti dell'uomo*, Giuffre, Milano, 2012.

2 See Spigno I., *La ejecución de las decisiones del Tribunal Europeo de Derechos Humanos en Italia*, cit., 274.

3 This approach has also been confirmed in the Constitutional Court's subsequent judgements: see *ex plurimis* decision no. 129/2008.

4 Between 1959 and 2016, the ECtHR has made pronouncements on 2,351 judgments involving the Italian State, and in 1,791 judgments (that is, more than the 76%), the ECtHR found at least one violation of a right or freedom recognised in the Convention. However, between 2014 and 2016, there was a significant reversal in this negative trend, both in the number of judgments issued against Italy and in the number of pending cases, which have dropped considerably.

5 See the "Introduction" in this Volume.

The context: The right to vote and its limitations in the Italian constitutional order

The right to vote is provided for in Art. 48 of the 1948 Italian Constitution. According to this disposition, any citizen, male or female, who is 18 years old can vote, wherever they reside.[6] Nevertheless, only those aged 25 years or older can vote in the Senate elections according to Art. 58 of the constitutional text. Art. 48 also establishes that the vote is personal (voting by proxy is excluded) and equal (according to the basic principle of any democratic system, which excludes the possibility of having multiple votes), free (the law prohibits and sanctions the coercions that may derive from the exercise of certain functions – public officials, ministry of worship, etc. – and considers the giving of money and food a crime in the run-up to the elections), and secret (in order to guarantee the significant freedom in its exercise, except for people with visual disabilities who can vote while accompanied inside the voting booth). According to the Italian Constitution, the exercise of the right to vote is a civic duty. This is an ambiguous formulation because it is not a proper legal duty, and there are no sanctions against those who do not vote. Consequently, abstention is also perfectly admissible and lawful.[7]

The right to vote[8] cannot be restricted, except in a few cases explicitly indicated by Art. 48, namely: due to civil incapacity; or where a final criminal sentence has been imposed and all appeals have been exhausted; or in cases of "moral unworthiness" under the definition laid down by law in which there is a specific reference to the loss of voting rights.

In the application of this provision, Art. 2 of the *Testo unico delle leggi per la disciplina dell' elettorato attivo e per la tenuta e la revisione delle liste elettorali* (hereinafter the *Testo Unico*)[9] people in the following situations are excluded

6 With a change made by Art. 1, Constitutional Law no. 1, 17 January 2000 (Amendment to Art. 48 of the Constitution concerning the establishment of the foreign constituency for the exercise of the right to vote of Italian citizens residing abroad), citizens residing abroad can exercise their right to vote. A constituency of Italians abroad shall be established for elections to the two Houses of Parliament; the number of seats of such constituency is outlined in a constitutional provision according to criteria established by law.

7 On the right to vote in the Italian Constitution see *ex plurimis* Lavagna C., *Il sistema elettorale nella Costituzione italiana*, in Riv. trim. dir. pubbl., 1952, 870. See also Chessa O., *Voto popolare e sistema elettorale nella Costituzione italiana*, in Rivista AIC, 3, 2017, 1–31 and Rubechi M., *Il diritto di voto: Profili costituzionali e prospettive evolutive*, G Giappichelli Editore, Torino, 2017.

8 To be interpreted as the right to vote as well as the right to be voted for. Despite the fact that Art. 48 makes explicit reference to the active electorate, the general principle of the Italian legal system is that of all voters' eligibility. The Constitution provides for some specific restrictions regarding age, indicating that to be elected to the Chamber of Deputies, one must be 25 years old (Art. 56, para. 3), while in order to be elected to the Senate, one must be at least 40 years old (Art. 58, para. 2). For the rest, reference is made to the electoral capacity concept whereby if the active electorate is lost, the passive one is also lost.

9 Presidential Decree no. 223, 20 March 1967, Consolidated legislation for the regulation of active electorate and the maintenance and revision of electoral lists.

from the right to vote: those who are subject, under specific measures, to prison security measures or to probation or the prohibition of residence in one or more municipalities or one or more provinces, according to Art. 215 of the Criminal Code, for as long as the measures are due to last;[10] people sentenced to a punishment which imposes on them a lifetime ban on entering public office; and people subject to a temporary ban from public offices for the entire time of its duration.[11] Furthermore, Art. 2, letter b) also excludes from the category of voters those who are subject, by a final decision, to the preventive measures referred to in Legislative Decree no. 159/2011[12] for the whole duration of the measures themselves.

The original version of Art. 2 of the *Testo Unico* contained a broader catalogue of people excluded from the possibility of exercising the right to vote, mainly relating to civil incapacity,[13] including for people with mental disabilities,[14] and bankrupt traders. This last limitation was repealed in 2006;[15] nevertheless, various cases have reached the ECtHR, which declared Italy responsible for violations on 13 occasions, as will be analysed in the following paragraph.

Analysis of the selected judgments

Judgments related to bankruptcy

Italy has been declared internationally responsible 13 times by the ECtHR for violations of Art. 3, Protocol 1 due to the legislation, in force at that time, and

10 According to Art. 215 of the Criminal Code: "Personal security measures are divided into custodial and non-custodial. The following are prison security measures: 1) assignment to an agricultural colony or a workhouse; 2) admission to a nursing and custodial home; 3) admission to a judicial asylum; 4) admission to a judicial reformatory. Non-custodial security measures are: 1) probation; 2) the ban on residing in one or more municipalities or one or more provinces; 3) the ban on attending taverns and public outlets serving alcoholic beverages; 4) the expulsion of a foreigner from the state. When the law establishes a security measure without specifying the specific type, the judge orders that probation be applied unless, in the case of a convicted felon, he decides to order his/her assignment to an agricultural colony or a house of work."

11 On this point, see in more detail *infra*.

12 Art. 2, letter b) of the *Testo unico* explicitly refers to Art. 3 of Law no. 1423, 27 December 1956, as most recently amended by article 4 of Law no. 327, 3 August 1988. However, Legislative Decree no. 159, 6 September 2011, explicitly repealed Law no. 1423/1956 and stated from its date of entry into force, the references to the provisions contained in the Law no. 1423/1956, wherever present, are understood to refer to the corresponding provisions contained therein (Art. 116).

13 See Dalla Balla F., *Come vota il civilmente incapace? Un caso concreto, due soluzioni apparenti, una proposta interpretativa*, in Forum di Quad. Cost., 2014, 14.

14 This provision was repealed by Art. 11, para. 1 of Law no. 180, 13 May 1978, thus eliminating from the Italian system any residual cause of limitation of the right to vote for civil incapacity. The interdict, therefore, holds the right to vote: the recognition, even for people with mental disabilities, of political rights represents a moment of maturity and democratic and civil progress.

15 See Legislative Decree no. 5, 9 January 2006. Generally, on this reform, see Ambrosini S. (ed.), *La riforma della legge fallimentare : profili della nuova disciplina*, Zanichelli, 2006.

later repealed in 2006, according to which bankrupt merchants were unable to vote (as long as the bankruptcy state lasted, but no later than five years from the date of the bankruptcy judgment).[16]

Most of the judgments date back to 2006 when the legislation had already been repealed.[17] These are rather repetitive cases, first in terms of the factual circumstances of the deprivation of the vote and the arguments advanced by the applicants regarding the violation of their rights, since the restriction on the right of bankrupts to exercise their electoral rights was based on the idea that the bankrupt was always criminally liable for the bankruptcy. According to the applicants, the measure in question should be considered as having no purpose other than to punish the bankrupt, and for this reason, it had to be considered anti-democratic in a modern context and to have diminished the human dignity of the person concerned.

These cases are somewhat repetitive also as far as the State's arguments justifying the compatibility of the legislation at stake and its application are concerned. More specifically, the Italian Government argued that States are afforded a wide margin of appreciation in choosing how to regulate the electoral rights provided in by Art. 3 of Protocol 1. Moreover, the restriction in question was limited to a specific period – five years following the bankruptcy order – so it should not have been considered contrary to the ECHR as it did not affect the right to vote in a disproportionate way.

The arguments developed by the ECtHR to declare the incompatibility of the legislation under consideration and the State international responsibility are also repetitive.

First of all, the Court reiterated its previous case law stating that even if not explicit, Art. 3 of Protocol 1 recognises that States must

16 See the cases: *Albanese* (23 March 2006, Application no. 77924/01); *Vitiello* (23 March 2006, Application no. 77962/01); *Bova* (24 May 2006, Application no. 25513/02); *Pantuso* (24 May 2006, Application no. 21120/02); *Collarile* (8 June 2006, Application no. 10644); *Chiumento* (29 June 2006, Application no. 3649); *La Frazia* (29 June 2006, Application no. 3653/02); *Vertucci* (29 June 2006, Application no. 29871/02); *Vincenzo Taiani* (13 July 2006, Application no. 3638/02); *Taiani* (20 July 2006, Application no. 3641/02); *Melegari* (13 November 2007, Application no. 17712/03); *Viola & others* (8 January 2008, Application no. 7842/02); and *Collarile & others* (18 December 2012, Applications no. 10652/02, 21532/05, 37211/05, 6723/06, 12373/06, 13553/06, 23446/06, 28978/06, 29698/06, 29699/06, 29704/06, 23003/06, 25473/06 et 29693/06).

17 In 2006, Italy has been declared international responsible for the violation of Art. 3, Protocol no. 1 10 times (in the following cases: *Albanese*, *Vitiello*, *Bova*, *Pantuso*, *Collarile*, *Chiumento*, *La Frazia*, *Vertucci*, *Vincenzo Taiani* and *Taiani*), one time in 2007 (in the *Melegari* case), one time in 2008 (in the *Viola & others* case) and the last one in 2012 (in the *Collarile & others* case). In fact, a violation of Art. 3 Protocol no. 1 was also invoked in the *Lepore* (Application no. 43466/04), *Ciccolella* (Application no. 314/04), *Citarella* (Application no. 28466/03) and *Mazzon* (Application no. 896/04) cases. In all these cases, the Court dismissed the action as being filed too late.

hold free elections at reasonable intervals by secret ballot, under conditions which will ensure the free expression of the opinion of the people in the choice of the legislature, also the subjective rights to vote and to stand for election.[18]

These individual rights are fundamental to establishing and maintaining "the foundations of an effective and meaningful democracy governed by the rule of law."[19]

Even if those rights are crucial, they are not, however, absolute. Contracting States have a wide margin of appreciation in their internal legal orders to establish regulations on the right to vote and the conditions to stand for election, but as a last resort, the ECtHR must determine whether these regulations meet the requirements established by Protocol 1. According to the Court, States' regulations and conditions must not curtail the rights related to Art. 3, Protocol 1 by affecting their deepest essence and, in a way, that deprives them of their effectiveness. In this sense, and despite the silence of Article 3, Protocol 1, those regulations must pursue a legitimate aim throughout and not use disproportionate means.[20]

Within this general framework, in the cases against Italy, the ECtHR observed that the Italian legislation which deprived people who had been declared bankrupt from the exercise of the right to vote for as long as the bankruptcy state lasted, but no later than five years from the date of the bankruptcy decision, represented an interference with the applicant's electoral rights guaranteed by Art. 3, Protocol 1, due to the incompatibility of the aim pursued by the legislative measure at stake. Article 3 of Protocol 1 does not specify or limit the aims which a measure must pursue to be considered compatible and, according to the previous ECtHR case law, a wide range of purposes may therefore be compatible with Article 3.[21] For example, preventing crime and enhancing civic responsibility and respect for the rule of law has been considered a legitimate aim to be pursued throughout the restriction of prisoners' voting rights.[22]

However, according to the Court, the restriction of electoral rights for those declared bankrupt "is an essentially punitive measure designed to belittle and punish the persons concerned, demeaning them as individuals for no other reason than their having been the subject of civil bankruptcy proceedings."[23] According to the Strasbourg Court, a legislative measure whose purpose is to belittle persons who have

18 The previous ECtHR case law on this point is quite clear: see *Mathieu-Mohin and Clerfayt v. Belgium*, 2 March 1987, Application no. 9267/81, para. 51.

19 This approach was already established in the Grand Chamber judgment *Hirst v. the United Kingdom (no. 2)*, 6 October 2005, Application no. 74025/01, para. 58.

20 In the same sense, see ECtHR, *Gitonas and Others v. Greece*, 1 July 1997, Application no. 18747/91, para. 39; *Aziz v. Cyprus*, 22 June 2004, Application no. 69949/01, para. 25; and *Hirst*, cit., para. 62)

21 See *Hirst*, cit., para. 74, and, for example, *Podkolzina v. Latvia*, 9 April 2002, Application no. 46726/99, para. 33.

22 See *Hirst*, cit.

23 See *ex plurimis* ECtHR, *Campagnano*, cit., para. 48.

been declared bankrupt, reprimanding them for merely having been declared insolvent, irrespective of whether they have committed an offence,[24] cannot be considered as pursuing a legitimate aim. As the Court itself stressed, "voting is not a privilege but a right guaranteed by the Convention."[25] This conclusion rendered it unnecessary for the Court to analyse if this aim was intended to be pursued throughout proportionate means or not and, based on these common considerations, in all the cases in which Art. 2, para. 1, letter b) of the *Testo Unico* was at stake, the ECtHR considered that there had been a violation of Art. 3, Protocol 1.

Judgments related to the application of public security prevention measures

The ECtHR declared Italy internationally responsible for the violation of Art. 3 of Protocol 1 in two cases based on limitations to the right to vote linked to the application of public security special surveillance prevention measures.

In the first one, the *Labita v. Italy*[26] case, the applicant, Benedetto Labita, was arrested on April 21, 1992, on charges of belonging to the mafia organisation in the town of his residence, Alcamo. Labita was placed in pre-trial detention and subject to the harsh prison regime provided for by Art. 41-bis of the penitentiary system.[27] Two years later, he was fully acquitted "for not having committed the crime."[28] This disposal was later confirmed on appeal. Following the acquittal, he was subjected to special public security surveillance measures and removed from the electoral roll ex Law 575/1965, according to which "preventive measures in the form of an order for special supervision, compulsory residence or exclusion may be imposed on persons against whom there is evidence (indiziati) that they belong to a mafia-type organisation."[29]

In the application presented to the ECtHR, the applicant considered that removing his name from the electoral roll, despite his acquittal, represented a violation of Article 3 Protocol 1. According to the Italian Government, the removal

24 *Ivi*, para 49. See, mutatis mutandis, *Sabou and Pircalab v. Romania*, 28 September 2004, Application no. 46572/99, para. 48.

25 See *Hirst*, cit., para. 75.

26 ECtHR, *Labita v. Italy*, 6 April 2000, Application no. 26772/95.

27 This provision, introduced by Law no. 663 of 1986 in the penitentiary system, provides for so-called "hard-prison" (*carcere duro*). It is a particularly severe type of detention. Whoever is subjected to this regime, usually those affiliated with criminal organisations, is detained in a single cell and does not have access to the common areas of the prison, and indeed are even expected to take their hour of air in total isolation. See Della Bella A., *Il carcere duro" tra esigenze di prevenzione e tutela dei diritti fondamentali. Presente e futuro del regime detentivo speciale ex art. 41 bis O.P.*, Giuffrè, Milano, 2016.

28 According to the formula contained in Art. 530 of the Italian Criminal Code.

29 See ECtHR, *Labita*, cited above, para. 107. Law 575/1965, titled "Provisions against mafia-type criminal organizations, including foreign ones," extended the measures of prevention established by Law no. 1423/1956 to subjects suspected of belonging to mafia associations, in application of Article 32 of *Testo Unico*.

of Mr. Labita from the electoral roll was intended to prevent the criminal organisation (the Mafia) from exerting influence over the representative colleges. In this sense, and taking into account the real risk that persons suspected of belonging to the Mafia exercise their right to vote in favour of other members of this criminal organisation, the temporary removal of Mr. Labita from the electoral lists should not be considered as disproportionate.

In its decision, the European Commission of Human Rights had concluded that the measure applied to Mr. Labita was disproportionate, in particular because the applicant had been acquitted from the penal charges, and the removal of his name from the electoral roll would have been represented a severe danger to him of being alienated from society.

The ECtHR recalled its previous case law on Art. 3, Protocol 1; more specifically, the European judge referred to the consideration that, within their margin of appreciation, member States have to take sufficient care to ensure that national regulations do not curtail the rights recognised in such disposition, to such an extent as to impair their very essence and to deprive them of their effectiveness. National regulations must pursue a legitimate aim throughout proportionate means,[30] always considering that in the last resort, the ECtHR is uncharged to verify whether these regulations meet the requirements established by Art. 3, Protocol 1 and the jurisprudential principles elaborated around it.

More specifically, in the *Labita* case, the ECtHR, in the analysis of the compatibility of the measure at stake, and in particular in analysing the legitimacy of the aim pursued and of the proportionality of the means used to reach it, considered that there is no doubt that "temporarily suspending the voting rights of persons against whom there is evidence of Mafia membership pursues a legitimate aim."[31] In the specific case, the public security special surveillance prevention measures had been imposed during the trial, but were not applied until the trial was over, and once the applicant had been acquitted on the ground that, "he had not committed the offence." This late application was made when there was no "suspicion" that the applicant belonged to the Mafia. Based on this argument, the Court considered that the aim of the measure was legitimate, but the means used to apply it were disproportionate, thereby concluding that Article 3 of Protocol 1 had been violated.

On the same lines, the second case in which the ECtHR declared Italy internationally responsible for the violation of Article 3, Protocol 1, in relation to public security special surveillance prevention measures, is the *Vito Sante Santoro* case.[32] The applicant, Mr. Vito Sante Santoro, between 1991 and 1994, was accused on several occasions of receiving stolen property. In March 1994, a preventive

30 See ECtHR, *Labita*, cit., para. 201 and *Gitonas and Others v. Greece*, cit., para. 39, and the judgment of the Grand Chambre *Matthews v. the United Kingdom*, 18 February 1999, Application no. 24833/94, para. 63.

31 See ECtHR, *Labita*, cit., para. 203.

32 ECtHR, *Vito Sante Santoro v. Italy*, 1 July 2004, Application no. 36681/97.

measure was imposed on him, and he was placed under public security special surveillance: the order was presented to the local police in April 1994 and was complied with in May 1994. It was only in January 1995 that the Local Electoral Committee decided to withdraw him from the electoral roll. Santoro therefore had his electoral rights suspended between January 10 and July 28, 1995 and was subsequently to be re-registered on the local electoral roll. However, months later, in 1995, the mayor of Ostuni (the city where Mr. Santoro lived) declared that the local police had determined that Santoro should have one more year of special supervision. In December 1995, the mayor declared Santoro ineligible for another year. As a result of these two periods of disqualification, Santoro was deprived of the right to vote first in the elections to the Regional Council in April 1995, and then in the elections to the National Parliament in April 1996.

According to the applicant, the disenfranchisement after 2 May 1995 was unlawful, as it was ordered based on a prevention measure of public security special surveillance, which had already expired. On the contrary, in the Government's opinion, the disenfranchisement was lawful in so far as it had to be regarded as the consequence of a lawfully imposed special supervision measure.

The ECtHR determined that the deprivation of Santoro's the right to vote was a violation of Article 3 of Protocol 1 and noted an "excessive" delay of nine months between April 1994 and January 1995 in its application. According to the Court, some delay in complying with the enforcement of a domestic court's decision is often inevitable; however, it must be kept to a minimum.[33] However, more than nine months between the date on which the order imposing the prevention measure was forwarded to the prefect (the authority which applies the prevention measures) and the date on which the applicant was disenfranchised was considered by the Court as "excessive,"[34] thus affecting the applicant's ability to vote both in the national and regional elections.[35] If Santoro had been immediately suspended from his right to vote for one year, the Court reasoned, his period of suspension would have ended one year before both regional and national elections, and he could have voted in the two electoral competitions.

Analysis of the legal and economic impact of the implementation of ECtHR on Art. 3, Protocol 1 on Italian legal order

Execution of judgments related to bankruptcy

In the 13 decisions on bankruptcy in which Italy's international responsibility was declared, the ECtHR, as far as the reparations of non-pecuniary damages and moral prejudices produced by, among the others, the violation of Art. 3 of Protocol 1 are concerned, usually holds that the finding of a violation constitutes

33 *Ivi*, para 57.
34 *Ivi*, para 58.
35 *Ivi*, para 59.

by itself sufficient just satisfaction for the harm sustained by the applicant, dismissing the applicant's claim for just satisfaction.[36] In some cases,[37] the Court has ordered the member State to pay a specific amount of money in terms of moral damages, to be intended for all the violations committed.

Although the number of judgments is not sufficient as to be able to identify a serial or structural violation,[38] the fact that these are repetitive cases and that the Court has decided them within a limited period (most of them in 2006) identifies a problem linked to a specific area of legislation on which the Italian State, if the Court had ruled on other cases, would have to intervene.

In fact, by the time that the Court had ruled on the cases mentioned above, the Italian State had already resolved the issue, repealing the internal legislation establishing limits to the electoral rights of people declared bankrupt, with Legislative Decree no. 5/2006. Consequently, it cannot be concluded that the 2006 Italian legislation, which repealed letter a of Art. 2 of the *Testo Unico* took place as a result of a desire to implement the judgments of the Court. In all likelihood, we are facing a situation in which the general European social and economic context somehow anticipated this compliance, which the Committee of Ministers (CM) itself then ratified to consider the execution of these cases closed.[39]

In any case, in order to fully understand the economic/legal meaning of this "anticipated compliance" it is necessary to understand the rationale of the 2006 reform. Until 2006, bankruptcy proceedings were regulated by the 1942 Bankruptcy Law.[40] For a long time, Italian law considered bankruptcy as a case of "moral unworthiness" and the corresponding legislation punished the bankrupt heavily so as to remove him/her from the commercial affairs engaged

36 See *Campagnano*, *Vitiello*, *Viola & others*, *Albanese*, all cit.

37 In *Chiumento*, *Bova*, *Pantuso*, *Melegari*, *La Frazia*, *Taiani*, *Vincenzo Taiani* and *Vertucci* cases, all cit., even where the ECtHR dismissed the claim for just satisfaction, it required the payment of a specific amount in accordance with Article 44 para. 2 of the ECHR (usually EUR 1,500) for moral damages moral and 2,000 EUR for costs and expenses, plus any tax that may be due. In the *Collarile & others* case the Court required the payment of EUR 20,000, plus any tax that may be due, for non-pecuniary damage, and of EUR 500 (five hundred euros), plus any amount that may be payable as tax by the applicants, for the costs and expenses of each application.

38 Sul punto sia consentito rinviare a Spigno I., *La ejecución de las decisiones del Tribunal Europeo de Derechos Humanos en Italia*, cit., 276 ff.

39 In this sense, in fact, the Committee of Ministers of the Council of Europe (CM) considered the pending issues concerning the limitations on the free exercise of personal rights by the person declared bankrupt following the adoption of the new regulations on insolvency procedures as definitively closed, with Résolution intérimaire CM/ResDH (2007) 27, 4 April 2007 in which, among other things, the CM "*se félicite de l'adoption de la réforme de 2006 sur les procédures de faillite et de ses effets immédiats.*" See Presidenza del Consiglio dei Ministri, Dipartimento affari giuridici e legislativi, *Relazione al Parlamento. L'esecuzione delle pronunce della Corte europea dei diritti dell'uomo nei confronti dello Stato italiano legge 9 gennaio 2006, no. 12*, 2008, 81.

40 See Royal Decree no. 267 of 16 March 1942, *Disciplina del fallimento, del concordato preventivo, dell'amministrazione controllata e della liquidazione coatta amministrativa*.

in prior to the declaration of bankruptcy.[41] Thus, a repressed figure of the bankrupt debtor emerged due to the severe limitations he/she had to endure, not to mention the social discrimination he/she ensued.[42] On a personal level, the declaration of bankruptcy-imposed limitations on the freedom of the bankrupt person; and further, it precluded them from being the beneficiary of certain individual rights, relationships, or offices (so-called special incapacities),[43] including the limitation of the right to vote.

The constitutionality of this last limitation has been challenged on various occasions. First of all, the constitutional review of the legislation creating this provision was raised with reference to Arts. 48 and 3 of the Constitution at the beginning of the 1970s. On that occasion, the Court declared the question unfounded since "the bankrupt undergoes a decrease in the bankrupt capacity regardless of the reasons for the failure and is based on a distrust of the juridical order towards him." Besides, the Court stated that

> it is not irrational that, without regard to facts that led to the failure, the bankrupt is also deprived of the electoral capacity, under the species of moral indignity, because the electorate, concerning rights attributed in the general interest, presupposes in the citizen qualities adequate to the very high civic scope of its content: [in this sense] there is a perfect coincidence between active electoral capacity and passive electoral capacity, so the former must be attributed only if the latter can be attributed (Constitutional Court decision no. 43/1970).

A new question of the constitutional legitimacy of Art. 2 first paragraph, letter a) of the *Testo Unico* was raised again in the 1990s regarding Art. 3 of the Constitution.[44] On this occasion, the Court declared its manifest inadmissibility due to irrelevance in the a quo judgment (order no. 327 of 1996).

41 See Bonsignori A., *Il fallimento*, CEDAM, Padova, 1986, 340–342.

42 According to the Bankruptcy Law, the declaration of bankruptcy resulted in a whole series of effects, not only of a financial nature, but also of a personal nature (see Arts. 48–50 of this legislation).

43 The person declared bankrupt suffered limitations as regards the freedom and secrecy of their correspondence (Article 15 of the Constitution) and their freedom of movement and residence (Article 16 of the Constitution), while the special incapacities, to which he/she was, and still is, subject due to their bankruptcy, are only those expressly established by law, which for the most part are outside the bankruptcy law, including the limitation of the right to vote (as established in Art. 2, letter a of the *Testo Unico*).

44 Meanwhile, Art. 2, para 1., letter a), of the *Testo Unico*, was replaced by Art. 1 of the Law no. 15 of 16 January 1992 (Amendments to the consolidated text of the laws for the regulation of the active electorate and for the maintenance and revision of electoral lists, approved by decree of the President of the Republic March 20, 1967, no. 223, and to the consolidated text of the laws containing rules for the election of the Chamber of Deputies, approved by decree of the President of the Republic March 30, 1957, no. 361). This amendment replaced the expression "bankrupt merchants, as long as the state of bankruptcy lasts, but no later than five years from the date of the decree declaring the bankruptcy" with "those who are declared bankrupt while the state of bankruptcy lasts, but no later than five years from the date of the bankruptcy judgment."

However, cultural, social, and economic conditions at the beginning of the 21st century have profoundly changed and provided a greater need and urgency to equip the legal system with adequate and coherent tools to ensure that the Italian position is in line with the requirements of the European Action Plan, that is to say, to ensure that internal growth corresponds to that required by the EU. It is this which pushed the Italian legislators to adopt Legislative Decree no. 5/2016 containing measures aimed at relaunching economic, social, and territorial development.[45]

Finally, the issue of people declared bankrupt losing the right to vote has completely disappeared with the express repeal of the aforementioned provision of Art. 2, para 1, letter a) of the *Testo Unico*,[46] in respect of all bankruptcies, even where an individual was declared bankrupt before the reform. Finally, the Constitutional Court, with decision no. 39 of 2008, also eliminated the inequality of treatment between bankruptcies before the 2006 reform and those who benefit from the new limitation regime.[47] In particular, the Court declared the constitutional illegitimacy of articles 50 and 142 of the Bankruptcy Law in the

45 More specifically, in the implementation of the Delegated Law no. 80 of 14 May 2005, Legislative Decrees no. 5 of 9 January 2006 and no. 169 of 12 September 2007, on the discipline of bankruptcy, arrangement with creditors and compulsory administrative liquidation (significantly modifying Royal Decree no. 267 of 1942, text still in force on bankruptcy proceedings), where approved. Legislative Decrees no. 5 of 2006 and no. 169 of 2007, among other things, have provided for a different discipline of the legal and personal incapacity of the subject to the bankruptcy procedure, on which the ECtHR had expressed several times through decisions that had affirmed the non-compliance with the ECHR of the previous discipline (and in particular, on the prohibition of departing from one's own residence without the permission of the presiding judge; on the prohibition of registration in the register of companies even after the conclusion of the procedure and as long as the rehabilitation and cancellation from the bankruptcy register had not occurred; on the removal from the subject of all correspondence addressed to him, without distinguishing between personal correspondence and correspondence relating to the operation of the company) and found a violation of Arts. 8 and 13 of the ECHR and articles 2 of Protocol no. 4, and 1 of Protocol no. 1. The reform law has specifically affected these aspects, with provisions which, among other things, have: a) eliminated the bankruptcy register and established that with the closure of the bankruptcy procedure the effects of the bankruptcy on the bankrupt's assets cease and the consequent personal incapacity of the same (Art. 120, Legislative Decree no. 5 of 2006); b) excluding the need for the authorisation of the judge in order to leave the home and only the communication of the change of residence or domicile is required for this purpose (Article 49 of the amended text of Royal Decree no. 267 of 1942); c) excluding the obligation to deliver to the bankruptcy trustee correspondence concerning the personal and private sphere of the bankrupt (Article 48 of the amended text of Royal Decree no. 267 of 1942); d) governed in a different way the personal property regime of the bankrupt (article 46).

46 Established by Art. 152, para. 1, letter a), of the Legislative Decree no. 5 of 2006.

47 On this decision see Mastroianni R., *La sentenza della Corte cost. no. 39 del 2008 in tema di rapporti tra leggi ordinarie e CEDU: anche le leggi cronologicamente precedenti vanno rimosse dalla Corte costituzionale?*, in Forum dei Quaderni Costituzionali, 2008, and Sciarabba V., *Il problema dei rapporti tra (leggi di esecuzione di) vincoli internazionali e leggi precedenti nel quadro della recente giurisprudenza costituzionale*, in Forum dei Quaderni Costituzionali, 2008.

text in force before the 2006 reform, which the ECtHR had found to be contrary to Art. 8 of the ECHR, as they are products of unnecessary interference in private and family life in a democratic society.

Execution of the decisions on special public security surveillance prevention measures

With reference to the reparation measures dictated in the two judgments analysed above, in which the ECtHR declared the Italian State's international responsibility for the disproportionate application of the public security special surveillance prevention measures, the following should be specified. In the *Labita* case, the Court required the State to pay the applicant, within three months, ITL 75,000,000 (seventy-five million Italian lire) in respect of non-pecuniary damage[48] and ITL 6,000,000 (six million Italian lire) for costs incurred at the hearing before the Court. Moreover, given that the violation in the *Labita* case was linked to an erroneous application of the legislation on public security special surveillance prevention measures by the judicial authorities, the CM found that, with reference to the general measures, the Superior Council of Magistracy organised a thematic seminar in 2005. Furthermore, the Labita judgment has also been published in several legal journals, including "Documenti Giustizia, 2000, no 1/2," and was sent to the Superior Council of the Magistracy, which has jurisdiction over the training of judges.[49]

In the *Vito Sante Santoro* case, the ECtHR required the State to pay the applicant, within three months from the date on which the judgment became final,[50] EUR 2,000 (two thousand euros) in respect of non-pecuniary damage, EUR 5,500 (five thousand five hundred euros) in respect of costs and expenses, and any tax that may be chargeable on the above amounts. Since there were no structural violations, the Court did not prescribe general measures. The CM declared that the execution of this case had been complied with in 2010 with Resolution CM/ResDH(2010)213.[51]

Nevertheless, the analysis of the execution of these judgments cannot be limited to verifying the fulfilment by the State of what is established by the Court (which in this specific case requires the payment of sums of money) but must be carried out in a broader context. Even if in the two cases under consideration,

48 See Resolution CM/ResDH(2009)83. See also Presidenza del Consiglio dei Ministri, Dipartimento affari giuridici e legislativi, *Relazione al Parlamento. L'esecuzione delle pronunce della Corte europea dei diritti dell'uomo nei confronti dello Stato italiano legge 9 gennaio 2006, n.12*, 2009, 126 ff.

49 *Ivi*, 129.

50 Cfr. Art. 44, para 2 ECHR.

51 See also Presidenza del Consiglio dei Ministri, Dipartimento affari giuridici e legislativi, *Relazione al Parlamento. L'esecuzione delle pronunce della Corte europea dei diritti dell'uomo nei confronti dello Stato italiano legge 9 gennaio 2006, n.12*, 2010, 113.

the ECtHR did not enter into the heart of the question, not deciding on the compatibility in particular of the public security special surveillance prevention measures and the restrictions on fundamental rights that these entail (as it did in the 1980 judgment in the *Guzzardi v. Italia* case),[52] the matter presents severe problems of compatibility (recently highlighted by the ECtHR itself in the recent de *Tommaso v. Italy*[53] decision).

Therefore, in the following pages, we will analyse some recent jurisprudential and legislative developments that correct some of the distortions linked to the application of the legislation on public security special surveillance prevention measures. These recent developments represent a form of early execution of a possible future declaration of Italy's international responsibility (however, already partly anticipated by the ECtHR itself in the *de Tommaso* case).

Prevention measures are special-preventive measures generally contemplated by contemporary criminal systems. From a formal point of view, they are administrative measures aimed at avoiding the future commission of crimes by specific categories of subjects considered to be socially dangerous. These are *ante delictum* or *praeter delictum* measures,[54] since they are applied regardless of whether there has been a previous crime committed. The doubts about their constitutionality and/or compatibility concern the controversial nature of the imposition of "penalties on the basis of suspicion" (in fact, they are used as a substitute for an impracticable criminal repression due to the lack of normal probative conditions),[55] the alleged lack of scientific evidence in the current cases of danger; and of the criteria for identifying the predicted danger; and finally, their recognised ineffectiveness in terms of the preventive purpose.[56]

The application of personal preventive measures leads to, among other consequences, the loss of the right to vote in case of moral unworthiness (according to Art. 48, last para. of the Constitution). They have accompanied the Italian legal system's history since its inception[57] and are now organically governed by

52 ECtHR, *Guzzardi v. Italy*, 6 November 1980, Application no. 7367/76.

53 ECtHR, *de Tommaso v. Italy*, 23 February 2017, Application no. 43395/09. See Viganò F., *La Corte di Strasburgo assesta un duro colpo alla disciplina italiana delle misure di prevenzione personali. Corte Edu, Grande Camera, sent. 23 febbraio 2017, de Tommaso c. Italia*, in Diritto Penale Contemporaneo, 3, 2017, 370–382. See also Maugeri A., *Misure di prevenzione e fattispecie a pericolosità generica: la Corte europea condanna l'Italia per la mancanza di qualità della "legge," ma una rondine non fa primavera*, in Diritto Penale Contemporaneo, 3, 2017, 33.

54 See Bricola F., *Forme di tutela "ante delictum" e profili costituzionali della prevenzione*, in AA. VV., Le misure di prevenzione (Atti del Convegno di Alghero – Centro Nazionale di prevenzione e difesa sociale), Giuffrè, Milano, 1975, also in Bricola F., *Scritti di diritto penale*, vol. I, tomo II, Giuffrè, Milano, 1997, 882–884.

55 *Ex plurimis* see Barile P., *Diritti dell'uomo e libertà fondamentali*, Il Mulino, Bologna, 1984, 138.

56 *Ex plurimis* see Nuvolone P., *Le misure di prevenzione nel sistema penale italiano*, in L'indice penale, 1973, 472–473.

57 The origins of this legislation date back to at least the 19th century, crystallised immediately after the unification of Italy in Law no. 2248 of 20 March 1865 (*Per l'unificazione amminis-*

Legislative Decree no. 159 of 2011.[58] The provisions contained in Legislative Decree no. 159 of 2011 are the result of a long and historic evolution, made through constitutional case law and normative reforms.

In its first year of activity, the Constitutional Court, through decision no. 2 of 1956, declared the unconstitutionality of those dispositions of the *Testo unico di pubblica sicurezza*,[59] regarding the compulsory execution of the repatriation order ordered by the *prefetto*.[60] Later on, with decision no. 11 of 1956, the constitutional judge declared the unconstitutionality of the admonition rule. In both cases, the decision was based on the incompatibility of the rules at stake with the "reserve of jurisdiction" provided for by Art. 13 of the Constitution to limit personal freedom.[61]

The legislator had, by December 1956, already promptly adapted to the rulings of the Court, through new organic preventive measures contained in Law no. 1423 of 1956. In its original version, the law indicated five different categories of people who could be affected by these measures: idlers and vagabonds; those known and habitually engaged in illicit trafficking; those inclined to commit a crime and those who, due to their conduct and standard of living, must consider themselves to be living habitually, even partially, with the proceeds of crimes or aiding and abetting; those believed to be engaged in the exploitation of prostitution, trafficking in women, bribery of minors, smuggling or drug trafficking; as

trativa del Regno d'Italia), annex B, which already conferred on the public security authority the power to order the measures of admonition, forced domicile (or police confinement) and repatriation. These measures were compulsory for people considered dangerous for society, even where there was no criminal sentence against them. Widely used in the Fascist era as an instrument of control and repression of political opponents, these measures – whose rules had meanwhile merged into the Royal Decree no. 773 of 18 June 1931 (*Testo unico di pubblica sicurezza*) – remained alive even after the entry into force of the Republican Constitution.

58 See Fiorentin F., *Le misure di prevenzione personali nel Codice antimafia, in materia di stupefacenti e nell'ambito di manifestazioni sportive*, Giuffrè, Milano, 2012, 28 and Filippi L., *Profili processuali: dalla proposta al giudizio di primo grado*, in Giurisprudenza italiana, 6, 2015, 1539 ff., 1545.

59 The reference is to the *Testo unico di pubblica sicurezza*: see *supra* nota no. 57.

60 The Constitutional Court was called upon to examine the legitimacy of the relative rules contained in the *Testo unico di pubblica sicurezza* by numerous referral orders from judges called to judge the criminal liability of persons accused of having violated the inherent provisions of preventive measures ordered by the police authority.

61 In particular, in decision no. 11/1956, the Constitutional Court underlined "that the warning order results in the individual being subjected to special police surveillance" and "through this provision a whole series of obligations are imposed on the warned person, to do and not to do, between which, that of not going out earlier and not going home after a certain time, is only one among the others that the special commission prescribes": all these effects entail a significant "restriction" on the right to personal freedom protected by Art. 13 of the Constitution, and as such removed – at the behest of the constituents – from the exclusive power of the police authority. See Nuvolone P., *Appunti e spunti tra precetti e sanzioni*, in Rivista italiana di diritto penale, 1956, 441 ff.

well as "those who habitually carry out other activities contrary to public morality and buon costume."

Regarding all of these categories, the law provided that the *prefetto*[62] could directly send a warning to the individual to change their behaviour and to order their repatriation using a compulsory travel document. At the same time, it entrusted to a court or tribunal – following the principle established by decision no. 11 of 1956 – the competence to have the most severe measure of special surveillance, to which the court itself could impose a prohibition on residing in one or more municipalities or provinces and, in cases of particular danger, the obligation to stay in a specific municipality. In any case, people subjected to preventive measures were considered morally unworthy once the measures became definitive and for its entire duration. Moreover, according to Art. 2, letter b, para. 1 of Presidential Decree no. 223, the person who faced any personal prevention measures was removed from the electoral roll.

The Italian legislators progressively extended the application of preventive measures: first of all, with Law no. 575 of 1965, and its subsequent modifications, preventive measures were extended to those "suspected of belonging to mafia-type associations." Secondly, Law no. 152 of 1975 (the so-called *legge Reale*) further broadened the scope of application to a wide area of subjects suspected to be involved in terrorist or subversive activities, of belonging to dissolved political associations or the fascist party, as well as to people already convicted of violations of the law on weapons and therefore considered, to have a greater propensity to commit more crimes of a similar nature.

The first signs of a more restrictive approach arrived in 1980, right at the height of the terrorist emergency that had taken hold at that time in Italy. Two significant judgments – one issued by the ECtHR and the other by the Italian Constitutional Court called attention to the need to protect the fundamental rights of people subject to preventive measures. In *Guzzardi v. Italy*,[63] the ECtHR stated that the application of the preventive measure of special surveillance with a residence order on an island unlawfully limited the applicant's freedom of movement and his personal freedom since it did not meet any of the exceptions provided for in the first paragraph of Art. 5 ECHR. More specifically, according to

62 The *prefetto*, in the Italian administrative system, is a monocratic body of the State, representative of the territorial government of provinces and metropolitan cities, in charge of an office called "prefecture-territorial government office," dependent on the Ministry of the Interior.

63 See ECtHR, *Guzzardi v. Italy*, cited above, para. 102 ff. This case originated from the application of the preventive measure of special surveillance with a residence order on the island of Asinara (Sardinia, Italy), under the suspicion that the applicant belonged to a mafia association under Law no. 575 of 1965. According to the ECtHR, the application of this measure not only limited the applicant's freedom of movement protected by Art. 2 Protocol no. 4 ECHR (at the time not yet ratified by Italy), but due to the particular narrowness of the space to which the applicant was confined, as well as the situation of substantial personal isolation in which he was forced to live, also represented a real deprivation of his personal freedom, provided in by Art. 5 ECHR.

the Court, the appellant's confinement could not be considered as a necessary measure "to prevent him from committing a crime" according to Art. 5, para. 1, letter c) since a deprivation of freedoms arranged for this purpose would necessarily have to be linked to a subsequent criminal trial, deliberated before the judicial authority and for a specific crime of which the subject was accused. A link that does not exist concerning preventive measures, the application of which is independent of the formulation of a criminal charge.

On the domestic front, through judgment no. 177 of 1980, the Constitutional Court declared incompatible with the principle of legality – considered on that occasion to also be applicable to personal prevention measures by Art. 13 and Art. 25, para. 3[64] of the Constitution – the applicability of preventive measures to those who

> for the events they have given rise to, give grounded reason to believe that they are inclined to commit a crime," due to the intolerable indeterminacy of this normative formula, considered such by "offering operators a space of uncontrollable discretion.

The legislative's reply arrived a few years later, with Law no. 327/1988 (on Rules on personal prevention measures), which eliminated the possibility for the court to order the obligation to stay in a municipality other than that of residence; and, additionally, reformulated the regulatory descriptions contained in Art. 1 of Law no. 1423 of 1956, eliminating the "vagabonds" and "idlers" from the list potential recipients of preventive measures. The Law also specified that the court should have carried out an evaluation of the subject's eligibility to be included in the categories described by the law based on "factual elements" (and not, therefore, based on mere rumours or suspicions).

This was an isolated trend because the following years' legislation continued along a line of progressive expansion of the categories of potential recipients of preventive measures.

These categories are now organically listed in Art. 4 of Legislative Decree no. 159 of 2011 and subsequent amendments.[65] According to Legislative Decree no. 159, prevention measures can be applied only to people who represent a danger to public safety. This dangerousness should be verified through their past criminal activities, which must be accompanied by further procedural verification, in terms of "significant probability of commission, in the future, of further criminal activities" (Art. 6, para. 1, Legislative Decree no. 159/2011). This evaluation must be based on "factual elements" rather than on "clues."

64 Art. 25, para. 3 of the Constitution states that "No restriction may be placed on a person's liberty save for as provided by law."

65 All the cases previously disseminated across several regulatory texts (which were not always easy to identify) were merged into Legislative Decree no. 159 of 2011.

Art. 4 contains a relatively long list of so-called "qualified" danger subjects (mainly people related to specific illegal activities). However, Art. 1, Legislative Decree no. 159 of 2011 contains few remaining categories of "generic" danger subjects,[66] among which subjects "habitually engaged in criminal trafficking" and to those "who habitually live, even partially, with the proceeds of criminal activities." The compatibility of these latter provisions was recently scrutinised, in line with international human rights law, by the Grand Chamber of the ECtHR in the *de Tommaso* case.[67] According to the Strasbourg Court, the provisions at stake did not meet the qualitative standards – in terms of precision, certainty, and predictability – that every regulation limiting the rights recognised by the ECHR or its protocols must respect.

In particular, the ECtHR stated that the relevant "factual elements" required had not been outlined either through legislation or by the Constitutional Court. Nor had there been a sufficient assessment of the danger that the person represented to society, the outcome of which can give rise to the application of the preventive measures. The ECtHR concluded that Art. 1 does not contain sufficiently detailed provisions of the types of conduct that should be considered to constitute a danger to society to avoid "an arbitrary interference" with the applicant rights.[68]

On the same lines, the Italian Constitutional Court, sharing this assessment of the excessive generality of the subjects indicated in Art. 1, letter a), of Legislative Decree n. 159 of 2011 (according to which preventive measures can be applied to "those who must be considered, based on factual elements, habitually engaged in criminal trafficking"), with decision no. 24/2019 declared the unconstitutionality of the disposition, which established the possibility of subjecting people who "must be considered, based on factual elements, habitually engaged in criminal trafficking" to public security special surveillance prevention measures (and to the measures preventing the confiscation of assets). According to the constitutional judge, the expression "criminal trafficking" is not, in particular, able to indicate with sufficient precision what criminal behaviours may give rise to the application of public security special surveillance (or confiscation of assets). It follows that there is a violation of the principle of legality (according to Art. 13 of the Italian Constitution), which requires that any restrictive measure of personal freedom or property of the individual is based on a law that precisely determines the conditions for its application.

66 Which were only partially remodelled following the intervention of this Court in 1980 and the legislator in 1988. See *supra*.

67 ECtHR, *de Tommaso v. Italy*, cited above.

68 *Ivi*, para. 117. The ECtHR reiterated that the provisions based on which the preventive measure that the applicant had drawn on had been adopted "did not indicate with sufficient clarity the scope or manner of exercise of the extensive discretion conferred on the domestic courts, and was therefore not formulated with sufficient precision to provide protection against arbitrary interferences and to enable the applicant to regulate his conduct and foresee to a sufficiently certain degree the imposition of preventive measures": para. 118.

On the other hand, the Court considered the provisions that allow the same measures to be applied to those who habitually live, even partially, with the proceeds of criminal activities, sufficiently precise, and therefore compliant with the principle of legality. According to the most recent jurisprudence, the measures in question can be applied only to those who, based on specific facts, can be considered to have committed, for a significant period, crimes that are the source of profits that have constituted their sole income, or at least a significant component of their income. Therefore, all these elements must be demonstrated by the public prosecutor or by the police authority in the preventive procedure so that the Court can apply special public security surveillance or the confiscation of assets allegedly acquired thanks to the criminal activities and of which the subject cannot justify the lawful origin. Finally, the Court specified that the sentence does not affect the rules that allow for the application of preventive measures against those accused of mafia crimes, terrorism, violations of the rules on weapons, sporting violence, corruption, and persecutory acts.[69]

With this decision, the Court has probably anticipated the execution of a future decision – already announced – by the ECtHR, thus allowing people who "must be considered, based on factual elements, habitually engaged in criminal trafficking" to be able to exercise, among others, the right to vote.

Conclusions: The sustainability of Italian democracy

How sustainable is Italian democracy? If we seek the answer to this question in the light of the legal impact of the implementation of the ECtHR judgments concerning the violation of political rights and electoral justice – and most particularly the analysis of the status of the implementation of the corresponding measures of reparation identified – we can identify reliable indicators to assess the status and sustainability of Italian democracy. First of all, with reference to economic sustainability: the violation of Art. 3, Protocol 1 represents a non-structural violation that did not require a significant economic outlay. Especially when compared to other sectors that represented a relatively high cost to the Italian State, Art. 3 of Protocol 1 has never been a problem. The sums paid to repair the few violations of this right are relatively small.

Secondly, both the lines identified – rulings on bankruptcy and those related to the application of preventive measures – are linked by a common thread represented by the fact that in both types of cases, we are faced with a theory of moral unworthiness which, as noted, the last paragraph of Art. 48 of the Constitution provides as a justification for limiting the right to vote. The choice of Italian democracy was, therefore, to protect itself against cases of moral unworthiness.

69 On this decision see Maugeri A. and Pinto de Albuquerque P., *La confisca di prevenzione nella tutela costituzionale multilivello: tra istanze di tassatività e ragionevolezza, se ne afferma la natura ripristinatoria (C. Cost. 24/2019)*, in Sistema penale, 2019.

The possibility of including moral indignity as an element of excluding persons from the right to vote was heatedly discussed during the debates in the Constituent Assembly.[70] Art. 48, in fact, in its original formulation, only contemplated limitations of the right to vote due to civil incapacity or as a result of the imposition of a final criminal sentence, where all possible appeals have been exhausted. On 21 April 1947, however, an ordinary bill on the management of the active electorate was presented to the Constituent Assembly, which provided for cases of exclusion from the vote for moral unworthiness (later approved with the Law no. 1058 of 7 October 1947). During its examination by the referring commission, it was found that this third category of exclusion from the vote could be maintained only if the text of the draft Constitution had included it in its definitive formulation. The amendment to the project of Art. 48 was therefore approved and undoubtedly marks the intention of the Constituent Assembly to give the notion of moral unworthiness a meaning that included, among other things, the status of bankruptcy, with reference to which, however, a minor degree of moral unworthiness was attributed in comparison to other cases of deprivation of the electoral right.[71]

A similar justification, as a theory of moral unworthiness, is the one at the basis of the exclusion of people who, as a result of being considered "dangerous to public safety," are subjected to personal prevention measures. The progressive coordinated work of national legislators and judges and the ECtHR circuit has ensured that the prevention needs of the legal system are adapted to the conditions of the sustainability of Italian democracy to avoid excessive limitations on a series of fundamental rights (as highlighted with the last reference to

70 In the draft of the Constituent Commission, this provision appeared in a substantially different form from the one later approved, because it lacked the proposition "or in the cases of moral unworthiness indicated by the law." Mr. Pietro Mastino proposed a broader formula referring to the law, while Mr. Giuseppe Micheli, president of the Commission for electoral laws, pointed out that Art. 2 of the draft that dictates the rules for the active electorate, presented to the Assembly on 21 April 1947, contained cases of exclusion from the vote for moral unworthiness that the Constitution would not have contemplated, with the consequence of a possible conflict between law and Constitution. To overcome this inconvenience, in the following session, the rapporteur Lina Merlin pointed out that it was appropriate to accept the observations of Mr. Micheli, making the provision more detailed (accepting a new formula proposed by Mr. Meuccio Ruini) than the Commission itself would have liked, in order not only to prevent discrepancies between the electoral law and the Constitution, but above all "to prevent that the legislator from tomorrow could impose incapacity or limitations to the right to vote for purely political reasons," which instead could have happened by accepting the Martino amendment (AC, 4152). The rapporteur Merlin then observed that the formula proposed by Mr. Ruini also implicitly included, among the cases of moral unworthiness, bankrupt merchants as well as "all those who are, pursuant to article 215 of the Criminal Code, subjected to prison security measures or probation": see Falzone V., Palermo F., Cosentino F., Orlando V. (eds.), *La Costituzione della Repubblica italiana illustrata con i lavori preparatori da Vittorio Falzone, Filippo Palermo, Francesco Cosentino. Con prefazione di Vittorio Emanuele Orlando*, Colombo, 1948, 94 ff.

71 See Constitutional Court decision no. 43/1970, cit.

the declaration of unconstitutionality in the Constitutional Court decision no. 24 of 2019). Consequently, while up until 1988, idles and vagabonds could be deprived of the right to vote; and up until 2019, also those people who "must be considered, based on factual elements, habitually engaged in criminal trafficking"; thanks to the interventions of the Constitutional and the European judges, the electorate, both active and passive, has expanded again to include those categories as well.

Thirdly, we can probably talk about cases of early execution of a partially announced incompatibility. This statement is clear with reference to the rulings on bankruptcy (as seen, the Italian State has been recognised as being internationally responsible on 13 occasions for the legislation that prevented persons declared bankrupt from exercising the right to vote, but the Italian legislator anticipated the European Court intervening in relation to this legislation and eliminated this limit even before the issuance of sentences). While a more in-depth analysis is required as regards the decisions related to the application of preventive measures, it is important to distinguish between the cases in which these measures are applied to people presumably belonging to criminal organisations and those applied to situations of generic danger that have nothing to do with the former.

As seen, preventive measures are aimed at guaranteeing the protection needs of the democratic system, whose roots can be found in the historical, social, cultural and political context, which justify their constitutionality and compatibility with the European Convention and. The constitutionality and compatibility with the Convention of the exclusion of certain persons involved in organised crime associations from exercising the right to vote have never been questioned, as demonstrated by the presence of other regulations that complete the panorama, such as the prohibition of propaganda during elections and the recently established crime of political–mafia electoral exchange.[72]

Fourthly, if examined within the parameters of Strasbourg, Italian democracy is also sustainable from a political point of view, given that if we take into consideration the various rulings of the ECtHR with which the legitimacy of some national laws that significantly affect the exercise of the right to vote, the political impact on the democratic circuit has not been particularly notable. This is demonstrated by the fact that the ECtHR has expressed itself by declaring the compatibility of the rule that provides for the loss of the right to vote with reference to criminal convictions (as provided for by Art. 48 of the Italian Constitution).

This limit is further specified by Art. 2 of the *Testo Unico* which refers to those sentenced to a punishment which imposes a lifetime ban on entering public office and those who are subject to temporary ban from public offices, for the entire time of the punishment duration and specified by Arts. 19 and 20 of the Penal

72 See Art. 416 *ter* of the Italian Criminal Code. See Amarelli G., *Una più chiara graduazione del disvalore delle condotte di contiguità mafiosa?*, in Diritto Penale Contemporaneo, 2, 2014, 4–23.

Code. In the light of this legal framework, a person who is sentenced to a prison sentence of not less than five years will be definitively deprived of the right to vote (and this regardless of the type of crime committed, and without the judge having the power to make any type of assessment in relation to the necessity and proportion of the measure).[73]

However, this legislation has never represented a problem of compatibility[74] and nor did the provisions of the so-called "Severino Law"[75] in the sense in which they regulate the reasons for ineligibility and forfeiture of certain public offices, including that of Senator of the Republic, against those who have been convicted of certain crimes.[76] No violation was found either with reference to the problematic profiles of Law no. 270 of 21 December 2005 (later declared unconstitutional by the Constitutional Court with decision no. 1 of 2014),[77] where it refrained from intervening in an issue strictly connected – electoral legislation – to the organisation of the state system, by leaving this and the development (and the reform) of the election systems to the sphere of state sovereignty, and leaving out, from the ECtHR's own sphere of competence, the matter of the "justiciability of political rights."[78]

It therefore seems clear that the challenge of Italian democracy in terms of sustainability is played not on the level of respect for the right to free elections provided for in Art. 3, Protocol 1, but rather on that of the balance between the defence of the democratic system and the tendency to guarantee greater inclusiveness.

73 The ban from public offices – which according to the provisions of Art. 28 para. 1 no. 1) of the Italian Criminal Code also involves the deprivation of the active and passive voting rights in all electoral rallies – is provided for by Art. 19 of the Italian Penal Code among the "accessory penalties" (these sanctions result directly from the sentence, falling – according to the provisions of Art. 20 Penal Code – among the criminal effects following the main sanction). The ban from public office can be lifelong or temporary: it is lifelong in the case of a sentence of life imprisonment or imprisonment of not less than five years; it is temporary in the case of a sentence of imprisonment of not less than three years (in which case the ban has a duration of five years) or in the case of a crime committed through an abuse of powers or through a violation of the duties inherent in a public function or a public service (in which case it has the same duration to that of the main sentence, pursuant to Art. 37 of the Penal Code).

74 See the ECtHR *Grand Chamber* decision *Scoppola v. Italy*, 22 May 2012, Application no. 126/05. On this case see Lang E., *A Disproportionate Response: Scoppola v. Italy (N. 3) and Criminal Disenfranchisement in the European Court of Human Rights*, in Am. U. Int'l L. Rev., 28, 2012–2013, 835 ff.

75 The reference is to Law no. 190 of 6 November 2012, on the prevention and repression of corruption. It is also known as the "Severino Law" from the name of the Minister of Justice, Paola Severino, the principal person responsible for this Law.

76 See the ECtHR *Grand Chamber* decision *Berlusconi v. Italy*, 27 November 2018, Application no. 58428/13.

77 On this decision see Milani G. and Spigno I., *Reflexiones sobre la declaratoria de inconstitucionalidad de la Ley Electoral: ¿Qué consecuencias tiene para el sistema democrático italiano?*, in Pedro Esteban Penagos López (ed.), Seguridad jurídica en el sistema democrático, Tirant lo Blanch, 2014, 209–245.

78 See ECtHR, *Saccomanno v. Italy*, 12 May 1999, Application no. 36719/97; on this decision see Trucco L., Saccomanno e altri c. Italia: anche per Strasburgo, tutte le strade portano al legislatore, in Quad. cost., 2012, 901–904.

Bibliography

Ambrosini S. (ed.), *La riforma della legge fallimentare: profili della nuova disciplina*, Zanichelli, 2006.

Barile P., *Diritti dell'uomo e libertà fondamentali*, Il Mulino, 1984, 138.

Bonsignori A., *Il fallimento*, CEDAM, 1986, 340–342.

Bricola F., *Forme di tutela "ante delictum" e profili costituzionali della prevenzione*, in AA. VV., Le misure di prevenzione (Atti del Convegno di Alghero - Centro Nazionale di prevenzione e difesa sociale), Giuffrè, 1975.

Bricola F., *Scritti di diritto penale, vol. I, tomo II*, Giuffrè, 1997, 882–884.

Chessa O., *Voto popolare e sistema elettorale nella Costituzione italiana*, in Rivista AIC, n. 3, 2017, 1–31.

Dalla Balla F., *Come vota il civilmente incapace? Un caso concreto, due soluzioni apparenti, una proposta interpretativa*, in Forum di Quad. Cost., 2014.

Falzone V., Palermo F., Cosentino F., Orlando V. (eds.), *La Costituzione della Repubblica italiana illustrata con i lavori preparatori da Vittorio Falzone, Filippo Palermo, Francesco Cosentino. Con prefazione di Vittorio Emanuele Orlando*, Colombo.

Filippi L., *Profili processuali: dalla proposta al giudizio di primo grado*, in Basile F. (ed.), in Le misure di prevenzione dopo il c.d. codice antimafia. Aspetti sostanziali e aspetti procedurali, in Giurisprudenza italiana, n. 6, 2015, 1545.

Fiorentin F., *Le misure di prevenzione personali nel Codice antimafia, in materia di stupefacenti e nell'ambito di manifestazioni sportive*, Giuffrè, 2012.

Lang E., *A Disproportionate Response: Scoppola v. Italy (N. 3) and Criminal Disenfranchisement in the European Court of Human Rights*, in Am. U. Int'l L. Rev., vol. 28, 2012–2013.

Lavagna C., *Il sistema elettorale nella Costituzione italiana*, in Riv. trim. dir. pubbl., 1952.

Mastroianni R., *La sentenza della Corte cost. n. 39 del 2008 in tema di rapporti tra leggi ordinarie e CEDU: anche le leggi cronologicamente precedenti vanno rimosse dalla Corte costituzionale?*, in Forum dei Quaderni Costituzionali, 2008.

Maugeri A., Pinto de Albuquerque P., *La confisca di prevenzione nella tutela costituzionale multilivello: tra istanze di tassatività e ragionevolezza, se ne afferma la natura ripristinatoria (C. Cost. 24/2019)*, in Sistema penale, 2019.

Milani G., Spigno I., *Reflexiones sobre la declaratoria de inconstitutionalidad de la Ley Electoral: ¿Qué consecuencias tiene para el sistema democrático italiano?*, in López P.E.P. (ed.), Seguridad jurídica en el sistema democrático, Tirant lo Blanch, 2014, 209–245.

Nuvolone P., *Appunti e spunti tra precetti e sanzioni*, in Rivista italiana di diritto penale, 1956, 441.

Nuvolone P., *Le misure di prevenzione nel sistema penale italiano*, in L'indice penale, 1973, 472–473.

Rubechi M., *Il diritto di voto: Profili costituzionali e prospettive evolutive*, in G Giappichelli Editore, 2017.

Sciarabba V., *Il problema dei rapporti tra (leggi di esecuzione di) vincoli internazionali e leggi precedenti nel quadro della recente giurisprudenza costituzionale*, in Forum dei Quaderni Costituzionali, 2008.

Spigno I., *La ejecución de las decisiones del Tribunal Europeo de Derechos Humanos en Italia*, in von Bogdandy, A. et al. (eds.), Cumplimiento e impacto de las sentencias de la Corte Interamericana y el Tribunal Europeo de Derechos Humanos. Transformando realidades, Instituto Max Planck de Derecho Público Comparado y Derecho Internacional Público, Instituto de Estudios Constitucionales del Estado de Querétaro, Instituto de Investigaciones Jurídicas, Universidad Nacional Autónoma de México, 2019, 265–316.

Trucco L., *Saccomanno e altri c. Italia: anche per Strasburgo, tutte le strade portano al legislatore*, in Quad. cost., 2012, 901–904.

6 Democracy and political participation in the countries of the former Yugoslavia

A complicated combination under the lens of the European Court of Human Rights

Francesca Pirola

The relationship between the European Court of Human Rights and the former Yugoslav States: A brief overview

The issue of the sustainability of the democratic rule within the "powder keg of Europe" is a thorny one for a number of reasons. In such multicultural and multi-ethnic environment, defined by an unstable democratic tradition, such as the former Yugoslav region, the establishment of a full-functioning constitutional, and institutional order represents the determinative step of a successful democratisation starting some decades ago. During such a process, it is argued that the European Court of Human Rights provided a fundamental role in the correct implementation of the principle of universal suffrage, as a condition *sine qua non* of any legitimate constitutional democracy. By way of background, to evaluate the effective impact of the "democratic arguments" flowing from its jurisprudence, it is nevertheless necessary to begin with some introductory considerations.

Political competition in the former Yugoslav area has always been different to that in other countries of the Eastern Bloc, especially due to social-economical peculiarities of the region.[1] Following the fall of the Iron Curtain, such divergences became even more clear, especially where political competition fuelled with ethnic rivalries turned the region into the stage for a brutal armed conflict, exacerbating such gross violations of the most fundamental individual freedoms, which those in the Yugoslav authoritarian rule had already previously been perpetuating: while this latter "[had not put] in the first place human rights and [had not defined] any clear legal restrictions applying to government authorities and their violence,[2] the regional war which burst out in the early 1990s witnessed ethnic cleansing, massive killings, and even genocide.

1 Džankić J., *The Politics of Inclusion and Exclusion: Citizenship and Voting Rights in Bosnia and Herzegovina*, in International Peacekeeping, 22, 2015, 528.

2 *Republika Slovenija Ustavno Sodišče, Številka*: U-I-158/94, judgment of 9 March 1995, (Constitutional Court of the Republic of Slovenia declaring a decision of unconstitution-

DOI: 10.4324/9781003229247-8

In such a context, it should come as no surprise that the accession to the Council of Europe (hereinafter "CoE") and, consequently, the incorporation of the European Convention on Human Rights ("ECHR" or "the Convention") within the former Yugoslav countries' jurisdiction has been welcomed as a fundamental step in incentivising the troubled process of democratisation.[3] The acceptance of the new undertakings flowing from the CoE – first of all, the respect for the ideal of democracy – indeed served the fundamental objective of averting the threat of a new repressive totalitarian regime. Undoubtedly, borrowing former President Spielmann's words, "*joining the Council, accepting its values and aims, integrating into its structures, and accepting its core human rights treaties would be part of* [the former Yugoslav countries'] *transition, not the reward for it.*"[4] These considerations aid us in explaining the primary importance attached to the Convention and, in general, the direct application international treaties are attributed, especially when it comes to the protection of human rights.[5]

Moreover, since the lack of a democratic tradition represented a common problem shared by all six States concerned, it was a widespread assumption that only an external and autonomous authority – such as the European Court of Human Rights (hereinafter: "ECtHR" or "Court") – could be considered the most legitimate institution to guide the shift to constitutional democracies.[6]

As for the impact of its jurisprudence, it is undeniable that the ECtHR exercised a pivotal influence within the respective domestic legal systems, by contributing to the consolidation of a higher standard of safeguard of individual liberties, as well as an enhanced cohesion around universal European fundamental values. Yet, statistical data tends to suggest a patent divergence between the

ality of the Agency of the Republic of Slovenia for Payment Operations internal organisation).

3 Slovenia was the first Former Yugoslav state to join the Council of Europe in 1993, followed shortly after by Macedonia, in 1995, and Croatia, in 1996. Bosnia and Herzegovina became a member of the Council of Europe only in 2002, while the State Union of Serbia and Montenegro acceded to it in 2003. After Montenegro's declaration of independence, in 2006, Montenegro was admitted as an independent state in 2007. On the applicability of the European Convention of Human Rights in Kosovo, see for example Milanović M., Papić T., *The Applicability of the ECHR in Contested Territories*, in International & Comparative Law Quarterly, 67, 4, 2018, 779 ff.

4 Spielmann D., *President's Opening Remarks (Seminar on Impact of ECHR in Eastern Europe)*, Strasbourg, 18 February 2013 www.echr.coe.int/Documents/Speech_20130218_Spielmann_ENG.pdf.

5 See Constitution of Bosnia and Herzegovina, Art. II (2); Constitution of the Republic of Croatia, Art. 141; Constitution of Montenegro, Art. 9; Constitution of Serbia, Art. 18; Constitution of Slovenia, Art. 8.

6 For further analysis, see Motoc I., Ziemele I. (eds.), *The impact of the ECHR on the democratic change in Central and Eastern Europe. Judicial Perspectives*, Cambridge University Press, Cambridge, 2016; on the same subject, see Keller H, Stone Sweet A. (ed.), *A Europe of rights: the impact of the ECHR on national legal systems*, Oxford University Press, Oxford, 2008.

fundamental freedoms as enshrined in the Convention and their effective application at national level.[7]

A comprehensive analysis of such findings goes beyond the scope of this chapter; yet, it is fairly safe to affirm that the incapacity of domestic authorities to exhaustively internalise the conventional guarantees coupled with the institutional unwillingness to respond to structural democratic frailties indeed represents one of the root causes of the poor level of execution of ECtHR's judgments to date.[8] As regards cases transmitted to the Committee of Ministers of the CoE for supervision, since the entry into force of the Convention, in Bosnia and Herzegovina only 70 out of 107 have been closed definitively, while in Serbia only 450 cases out of 507 and in Croatia 398 cases out of 481 have met with the same destiny. A slightly better position is that of North Macedonia (282 cases out of 317), Montenegro (63 closed cases out of 67) and Slovenia (332 cases out of 345).[9]

Narrowing the scope of investigation to that case-law specifically dealing with the right to free elections – as protected under Art. 1 of Protocol 3 – the main concerns shown by the Court have been related to the lack of effective political participation within the domestic legal systems under scrutiny; more specifically, two main issues have tested the ECtHR's authority.

The first challenge former Yugoslav States had to face pertains to the difficult objective of nourishing a civic identity of their own without weighing on ethnic minorities' effective participation in public and political matters. As a matter of fact, the failure to reach a satisfying compromise has led to the result that, rather than a means by which to guarantee effective political participation, elections have often exhibited their discriminatory nature for national minorities.[10]

In this respect, the example of Bosnia and Herzegovina is emblematic: here, in contradiction to the very basic democratic principle, the individual's enjoyment of civil and political rights is limited by the peculiar combination of territorial and consociational elements envisaged in the constitutional principle "one

7 Between 1959–2019, 76 judgments out of 83 have found Bosnia and Herzegovina in violation, 325 out of 412 have found a violation imputable to Croatia, 48 judgments out of 53 have found Montenegro in violation, while North Macedonia have been found in breach 145 times out of 165; Serbia have been found in violation 195 times out of 216, while Slovenia have been found to be in breach of the Convention 338 times out of 368. Nevertheless, the total number of applications decided in the same period of time is much higher: for instance, 9,967 claims have been lodged against Bosnia and Herzegovina, and 15,682 complaints have concerned Croatia and 30,283 applications have been submitted against Serbia. For further details, see *ECHR Overview 1959–2019* www.echr.coe.int/Documents/Overview_19592019_ENG.pdf.

8 On the topic see among others Černič J.L., *A Glass Half Empty? Execution of Judgments of the European Court of Human Rights in Central and Eastern Europe*, in Baltic Yearbook of International Law Online, 15, 2016, 285 ff.

9 See CoE, *Country Factsheets*. Available at www.coe.int/en/web/execution/country-factsheets.

10 On the specific subject of the safeguard of voting rights of minorities and the role of ethnicity in elections in the post-Yugoslav space, see Hardman H., Dickson B., *Electoral rights in Europe: advances and challenges*, Routledge, London, 2017.

state – two entities – three nations."[11] Pursuant to this, a fundamental role in the system of vertical separation of powers between Bosnia and Herzegovina and its two federal units (so-called "Entities") – namely, the Federation of Bosnia and Herzegovina and Republika Srpska – is played by those who the Preamble defines as "the constituent peoples," that is the main ethnic communities living in the country: Bosniaks, Serbs, and Croats. Around these three ethnic communities, a power-sharing system has been set up aimed at safeguarding their groups' interest. However that same system side lines from active political participation both the "Others" (i.e. those who do not declare themselves as one of the three abovementioned ethnic groups) and constituent peoples who are residents of an entity different from that where their ethnic group forms a majority.[12]

Another issue the Court of Strasbourg has had to face originated from the domestic authorities' incapacity to deal with the previous status quo and, more specifically, with delays in the transformation from communism to a constitutional democracy, especially as regards the role played by political parties within the system of democratic representation. In this respect, the practice of parties' control over parliamentary seats institutionalised by the 2006 Constitution of Serbia, known under the term "blank-form resignation" fell under the scrutiny of the Court of Strasbourg due to its potential destabilising impact upon the very basis of any representative democracy, i.e. the right of each elected parliamentarians to remain in office. The abovementioned mechanism presented itself as a "contract" between a certain political party and its members, pursuant to which every candidate elected on a party list was expected to sign an undated resignation letter and to deposit it with the leaders of the political party itself so that, in the case of dissent, the leader would simply have needed to fill in the date on the blank-form resignation to activate it.

As a result of this practice, political parties produced weak, replaceable MPs, and, consequently, a weakened parliament.[13] It is clear that, by imposing the

11 As cited in Seizovic Z., *Constitutional Reform in Bosnia and Herzegovina – Civil State of Constituent Peoples*, in Annals of the Faculty of Law of the University of Zenica, 1, 2007, 31; on the functioning of the principle see for example BRUNO M. M., *Bosnia and Herzegovina electoral system and ECHR, a conflicting relationship. Recent developments and European prospects*, in 7 International Journal of Rule of Law, Transitional Justice and Human Rights, 2016, 33 ff; Antloga A., *The right to stand for elections in the Constitution of Bosnia and Herzegovina as a basic political right in a post-conflict society*, in International Journal on Rule of Law, Transitional Justice and Human Rights, 10, 2019, 11 ff.

12 On the importance of the constituency of peoples as a collective right of ethnic communities, see for example Begić Z., Delić Z., *Constituency of peoples in the constitutional system of Bosnia and Herzegovina: Chasing fair solutions*, in International Journal of Constitutional Law, 11, 2, 2013, 447 ff; Tabaković Jašar S., *The impact of constituent peoples' principle on democratical transition and human rights protection in Bosnia and Herzegovina*, in International Journal on Rule of Law, Transitional Justice and Human Rights, 9, 2018, 37 ff.

13 Šturanović P., *Political parties and their influence on the parliamentary mandate after the fall of communism in Montenegro and Serbia*, in Studia Politica: Romanian Political Science Review, 18, 3, 2018, 423.

political party's rationale over the individual right to effective participation in the decision-making process, the rule of the "blank-form resignation" tended to emulate the dynamics previously embedded in the totalitarian regime. From this perspective, it became symptomatic of the "hybrid" nature of a country caught between past and future, that is between the political goal to depart from the pre-existing authoritarian rule and the incapacity to comply totally with the objective of full realisation of democratic constitutionalism.[14]

The analysis of the European Court of Human Rights' case-law

Equipped with this knowledge, the following paragraphs will turn to the analysis of selected cases specifically dealing with the abovementioned matters of concern, namely the safeguard of ethnic minority voting rights in Bosnia and Herzegovina and the limits to political participation deriving from the former "blank-form resignation" practice in Serbia.

The protection of ethnic minorities in political participation: The examination of the **Sejdić and Finci** *saga*

What is known as the "*Sejdić and Finci* saga" refers to the ECtHR case-law that challenged Bosnia and Herzegovina's (hereinafter "BiH") discriminatory domestic electoral system, which unjustifiably excludes ethnic minorities' rights to stand for election to the House of Peoples[15] and the Presidency.[16]

In accordance with the Constitution of BiH, taken in conjunction with the Election Act passed by the Parliamentary Assembly in 2001, a declaration of affiliation with one of the "constituent peoples" represents the prerequisite for an effective exercise of the passive voting right. While the right not to declare such an affiliation is granted to every potential candidate, the failure to do so is considered a waiver of the prerogative to be elected or appointed to the House

14 Beširevič V. (ed.), *Public Law in Serbia: Twenty Years After*, European Public Law Series, CI, 2002, 24–54.

15 The House of Peoples is the upper Chamber of the State Parliament, composed of 10 Bosniak and Croat members appointed by the cantonal parliaments of the Federation of Bosnia and Herzegovina, and of 5 Serbs elected by the National Assembly of Republika Srpska. The House of Peoples shares equal legislative powers with the lower parliamentary branch, called the House of Representatives, composed of 28 members affiliated with the Bosniak and Croat ethnic communities, elected by the residents of the Federation of Bosnia and Herzegovina, and of 15 Serbs elected by the citizens residing in the Republika (Constitution of Bosnia and Herzegovina, Art. IV).

16 The Presidency is the collective Head of State, which shares the executive power with Council of Ministers. Its composition strictly respects the same territorial rule followed by the bicameral State Parliament: Bosniak and Croat members are elected directly by the residents of the Federation of Bosnia and Herzegovina, while the Serb member is elected by the citizens residing in Republika Srpska (Constitution of Bosnia and Herzegovina, Art. V).

of Peoples and the Presidency.[17] As a result, Bosnian citizens are left with a non-equal condition, with those who fail to meet the requirement above deprived of their right to vote.

The following pages hence are aimed at illustrating each of the "chapters" of the *Sejdić and Finci judicial* saga – that is the five cases examined by the judges of Strasbourg – so as to evaluate the Court's response vis-à-vis the discriminatory effect resulting from the Bosnian electoral system.

Sejdić and Finci v. Bosnia and Herzegovina

In 2009, the Strasbourg judges were called upon to rule on the exclusion of two Bosnian citizens' passive voting rights for the first time.[18] The applicants, Mr Dervo Sejdić and Mr Jakob Finci, were two prominent public figures who took issue with their ineligibility to stand for election to the House of Peoples or the Presidency of Bosnia and Herzegovina on the grounds that they described themselves to be of Roma and Jewish origin respectively. As regards the ineligibility to stand for election to the House of Peoples, the applicants invoked Art. 14 of the Convention taken in conjunction with Art. 3 of Protocol 1,[19] Art. 3 of Protocol 1 taken alone[20] and Art. 1 of Protocol 12;[21] while concerning the ineligibility to stand for election to the Presidency, they relied only on Art. 1 of Protocol 12.

Before the Court, the Bosnian Government invoked a wide margin of appreciation in its favour, in particular referring to the Court's precedent of *Ždanoka v. Latvia*,[22] where the Strasbourg judges had declared that:

> *States enjoy considerable latitude in establishing constitutional rules on the status of members of parliament, including criteria governing the eligibility to*

17 See Constitution of Bosnia and Herzegovina, Arts. IV and V and Election Act 2001, section 4.19; as for the determination of one's ethnicity, the Constitution contains no objective criteria, so that it is assumed the former Yugoslav system of self-classification still operates.

18 ECtHR, *Sejdić and Finci* v *Bosnia and Herzegovina*, Applications nos. 27996/06 and 34836/06, 2 December 2009.

19 According to Art. 14 of the Convention "the enjoyment of the rights and freedoms set forth in this Convention shall be secured without discrimination on any ground such as sex, race, colour, language, religion, political or other opinion, national or social origin, association with a national minority, property, birth or other status."

20 Art. 3 of Protocol 1 reads "the High Contracting Parties undertake to hold free elections at reasonable intervals by secret ballot, under conditions which will ensure the free expression of the opinion of the people in the choice of the legislature."

21 Art. 1 of Protocol 12 provides for a general prohibition of discrimination, stating that "the enjoyment of any right set forth by law shall be secured without discrimination on any ground such as sex, race, colour, language, religion, political or other opinion, national or social origin, association with a national minority, property, birth or other status" (para. 1) and that "no one shall be discriminated against by any public authority on any ground such as those mentioned in paragraph 1" (para. 2).

22 ECtHR, *Ždanoka* v *Latvia*, Application no. 58278/00, 17 June 2004.

> *stand for election ... these criteria vary[ing] in accordance with the historical and political factors specific to each State.*[23]

In addition, it was maintained that the contested constitutional provisions should be assessed against the peculiar historical background in which they were adopted. In fact, the Constitution of Bosnia and Herzegovina was adopted as an Annex (Annex IV)[24] to the 1995 General Framework Agreement for Peace in Bosnia and Herzegovina (hereinafter, "the Dayton Agreement"), initiated at Dayton on 21 November 1995 and signed in Paris on 14 December 1995; hence, as part of a peace treaty, it was primarily focused on the paramount objective of restoring peace in the country and, more specifically, to preserving the fragile cohabitation between the three main ethnicities, namely Bosniaks, Serbs, and Croats in the early post-conflict stage.

From the government's perspective, therefore, the fragile equilibrium of power reached between the three "constituent peoples" not only warranted the inclusion of the contested provisions, but also represented an on-going challenge, since the "*time was still not ripe for a political system which would be a simple reflection of majority rule, given, in particular, the prominence of mono-ethnic political parties and the continued international administration of Bosnia and Herzegovina*";[25] in the light of the above, their preservation within the domestic constitutional framework would inevitably be endorsed by the existence of an objective and reasonable justification.

Turning to the Court's reasoning, the Grand Chamber began its analysis by taking the ethnic issue into careful consideration. More specifically, it acknowledged that, at the time of the entry into force of the Constitution, the exclusion of representatives from political participation of the communities other than the "constituent peoples" – such as, for instance, Roma and Jewish groups – "*pursued at least one aim which is broadly compatible with the general objectives of the Convention, as reflected in the Preamble to the Convention, namely the* restoration of peace" in the aftermath of "*a brutal conflict marked by genocide and ethnic cleansing.*"[26]

Nevertheless, the Grand Chamber did not embrace the argument put forward by the Bosnian Government, since the maintenance of such an "emergency" system perpetuating the absolute exclusion of ethnic minorities in exercising their right to vote could not but amount to a form of racial discrimination, that is to "*a particularly egregious kind of discrimination* ... [which], *in view of its*

23 *Ibid.*, para 83; see also ECtHR, *Mathieu-Mohin v. Belgium*, Application no. 9267/81, 2 March 1987; ECtHR, *Melnychenko v Ukraine*, Application no. 17707/02, 19 October 2004.

24 The Constitution of Bosnia and Herzegovina represents a unique example of an externally imposed constitutional framework, albeit the Parliamentary Assembly was granted the power to amend it (Art. X).

25 *Sejdić and Finci*, cited above, para. 34.

26 *Ibid.*, para. 45.

perilous consequences, requires from the authorities special vigilance and a vigorous reaction"[27] and which entails a strict requirement of proportionality to be satisfied.

In assessing the restriction's reasonableness, "time" indeed represented a determinative factor in reaching the conclusion that the contested provisions in any event did not satisfy the requirement above. First of all, the Grand Chamber noted a series of significant positive developments which BiH had undergone after the Dayton Agreement.[28] In addition, the judges of Strasbourg took the opportunity to emphasise the specific obligation on the respondent State, arising since it became a member of the Council of Europe in 2002 and, more specifically, since the agreement it had reached to "*review within one year, with the assistance of the European Commission for Democracy through Law (Venice Commission), the electoral legislation in the light of Council of Europe standards, and to revise it where necessary.*"[29]

Additionally, the Court strongly pointed out the existence of alternative mechanisms of power-sharing which would allow for the pursuit of the aim of the integration of ethnic minorities into the political system of representation without necessarily jeopardising the interest of "constituent peoples" and without necessarily abandoning the BiH peculiar post-conflict institutional framework.[30]

In conformity with such findings, the applicants' continued ineligibility to stand for election to the House of Peoples of Bosnia and Herzegovina lacked an objective and reasonable justification and, accordingly, it was found to be in violation of Art. 14 taken in conjunction with Art. 3 of Protocol 1. Not only that, but for the same reasons outlined above, the Court held that the constitutional precondition of the affiliation with a "constituent people" so as to stand for election to the Presidency amounted to a discriminatory difference in treatment, prohibited by Art. 1 of the Protocol 12.[31]

Accordingly, BiH was required to pay the applicants 1,000 and 20,000 euros respectively as just satisfaction under Art 41 of the Convention in respect of costs and expenses.

Zornić *and* Šlaku

As regards the "after-effects" of the judgment, immediate expectations were raised among both academics and the international community; notwithstanding the fact that the Strasbourg judges had not prescribed any specific measures as part of the implementation of the ruling, the *Sejdić and Finci v. Bosnia and Herzegovina* case was nevertheless rather meaningful for two relevant aspects: not

27 *Ibid.*, para. 43.
28 *Ibid.*, para. 47.
29 *Ibid.*, para. 49.
30 *Ibid.*, para. 48.
31 *Ibid.*, paras. 53–56.

only did it mark the first application of the general prohibition of discrimination prescribed by Art. 1 of Protocol 12 – thus opening what was awaited as a new promising chapter of the ECtHR's jurisprudence – but also, and even more significantly, it represented a unique case where the Court intruded upon a States' domestic constitutional framework so as to rule on its incompatibility with the Convention.

Despite the general favour the judgment was welcomed with, its legal impact was nonetheless overestimated and, in both 2014 and 2016, the judges of Strasbourg were charged again with the task of ruling on the discriminatory practices represented by the parts of the Bosnian electoral system still in force.

The first dispute in concern arose from the application of Mrs Azra Zornić,[32] a Bosnian citizen, claiming the violation of her passive right to vote due to her ineligibility to run for election to the House of Peoples and the Presidency of Bosnia and Herzegovina in 2002. A clear resemblance to the factual circumstances of the *Sejdić and Finci* case is easily spotted, with the only difference being that, in the present case, the applicant's exclusion was grounded on her refusal to affiliate with "constituent people" rather than on her identification with another ethnic community. The second case[33] originated in a complaint lodged against Bosnia and Herzegovina by Mr Samir Šlaku, a political activist, whose "passive" electoral right was denied due to his belonging to BiH's Albanian ethnic minority. As with the *Sejdić and Finci* case, both Mrs Zornić and Mr Šlaku relied on Art. 3 of Protocol 1 taken alone and in conjunction with Art. 14 of the Convention, and on Art. 1 of Protocol 12 as well.

Since the reasoning largely followed the previous assessments enshrined in the *Sejdić and Finci* judgment, the legal importance of *Zornić* and *Šlaku* cases mainly flows from the Court's application of Art. 46 of the Convention. As a matter of fact, both cases were considered under such a disposition as interpreted in the light of Art. 1 of the Convention, which "*imposes on the respondent State a legal obligation to implement, under the supervision of the Committee of Ministers, appropriate general and/or individual measures to secure the right of the applicant which the Court found to be violated" as well as the right of the "persons in the applicant's position, notably by solving the problems that have led to the Court's findings.*"[34]

Pursuant to this, the Court emphasised that the violation of the two petitioners' right to stand for election in the House of Peoples and the BiH Presidency represented nothing but "*the direct result of the failure of the authorities of the respondent State to introduce measures to ensure compliance with the judgment in Sejdić and Finci,*" that is "*constitutional and legislative proposals to put an end to the current incompatibility of the Constitution and the Electoral Law*" with the conventional standards; this situation contributed as an "*aggravating factor as regard the State's responsibility under the Convention for an existing or past state of*

32 ECtHR, *Zornić* v *Bosnia and Herzegovina*, Application no. 3681/06, 15 July 2014.

33 ECtHR, *Šlaku* v *Bosnia and Herzegovina*, Application no. 56666/12, 26 May 2016.

34 *Zornić*, cited above, para 39; *Šlaku*, cited above, para 36.

affairs" but also *was seen as a "threat to the future effectiveness of the Convention machinery.*"[35]

Consequently, and "*in view of the need to ensure effective political democracy,*" the Court considered that

> *the time has come for a political system which [would] provide every citizen of Bosnia and Herzegovina with the right to stand for elections to the Presidency and the House of Peoples of Bosnia and Herzegovina without discrimination based on ethnic affiliation and without granting special rights for constituent people to the exclusion of minorities;*[36]

in addition and in accordance with the paramount objective to guarantee an effective representation to ethnic minorities, the Court urged "*the speediest and most effective resolution of the situation in a manner which complies with the Convention's guarantees,*" and expressed its expectation that "*that democratic arrangements* [would] *be made without further delay.*"[37]

No pecuniary reward was granted to the applicants. Yet, the relevance of these two cases lies in the circumstance that, unlike in *Sejdić and Finci v. Bosnia and Herzegovina*, the Court explicitly refers to the imperative to introduce legislative and constitutional amendments so as to put an end to the violation which had occurred, further emphasising the legal obligation of the compliance with its judgments, albeit the Court's indications remained unfollowed.

Pilav *and* Pudarić

The next chapter of the Sejdić and Finci saga is constituted by *Pilav v. Bosnia and Herzegovina*:[38] the 2016 dispute saw the Grand Chamber challenging the restrictive character of the ethnocentric BiH electoral system which manifested itself in the need to meet ethnic origin and place of residence requirements in order to exercise passive suffrage.

The applicant, Mr Ilijaz Pilav, was a Bosniac-affiliated citizen residing in the town of Srebrenica, in Republika Srpska. Since the Bosnian electoral system[39] expressly provides that the presidential candidate from that Entity must be a Serb, his attempts to put forward his candidacy for both the 2006 and 2010 elections to the Presidency of Bosnia and Herzegovina were rejected by the Central Election Commission of BiH. The dismissal of Mr Pilav's candidature was endorsed by the same Constitutional Court of BiH, which held[40] that there had been no violation

35 *Zornić*, cited above, para 40; *Šlaku*, cited above, para 37.

36 *Zornić*, cited above, para 43; *Šlaku*, cited above, para 40.

37 *Zornić*, cited above, paras 42–43; *Šlaku*, cited above, paras. 39–40.

38 ECtHR, *Pilav v. Bosnia and Herzegovina*, Application no. 41939/07, 9 June 2016.

39 Constitution of Bosnia and Herzegovina, Art. V; Election Act 2001, Art. 8.2. para 2.

40 *Ustavni sud Bosne i Hercegovine* (Constitutional Court of Bosnia and Herzegovina) decision no. AP 2678/0 *Stranka za Bosnu i Hercegovinu (Party for Bosnia and Herzegovina) and Mr Ilijaz Pilav.*

of the appellant's right on the grounds that the above exclusion was reasonably "*justified by the … specific nature of [BiH] constitutional order*" as well as by *"the current constitutional and law arrangements*," given that it served a legitimate aim, it did not place an excessive burden on the candidate and it was "*proportionate to the objectives of the general community in terms of preservation of the established peace.*.[41]

Faced with two unbearable options, either to move to the Federation of Bosnia and Herzegovina (thereby giving up the chance to serve his community in the place of residence) in order to effectively exercise his right, or to accept a status of second-class citizen in Republika Srpska, the applicant took issue with the legal impossibility for him to stand for election to the Presidency of Bosnia and Herzegovina and to vote for a member of his own community to be elected to this office.

The case differentiates itself from the previous ones analysed above in two relevant aspects. Firstly, as underlined by the Bosnian Government, unlike the applicants in *Sejdić and Finci*, Mr Pilav belonged to one of "the constituent people" (i.e. Bosniaks); hence, allegedly, he was not treated differently compared to members of the other two main ethnic communities on the grounds that "*the territorial restriction in question applied to Serbs and Croats as well*"[42] and that the applicant's right to vote and stand for elections was "*not restricted to the extent of impairing* [its] *very essence.*"[43]

Secondly, in line with the non-legislative nature of the Head of State of BiH, the applicant only invoked the general prohibition of discrimination (Art. 1 of Protocol 12) and not the right to free elections. Even though, the Court reiterated that the residence requirement is not per se disproportionate or irreconcilable with the underlying purposes of the right to free elections protected under Art. 3 of Protocol 1, as the enjoyment of the right to vote and to stand for election could depend on the nature and degree of the links that existed between the individual applicant and the legislature of the particular country.[44] Despite noting that, in the specific case under examination, the Court recognised that the Presidency of Bosnia and Herzegovina was a political body of the State – and not of the Entity – whose decisions could potentially affect all citizens of Bosnia and Herzegovina. Therefore, although the petitioner was involved in political life in Republika Srpska, he was also clearly concerned with the political activity of the collective Head of State.[45]

While it was true that the residence requirement in question applied to all the "constituent peoples" equally, the Court concluded that the applicant was indeed subject to such differentiation of treatment if compared to Serbs living in the Republika Srpska, which could not be upheld in the light of the reasons already examined in *Sejdić and Finci*. Hence, and notwithstanding the difference

41 *Ibid.*, para 22.
42 *Pilav*, cited above, para 23.
43 *Ibid.*, para 32.
44 *Ibid.*, para 44.
45 *Ibid.*, para 45.

between the current dispute and the previous cases, the Court concluded that the requirement of residence as combined with the individual's ethnic origin provided grounds of distinction which inevitably fell within the scope of the general principle of non-discrimination, thus amounting to discriminatory treatment in breach of Art. 1 of Protocol 12. Furthermore, BiH was ordered to pay the applicant 6,607 euros as just satisfaction in respect of costs and expenses.

Finally, the 2016 judgment reasoning was very recently relied upon in *Paunović v. Bosnia and Herzegovina* case,[46] concerning (once again) the applicant's ineligibility to stand for election to the Presidency of Bosnia and Herzegovina. The factual circumstances are the same as those in *Pilav* case, but reversed. In 2018, Mr Paunović, a Serb politician residing in the Federation of Bosnia and Herzegovina, saw his candidacy rejected on the grounds that, contrary to sections 4.2(1) and 8.1(2) of the Elections Act 2001, he was not registered in the Central Voters Register in Republika Srpska.

By way of observation, not only did the ECtHR reiterate that a "*similar constitutional precondition had already been found to amount to a discriminatory difference in treatment in breach of Art. 1 of Protocol 12 in Pilav*,"[47] but it also took the opportunity to expressly offer a reminder that

> *no legal provision of domestic law should be interpreted and applied in a manner incompatible with States' obligations under the Convention …, particularly if that would be inconsistent with the prohibition of discrimination and more broadly with the principles underlying the Convention*,

especially in a respondent State (such as Bosnia and Herzegovina), "*whose own Constitution accords the Convention priority over all other law*."[48]

Undoubtedly, the consideration that no fact or persuading argument were found so as to diverge from the prior case-law on the subject led to the inevitable conclusion that there had been a violation of Art. 1 of Protocol 12 to the Convention.

The limits to the individual's effective participation: The Practice of "blank-form resignation" in the Paunović and Milivojević v. Serbia *case*

The introduction to this chapter already mentioned that the ECtHR's case-law dealing with the right to free elections in Serbia untangled another problematic aspect of political participation in former Yugoslav countries, namely political parties' control over the mandate of elected MPs. More specifically, it is the "blank-form resignation" practice falling under the scope of scrutiny of the European

46 ECtHR, *Pudarić* v *Bosnia and Herzegovina*, Application no. 55799/18, 8 December 2020.
47 *Ibid*., para 26.
48 *Ibid*., para 27.

Court, which in the *Paunović and Milivojević v. Serbia* case[49] was found not to be in line with the individual's voting rights as guaranteed under the Convention.

The dispute originated in the alleged violation of the applicants' right to free elections on account of the termination of their parliamentary mandate in breach of Art. 3 of Protocol 1 as well as of the lack of an effective remedy in violation of Art. 13 taken in conjunction with Art. 3 of Protocol 1.

As regards the factual circumstances, during the 2003 Parliament elections,[50] the two Serbian applicants, Mr Goran Paunović and Ms Ksenija Milivojević, were elected on behalf of their political party called G17 PLUS; however, before the ballot, the party had required all the candidates to sign undated resignation letters to be entrusted to the party, providing it with the power to replace its members, if necessary. In early May 2006, following political divergences, and even though the applicants had officially declared their intention to retain their seats in the National Assembly, the head of the party dated the applicant's resignation letters and remitted them to the President of Parliament. Contextually, Mr Paunović personally informed the Parliamentary Committee on Administrative Affairs of his real intention, claiming that his prior resignation was to be considered null and void since it was not delivered in person to the President of Parliament and therefore carried out in breach of the applicable domestic legislation.

Faced with the Committee's decision asserting the effective genuine nature of his resignation, as well as with the decisions of both the Supreme Court and the Constitutional Court in dismissing his complaint, Mr Paunović[51] took the view that the abrupt termination of his office gave rise to an unjust interference with his right to stand for election in violation of Art. 1 of Protocol 3, and that his attempts to obtain redress before the domestic courts had proved futile in contrast with Art. 13 of the Convention taken in conjunction with Art. 1 of Protocol 3.

The legal relevance of the case under scrutiny is remarkable: firstly, it represented an example of the application of the provision as guaranteeing not only the individual's right to vote and to stand for election, but also to sit as a member of parliament once elected as well. Secondly, for the first time, the ECtHR was called upon to rule on its lawfulness under domestic law and its accordance with the applicable legal rules of the termination of parliamentary office in the context of party control of seats. In this respect, the Court began its assessment by reiterating that, even though no legal basis for the impugned measure is required under Art. 3 of Protocol 1,

49 ECtHR, *Paunović and Milivojević* v *Serbia*, Application no. 41683/06, 24 May 2016.

50 Parliamentary elections in Serbia tend to favour the prevalence of political parties over the individuals: in fact, they are held on the basis of a proportional representation system in which voters choose between lists of candidates put forward by the political forces or coalitions, and not directly for individual contestants.

51 The second applicant's complaint was struck out of the Court's list of cases under Art. 37 para 1.

> *the rule of law, one of the fundamental principles of a democratic society, is inherent in all the Articles of the Convention and its Protocols [and] entails a duty on the part of the State to put in place a framework of legislation and as appropriate, subordinate legislation, for securing its obligations under … Article 3 of Protocol 1 in particular.*[52]

In the specific case of Serbia, the Court recognised the existence of a specific domestic legislation that had been put in place pursuant to such an international undertaking, specifying that a parliamentary mandate belonged to an MP personally, not to the political party on whose list he or she was elected,[53] and expressly stating that an MP, when tendering his or her resignation, had to do so in writing and to hand it personally to the President of Parliament.[54]

On such a premise, the Court unanimously concluded that the termination of the applicant's mandate was conducted in breach of the petitioner's genuine will, which fell outside the applicable legal framework, and was therefore declared in conflict with the right to free elections as set in Art. 3 of Protocol 1. Moreover, the lack of review of the post-election dispute by the Supreme Court and the Constitutional Court due to the dismissal of the applicant's complaints without any examination of their merits was found to be in violation of Art. 13 of the Convention taken in conjunction with Art. 3 of Protocol 1.

Accordingly, the applicant was awarded 4,600 euros in respect of pecuniary damage and 5,400 in respect of costs and expenses.

The implementation of the democratic arguments at the national level: An analysis of the state of execution of the Court's case-law

In all the cases under inquiry, the Court delivered judgments, the execution of which necessarily requires a "political decision" entailing the prescription of either constitutional/legislative adjustments or the modification of the existing legal-political practice at domestic level. As further analysed below, the "sensitiveness"

52 *Paunović and Milivojević*, cited above, para 61.

53 The initial version of Art. 88 of the Election of Members of Parliament Act provided that the mandate of an elected MP would expire if the person ceased to be a member of the political party or coalition on whose list of candidates he or she he had been elected. However, those provisions were abrogated by the Constitutional Court of Serbia on 27 May 2003. In particular, this latter emphasised that the mandate of an elected MP belonged to the MP personally, and not to the political party and that, once elected, the candidates should be accountable primarily to the voters only. This flows from the fact that they hold a mandate from the people, not from their party. The fact that an MP has resigned from the party or been expelled should not therefore lead to their expulsion from parliament. There is no constitutional obligation on MPs to resign if they have political disagreements with their party, even if they are expelled from it; see *Ustavni sud Republike Srbije* (Constitutional Court of Serbia) decision IU no. 197/2002.

54 Parliamentary Rules of Procedure, Art. 230.

of the object of scrutiny helps to explain the wide margin of appreciation left to the respondent States in the identification of the most appropriate measures necessary to abide by the Court's judgments, albeit under the supervision exercised by the Committee of Ministers of the CoE; it also ascribes a particular weight to the issue of "execution."

On the one hand, the involvement of the Court in such issues as the functioning of the *demos* and political competition is not exempt from criticism, despite the imperative of the implementation of its rulings. In this respect, the words of Judge Bonello are emblematic: in his dissenting opinion to the *Sejdić and Finci* ruling,[55] the Strasbourg judge sharply criticised the Court for behaving like an "uninvited guest," taking it upon itself to disrupt the "*filigree construction extinguish[ing] the inferno that had been Bosnia and Herzegovina.*"[56] In particular, Bonello wrote that

> *the Court has almost unlimited powers when it comes to granting remedies to established violations of Convention-acknowledged human rights – and that surely is as it should be. But do these almost unlimited powers include that of undoing an international treaty, all the more so if that treaty was engineered by States and international bodies, some of which are neither signatories to the Convention nor defendants before the Court in this case? More specifically, does the Court have jurisdiction, by way of granting relief, to subvert the sovereign action of the European Union and of the United States of America, who together fathered the Dayton Peace Accords, of which the Bosnia and Herzegovina Constitution – impugned before the Court – is a mere annex? I do not offer facile answers to these questions, but believe them to be cogent enough for the Court to have tackled them preliminarily and in some depth. It did not.*[57]

On the other, it might bear in mind the declaratory nature of the ECtHR's judgments, meaning that the credibility of the human rights protection system as enshrined in the Convention still depends to a great extent on the State's fulfilment of their international obligations under the CoE. But, if the effectiveness of the European Court's action strictly relies on the State's collaboration, the inherent "political nature" of the European case-law intruding upon the institutional system of democratic representation inevitably makes the risk that the ECtHR's rulings fall on deaf ears even more real.

Equipped with such preliminary considerations, the following pages will turn to the evaluation of the current status of implementation of the Court's case-law under examination, especially focusing on the economic and legal consequences within the domestic legal systems.

55 *Sejdić and Finci*, cited above, dissenting opinion of Judge Bonello.
56 *Ibid.*
57 *Ibid.*

The cost of deference

On the subject of the economic impact of the implementation of the ECtHR jurisprudence at the national level in Serbia and in Bosnia and Herzegovina, two different sets of considerations are possible. The first one pertains to the quantum to be remitted to the injured party, while the second focuses on the willingness – or, conversely, the reluctance – of the Respondent States to comply with the pecuniary measures.

With regard to the first concern, the "pecuniary" obligations flowing from the rulings analysed above have been shown to be rather modest. As for the applicants' claim for just satisfaction under Art. 41 of the Convention, in all the following cases, *Paunović and Milivojević*, *Sejdić and Finci*, *Šlaku* and *Pilav*, the judges of Strasbourg concluded that, in the light of the factual circumstances under dispute, the finding of a violation was considered to constitute a sufficient just satisfaction in respect of non-pecuniary damage suffered by the applicants,[58] while Ms Zornić submitted no request in this regard and Pudarić's claim was dismissed.[59]

With respect of pecuniary damages, it was only in *Paunović and Milivojević* that the applicant was awarded the entire sum claimed – notably 4,600 euros – this amount corresponding to the net salary and allowances to which he would have been entitled as an MP for the period between 16 May 2006 and 14 February 2007, when the mandates of all MPs in the Parliament came to an end due to new election.[60] Meanwhile, both Mr Šlaku's and Mr Pilav's requests were rejected due to the lack of any causal link between the violation found and the pecuniary damage alleged,[61] while in the other two cases (*Sejdić and Finci* and *Zornić*) no such claim was submitted.[62]

The other sum to be occasionally remitted regards the reimbursement of the costs and expenses of the proceedings; in this respect, the Court considered it reasonable to award Mr Paunović the sum of 5,400 euros to cover costs under all heads;[63] in *Sejdić and Finci*, the Court required the respondent State to pay the first applicant 1,000 euros and the second was granted a more considerable sum, that is 20,000 euros,[64] while Mr Pilav was awarded 6,607 euros.[65] Lastly, both the applicants Šlaku and Zornić were awarded no pecuniary sum.[66]

The modest entity of just satisfaction required may constitute one of the reasons behind the prompt fulfilment of the state's obligations under Art. 41 of the

58 *Paunović and Milivojević*, cited above, para 84; *Pilav*, cited above, para 54; *Sejdić and Finci*, cited above, para 63; *Šlaku*, cited above, para 44.

59 *Zornić*, cited above, para 45.

60 *Paunović and Milivojević*, cited above, para 81.

61 *Pilav*, cited above, para 54; *Šlaku*, cited above, para 44.

62 *Sejdić and Finci*, cited above, para 62; *Zornić*, cited above, para 45.

63 *Paunović and Milivojević*, cited above, para 87.

64 *Sejdić and Finci*, cited above, paras 64–66.

65 *Pilav*, cited above, para 57.

66 *Šlaku*, cited above, para 45; *Zornić*, cited above, para 45.

Convention; in fact, both Bosnia and Herzegovina and Serbia paid the injured party the sum respectively required. The Serbian authorities communicated that the amount of just satisfaction awarded by the European Court had been disbursed to the applicants on 20 September 2016.[67] In relation to Mr Sejdić and Mr Finci, they were both awarded the amount prescribed within the thee-month time limit, while on 5 December 2016, the Bosnian ministry of Finance and Treasury made the payment of just satisfaction to Mr Pilav.[68]

Domestic reforms

Bosnia and Herzegovina

22 December 2019 saw the disturbing celebration of the 10th anniversary of the delivery of *Sejdić and Finci* judgment; since that time, despite the continuing rhetoric on the imperative for reform, no concrete steps have been taken in order to adjust the domestic constitutional and legislative framework to match conventional requirements.[69] Consequently, the current situation is still characterised by the Committee of Ministers as a manifest breach of Bosnia and Herzegovina's unconditional obligations under the European Convention on Human Rights, and thus also of its undertakings as a Member State of the Council of Europe, putting at risk the democratic unfolding of the 2022 national elections.

Vis-à-vis BiH's discriminatory representative regulation, the international community's response has been prominent; reports have been published and suggestions have been advanced by a variety of interlocutors such as the UN Human

67 See DH-DD (2017)422 *Communication from Serbia concerning the case of PAUNOVIC and MILIVOJEVIC v. Serbia*, Application no. 41683/06).

68 See DH-DD (2017)380 *Communication from Bosnia and Herzegovina concerning the case of SEJDIC AND FINCI v. Bosnia and Herzegovina*, Application no. 27996/06.

69 The ECtHR has recently ruled on *Baralija v. Bosnia and Herzegovina* case (Application no. 30100/18, 29 October 2020) concerning the State's failure to fulfil its positive obligation to adopt measures to hold democratic elections in Mostar, in breach of the general principle of non-discrimination (Art. 1 of Protocol 12). The European Court noted that local elections in Mostar were last held in 2008; since 2012 the city has been governed solely by a mayor who, having only a "technical mandate," did not enjoy the required democratic legitimacy, leading to the applicant's unjustified inability to vote or to stand in any such elections due to his place of residence. This situation was found to be the consequence of the non-implementation of the Constitutional Court's decision and ancillary orders of 2010, which declared certain sections of the Election Act 2001 and the Statute of the City of Mostar unconstitutional and ordered their amendment. Therefore, having regard to the rule of law issue deriving from the failure to abide by the final, binding decisions of the Constitutional Court, the judges of Strasbourg indicated under Art. 46 that "the respondent State must, within six months of the date on which the present judgment becomes final, amend the Election Act 2001 in order to enable the holding of local elections in Mostar. Should the State fail to do so, the Court notes that the Constitutional Court, under domestic law and practice … , has the power to set up interim arrangements as necessary transitional measure" (para 62). Yet, in the two months since the ECtHR's decision became final (on 29 January 2020), the Bosnian Constitutional Court has not taken any action.

Rights Council, the European Commission for Democracy through Law (Venice Commission), non-governmental organisations, and, of course, the Council of Europe.

As far as the latter is concerned, considering the violations found by the Court, the Committee of Ministers of CoE has always considered that a number of amendments to the Constitution of BiH and its electoral legislation should be adopted for the execution of the Sejdić and Finci judgments group. In relation to that, three interim resolutions were adopted – in 2010, 2011, and 2013 respectively – and numerous decisions were also taken, calling on the authorities and political leaders of BiH to change the domestic electoral legislation and amend the provisions of the Constitution "as a matter of priority," so that "*the functioning of democratic institutions in the country and citizens' confidence in them would be enhanced.*"[70] The Committee also reiterated "*that failure to do so would not only amount to a manifest breach of obligations under Art. 46, paragraph 1, of the Convention but could also potentially undermine the legitimacy and the credibility of the country's future elected bodies.*"[71]

In addition, emphasis was placed on the fact that the execution of the ECtHR's judgments not only constituted a legal obligation of the State, but also fell within the "*particular responsibility of the authorities and political leaders of BiH … having regard also to the bearing that this matter has on [the State]'s prospect for European integration*":[72] the implementation of the ECtHR's case-law hence appears to be – even if not expressly – one of the key pre-requisites for submitting a credible membership application, as much as one of the more foreseeable human conditions attached to EU candidacy; on such a premise, since 2010, a high-level EU–BiH negotiation has been underway to support the enforcement of the *Sejdić-Finci* group.

Furthermore, the Parliamentary Assembly of the CoE has adopted several Resolutions and Recommendations urging the BiH authorities to adopt the required constitutional amendments and legislative reforms so as to ensure a fully functioning political democracy.[73]

Notwithstanding the Committee's interventions and the extensive support offered to the domestic relevant political actors, none of these have been availed of and, consequently, the effectiveness of the Court of Strasbourg's action has been greatly deflated. Looking at the aftermath of *Sejdić and Finci*, the biggest challenge for Bosnia and Herzegovina has been the search for the best way of enforcement, since the Court had not specified this in its ruling to any great

70 See CM/ResDH(2011) 291.

71 See CM/ResDH(2013) 259.

72 See CM/ResDH(2012) 233.

73 Resolutions no. 1701(2010) *Functioning of democratic institutions in Bosnia and Herzegovina*; Resolutions no. 1725(2010) *Urgent need for constitutional reform in Bosnia and Herzegovina*; Resolution no. 1855 (2012) *The functioning of democratic institutions in Bosnia and Herzegovina*; Recommendation no. 2025(2013) *The functioning of democratic institutions in Bosnia and Herzegovina.*

extent. Ever since the adoption of the Grand Chamber's judgment, every effort which has been put forward by the relevant Bosnian authorities in the attempt to secure the harmonisation of the domestic constitutional framework and the legislative electoral system with conventional standards has failed to meet political consensus among the wider political forces.

Suffice to mention that, towards the end of 2015, only two significant initiatives to introduce the necessary constitutional amendments were submitted, and even so both of them have been demonstrated to be political flops. The 2008 "Prud Process" ended before a debate on concrete reform proposals had actually started, while the 2009 "Butmir Process" was quickly set aside on the grounds that it failed to secure the accord of key domestic political stakeholders.[74]

Moreover, even under the strict supervision of the Committee of Ministers of the Council of Europe, the relevant Bosnian authorities have repeatedly struggled to respect all the timeframes set to introduce the necessary constitutional and legislative adjustments. This can best be illustrated by briefly looking at few examples; hence, for instance, when the supervision by the Committee of Ministers of the CoE took place for the first time, in 2010, it was observed that the Working Group appointed by the Council of Minister of BiH to implement the "Action Plan for the Enforcement of Judgment in *Sejdić and Finci* against BiH" had not succeeded in meeting the deadline for reaching an agreement on proposed adjustments.[75]

The following year, another supervisory session of the Council of Ministers of the CoE passed without any change to the situation of the country's discriminatory electoral system. No political agreement was found among the six proposals for the amendment of the Constitution of BiH revealed by the updated information on the Action plan. Meanwhile the new "Interim Joint Commission" taking the place of the prior working group did not have much more success than its predecessor in meeting the deadline set in December 2011 and, subsequently, in August 2012.[76] Three years later, in 2015, due to lack of political agreement, the same unfortunate destiny befell the attempt to appoint a Task Force aimed at drafting the constitutional amendments that would be forwarded to the Council of Ministers of BiH.[77]

74 To be precise, the first comprehensive attempt at reforming Dayton constitutional framework came about in 2005 under the name "April Package" (see Hays D., Crosby J., *From Dayton to Brussels Constitutional Preparations for Bosnia's EU Accession*, 2006 Special Report, www.usip.org/sites/default/files/SRoct06_2.pdf); unfortunately, it fell two votes short of reaching the required two-thirds majority. For further information concerning this "closed-door negotiations" among the most important parties, see also Zdeb A., *Prud and Butmir Processes in Bosnia and Herzegovina: Intra-ethnic Competition from the Perspective of Game Theory*," in Ethnopolitics, 16, 2017, 369 ff.

75 See DH – DD (2011)915E *Communication from Bosnia and Herzegovina concerning the case of SEJDIC AND FINCI v. Bosnia and Herzegovina* (Application no. 27996/06).

76 See DH-DD (2012)774 *Communication from Bosnia and Herzegovina concerning the case of SEJDIC AND FINCI v. Bosnia and Herzegovina* (Application no. 27996/06).

77 See DH-DD (2016)1154 and DH-DD(2017)380 *Communications from Bosnia and Herze-*

In all the cases briefly illustrated above, the key obstacle in the adoption of any necessary amendment has been posed by the inability and unwillingness of the relevant actors to confront the high degree of penetration of ethnic agendas within the domestic institutional system. The removal of the exclusionary aspects of the contested provisions, and the consequent proliferation of subjects entitled to be actively involved in the political competition of the country, would in fact undermine the existing power balance among the three main ethnic groups established by the Dayton Agreement. It thus would alter the current tri-partite institutionalisation of the party system, weakening the ethno-federal model the whole state-functioning is based on. In other words, "Bosnia's Gordian Knot"[78] – as the International Crisis Group defines it, the impossibility of putting the BiH Constitution and the electoral system in line with international standards – is the direct outcome of "the combination of the country's fragile statehood" underpinned by the lack of any democratic traditions and further enhanced by the "static nature of political competition in the country"[79] as that embedded in the post-conflict Constitution of BiH.

In the attempt to follow the indications provided by the European Court in order to definitively abandon the special ethnic-rule discriminating against the "Others" as well as the "constituent people" living outside "their own entity," a significant step forward was made by the Bosnian Constitutional Court in March 2015, when for the first time[80] it declared the unconstitutionality of the Electoral Law in so far as the mechanism of election of the vice president position of the two Entities was concerned.[81] More specifically, in excluding those

govina concerning the case of SEJDIC AND FINCI v. Bosnia and Herzegovina (Application no. 27996/06).

78 International Crisis Group, *Bosnia's Gordian Knot: Constitutional Reform*, 2012 Europe Briefing, www.crisisgroup.org/en/regions/europe/balkans/bosnia-herzegovina/b068-bosnias-gordian-knot-constitutional-reform.aspx.

79 As cited by Džankić J., cited above, 527.

80 In its previous case-law, the Constitutional Court of BiH had declared inadmissible both the question of compatibility of Art. V of the Constitution of Bosnia and Herzegovina and the Election with the European Convention of Human Rights, arguing that while the Convention has priority over ordinary legislation in Bosnia, according to Art. II(2), it is not superior to the Constitution or the legislation such as the Election Law deriving from it (see *Ustavni sud Bosne i Hercegovine* (Constitutional Court of Bosnia and Herzegovina) decisions U-5/04, 27 January 2006 and U-13/05, 26 June 2006); in a third decision, the claim was refused on the merits on the grounds that the Constitution and Election Law could still be justified since they pursue the legitimate goal to preserve peace in Bosnia and Herzegovina by strengthening the position of the "three constituent peoples" with the help of an exclusive power-sharing arrangement; the Court also recognised that the contested restrictions were still proportionate to the objectives of general community in terms of preservation of the established peace and continuation of dialogue (see *Ustavni sud Bosne i Hercegovine* (Constitutional Court of Bosnia and Herzegovina) Decision AP-2678/06, 29 September 2006).

81 See Dicosola M., *The Constitutional Court of Bosnia and Herzegovina declares the system of ethnic federalism of the Entities inconsistent with the principle of non-discrimination: much ado about nothing?* in Diritti Comparati, 2015.

who did not affiliate with one of the "constituent peoples" from the possibility of exercising the presidential and vice-presidential functions, the ethnic-federalism-featured electoral systems of Republika Srpska[82] and the Federation of Bosnia and Herzegovina,[83] and that one set in the Electoral Law of Bosnia and Herzegovina[84] were found to be inconsistent with the principle of non-discrimination as embedded by Art. II(4) of the BiH Constitution and Art. 1 of Protocol 12.[85] Notably, the Bosnian Constitutional Court largely relied on the *Sejdić and Finci* ruling so as to observe what follows. Notwithstanding that such a system of power-sharing in which members of "Others" are excluded from accessing a number of public offices was indisputably used to pursue a legitimate goal reflected in the preservation of peace and the building of trust between the former conflicting parties, the differential treatment based on ethnic origin was to be found without objective and reasonable justification. More specifically, the Constitutional Court ruled that

> [w]*hen one considers, on the one hand, the principles of the rule of law, the standards of human rights and the obligation of non-discrimination in their enjoyment and protection, the positive development made by BiH ever since the signing of the Dayton Agreement, the international obligations it assumed also in the area of exercising and protecting human rights, and the clear commitment to the further democratic development, the exclusion of "Others" from exercising one of the human rights which constitutes the foundation of a democratic society can no longer represent the only way in which to achieve the legitimate goal reflected in the preservation of peace. Particularly so when one bears in mind that such an exclusion was established expressly on ethnic affiliation, which cannot be objectively justified in the contemporary democratic societies built on the principles of pluralism and respect for different cultures, which BiH society is and which it aspires to.*[86]

The importance of this ruling should not be overestimated, though. The scrutiny of the Constitutional Court was in fact restricted to the mere consistency of the provisions of the Constitutions of the Entities – that "are not identical to any provision of the Constitution of BiH"[87] – with the Constitution of BiH. Even more importantly, being aware of the challenging nature of the process of constitu-

82 Constitution of the Republika Srpska, Art. 80(2)(4).

83 Constitution of the Federation of Bosnia and Herzegovina, Art. IV.B.1, 2(1) and (2).

84 Election Act 2001, Arts. 9.13, 9.14, 9.16, and 12.3.

85 On the contrary, the request to find a violation of the right to vote, according to Art. 14 of the Convention taken in conjunction with Art. 3 of Protocol 1, was dismissed as ill-found, due to the fact that the President of Republika Srpska and President of the Federation of BiH do not constitute a "legislature" within the meaning of Art. 3 of Protocol 1.

86 *Ustavni sud Bosne i Hercegovine* (Constitutional Court of Bosnia and Herzegovina) decisions U-14/012, 26 March 2015, para 71.

87 *Ibid.*, para 48.

tional reform which follows the ECtHR's directions, no direct effect was attached to the above declaration of unconstitutionality, so that the "Constitutional Court [would] not quash the aforementioned provisions" and

> [would] *not order ... to harmonize the aforementioned provisions until the adoption, in the national legal system, of constitutional and legislative measures removing the current inconsistency of the Constitution of Bosnia and Herzegovina and Election Law with the European Convention, which was found by the European Court.*[88]

In this respect, since a wide margin of deference was awarded to the Parliamentary Assembly of BiH, the constitutional review still remained meaningless in front of the negligence of the Parliament. A significant obstacle to an effective legislative action was found in the complex procedure of protection of the so-called "vital national interest," which entitles any of the three "constituent people" to declare a veto and to prevent the adoption of any proposal that is considered destructive of their specific group rights and interests.[89]

As a result of either the persistent lack of active involvement of the relevant political actors or the political impasse within the legislative branches, all the General Elections in BiH, in 2010, 2014, and 2018 – at which the voters at the state level elected the President, the BiH House of Representatives and by indirect elections the BiH House of Peoples – they all had been held in accordance with the same ethnic-discriminatory regulatory framework; meanwhile, the execution of the *Sejdić and Finci* group of judgments remains pending.

It is emblematic that, in respect of the tenth year of failing to comply with the ruling of the European Court of Human Rights in the *Sejdić and Finci v. Bosnia and Herzegovina* case, the relevant appellants have decided to prepare an open letter[90] in which they observed that "[t]he state of Bosnia and Herzegovina has not eliminated the discrimination and implemented the rulings" and further noted that:

> *The process of constitutional change has never really begun where it should take place – in the Parliamentary Assembly of Bosnia and Herzegovina ... Postponing the implementation and politicizing the constitutional discrimination by focusing on resolving other, essentially ephemeral, current political "issues," accompanied with constant and overt threats of obstruction in decision making and conflicts has become the only way to discuss the constitutional amendments in Bosnia and Herzegovina. At the same time, elections take place in which the*

88 *Ibid.*, para 74.

89 Constitution of Bosnia and Herzegovina, Art IV (3).

90 Zornić A., Finci J., Pudarić S., Pilav I., *Open Letter: UNTIL WHEN?*, 2019. Available at https://womencitizensforconstitutionalreform.wordpress.com/2019/12/20/open-letter-when/.

> *citizens of Bosnia and Herzegovina are deprived of their fundamental rights. Contrary to EU recommendations, Council of Europe resolutions, opinions of the Venice Commission, the primacy of the European Convention on Human Rights, and the European Court of Human Rights, the existing political system in Bosnia and Herzegovina has served for ten years now to incite and deepen the mistrust among the peoples, which prevents the country from becoming democratic. As a result, society is held hostage in a state of collective intolerance and in the lack of organised force to lead and win the struggle for the implementation of the rulings. Nothing happens in reality; it is to note that, on one hand, political oligarchies in power are hampering the implementation and, on the other hand, all parties pledge their support for the implementation. However, none of them has taken any steps towards the implementation.*[91]

Lastly, delegates of the negotiations on the formation of the government following to the 2018 general elections have negatively impacted on the country's legislative progress throughout the whole of 2019, substantially hampering the co-operation in the electoral reform sector.[92] Only very recently, in December 2019, did the appointment of the Council of Ministers represent a first positive sign for the further advancement of the necessary political and legal reform, just in time for the next election in 2022.

Serbia

In *Paunović and Milivojević v. Serbia*, the violations concerned resulted from the inadequate practice of Parliament leading to the termination of the applicants' mandate in breach of the domestic legislation. Additionally, the Court of Strasbourg recognised the lack of an effective remedy for the applicants to challenge the breach of their passive electoral rights.

Following the facts of the case – which took place in May 2006 – a new Constitution was adopted and entered into force in November 2006. With reference to the subject of parliamentary mandates, in particular, the new constitution allowed MPs to put their mandate irrevocably at the disposal of the political party of which they were a member at the time they were elected (the so-called "imperative mandate");[93] hence, the Serbian Constitution directly challenged the views of the Constitutional Court that had prohibited such a practice.[94] Against this background, the positive influence of the ECtHR's judgment can be evaluated at the domestic level, through an analysis of those constitutional reforms and variations adopted by the relevant authorities accordingly.[95]

91 *Ibid.*

92 See GR-DEM(2020)9 *Council of Europe Action Plan for Bosnia and Herzegovina* 2018–2021.

93 Constitution of Serbia 2006, Art. 102 para 2.

94 See *Ustavni sud Republike Srbije*, cited above

95 See DH-DD (2017)422, cited above

First of all, on 28 November 2007, the Constitutional Court Law was adopted, entitling such a Court exclusive jurisdiction to examine electoral disputes, including those concerning the early termination of parliamentary mandate. Furthermore, in the light of the Parliamentary Assembly of the Council of Europe reprimands[96] urging the abrogation of the controversial provisions, in 2011 the Act on Altering and Amending the Act on Election of Members of Parliament was adopted, abolishing "party-administered mandates" and blank resignations. Such a legislative amendment has been welcomed with great favour by the Parliamentary Assembly of the CoE, which in 2012 expressly congratulated Serbia for bringing "the system of allocation of mandates in the parliament into line with European standards."[97] Moreover, it was reported that, following the outcome of this case, the early termination of parliamentary mandates was a rare occurrence. In particular, only seven such cases are known as of April 2017 and all of them were carried out in strict conformity with the applicable domestic law.[98]

Secondly, in relation to measures aimed at introducing an effective remedy, the 2006 Constitution of Republic of Serbia[99] introduced a constitutional appeal to be lodged against individual decisions or actions of State bodies adopted in breach of human rights guaranteed by the Constitution, once other legal remedy have already been exhausted or have not been prescribed. Pursuant to the 2007 Constitutional Court Act mentioned above, such a remedy may be aimed not only at suppressing the impugned decision but also at granting specific measures in order to provide redress to the appellant for any adverse consequences sustained as a result of this violation and, more specifically, to request compensation for the damage sustained.[100]

In the light of the above, on 14 June 2017 at the 1289th meeting of the Ministers' Deputies, the CoM recognised that all the measures required by Art. 46, paragraph 1 have been adopted by Serbia and decided to close the examination thereof.[101]

Conclusions

The overall analysis above was aimed at investigating the economic and legal impact of the ECtHR case-law in countries of the former Yugoslavia so as to provide a

96 See Resolution 1619(2008) *State of democracy in Europe Functioning of democratic institutions in Europe and progress of the Assembly's monitoring procedure.*
97 See Resolution 1858(2012) *The honouring of obligations and commitments by Serbia.*
98 See DH-DD (2017)422, cited above, para. 19.
99 Constitution of Serbia 2006, Art. 170.
100 The first decision establishing a violation of the Constitution had been adopted on 10 July 2008, where the Constitutional Court quashed the decisions adopted by the lower courts as well as the Supreme Court and held that financial compensation for the damage suffered by the appellant had been warranted (See *Vinčić*, App. no. 44698/06, Constitutional Court of Serbia, 1 December 2009).
101 Resolution CM/ResDH(2017)193.

comprehensive evaluation of the status of how the democratic arguments' flowing from European jurisprudence are received. Since this chapter adopted a typical cross-national perspective, especially in the first part which intentionally tried to encapsulate the phenomenon under scrutiny – i.e. the implementation of the ECtHR's indication into domestic legal systems – considerations have been made on the common trends within the whole of the former Yugoslavia.

In this regard, a first point of departure was the assumption of the unchallenged legitimacy of the European Court as a regional "driver of human rights" following the progressive accession to the Council of Europe of Bosnia and Herzegovina, Croatia, Montenegro, North Macedonia, Serbia, and Slovenia at the dawn of their democratisation. Indeed, the Strasbourg jurisprudence played a pivotal role in shaping their domestic law and politics around a universal standard of protection of fundamental liberties in the face of gross violations perpetuated during the armed conflict in the Nineties and, even before that, by the former Yugoslav regime.

Yet, during the last decade, the countries above have had to face several obstacles to the establishment of fully functioning constitutional democracies, as witnessed by the increasingly high number of individual applications lodged before the Court. On this premise, the main question addressed in this chapter was to assess whether or not States have made the necessary fundamental structural adjustments in response to the judgments of the Court, in order to comply with the conventional guarantees and standards.

To this effect, a study confined to the specific case-law dealing with the guarantee of political rights and electoral justice in Bosnia and Herzegovina and in Serbia – the only two former Yugoslav countries ever convicted in relation to electoral matters – shows a rather nuanced scenario. In these States the regulation of enfranchisement has been shown to be one of the crucial mechanisms of inclusion or, on the contrary, of exclusion in relation to access to the democratic system of representation

As regards Serbia, in *Paunović and Milosević v. Serbia*, the Court had to face the widely tolerated practice of "blank-form resignation" and its effect of frustrating the individual's right to participate effectively in decision making, once elected. This technique is akin to a form of imperative mandate *largo sensu*, deriving the mandate's holder prerogatives from the political party's direction and rationale.

The case in question is legally relevant on the grounds that, for the first time, the Court had to rule on its lawfulness under domestic law and its accordance with the applicable legal rules of the termination of parliamentary office in a context of party control seats. The abrupt cessation of the applicant's mandate was found to have been conducted in breach of the applicable legal framework, as well as in contrast with the right to free elections as set in Art. 3 of Protocol 1. Additionally, the lack of review of the post-election dispute was found to amount to a breach of Art. 13 of the Convention taken in conjunction with Art. 3 of Protocol 1.

The judgment was successfully implemented at the national level. As a matter of fact, Serbia paid the applicant the amount awarded in respect of just satisfaction under Art. 41 within the timeframe set by the Court and further adopted the necessary structural amendments to put an end to the odious practice above. Notwithstanding the undoubted positive impact at the national level, it is nevertheless important not to overestimate the Court action's effectiveness. *Paunović and Milosević v. Serbia* represents an isolated case and, as such, cannot be considered as exhaustive for the purposes of this chapter.

An even more worrying situation is that featuring in Bosnia and Herzegovina, where a fully functioning *demos*-participation in the system of representation is still an open challenge for the Court, whose action throughout that time did not have the effects anticipated. The *Sejdić and Finci v. Bosnia and Herzegovina* case represents a landmark, in which an international Court has challenged the constitutional foundations of a respondent State so as to impose the petitioners' claim, over and above the politico-historical reasons put forward by the relevant domestic authorities. By means of reference to the principle of non-discrimination (Art. 14) taken in conjunction with the right to free elections as set in Art. 3 of Protocol 1, or alternatively to Art. 1 of Protocol 12, five consecutive times (*Sejdić and Finci v. Bosnia and Herzegovina*, *Zornić*, *Šlaku*, *Pilav*, and *Pudarić*) the ECtHR has consistently declared the BIH electoral system to be discriminatory towards those ethnic minorities other than the so-called "constituent peoples" (i.e. Bosniaks, Croats, and Serbs), illegitimately disfranchising and excluding them from the possibility of exercising parliamentary and presidential offices.

Nevertheless, the Court's "revolutionary" action has not been immune to critics questioning the possibility of imposing legal reforms of such a nature and, more importantly, pointing out a shift to a more "paternalistic grip" by the ECtHR over the public affairs of the respondent States. An immediate question then arises: was it worth it? The resilience of Bosnian authorities and the consequent perpetuation of the same status quo for more than a decade seems to point to answering that in the negative. While Bosnian domestic authorities have had no problem with complying with the Court's requirements in respect to the just satisfaction to be afforded to the injured parties, as far as constitutional and legislative reforms are concerned, no consensus has been reached by the domestic relevant actors, thus aggravating the internal political stalemate of the county.

Indeed, it is undoubtedly remarkable that the Court attempted to detach itself from its previously "prudent" case-law dealing with the right to free elections. Since *Sejdić and Finci v. Bosnia and Herzegovina*, by means of reference to its application of the principle of non-discrimination in relation to a subject traditionally belonging to the State's sovereign domain – namely domestic elections – the Strasbourg judges have in fact been able to take the individual's ethnic identity choice into account to evaluate the electoral system as designed and, certainly, to narrow the (otherwise) wide margin of appreciation States are normally granted.[102]

102 As explained in Graziadei S., *Democracy v Human Rights? The Strasbourg Court and the Challenge of Power Sharing*, in European Constitutional Law Review, 12, 2016, 54 ff.

Yet, it could be argued that the Court's intrusion within the "mined terrain of Bosnian political structure" has not dovetailed with a proper identification of the actors, the processes, and the timeframe necessary for the implanting of its ruling within the domestic legal system, therefore leaving an open room for legal ambiguity and uncertainty. In this sense, the persistence of such a dangerous political stalemate is patently symptomatic of the fact that not even the CoE bodies are almighty and that there is a clear difference between "what is principled" in theory and "what is possible" in practice.[103]

Bibliography

Antloga A., *The right to stand for elections in the Constitution of Bosnia and Herzegovina as a basic political right in a post-conflict society*, in International Journal on Rule of Law, Transitional Justice and Human Rights, 10, 2019, 11f.

Belle C., *Power-sharing and human rights law*, in International Journal of Human Rights, 17, 2, 2013, 204–237.

Begić Z., Delić Z., *Constituency of peoples in the constitutional system of Bosnia and Herzegovina: Chasing fair solutions*, in International Journal of Constitutional Law, 11, 2, 2013, 447–465.

Beširevič V. (ed.), *Public law in Serbia: Twenty years after*, European Public Law Series, CI, 2002, 24–54.

Černič J.L., *A glass half empty? Execution of judgments of the european court of human rights in Central and Eastern Europe*, in Baltic Yearbook of International Law Online, 15, 2016.

Bruno M.M., *Bosnia and Herzeogvina electoral system and ECHR, a conflicting relationship. Recent developments and European prospects*, in International Journal of Rule of Law, Transitional Justice and Human Rights, 7, 2016.

Dicosola M., *The Constitutional Court of Bosnia and Herzegovina declares the system of ethnic federalism of the Entities inconsistent with the principle of non-discrimination: much ado about nothing?*, in Diritti Comparati, 2015.

Džankić J., *The Politics of Inclusion and Exclusion: Citizenship and Voting Rights in Bosnia and Herzegovina*, in International Peacekeeping, 22, 2015.

Graziadei S., *Democracy v Human Rights? The Strasbourg Court and the Challenge of Power Sharing*, in European Constitutional Law Review, 12, 2016.

Hardman H., Dickson B., *Electoral rights in Europe: Advances and challenges*, Routledge, London, 2017.

Keller H., Stone Sweet A. (eds.), *A Europe of rights: The impact of the ECHR on national legal systems*, Oxford University Press, Oxford, 2008.

Milanović M., Papić T., *The applicability of the ECHR in contested territories*, in International & Comparative Law Quarterly, 67, 4, 2018, 779–800.

Motoc I., Ziemele I. (eds.), *The impact of the ECHR on the democratic change in Central and Eastern Europe. Judicial Perspectives*, Cambridge University Press, Cambridge, 2016.

103 These words are borrowed from Belle C., *Power-sharing and human rights law*, in International Journal of Human Rights, 17, 2, 2013, 204 ff.

Seizovic Z., *Constitutional Reform in Bosnia and Herzegovina - Civil State of Constituent Peoples*, in Annals of the Faculty of Law of the University of Zenica, 1, 2007.

Šturanović P., *Political parties and their influence on the parliamentary mandate after the fall of communism in Montenegro and Serbia*, in Studia Politica: Romanian Political Science Review, 18, 3, 2018, 423–445.

Tabaković Jašar S., *The impact of constituent peoples' principle on democratical transition and human rights protection in Bosnia and Herzegovina*, in International Journal on Rule of Law, Transitional Justice and Human Rights, 9, 2018, 37–45.

Zdeb A., *Prud and Butmir Processes in Bosnia and Herzegovina: Intra-ethnic Competition from the Perspective of Game Theory*, in Ethnopolitics, 16, 2017, 369–387.

7 At any cost?

The economic and legal response of Romania to the European Court of Human Rights Judgments relating to Art. 3 of Protocol 1 to the European Convention on Human Rights

Francesca Mussi *

Introduction

Free and fair elections are crucial for the legitimacy of democratic States and are protected as a human right. Jurisprudence and scholarship have often emphasised the connection between democracy and human rights.[1] For example, the European Convention on Human Rights (ECHR, or the Convention) was designed to "maintain and promote the ideals and values of a democratic society."[2] Indeed, according to the European Court of Human Rights (ECtHR or the Court) democracy is the only political model contemplated by the Convention and the only one compatible with it.[3] This notwithstanding, at the time of the drafting of the Convention, States parties were not able to agree on an article defining the concept of effective political democracy.[4] Thus, it was not until 20 March 1952 that Art. 3 of Protocol 1 to the ECHR was introduced and which reads as follows: "The High Contracting Parties undertake to hold free elections at reasonable intervals by secret ballot, under conditions which will ensure the free expression of the opinion of the people in the choice of the legislature."

* The author would like to thank the editors for kindly reviewing an earlier version of this manuscript and providing valuable suggestions and comments.

1 See, among others, CHARLESWORTH H., *International Legal Encounters with Democracy*, in Global Policy, 8, 6, 2017, 34 ff.; BESSON S., *Human Rights and Democracy in a Global Context: Decoupling and Recoupling*, in Ethics & Global Politics, 4, 1, 2011, 19 ff.; CHRISTIANO T., *The Constitution of Equality*, Oxford University Press, Oxford, 2008.

2 See ECtHR, *Kjeldsen, Busk Madsen and Pedersen v. Denmark*, Applications nos. 5095/71; 5920/72; 5926/72, judgment 7 December 1976, para. 53; *Soering v. the United Kingdom*, Application no. 14038/88, judgment 7 July 1989, para. 87.

3 ECtHR, *United Communist Party of Turkey and Others v. Turkey*, Application no. 19392/92, judgment 30 January 1998, para. 45.

4 MARKS S., *The European Convention on Human Rights and its "Democratic Society,"* in British Yearbook of International Law, 66, 1, 1995, 221–224.

DOI: 10.4324/9781003229247-9

Although this formulation can be regarded as "an unsatisfactory text, which is the result of a compromise, and which continues to give rise to problems of interpretation,"[5] the right to free and fair elections is well-established and has often been reiterated in ECtHR case-law as an imperative to democracy. Despite its fundamental importance, the right in question is not absolute,[6] as States may impose limitations albeit, however, they must not be arbitrary or disproportionate and impair its very essence.[7] This has led to an increase in the number of violations of Art. 3 of Protocol 1 to the ECHR, which, contrary to what might be expected, are not country-specific. Indeed, whilst the problem is particularly acute in a few ECHR States parties, it is by no means limited to them. This notwithstanding, as has been rightly observed, a finding of a violation of the ECHR by the ECtHR is not the end in itself.[8] Judgments can also be seen as a promise for the future, and it is clear that they would have little value without compliance and enforcement. The execution of judgments of the Court, which is mandatory under Art. 46 ECHR for the States that have ratified it, is therefore important not only for the overall credibility of the human rights protection system in Europe but also, for the purposes of the present analysis, with regard to the impact of the ECtHR's case-law on electoral matters across the different Council of Europe Member States.

In light of the above circumstances, the present contribution aims at focusing on the case of Romania – a State that has been found responsible for violating Art. 3 of Protocol 1 to the ECHR for automatically disenfranchising those who are incarcerated and, separately, for introducing new requirements shortly before elections were due to take place with the aim of depriving opposition and minorities groups of an opportunity to organise their activities in such a way as to be able to satisfy the eligibility criteria introduced as a result of the new legislation – in order to assess the response, from an economic and legal perspective, that it has taken to ensuring the execution of the ECtHR judgments which concern a violation of the right to free elections, and, additionally, to verify whether or not it has complied with them. On the basis of the data presented, this essay will also evaluate to what extent the Court's case-law concerning Article 3 of Protocol 1 to

5 Rainey B., McCormick P., Ovey C., *Jacobs, White and Ovey: The European Convention on Human Rights*, Oxford University Press, Oxford, 2006, 388.

6 The ECtHR has determined that there are 'implied limitations' to Article 3 of Protocol 1 to the ECHR: see, among others, [GC] *Sitaropoulos and Giakoumopoulos v. Greece*, Application no. 42202/07, judgment 15 March 2012, para. 64, where it held that "[g]iven that Article 3 of Protocol No. 1 is not limited by a specific list of 'legitimate aims' such as those enumerated in Articles 8 to 11 of the Convention, the Contracting States are free to rely on an aim not contained in such a list to justify a restriction, provided that the compatibility of that aim with the principle of the rule of law and the general objectives of the Convention is proved in the particular circumstances of a case."

7 ECtHR [GC], *Yumak and Sadak v. Turkey*, Application no. 10226/03, judgment 8 July 2008, para. 118.

8 Tulkens F., *Execution and Effects of Judgments of the European Court of Human Rights: The Role of the Judiciary, Dialogue between Judges*, Council of Europe Publishing, Strasbourg, 2006, 12.

the ECHR is able to influence reform of policy on prisoner voting rights and the representation of opposition and national minorities in Romania. To this end, the present contribution first provides a brief overview of the status of the ECHR and the impact of the ECtHR's case-law on the Romanian legal system. Thereafter, it analyses the judgments of the ECtHR in which the Court has found violations of Art. 3 of Protocol 1 to the ECHR, which Romania has undertaken to comply with through the adoption of the necessary execution measures, in accordance with Art. 46 of the Convention. Finally, it explores what measures have been taken at the national level to give effect to the ECtHR's judgments on the right to free elections cases and discusses whether they can be considered sufficient to satisfy the ECtHR's criteria, with which they must comply.

The status of the ECHR and the position of the ECtHR's case-law in the Romanian legal system: "Theory Is When You Know Everything, but Nothing Works"

As is well known, the ECHR leaves it to the States parties to decide how to comply with their duty to implement the provisions of the Convention. Indeed, as stated specifically by the ECtHR, the ECHR does not lay down for the States parties "any given manner for ensuring within their internal law the effective implementation" of any of the rights and freedoms guaranteed.[9] Moreover, in the *James and Others*[10] and in the *Lithgow and Others* cases,[11] the ECtHR held that States are not requested to incorporate the Convention into domestic law,[12] but that "the substance of the rights and freedoms set forth must be secured under the domestic legal order, in some form or another, to everyone within the jurisdiction of the Contracting States."[13]

The mere incorporation of the ECHR into a domestic legal system is, therefore, neither able to solve all the issues related to its application, nor to guarantee the faithful and effective application of the Convention in the domestic legal system of the States parties.[14] Thus, it is important to analyse the status of the ECHR in domestic legal orders,[15] assuming that the strength of the impact of

9 ECtHR, *Swedish Engine Drivers Union v. Sweden*, Application no. 5614/72, judgment 6 February 1976, para. 50.

10 ECtHR, *James and Others v. the United Kingdom*, Application no. 8793/79, judgment 21 February 1986.

11 ECtHR, *Lithgow and Others v. the United Kingdom*, Applications nos. 9006/80, 9262/81, 9263/81, 9265/81, 9266/81, 9313/81, 9405/81, judgment 8 July 1986.

12 ECtHR, *James and Others v. the United Kingdom*, supra note 10, para. 84; *Lithgow and Others v. the United Kingdom*, supra note 11, para. 205.

13 ECtHR, *Soering v. the United Kingdom*, supra note 2, para. 120.

14 In this sense see Caligiuri A., Napoletano N., *The Application of the ECHR in the Domestic Systems*, in Italian Yearbook of International Law, 20, 2010, 126.

15 Much has been written on this issue. See, among others, Martinico G., Pollicino O. (eds.), *The National Judicial Treatment of the ECHR and EU Laws. A Comparative Constitutional Perspective*, Europa Law Pub Netherlands, Groningen, 2010; Keller H., Stone Sweet A.

the Convention on the national legal system mainly depends on two aspects. On the one side, the position of the ECHR in the domestic hierarchy of sources of law, that is to say, whether it has a *supra*-legislative status in domestic legal orders and, therefore, prevails over conflicting national laws enacted before or after the ratification and the entry into force of the Convention itself; on the other side, the self-executing character of the ECHR rules and the possibility that the Convention rights be directly enforced by national courts.[16]

As far as the relationship between the domestic and international legal systems is concerned, although there is some controversy,[17] Romania's legal order has some undeniably monist features. The incorporation of international treaties into the Romanian legal system is expressly stated in Art. 11.2 of the 1991 Constitution of Romania,[18] which reads that "[t]reaties lawfully ratified by Parliament shall form an integral part of the domestic legal order." In light of the aforementioned provision, which refers also to the ECHR, as it is included in the "treaties" chapter, one can thus conclude that the ECHR, to which Romania has been a party since June 1994[19] – only three years after the adoption of its first post-revolution Constitution – is automatically incorporated into the national legal system. Regarding its rank in the hierarchy of sources of laws, the Romanian Constitution recognises that international human rights treaties have a role which is complementary to the Constitution and enjoy supremacy over national legislation. Indeed, according to Art. 20:

> [The] constitutional provisions on citizens' rights and liberties shall be interpreted and applied in accordance [...] with the covenants and other treaties to which Romania is a party. [...] In the event of conflict between the covenants and treaties on fundamental human rights to which Romania is a party and domestic laws, the international instruments shall prevail.

(eds.), *A Europe of Rights. The Impact of the ECHR on National Legal Systems*, Oxford University Press, Oxford, 2008; Blackburn R., Polakiewicz J. (eds.), *Fundamental Rights in Europe. The European Convention on Human Rights and Its Member States, 1950–2000*, Oxford University Press, Oxford, 2001.

16 In this sense see Cataldi G., "La natura *self-executing* delle norme della CEDU e l'applicazione delle sentenze della Corte europea negli ordinamenti nazionali" in Caligiuri A., Cataldi G., Napoletano N. (eds.), *La tutela dei diritti umani in Europa tra sovranità statale e ordinamenti sovranazionali*, Cedam, Padova, 2010, 565 ff.

17 For authors who consider Romania to be a dualist State, see Deaconu S., *Drepturile şi libertăţile fundamentale în sistemul constituţional românesc*, in Revista română de drept privat, 4, 2011, 48. For authors considering Romania to be a monist State, see Corlăţean T., *Constitution of Romania as an Instrument for Incorporating International Standards of Human Rights Protection*, in Revista de Drept Public (Supliment pe anul 2014), 2014, 100; Heyns C., Viljoen F., *The Impact of the United Nations Human Rights Treaties on the Domestic Level*, Martinus Nijhoff Publishers, The Hague, 2002, 7.

18 The text of the Romanian Constitution is available at www.wipo.int/edocs/lexdocs/laws/en/ro/ro021en.pdf.

19 On the accession process, see Donald A., Leach P., *Parliaments and the European Court of Human Rights*, Oxford University Press, Oxford, 2016, 195–198.

Furthermore, Art. 3 ("The application with priority of international instruments pertaining to human rights") of the Code of Civil Procedure (Law 134/2010, effective 15 February 2013) requires that its provisions pertaining to human rights shall be interpreted and applied in conformity with the Constitution, the Universal Declaration on Human Rights, and other human rights treaties to which Romania is a party, and that in case of inconsistency between international human rights instruments and the Code, the international norms have priority, except when the national law is more favourable.[20]

Regarding the self-executing character of the ECHR rules and the possibility that the Convention rights be directly enforceable by the Romanian courts, according to Art. 11.2 of the Constitution, the Convention may be used directly in the domestic legal system. In addition, the practice of Romanian institutions has consistently shown that national courts have admitted and accepted the "self-executing" nature of the provisions of the ECHR.[21]

The above considerations also apply to the position of the ECtHR's case-law in the Romanian legal order. Indeed, the system of the protection of human rights developed in the framework of the Council of Europe is a mixed system in terms of its sources, as it is based on written law (the Convention) and judicial precedents (the ECtHR case-law).[22] The Convention and its protocols may be correctly read and applied only by referring to the jurisprudence of the Strasbourg Court. As a result, in Romanian domestic law, the ECtHR case-law has the same position held by the provisions of the Convention and, therefore,

20 The text of the Romanian Code of Civil Procedure is available at https://elrc-share.eu/repository/browse/romanian-new-civil-procedure-code/017a4441ad8811e6bfe700155d0205025fe5a8c9bca9437f9107068080738a32/.

21 See the relevant examples mentioned in CORLĂŢEAN T., *Considerations regarding the Authority of the European Convention on Human Rights and Fundamental Freedoms and of the European Court on Human Rights Jurisprudence on the National Law Systems in Some of the Member States*, in International Law Review, 1, 2011, 27–28.

22 In its ruling rendered in the case *Cossey v. the United Kingdom*, Application no. 10843/84, judgment 27 September 1990, para. 35, the Court declared that it "is not bound by its previous judgments [...]. However, it usually follows and applies its own precedents, such a course being in the interests of legal certainty and the orderly development of the Convention case-law." Ten years later, in the judgment rendered in the case *Chapman v. the United Kingdom*, Application no. 27238/95, judgment 18 January 2001, the ECtHR considered that "while it is not formally bound to follow any of its previous judgments, it is in the interests of legal certainty, foreseeability and equality before the law that it should not depart, without good reason, from precedents laid down in previous cases" (para. 70). For a thorough analysis, see PALANCO A., *Le précédent dans la jurisprudence de la Cour européenne des droits de l'homme*, Bruylant, Bruxelles 2019; WILDHABER L., "Precedent in the European Court of Human Rights," in MAHONEY P. et al. (eds.), *Protecting Human Rights: The European Perspective*, Heymann, Köln, 2000, 1529 ff.; SUNDBERG F.G.E., *The European Experience of Human Rights Proceedings: The Precedent Value of the European Court's Decisions*, in Akron Law Review, 20, 1987, 629 ff.

is directly applicable and possesses complementary constitutional force, as well as over-legislative force.[23]

With such a generous constitutional framework, providing for the ECHR and the ECtHR case-law to be directly applicable and giving them *supra*-legislative status, one could legitimately expect that the ECHR system has substantially brought a state-level improvement in the considered national legal order, thus contributing significantly to the promotion and protection of fundamental rights in Romania. Unfortunately, this has not in fact happened. On the contrary, statistics and monitoring reports focusing on Romania indicate the seriousness of the human rights problems in evidence, both in terms of their number and severity, and the implementation of the relevant ECtHR judgments against it.[24]

In December 2020, Romania accounted for 12,5% of applications pending before the ECtHR (7,561), the fourth largest total in the Council of Europe after the Russian Federation, Turkey, and Ukraine.[25] From the time of Romania's ratification of the ECHR in 1994 to the end of December 2020, there were 77,451 applications decided against Romania; again, this was the fourth highest after the Russian Federation, Turkey, and Italy.[26]

In 2020, there were 82 adverse judgments concerning Romania, the fourth highest in the Council of Europe after the Russian Federation, Turkey, and Ukraine.[27] Since when Romania ratified the Convention up to the end of 2020, it was the target of 1,578 adverse judgments, or 7% of all judgments that have found at least one violation of the ECHR by a State party.[28] Around 300 of these concerned substantive or procedural violations of Art. 3 ECHR (prohibition of torture and inhuman or degrading treatment or punishment). Almost half arose from violations of Art. 6 ECHR (right to a fair trial). Six of these related to violations of Art. 3 of Protocol 1 to the ECHR (right to free elections).

23 See CORLĂŢEAN, supra note 21, 27.

24 According to some legal scholars, Romania's bad implementation record is a consequence of domestic implementation structures – with limited political clout, resources, and ability to influence the law – and policy-making processes. This is confirmed by the fact that implementation arrangements are dominated by the Office of the Government's Agent, a body functioning within the Ministry of Foreign Affairs, which simultaneously represents the State before the ECtHR and is responsible for implementing its adverse rulings. These two roles reflect conflicting commitments that may undermine execution: the same body that defends the State against alleged rights violations must also ensure that national authorities institute effective measures to remedy such violations when they are detected by the ECtHR. See ANAGNOSTOU D., MUNGIU-PIPPIDI A., *Domestic Implementation of Human Rights Judgments in Europe: Legal Infrastructure and Government Effectiveness Matter*, in European Journal of International Law, 25, 1, 2014, 222–223.

25 Council of Europe, Annual Report 2020 of the European Court of Human Rights, 2021, 156, available at www.echr.coe.int/Documents/Annual_report_2020_ENG.pdf.

26 European Court of Human Rights, Overview: 1959–2020, February 2021, 5, available at www.echr.coe.int/Documents/Overview_19592020_ENG.pdf.

27 See Council of Europe, *Annual Report 2020*, supra note 25, 163.

28 Ibid., 165.

In respect of implementation, according to the latest information available, Romania accounted for 284 cases pending before the Committee of Ministers at the end of 2019 (in comparison with 309 in 2018);[29] of which 23 had been pending for more than 5 years.[30] In the Committee of Ministers' list of worst-offending States with cases under enhanced supervision (on the basis of the number of leading cases), Romania ranked fourth.[31]

According to the latest report of the Parliamentary Assembly of the Council of Europe (PACE) Rapporteur on the implementation of the ECtHR judgments,[32] there are a number of cases (or groups of cases) exposing structural or systemic problems. These are outstanding issues relating to the failure to restore or compensate for nationalised property,[33] which led to the first pilot judgment rendered against Romania;[34] the excessive length of civil and criminal proceedings and the lack of an effective remedy;[35] the non-enforcement of domestic judicial decisions;[36] poor conditions of detention;[37] the ineffectiveness of criminal investigations into the violent suppression of anti-government demonstrations relating to the fall of the Communist regime;[38] the lack of appropriate legal protection and medical and social care for vulnerable persons with mental disabilities;[39] the inadequate management of psychiatric conditions of detainees in prison;[40] and the conviction of a whistle-blower for having disclosed information on the illegal secret surveillance of citizens by the intelligence service and the lack of safeguards in the statutory framework governing secret surveillance.[41]

29 Council of Europe, 13th Annual Report of the Committee of Ministers, Supervision of the Execution of Judgments and Decisions of the European Court of Human Rights 2019, 62, available at https://rm.coe.int/annual-report-2019/16809ec315.

30 Ibid., 74.

31 Ibid.

32 PACE, Committee on Legal Affairs and Human Rights, Implementation of the Judgments of the European Court of Human Rights, 10th Report: Romania, Doc. AS/Jur (2019) 52, 12 December 2019 (Rapporteur: Constantinos Efstathiou), paras. 4–36, available at www.assembly.coe.int/LifeRay/JUR/Pdf/DocsAndDecs/2019/AS-JUR-2019-52-EN.pdf.

33 ECtHR, *Străin and Others v. Romania*, Application no. 57001/00, judgment 21 July 2005.

34 ECtHR, *Maria Atanasiu and Others v. Romania*, Applications nos. 30767/05 and 33800/06, judgment 12 October 2010.

35 ECtHR, *Vlad and Others v. Romania*, Applications nos. 40756/06, 41508/07 and 50806/07, judgment 26 November 2013.

36 ECtHR, *Ruianu v. Romania*, Application no. 34647/97, judgment 17 June 2003; *Săcăleanu v. Romania*, Application no. 73970/01, judgment 6 September 2005; *Strungariu v. Romania*, Application no. 23878/02, judgment 29 September 2005.

37 ECtHR, *Bragadireanu v. Romania*, Application no. 22088/04, judgment 6 December 2007.

38 ECtHR, *Association "21 December 1989" v. Romania*, Applications nos. 33810/07 and 18817/08, judgment 24 May 2011.

39 ECtHR [GC], *The Centre for Legal Resources on behalf of Valentin Câmpeanu v. Romania*, Application no. 47848/08, judgment 14 July 2014.

40 ECtHR, *Ticu v. Romania*, Application no. 24575/10, judgment 1 October 2013.

41 ECtHR, *Bucur and Toma v. Romania*, Application no. 40238/02, judgment 8 January 2013.

Notwithstanding these areas of continuing concern, judgments of the ECtHR have led to significant – albeit, in some cases, still incomplete – legal and policy reforms in Romania. Some legal scholars have identified four areas in which ECtHR judgments have had the greatest influence: prosecutorial powers; the powers of the intelligence services; the restitution of nationalised property; and freedom of expression.[42] The following sections will focus on a group of final judgments in which violations of Art. 3 of Protocol 1 to the ECHR were found, as a premise to subsequently assessing if and to what extent Romania has responded to the findings and executed the measures required. With this in mind, particular attention will be paid to the reasoning developed by the ECtHR with regard to the "democratic argument" and the measures of reparation indicated.

The right to free elections in the ECtHR's judgments against Romania

As of February 2021, there are seven final judgments of the ECtHR where it found violations of Art. 3 of Protocol 1 to the ECHR, which Romania has undertaken to comply with through the adoption of the necessary execution measures. Among them, three deal with the automatic imposition of the penalty of disenfranchisement as a direct consequence of incarceration, while the other four judgments concern the effective participation of minorities and opposition parties in public affairs and public life, with specific regard to the introduction of new requirements shortly before the date of the elections which sought to deprive them of an opportunity to organise their activities in such a way as to be able to satisfy the eligibility criteria introduced as a result of the new legislation.

As far as the automatic withdrawal of prisoners' voting rights is concerned, the first judgment was rendered by the ECtHR on 13 November 2012 in the case *Cucu v. Romania*.[43] On 21 November 2001, the Bucharest Appeal Court found the applicant guilty of robbery and 2 traffic offences and sentenced him to 11 years' imprisonment. In addition, through the application of Art. 71 of the Romanian Criminal Code, according to which prisoners sentenced to a term of imprisonment are also given an accessory punishment prohibiting them from exercising certain rights listed in Art. 64, including the right to vote,[44] his right to vote and to be elected was withdrawn during the execution of the prison sentence as a complementary sanction. The applicant complained under Art. 3 ECHR about the detention conditions in the Jilava and Giurgiu penitentiaries; under Art. 6, paragraphs 1 and 8, with reference to the impossibility of receiving visits

42 See, among others, Bogdan D., Mungiu-Pippidi A., "The Reluctant Embrace: The Impact of the European Court of Human Rights in Post-Communist Romania," in Anagnostou D. (ed.), *The European Court of Human Rights: Implementing Strasbourg's Judgments on Domestic Policy*, Edinburgh University Press, Edinburgh, 2013, 74.

43 ECtHR, *Cucu v. Romania*, Application no. 22362/06, judgment 13 November 2012.

44 See Romanian Criminal Code (Law No 286/2009), as amended in 2017, available at legislatie.just.ro/Public/DetaliiDocument/109855.

from his common-law wife; and, for the purposes of the present analysis, under Art. 3 of Protocol 1 to the ECHR as regards the automatic withdrawal of his voting rights.

Leaving aside considerations about the alleged violations of Arts. 3 and 6, paragraphs 1 and 8 ECHR, as far as the purported violation of Art. 3 of Protocol 1 to the ECHR is concerned, the ECtHR recalled its previous case-law,[45] stating that the rights guaranteed by that provision are crucial to establishing and maintaining the foundations of an effective and meaningful democracy governed by the rule of law and a general, automatic and indiscriminate restriction on the right to vote applied to all convicted prisoners serving sentences is incompatible with the above provision.[46] In addition, the Court noted that it had already found in respect of Romania a violation of Art. 3 of Protocol 1 to the ECHR on account of an automatic withdrawal of the right to vote as a secondary penalty to a prison sentence and of the lack of competence of the courts to proceed with a proportionality test on that measure.[47] In light of the above, the ECtHR concluded that in the *Cucu* case there had been, among others, a violation of Art. 3 of Protocol 1 to the ECHR, and, pursuant to Art. 41 ECHR, ordered Romania to pay the applicant the sum of EUR 13,000 in respect of non-pecuniary damage, plus EUR 4,000 in respect of costs and expenses. The Court allowed the Romanian government a period of three months to execute the judgment from the date on which it became final.

The second relevant judgment was delivered by the ECtHR on 27 October 2015 in the case *Branduse v. Romania (no. 2)*.[48] The applicant was serving a prison sentence for fraud, imposed by two decisions of the Timişoara Court of Appeal of 14 August 2002 and 11 November 2004 respectively. On 30 November 2008, the applicant was not allowed to vote in the parliamentary elections and, despite his requests for clarification, the prison authorities failed to provide him with confirmation as to whether he was entitled to vote. The applicant complained under Art. 3 ECHR about the conditions of his detention in Jilava prison, and under Art. 3 of Protocol 1 to the ECHR, due to the fact he had not been allowed to vote in the parliamentary elections of 30 November 2008.

With regard to the alleged violation of Art. 3 of Protocol 1 to the ECHR, the ECtHR reiterated that the above provision guarantees subjective rights, including the right to vote and to stand for election.[49] It further noted that the rights guaranteed by this provision are crucial to establishing and maintaining the foun-

45 ECtHR [GC], *Hirst v. the United Kingdom (no. 2)*, Application no. 74025/01, judgment 30 March 2004, paras. 58 and 82. Similarly [GC], *Scoppola v. Italy (no. 3)*, Application no. 126/05, judgment 22 May 2012, paras. 96, 108 and 109.

46 Para.109 of the judgment.

47 Para.111 of the judgment. See also *Calmanovici v. Romania*, Application no. 42250/02, judgment 1 July 2008, para.153.

48 ECtHR, *Brânduşe v. Romania (no. 2)*, Application no. 39951/08, judgment 27 October 2015.

49 Ibid., para. 44.

dations of an effective and meaningful democracy governed by the rule of law and that the right to vote is not a privilege.[50] In addition, the Court highlighted that universal suffrage cannot be considered a privilege in the 21st century, as the presumption in a democratic State has to be in favour of inclusion.[51] The ECtHR further recalled its previous case-law[52] stating that, when disenfranchisement affects a group of people generally, automatically, and indiscriminately, based solely on the fact that they are serving a prison sentence, irrespective of the length of the sentence and irrespective of the nature or seriousness of their offence and their individual circumstances, it is not compatible with Art. 3 of Protocol 1 to the ECHR.[53] As far as Romania is concerned, the Court noted once again that it has already found a similar restriction to be incompatible with the requirements of the above provision in so far as, according to Romanian law as it was applied by the domestic courts at that time, all convicted prisoners serving prison sentences received a secondary penalty in the form of a general, automatic, and indiscriminate restriction on the right to vote.[54] In light of this, the Court concluded that, also in the case in question, there had been a violation of Art. 3 of Protocol 1 to the ECHR, as the disenfranchisement was imposed as a direct consequence of incarceration, without an individual assessment of the applicant's specific situation by the courts. As a result, according to Art. 41 ECHR, it ordered Romania to pay the applicant the sum of EUR 1,500 in respect of non-pecuniary damage for the violation of Art. 3 ECHR, but no additional award was made for the violation of Art. 3 of Protocol 1 to the ECHR. The Court allowed the Romanian government a period of three months to execute the judgment from the date on which it became final.

The last judgment against Romania concerning the automatic imposition of the penalty of disenfranchisement as a direct consequence of incarceration was delivered on 17 January 2017 in the *Nenciu v. Romania* case.[55] On 24 June 1999, the Călăraşi County Court convicted the applicant of burglary, rape, and murder, and sentenced him to 25 years' imprisonment. In addition, through the application of Art. 71 of the Romanian Criminal Code, his right to vote and to be elected was withdrawn during his detention. The applicant complained under Art. 3 ECHR about the inadequate conditions of his detention in prison and under Art. 3 of Protocol 1 to the ECHR in relation to his automatic and complete disqualification from exercising his right to vote, arguing that his case was identical to that of *Cucu*. The reasoning of the ECtHR with regard to the alleged violation of Art. 3 of Protocol 1 to the ECHR was identical to that developed in the above-discussed *Branduse* case. Similarly, the Court found a violation of

50 Ibid.
51 Ibid.
52 ECtHR [GC], *Hirst v. the United Kingdom (no. 2)*, supra note 45, para. 82.
53 Para. 45 of the judgment.
54 Ibid., para. 46.
55 ECtHR, *Nenciu v. Romania*, Application no. 65980/13, judgment 17 January 2017.

the above article, as the disenfranchisement was imposed as a direct consequence of his incarceration, without an assessment by the courts of the applicant's individual circumstances. Therefore, pursuant to Art. 41 ECHR, the ECtHR ordered Romania to pay the applicant the sum of EUR 14,400 in respect of non-pecuniary damage for the violation of Art. 3 ECHR plus EUR 2,585 in respect of costs and expenses. No additional sums were awarded for the violation of Art. 3 of Protocol 1 to the ECHR. The Court allowed the Romanian government a period of three months to execute the judgment from the date on which it became final.

As anticipated, on several occasions the ECtHR has declared Romania to be in violation of Art. 3 of Protocol 1 to the ECHR as a consequence of the introduction of new legislative requirements shortly before the date of the elections with the aim of depriving minorities and opposition parties of an opportunity to fully participate in public affairs and public life.

In this regard, the first judgment was delivered on 2 March 2010 in the *Grosaru v. Romania* case.[56] The applicant was a candidate in the parliamentary elections of November 2000, when he stood for the seat assigned to the Italian minority in Romania. The Central Electoral Office, on the basis of the 1992 Law on Elections to the Chamber of Deputies and the Senate, granted the parliamentary seat belonging to the Italian minority to the "Italian Community of Romania." Although the applicant was the candidate from the organisation who had obtained the most votes, the Central Electoral Office allocated the seat in Parliament to another member of the organisation, who had stood for election on another single-candidate list and had secured less votes, but in a single constituency. The applicant challenged the decision that allocated the parliamentary seat to another candidate before the Central Electoral Office, which dismissed his request. He then challenged this decision before the same Central Electoral Office, which consisted of a panel composed of 6 judges and 12 representatives of political parties and declared his appeal inadmissible. Appeals to both the Supreme Court and the Constitutional Court were also declared inadmissible. The applicant complained under Art. 3 Protocol 1 of the ECHR that the authorities had refused to allocate him a seat as an MP representing the Italian minority in the parliamentary elections of 2000 and under Art. 13 ECHR taken in conjunction with Art. 3 of Protocol 1 to the ECHR that he had had no effective remedy by which to challenge the authorities' refusal to allocate him the parliamentary seat for the Italian minority and, as a result, that there had been a violation of the freedom of expression of the opinion of the people as to the choice of legislative body.

With regard to the alleged violation of Art. 3 of Protocol 1 to the ECHR, the ECtHR reiterated that the rights guaranteed under the above provision are crucial to establishing and maintaining the foundations of an effective and meaningful democracy governed by the rule of law, but are not absolute – as, in principle, there is room for "implied limitations" – and States parties must be given a

56 ECtHR, *Grosaru v. Romania*, Application no. 78039/01, judgment 2 March 2010.

margin of appreciation in this sphere.[57] However, as observed by the Court, the conditions must not curtail the rights in question to such an extent as to impair their very essence and deprive them of their effectiveness; they must be imposed in pursuit of a legitimate aim; and the means employed must not be disproportionate.[58] The ECtHR preliminarily noted that, unlike the majority of judgments it had delivered on electoral matters, the *Grosaru* case did not concern conditions of eligibility but rather the allocation of a parliamentary seat, that is to say, a post-electoral rights matter.[59] It further observed that the 1992 Law on Elections to the Chamber of Deputies and the Senate does not clearly set out the procedure to be followed in assigning the parliamentary seat which is set aside for the winning organisation representing a national minority, and that the guarantees through which an impartial challenge could be brought against the authorities' refusal to allocate him the parliamentary seat for the Italian minority were not sufficient.[60] The ECtHR thus concluded that there had been a violation of Art. 3 of Protocol 1 to the ECHR taken alone and together with Art. 13. Consequently, pursuant to Art. 41 ECHR, it awarded the applicant the sum of EUR 5,000 in respect of non-pecuniary damage. The Court allowed the Romanian government a period of three months to execute the judgment from the date on which it became final.

The second judgment which deserves to be considered is that delivered on 21 April 2015 in the *Danis and Association of Ethnic Turks v. Romania* case.[61] The case concerned the applicant association's inability to meet the requirements for standing in the parliamentary elections of 30 November 2008, following the entry into force of a new electoral law only seven months before the elections. The association had taken part in the November 2004 parliamentary elections but failed to win the seat reserved for the Turkish minority, which had gone to another Turkish minority association, that had polled a slightly higher number of votes. On 16 March 2008, a new electoral law entered into force, requiring national minority organisations not represented in Parliament to have been granted charitable status in order to be able to stand for election. The association decided to stand in the parliamentary elections scheduled for November 2008, but did not apply for charitable status, as it did not satisfy some of the conditions. After the Central Electoral Bureau's refusal of the association's candidature, the applicants applied to the Bucharest County Court for judicial review of that decision. The Court referred the question to the Constitutional Court, which dismissed the applicants' objection. In a judgment delivered on 14 November 2008, the County Court dismissed the applicants' claim; the judgment was upheld on appeal. The applicants then complained under Art. 14 (prohibition

57 Ibid., para. 43.
58 Ibid., para. 44.
59 Ibid., para. 46.
60 Ibid., paras. 49–56.
61 ECtHR, *Danis and Association of Ethnic Turks v. Romania*, Application no. 16632/09, judgment 21 April 2015.

of discrimination) in conjunction with Art. 3 of Protocol 1 to the ECHR, stating that their right to stand as candidates in parliamentary elections had been infringed.

The reasoning of the ECtHR is similar to that developed in the above-discussed *Grosaru* case, as it reiterated that the rights guaranteed under Art. 3 of the Protocol 1 to the ECHR, albeit fundamental, are not absolute and can be subjected to "implied limitations."[62] The Court, however, observed that the introduction of new requirements shortly before the date of the elections can result in the automatic disqualification of opposition parties and coalitions enjoying significant popular support, and thus benefit political formations currently in power.[63] According to the Court, such a practice is incompatible with the democratic order and undermines citizens' trust in their country's public authorities. The ECtHR noted that the law governing the elections scheduled for 30 November 2008 had come into force on 16 March 2008, leaving approximately seven months for the applicants to put themselves forward for election.[64] Therefore, the authorities had not given the applicants the opportunity to organise their activities in such a way that they could be granted charitable status, as it had been objectively impossible for them to obtain that status and thus satisfy the eligibility requirement under the new electoral law.[65] Consequently, the Court concluded that there had been a violation of Art. 14 of the Convention in conjunction with Art. 3 of Protocol 1 to the ECHR and held that the finding of a violation constituted in itself sufficient just satisfaction for the non-pecuniary damage sustained by the applicants.

The third judgment was delivered on 15 December 2015 in the *Ofensiva Tinerilor v. Romania* case.[66] The case concerned the refusal of the Romanian authorities to register the applicant association's list of candidates for the parliamentary elections. The applicant association sought the annulment of the Central Electoral Board's rejection of the applicant's candidates in the High Court of Cassation and Justice, but the Court's Civil Division declared the association's claim inadmissible. The applicant association then lodged a new claim for the annulment of the Board's decision in the Bucharest Court of Appeal. The case was transferred to the Civil Division of the High Court which, without summoning the parties, dismissed the action on the ground that the judgment of the High Court of Cassation and Justice was final. The association lodged an appeal on points of law, which were declared inadmissible. Relying in particular on Art. 3 of Protocol 1 ECHR, the applicant association complained about the decision of the Romanian authorities to refuse to register its list of candidates for the parliamentary elections and its inability to challenge that decision in the domestic courts. In addition, the applicant association complained under Art. 13 ECHR,

62 Ibid., para. 38.
63 Ibid., para. 45.
64 Ibid., para. 48.
65 Ibid., para. 54.
66 ECtHR, *Ofensiva Tinerilor v. Romania*, Application no. 16732/05, judgment 15 December 2015.

in conjunction with Art. 3 of Protocol 1 that it had had no effective remedy by which to challenge the decision of the Central Electoral Board; under Art. 14 in conjunction with Art. 3 of Protocol 1 to the ECHR that, differently from other parties, its list of candidates for the parliamentary elections was not automatically accepted and under Art. 11 (right to freedom of assembly and association) that the refusal of the Romanian authorities to register the applicant association's list of candidates had violated its right to freedom of association.

For the purposes of the present contribution, as far as Art. 3 of Protocol 1 to the ECHR is concerned, the ECtHR once again reiterated that the rights guaranteed under the above provision, albeit fundamental, can be subjected to "implied limitations" and States parties enjoy a wide margin of appreciation in establishing eligibility conditions.[67] With regard to the right to stand for election, the Court further admitted that it is particularly cautious in its assessment of the restrictions, as they must not infringe upon the essence of the right and must be surrounded by sufficient guarantees to avoid arbitrariness.[68] In the instant case, the ECtHR recognised that the electoral law established unclear eligibility conditions for organisations of ethnic minorities to lodge their candidates and a lack of sufficient safeguard for the impartiality of the supervisory body responsible for examining the candidate's list, thus finding a violation of Art. 3 of Protocol 1 to the ECHR.[69] In this regard, the ECtHR concluded that the finding of a violation constituted sufficient just satisfaction for the non-pecuniary damage.

The most recent judgment was delivered on 24 March 2020 in the *Cegolea v. Romania* case.[70] The case concerned the refusal of the Romanian authorities to award the applicant's foundation charitable status, which was a requirement under the Electoral Act in order for the applicant to be allowed to stand as a candidate in the parliamentary elections of 9 December 2012, on behalf of the foundation, as an organisation representing the Italian minority. In May 2012, the Government's Secretariat General registered the application and forwarded it to the Department for Inter-ethnic Relations (DIR) and to the Ministry of Culture and National Heritage for their opinion. The former refused the foundation's application for charitable status. The applicant appealed against that decision, without success. In July 2012, Law no. 145/2012 amending Government Order no. 26/2000 on associations and foundations entered into force. The amendments related mainly to the provisions concerning the granting of charitable status. In October 2012, the applicant sought to register as a candidate for the foundation in the parliamentary elections, but her candidature was not registered because the foundation did not have charitable status. She then appealed against that decision to the County Court, which, despite dismissing her appeal on the grounds that the foundation lacked charitable status, allowed the applicant's

67 Ibid., para. 51.
68 Ibid., para. 52.
69 Ibid., paras. 59–60.
70 ECtHR, *Cegolea v. Romania*, Application no. 25560/13, judgment 24 March 2020.

request to apply to the Constitutional Court. The Constitutional Court declared her plea of unconstitutionality inadmissible. A few days later the deadline for registering as a candidate in the parliamentary elections of 9 December 2012 expired. In January 2013, the applicant was informed of the Ministry's reply. The latter explained that, when the application had been submitted and examined, the foundation had satisfied the statutory criteria for the granting of charitable status. However, after the entry into force on 1 August 2012 of Law no. 145/2012 amending Order no. 26/2000, new criteria had been established which the foundation did not satisfy. The applicant then complained under Art. 3 of Protocol 1 to the ECHR read in conjunction with Art. 14 that her candidature had been subject to additional conditions compared with those imposed on the candidate already representing the Italian minority in the Romanian Parliament, who had simply been required to renew his candidature for the December 2012 elections without any further conditions being attached.

As far as Art. 3 Protocol 1 to the ECHR is concerned, the ECtHR once again reiterated that the rights guaranteed under the above provision can be subjected to "implied limitations," which, however, must not infringe their essence and must be surrounded by sufficient guarantees to avoid arbitrariness.[71] It also recognised that similar issues had already been examined in the aforementioned and discussed case of *Danis and Association of Ethnic Turks*. Nevertheless, the Court noted that the present case differed from the latter from the formal point of view, with regard to the legal conditions necessary to obtain charitable status after the entry into force of Law no. 145/2012 amending the Order no. 26/2000 on 29 July 2012.[72] The criteria to be met in order to apply for charitable status had been amended less than five months before the elections of 9 December 2012 and after the foundation had made its application. According to the Court, Order no. 26/2000 had therefore had a direct impact on the national legislation.[73] In addition, the ECtHR noted that Order no. 26/2000 laid down time-limits of 60 and 90 days respectively within which the competent administrative authority and the Ministry were required to deal with applications for charitable status.[74] The Government had not made clear whether those time-limits were indicative or binding. However, while the DIR had replied before the deadline, the Ministry had done so after the elections had taken place, taking differing positions on the criteria to be satisfied by the foundation.[75] In light of the lack of effective judicial scrutiny to protect against arbitrariness and the wide discretion enjoyed by the State in granting charitable status even where the requesting association or foundation fulfilled the statutory criteria, the ECtHR held that the difference in treatment to which the applicant had been subjected compared

71 Ibid., paras. 40–42.
72 Ibid., para. 46.
73 Ibid., para.55.
74 Ibid., para.57.
75 Ibid., para.58.

with the national minority organisations already represented in Parliament had been insufficiently justified in relation to the legitimate aim pursued (to ensure that organisations were properly representative and to encourage only serious candidates to stand). Therefore, the Court found that there had been a violation of Art. 14 of the Convention read in conjunction with Art. 3 of Protocol 1 to the ECHR, and held that the finding of a violation constituted in itself sufficient just satisfaction for the non-pecuniary damage sustained by the applicant.

The economic and legal response of Romania to judgments relating to Art. 3 of Protocol 1 to the ECHR

Having reviewed the relevant final judgments, it is essential to analyse Romania's responses to the ECtHR's rulings on prisoners' right to vote and the late changes to the electoral law aimed at depriving opposition and minority parties of an opportunity to organise their activities and discuss whether or not the concerned State has complied with them, as recognised by the Committee of Ministers of the Council of Europe. Attention will be devoted to the economic and legal measures taken by Romania to implement the above analysed ECtHR's judgments, in order to verify whether they can be considered sufficient to satisfy the ECtHR's criteria with which they must comply.

As far as prisoners' right to vote is concerned, in February 2007, a few years after the ECtHR's seminal judgment in the case *Hirst v. the United Kingdom (no. 2)*[76] recognised that a blanket ban on prisoner voting breached the Convention, albeit without specifying what *would* be ECHR-compliant, and in spite of the fact that at the time there was no any specific ECtHR's judgment against Romania, the High Court of Cassation and Justice of Romania had the opportunity to present its own legal position on the application of the ancillary penalty of the prohibition of the right to vote. It expressed the view that prisoners' disenfranchisement should only be imposed by a court decision, following a debate by the parties and after the examination of its compliance with the proportionality principle.[77] Furthermore, in a decision delivered in the interest of clarifying the law in November 2007, the High Court of Cassation and Justice stated that an assessment of the criteria set by Art. 71, para. 3 of the Criminal Code needs before an order can be made to apply the ancillary penalties stipulated by Arts. 64 a) (first thesis) – c) taken in conjunction with Art. 71 of the Criminal Code, and no automatic decision should be made in this respect.[78] This means that domestic courts should assess whether it is necessary to impose the ancillary and

76 ECtHR [GC], *Hirst v. the United Kingdom (no. 2)*, supra note 45.

77 See the information provided in the Romania's Revised Action Report of 13 December 2013: Communication from Romania concerning the Calmanovici Group of Cases against Romania (Application no. 42250/02), DH-DD (2013)1341, 13 December 2013, available at search.coe.int/cm/pages/result_details.aspx?objectid=09000016804a2651.

78 Ibid.

complementary penalties, including the prohibition of electoral rights, on a convicted person in each individual case by taking into account the facts and personal circumstances of the defendants.[79] Although the ECtHR acknowledged the judgment of the High Court of Cassation and Justice, it nevertheless found a violation of the right to vote of the applicants in the cases of *Cucu v. Romania*, *Brânduse v. Romania (no. 2)*, and *Nenciu v. Romania*, as the High Court of Cassation and Justice's decision only became mandatory for domestic courts in July 2008, after the applicants' conviction and sentencing in all three of these cases. The ECtHR awarded the applicants just satisfaction for non-pecuniary damage in all the above cases (in the case of *Cucu* only with regard to the declared violation of Article 3 of Protocol 1 to the ECHR, while in the other cases as a consequence of a violation of Article 3 ECHR, as the Court considered that the finding of a violation of the right to free elections constituted in itself sufficient just satisfaction). The sums awarded were paid within the deadlines indicated in the Court's judgments. The Committee of Ministers has exercised its supervision duty with regard to prisoner disenfranchisement cases and closed its formal supervision of Romania with regard to the cases of *Cucu*[80] and *Brânduse (no. 2)*,[81] since no other individual measures were required, and the general measures had already been examined in the *Calmanovici* group of cases.[82]

Unlike the above cases, the execution of the judgment in the case *Nenciu v. Romania* is still pending. The national authorities submitted an action plan in this case on 11 September 2017.[83] According to the document provided, with regard to individual measures and as previously anticipated, Romania paid the applicant the sum awarded under Art. 41 ECHR for non-pecuniary damage within the deadlines indicated in the Court's judgment. In addition, at the date of the action plan, the translation of the ECtHR's judgment into Romanian was underway. As at the date of its completion, the applicant can request the publication of the translated judgment in the Official Gazette and then lodge a request

79 Ibid.

80 Committee of Ministers of the Council of Europe, Resolution on Execution of the Judgments of the European Court of Human Rights: 4 Cases against Romania, CM/ResDH(2017)291, 21 September 2017, available at https://rm.coe.int/168074cb8f.

81 Committee of Ministers of the Council of Europe, Resolution on Execution of the Judgments of the European Court of Human Rights: 121 Cases against Romania, CM/ResDH(2018)108, 15 March 2018, available at hudoc.exec.coe.int/eng#{%22EXECIdentifier%22:[%22001-181972%22]}.th.

82 ECtHR, *Calmanovici v. Romania*, Application no. 42250/02, judgment 1 July 2008. On the execution of the judgment see also Committee of Ministers of the Council of Europe, Resolution on Execution of the Judgments of the European Court of Human Rights: 8 Cases against Romania, CM/ResDH(2014)13, 5 February 2014, available at https://hudoc.exec.coe.int/ENG#{%22EXECIdentifier%22:[%22001-142771%22]}.

83 Romania's Action Report of 11 September 2017: Communication from Romania concerning the case of Nenciu v. Romania (Application no. 65980/13), DH-DD(2017)1044, 25 September 2017, available at https://rm.coe.int/CoERMPublicCommonSearchServices/DisplayDCTMContent?documentId=090000168074f156.

for a revision of the court decision which had automatically deprived him of his voting rights. The action plan is all the more relevant in so far as it also provides information concerning general measures aimed at preventing similar human rights infringements from recurring. As regards the violation of Art. 3 of Protocol 1 to the ECHR, the authorities highlighted the historical context of the violation and recalled that in 2007 the High Court of Cassation and Justice found that the ban on a prisoner's voting rights could only be imposed by a court decision, after being debated by the parties and after examination of its compliance with the proportionality principle.[84] This ruling became mandatory on all domestic courts from 18 July 2008. Since the consequences of an automatic ban on voting rights previously applied may continue in some cases, the authorities indicated that they were assessing the scale of this problem and the measures to be taken in this context and that they would keep the Committee of Ministers informed of any further developments.[85]

Despite the violations of Art. 3 Protocol 1 to the ECHR found in the cases of *Cucu*, *Brânduse (no. 2)* and *Nenciu*, which can be regarded as the "late side effects" of the previous automatic imposition of the penalty of disenfranchisement on detainees, Romania seems to have adopted an overall rights-based policy for prisoners' voting, as the sentencing courts now hold the power to assess prisoners' disenfranchisement in individual cases. Indeed, although the intervention of a judge is not a *sine qua non* requirement of an acceptable restriction upon the right of prisoners to vote under the Convention,[86] the ECtHR held that it is "in principle likely to guarantee the proportionality of restrictions on prisoners' voting rights."[87] In this respect, the prisoners' disenfranchisement system in Romania not only provides adequate safeguards to ensure that prisoners are not automatically and indiscriminately denied the right to vote, but it is also beyond what is required to satisfy the ECtHR's criteria for an acceptable restriction on prisoners' voting rights under Art. 3 of Protocol 1 to the ECHR.[88]

As discussed in the previous section of the present contribution, the ECtHR found violations of Art. 3 of Protocol 1 to the ECHR also with regard to the effective participation of minorities and opposition parties in public affairs and the lack of an effective remedy in electoral matters in the cases of *Grosaru v. Romania*, *Danis and Association of Ethnic Turks v. Romania*, *Ofensiva Tinerilor v. Romania*, and *Cegolea v. Romania*. The ECtHR awarded the applicants just satisfaction for non-pecuniary damage only in the first of the above cases and the sums awarded were paid within the deadlines indicated in the Court's judgment, while in the other cases it concluded that no individual measures were

84 Ibid.

85 Ibid.

86 ECtHR, *Scoppola v. Italy (no 3)*, supra note 45, paras. 97–102; *Anchugov and Gladkov v. Russia*, Applications nos. 11157/04 and 15162/05, judgment 4 July 2013, para. 107.

87 ECtHR, *Scoppola* v. *Italy (no 3)*, supra note 45, para. 99.

88 See Celiksoy E., *Execution of the Judgments of the European Court of Human Rights in Prisoners' Right to Vote Cases*, in Human Rights Law Review, 20, 3, 2020, 557.

necessary, as the finding of a violation constituted sufficient just satisfaction for the non-pecuniary damage. Leaving aside the case of *Cegolea*, which is currently pending as the judgment only became final on 24 July 2020, the Committee of Ministers has exercised its supervision duty and brought it to a close for Romania with regard to the cases *Grosaru*,[89] *Danis and Association of Ethnic Turks*,[90] and *Ofensiva Tinerilor*.[91] Unlike the case of *Danis and Association of Ethnic Turks*, whose implementation did not require any particular measure other than the translation and dissemination of the judgment – as the facts related very specifically to the parliamentary elections of 2008 and the ECtHR did not question the electoral law itself, or the opportunity of introducing different eligibility conditions for candidates – the cases of *Grosaru* and *Ofensiva Tinerilor* are particularly relevant, as they provide information concerning the general measures to be adopted in order to prevent similar human rights infringements from recurring. According to the data available in the action report provided by Romania in the former case,[92] legislative reform was adopted in 2015 and the law in force at the material time (Law no. 68/1992) was repealed by a new law (Law no. 208/2015) concerning the election of the Senate and the Deputies Chamber of Deputies and the functioning of the Permanent Electoral Authority. As regards the requirement of clarity of the legal regulations applicable in the electoral field, Law no. 208/2015 clarifies that the mandate of deputy will be allocated to the ethnic minority organisation which secures the greatest number of votes at the national level. With regard to the right to an effective remedy before the national courts, the action report notes a binding decision issued by the Constitutional Court on 14 September 2004, which declared that the rulings delivered by the Central Electoral Bureau are defined as jurisdictional administrative acts and thus can be challenged before the ordinary administrative courts.[93] In addition, the document highlights that, according to Law no. 208/2015, the decisions by the electoral bureaux are made in the context specific to electoral activities and

89 Committee of Ministers of the Council of Europe, Resolution on Execution of the Judgment of the European Court of Human Rights: Grosaru against Romania, CM/ResDH(2016)322, 9 November 2016, available at https://hudoc.echr.coe.int/app/conversion/docx/pdf?library=ECHR&id=001-168993&filename=CEDH.pdf.

90 Committee of Ministers of the Council of Europe, Resolution on Execution of the Judgment of the European Court of Human Rights: Danis and the Association of Ethnic Turks against Romania, CM/ResDH(2016)130, 7 June 2016, available at https://hudoc.echr.coe.int/eng#{%22itemid%22:[%22001-164015%22]}.

91 Committee of Ministers of the Council of Europe, Resolution on Execution of the Judgment of the European Court of Human Rights: Ofensiva Tinerilor against Romania, CM/ResDH(2017)9, 18 January 2017, available at https://rm.coe.int/native/09000016806dcd58.

92 Romania's Action Report of 13 September 2016: Communication from Romania concerning the case of Grosaru against Romania (Application no. 78039/01), DH-DD(2016)1073, 4 October 2016, available at https://search.coe.int/cm/Pages/result_details.aspx?ObjectID=09000016806aa9c0.

93 Ibid.

can be contested in court by the interested parties pursuant to the administrative legislation.[94]

Moreover, the action report provided in the case of *Ofensiva Tinerilor* is interesting in this regard.[95] According to it, the applicable law in force at the material time (Law no. 373/2004), which established rather unclear eligibility conditions imposed on organisations belonging to ethnic minorities to be able to lodge their candidature, was modified by Law no. 208/2015 regarding the election of the Senate and the Deputy Chamber and the functioning of the Permanent Electoral Authority.[96] It established detailed conditions for the participation of organisations belonging to ethnic minorities that are not represented in the Parliament, the sole criteria being the recognition of the public utility of the government decision and a minimum number of citizens that have declared themselves to belong to the respective national minority at the last census. The role of the Central Electoral Bureau is limited to verifying these conditions. As regards the lack of impartiality of the bodies competent to examine the legal requirements to be complied with when submitting a candidature, Law no. 208/2015 states that the decisions of the Central Electoral Bureau are not final and can be contested in court.[97]

Also, with regard to the right to stand in elections, Romania seems to have adopted an overall approach aiming at effectively guaranteeing and strengthening the equal participation of organisations belonging to opposition and minorities groups. It is true that the ECtHR has traditionally been more cautious in its assessment of restrictions under this aspect of Art. 3 of Protocol 1 to the ECHR than when it has been called upon to examine restrictions on the right to vote, admitting that the proportionality test is more limited and States thus enjoy a broader margin of appreciation in respect of the "passive" aspect.[98] Nevertheless, the Court has recognised that, even though the margin of appreciation usually afforded to States as regards the right to stand for election is a broad one, where a difference in treatment is based on race, colour or ethnicity, the notion of objective and reasonable justification must be interpreted as strictly as possible.[99] In this regard, the electoral legislation in Romania as amended in 2015 provides adequate safeguards to ensure that minority groups are not unreasonably and disproportionately denied the right to stand in elections, as it clearly identifies

94 Ibid.

95 Romania's Action Report of 27 September 2016: Communication from Romania concerning the case of Ofensiva Tinerilor against Romania (Application no. 16732/05), DH-DD(2016)1109, 10 October 2016, available at https://search.coe.int/cm/Pages/result_details.aspx?ObjectID=09000016806ac956.

96 Ibid.

97 Ibid.

98 ECtHR, *Etxeberria and Others v. Spain*, Application no. 74016/12, judgment 7 October 2014, para. 50; *Davydov and Others v. Russia*, Application no. 75947/11, judgment 30 May 2017, para. 286.

99 ECtHR [GC], *Sejdić and Finci v. Bosnia-Herzegovina*, Applications nos. 27996/06 and 34836/06, judgment 22 December 2009, para. 44.

eligibility conditions and affords sufficient safeguards against arbitrariness, admitting that powers of the executive authorities can be scrutinised by courts. This seems to be in line with what is required to satisfy the ECtHR's criteria for an acceptable restriction under Art. 3 of Protocol 1 to the ECHR.

Conclusion

Over the past years, Romania has proven to have a poor human rights record, as is confirmed not only by the high violations rate in the ECHR system, but also in terms of the implementation performance of the ECtHR judgments imposed against it.

If this works as a rule, the above analysis has shown that things change when it comes to violations of the right to free elections, as set out in Art. 3 of Protocol 1 to the ECHR. Indeed, as of February 2021, Romania has undertaken to comply with seven final judgments where violations of the above provision were found, and the Committee of Ministers has brought its supervision to a close with regard to five of them. Two cases are still pending, one concerning automatic disenfranchisement for prisoners, and the other, which became final only on 24 July 2020, regarding the participation of opposition and minority groups to public life.

The analysis undertaken has shown that it may be seen as encouraging that Romania has implemented the judgments of the ECtHR, not only by means of individual measures (mainly the payment of the sums awarded by the Court as just satisfaction) but also through the adoption of general measures aimed at preventing violations similar to those found by the Court. With regard to this last aspect, particularly remarkable is the loyal and careful approach that has been taken to execution by Romania, which overall results in the ECHR standards having a strong impact at the national level. While normally only the respondent State to the case is bound by the judgment – and therefore has an obligation to take general measures – as far as the automatic withdrawal of prisoners' voting rights is concerned, the Romanian High Court of Cassation and Justice spontaneously took into account the interpretation of the Convention as expressed in the ECtHR's judgment in the case of *Hirst (no. 2)*, thus providing a good illustration of how the ECtHR's case-law may enjoy a persuasive authority for the domestic courts, and have a preventive effect, because States are aware that they risk condemnation.[100] This relates to the *erga omnes* effect of the judgments,

100 On the persuasive authority of ECtHR's judgments and decisions for other States than those party to the proceedings, see, among others, ARNARDÓTTIR O.M., Res Interpretata, Erga Omnes *Effect and the Role of the Margin of Appreciation in Giving Domestic Effect to the Judgments of the European Court of Human Rights*, in European Journal of International Law, 28, 3, 2017, 819 ff.; BODNAR A., "*Res Interpretata*: Legal Effect of the European Court of Human Rights' Judgments for Other States Than Those Which Were Party to the Proceedings," in HAECK Y., BREMS E. (eds.), *Human Rights and Civil Liberties in the 21st Century*, Springer, Dordrecht, 2014, 223 ff.; BESSON S., "The *Erga Omnes* Effect of Judgments of the European Court of Human Rights: What's in a Name?", in BESSON S.

which may be deducted from the obligation to "secure" the rights of the ECHR under Article 1. In light of this, it is not surprising therefore that, after the decision of the High Court of Cassation and Justice, the domestic courts' practice has improved to the point that the ECtHR has found Romania in violation of Art. 3 Protocol 1 to the ECHR with regard to prisoners' voting rights in a very limited number of judgments, all of which arose from cases where the applicants' conviction have been imposed before the intervention of the High Court of Cassation and Justice. It is little wonder that the examined ECtHR judgments were also executed without any major issues.

The acceptance of the influence of the ECHR and the Court's case-law by Romanian authorities clearly emerges also from the way they have ensured the execution of the ECtHR's judgments concerning disputes over the effective participation of minorities and opposition groups in public life and the lack of judicial review as regards the interpretation of the electoral legislation. This has been done, on the one hand, by the Romanian Parliament through the adoption of a new electoral law which governs the allocation of parliamentary seats to the representatives of the national minorities and has established a Permanent Electoral Authority and the Central Electoral Bureau as two autonomous bodies, and, on the other hand, by the Constitutional Court, which has modified its jurisprudence and declared that the decisions of the Central Electoral Bureau are jurisdictional administrative acts and can be contested in court by the interested parties before the ordinary administrative courts. While national courts frequently refer to the ECtHR's case-law and their methods of review and argumentation in cases about fundamental rights often appear to be modelled on the standards developed by the Court,[101] it is important to highlight the collaborative approach of the Romanian law makers, which did not hinder the execution of the ECtHR's judgments concerning questions which pertain to the sovereignty of parliaments and are perceived as political.

Further, the closures of cases may be seen as positive since the Committee of Ministers has endorsed the reforms undertaken by Romania as sufficient to ensure the implementation of the ECtHR's judgments concerning prisoner voting rights and the parliamentary representation of minority and opposition groups.

Finally, the ECtHR rulings analysed provided an opportunity for the Committee of Ministers to reaffirm its commitment to supervision of the

(ed.), *The European Court of Human Rights after Protocol 14: Preliminary Assessment and Perspectives*, Schulthess, Geneva, 2011, 125 ff.; Klein E., "Should the Binding Effect of the Judgments of the European Court of Human Rights Be Extended?", in Mahoney P. et al. (eds.), *Protecting Human Rights: The European Perspective*, Heymann, Köln, 2000, 705 ff.; Lambert-Abdelgawad É., *Les effets des arrêts de la Cour européenne des droits de l'homme*, Bruylant, Bruxelles, 1999.

101 See Bjorge E., *National Supreme Courts and the Development of ECHR Rights*, in International Journal of Constitutional Law, 2011, 5–31; Helfer L.R., *Redesigning the European Court of Human Rights: Embeddedness as a Deep Structural Principle of the European Human Rights Regime*, in European Journal of International Law, 19, 1, 2008, 125–159.

execution of judgments, which ensures that States are implementing the Court's judgments in a manner which makes the protection of the Convention rights practical and effective. In this regard, the closure of the cases of *Cucu*, *Brânduse (no. 2)*, *Grosaru*, *Danis and Association of Ethnic Turks* and *Ofensiva Tinerilor*, with the adoption of general measures capable of resolving the structural problem and preventing similar violations from reoccurring, is particularly relevant for the sake of the credibility of the ECHR system, as it concerns an area in which the margin of appreciation of States is particularly wide.

Bibliography

ANAGNOSTOU D., MUNGIU-PIPPIDI A., *Domestic Implementation of Human Rights Judgments in Europe: Legal Infrastructure and Government Effectiveness Matter*, in European Journal of International Law, 25, 2, 2014, 205–227.

ARNARDÓTTIR O.M., Res Interpretata, Erga Omnes *Effect and the Role of the Margin of Appreciation in Giving Domestic Effect to the Judgments of the European Court of Human Rights*, in European Journal of International Law, 28, 3, 2017, 819–843.

BESSON S., *Human Rights and Democracy in a Global Context: Decoupling and Recoupling*, in Ethics & Global Politics, 4, 1, 2011, 19–50.

BESSON S., "The *Erga Omnes* Effect of Judgments of the European Court of Human Rights: What's in a Name?", in BESSON S. (ed.), *The European Court of Human Rights after Protocol 14: Preliminary Assessment and Perspectives*, Schulthess, Geneva, 2011, 125.

BLACKBURN R., POLAKIEWICZ J. (eds.), *Fundamental Rights in Europe. The European Convention on Human Rights and Its Member States, 1950–2000*, Oxford University Press, Oxford, 2001.

BODNAR A., "*Res Interpretata*: Legal Effect of the European Court of Human Rights' Judgments for Other States Than Those Which Were Party to the Proceedings", in HAECK Y., BREMS E. (eds.), *Human Rights and Civil Liberties in the 21st Century*, Springer, Dordrecht, 2014, 223.

BOGDAN D., MUNGIU-PIPPIDI A., "The Reluctant Embrace: The Impact of the European Court of Human Rights in Post-Communist Romania", in ANAGNOSTOU D. (ed.), *The European Court of Human Rights: Implementing Strasbourg's Judgments on Domestic Policy*, Edinburgh University Press, Edinburgh, 2013, 71.

CALIGIURI A., NAPOLETANO N., *The Application of the ECHR in the Domestic Systems*, in Italian Yearbook of International Law, 20, 2010, 125–159.

CATALDI G., "La natura *self-executing* delle norme della CEDU e l'applicazione delle sentenze della Corte europea negli ordinamenti nazionali", in CALIGIURI A., CATALDI G., NAPOLETANO N. (eds.), *La tutela dei diritti umani in Europa tra sovranità statale e ordinamenti sovranazionali*, Cedam, Padova, 2010, 565.

CELIKSOY E., *Execution of the Judgments of the European Court of Human Rights in Prisoners' Right to Vote Cases*, in Human Rights Law Review, 20, 3, 2020, 555–581.

CHARLESWORTH H., *International Legal Encounters with Democracy*, in Global Policy, 8, 6, 2017, 34–43.

CHRISTIANO T., *The Constitution of Equality*, Oxford University Press, Oxford, 2008.

CORLĂŢEAN T., *Considerations regarding the Authority of the European Convention on Human Rights and Fundamental Freedoms and of the European Court on Human

Rights Jurisprudence on the National Law Systems in Some of the Member States, in International Law Review, 1, 2011, 1.

Corlăţean T., *Constitution of Romania as an Instrument for Incorporating International Standards of Human Rights Protection*, in Revista de Drept Public (Supliment pe anul 2014), 2014, 91–105.

Deaconu S., *Drepturile şi libertăţile fundamentale în sistemul constituţional românesc*, in Revista română de drept privat, 4, 2011, 32–55.

Donald A., Leach P., *Parliaments and the European Court of Human Rights*, Oxford University Press, Oxford, 2016.

Helfer L.R., *Redesigning the European Court of Human Rights: Embeddedness as a Deep Structural Principle of the European Human Rights Regime*, in European Journal of International Law, 19, 1, 2008, 125–159.

Heyns C., Viljoen F., *The Impact of the United Nations Human Rights Treaties on the Domestic Level*, Martinus Nijhoff Publishers, The Hague, 2002.

Keller H., Stone Sweet A. (eds.), *A Europe of Rights. The Impact of the ECHR on National Legal Systems*, Oxford University Press, Oxford, 2008.

Klein E., “Should the Binding Effect of the Judgments of the European Court of Human Rights Be Extended?”, in Mahoney P. et al. (eds.), *Protecting Human Rights: The European Perspective*, Heymann, Köln 2000, 705.

Lambert-Abdelgawad É., *Les effets des arrêts de la Cour européenne des droits de l’homme*, Bruylant, Bruxelles, 1999.

Marks S., *The European Convention on Human Rights and its ‘Democratic Society’*, in British Yearbook of International Law, 66, 1, 1995, 209–238.

Martinico G., Pollicino O. (eds.), *The National Judicial Treatment of the ECHR and EU Laws. A Comparative Constitutional Perspective*, Europa Law Pub Netherlands, Groningen, 2010.

Palanco A., *Le précédent dans la jurisprudence de la Cour européenne des droits de l’homme*, Bruylant, Bruxelles, 2019.

Rainey B., McCormick P., Ovey C., *Jacobs, White and Ovey: The European Convention on Human Rights*, 8th edn., Oxford University Press, Oxford, 2006.

Sundberg F.G.E., *The European Experience of Human Rights Proceedings: The Precedent Value of the European Court’s Decisions*, in Akron Law Review, 20, 1987, 629.

Tulkens F., *Execution and Effects of Judgments of the European Court of Human Rights: The Role of the Judiciary, Dialogue between Judges*, Council of Europe Publishing, Strasbourg, 2006.

Wildhaber L., “Precedent in the European Court of Human Rights”, in Mahoney P. et al. (eds.), *Protecting Human Rights: The European Perspective*, Heymann, Köln, 2000, 1529.

8 Right to vote and the right to have the last word

Russia and the European Court of Human Rights facing political rights

Simone Penasa

Introduction and context: The slow but steady encroachment of the Russia–ECtHR relationship through the lens of political rights protection

Russia is used to being one of the main "targets" for the European Court of Human Rights (ECtHR). According to the latest statistics provided by the ECtHR, Russia is the Member State which is the second most challenged before the Court.[1] At the same time, in the specific context of political rights, guaranteed especially by Article 3 of the Protocol 1, only in six cases has Russia been found to be in violation of the rights enshrined in this article. Thus, from a quantitative viewpoint it may appear bizarre to focus on this specific issue. Nevertheless, taking this perspective is crucial in order to understand the effective guarantee of the rule of law in the national order under analysis. As the specific analysis will show, the ECtHR's case-law in this context provided one of the more powerful triggers for the 2015 reform which entitled the Russian Constitutional Court to bar compliance with an ECtHR judgment where the latter is considered contrary to the Russian Constitution. Before entering into an in-depth analysis of the ECtHR's case-law involving Russia in the context of political rights, as enshrined in Art. 3 of Protocol 1, it is worth providing some general context in order to outline the evolution of the relationship between the CoE's framework of human rights protection and the Russian legal system. In order to do so, it is necessary to clarify the constitutional status through which international treaties are acknowledged at the constitutional level, as the concrete meaning and substantial scope of application of its constitutional basis (Art. 15, para 4, Russian Constitution) has been subject to very different interpretations among Russian and foreign scholars, as well as by the same Russian Constitutional Court.[2]

1 Source: Committee of Ministers, *Supervision of the execution of judgments and decisions of the European Court of Human Rights* (13th Annual Report of the Committee of Ministers 2019, Council of Europe, 2020).

2 On the general role of the Russian Constitutional Court in implementing human rights protection framework, see Khozikova E.S., Yakovlev K.L., Ezhevski D.O., Korabelnikova Y.L., *The Role of the Constitutional Court of Russian Federation in the Mechanism of Human Rights*

DOI: 10.4324/9781003229247-10

According to Art. 15, paragraph 4, of the Russian Constitution,

> Universally recognised principles and norms of international law as well as international agreements of the Russian Federation should be an integral part of its legal system. If an international agreement of the Russian Federation establishes rules, which differ from those stipulated by law, then the rules of the international agreement shall be applied.

Principles enshrined in this article have been given very different legal meanings, due essentially to a lack of a formal declaration of "constitutional supremacy."[3] Thus, though it is undisputed that the European Convention enjoys a priority rule before Russian federal laws, binding national courts not to apply the latter when a clash with the former raises (except when national laws provide for a higher level of protection),[4] on the contrary, the priority mechanism enforceable in case of conflict with the Constitution remains uncertain and open to debate by both legal scholars and the Russian courts, at least until the constitutional reform occurred in 2015 (see below). In very general terms, there is a variety of different meanings for the terms "national law" contained in Art. 15 of the Russian Constitution. They range from the identification of the absolute supremacy of the Constitution, according to an approach which seems to evoke the counter-limits theory in the European law context,[5] to the enforcement of the *pacta sunt servanda principle*, according to which States may not invoke national law – not even the Constitution – in order to justify the failure to enforce international treaty law.[6]

However, it must be underlined that, although no consensus is detectable, prevailing opinion favours the recognition of the primacy of the Constitution over international agreements.[7] The Russian Constitutional Court (RCC) has also floated between different interpretations, until it eventually came to embrace the theory of the constitutional supremacy in the leading case of N21-P.[8] It is worth noting that the consolidation of the RCC's case-law occurred in the context of clarifying the relationship between the ECtHR's judgments against Russia and national sources of law. It occurred progressively, as in previous cases the Court

---

Provision and Support: International and Domestic Aspects, in European Research Studies Journal, 2, 2018, 79–88.

3 STARZHENETSKIY V., "The Execution of ECtHR Judgments and the 'Right to Object' of the Russian Constitutional Court," in BREUER M. (ed.), *Principled Resistance to ECtHR Judgments – A New Paradigm?*, Berlin-Heidelberg, Springer, 2019, 249.

4 *Ibid.*

5 Critically on this GUAZZAROTTI A., *La Russia e la CEDU: i controlimiti visti da Mosca*, in Quaderni costituzionali, 2, 2016, 385.

6 STARZHENETSKIY V., *The Execution of ECtHR Judgments and the "Right to Object" of the Russian Constitutional Court*, cited above, 250.

7 AKSENOVA M., MARCHUK I., *Reinventing or rediscovering international law? The Russian Constitutional Court's uneasy dialogue with the European Court of Human Rights*, in I·CON, 16, 2019, 1335.

8 Russian Constitutional Court, judgment no. N21-P/2015, 14 July 2015.

stated that a judgment against Russia creates "international legal obligations not only to pay just satisfaction (…), but also to take other measures of general and individual character in order to put an end to violations."[9] Following this judgment, the RCC has progressively shifted towards more of a "sovereignty approach,"[10] which was aimed at guaranteeing the supremacy of the Constitution, as interpreted and enforced by the same Constitutional Court.[11] In order to do so, it claimed the power to assess whether an ECtHR's judgment against Russia goes against the Constitution and thus whether the former should be declared non-executable within the national legal order, when the incompatibility cannot be overcome and the non-execution is the only way to guarantee the Constitution's prevalence.

Also in the light of this process, it is possible to structure the ECHR–Russia relationship into what could be described as different "seasons," each of which recalls the progressive steps made by the RCC.[12] They have led to a gradual divergence over the interpretation of both the nature and functions of the ECHR between the ECtHR and Russian authorities. In very succinct terms, it is possible to identify at least three phases, through which the determination of the ECtHR's case-law on Art. 3, Protocol 1, ECHR, has played a decisive role, as the analysis provided below will show. While Russia's ratification of the ECHR has been defined as the "apogee" of the process of borrowing "Western patterns of the rule of law, human rights, and liberalism,"[13] opening up a decade of productive cooperation, the whole relationship has also been qualified as an "uneasy partnership,"[14] and a "non-linear process."[15] If interpreted through the lens of the ECtHR–RCC understanding of the very essence of the European Convention, it is possible to trace "Russia's growing resistance to the ECtHR"[16]

9 RCC, judgment no. N4-P/2010, 26 February 2010. See Starzhenetskiy V., *The Execution of ECtHR Judgments and the "Right to Object" of the Russian Constitutional Court*, cited above, 251.

10 Górski M., *Quo Vadis, Russia? On the Country's Recent Approach Towards Implementing Judgments of the European Court of Human Rights*, in Comparative Law Review, 23, 2017, 142.

11 Starzhenetskiy V., *The Execution of ECtHR Judgments and the "Right to Object" of the Russian Constitutional Court*, cited above, 257.

12 For a description of different phases which characterise the relationship between Russia and the European human rights system, see Benedek W., "Russia and the European Court of Human Rights: some general conclusions," in Mälksoo L., Benedek W. (eds.), *Russian and the European Court of Human Rights. The Strasbourg effect*, Cambridge University Press, Cambridge, 2017, 387–389.

13 Starzhenetskiy V., *The Execution of ECtHR Judgments and the "Right to Object" of the Russian Constitutional Court*, cited above, 246; see also Górski M., *Quo Vadis, Russia? On the Country's Recent Approach Towards Implementing Judgments of the European Court of Human Rights*, cited above, 153.

14 Nelaeva G., Khabarova E.A., Sidorova N.V., *Russia's Relations with the European Court of Human Rights in the Aftermath of the Markin Decision: Debating the "Backlash,"* in Human Rights Review, 21, 2020, 95.

15 Starzhenetskiy V., *The Execution of ECtHR Judgments and the "Right to Object" of the Russian Constitutional Court*, cited above, 255.

16 *Ibid.*

back to the clash between the RCC's originalist – better described as, sovereignty-based – approach to the interpretation of the Convention, and the more evolutionary approach implemented by the ECtHR, which is linked with the identification of the Convention as a living instrument.[17] The more the latter has been consolidated by the ECtHR, the more the former has characterised the RCC's case-law on the assessment of the binding nature of the ECtHR's judgments. This element, together with the feeling, manifested by the RCC,[18] that there was a risk of substantial subordination to the ECHR mechanism, contributed to fuelling the season of resistance which started from the turning-point case of *Markin v. Russia*,[19] which was the first case where a disagreement between the two courts arose.[20] The RCC claimed that there were limits to the scope and intensity of the ECtHR's scrutiny and subsequently claimed that it was competent to assess conflicts between the two jurisdictions and ultimately the power to declare non-executable the ECtHR's judgment.[21] In a subsequent judgment,[22] which further strengthened this approach, the Constitutional Court claimed the duty

> in the event of [the] emerging of any collisions in this field (…) to give preference to the requirements of the Constitution of the Russian Federation and thereby not follow literally the judgment of the European Court of Human Rights in the event of its execution contradicts constitutional values.[23]

17 Kahn J., *The Relationship between the European Court of Human Rights and the Constitutional Court of the Russian Federation: Conflicting Conceptions of Sovereignty in Strasbourg and St Petersburg*, in The European Journal of International Law, 30, 2019, 939, according to whom "the ECtHR's evolutive interpretations changed the convention's meaning in ways that Russia could not have accepted – because it was in conflict with its law – at the relevant time of agreement." Nelaeva G., Khabarova E.A., Sidorova N.V., *Russia's Relations with the European Court of Human Rights in the Aftermath of the Markin Decision: Debating the "Backlash,"* cited above, 104, refer to the abuse of ECtHR's right of evolutionary interpretation of the Convention, by referring to the RCC's line of reasoning.

18 Kahn J., *The Relationship between the European Court of Human Rights and the Constitutional Court of the Russian Federation: Conflicting Conceptions of Sovereignty in Strasbourg and St Petersburg*, cited above, 941 utilises the expression of "RCC's confrontational rejection of 'subordination'".

19 ECtHR, *Markin v. Russia*, Application no. 30078/06, 7 October 2010. See Vaypan G., *Acquiescence Affirmed, Its Limits Left Undefined: The Markin Judgment and the Pragmatism of the Russian Constitutional Court vis-à-vis the European Court of Human Rights*, in Russian Law Journal, 2, 3, 2014, 130–139.

20 See Issaeva M., Sergeeva I., Suchkova M., *Enforcement of the judgments of European Court of Human Rights in Russia: recent developments and current challenges*, in Sur international journal on human rights, 8, 2011, 78.

21 RCC, judgment no. N27-P/2013, 6 December 2013. See Mäger K., *Enforcing the Judgments of the ECtHR in Russia in Light of the Amendments to the Law on the Constitutional Court*, in Juridica International, 24, 2016, 17.

22 RCC, judgment no. N21-P/0215, 14 July 2015.

23 See critically the Venice Commission's Opinion no. 832/2015 *Final Opinion on the Amendments to the Federal Constitutional Law on the Constitutional Court* (2016).

This led to the opening of the "right to object" season, in which an *ad hoc* amendment to the federal constitutional Law on the Constitutional Court[24] went on to ratify the mechanism already designed by the RCC, which had by then acquired a veto power over the compatibility of the ECtHR's rulings and constitutional provisions or values.[25] Thus, the RCC had the ability to block the execution of an ECtHR judgment when, according to its own evaluation, two conditions were met: an ECtHR ruling goes against the Constitution and the alternative solution proposed would be "impossible to implement"[26] in a way that did not infringe upon essential constitutional rules and values.[27]

Since then, RCC has made use of this mechanism twice, thus confirming that the evolution of the relationship with the ECtHR can be intended to be viewed from a twofold perspective.

From an institutional perspective, it can be viewed as the enactment of the international relations idea of "sovereign democracy,"[28] which typically for the Russian legal system, aims at "securitizing" domestic legal traditions against non-native ideas.[29] The RCC has tried to compare its own approach with a more general confrontational trend with the ECtHR seen with many others Member States (such as the UK, Germany, and Italy). Nevertheless, the two waves do not appear to be directly comparable, as other States have never questioned the enforceability of ECtHR judgments in itself.[30] From a case-oriented perspective, this

24 Federal Constitutional Law "On Constitutional Court" N 7-FKZ, 14 December 2015. See Mäger K., *Enforcing the Judgments of the ECtHR in Russia in Light of the Amendments to the Law on the Constitutional Court*, cited above, 19; and Bowring B., "Russia's cases in ECtHR and the question of implementation," in Mälksoo L., Benedek W. (eds.), *Russian and the European Court of Human Rights. The Strasbourg effect*, cited above, 190–193.

25 Starzhenetskiy V., *The Execution of ECtHR Judgments and the "Right to Object" of the Russian Constitutional Court*, cited above, 260–261.

26 Chaeva N., *The Russian Constitutional Court and its Actual Control over the ECtHR Judgement in Anchugov and Gladkov*, in EJIL: Talk!, 26 April 2016 (URL: www.ejiltalk.org/the-russian-constitutional-court-and-its-actual-control-over-the-ecthr-judgement-in-anchugov-and-gladko/).

27 See Venice Commission (21) 8, according to which "The Constitutional Court may therefore be asked (only) to assess whether a specific form or modality (measure) of execution raises an issue of constitutionality (such cases should be rather exceptional)." Caligiuri A., *La recente giurisprudenza costituzionale russa sui rapporti tra Convenzione europea dei diritti umani e ordinamento interno*, in Diritti umani e diritto internazionale, 3, 2016, 706, refers to the "essential core" of a constitution.

28 Mäger K., *Enforcing the Judgments of the ECtHR in Russia in Light of the Amendments to the Law on the Constitutional Court*, cited above, 21.

29 Górski M., *Quo Vadis, Russia? On the Country's Recent Approach Towards Implementing Judgments of the European Court of Human Rights*, cited above, 153.

30 See again Venice Commission, *Final Opinion on the Amendments to the Federal Constitutional Law on the Constitutional Court*, cited above, 8; Aksenova M., Marchuk I., *Reinventing or rediscovering international law? The Russian Constitutional Court's uneasy dialogue with the European Court of Human Rights*, cited above, 1332, who consider the analogy with other countries "misleading." Górski M., *Quo Vadis, Russia? On the Country's Recent*

attitude appears to manifest as a more moderate and balanced implementation, as the RCC is used to referring to the need for a dialogue and a fair implementation of the ECtHR's judgments, as far as is achievable *via* interpretation. It is remarkable that, in assessing the domestic effect of the *Anchugov* case, the RCC tried to provide an interpretation consistent with both the ECHR and of Art. 32.4 of the Russian Constitution and to achieve a compromise between the constitutional identity and the international duties arguments by finding a "cautious way" to declare non-executable the ECtHR's judgment.[31] Undoubtedly, even if we adhere to an *in bonam partem* interpretation of Russian attitudes to the ECHR framework of human rights protection, the overall feeling is that Russian authorities have aimed to put pressure on the ECtHR, by making clear that the authority of the latter may now be openly dismissed by the highest judicial authority of a CoE Member State, thus undermining the scope of Art. 46 of the ECHR[32] and the power of penetration into the national legal system of the evolutionary interpretation of the Convention.

If we try to contextualise the evolution towards a more muscular and even sovereign(tist) approach to the ECHR framework, the analysis of the caseload involving Russia becomes relevant, from the perspective of both the total number and non-implemented judgments. According to the ECtHR's Annual Report 2019,[33] Russia has the highest number of pending cases before the Court (15,037), which represents 25% of the total workload. With regard to the number of violations which have been declared, in 2019 Russia has been found responsible for at least 1 violation in 186 cases across a total number of judgments which runs to 198. For the sake of this analysis, in 2019 Art. 3, Protocol 1, has not yet been applied against Russia. If we consider the total number of violations per Member State in the period covered by the 2019 Annual Report (1959–2019), only Turkey achieved a higher rank in the number of violations declared compared to Russia (3,225 violations against 2,551).

With specific regard to the right to free elections, Russia has been found in violation of Art. 3, Protocol 1, in six cases, which puts it outside the most condemned Member States.[34] From a more political and institutional perspective, it is worth noting that the President of the European Court of Human Rights in the Foreword to the Annual Report highlighted how crucial it was for the Council of Europe that the Parliamentary Assembly and the Committee of Ministers opted

---

Approach Towards Implementing Judgments of the European Court of Human Rights, cited above, 158, recalls the "specificity of the Russian approach."

31 Aksenova M., Marchuk I., *Reinventing or rediscovering international law? The Russian Constitutional Court's uneasy dialogue with the European Court of Human Rights*, cited above, 1337.

32 Marchuk I., *The Tale of Yukos and of the Russian Constitutional Court's Rebellion against the European Court of Human Rights*, in Rivista AIC, 6, 2017, 12, recalls the risk that the RCC will allow "cherry pick[ing of] decisions to be enforced on the territory of Russia".

33 ECHR, *Annual Report 2019* (2020).

34 Azerbaijan, 25; Italy, 17; Turkey, 11; United Kingdom, 8.

for Russia's continued membership of the Council of Europe. As stressed by the President,

> The fact that almost one quarter of all applications currently pending before the Court concern the Russian Federation gives some idea of the scale of the consequences Russia's departure from the Organisation would have had for a large number of applicants. Such an eventuality would have represented a serious setback for human rights in that part of our continent.[35]

These remarks, which link the institutional backlashes involving Russia and the effective protection of fundamental rights of its citizens, are based on two further elements, related respectively to the percentage of judgments effectively implemented by Russian authorities and to the diplomatic actions taken by Russia as a CoE Member State.

On one hand, according to the 2020 Report on "The implementation of judgments of the European Court of Human Rights,"[36] Russia, is among the Member States which have the highest number of non-implemented Court judgments and still face serious structural or complex problems, some of which have not been resolved for over ten years. Accordingly, Russia is also the Member State with the largest number of pending cases before the Committee of Ministers (1,663 in 2019; 1,585 in 2018). All the more, at the end of 2019 Russia was the State with more leading cases which had been pending for more than 5 years under enhanced supervision before the Committee of Ministers (38, together with Ukraine; 26). At the same time, in January 2019 the lower House of the Russian Parliament – the State Duma – voted not to send a delegation to the Council's Parliamentary Assembly and not to pay their financial contributions to the Council of Europe (€30 million), thus confirming a political standoff which started in 2017.[37] After having analysed the institutional and legal framework which characterises the relationship between Russia and the Council of Europe, the next section will be devoted to a categorisation of case-law linked to Art. 3, Protocol 1, of the Convention.

Analysis of the selected judgments: A categorisation of Art. 3, Protocol 1 case-law against Russia

As already anticipated, the ECtHR's case-law against Russia under the scope of Art. 3, Protocol 1, is not extensive. Russia has been found in violation of the right

35 ECHR (31) 7.

36 Committee on Legal Affairs and Human Rights, *The implementation of judgments of the European Court of Human Rights* (15 July 2020) 3, Parliamentary Assembly, Rapporteur Mr Constantinos Efstathiou, Doc. 15123.

37 From a broader perspective, on the possible political impact of the status of being a big payer within the CoE, see Fura E., Maruste R., "Russia's impact on the Strasbourg system, as seen by two former judges of the European Court of Human Rights," in Mälksoo L., Benedek W. (eds.), *Russian and the European Court of Human Rights. The Strasbourg effect*, cited above, 228.

to free elections only six times. At the same time, we have already stressed how influential the case-law in this context has been in terms of the reconfiguration of the RCC's scrutiny over the binding nature of ECtHR's judgments. Having said that, this section will categorise the existing case-law into three categories, taking as a distinctive parameter the specific right allegedly violated: firstly, the right to stand for election, from the perspective of both political parties and individual candidates; secondly, the right to vote, with a specific focus on cases concerning the disenfranchisement of prisoners; thirdly, the right to a democratic and fair electoral process, where it becomes central to the connection between the guarantees set forth by Art. 3, Protocol 1, and other freedoms, such as the freedom of expression or the freedom of press.

First category: The right to stand for the election and the right to vote for a favourite political party

There are three cases where Russia has been condemned for at least one violation within this category. Among them, a preliminary distinction must be introduced between suggested violations of the right for political parties to take part to elections, on the one hand, and the freedom to vote of citizens, which can be allegedly be infringed in the case of an illegitimate exclusion of a party from an election.[38] Within the scope of the right to stand for the election, a further distinction must be made between the political party's right to participate in elections, on the one hand, and the individual right to stand for as candidate within an electoral list.

Both rights, and their inner ramifications, are covered by Art. 3, Protocol 1, ECHR, as interpreted by the European Court, as in its case-law it has consistently affirmed that "implicit in Article 3 of Protocol No. 1 are the subjective rights to vote and to stand for election."[39] At the same time, the Court specifies that those rights are "not absolute,"[40] as there may be legitimate limitations and conditions for their exercise, in the determination of which Member States enjoy a wide margin of appreciation, as far as they do not affect "their very essence and deprive them of their effectiveness."[41] As will become clear after our case-by-case analysis, the level of scrutiny that the ECtHR applies to the two rights, that is – to stand for and to vote in the elections – is rather divergent. It is quite strict, when it comes to verifying the compatibility with the ECHR of a State's regulation and praxis where it aims at limiting the right of political parties or individual candidates to participate in elections, especially when procedural rules are in place to govern the right to take part to the election; on the contrary, it becomes broader when the individual right to vote for a preferred political party is involved, as the right

38 See the case ECtHR, *Russian Conservative Party of Entrepreneurs and Others v. Russia*, Applications nos. 55066/00 and 55638/00, 11 January 2007.

39 *Ibid.*, para. 48.

40 *Ibid.*

41 *Ibid.*

is allegedly being limited by the exclusion of the latter from political elections. This trend clearly emerges from the analysis of selected cases under this category.

In *Russian Conservative Party of Entrepreneurs and Others v. Russia*, the RCPE, a nationwide political party recognised by the law, and one of its candidates, were excluded from the elections to the State Duma of the Federal Assembly of the Russian Federation in 1999 by a decision of the Central Electoral Commission. The Commission refused to register the applicant party's list, as a consequence of the submission – required by the Elections Act – of "substantially inaccurate information about their income and property" made by 17 list candidates and accordingly it excluded them from the list. As one of them was the number two candidate on the list, the Central Electoral Commission refused to register the applicant party's list, by implementing the Elections Act provisions according to which

> if withdrawal of one or more candidates listed in the top three positions in the nationwide section of the approved federal list of candidates occurs (…), the Central Electoral Commission shall refuse to register the federal list of candidates or shall cancel such registration.[42]

The Commission's decision was only partially confirmed by the first-instance court (the Civil Division of the Supreme Court of the Russian Federation), which agreed with excluding the individual candidates, but declared unlawful the refusal to register the list in its entirety.[43] A key-argument was the interpretation of the term "withdraw" provided by the Elections Act, which the Civil Division interpreted in a narrow way, thus concluding that the term refers exclusively to a candidate's "voluntary" withdrawal and thus does not apply to a situation where one of the top three candidates had been struck off the list by a Commission's decision.[44] As a consequence, the Commission allowed the registration of the applicant party's list. More recently, on the initiative of the deputy Prosecutor General of the Russian Federation in the framework of a supervisory-review before the Presidium of the Supreme Court,[45] a broader interpretation of "withdrawal" was preferred by the Supreme Court, which agreed with the Prosecutor General in interpreting it as a "generic term which applied to any situation where a candidate was struck off the list."[46] The Presidium's ruling is binding for the Electoral Commission, which does not have any discretionary power in implementing it, and thus it was obliged as a matter of law to reverse its previous ruling and

42 Elections Act, Sec. 51. See ECtHR, *Russian Conservative Party of Entrepreneurs and Others v. Russia*, cited above, para. 35.

43 *Ibid.*, para. 13.

44 *Ibid.*

45 It is worth mentioning the influence exercised over the judiciary by political powers in Russia (see Tarchi R., *Sistema delle fonti e poteri normative dell'esecutivo in una forma di governo iper-presidenziale: il caso della Federazione Russa*, in Osservatorio sulle Fonti, 3, 2018, 23).

46 ECtHR, *Russian Conservative Party of Entrepreneurs and Others v. Russia*, cited above, para. 17.

therefore refused the applicant party's registration.[47] It is worth mentioning, in the light of the possible violation of Art. 13 ECHR (right to an effective remedy), that after the case the Russian Constitutional Court declared unconstitutional the part of the Elections Act, which provided for the refusal or cancellation of a party's registration in the event of the withdrawal of one of the top three candidates on the list, on the grounds that it amounted to a restriction on the other candidates' right to stand for election and on the citizens' right to vote for them.[48]

The ECtHR stuck to its own previous case-law and addressed the issue on its merits – the compatibility of the exclusion of both the party list and the individual candidate – and on the grounds of the existence of an effective remedy against the national bodies' decision. Accordingly, the European Court identified the issue in the respect of procedural fairness and legal certainty within the process for determining the eligibility to participate in the election.[49] By assuming a procedural perspective, the Court made safe Member State's discretionary power in selecting the most adequate electoral procedure in the light of its legal, political, and cultural background.[50] Once having confirmed that States' authorities have a wide margin of appreciation, the assessment of the respect of standards, such as legal certainty, which are very close to the very essence of a democratic legal order, becomes essential for the Court. Thus, the ECtHR recalled the principle according to which "Higher courts'" power to quash or alter binding and enforceable judicial decisions should be exercised for the correction of fundamental defects,[51] and not merely in the case of the existence of the mere possibility of two views on the same subject. In the case at hand, the fact that a national authority which was not part of the main proceedings – the deputy Prosecutor General – requested on its own motion to obtain a fresh determination of the issue that had been already settled by the Supreme Court's competent Division, shows that "the domestic authorities violated the principle of legal certainty in the procedure for determining the applicant party's and the second applicant's eligibility to stand in the elections."[52]

The ECtHR moved on to assessing whether the decision to exclude the list from the election was proportionate to the legitimate aim pursued, which in this instance was enabling voters to make an informed choice and to promote the overall fairness of elections by obliging candidates to disclose information on their property, earnings, and sources of income.[53] The Court assessed that this requirement did not appear *per se* unreasonable or arbitrary and nor did excluding a candidate that had intentionally omitted or misrepresented the required

47 *Ibid.*, para. 19.
48 *Ibid.*, para. 22.
49 *Ibid.*, para. 58.
50 *Ibid.*, para. 49.
51 *Ibid.*, para. 58.
52 *Ibid.*, para. 60.
53 *Ibid.*, paras. 61–62.

information from the list.[54] Nevertheless, in the case at hand, neither the applicant party nor the individual applicant was found to be in breach of the electoral laws, thus they were "sanctioned for circumstances which were unrelated to their own law-abiding conduct and were also outside their control."[55] This outcome, even in the light of the State's wide margin of appreciation, resulted in a disproportionate outcome, compared with the legitimate aim pursued, as stated also by the Russian Constitutional Court.[56] It inevitably led to the violation of Art. 3, Protocol 1, in respect of both the applicant party and the individual candidate.[57]

As anticipated, the Court did not consider illegitimate the aim pursued through the withdrawal mechanism, in light of both the wide margin of appreciation which States enjoy in regulating their own democratic and electoral process, and the reasonable aim of ensuring the truthful disclosure of the candidates' financial position, and promoting the integrity of electoral blocs or unions, as well as the overall fairness of elections. What was disproportionate is to extend the effects of such a violation not only to those candidates that clearly acted against the law, but to the entire party's list and therefore to all other candidates that had acted fairly. Significantly, the ECtHR recalled the Russian Constitutional Court' reasoning, where it considered that "disqualification of candidates and entire electoral alliances for reasons unrelated to their conduct unduly impaired their passive voting rights."[58]

In relation to compliance with Art. 13 of the Convention, the Court concluded that the applicants were denied an effective remedy, as the supervisory-review judgment of the Presidium of the Supreme Court was final, and no appeal mechanism was provided by the Russian legal order.[59] Specifically, only another supervisory-review judgment, which could only be activated by a motion of the deputy Prosecutor General and thus was not at applicants' disposal, would have provided a new assessment of the case. Thus, the remedy, even if formally provided by Russian law, was not effectively accessible to the applicants.

Even if the conventional grounds for the violation was Art. 13 ECHR, the lack of an effective remedy against the unlawful decision, which had the capacity to negatively impact on the effective exercise of the political rights by the political parties and the individuals represents, albeit indirectly a block against the effective implementation of the scope of Art. 3, Protocol 1. It may lead to the conclusion that Art. 3, Protocol 1, is able to be expressed not only in a multidimensional way, in light of the plurality of rights which have been derived from it by the ECtHR's case-law, but also an interdependent one, if we consider all the interactions which appear from its specific implementation and guarantee with other

54 *Ibid.*, para. 64.
55 *Ibid.*, para. 65.
56 *Ibid.*, para. 66.
57 *Ibid.*, para. 67.
58 *Ibid.*, para. 66.
59 *Ibid.*, para. 87.

conventional rights (such as the right to an effective remedy and, as we will see below, freedom of expression).

As anticipated, the stance of the ECtHR towards the alleged unjustified interference with the applicant party's supporter's right to vote, as a result of the exclusion of the party's list from the election, has been quite opposite. Responding to the third applicant's argument, according to which they were forced to change their voting preference, or alternatively to not cast their vote in the election at all, the Court started its reasoning by distinguishing this case from its precedents, where the disenfranchisement due to restrictions on the right to vote in law or in practice was the reason of the application.[60] Here, the supposed infringement derives from the fact that the third applicant couldn't cast his vote for a party of his choosing. According to the Court, the mere "frustrating voting intention" is not capable of grounding an arguable claim under the scope of Art. 3, Protocol 1, if the electoral system is able to provide – *de jure* and *de facto* – adequate substantial and procedural guarantees of the democratic nature of electoral process. By doing so, the Court listed a non-exhaustive catalogue of measures which are required to guarantee the right to vote, which become relevant also beyond the specific case at stake. Specifically, the free expression of people's opinion through ballots is assured by: the "participation of a plurality of political parties representing the different shades of opinion to be found within a country's population";[61] adequate and sufficient information about candidates are available to voters during the electoral campaign; the absence of any form of pressure or undue inducement in voting choices; the freedom to cast the vote "against all candidates" or a blank ballot.[62] In the specific case at stake, none of the previous conditions were lacking, thus the mere impossibility of voting for the favoured list is not per se sufficient to amount to a violation of the applicant's right to vote (para. 81). According to the Court's ruling, therefore, the mere intention to vote is not covered by Art. 3, Protocol 1, unless it is proved that evoked guarantees have not been concretely satisfied.[63]

Krasnov and Skuratov v. Russia[64] belongs to the first line of allegations and more precisely to the sub-group of cases represented by an applicant's exclusion from the elections, due to a failure to satisfy the personal information disclosure obligation required in order to be registered as a candidate.

Aside from the specific characteristics of the two applicants' cases, the Court grounded its reasoning on three common parameters: the nature of the required information; the good-faith of the applicant in managing the required personal information, even if the disclosure is *in concreto* defective, incomplete or even

60 *Ibid.*, para. 74.

61 *Ibid.*, para. 79.

62 *Ibid.*, para. 80.

63 It is worth mentioning that a similar application was dismissed in the context of *Yabloko Russian United Democratic Party and Others v. Russia*, see below.

64 ECtHR, *Krasnov and Skuratov v. Russia*, Applications nos. 17864/04 and 21396/04, 19 July 2007.

erroneous; and ultimately, the capacity it has to adversely affect the voters' ability to make an informed choice. With regard to the soundness of the requirement provided by Russian Elections Act and in line with the Russian Conservative Party case, the ECtHR confirms that "requiring a candidate for election to the national parliament to submit truthful information on their employment and party affiliation is a legitimate aim." The Court then considered the behaviour of the two applicants in the context of the above conditions. On the one hand, it considered that the first applicant did not act in good-faith in relation to his employment status – specifically by claiming that he was still carrying out a relevant administrative position at the local level, even if it was clear that he already ceased doing that work – and that the untrue information was not provided in good-faith, thus he had "knowingly submitted untrue information on his employment."[65] This unethical conduct becomes relevant in the finding that there was no violation of the first applicant's right to stand for elections once the Court assessed a causal link between the disclosure of false information, on the one hand, and the negative impact on voters' ability to make an informed electoral choice, on the other hand.[66] This conclusion is further strengthened by the nature of the information, which related to the office of the head of the district council where the elections were organised, which according to the Court was not a matter of indifference for the voters, all of whom were local residents.

The ECtHR reached an entirely different conclusion with regard to the second applicant's case, in which they were excluded by the local electoral commission for having declared themselves the head of a university department, instead of their real position as a professor within the same entity.[67] Contrary to the first applicant, according to the Court the criterion of the good-faith had been fulfilled by the second applicant and, in the light of the nature of the information,

> it could not be seriously maintained that the difference between the positions of professor and acting head of the same department was capable of misleading the voters. In any event, the second applicant was a well-known public figure because of his past employment as the Prosecutor General of the Russian Federation.[68]

It led the Court to conclude that a reasonable relationship of proportionality between that measure and the legitimate aim was lacking, thus it declared a breach of Art. 3, Protocol 3.

In *Yabloko Russian United Democratic Party and Others v. Russia*[69] the ECtHR was confronted again with the issue of the compatibility with Art. 3,

65 *Ibid.*, para. 49.
66 *Ibid.*, para. 50.
67 *Ibid.*, para. 58.
68 *Ibid.*, para. 62.
69 ECtHR, *Yabloko Russian United Democratic Party and Others v. Russia*, Application no. 18860/07, 8 November 2016.

Protocol 1, ECHR, of their exclusion of the applicant party's electoral list from the election, due to the fact that the regional party conference which called for the selection of candidates and the forming of party electoral lists was composed only of registered party members, and not party members in general, in breach of the Elections Act which guarantees equal rights of participation in party activities for all members. The case is especially relevant because it involves the limits and conditions that national laws may legitimately impose upon the political parties' right to freely organise their own internal organisation and activities, which contributes to establishing and maintaining the foundations of an effective and meaningful democracy governed by the rule of law. Similarly, in this case, the Court confirmed that Member States have a wide margin of appreciation in organising and running electoral systems and it therefore limited its scrutiny to two specific criteria: whether there had been arbitrariness or a lack of proportionality; and, whether the restriction had interfered with the free expression of the opinion of the people.[70]

As in previous cases, it seems that the protection of parties or candidates' rights is conceived by the Court as required for a major aim, that is to guarantee the fairness, impartiality and transparency of electoral procedures and the ability of voters to make free and non-biased electoral choices. In the light of this,

> the Court accepts that in certain cases, the States' margin of appreciation may include a right to interfere – subject to the condition of proportionality – with an association's internal organisation and functioning in the event of non-compliance with reasonable legal formalities applying to its establishment, functioning or internal organisational structure.[71]

However, in the case at stake, the Court must assess whether cancelling the registration of a party list for the reasons mentioned above is compatible with the principle of the rule of law, especially when legislative requirements are able to extensively affect the internal organisation of a political party and thus interfere with its autonomy. According to the Court, the applicant party's internal acts clearly provided for a difference between members and registered members with regard to their participation to nomination of candidates. All the more, the procedure was sufficiently transparent to ensure that every party member could determine the scope of his or her participation in its work by choosing whether or not to register with the local offices. Taking also into account that no complaints had been made by party members challenging the candidates selection procedure, the exclusion of the party list for solely formalistic reasons appears to the Court to be "clearly disproportionate."[72] For the sake of the influence that democratic principles produce in the Court's reasoning, such an exclusion "interfered dis-

70 *Ibid.*, para. 68.
71 *Ibid.*, para. 71.
72 *Ibid.*, para. 80.

proportionately with the party's own internal organisation, which followed the principles of transparency and representation, and resulted in its inability to participate in the regional elections," thus provoking a violation of Art. 3, Protocol 1, of the Convention.[73]

The right to vote: The case of prisoners' disenfranchisement

We have already referred to *Anchugov and Gladkov v. Russia*[74] as one of the cases (together with *Yukos*) which triggered the shift within the RCC case-law, ultimately leading to the reform of the Act on the Constitutional Court which gave the RCC the power to declare, under specific conditions, the ECtHR's judgment unenforceable. Here the case will be analysed in light of the assessment of the impact on the determination of the specific scope of the right to vote covered by Art. 3, Protocol 1, in the specific context of prisoners' rights.

As mentioned, this case is part of a long-lasting judicial stream which is confronting the ECtHR and Member States. Within this case-law, the distinctive element of *Anchugov* is that the disenfranchisement of prisoners has a constitutional nature, as Art. 32.3 of the Russian Constitution provides that "citizens detained in a detention facility pursuant to a sentence imposed by a court shall not have the right to vote or to stand for election." In this respect, the ECtHR tried to defuse the risk of a full-frontal clash with a Member State's Constitution, and indirectly with its Constitutional Court, by specifying that

> the Court's task in the present case is not to review, *in abstracto*, the compatibility with the Convention of the relevant provisions of Article 32 of the Russian Constitution, but to determine, *in concreto*, the effect of those provisions on the applicants' rights secured by Article 3 of Protocol 1 to the Convention.[75]

At the same time, it is resolute in affirming the general principle enshrined in Art. 3, Protocol 1, according to which "any departure from the principle of universal suffrage risks undermining the democratic validity of the legislature thus elected and the laws it promulgates" and that "exclusion of any group or categories of the general population must accordingly be reconcilable with the underlying purposes of Article 3 of Protocol No. 1." Nevertheless, a "severe measure of disenfranchisement" can be compatible with the Convention, as long as a discernible and sufficient link between the sanction and prisoners' conduct and circumstances is detectable, in the light of the proportionality test.[76] In interpreting

73 *Ibid.*, para. 81.
74 ECtHR, *Anchugov and Gladkov v. Russia*, Applications nos. 11157/04 and 15162/05, 4 July 2013.
75 *Ibid.*, para. 52.
76 *Ibid.*, para. 97.

the concrete scope of Art. 32.3, RC, the ECtHR did not adhere to the competent national court's interpretation of the ban. According to the national court, and later also the Constitutional Court, the constitutional provision applies only to those prisoners convicted of particularly serious offences and sentenced to a term of imprisonment of more than five years. In the ECtHR's view, this interpretation goes against the wording of Art. 32 RC and no domestic case-law has been adduced to confirm this view.[77] Thus, by interpreting literally the ban set forth by the Russian Constitution, the ECtHR concluded that the measure, even if aiming at achieving a legitimate aim (to enhance civic responsibility and respect for the rule of law and to ensure the proper functioning and preservation of civil society and a democratic regime), was disproportionate in its specific scope, as it is designed in a way which imposes a blanket restriction on all convicted prisoners serving their prison sentence.[78] According to the Court, therefore, it is not possible to establish any direct link between the facts of any individual cases and the removal of the right to vote, for instance in terms of the proportionality of disenfranchisement in the light of the particular circumstances of each case.

The supposed existence of a judicial praxis aimed at limiting the ban on voting rights only to convicted prisoners serving their custodial sentence in prison for particularly serious offences and sentenced to a term of more than five years[79] is not proved by any evidence, and there isn't any proof that the link between the sanction and the disenfranchisement is routinely taken into account by Russian courts. In declaring a violation of Art. 3, Protocol 1, due to the establishment of a blanket ban on prisoners' right to vote, it is worth mentioning that the ECtHR does not accept the sovereignty-based argument according to which the ban would fall outside the Court's scrutiny as it must be considered as the expression of "Russia's current democratic vision," profoundly rooted in the State's political history.[80] By highlighting that "the right to vote is not a privilege" and that the presumption in a democratic State must be in favour of inclusion and universal suffrage, the ECtHR seems – at least between the lines – to question the compatibility of this declaration of Russian constitutional identity when compared with the very essence of the European rule of law.

Anticipating an element which will be further developed in next section, the ECtHR leaves to the national authorities the right "to choose, subject to supervision by the Committee of Ministers, the means to be used in its domestic legal order in order to discharge its obligation under Article 46 of the Convention."[81] Among the potential implementable remedies, the Court suggests – the main interlocutor being the Russian Constitutional Court – favouring the interpretation of Art. 32 of the Russian Constitution in harmony with the Convention, in

77 *Ibid.*, para. 102.
78 *Ibid.*, para. 105.
79 *Ibid.*, para. 101, as alleged by respondent State.
80 *Ibid.*, para. 103.
81 *Ibid.*, para. 111.

order to coordinate their effects and avoid any conflict between them (para. 111). As we saw above, the Russian Constitutional Court did not follow this route and chose to start an open confrontation about the "ownership" of the right to the last word in assessing the compatibility – and thus the priority – between constitutional and conventional duties. In *Isakov and Others v. Russia*,[82] where a group of applicants raised the same issue of being barred from voting in elections as a consequence of their status as convicted prisoners, the ECtHR plainly confirmed the *Anchugov* reasoning and ruling.

The right to a democratic and fair electoral process: The inner link with other conventional freedoms

The third group of cases is related to the duty of Member States to guarantee the fairness, transparency, and accountability of the democratic process, especially during the electoral campaign and the processing of electoral results. They are especially relevant because they involve the effective enactment of both substantial and procedural measures which are functional to the exercise of the right to stand for the election and the right to vote. They show furthermore the existing link with other freedoms guaranteed by the Convention, such as freedom of expression and the freedom of the press during electoral campaigns, and the right to an effective remedy, against a possible violation of the rules during the counting of the electoral votes.

In *Davydov and Others v. Russia*[83] a group of applicants assumed that during local and federal elections which took place in St Petersburg in 2011, in which they participated as candidates, as well as voters and members of electoral commissions, that electoral commissions had falsified results by systematically assigning more votes to the ruling Yedinaya Rossiya (ER) party and its candidates, and stripping the opposition parties and candidates of their votes. According to the ECtHR's case-law, the manner in which the elections results are reviewed and potentially contested also falls within the scope of Art. 3, Protocol 1. In order that transparency, impartiality, and independence from political manipulation are guaranteed, the process of counting and formalising election results is crucial and thus national competent authorities must comply with a number of recommendations while performing these duties.[84] The observation by members across the whole political spectrum, including the opposition, represents an essential requirement for ensuring voters' freedom to express their will and the need to combat electoral fraud. Thus, the compliance of the whole electoral process with these principles is part of the common principles of the European constitutional heritage, which form the basis of any genuinely democratic society,

82 ECtHR, *Isakov and Others v. Russia*, Applications nos. 54446/07 and 23 others, 4 July 2017.

83 ECtHR, *Davydov and Others v. Russia*, Application no. 75947/11, 30 May 2017.

84 *Ibid.*, para. 283.

and it guarantees the freedom to cast a vote in universal, equal, free, secret and direct elections.[85]

When it came to implementing such a standard, the Court, however, took into consideration the highly technical nature of the vote-counting procedure, thus requiring less stringent scrutiny, in which a violation can only occur in the event that two conditions are met: if there is evidence of procedural breaches that would be capable of thwarting the free expression of the opinion of the people, for instance through a gross distortion of the voters' intent; and, where such complaints have received no effective examination at the domestic level.[86] In the case in question, a number of *de facto* elements which characterised the recounting process – such as the proven absence of transparency and notification at the level of territorial commissions, the widespread absence of opposition parties' representatives when the decision to conduct recounts were taken and also when the recounts took place, the systematic recounting of votes on a massive scale, the speed of recounting procedures, the relevant number of votes reassigned after recounting systematically favouring leading party – led the Court to conclude that the fairness of the elections had been seriously compromised by the procedure in which votes had been recounted, potentially leading to a "gross distortion of the voters' intentions."[87]

As to the second requirement – the effective examination of applicants' complaints by the national authorities – the ECtHR found a widespread negligence in seriously assessing the evidence pointing to gross and widespread breaches of procedure and transparency requirements, which led national courts essentially to endorse the electoral commission's decision without performing any real examination of the reasons for complaints. Thus, "domestic courts did not ensure a procedure which could comply with the requirement to provide sufficient guarantees against arbitrariness in the review of an arguable claim of serious violations of electoral rights."[88] Therefore, the Court declared a violation of the individuals' right to free elections guaranteed under Art. 3, Protocol 1, in its active and passive dimension, insofar as an effective examination of complaints of serious irregularities in the procedure in which votes were recounted had not been provided by competent national authorities.

In *Communist Party of Russia and Others v. Russia*,[89] the applicant party alleged a violation of Art. 3, Protocol 1, due to the biased coverage of the 2003 parliamentary election campaign by the major TV stations, which was unfair to opposition parties and candidates as TV channels in fact campaigned for the ruling party (United Russia). They grounded their complaints on both statistical data on the airtime reserved to each running party and on the fact that news

85 *Ibid.*, para. 285.
86 *Ibid.*, para. 288.
87 *Ibid.*, para. 311.
88 *Ibid.*, para. 334.
89 ECtHR, *Communist Party of Russia and Others v. Russia*, Application no. 29400/05, 19 June 2012.

and informational TV programmes were not neutral in providing information to citizens. In sum, the applicants claimed that the "*de jure* neutrality of five nationwide channels did not exist *de facto*."[90]

The Court did not assert any breach of Art. 3, Protocol 1. The Court's reasoning tackled three issues, none of which is considered well-grounded. Firstly, the ECtHR agreed with the Russian Supreme Court that there was no evidence able to reasonably support the existence of a manipulation of media by the government and that it was, as a matter of principle, very difficult to quantify the effect of media coverage on election's results.[91] Secondly, according to the ECtHR, the State adequately fulfilled its positive obligation under Art. 3, Protocol 1, to ensure that "media coverage by the State-controlled mass-media was balanced and compatible with the spirit of 'free elections'" by ensuring the availability of a domestic system for the effective examination of individual complaints in matters concerning electoral rights (in the case at hand, the access to the Supreme Court).[92] Thirdly, as to the State's substantive positive obligations, Russia had positively fulfilled the duty to secure a pluralism of views by guaranteeing – through a system of free spaces for political communication on the major State-controlled TV media – to the opposition parties "at least minimum visibility."[93]

The reference to a minimum standard of pluralism seems to suggest that the Court, after having reaffirmed the State's wide margin of appreciation and the existence of different democratic visions which may characterise each Member State, applied a fairly broad – even weak – scrutiny of the assessment of both the legislative and *de facto* system of political broadcasting during the electoral campaign. The same cautious approach characterises also the scrutiny of the guarantee of the neutrality of the audio-visual media. According to the Court, no violation of this "duty of neutrality"[94] is appreciable, as the respondent State "took certain steps to guarantee some visibility of opposition parties and candidates on Russian TV and secure editorial independence and neutrality of the media," even if the same Court "admits" that "probably, these arrangements did not secure de facto equality of all competing political forces in terms of their presence on TV screens."[95] Notwithstanding this, the divergence between *de jure* and *de facto* neutrality and pluralism does not achieve a sufficient level of relevance so as to trigger a violation of the State's positive obligation. Even if coming to an opposite result compared to the previous one, this case seems to confirm that when it is called upon to evaluate States' organisation of electoral processes, the ECtHR makes reference to the wide national margin of appreciation to confine itself to merely assessing the procedural legality of measures implemented, on the one hand, and the existence of an effective and fair judicial remedy to which interested

90 *Ibid.*, para. 112.
91 *Ibid.*, paras. 116–119.
92 *Ibid.*, para. 124.
93 *Ibid.*, para. 126.
94 *Ibid.*, para. 127.
95 *Ibid.*, para. 128.

parties or candidates shall appeal against possible violations and failures within different phases of the electoral process, on the other hand.

As to reparation measures following the violation of Art. 3, Protocol 1, the Court is used, at least within the case-law analysed, to acknowledging applicants' monetary just satisfaction, as occurred in *Russian Conservative Party* (RUR 2,315,520 in respect of pecuniary damage), *Krasnov and Skutarov* (to the second applicant, EUR 8,000 in respect of non-pecuniary Damage) and *Davydov* (EUR 7,500 each, plus any tax that may be chargeable, in respect of non-pecuniary damage, to Mr Davydov, Mr Belyakov, Mr Truskanov, and Ms Pushkareva). On the contrary, no just satisfaction was required in *Yabloko*, as applicants did not submit a claim for just satisfaction. *Anchugov and Gladkov* represents an exception within the case-law. This is accurate not only for the systemic consequences which the ECtHR's judgment contributed to producing within the Russian legal order, but also for the Court's ruling, which did not recognise any just satisfaction for the appellants, arguing that "the finding of a violation constitutes in itself sufficient just satisfaction for any non-pecuniary damage sustained by the applicants" and dismissing their claim for pecuniary damages. At the same time, as a general measure, the Court asked the State to choose, among various approaches to addressing the issue of disenfranchisement and subject to supervision by the Committee of Ministers, the means to be used in its domestic legal order in order to discharge its obligation under Article 46 of the Convention. Thus, it left it to the respondent Government to explore all the possible ways it could act to meet that obligation and to decide whether their compliance with Art. 3 of Protocol No. 1 could be achieved through some form of political process (such as the amendment of the relevant constitutional provision or legislative reform) or by interpreting the Russian Constitution in harmony with the Convention in such a way as to coordinate their effects and avoid any conflict between them.

Analysis of the legal and economic impact of the implementation of ECtHR judgments at the national level

In this section, we will briefly tackle the level of implementation of judgments analysed above, and then we will also focus on the legislative and institutional impact that they have produced within the Russian system. Inevitably, Anchogov and Gladkov case will be the object of special consideration, as the ECtHR explicitly asked the Russian authorities to implement general measures in order to guarantee the full respect of Art. 46 ECHR and more broadly the physiology of the relationship between the ECtHR and the RCC.

As to the first dimension, in both *Russian Conservative Party* and *Krasnov and Skuratov* pecuniary and non-pecuniary damages were diligently paid. Although the judgments did not require any specific individual or general measure to be implemented by Russia, it must be underlined that with regard to *Russian Conservative Party*, the Russian Constitutional Court declared unconstitutional the national provision which was the source of the violation (Section 51.11, 1999 Elections Act), thus according to the Council of Ministers the source of the violation has been eliminated and no further general measures are necessary in this respect.[96] With regard to *Krasnov and Skuratov*, legislative reform clarified the consequences of a failure to submit accurate information by a potential candidate for elections about his or her curriculum vitae. In these cases, the election commissions now have the duty to provide a candidate with an opportunity to correct or submit the relevant information.[97] According to the quoted Resolution,

> the law is now clear and does not allow the authorities to refuse or cancel the registration of a candidate to stand for federal parliamentary elections on the ground of having submitted inaccurate information about his or her curriculum vitae.

If with regard to *Yabloko*[98] and *Davydov*[99] the Committee of Ministers does not publish any Report on the ongoing state of the judgments' implementation, with regard to *Anchugov and Gladkov* it reached a final evaluation which seems to have put an end, at least in terms of judgment's implementation, to the "saga" between the ECtHR and the RCC. As already mentioned, in the latter case no individual measure was required. Instead, the ECtHR asked Russia to adopt general measures in order to relax the absolute ban for prisoners' vote enshrined in the Constitution. In its final Resolution,[100] the Committee of Ministers acknowledged that the Russian Constitutional Court, even if it activated a blocking mechanism with regard to the judgment's execution at the national level, it suggested the possibility that the federal legislature could optimise the criminal punishment system, so that some criminal sanctions, even if entailing a compulsory restriction of freedom, would not involve restrictions on voting rights. On January 2017, a new category of criminal punishment – community work – was introduced into the Criminal Code in cases of non-serious or medium gravity offences (or if a serious offence is committed for the first time). According to Russian criminal law, community work does not amount to a measure depriving the individual of their freedom (Criminal code, Art. 43–59), even if the condemned person is not allowed to leave the correctional centre without the permission of the competent authorities (Art. 60.4). This reform, together with other minor measures aimed

96 Resolution CM/ResDH(2018)17, *Execution of the judgments of the European Court of Human Rights Two cases against Russian Federation*, adopted by the Committee of Ministers on 10 January 2018 at the 1303rd meeting of the Ministers' Deputies.

97 Basic Guarantees of Electoral Rights Act, as reformed in 2016, Sec. 38 (1.1).

98 See info at https://hudoc.exec.coe.int/eng#{%22tabview%22:[%22document%22],%22EXECIdentifier%22:[%22004-47003%22]}.

99 See info at https://hudoc.exec.coe.int/eng#{%22fulltext%22:[%22davydov%22],%22EXECDocumentTypeCollection%22:[%22CEC%22],%22EXECIdentifier%22:[%22004-48323%22]}.

100 See info at https://hudoc.exec.coe.int/eng#{%22tabview%22:[%22document%22],%22EXECIdentifier%22:[%22004-14110%22]}.

at decreasing the number of convicted persons and thus the number deprived of the right to vote, contributed to reducing the prison population by 7% in 2018 (compared to 2017) and by 17.2% (compared to 2013). For all these reasons, the Committee of Ministers concluded that the blanket ban on prisoners' right to vote can no longer be considered in place and that, also in the light of the wide margin of appreciation to be provided to States in this context, the measures adopted by Russian authorities appear to be capable of guaranteeing the adequate execution of the *Achugov* judgment. [101]

Conclusion: The last word or parallel worlds? Procedural scrutiny as a medium between sovereignty-based and evolutionary theories of the ECHR

We started this contribution by suggesting that it might sound "bizarre" to focus on Russia's engagement with Art. 3, Protocol 1, before the ECtHR, taking into account the limited number of violations in this context compared with the traditional role of the "prime target" of Russia within the ECtHR's case-law. Notwithstanding this, the analysis carried out from a broader and institutional perspective, and with a specific focus on judgments connected with Art. 3, Protocol 1, has shown that if this feeling can be justified when limiting the focus to a quantitative assessment, it becomes quite the opposite if the limited number of judgments is assessed in the light of both its impact on the internal constitutional order and its relevance within the ECtHR case-law on political rights.[102]

If we quantitatively look at the cases analysed, we can conclude that they are number very few and the judgments are usually executed by Russian authorities. This is true if we consider the enactment of individual measures, which – as we saw above – are not so frequent, as the ECtHR seems to be used to considering that the finding of a violation constitutes in itself sufficient just satisfaction for any non-pecuniary damage sustained by the applicants. But it is also true if we look to what can be defined as the "spontaneous" adaptation to ECtHR's judgments, particularly in the absence of a formal request to implement general measures. This has occurred through the declaration of the unconstitutionality of provisions which were the reason for ECHR's violation and the subsequent adaptation of national laws in line with the ruling of the Court. This outcome is even more significant when compared with the general attitude of Russia in guaranteeing the effective implementation of the ECtHR's judgments, as it – according to the Parliamentary Assembly Report on The implementation of judgments of the European Court of Human Rights (2020) – is routinely among the group of

101 See Padskocimaite A., *Case Closed, but what about the Execution of the Judgment? The closure of Anchugov and Gladkov v. Russia*, in EJIL: Talk!, 30 October 2019.

102 And also from the perspective of the broader condition of political opponents in Russia and the consequent ECtHR' case-law, see Lizzi L., *The (mal)functioning of the Russian justice system in cases involving political opponents and the European Court of Human Rights*, in La Comunità Internazionale, 1, 2017, 59–82.

Member States with "the highest number of non-implemented Court judgments and still face serious structural or complex problems, some of which have not been resolved for over ten years."[103]

Within this framework, *Anchugov* can be considered as the exception. But, as clarified, it represents an exception which contributed to triggering the most remarkable shift in Member State–ECtHR relationships in terms of ownership of the right to the last word over the binding nature and in general the effective enforceability of ECtHR's judgments at the national level. As shown, legal scholarship is divided in interpreting the confrontation which involved the Russian Constitutional Court and the ECtHR and in particularly the exact extent and scope of both the RCC's 2016 ruling and the related legislative reform. After having ascertained the attitude of the Committee of Ministers to the execution of the *Anchugov* ruling by the Russian Constitutional Court,[104] it seems that there are two ways of reading it.[105]

From a formalistic stance, Russian authorities have taken a diplomatic approach, as the interpretation provided by the Constitutional Court of Art. 32.3 RC at least allowed the constitutionally oriented execution of *Anchugov*.[106] This interpretation would be sealed by the closure of the Action Report against Russia by the Committee of Ministers, which concluded that the blanket ban on prisoners' right to vote can no longer be considered to be in place in Russia. According to this perspective, the RCC tried to provide for an interpretation consistent with both the ECHR and of the Russian Constitution and to reconcile the safeguard of the Russian "constitutional identity" and the fulfilment of its "international duties," by finding a cautious way – at least *in abstracto* – to declare non-executable the ECtHR's judgment.[107] Instead, a more context-driven approach may lead to understanding the events in the light of the State's desire to impose a sovereignty-based conception of the relationship with the ECHR system, with the aim of challenging the idea of the Convention as a living instrument, or at least to subordinate this evolutionary approach to States' approval, and to claim the right

103 Committee on Legal Affairs (34) 3.

104 As we saw above, the Committee acknowledged that the combination of the RCC's ruling and subsequent legislative reforms was capable of guaranteeing the adequate execution of ECtHR's judgment.

105 For an in-depth analysis from a different perspective, see Blankenagel A., *The Relationship between the European Court of Human Rights and the Constitutional Court of the Russian Federation: A Reply to Jeffrey Kahn*, in The European Journal of International Law, 3, 2019, 961–969, that is more incline to accept the RCC's perspective.

106 Aksenova M., Marchuk I., *Reinventing or rediscovering international law? The Russian Constitutional Court's uneasy dialogue with the European Court of Human Rights*, cited above, 1337, state that it "can be implemented in what concerns general measures ensuring fairness, differentiation, and proportionality of the restrictions on voting rights." Caligiuri A., *La recente giurisprudenza costituzionale russa sui rapporti tra Convenzione europea dei diritti umani e ordinamento interno*, cited above, 710, refers to a compromise positively evaluated by the Venice Commission.

107 *Ibid.*

to object to the execution of the ECtHR's judgments, even if this institutional "weapon" is conceived and enforced as a last resort tool.[108]

If we look to the ECtHR's reasoning, from the cases analysed above it is possible to derive some general conclusions related to the nature and intensity of the scrutiny implemented by the same Court when assessing the State's choice in the context of electoral process and their impact on parties, candidates and voters' political rights.

The Court never assesses the State's choice *in abstracto*, as it constantly affirms the existence of a wide margin of appreciation according to which States remain free to select the electoral system most suitable and adequate for their own "democratic vision."[109] It emerges from the analysis of these cases that the Court is inclined to consider legitimate the aims pursued by the measures subject to scrutiny, even when they may lead to a limitation of applicants' rights: to ensure the truthful disclosure of the candidates' financial position and promoting the integrity of electoral blocs or unions, as well as the overall fairness of elections (*Russian Conservative Party*); to guarantee fairness, impartiality, and transparency of electoral procedures, and the ability of voters to make free and non-biased electoral choices (*Yabloko*); to enhance civic responsibility, respect for the rule of law, and ensure the proper functioning and preservation of civil society and democratic regime (*Anchugov*); to guarantee the freedom of casting a vote in universal, equal, free, secret, and direct elections (*Davydov*); and to secure a pluralism of views (*Russian Communist Party*).

Accordingly, the Court's assessment is limited to verifying whether the measures enacted are able to impair the "very essence" of rights guaranteed under Art. 3, Protocol 1, and to "deprive them of their effectiveness."[110] In performing this assessment, the Court seems to prefer a procedural approach, which quite often is aimed at verifying whether an effective judicial remedy against potentially illegitimate measures was enforceable by the applicants. This happened for instance in *Russian Conservative Party*, where the lack of an effective remedy against the unlawful decision led to a negative impact on the effective exercise of the political rights of parties and individuals representing, at least an indirect block to the effective implementation of the scope of Art. 3, Protocol 1. In addition, when it is called to evaluate how States have organised their electoral processes, the ECtHR use the reference to the wide national margin of appreciation to confine itself to merely assessing the procedural legality of measures implemented, on the one hand, and the existence of an effective and fair judicial remedy to which interested parties or candidates are able to appeal against possible violations and failures within different phases of the electoral process. The existence of effective

108 Dzehtsiarou K., Golubok S., Timofeev M., *Imaginary Dialogue and Fictitious Collaboration: Russian Response to the Prisoner Voting Judgment*, in ECHR Blog, 29 April 2016 (URL: http://echrblog.blogspot.com/2016/04/) highlight that the RCC's "gesture is strongly symbolic" and involves "the integrity and legitimacy of the Strasbourg system."

109 *Anchugov* para. 95.

110 *Ibid.*, para. 96.

remedies acts as *fil rouge* between the cases analysed: it can become relevant as direct parameter in the Court's assessment (Art. 13 ECHR), as well as a standard for assessing State's compliance of duties deriving from Art. 3, Protocol 1.

Bibliography

AKSENOVA M., MARCHUK I., *Reinventing or rediscovering international law? The Russian Constitutional Court's uneasy dialogue with the European Court of Human Rights*, in I·CON, 16, 2019, 1335.

BENEDEK W., "Russia and the European Court of Human Rights: some general conclusions", in MÄLKSOO L., BENEDEK W. (eds.), *Russian and the European Court of Human Rights. The Strasbourg effect*, Cambridge University Press, Cambridge, 2018.

BLANKENAGEL A., *The Relationship between the European Court of Human Rights and the Constitutional Court of the Russian Federation: A Reply to Jeffrey Kahn*, in The European Journal of International Law, 3, 2019, 961–969.

BOWRING B., "Russia's cases in ECtHR and the question of implementation", in MÄLKSOO L., BENEDEK W. (eds.), *Russian and the European Court of Human Rights. The Strasbourg effect*, Cambridge University Press, Cambridge, 2018.

CALIGIURI A., *La recente giurisprudenza costituzionale russa sui rapporti tra Convenzione europea dei diritti umani e ordinamento interno*, in Diritti umani e diritto internazionale, 3, 2016, 703–711.

CHAEVA N., *The Russian Constitutional Court and its Actual Control over the ECtHR Judgement in Anchugov and Gladkov*, in EJIL: Talk!, 26 April 2016.

DZEHTSIAROU K., GOLUBOK S., TIMOFEEV M., *Imaginary Dialogue and Fictitious Collaboration: Russian Response to the Prisoner Voting Judgment*, in ECHR Blog, 29 April 2016.

FURA E., MARUSTE R., "Russia's impact on the Strasbourg system, as seen by two former judges of the European Court of Human Rights", in MÄLKSOO L., BENEDEK W. (eds.), *Russian and the European Court of Human Rights. The Strasbourg effect*, Cambridge University Press, Cambridge, 2018.

GÓRSKI M., *Quo Vadis, Russia? On the Country's Recent Approach Towards Implementing Judgments of the European Court of Human Rights*, in Comparative Law Review, 23, 2017, 139–158.

GUAZZAROTTI A., *La Russia e la CEDU: i controlimiti visti da Mosca*, in Quaderni costituzionali, 2, 2016, 383–386.

ISSAEVA M., SERGEEVA I., SUCHKOVA M., *Enforcement of the judgments of European Court of Human Rights in Russia: recent developments and current challenges*, in Sur International Journal On Human Rights, 8, 2011, 67–89.

KAHN J., *The Relationship between the European Court of Human Rights and the Constitutional Court of the Russian Federation: Conflicting Conceptions of Sovereignty in Strasbourg and St Petersburg*, in The European Journal of International Law, 30, 2019, 933–959.

LIZZI L., *The (mal)functioning of the Russian justice system in cases involving political opponents and the European Court of Human Rights*, in La Comunità Internazionale, 1, 2017, 59–82.

MÄGER K., *Enforcing the Judgments of the ECtHR in Russia in Light of the Amendments to the Law on the Constitutional Court*, in Juridica International, 24, 2016, 14–22.

MARCHUK I., *The Tale of Yukos and of the Russian Constitutional Court's Rebellion against the European Court of Human Rights*, in Osservatorio AIC, 6, 2017, 1–12.

NELAEVA G., KHABAROVA E.A., SIDOROVA N.V., *Russia's Relations with the European Court of Human Rights in the Aftermath of the Markin Decision: Debating the "Backlash"*, in Human Rights Review, 21, 2020, 93–112.

PADSKOCIMAITE A., *Case Closed, but what about the Execution of the Judgment? The closure of Anchugov and Gladkov* v. *Russia*, in EJIL: Talk!, 30 October 2019.

STARZHENETSKIY V., "The Execution of ECtHR Judgments and the 'Right to Object' of the Russian Constitutional Court", in BREUER M. (ed.), *Principled Resistance to ECtHR Judgments – A New Paradigm?*, Springer, Berlin-Heidelberg, 2019.

TARCHI R., *Sistema delle fonti e poteri normative dell'esecutivo in una forma di governo iper-presidenziale: il caso della Federazione Russa*, in Osservatorio sulle Fonti, 3, 2018, 1–30.

VAYPAN G., *Acquiescence Affirmed, Its Limits Left Undefined: the Markin Judgment and the Pragmatism of the Russian Constitutional Court vis-à-vis the European Court of Human Rights*, in Russian Law Journal, 2, 3, 2014, 130–140.

9 Democracy and the right to free elections in Turkey

What role for the European Court of Human Rights?

*Valentina Rita Scotti**

A protected democracy with authoritarian drifts

Since its establishment as a Republic (1923), Turkey has built a "democracy under custody" mainly controlled by the military and other institutions, such as the Judiciary, forming the so-called Republican Alliance.[1] It is for this reason that every time the pillars upon which the republican system was founded have been endangered by divergent political majorities, the Army has intervened with declarations – and when that proved insufficient – by staging coups d'état, following which a new Constitution was approved.[2] This trend engendered a minimalist approach to constitutionalism[3] and the establishment of a "militant democracy," according to which strong limits have been introduced to the freedom of expression and to engage in any political discourse which has the potential to harm the integrity of the State[4] or the principle of secularism.[5]

* Associate Professor in Comparative Public Law, European Law and Governance School – EPLO, Athens, Greece.

1 Belge C., *Friends of the Court: The Republican Alliance and Selective Activism of the Constitutional Court in Turkey*, in L. & Soc. Rev., 2006, 40, 653, 671–674, Narli N., *Civil–Military Relations in Turkey*, in Turkish Studies, 2000, 12, 107; Hale W., *The Turkish Army in Politics, 1960–73*, in Finkel A., Sarman N. (eds), *Turkish State, Turkish Society*, London, 1990, 53.

2 The 1961 and 1982 Constitutions were indeed approved after military coups d'état. For details on the Turkish constitutional history, see Özbudun E., Gençkaya Ö.F., *Democratization and the Politics of Constitution-Making in Turkey*, Budapest, 2009, 7.

3 See Isiksel T., *Between text and context: Turkey's tradition of authoritarian constitutionalism*, in International Journal of Constitutional Law, 2013, 13, 702.

4 The obsession with the integrity of the State originates both from the difficulties the founding elite had in having the current territory recognised as a Republic at the time of the disintegration of the Ottoman Empire (Treaty of Sevres – 1921), and from the controversial clauses relating to ethnic and religious minorities in the Treaty of Lausanne (1923). See Schmid D., *Turquie: le syndrome de Sèvres, ou la guerre qui n'en finit pas*, in Politique étrangère, 2014, 1, 199.

5 It is a pillar principle in Turkish constitutional history because it was on the basis of this that the country could distance itself from its Ottoman past. See Üksül Z.Ö., *L'affirmation de la laïcité en Turquie: un gage de modernité*, in Politique et sécurité internationales, 1999, 3, 20. For a comment on the limits the protection of this principle entailed for democracy, see also Ertan A., *The Tension between Secularism and Democracy in Turkey: Early Origins, Current*

DOI: 10.4324/9781003229247-11

The 1982 Constitution, currently in force, still bears the signs of this authoritarian spirit[6] in spite of the process of reforms it went through at the end of the 1990s. It is worth noting that most of the democratising reforms which came about during the so-called "reformist decade" (2000–2010) were realised by the religiously inspired *Adalet ve Kalkinma Partisi* (Justice and Development Party – AKP), whose interest in reforming the legal system's approach to secularism also opened up the dialogue with minorities, including the secessionist groups among Kurds.[7] Nevertheless, during the last decade of the 21st century, a decisive U-turn characterised AKP's policies, which sought to deeply exploit the authoritarian spirit of the 1982 Constitution in order to secure power. Indeed, the Executive has been empowered at the expense of the Grand National Assembly of Turkey (GNAT),[8] and notably at the expense of the political opposition's negotiating margins. During the war in Syria, the attempts to solve the Kurdish issue were also terminated and assimilationist policies were renewed in the framework of the territorial control of the south-eastern border.

The dialogue on the issue of democracy between Turkey and the European Court of Human Rights (henceforth ECtHR or the Court) should be framed in this context. Notably, the present contribution aims at assessing to what extent the judgments against Turkey for a violation of Art. 3 of Protocol 1 of the European Convention of Human Rights (ECHR) impinge on the domestic legislation and whether they have acted as a stimulus for the reforms within the wider framework of the CoE monitoring system. With this aim, an overview of the relationship between Turkey and the Strasbourg system, as well as of the relevant Turkish domestic legislation, is provided. Subsequently, an analysis will be carried out of the judgments in which a violation of Art. 3 of Protocol 1 has been found. Methodologically, the analysis of these cases focuses only on the arguments concerning the violation of Art. 3 of Protocol 1 with limited references to the alleged violation of other ECHR provisions. The aim is to underscore the inconsistencies of the Turkish legislation with the right to free elections according to the current interpretation of the ECtHR, contributing to the existing scholarship by questioning whether the costs deriving from the failure to implement the CoE's standard of democracy have impinged on the introduction of systemic reforms. In this vein, a section is devoted to dealing with the Turkish mechanism of compliance with the ECtHR's judgments and its functioning in the implementation

Legacy, in European View, 2007, 6, 11.

6 The renowned Turkish scholar Bülent Tanör defined the 1982 Constitution as a dysfunctional one (see Tanör B., *Türkiye'nin Insan Hakları Sorunu* Istanbul, 1990, 352).

7 See Pusane Ö.K., *Turkey's Kurdish opening: Long awaited achievements and failed expectations*, in Turkish Studies, 2014, 15, 81.

8 See the 2017 constitutional amendment (law no. 6771, 16 April 2017) introducing a very peculiar form of presidentialism apparently inspired by the US archetype, but lacking several checks and balances typical of the US system. For a comment on it, see Scotti V.R., *Presidentialism in Turkey. A First Appraisal of 2017 Constitutional Reform*, in DPCE online, 2017, 2, 251.

of the examined cases, namely with regard to the payment of the compensations the Court has required. Concluding remarks will discuss the effectiveness of these financial tools in increasing the protection of the right to free elections.

Turkey and the European Court of Human Rights

The Council of Europe embodies Turkey's first institutional tie with Europe after World War II. Turkey was invited to join the organisation (together with Greece and Iceland) in August 1949, and it quickly ratified the Statute of the Council of Europe on 13 April 1950.

Since its inception, Turkey – which was de facto neutral during the conflict – contributed to the efforts to take Europe out of the post-war psychology by actively upholding the idea of European integration at intergovernmental and parliamentary platforms. Furthermore, Turkish MPs participated in the Parliamentary Assembly of the Council of Europe (PACE) following its establishment and contributed to building the common European identity and vision. At the same time Turkey was ratifying the Statute, it also cooperated with drafting the ECHR, which entered into force in 1953. Turkey ratified the Convention through law no. 6366 of 10 March 1954 and it entered into force in the country on 18 May 1954. However, for a long time, the only viable option for bringing a petition against Turkey was through interstate complaints, as the right of individuals to bring complaints to the ECtHR was only allowed on 28 January 1987. The recognition of the binding effect of the Court's judgments followed in 1989.

In the words of the then President of the European Commission of Human Rights, Sir Humphrey Waldock, pronounced at the moment of the entry into force of the Court's jurisdiction, the ratification of the right to make an individual application meant the recognition of the Convention as a European Bill of Rights. Confirming this role for the ECHR, as well as the relevance of the other Treaties and Conventions on human rights, in 2004 Art. 90 of the 1982 Constitution was amended to clarify that the treaties on human rights duly ratified by the GNAT, due to their special content, acquire the rank of statutory law in the hierarchy of the sources of law, but cannot be subject to judicial review.[9] Art. 90 also clarifies that in the case of a conflict between international agreements, duly put into effect, concerning fundamental rights and freedoms – such as the ECHR – and the domestic laws due to differences in provisions on the same matter, the provisions of international agreements shall prevail.[10] Furthermore, the content of the 2004 constitutional amendment was interpreted as implying the superiority of the treaties on human rights and fundamental freedoms over the Constitution

9 Constitutional Law no. 5170, 22 May 2004.

10 This constitutional amendment sits in the middle of a huge debate on the role of the ECHR in the domestic system, discussed by scholars since its ratification, and contrasted with the 1988 decision of the Constitutional Court (E1987/2 K1988/3, 28 January 1988) affirming its competence in checking the constitutionality of the laws ratifying international agreements.

and was hailed by some scholars as a "significant step towards full democratic rule in Turkey."[11] It also involved the Court of Cassation and the Council of State in the assessment of the compliance of statutory laws with the ECHR and with other treaties on human rights. [12]

The 2010 constitutional amendment, specifically the part reforming the composition and the functioning of the Constitutional Court introducing the individual petitions, confirmed the relevance of the ECHR as a source of law when it established that individuals can claim a violation of the rights provided in the ECHR and recognised in the Constitution (Art. 148 of the Constitution).[13] Besides the formal recognition of the Convention as a source of law, however, Turkish judges have seldom relied on ECtHR case-law, especially when it does not concern Turkey.[14] The introduction of the individual complaint mechanism only partially changed this approach,[15] allowing several critics to suggest that rather than genuinely seeking to introduce stronger tools for rights' protection, the authorities envisaged it as a means to further hamper the right to appeal to the ECtHR in the light of the rule of the previous exhaustion of domestic remedies (Art. 35 ECHR). The amendment once again changed the mechanism of the adjudication of rights and made the Constitutional Court the sole body entitled to assess if there had been a violation of the ECHR. Furthermore, the amendment reduced the possibility to seek remedies in Strasbourg for violations occurred in Turkey. Indeed, with Art. 35 ECHR, the Strasbourg system has been imagined as a standard-setter for rights' protection ancillary to the procedural and substantive domestic mechanisms.[16] Thus, the ECtHR acts as a Court of

11 See Dutheillet de Lamothe O. (ed), *Draft Report on Case-law regarding the supremacy of international human rights treaties*, Venice Commission, no. 304, 2004.

12 See, i.e., Court of Cassation, Plenum Civil Section, E2005/9-320, 25 May 2005; IX Penal Section of the Court of Cassation, K 2005/355, 13 July 2004, Plenum Penal Section Court of Cassation E2005/7-24, 24 May 2005. See also Council of State XIII Chamber E2005/588, 8 February 2005; V Chamber E2004/291 K2004/3370, 29 September 2004.

13 On this mechanism, introduced in 2010, see Scotti V.R., *Il ricorso individuale in Turchia: fra riforma dell'ordinamento e influenze esterne*, in Decaro C., Lupo N., Rivosecchi G. (eds), *La "manutenzione" della giustizia costituzionale. Il giudizio sulle leggi in Italia, Spagna e Francia*, Torino, 2012, 301–314; Göztepe E., *Türkiye'de Anayasa Mahkemesi'ne Bireysel Başvuru Hakkının (Anayasa Şikayeti) 6216 Sayılı Kanun Kapsamında Değerlendirilmesi*, in Türkiye Barolar Birliği Dergisi, 2011, 95, 13.

14 This has formed part of a previous research work. See Scotti V.R., *Il costituzionalismo in Turchia tra circolazione dei modelli e influenze sovrastatali*, Sant'arcangelo di Romagna, 2014, Ch. 5. The research showed that Turkish judges are quite reluctant to use – or at least to openly show they are using – the comparative method and seldom rely, not always through effective interpretations, on the ECtHR jurisprudence, only very rarely directly quoting a specific decision.

15 For some elements on the impact of the individual complaint in Turkey, see *The Impact of the Right to Individual Petition on Constitutional Interpretation, Interpretation of International Law and the Turkish Judicial System: a Qualitative and Comparative Analysis of the Judgements of the Turkish Constitutional Court between 2012–2017*, TUBİTAK Project (https://anayasatakip.ku.edu.tr/).

16 See Sudre F., *Droit International et européen des droits de l'homme*, Paris, 2005, 290.

last resort, especially when the possibility for individual complaints to be made at the domestic level exists, as it has in Turkey since 2010.[17] As a consequence, several cases that would have reached the ECtHR before 2010, thenceforth were decided by the Constitutional Court or were rejected by the ECtHR because the applicant had failed to exhaust domestic remedies. This dynamic proved of particular importance with regard to the adjudication of the claims arising during the state of emergency (2016–2018).[18]

Finally, the 2010 amendment is important for the consequences it had on the domestic management of the applications to the ECtHR. Indeed, in accordance with the Cooperation Protocol between the Ministry of Justice and the Ministry of Foreign Affairs, which came into force on 1 March 2012, applications arising from domestic law issues and the execution of the judgments rendered on these applications are followed by the Ministry of Justice. Applications communicated to the Government before the effective date of the Protocol or applications or judgments which relate to foreign policy and international relations of Turkey are followed by the Ministry of Foreign Affairs.

Due to the very high number of violations ascertained,[19] Turkey, together with Italy and Russia, has been labelled as a serial violator. Indeed, it is possible to individuate groups of decisions underlying systemic lack of rights protection: right to life connected to the prohibition of torture and cruel and inhuman treatments or punishments (Arts. 2 and 3 ECHR); right to a fair trial and to effective remedies (Arts. 6 and 13 ECHR); right to liberty and security (Art. 4 ECHR); right to property (Art. 1 Prot. 1 to ECHR); freedom of expression (Art. 10 ECHR). Although less relevant numerically, the decisions concerning the use of religious symbols are fundamental for understanding the dialogue between Turkey and the CoE. Finally, domestic decisions on the ban of political parties should be mentioned because they ground claims of violations of the freedom of association (Art. 11 ECHR) often representing the premise for applications denouncing violations of Art. 3 of Protocol 1.

The domestic rules on political parties represent another pillar for the abovementioned authoritarian drifts hidden by the aspiration of protecting democracy. Indeed, according to Art. 68.4 of the 1982 Constitution:

> The statutes and programs, as well as the activities of political parties, shall not be contrary to the independence of the State, its indivisible integrity with its territory and nation, human rights, the principles of equality and rule of

17 As several cases concerning Turkey have shown, this may have a twofold consequence. On the one hand, it may decrease the legitimacy of domestic courts when their decisions conflict with those of the ECtHR; on the other hand, it may encourage cooperation among jurisdictions. De Schutter O., *La cooperation entre la CEDH et le juge national*, in Revue belge de droit international, 1997, 1, 21.

18 Scotti V.R., *Il golpe in Turchia e la Corte europea dei diritti umani: brevi note critiche sulle decisioni di irricevibilità per il mancato previo esperimento dei ricorsi interni*, in Rivista AIC, 2017, 1.

19 See the data available at www.echr.coe.int/Documents/Stats_violation_1959_2019_ENG.pdf.

> law, the sovereignty of the nation, the principles of the democratic and secular republic; they shall not aim to promote or establish class or group dictatorship or dictatorship of any kind, nor shall they incite citizens to crime.

Should a party fail to comply with this instruction, Art. 69.6 Const. (as amended in 2001) allows the Constitutional Court to dissolve the party when it can be proved that the actions in violation of Art. 68.4:

> are carried out intensively by the members of that party or the situation is shared implicitly or explicitly by the grand congress, general chairpersonship or the central decision-making or administrative organs of that party or by the group's general meeting or group executive board at the Grand National Assembly of Turkey or when these activities are carried out in determination by the abovementioned party organs directly.

It is worth emphasising that the constitutional amendment introduced through law no. 4709 of 3 October 2001 provided that:

> Instead of dissolving it permanently in accordance with the above-mentioned paragraphs, the Constitutional Court may rule the concerned party to be deprived of state aid wholly or in part with respect to the intensity of the actions brought before the court (Art. 69.7).

Before the entry into force of the 2001 constitutional amendment, the provisions for dissolving political parties were applied several times to pro-Kurdish parties, as well as to parties declaring a religious inspiration.[20] After the amendment, the procedure for dissolving a religiously inspired party was used against the AKP, although the Constitutional Court only decided to punish the party's activities – which conflicted with the principle of secularism – by depriving it of access to state funds for political parties.[21] The Court's decision was hailed as a first step to weakening Turkish militant democracy. Nevertheless, this optimism was quickly dampened a few months later, when the Court banned the pro-Kurdish Party for a Democratic Society (*Demokrat Türkiye Partisi* – DTP), which – up to 2021 – was the last party to be dissolved.[22]

The dissolution of a political party also leads to the exclusion of its members from political life. Indeed, members of a dissolved political party shall not be founders, members, directors, or supervisors of any other party for a period of five years from the date of publication of the Constitutional Court's final decision

20 For an overview, see Hakyemez Y.S., Akgun B., *Limitation on the Freedom of Political Parties in Turkey and the Jurisdiction of the European Court of Human Rights*, in Mediterranean Politics, 2002, 7, 54.

21 Constitutional Court K2009/3 E2002/3, 7 October 2009.

22 Constitutional Court, K 2009/4 E2007/1, 11 December 2009.

in the Official Gazette (Art. 69.9 of the Constitution).[23] Furthermore, Art. 84.2 of the Constitution states that the loss of parliamentary membership, through a settled judicial sentence or the deprivation of legal capacity, takes effect after the GNAT's plenum has been notified of the final judicial decision on the matter.

Since 2016, loss of membership can also occur because of the lifting of an MP's parliamentary immunity. According to Art. 83.2 of the Constitution, an MP shall not be detained, interrogated, arrested, or tried unless the GNAT decides otherwise. Dossiers put together during their time in office, however, can be used to prosecute them once their term comes to an end. For a long time, the possibility of narrowing the margins of parliamentary immunity has been at the centre of the Turkish political debate. This is both because of people's distrust towards corrupt political elites and the will of the dominant political forces to control those political opinions conflicting with the tenets of the Constitution.[24] On the lifting of parliamentary immunity in fact, an overall agreement existed between the AKP and the main opposition party – the heir to the Kemalist tradition, the *Cumhuriyet Halk Partisi* (Republican People's Party – CHP)[25] – to reduce the extent of the level of freedom of speech for members of pro-Kurdish parties. The revamp of secessionist terrorism with the attacks in 2016 provided the perfect occasion to deal with the issue. On 20 May 2016, a constitutional amendment[26] added to the Constitution a provisional Art. 20 suspending the abovementioned guarantees of Art. 83 and allowing for the prosecution of the MPs under investigation, even though it started before the entry into force of the amendment.

This amendment should be read against the background of the current authoritarian drift. Given the majority the AKP holds with the party-in-coalition MHP (*Milliyetçi Hareket Partisi* – Party of the Nationalist Movement), it has sufficient control to ensure the authorisation of the GNAT to allow the prosecution of MPs belonging to the opposition. This is indeed what is happening against MPs belonging to the pro-Kurdish *Halkların Demokratik Partisi* (Peoples' Democratic Party – HDP)[27] and its sister party *Demokratik Bölgeler*

23 For a comment on the provisions about the dissolution of political parties and their adjudication at the domestic and ECtHR level, see Özbudun E., *Party prohibition cases: different approaches by the Turkish constitutional court and the European Court of Human Rights*, in Democratization, 2010, 1, 125.

24 On this debate, see Özbudun E., *Constitutional Debates on Parliamentary Inviolability in Turkey*, in European Constitutional Law Review, 2005, 11, 2; Sevinç M., *Türkiye'de Milletvekillerinin Dokunulmazliklari*, Istanbul, 2004; Kocan G., Wigley S. *Democracy and the Politics of Parliamentary Immunity in Turkey*, in New Perspectives on Turkey, 2005, 121.

25 The CHP also considered that narrowing the parliamentary immunity could have had a boomerang effect on AKP, due to its religious inspiration which they conceive as contrary to the secularism constitutionally entrenched.

26 See constitutional law no. 6718, 20 May 2016. It was approved with a majority of 348 out of 550 MPs; therefore, there was no need for a constitutional referendum and the law entered into force after the presidential ratification.

27 In March 2021, however, an indictment has been filed for the dissolution of the catch-all pro-Kurdish party HDP. The decision of the Constitutional Court is still awaited (June 2021).

Partisi (Democratic Regions Party – DBP). Nevertheless, it has also had a boomerang effect, with the ability to lift parliamentary immunity also transformed into a tool to blackmail the CHP opposition.

For an analysis of the violations of Art. 3 of Protocol 1, finally, the legislation limiting the right to vote for people convicted of crimes should be considered. Indeed, according to Art. 53 of the Criminal Code, individuals convicted for crimes intentionally committed, notwithstanding the nature of the crime, are subject to disenfranchisement for the entire duration of the sentence handed down, thus meaning they lose both their active and passive electoral rights, even if they are then placed on conditional release.

Analysis of the relevant judgments

Until 2020, only 17 applications had been lodged against Turkey for a violation of Art. 3 of Protocol 1, alone or jointly with other ECHR provisions; in 11 of them, the ECtHR has found a violation. Overall, three different groups of applications can be showcased: 1) applications deriving from a previous dissolution of a political party, either for having pursued secessionist aims (i.e., in the *Sadak* saga and in *DTP and others* case) or for religious inspiration (i.e., in the cases connected to the dissolution of the *Fazilet Partı*); 2) applications of individuals whose electoral rights were restricted because they were subject to a conviction; 3) the *Demirtaş* case, connected with the constitutional amendment on parliamentary immunity, which, after the Grand Chamber's final decision, may represent the leading case for a range of rulings against Turkey for the violation of Art. 3 of Protocol 1.

The Sadak *saga*

Summary of the cases

Following the dissolution of the pro-Kurdish Democracy Party (DEP) on 16 June 1994 on the ground that it undermined the territorial integrity of the State and national unity, the Turkish Constitutional Court (*Anayasa Mahkemesi* – AYM) established, as a secondary measure, that the party would forfeit all the parliamentary seats held by its members and that some of them would be charged separately with sharing separatist propaganda or of being a member of an armed group. After having exhausted all domestic remedies, in 1995 13 of the forfeited MPs lodged applications[28] complaining that they had been forced to vacate their parliamentary seats (*Sadak no. 2*). Subsequently, on 24 October 2007, as a result of the conviction they received, Mehmet Hatip Dicle and Selim Sadak, who were among the applicants in *Sadak no. 2*, claimed a violation of Art. 6.2 ECHR and

28 *Sadak and Others v. Turkey (No. 2)*, Apps nos. 25144/94, 26149/95 to 26154/95, 27100/95 and 27101/95 (ECtHR, 6 November 2002).

of Art. 3 of Protocol 1.[29] This application originated from the execution of the judgment in *Sadak and Others v. Turkey (no. 1)*.[30]

Indeed, Dicle and Sadak were arrested respectively on 2 March 1994 and 1 July 1994, and on 8 December 1994 the Ankara State Security Court sentenced them to 15 years' imprisonment for belonging to an illegal organisation (Art. 168 § 2, Penal Code). On 26 October 1995, the Court of Cassation upheld that judicial decision. Nevertheless, in *Sadak no. 1*, the ECtHR ruled that there had been a violation of the right to a fair hearing (17 July 2001) and, in line with the follow-up resolutions of the Committee of Ministers of the Council of Europe,[31] the applicants had the criminal proceedings reopened on 4 February 2003.[32] Pending the new trials, they were released in compliance with the principle of the presumption of innocence. According to the provisions of the by then revised Criminal Code (Art. 314.2), on 27 February 2008, the Court of Cassation finally sentenced them to a prison term of seven years and six months, from which the period they had already served under conviction had to be deducted, de facto meaning that they had completed the full prison term to which they had been sentenced. Before the Court of Cassation had handed down this sentence, however, on 9 June 2007 Dicle and Sadak had their candidacy for the 2007 parliamentary elections rejected by the Supreme Board of Elections (*Yüksek Seçim Kurulu* – YSK). Indeed, with regard to the conditions which candidates had to meet for the 2007 elections, the YSK had established that individuals who had been convicted of a crime also had to provide a document certifying that they had recovered their civil rights and that the conviction was a *res judicata*, alongside their application for candidacy. Pending the Court of Cassation's final decision and despite the fact that according to the Criminal Code they could not receive a harsher conviction, the applicants were unable to obtain the documents for the candidacy and were therefore considered ineligible.

Democratic argument

With regard to Art. 3 of Protocol 1, in *Sadak no. 2* the applicants insisted on the role of elected representatives in a pluralist, democratic, and parliamentary system, and underscored that they had not tried to harm the integrity of the State, but had simply wanted to promote the introduction of legislation aimed at protecting the Kurdish identity, namely the Kurdish language and culture. Furthermore, they referred to the Resolution of 30 June 1994 in which the PACE made observations on the DEP's

29 *Dicle and Sadak v. Turkey*, App no. 48621/07 (ECtHR, 16 June 2015).

30 *Sadak and Others v. Turkey (no. 1)*, Apps nos. 29900/96, 29901/96, 29902/96 and 29903/96 (ECtHR, 17 July 2001).

31 Committee of Ministers, *Interim Resolution* ResDH(2002)59, 30 April 2002, and *Interim Resolution* ResDH(2004)31, 6 April 2004.

32 See Act no. 4793, 3 February 2003, adding to Art. 327 of the Code of Criminal Procedure (CPP) a new paragraph 6 providing for the reopening of criminal proceedings following a finding of a violation by the European Court of Human Rights.

dissolution[33] to emphasise that pluralism in a democratic society requires the free expression of all opinions even if they do not correspond with those expressed by the Government. In this light, the applicants maintained that the forfeiture of their parliamentary seats prevented a part of the population from participating in political debate and thus led to an infringement of Art. 3 of Protocol 1. Conversely, the Government reiterated that the forfeiture of the applicants' seats had been the consequence of the DEP's dissolution and was in line with the relevant constitutional provisions.

The ECtHR pointed out that Art. 3 of Protocol 1 guarantees the subjective rights to vote and to stand for election, and, once elected, to sit as a Member of Parliament (henceforth, MP). These rights, however, are not absolute and States have a wide margin of appreciation in this sphere. Hence, it is for the Court to determine whether the limits a State can introduce do not curtail the rights in question to such an extent as to impair their very essence and deprive them of their effectiveness. Therefore, limits must be imposed in the pursuit of a legitimate aim and through means that are not disproportionate. In the instant case, the ECtHR noted that, even confirming the Government's position that the dissolution of the party and the forfeiture of seats serve multiple legitimate aims, the measures being introduced were too severe and therefore not proportionate to the aims. Thus, the ECtHR found a violation of Art. 3 of Protocol 1 and considered it unnecessary to examine the claims for a violation of Arts. 6.1, 7, 9, 10, 11, and 14 ECHR and of Art. 1 of Protocol no. 1.

In *Dicle and Sadak*, the focus was on the violation of Art. 3 of Protocol 1, which came about due to the prevention of individuals standing for election as a result of an arbitrary application of the domestic law. The Government considered that the Supreme Board of Elections' decision to exclude the applicants' candidacy was connected to the fact that, at the moment of their request, the reopened trial was pending, and the previous sentence of 15 years had not been served yet. In addition, the Government underscored the temporary measure of this exclusion, mentioning that the applicants had been allowed to put themselves forward for candidacy in the 2011 elections. Applying the same test already used in *Sadak no. 2* and recalling its decision in *Yumak and Sadak*[34] in 2008, the ECtHR upheld the violation of Art. 3 of Protocol 1.

It is noteworthy that Judges Spano and Kjølbro wrote a Joint Partly dissenting opinion in which, relying on a different understanding of the relevance of the Court of Cassation's decision in the mechanism of trials re-examination, they did not find a violation both of Art. 6.2 and of Art. 3 of Protocol 1.

Costs of the rulings

In *Sadak no. 2*, the ECtHR considered that, because of the forfeiture of their parliamentary seats, the applicants suffered pecuniary damage, which however

33 PACE, *Resolution on the Consequences of the dissolution of the Party for Democracy (DEP) in Turkey*, no. 1041 (1994).

34 *Yumak and Sadak v. Turkey* App no. 10226/03 (ECtHR [GC], 8 July 2008).

could not exactly be assessed, as well as non-pecuniary damage, which the finding of a violation was not sufficient to redress. Hence, deciding on an equitable basis (Art. 41), the Court awarded EUR 50,000 to each applicant. In the light of the evidence in its possession, with regard to expenses, the Court also awarded 7 applicants the amount of EUR 10,500 and a further 6 others EUR 9,000.

In *Dicle and Sadak*, the applicants only claimed for moral damages (EUR 50,000 each), which the ECtHR reduced to EUR 12,000 in total, plus a minimum amount of EUR 715 by way of expenses because the applicants had failed to prove the amount claimed.

The dissolution of the Fazilet Partı: Kavakçi,[35] *Silay,*[36] *Sobaci,*[37] *and Ilicak*[38]

Summary of the cases

Kavakçi is the leading case for a series of judgments originating from the forfeit of the parliamentary seats of the members of the *Fazilet Partı* dissolved in 1999. Indeed, Merve Safa Kavakçi appealed to the ECtHR on 28 May 2008 alleging a violation of her freedom of religion (Art. 9 ECHR) as well as of her right to political participation stemming from Art. 6.1 ECHR and Art. 3 of Protocol 1 ECHR. Finally, she alleged a violation of her freedom of expression (Art. 14 ECHR). The applicant, who opened a debate on the use of the veil in public institutions by appearing veiled at the oath for her mandate as an MP – at which point the procedure for banning the party began – lost the right to participate in political activities for five years along with four other members of the party, and saw her parliamentary office terminated by the Constitutional Court as an ancillary measure to the party's dissolution. In addition, following Art. 25a of the Citizenship Law,[39] she was deprived of her Turkish citizenship, as it was alleged that she had acquired American citizenship without the prior agreement of the Turkish authorities. The deprivation of her Turkish nationality also led to the loss of her right to serve as an MP in the future. On this point, the Inter-Parliamentary Union (IPU) intervened in support of the applicant. The IPU reminded the Court that the parliamentary mandate is essential to enable political participation and that the Turkish legislation lacked a provision establishing for the loss of the mandate in the event that the conditions for eligibility are lost. Furthermore, the IPU stated that in the case of double citizenship, the Turkish authorities generally provide for a form to be filled in, in order to redress the lack of previous authorisation. Because this was not provided to Kavakçi, the IPU maintained that the applicant was discriminated against.

35 *Kavakçi v. Turkey* App no 71907/01 (ECtHR, 5 April 2007).
36 *Silay v. Turkey* App no. 8691/02 (ECtHR, 5 April 2007).
37 *Sobaci v. Turkey* App no 26733/02 (ECtHR, 29 November 2007).
38 *Ilicak v. Turkey* App no 15394/02 (ECtHR, 5 April 2007).
39 See Citizenship Law no. 403, 22 February 1964.

In separate applications, Bekir Sobacı, Ayse Nazli Ilicak, and Mehmet Silay claimed a violation of Art. 3 of Protocol 1 deriving from the termination of their parliamentary office as members of a dissolved party. Silay also claimed damages because of the confiscation of 5,000 copies of his book during the proceedings for the party's dissolution.

Democratic argument

In the leading case, the ECtHR considered it necessary to examine in detail the potential violation of Art. 3 of Protocol 1 because it protects the most inherent elements of democracy, such as the right to be elected and the right of the voters to decide on their representatives. Because limits to these rights should be carefully introduced, according to the ECtHR the measures adopted against the applicant were seen as not being proportionate to the aim of protecting secularism – albeit the Court recognised this as a serious motive for limiting political rights – and a violation of Art. 3 of Protocol 1 was declared.

The Court also used the proportionality test in the other cases and affirmed that the termination of the parliamentary office infringes voters' right to select their representative and violates Art. 3 of Protocol 1, making it unnecessary to decide on the other alleged violations.

Costs of the rulings

In *Kavakçi*, the Court rejected the applicant's request of EUR 150,000 for the salary lost due to the termination of her mandate because it did not see a link between the violation and the alleged material damage. It further considered that the recognition of the violation was sufficient to compensate for the moral damage. However, the ECtHR required Turkey to pay EUR 4,000 in expenses.

The same approach was followed in *Silay* and *Ilicak*, the ECtHR respectively requiring EUR 3,000 and EUR 5,000 of compensation for the expenses while rejecting the request for compensation for material and moral damages. In *Sobaci*, the Court rejected the claim for compensation for expenses because the applicant had failed to justify the claim.

Voting rights and detention: Söyler[40] *and Vural*[41]

Summary of the cases

Ahmet Atahür Söyler was a businessman convicted for having drawn void cheques and sentenced to prison for 4 years, 11 months and 26 days,[42] before being released on probation after almost 2 years in prison.

40 *Söyler v. Turkey* App no. 29411/0720 (ECtHR, 20 January 2014).

41 *Murat Vural v. Turkey* App no. 9540/07 (ECtHR, 1 January 2015).

42 Law No. 3167 on Cheques, repealed in 2012.

Murat Vural was an unemployed teacher who decided to express his resentment towards Atatürk, the founder of the Turkish Republic, by pouring paint on some Atatürk's statues in the town of Sincan. According to Law no. 5816 on Offences Committed against Atatürk, he was sentenced to a total prison term of 13 years, 1 month and 15 days. In 2013, however, he was released on probation.

In accordance with Art. 53 of the Criminal Code, both of them were prevented from voting for the duration of the period they were sentenced to, notwithstanding the fact that they had been granted conditional release. For this reason, they applied to the ECtHR claiming a violation of Art. 3 of Protocol 1.

Democratic argument

The Court applied the proportionality test for assessing whether the limitation curtailed the right to vote to such an extent as to impair its very essence and deprive it of effectiveness, having already established in its previous jurisprudence that:

> an indiscriminate restriction applicable automatically to prisoners, irrespective of the length of their sentence and irrespective of the nature or gravity of their offence and their individual circumstances, must be seen as falling outside any acceptable margin of appreciation, however wide that margin might be, and as being incompatible with Art. 3 of Protocol No. 1.[43]

In the cases at hand, the applicable domestic legislation disenfranchises individuals convicted of having intentionally committed an offence for the duration of the prison term established, even though they are then released on probation. Because of this, the Court considered the Turkish approach to the disenfranchisement of convicted individuals as incompatible with Art. 3 of Protocol 1 and, because it continues for the duration of the sentence even if the individual is on conditional release, the ECtHR judged the latter to be harsher and more far-reaching than the other previously examined system of convict disenfranchisement. Finally, the Court underscored that the element of "intent" provided for in Art. 53 of the Criminal Code as a criterion for distinguishing those who face disenfranchisement is neither sufficient to ensure the protection of the right to vote nor does it create a sufficient connection between the conduct and the sanction.

Hence, in both *Söyler* and *Vural*, the ECtHR confirmed a violation of Art. 3 of Protocol 1.

Costs of the rulings

In *Söyler*, though the applicant claimed EUR 3,000 for non-pecuniary damages, the Court agreed with the Government and considered that the finding

43 *Hirst (no. 2) v. UK* App no. 74025/01 (ECtHR [GC], 6 October 2005). See also *Frodl v. Austria* App no. 20201/04 (ECtHR, 4 October 2010) and *Scoppola v. Italy (no. 3)* App no. 126/05 (ECtHR [GC], 22 May 2012).

of a violation constituted sufficient just satisfaction. Conversely, with regard to expenses, the ECtHR awarded EUR 3,000 from which the EUR 850 granted to the applicant by way of legal aid under the Council of Europe's legal aid scheme had to be deducted.

In *Vural*, instead, the Court rejected the request for pecuniary damages as well as for the reimbursement of the costs and expenses incurred before the domestic courts and the ECtHR, but awarded EUR 26,000 for non-pecuniary damages. With regard to this allocation, the partially dissenting/partially concurring opinion of Justice Sajo should be noted. Indeed, though he mainly focused on the way the ECtHR applied the proportionality test for assessing the violation of Art. 10 ECHR the applicant claimed, Justice Sajo dissented also from the decision not to award compensation for pecuniary damages. Indeed, he envisaged a direct link between the incarceration and the loss of income as well as between the impossibility of serving as a civil servant as a result of the applicant's conviction and the loss of future income.

The last party dissolution: The case of the Party for a Democratic Society

Summary of the case

As a consequence of the forfeiture of their parliamentary seat as a result of the dissolution of the Party for a Democratic Society (DTP) on 11 December 2009 due to secessionist activities linked to the pro-Kurdish terrorist group PKK, Turk and Tugluk, plus another eight applicants, made a claim for a violation of Art. 11 ECHR and of Art. 3 of Protocol 1. [44]

Democratic argument

Although the ECtHR applied the already noted proportionality test, this case is relevant for the discussion it started about the domestic provisions on the dissolution of parties. Indeed, looking at the reasoning of the AYM and at the evidence on which it grounded the link between the PKK programme and that of the DTP, the ECtHR highlighted that the DTP programme, calling for non-violent solutions and a participative method to solving the Kurdish issue, was evidently against the principles outlined in the Turkish Constitution about the integrity of the State, but was not against the conception of democracy as enshrined in the ECHR. Similarly, the ECtHR recognised that the DTP's failure to distinguish itself from the PKK led to the State intervention aimed at protecting national security and fighting internal terrorism, but it considered that the party's dissolution was not proportionate to this aim. Once the dissolution of the party

44 *Party for a Democratic Society (DTP) and others v. Turkey* Apps no. 3840/10, 3870/10, 3878/10, 15616/10, 21919/10, 39118/10 and 37272/10 (ECtHR, 6 June 2016).

was framed as a violation of the Convention, *a fortiori* the ancillary measure providing for the termination of the mandate of MPs was also deemed not to be proportionate.

Costs of the ruling

Recognising material damage in the fact that the applicants did not receive their salary as MPs due to the forfeiture of their seat, as well as moral damages that the mere recognition of the violation could not remedy, because of the difficulty of calculating the actual loss, the ECtHR decided to allocate EUR 30,000 to each of the applicants for moral and material damages. In addition, EUR 7,500 was allocated as compensation for the moral prejudice Ay, a member of the DTP's Executive Board, suffered because of the party's dissolution. With regard to expenses, the applicants were also granted EUR 3,000 together, with EUR 1,000 for Ay.

The new rules on parliamentary immunity: The **Demirtaş no. 2** *case*

Summary of the case

Selahattin Demirtaş applied to the ECtHR on 20 February 2017 claiming that his pre-trial detention breached Arts. 5, 10, and 18 ECHR, as well as Art. 3 of Protocol 1. The Council of Europe Commissioner for Human Rights exercised his right to intervene in the proceedings and submitted written comments, as did the Inter-Parliamentary Union (IPU) and the non-governmental organisations ARTICLE 19 and Human Rights Watch.

The applicant, who was one of the co-chairs of the pro-Kurdish Peoples' Democratic Party (HDP), was an MP between 2007 and 2018 and in the 2014 and 2018 presidential elections had received respectively 9.76% and 8.32% of the votes. His party was involved in the 2015 turmoil that started with the *Daesh* attack on Kobani and led to the end of the abovementioned solution process for the Kurdish question launched in 2012. Notably, on 4 November 2016, the applicant was arrested at his home, taken into police custody, and then placed in pre-trial detention for having membership of an armed terrorist organisation and for incitement to commit an offence.

Although the applicant lodged more than 15 objections against his pre-trial detention, the Turkish courts considered it a necessary and proportionate measure given the alleged offences, for which the public prosecutor had asked for a sentence of between 43 and 142 years' imprisonment. On 17 November 2016, the applicant also lodged an individual application with the Constitutional Court, declared inadmissible in 2017,[45] for a violation of his right to liberty and security

45 *Selahattin Demirtaş* [GK], B. No: 2016/25189, 21 December 2017.

and his right to engage in political activities. Assuming that he had been arrested, taken into police custody, and placed in pre-trial detention on account of the political speeches he had made as an MP and co-chair of a political party, he also alleged a violation of his freedom of expression. Lastly, he maintained that his continued pre-trial detention amounted to a violation of the right to free elections (Art. 3 of Protocol 1) given his status as an MP.

Because the pre-trial detention hampered his participation in the 2018 presidential electoral campaign, on 29 May 2018 the applicant lodged another individual petition with the Constitutional Court alleging a violation of Arts. 5 and 10 ECHR and of Art. 3 of Protocol 1. Then, following the Grand Chamber decision (20 December 2020), another application was lodged claiming for the respect of the latter by Turkish authorities.

Democratic argument

The case raises important questions with regard to the rules on parliamentary immunity, as well as the possibility of interpreting Art. 3 of Protocol 1 as entailing not only a right to be elected but to exercise political activities after the election.

Indeed, the applicant lamented that the pre-trial detention hampered his ability to engage in political activity, moreover damaging the wider activity of the party he led. Conversely, the Government maintained that Art. 3 of Protocol 1 did not impose on States a duty to recognise a right to engage in political activities and that in any case the applicant had not lost his status as an MP because of the pre-trial detention, but because of the lifting of the parliamentary immunity which followed an authorised parliamentary procedure.

Recalling the reasoning of the Chamber,[46] the Grand Chamber, issuing the final decision,[47] considered that the Commission for Democracy through the Law, a.k.a. Venice Commission, had already pointed out[48] that the Turkish rules on parliamentary immunity introduced in 2016, allow for *ad homines* measures because they can affect matters already pending. The same point was made by the Commissioner for Human Rights in the Memorandum on freedom of expression and media freedom in Turkey issued on 15 February 2017. Then, it stated that democracy also means having a functioning Parliament, which cannot be a reality if MPs can be deprived of their right to their seat as such at any moment. Hence, the ECtHR underscored that pre-trial detention is a measure the Convention and the Protocol do not exclude *per se*, but only when it is not necessary and proportionate. On this ground, the Chamber rejected the Government's arguments on the interpretation of Art. 3 of Protocol 1 and highlighted the domestic courts' failure to consider that the applicant was not a simple MP, but a party leader

46 *Selahattin Demirtaş v. Turkey (No. 2)*, App no. 14305/17 (ECtHR, 18 September 2019).

47 *Selahattin Demirtaş v. Turkey (No. 2)*, App no. 14305/17 (ECtHR, 22 December 2020).

48 Venice Commission, *Opinion on the constitutional amendment allowing for the lift of the parliamentary immunity*, CDL-AD(2015)013, 19 June 2015.

"whose performance of his parliamentary duties required a high level of protection." Instead, the Turkish judicial authorities deprived the applicant of all the opportunities he had to devote himself to his parliamentary responsibilities without explaining why an alternative measure to detention would have been insufficient in the applicant's particular case, even though such measures are provided for by domestic law. Being an unjustified interference with the free expression of the opinion of the people and with the applicant's right to be elected and to sit in Parliament, the ECtHR declared a violation of Art. 3 of Protocol 1.

Costs of the ruling

The applicant claimed TRY 59,614.04 for pecuniary damages, corresponding to the cost of the air tickets paid for by his wife, daughters, parents, and sister to visit him in prison, which the Chamber rejected due to a lack of direct link between the violations found and the pecuniary damage claimed. He also claimed EUR 250,000 for non-pecuniary damages, which the ECtHR agreed with up to a level of EUR 10,000. Finally, for costs and expenses, the Chamber awarded EUR 15,000. In front of the Grand Chamber, then, the applicant claimed EUR 25,800 for his representatives' expenses, plus TRY 40,332 for translation expenses, which were awarded in full.

The Legal and economic impact of the ECtHR judgments

The duty to comply with the ECtHR's judgments means that States have to provide for a fair remedy. This may acquire the form of a payment within three months from the judgment. Should the ECtHR deem the payment insufficient, it may also impose specific measures to provide redress for the violation and/or to avoid its repetition. With regard to the payment, the Committee of Ministers (Art. 50 ECHR) is provided with a monitoring role, which has encouraged the ECtHR to highlight systemic malfunctioning in its rulings so as to better support serial violators, such as Turkey, in reforming their legal system.[49]

In order to respect these duties, Turkey has established a mechanism centred on the Ministry of Justice – Human Rights Department, which coordinates the defence before the ECtHR, even providing the lawyers and the legal experts involved in the matter, communicates the final decision of the Court to the other national authorities involved in the case and proposes the measures to be enacted in order to implement the judgment. Along with these activities, the Ministry works in coordination with other authorities who may potentially be involved in ensuring the violation is redressed and eliminating its systemic causes, if any.

49 Committee of Ministers, Resolution no. 2004–3, 20 October 2004. For a critical approach on the Committee's monitoring activity, see Ferrer Lloret J., *La ejecución de las sentencias del TEDH relativas a la Federación de Rusia y a Turquía: ¿han fracasado las reformas del Protocolo 14?*, in Revista de Derecho Comunitario Europeo, 2018, 61, 853.

The Ministry also works with the Ministry of Economy and Finance in relation to the payment of compensation. Notably, to comply with the need to pay compensation for the judgments confirming violations of the ECHR so frequently, in 2013 Turkey developed specific legislation,[50] according to which a Commission was established to determine the amount of compensation due when the ECtHR's judgments fail to be executed or are not executed in due time.

With specific regard to the execution of the judgments, the competent office is the Office for the Execution of Decisions of the Ministry of Justice – Human Rights Department. When the decision of the ECtHR arrives at the Office, it is charged with developing an Action Plan or a Report to be submitted to the Council of Europe within six months from the finalisation of the ECtHR judgment and providing information about the files in progress. Once the Committee of Ministers of the Council of Europe considers the judgment executed, the file is closed.

At the internal level, the Office for the Execution of Decisions of the Ministry of Justice – Human Rights Department coordinates all the other domestic institutions involved in the execution of the judgment, including the Ministry of Finance, which provides the budget for the remediation. The Office is also entitled to publish the decisions in Turkish for the authorities involved.

In 2019, the Office completed the execution of 732 decisions with 80 Action Reports and 11 Action Plans; as of the beginning of 2020, the number of enforced proceedings was 687.[51]

The implementation of the judgments on the right to free elections

With regard to the judgments on the violation of Art. 3 of Protocol 1, the financial impact of the compensation payments required by the ECtHR is summarised in the following table (see Table 9.1).

Overall, Turkey respected the judgments and implemented them within due time. For instance, the 2001 amendment to Art. 69 of the Constitution, specifying the circumstances under which actions or statements of members of a political party may be attributed to the party and providing for less stringent sanctions than the party's dissolution, contributed to the closure of the implementation of *Kavakci* and of the repetitive cases *Silay*, *Sobaci* and *Ilicak*, which were connected with the dissolution of the *Fazilet Parti*.[52] Similarly, though a Final Resolution from the Committee of Ministers is still awaited, the amendment of Art. 69 can be considered to be a sufficient general measure to ensure the closure of the file in the case *DTP and others*, especially considering that in 2010 Art. 84.5 on the

50 See Law on Compensation of Some Applications Made to the European Court of Human Rights No. 6384, 9 January 2013.

51 Data available on the website of the Human Rights Department (http://inhak.adalet.gov.tr/).

52 See Committee of Ministers, Final Resolution CMResDH(2010)184, 2 December 2010.

Table 9.1 Costs of the compensations

Case	*Costs in Euro*
SADAK AND OTHERS v. TURKEY (no. 2)	777,500
ILICAK v. TURQUIE	5,000
KAVAKÇI v. TURQUIE	4,000
SILAY v. TURQUIE	3000
SOBACI v. TURQUIE	0
SÖYLER v. TURKEY	2,150
MURAT VURAL v. TURKEY	26,000
DİCLE AND SADAK v. TURKEY	12,715
DTP and OTHER v. TURQUIE	71,500
SELAHATTİN DEMİRTAŞ v. TURKEY (no. 2)	56,900
TOTAL	**958,765**

loss of parliamentary office was amended to allow MPs whose statements and activities led to the dissolution of the party to pursue their political activities as independent deputies.

The files have also been closed for *Söyler* and *Vural* following the payment of the just satisfaction. Furthermore, in the Action Plan for *Söyler* submitted on 3 December 2014, the Turkish authorities underscored that the Supreme Board of Elections had started a trend of allowing prisoners convicted of negligence offences, those released on probation, or on conditional release, or subject to suspended sentences to vote. The approach of the Supreme Board of Elections couples with the decision of the Constitutional Court partially annulling Art. 53 of the Criminal Code, holding that by extending the ban on voting beyond the period actually served in prison it had exceeded the restriction defined in the Constitution.[53] This decision means that only persons convicted of intentional offences and currently serving their sentence in prison are denied the right to vote, thus allowing the Committee of Ministers to close the file.[54]

With regard to the implementation of these judgments, it is finally worth noting that the Turkish authorities provided for their translation and dissemination among the relevant domestic authorities, both to assist with the implementation and for training purposes.

Conversely, the *Sadak* saga remains open. Notably, the file for the case *Sadak no. 2* has been closed because Turkey has paid the required amount of compensation to the applicants. Yet, *Dicle and Sadak* remains an open file. An Action Plan was received in July 2016 confirming the payment of the just satisfaction and the fact that the Assize Court had already refused the request to reopen

53 Constitutional Court, E 2014/140 K 2015/85, 8 October 2015.
54 See Committee of Ministers, Final Resolution CM/ResDH(2019)147, 6 June 2019.

the proceedings before the ECtHR's judgment.[55] Furthermore, with regard to the assessed violation of Art. 3 of Protocol 1, the Supreme Electoral Board has refused the applicants' candidatures because of their convictions, in spite of the reopening of the proceedings and of the fact that they were pending at the time of the elections.

Similarly, the *Demirtaş* case is still pending and is engendering important clashes between Turkey and CoE authorities. Soon after the decision of the Chamber, indeed, President Erdoğan declared that Turkey is not bound by the Court's decision. Adopting the same approach, after the final decision of the Grand Chamber, the Ankara 7th Criminal Court of Peace rejected the request for release, considering that there was no change in Demirtaş' legal status. As a consequence, the Committee of Ministers urged Turkey to implement the judgment and release the applicant,[56] however without success.

Concluding remarks: Democracy does not cost enough

Since its Preamble, the ECHR affirms the pillar role of liberal democracy in the common heritage CoE member States share. Building on this, the ECtHR has developed a solid jurisprudence for contrasting undemocratic behaviours among member States.[57] In the post-Cold War era, the ECtHR further focused on member States' internal democracy and provided for more rulings on the substantive guarantee to rights connected with democracy.[58] In this respect, the Court developed the benchmark test – "necessary in a democratic society" – assessing the extent of the margin of appreciation States may enjoy in the limitations to rights with the aim of protecting democracy. Nevertheless, democracy does not find a single ECHR article openly stating that States have a duty to comply with it, and its protection results from a combination of different articles: the joint application of Arts. 10 and 11 ECHR respectively on freedom of expression and association; the application of Art. 17 ECHR while deciding on cases' admissibility; the violation of Art. 3 of Protocol 1.[59]

This article has often been deemed the weaker form of protection for democracy,[60] though the ECtHR has exploited it in order to transform a state

55 See Committee of Ministers, Communication from Turkey in the case of Dicle and Sadak against Turkey (Application No. 48621/07), DH-DD(2016)848, 25 July 2016.

56 See Committee of Ministers, 1398th (Human Rights) meeting, 9–11 March 2021.

57 See, i.e., Kjeldsen, *Busk Madsen and Pedersen v. Denmark*, Apps no. 5095/71, 5920/72 and 5926/72 (ECtHR, 7 December 1976), *Klass and Others v. Germany* App no 5029/71 (ECtHR, 6 September 1978), *Soering v. United Kingdom* App no. 14038/88 (ECtHR, 7 July 1989).

58 See *The United Communist Party of Turkey v. Turkey* App. No 133/1996/752/951 (ECtHR [GC], 30 January 1998). See also Aydin Ö., *Serbest Seçim Hakkı Ve Kişinin Siyasal Etkinliklerinin Kısıtlanması Sorunu*, in Uyuşmazlık Mahkemesi Dergisi, 2020, 15, 69.

59 *Hasan and Chaush v. Bulgaria*, App no. 30985/96 (ECtHR, 26 October 2000).

60 See, i.e., Zand J., Keser H., *Democracy is One of the Main Features of the European Convention on Human Rights*, in Gazi Üniversitesi Hukuk Fakültesi Dergisi, 2013, 4, 183, at 193.

obligation into a subjective right.[61] Furthermore, while ruling on a violation of Art. 3 of Protocol 1, the ECtHR has applied a test mainly focused on the arbitrariness of the limitations introduced and on their proportionality with the aim to be achieved, especially when the disqualification of individuals from the passive right to vote was in question. The latter certainly represents the main group of applicants against Turkey, the violation of their passive electoral rights deriving from the very stringent legislation established in the framework of a militant democracy. Among them, confirming a trend already observed when adjudicating on the dissolution of political parties, the Court seems to draw a distinction between the applicants belonging to the Kurdish minority and those challenging the Turkish principle of secularism, as if the preservation of the latter widens the State's margins of appreciation. Indeed, in the *Sadak* saga, the ECtHR seems to prefer the recognition of moral damages instead of allotting compensation for the loss of salary deriving from the forfeiture of the seat, while in *Kavakci* and in the other cases of this group, the ECtHR is more restrictive about the recognition of compensation. This distinction is even more evident when recalling that in *DTP and others* the damages deriving from the loss of the parliamentary salary were recognised.

This recognition, occurring chronologically with the last ruling, probably underscores a new trend for the ECtHR, which may have considered the position of the dissenting Justice Sajo in *Vural*, having blamed the Court for failing to understand the link between the violation and the loss of income. In a general overview, however, for the time being, the ECtHR seems not to rely on financial tools to push Turkey into adopting reforms for removing the systemic basis for the violations.

Though in this essay only the judgments ascertaining violations have been analysed, it can be underscored that important questions on the content of Art. 3 of Protocol 1 have also been raised on the occasion of the other applications against Turkey in which the ECtHR considered Art. 3 of Protocol 1 not to have been violated. This is for instance the case in *Oran*,[62] when the ECtHR decided that Art. 3 of Protocol 1 had not been violated by the Turkish legislation, which enabled Turkish voters living abroad to vote in polling stations set up in customs posts only for political parties and not for independent non-party candidates. The Court considered the limitation justified by the need to limit the influence of citizens resident abroad in elections on issues which primarily affect persons living in the country, and considered that the limitation pursued the legitimate aim of enhancing democratic pluralism, while preventing the excessive and dysfunctional fragmentation of candidatures, thereby strengthening the expression of the opinion of the people in the choice of the legislature. Furthermore, Art. 3 of Protocol 1 was called into question in the first *Sadak* decision, which started the

61 See Ruiz Robledo A., *The Construction of the Right to Free Elections by the European Court of Human Rights*, in Cambridge International Law Journal, 2018, 7, 225.

62 *Oran v. Turkey* App no. 28881/07, 37920/07 (ECtHR, 15 April 2014).

saga discussed here. Indeed, in *Yumak and Sadak v. Turkey*, the ECtHR, while stating that the 10% electoral threshold appeared to be excessive and recommending that it be lowered to increase the transparency of the electoral process, did not envisage a violation of Art. 3 of Protocol 1 because of the existing corrective measures, such as the possibility of creating electoral coalitions.

On the Turkish legislation on political parties, finally, it is worth adding that the Venice Commission has deeply discussed the measures for the dissolution of political parties both in general Guidelines for CoE member States[63] and in a devoted Opinion.[64] In the Conclusions of the latter document, the Venice Commission highlighted that, when comparing Turkey with other European "protected democracies," the list of substantive criteria applicable to the constitutionality of political parties goes beyond the legitimate criteria, that the procedure for initiating decisions on party prohibition or dissolution makes this initiative more arbitrary and less subject to the democratic control than in other European countries and that the tradition for regularly applying the rules on party closure to an extent that has no parallel in any other European country demonstrates that this is not regarded as an extraordinary measure. Therefore, the Turkish system has been considered not to be in line with Art. 11 ECHR. However, structural issues have not been observed with regard to the limitations to the electoral rights as protected in Art. 3 of Protocol 1.

Structural issues also do not exist in terms of the implementation of the judgments, which Turkey progressively conceived as a part of the natural evolution of the process of rights' adjudication, as the 2012 decision to move the implementation of the ECtHR judgments from the competences of the Minister for Foreign Affairs – thus making of them a matter concerning the international standing of the country – to the competences of the Minister for Justice seems to prove.

Overall, conclusively, the analysis of the judgments issued up to 2020 showcases that the Turkish authorities seem to have very few difficulties in complying with the ECtHR's judgments in this field and that the latter are not related to the amount of the compensation required, which Turkey has paid within due time. If at all, the still-pending execution of *Dicle and Sadak* and *Demirtaş* prove that the issues mostly reside in the reluctance to accept the potential infringement of national sovereignty underlying the imposition of reopening trials, especially when they concern individuals condemned for having attacked on the integrity of the State. In fact, given the role secularism and the protection of the integrity of the State has had on the country's history, state authorities, and namely the Judiciary because of its important role in the Republican Alliance, have struggled to protect the rights of religious groups and Kurds consistently

63 Venice Commission, *Guidelines on prohibition and dissolution of political parties and analogous measures*, CDL-INF (2000)001, 10 January 2000.

64 Venice Commission, *Opinion on the Constitutional and Legal Provisions Relevant to the Prohibition of Political Parties in Turkey*, CDL-AD (2009)006, 13 March 2009. It should be underscored that since this opinion was issued Turkey has not started any other procedure for dissolving a political party.

with the ECHR. Whether the new elite in power has progressively extended its tutelage on (some) religious groups, Kurdish secessionist movements and their cognate groups are instead still conceived as the main threat to the stability of the State.

Bibliography

BELGE C., *Friends of the Court: The Republican Alliance and Selective Activism of the Constitutional Court in Turkey*, in L. & Soc. Rev., 2006, 40, 653.

DE SCHUTTER O., *La cooperation entre la CEDH et le juge national*, in Revue belge de droit international, 1997, 1, 21.

DUTHEILLET DE LAMOTHE O. (ed.), *Draft Report on Case-law regarding the supremacy of international human rights treaties*, Venice Commission, 2004, 304.

ERTAN A., *The Tension between Secularism and Democracy in Turkey: Early Origins, Current Legacy*, in European View, 2007, 6, 11.

FERRER LLORET J., *La ejecución de las sentencias del TEDH relativas a la Federación de Rusia y a Turquía: ¿han fracasado las reformas del Protocolo 14?*, in Revista de Derecho Comunitario Europeo, 2018, 61, 853.

GÖZTEPE E., *Türkiye'de Anayasa Mahkemesi'ne Bireysel Başvuru Hakkının (Anayasa Şikayeti) 6216 Sayılı Kanun Kapsamında Değerlendirilmesi*, in Türkiye Barolar Birliği Dergisi, 2011, 95, 13.

HAKYEMEZ Y.S., AKGUN B., *Limitation on the Freedom of Political Parties in Turkey and the Jurisdiction of the European Court of Human Rights*, in Mediterranean Politics, 2002, 7, 54.

HALE W., *The Turkish Army in Politics, 1960–73*, in FINKEL A., SARMAN N. (eds.) Turkish State, Turkish Society, London, 1990, 53.

ISIKSEL T., *Between text and context: Turkey's tradition of authoritarian constitutionalism*, in International Journal of Constitutional Law, 2013, 13, 702.

KOCAN G., WIGLEY S. *Democracy and the Politics of Parliamentary Immunity in Turkey*, in New Perspectives on Turkey, 2005, 33, 121.

NARLI N., *Civil–Military Relations in Turkey*, in Turk. Stud. 2000, 12, 107

ÖZBUDUN E., *Constitutional Debates on Parliamentary Inviolability in Turkey*, in European Constitutional Law Review, 2005, 11, 2.

ÖZBUDUN E., GENÇKAYA Ö.F., *Democratization and the Politics of Constitution-Making in Turkey*, Budapest, 2009.

PUSANE Ö.K., *Turkey's Kurdish opening: Long awaited achievements and failed expectations*, in Turkish Studies, 2014, 15, 81.

RUIZ ROBLEDO A., *The construction of the right to free elections by the European Court of Human Rights*, in Cambridge International Law Journal, 2018, 7, 225.

SCHMID D., *Turquie : le syndrome de Sèvres, ou la guerre qui n'en finit pas*, in Politique étrangère, 2014, 1, 199.

SCOTTI V.R., *Il costituzionalismo in Turchia tra circolazione dei modelli e influenze sovrastatali*, in Sant'arcangelo di Romagna, 2014.

SCOTTI V.R., *Il ricorso individuale in Turchia: fra riforma dell'ordinamento e influenze esterne*, in DECARO C., LUPO N., RIVOSECCHI G. (eds), La "manutenzione" della giustizia costituzionale. Il giudizio sulle leggi in Italia, Spagna e Francia, Torino, 2012, 301–314.

SCOTTI V.R., *Il golpe in Turchia e la Corte europea dei diritti umani: brevi note critiche sulle decisioni di irricevibilità per il mancato previo esperimento dei ricorsi interni*, in Rivista AIC, 2017, 1.

SCOTTI V.R., *Presidentialism in Turkey. A first appraisal of 2017 Constitutional Reform*, in DPCE Online, 2017, 2, 251.

SEVINÇ M., *Türkiye'de Milletvekillerinin Dokunulmazliklari*, Istanbul, 2004.

SUDRE F., *Droit International et européen des droits de l'homme*, Paris, 2005, 290.

TANÖR B., *Türkiye'nin Insan Hakları Sorunu Istanbul*, 1990, 352.

ÜKSÜL Z.Ö., *L'affirmation de la laïcité en Turquie: un gage de modernité*, in Politique et sécurité internationales, 1999, 3, 20.

ZAND J., KESER H., *Democracy is One of the Main Features of the European Convention on Human Rights*, in Gazi Üniversitesi Hukuk Fakültesi Dergisi, 2013, 4, 183, 193.

10 Prisoners' voting rights and the long-lasting political resistance to the implementation of the European Court of Human Rights' judgments

Alessandra Osti

Introduction

The UK is one of the founding States of the Council of Europe, having ratified the Statute of the Council of Europe in 1949 and the European Convention on Human Rights (hereafter the ECHR) in 1951. However, its relationship with the Council of Europe, and especially with the European Court of Human Rights (hereafter the ECtHR), has often been less than idyllic.[1]

The coming into force of the Human Rights Act 1998 (HRA), which incorporated the Convention into domestic law, has granted the effective protection of the human rights enshrined in the ECHR at the national level, but – at the same time – it has led to greater conflict between the UK and the ECtHR. That conflict is particularly evident (thanks to the media, the Government, and members of Parliament) when the Strasbourg court rules against the UK on controversial political issues, such as the blanket ban on prisoner voting, which will be discussed in this chapter. The negative "sentiment" characterising public opinion against the ECtHR, which is mainly down to media misinformation, has often been exploited by politicians who propose changes in human rights law in order to "bring rights back home." In the run up to the general election in May 2015, the Conservative Party promised to replace the HRA with a British Bill of Human Rights and to alter the relationship between the UK and the ECtHR in order to put an end to the expansion of the ECHR into new areas and to curb the Strasbourg court's attempts to "overrule" British law and judgments.[2] Although the Conservative Party won the May 2015 general election, its "revolutionary"

1 The relationship between the UK and the Convention system is deeply described in ZIEGLER K.S., WICKS E., HODSON L. (eds.), *The UK and European Human Rights – A Strained Relationship?*, Hart Publishing, 2015. See also: JAY Z., *Keeping rights at home: British conceptions of rights and compliance with the European Court of Human Rights*, in The British Journal of Politics and International Relations, 19, 4, 2017, 842–860.

2 See Conservative Party Manifesto 2015, in particular at 62. at: http://ucrel.lancs.ac.uk/wmatrix/ukmanifestos2015/localpdf/Conservatives.pdf.

DOI: 10.4324/9781003229247-12

plan was stopped by the (unexpected) result of the *Brexit* referendum which changed the Government's priorities.

If we look to the statistical reports published by the ECtHR,[3] it can be clearly observed that the clash between the UK and the ECtHR is based almost entirely on political reasons and thus is not supported by real data. Indeed, from its initial establishment in 1959 until the end of 2018, the number of applications made against the UK are in fact very low and there has been a general downward trend in the numbers since 2010. By population, the UK has the fewest applications of all States at 5 per million people, in a population of 52 per million. Furthermore, the most interesting data concerns the number of adverse judgments handed down in UK cases: from 2014 to 2018 there were only 18. Even if we look at the Annual Report of the Committee of Ministers on the "Supervision of the execution of judgments and decisions of the European Court of Human Rights,"[4] we can observe that from the data concerning the execution of the ECtHR's Judgments, that the UK Government's response have been very good and that, for instance, in 2018 there were only 12 cases pending before the Committee of Ministers.

The good performance of the UK within the ECHR system, which has been highlighted, is partly down to the mechanisms enshrined in the HRA 1998. We can mainly identify three mechanisms which are intended to enhance the respect of Human Rights at the national level: (i) the statement of compatibility, (ii) the interpretation of legislation, and (iii) the declaration of incompatibility. It is worth noting that all the aforementioned mechanisms recognise the long-held doctrine of parliamentary sovereignty since only Parliament can decide whether or not to repeal or amend legislation.

Specifically, (i) under Section 19 of the HRA, any Minister who is in charge of a Bill in both Houses of Parliament, before the Second Reading of the Bill, *must* make a statement on the compatibility of the Bill with human rights. This statement represents the personal opinion of the Minister introducing the Bill and it is not binding on Parliament or the courts, but rather it is aimed at encouraging Ministers and the civil service to consider the human rights implications of proposed legislation before it is introduced. Therefore, the statement of compatibility serves to trigger a parliamentary debate and affects the quality of legislation. (ii) Under Section 3(1), anyone interpreting the law (courts, tribunals, or public authorities) must read primary legislation and subordinate legislation in a way which is compatible with the Convention rights, if it is possible to do so. Lastly, (iii) under section 4 of the HRA, a higher court (such as the High Court, Court of Appeal, or Supreme Court) which considers that a provision in an Act of Parliament is incompatible with human rights can make a declaration of incompatibility. The declaration of incompatibility does not directly affect the

3 Statistics are available at https://echr.coe.int/Pages/home.aspx?p=reports.

4 The Annual Report 2018 of the Committee of Ministers is available at: www.coe.int/en/web/execution/annual-reports.

legislation in question, but it serves to open up a "dialogue" in which Parliament can decide if and how to respond.

Despite the good performance by the UK within the Convention system and the well-functioning mechanisms provided by the HRA, the prisoners' voting right issue has, for almost 15 years, been the embers in the ashes, ready to flare up into the fire of political conflict. And the reason is quite obvious: the issue touches upon the societal values of the community and the foundation of democracy.

The prisoners' voting saga[5]

In this paragraph we will consider the prisoners' voting saga, looking especially to the jurisprudence of the ECtHR as regards the UK during the period 2004–2020. However, it is important to bear in mind that, during that period, the ECtHR has dealt with a number of other cases concerning the issue of prisoner disenfranchisement from other States, namely Austria,[6] Bulgaria,[7] Georgia,[8] Italy,[9] Romania,[10] Russia,[11] and Turkey.[12] Only the Italian system of prisoners' voting was considered to be congruent with the Convention right to vote,[13] while

5 The expression "prisoner voting saga" is coined by Bates E., *Analysing the Prisoner Voting Saga and the British Challenge to Strasbourg*, in Human Rights Law Review, 14, 3, 2014, 503–540. On this "saga," among the others, see also: Weston J., *A Ban Behind Bars: A Critical Analysis of Britain's Blanket Ban on Prisoner Voting*, in Ordines, 1, 2017, 68–123; Dzehtsiarou K., "Prisoner Voting Saga: Reasons for Challenges," in Dickson B. and Hardman H. (eds.), *Electoral Rights in Europe Advances and Challenges*, Routledge, London and New York, 2017.

6 ECtHR, *Frodl v. Austria*, Application no.20201/04, 8 April 2010.

7 ECtHR, *Kulinski and Sabev v. Bulgaria*, Application no.63849/09, 21 July 2016.

8 ECtHR, *Ramishvili v. Georgia*, Application no.1704/06, 27 January 2009.

9 ECtHR, *Scoppola v. Italy (No 3)*, Application no. 126/05, 22 May 2012.

10 ECtHR, *Calmanovici v. Romania*, Application no. 42250/02, 1 July 2008.

11 ECtHR, *Anchugov and Gladkov v. Russia*, Application Nos. 11157/04 and 15162/05, 4 July 2013; ECtHR, *Isakov and Others v. Russia*, Application no. 54446/07, 4 July 2017.

12 ECtHR, *Söyler v. Turkey*, Application no. 29411/07, 17 September 2013.

13 The Court, in the Italian case, stated that the Italian system has not the general, automatic, and indiscriminate character that led it, in the *Hirst (No. 2)* case, to find a violation of Article 3 of Protocol 1. In Italy, indeed, there is no disenfranchisement in connection with minor offences or those which, although more serious in principle, do not attract sentences of three years' imprisonment or more, regard being had to the circumstances in which they were committed and to the offender's personal situation. As a result, a large number of convicted prisoners are not deprived of the right to vote in parliamentary elections. Moreover, "under Italian law it is possible for a convicted person who has been permanently deprived of the right to vote to recover that right. Three years after having finished serving his sentence, he can apply for rehabilitation, which is conditional on a consistent and genuine display of good conduct and extinguishes any outstanding ancillary penalty (Articles 178 and 179 of the Criminal Code – see paragraph 38 above). In addition, the length of the sentence actually served may be reduced in accordance with the early release mechanism provided for in section 54 (1) of Law no. 354 of 1975, under the terms of which a reduction of forty-five days for every six months served is granted if the detainee takes part in the re-education scheme. This means that he can apply for rehabilitation and, where applicable, recover the right to

the other six countries were asked to change their policies on the disenfranchisement of prisoners, where this was applied automatically and indiscriminately.[14]

The leading case: Hirst v. United Kingdom

In 2001, three convicted prisoners challenged an Electoral Registration Officer's decision not to register them to vote. This rejection was based on the Representation of People Act 1983, as amended by the Representation of People Act 1985, which – at Schedule 3 (1) – reads that "a convicted person during the time that he is detained in a penal institution in pursuance of his sentence is legally incapable of voting at any parliamentary or local government election." In other words, any UK prisoners serving a custodial sentence, under the law, do not have the right to vote. The *ratio legis* of the ban enshrined in this statute is linked to the notion of "civic death," which dates back to the Forfeiture Act 1870, and which has consistently been renewed through the years on the basis that "prisoners should lose their right to vote while in detention because if you commit a crime that is serious, you should lose the right to have to say in how you are governed." The High Court dismissed the applications. One of the applicants, John Hirst, who – at that time – was serving a life sentence for having been convicted of a serious crime, asked the High Court to make a declaration of incompatibility under the HRA 1998. However, the High Court ruled that the right to vote is of high constitutional importance and it is a matter for Parliament to decide whether prisoners should vote and that Parliament has taken the view that convicted prisoners, for the period during which they are in custody, have forfeited their right to have a say in the way the country is governed. In the view of the High Court, the ban was compatible with the ECHR since the prisoners' disenfranchisement was one of the possible, rational, and fully legitimate political approaches to the issue.[15]

The case was then brought to the attention of the ECtHR which in 2004 ruled unanimously that the UK's blanket ban on prisoners' voting breached Article 3, Protocol 1 of the ECHR.[16] The Government, evidently, appealed that decision, which openly challenged a well-established political position.

---

vote at an earlier date. In the Court's opinion this possibility shows that the Italian system is not excessively rigid."

14 For an accurate and updated deepening of the mentioned jurisprudence, see: Celiksoy E., *Execution of the Judgments of the European Court of Human Rights in Prisoners' Right to Vote Cases*, in Human Rights Law Review, 20, 2020, 555–581.

15 [2001] EWHC Admin 239.

16 ECtHR, *Hirst United Kingdom*, Application no. 74025/01, 30 June 2004. It seems important here to remind ourselves of the wording of Article 3, Protocol 1. Under this article the Contracting States are obliged "to hold free elections at reasonable intervals by secret ballot, under conditions which will ensure the free expression of the opinion of the people in the choice of the legislature." The wording of this Article is different from all other substantive clauses in the Convention and its Protocols, and it does not directly grant individual rights and contains no other conditions for the elections, including in relation to the scope of a

The aforementioned facts had an impact on the national political debate: indeed, in 2004 the Prison Reform Trust and Unlock launched a campaign to secure the right to vote for prisoners, and in 2005, during the run up to the general election, the Liberal Democrats called for prisoners to be allowed to vote on the basis of their being citizens. However, those voices were relatively feeble at the political level: it is sufficient to remind ourselves that in the 2005 general elections the Lib Dems obtained only 61 Seats in the House of Commons, while Labour obtained 356 Seats. However, the political issue on prisoners voting was, at that point, still at an early stage and far from settled, since – shortly after the general election – the Grand Chamber ruled against the UK, holding by a majority of 12 to 5 that there was a breach of Article 3, Protocol No 1.[17]

The Grand Chamber, in its *Hirst (no. 2)* judgment, emphasised that the rights guaranteed under Article 3, Protocol 1 are crucial to establishing and maintaining the foundations of an effective and meaningful democracy governed by the rule of law, and that the right to vote, even though it is not absolute, is not a privilege. The Court reaffirmed as well that the margin of appreciation in this area is wide and that there are numerous ways of organising and running electoral systems depending on historical development, cultural diversity, and political thought. However, it found that the Representation of People Act 1983

> stripped of their Convention right to vote a significant category of people and it did it so in a way which was indiscriminate. It applied automatically to convicted prisoners in prison, irrespective to the length of their sentence and irrespective of the nature or gravity of their offence and their individual circumstances.

In other words: the UK's blanket ban on prisoners' voting was an automatic and indiscriminate restriction which fell outside any acceptable margin of

right to vote, other than the requirement that the free expression of the opinion of the people must be ensured. The Commission in its early case law did not consider that the Article granted individual rights, but then it changed its approach and the Court subsequently held that the Article does grant individual rights, including the right to vote, while at the same time recognising that such individual rights are not absolute but are open to implied limitations leaving the Contracting States *a wide margin of appreciation*, which is nonetheless subject to the Court's scrutiny. The Court must therefore satisfy itself that limitations do not curtail the rights in question to such an extent as to impair their very essence and deprive them of their effectiveness. See, among others: Bellamy R., "The democratic legitimacy of international human rights conventions: political constitutionalism and the *Hirst* case," in Føllesdal A., Schaffer J., & Ulfstein G. (eds.), *The Legitimacy of International Human Rights Regimes: Legal, Political and Philosophical Perspectives*, Cambridge University Press, Cambridge, 2013, 243–271.

17 ECtHR, *Hirst v. United Kingdom (no. 2)*, Application no. 74025/01, Grand Chamber, 6 October 2005.

appreciation.[18] The UK legislature therefore had the *duty* to decide on the choice of means for securing the rights by Article 3, Protocol 1.

Before going on with the case law on this issue, it is important to point out two preliminary considerations.

First of all, it is important to consider the facts of the case. The applicant, Mr Hirst, pleaded guilty to manslaughter and was serving a discretionary life sentence. The Court did not seem to take this factual element into consideration and merely focused, similarly to a Constitutional Court, on the general issue of prisoners' right to vote and on the law, without considering the fact that in all likelihood, even a less restrictive ban would have limited the applicant's right to vote given he was serving a life sentence.

Secondly, it is worth noting that the political debate, which was set off by the *Hirst (No. 2)* judgment, was partly focused on a constitutional issue only marginally linked with the right of prisoners to vote: this judgment, indeed, offered the opportunity to dispute the UK's relationship with the European Court of Human Rights, which was accused of seeking to impose its political views. Therefore, at the centre of the political debate was the bipartisan defence of the parliamentary sovereignty: i.e., Parliament's legislative authority cannot be overstepped by an international Court, which should not dictate the legislative agenda and which should not "suggest" the result of the legislative process. Those criticisms were even stronger considering the nature of the right at stake: in a case concerning the integrity of the electoral process and the essence of democracy itself the ECtHR should have borne in mind, as the minority judges wrote in the dissenting opinions, "that the Court is not a legislator and should be careful not to assume legislative functions,"[19] but rather that it should respect the wide margin of appreciation unless – and it was not the case here – restrictions to the right impair the very essence of the vote or are arbitrary.

Legislation expresses the sense of societal values of a community in relation to serious criminal behaviour and the right to vote in the society. The choice of Parliament on this issue is not merely symbolic, but rather it sends a clear message to people who are found guilty of serious crimes: they will be separated from society, which means that they will have the privileges of society removed from them, among which is the right to vote for their representative. The Westminster choice was clear and it had been reiterated in 1983, 1985, and most clearly in 2000 when the Government's proposal to amend the Representation of the People Act 2000 to permit remand prisoners and un-convicted mental patients to vote, was dismissed by Parliament. Why then should this clear and deliberate choice be changed?

18 *Ibidem*, at para. 82.

19 *Ibidem*, Joint dissenting opinion of judges Wildhaber, Costa, Lorenzen, Kovler and Jebens, at para. 6.

The pilot procedure: Green and M.T. v. United Kingdom

Coming back to the series of case law which follows the *Hirst (No. 2)* judgment, it is important to mention the *Greens and M.T. v. United Kingdom* judgment, delivered at the end of 2010, therefore five years later than the *Hirst* judgment. Here, the Strasbourg Court, since there had been no amendment in the national law, confirmed the continuing violation of Article 3, Protocol 1 ECHR and it clarified that the violation was due to the UK's failure to implement the previous judgment. The Court having considered the significant number of applications raising arguments similar to those in *Hirst* received shortly before the general election in 2010, made use of the pilot judgment procedure. As a result, the Court on one hand required the UK to amend the legislation concerning the contested blanket ban within six months of the *Greens and M.T.* judgment becoming final, while on the other hand it discontinued, for the same period of time, the examination of the pending applications concerning the same issue (approximatively 2,000) and in the event of compliance by the UK, those pending cases would have been struck out.

It is worth noting that the Court rejected the applicant's claim for compensation, holding that the finding itself of the violation constituted sufficient just satisfaction. Moreover, the Court made clear that, in general, claims for legal costs would be excluded from future cases, that is, assuming that an application was straightforward and did not require any legal assistance, even though in that specific case it awarded a total sum of 5,000 Euro for the applicants by way of reimbursement of legal costs and expenses. The Court, clearly, had sought to avoid any attempt by the applicants to take advantage of their situation by taking the case to the ECtHR with the sole aim of making money, that is to say, without any real interest in the voting issue. However, on the other hand, in doing so the Court lost an important tool for applying political pressure to ensure the execution of the judgment and a way to "condemn" the resistance to the application of the judgment which at that point had lasted nine years.

The six-month deadline was then extended in order to allow the UK to intervene as a third party in the Italian prisoner voting case *Scoppola (no. 3) v. Italy*, which was due to be heard by the Grand Chamber on 2 November 2011. In that hearing the UK Government asked the Court to revisit its previous decision and, in support of its claim, indicated that the compatibility of the legislation of the United Kingdom with the guidelines established in the *Hirst (No. 2)* case had been debated on 10 February 2011 in the House of Commons, but that the House had voted by 234 to 22 against narrowing the scope of section 3 of the Representation of the People Act 1983.

However, the position of the UK did not succeed and, in May 2012, the Grand Chamber gave its judgment which reaffirmed its ruling in *Hirst (No. 2)*. In the view of the Court, nothing had occurred or changed at the European and Convention levels since the *Hirst (No. 2)* judgment that might lend support to the suggestion that the principles set forth in that case should be re-examined. "On the contrary, analysis of the relevant international and European documents and comparative-law information reveals the opposite trend, if anything – towards fewer restrictions on convicted prisoners' voting rights." Therefore, when disenfranchisement affects a group of people generally, automatically, and indiscriminately, based solely on the fact that they are serving a prison sentence, irrespective of the length of the sentence and irrespective of the nature or gravity of their offence and their individual circumstances, it is not compatible with Article 3, Protocol 1. The UK was then granted a deferral of the deadline imposed by *Greens and MT*, and was given six months from 22 May 2012 to introduce proposals to address the blanket ban.

Other judgments and decisions related to the saga

There are other areas of case law concerning the right of prisoners to vote in the UK and those decisions will be shortly discussed here.

In 2014, in the case of *Firth and Others v. United Kingdom*,[20] a case concerning several prisoners who were automatically prevented from voting in the elections to the European Parliament held on 4 June 2009, the Strasbourg Court, even though it recognised the steps taken in the UK, with the publication of a draft bill and a report by the Parliamentary Joint Committee appointed to examine the bill, considered that those steps were not enough to amend the offending legislation and therefore declared, once again, a violation of Article 3, Protocol 1.

One year later, in *McHugh and Others v. United Kingdom*,[21] a case concerning 1,015 prisoners, the Court, after having considered that the relevant legislation had not yet been amended, concluded (again) that there had been a violation of conventional voting rights.

The Court, sitting as a Committee, confirmed the ruling again in 2016 and in 2019 with regard to prisoners who were prevented from voting in the European Parliament elections, the Scottish Parliament elections and the general election in the cases *Millbank and Others v. United Kingdom*[22] and *Miller and Others v. United Kingdom*.[23]

It is worth highlighting that the *Miller* judgment was decided following a move by the UK Government in 2018 – as will be discussed in more detail later – to adopt a number of administrative measures which the Committee of Ministers

20 ECtHR, *Firth and Others v. United Kingdom*, Application Nos. 47784/09, 47806/09, 47812/09, 47818/09, 47829/09, 49001/09, 49007/09, 49018/09, 49033/09 and 49036/09, 12 August 2014.

21 ECtHR, *McHugh and Others v. United Kingdom*, Application no. 51987/08, 10 February 2015.

22 ECtHR, *Millbank and Others v. United Kingdom*, Application nos. 44473/14, 58659/14, 70874/14, 71699/14, 73574/14, 73638/14, 73771/14, 73783/14, 73909/14, 73911/14, 74403/14, 74409/14, 75735/14, 75846/14, 2294/15, 18149/15, 24868/15, 26031/15, 26045/15, 28688/15, 32681/15 and 32685/15, 30 June 2016.

23 ECtHR, *Miller and Others v. United Kingdom*, Applications nos. 70571/14 and 6 others, 11 April 2019.

declared satisfactory enough to close the supervision of the execution concerning the *Hirst (No. 2)* group of cases. However, the Court considered that the violation referred to elections which preceded the package of measures adopted by the respondent Government in 2018 when the statutory ban on prisoners voting in elections was, by reason of its blanket character, incompatible with Article 3 of Protocol 1.

In order to give a complete picture of the Strasbourg jurisprudence on this issue, we need also to remind ourselves of three decisions on admissibility which helped to define the meaning and the applicability of Article 3, Protocol 1. We refer to the cases of *McLean and Cole v. United Kingdom* (2013),[24] *Dunn and Others v. United Kingdom* (2014),[25] and *Moohan and Gillon v. United Kingdom* (2017).[26] First of all, the Court clarified that it is not possible to complain about forthcoming elections: many relevant events may occur between the lodging of the applications and the date of the elections (for instance, release from detention, transfer to a psychiatric hospital, or even death). Moreover, not all types of voting are covered by Article 3, Protocol 1 of the Convention: indeed, the Court clarified that referenda[27] and local elections fall outside the scope of the Convention right and therefore declared inadmissible the application brought to Strasbourg by applicants, who were serving prison sentences, who contested that they were ineligible to vote in a nationwide referendum on the alternative vote on 5 May 2011, in the independence referendum organised in Scotland on 18 September 2014 and in various local elections. More specifically, the Court recalled that the word "legislature" in Article 3 of Protocol 1 does not necessarily mean the national Parliament: the word has to be interpreted in the light of the constitutional structure of the State in question. However, the legislative function of local authorities in the United Kingdom is restricted to the making of by-laws, which are applicable only in their local authority area, and the scope of this function is rigidly limited by statute. Furthermore, local authorities in the United Kingdom are the repositories of powers which are essentially of an administrative nature and concern the organisation and provision of local services. These powers are granted by a statute which closely and restrictively defines their field of application.

24 ECtHR, *McLean and Cole v. United Kingdom*, Application nos. 12626/13 and 2522/12, December 28 June 2013.

25 ECtHR, *Dunn and Others v. United Kingdom*, Application nos. 7408/09, 566/10, 578/10 et al., December 13 May 2014.

26 ECtHR, *Moohan and Gillon v. United Kingdom*, Application nos. 22962/15 and 23345/15, December 13 June 2017.

27 The Court has explained that in principle a referendum does not fall within the scope of Article 3 of Protocol 1 however, it takes account of the diversity of electoral systems in the various States. It has thus not excluded the possibility that a democratic process described as a "referendum" by a Contracting State could potentially fall within the ambit of Article 3 of Protocol 1. In order to do so the process would need to take place "at reasonable intervals by secret ballot, under conditions which will ensure the free expression of the opinion of the people in the choice of the legislature."

The long-running political resistance

After having considered and analysed the relevant ECtHR's jurisprudence, we will, at this point, consider the long process of the implementation of the selected judgments and we will try to evaluate the legal and economic impact of the development of this implementation at the national level.

Preliminarily, we can affirm that the economic impact of the prisoners' voting saga is to be considered quite limited for two sets of reasons. First of all, the Court avoided the granting of compensation to the applicants, holding that the finding itself of the violation constituted sufficient just satisfaction, and generally also rejected the claim for legal costs, assuming that application did not require any legal assistance. Therefore, the execution of the ECtHR's judgment did not have direct economic costs. Secondly, the UK electoral system allows postal and proxy voting, it is therefore not necessary to provide polling stations in prison (solution that may be more expensive).

Instead, as it has already been pointed out, the *Hirst* case raised a deep seated *political* debate about the relationship between the ECtHR and the UK and the defence of the principle of parliamentary sovereignty. The following analysis will provide evidence of the main parts of the debate and it will especially consider the most recent evolution of the process of executing the judgement. [28]

In the aftermath of the Grand Chamber judgment in the case *Hirst*, at the beginning of 2006, the then Lord Chancellor announced a public consultation on prisoners' voting rights in order to raise a debate and examine all the possible options. The consultation document, published at the end of the same year, did not hide the firm position of the Government, which believed that "individuals who have committed an offence serious enough to warrant a term of imprisonment, should not be able to vote while in prison." The two-stage consultation process should have helped the Government to identify a proposal which might have worked in practice even though, of course, Parliament was, ultimately, the appropriate place to debate and decide upon the issue, given it was so significant from a constitutional point of view. Unfortunately, after two years the consultation process remained stuck at the first stage and the Government had not introduced any draft legislation. The official position was that the prisoners' voting issue had to be discussed in a wider debate based on the Governance of Britain Green Paper, which at its core was a proposal for a national debate on citizenship and the linked rights and responsibilities. The Government kept the Committee of Ministers updated on progress towards the implementation of the

28 A complete report of the issue of prisoners' voting rights can be found in: A. Horne, I. White, *Prisoners' voting rights (2005 to May 2015)*, Standard Note no. 01764, 11 February 2015, House of Commons Library; N. Johnston, *Prisoners' voting rights: developments since May 2015*, Briefing Paper no. 07461, 18 August 2020, House of Commons Library, both the documents are available at www.parliament.uk/commons-library.

Hirst judgment, however it is not difficult to see that this was a political tactic aimed at slowing things down.

In December 2010, the UK's Coalition Government proposed an amendment to the law to allow prisoners serving less than four years in prison to vote. However, on 10 February 2011, the House of Commons voted by 234 to 22 against the proposal and in favour of the retention of the blanket ban enshrined in section 3 of *the Representation of the People Act* 1983.

Almost five years later, in 2015, the then Lord Chancellor Michael Gove highlighted, before the House of Lords Select Committee on the Constitution, the conflict of respecting both the judgment of the ECtHR and the sovereignty of Parliament to decide the issue of prisoners voting and concluded that in having to choose between the two important principles, the UK *must* respect the democratic principle of parliamentary sovereignty.[29] A very strong position which partially reflects the political resistance to the implementation of the ECtHR judgments. However, it can be observed that this resistance is not really a general one, but one that varies case by case. Examining the statistics helps us to understand that point: if we consider the Court's entire life time (up until 2018) we can see that the number of adverse judgments totals 315. By the end of 2018, the UK was responsible for a total of 12 of the total pending judgments before the Committee of Ministers (i.e., 12 out of the 315 adverse judgments whose implementation is still being supervised).

One year later, in December 2016, the UK Government gave a public commitment to the Committee of Ministers of the Council of Europe that it would propose solutions in order to address the prisoners voting issue raised by *Hirst (No. 2)* case. The political scenario was then slightly different from that seen in the past; the referendum on *Brexit* had changed priorities and the political resistance to the Convention system had been set apart. Following the general elections in 2017, the newly nominated Secretary of State for Justice, David Lidington, sought to address the problem concerning the prisoners' voting by making non-legislative proposals.

Specifically, he proposed two administrative changes while maintaining the general restriction on convicted prisoners in custody.

The first one was to explicitly notify prisoners that on conviction they would lose the right to vote: he intended to work with the judiciary in order to make clear to convicted criminals when they are sentenced that while they are in prison they cannot vote.

29 Bates E., "Democratic Override (or Rejection) and the Authority of the Strasbourg Court: The UK Parliament and Prisoner Voting," in Saul M., Føllesdal A., Ulfstein G. (eds.), *The International Human Rights Judiciary and National Parliaments: Europe and Beyond*, Cambridge University Press, Cambridge, 2017, 275–303; Hardman H., *In the name of parliamentary sovereignty: conflict between the UK Government and the courts over judicial deference in the case of prisoner voting rights*, in British Politics, 15, 2020, 226–250.

The second one was to amend Prison Service Guidance for prisoners released on temporary licence[30] and prisoners released on home detention curfew[31] in order to allow a limited number of convicted prisoners to vote. Indeed, in these cases, offenders are released back into the community and this step is usually linked with their full return to society: therefore, reinstating the civic right to vote is consistent with the general approach of the law.[32]

The Council of Europe Committee Ministers accepted the package of proposals submitted by the UK Government and considered them sufficient, if implemented, in order to comply with the *Hirst* group of judgments.[33] The UK Government committed to updating the Council of Europe on progress on 1 September 2018 and reported that

> a) prisoners on remand can vote; b) prisoners committed to prison for contempt of court can vote; c) prisoners committed to prison for defaulting on the payment of fines can vote; d) eligible prisoners released on temporary licence can vote; e) prisoners released on home detention curfew can vote.

It must be noted that the list of categories of prisoners allowed to vote is slightly misleading, since those in the "a," "b," and "c" categories were already allowed to vote when the ECtHR declared there to be a violation of Article 3, Protocol 1 in the *Hirst (No. 2)* case. Therefore, only two new categories of prisoners (namely "d" and "e") were effectively enfranchised and the impact of the changes were extremely limited, ultimately providing the right to vote to up to one hundred prisoners.[34] However, the Council of Europe confirmed that the case was closed.

The long-running dispute between the UK and Strasbourg has come to an end. Not probably the best end, but still an end.

30 Release on Temporary Licence ("ROTL") is the mechanism that enables prisoners to leave prison during the day to participate in certain activities (primarily related to employment), outside of the prison establishment. Most prisoners eligible to vote under this proposal would likely be on short sentences. Key to the possibility of ROTL is that the prisoner poses no risk to the community or the public.

31 Detention scheme whereby certain prisoners, who pose no risk to the public, are released from prison before the completion of their sentence to allow them to integrate back into society. Typically, such prisoners are required to remain in their designated home between 7 p.m. and 7 a.m. This scheme allows prisoners to live outside of prison, providing that they do not breach the rules of their curfew.

32 See at House of Commons Hansard, 2 November 2017, vol. 630 col. 1007 available online at: https://hansard.parliament.uk/commons/2017-11-02/debates/9E75E904-9B25-475F-87C4-DD8F3C4836C4/Sentencing.

33 Council of Europe, Committee of Ministers 1302nd meeting, 5–6 December 2017, pp. 171–173. Available at https://rm.coe.int/native/09000016807647ff.

34 See David Lidington statement in House of Commons Hansard, 2 November 2017, vol. 630 col. 1007, cit.

It is interesting to consider, in order to offer a complete picture, that the minor administrative changes adopted by the UK Government affect only general elections, since the responsibility for elections to the Scottish Parliament and National Assembly for Wales are devolved, including the question of those enfranchised to vote in those elections. Therefore, prisoner voting for devolved elections has been considered separately in both countries. The position of Scotland and Wales on the issue of prisoners' voting is, undoubtedly, much less rigid than that of the UK central Government. Indeed, the Scottish Government, after having rejected a proposal by Scottish Parliament's Equalities and Human Rights Committee which suggested removing the ban on prisoners in its entirety, preferred to extend the franchise only to prisoners sentenced to a term of 12 months or less. Therefore, under the *Scottish Elections (Franchise and Representation) Act* 2020, recently approved in February 2020, convicted prisoners serving a prison sentence of one year (or less) may register to vote in local and Scottish Parliamentary elections and are permitted to vote by post or proxy. In Wales the legislative process is still in progress and currently, prisoners in Wales cannot register to the vote. However, the Welsh Government is evaluating the possibility of allowing prisoners serving sentences of less than 4 years to register to vote in local elections and this, in its opinion, would affect nearly 1,900 prisoners.[35]

Conclusions: *Much Ado About Nothing*?

After the clamour of the long period of resistance, the epilogue of the prisoners' voting saga has arrived quietly. The rather weak solution proposed by the UK Government, exclusively in order to close a never-ending dispute, can be defined as minimalist compliance[36] and the minor administrative changes can be read as a demonstration of the UK's political resistance to an effective implementation of ECtHR judgments. Indeed, the Strasbourg Court has always and expressly emphasised (in the relevant jurisprudence aforementioned) the need to make a *legislative change* in order to put an end to the blanket ban on prisoners' right to vote enshrined in section 3 of the *Representation of People Act* 1983;[37] it has

35 Welsh Government, *Prisoners voting plans unveiled*, press release, 8 march 2020.

36 VON STADEN A., *Minimalist compliance in the UK Prisoner Voting Rights Cases*, November 2018. In the same direction of criticism: CELIKSOY A., *Execution of the Judgments of the European Court of Human Rights in Prisoners' Right to Vote Cases*, cited above, and ADAMS E., *Prisoners' Voting Rights: Case Closed?*, in Blog of UK Constitutional Law Association, 30 January 2019. Available at: https://ukconstitutionallaw.org/2019/01/30/elizabeth-adams-prisoners-voting-rights-case-closed/.

37 For example, in *Greens and M.T. v. United Kingdom* at para. 115 the Court affirmed that UK "must introduce legislative proposals to amend section 3 of the 1983 Act … with the view to the enactment of an electoral law to achieve compliance with the Court's judgment in *Hirst.*" In the following cases (*Firth and Others v. United Kingdom*, *McHugh and Others v. United Kingdom* and *Millbank and Others v. United Kingdom*) the Strasbourg judges stressed that the law had not been amended and held that "the statutory ban on prisoners voting in elections was, by reason of its blanket character, incompatible with article 3 of Protocol No 1 of the Convention."

never suggested an administrative change since the declared violation was deeply rooted in the statute due to the fact that the *statutory ban* applied automatically and indiscriminately to prisoners who were in detention. However, the UK has remained deaf to that statement and its political opposition has remained unmovable. Proof of what we have just affirmed can be found in the fact that the political opposition to the necessary legislative amendments has been reaffirmed recently in the Conservative Party's General Election Manifesto of 2019, where it was stated – even though it was not strictly necessary since the examination of prisoners' right vote case against the UK had already been closed – that the ban on prisoners voting from jail would be maintained.[38] It is worth noting that the latter's unnecessary clarification may be read as a targeted political warning sign for the ECtHR's future judgments on the same issue.

The UK's minimalist compliance to the ECtHR judgments has had at least three adverse consequences:

(i) a risky precedent for more problematic Countries (such as Russia and Turkey) adjudged to have violated Article 3, Protocol 1 of the Convention;
(ii) a conflict between the Strasbourg Court and the Committee of Ministers;
(iii) a minor impact on the prisoners voting in UK.

Let's try to delve into the details of the aforementioned problems.

First of all, *(i)* the endorsement by the Committee of Ministers of the administrative package of measures proposed by UK Government constitutes a detrimental precedent that has already been used by Russia and Turkey in order to persuade the Committee of Ministers to close its examination of their compliance on the right of prisoners to vote without any valuable legislative change. For instance, Turkish Authorities explicitly drew the Committee's attention to the Committee of Ministers' final resolution in the *Hirst* group of cases where it was decided that the examination concerning the same issue of prisoners' voting rights should be closed. The general measures taken by the UK Government in the *Hirst* group of cases, in the view of Turkish Authorities, were in line with the measures set by Turkish Legislation and practice, and therefore also had to be considered to be compatible with the Convention.[39] The Committee of Ministers, therefore, had to act consistently with its precedent and decided to close its examination, even though, in general, the Turkish democratic situation is not comparable with the British one. Similar considerations could be made with regard to Russia where, incidentally, the ban was enshrined in the Constitution and the Constitutional Court has already "contested" the execution of the ECtHR Judgment.

38 Conservative and Unionist Party Manifesto 2019, p. 19 available online.

39 See Communication from Turkey concerning the *Soyler* group of cases (Application no. 29411/07), paras. 32-34. Available online at: https://search.coe.int/cm/Pages/result_details.aspx?ObjectID=0900001680920439. See also Resolution CM/ResDH (2019)147 – Execution of the judgments of the European Court of Human Rights, adopted by the Committee of Ministers on 6 June 2019 at the 1348th meeting of the Ministers' Deputies.

Moreover, *(ii)* the view of the Strasbourg judges and the view of Committee of Ministers seem to differ quite significantly. While the Court has always asked for legislative change, the Committee of Ministers has endorsed an administrative (and rather bland) change. It might be that this conflict is going to remain unexploded since, under the Convention system,[40] the Committee of Ministers has the ultimate responsibility for supervising the execution of judgments, which is a political (and not judicial) tool conferred to a political organ. However, this consideration may be quite misleading in practice. Indeed, the Court maintains a role in the execution of judgments.[41]

It is up to the Court, for example, within the pilot procedure, to suggest the type of measures that the State might take in order to end a systematic violation of the Convention.[42] Indeed, in *Greens M.T. v. United Kingdom*, which applied the pilot judgment form, the Court has expressly asked the UK Government to put forward "legislative proposals intended to amend the 1983 Act (… *omissis*) in a manner which is Convention-compliant" within the wide margin of appreciation accorded. That means that the Court, recalling its subsidiarity role, provided the respondent Government with some guidance as to what is required for the proper execution of the present judgment, but it did it only with regard to the procedure (i.e., legislative amendment), leaving the UK Government free to evaluate the wide range of policy alternatives which were available.

Of course we have to bear in mind that the ultimate choice of the measures to be taken remains with the States under the supervision of the Committee of Ministers,[43] but at the same time we should consider whether the measures taken by the respondent State (and accepted by the Committee of Ministers) are compatible with the conclusions of the Court's judgment. The institutional balance between the Court and the Committee of Ministers can be seen as quite unstable: on one side the execution process cannot be limited by the Court's explicit indications because it would withdraw the flexibility needed by the Committee of Ministers to carry out its supervision, but on the other side the Committee's execution process cannot betray the spirit of the judgment. Until now the Court has followed the Committee when the latter accepted the execution measures, but things may change when future post reform cases on prisoners' voting rights will arise.

The latter considerations lead us to the next point.

40 Article 46, section 2, European Convention on Human Rights: "The final judgment of the Court shall be transmitted to the Committee of Ministers, which shall supervise its execution."

41 On the role that Strasbourg Court carries out in "supervising" execution, see, among others, Glas L. R., *The European Court of Human Rights supervising the execution of its judgments*, in Netherlands Quarterly of Human Rights, 37, 3, 2019, 228–244.

42 ECtHR, *Burmich and others v. Ukraine*, Application Nos. 46852 et al., Strike Out 12 October 2017, especially at para. 198.

43 ECtHR, *Ilgar Mammadov v. Azerbaijan* [GC], Application no. 15172/13, 29 May 2019, para. 182.

Indeed, *(iii)* we cannot avoid a consideration of the practical effects of the minor administrative changes introduced in the British system. Unfortunately, the Electoral Statistics, UK: 2019, published in May 2020, do not contain any data about prisoner voting, therefore it is not possible to carry out an accurate evaluation, rather we can only provide some reflections on the basis of general information.

In November 2019 (1 month before the general elections) there were nearly 90,000 total prisoners in the UK. Almost 25% of the total number of prisoners (regardless of the fact that they are in prison) are not eligible to vote because they are not UK citizens or they are underage. In *Green and M.T. v. United Kingdom* the Court affirmed that, at that time, there were approximately 2,500 applications to decide and observed that the number was going to grow with each relevant election. These numbers become quite interesting if we consider that the administrative changes were estimated to affect up to 100 offenders on temporary licence (at any election).[44]

It will be interesting to see if, facing these numbers and the difference of policies between devolved and general elections, the Strasbourg Court will say something or if the UK Government has had, on this issue, the last word. If so, this is *Much Ado About Nothing*.

Bibliography

Adams E., *Prisoners' Voting Rights: Case Closed?*, in Blog of UK Constitutional Law Association, 30 January 2019. Available at: https://ukconstitutionallaw.org/2019/01/30/elizabeth-adams-prisoners-voting-rights-case-closed/.

Bates E., *Analysing the Prisoner Voting Saga and the British Challenge to Strasbourg*, in Human Rights Law Review, 14, 3, 2014, 503–540.

Bates E., "Democratic Override (or Rejection) and the Authority of the Strasbourg Court: The UK Parliament and Prisoner Voting," in Saul M., Follesdal A., Ulfstein G. (eds.), *The International Human Rights Judiciary and National Parliaments: Europe and Beyond*, Cambridge University Press, Cambridge, 2017, 275–303.

Bellamy R., "The Democratic Legitimacy of International Human Rights Conventions: Political Constitutionalism and the *Hirst* Case," in Føllesdal A., Schaffer J. and Ulfstein G. (eds.), *The Legitimacy of International Human Rights Regimes: Legal, Political and Philosophical Perspectives*, Cambridge University Press, Cambridge, 2013, 243–271.

Celiksoy A., *Execution of the Judgments of the European Court of Human Rights in Prisoners' Right to Vote Cases*, in Human Rights Law Review, 20, 2020, 555–581.

Dzehtsiarou K., "Prisoner Voting Saga: Reasons for Challenges," in Dickson B. and Hardman H. (eds.), *Electoral Rights in Europe Advances and Challenges*, Routledge, London and New York, 2017.

44 See at House of Commons Hansard, 2 November 2017, vol. 630 col. 1007, cited above.

FRASER, J., *Inclusive Democracy: Franchise Limitations on Non-Resident Citizens as an Unjust Restriction of Rights under the European Convention on Human Rights*, in Utrecht Journal of International and European Law, 33, 84, 2017, 23–43.

GLAS L. R., *The European Court of Human Rights supervising the execution of its judgments*, in Netherlands Quarterly of Human Rights, 37, 3, 2019, 228–244.

HARDMAN, H., *In the Name of Parliamentary Sovereignty: Conflict Between the UK Government and the Courts Over Judicial Deference in the Case of Prisoner Voting Rights*, in British Politics, 15, 2020, 226–250.

HORNE A., WHITE I., *Prisoners' Voting Rights (2005 to May 2015)*, Standard Note no. 01764, 11 February 2015, House of Commons Library. Available at www .parliament.uk/commons-library.

JAY Z., *Keeping rights at home: British conceptions of rights and compliance with the European Court of Human Rights*, in The British Journal of Politics and International Relations, 19, 4, 2017, 842–860.

JOHNSTON N., *Prisoners' Voting Rights: Developments Since May 2015*, Briefing Paper no. 07461, 18 August 2020, House of Commons Library. Available at www .parliament.uk/commons-library.

VON STADEN A., *Minimalist Compliance in the UK Prisoner Voting Rights Cases*, November 2018.

WESTON J, *A Ban Behind Bars: A Critical Analysis of Britain's Blanket Ban on Prisoner Voting*, in *Ordines*, 1, 2017.

ZIEGLER K.S., WICKS E., HODSON L. (eds.), *The UK and European Human Rights – A Strained Relationship?*, Hart Publishing, 2015.

Part II

The Inter-American Court of Human Rights

11 The protection of the political rights of minorities in the ACHR

An analysis of the *Norin Catrimán* case and the right to political participation in the State of Chile

Laura Cappuccio

Chilean participation in the Inter-American system of protection of human rights: A clean break

On 22 November 1969 the State of Chile signed the American Convention on Human Rights upon its adoption. Yet, Chile only entered the Inter-American system of protection of human rights many years later. When the Convention entered into force, on 18 July 1978, Chile had still not yet become a member of the system.

In fact, during the years of dictatorship, Chile's international commitments in relation to the protection of human rights went unfulfilled, due to a lack of action in publishing and enacting them in the country.[1] With a view to countering this practice, the 1989 constitutional reform modified Art. 5 of the Constitution by adding a second paragraph specifically referencing the treaties on human rights:

> The exercise of sovereignty is limited by the respect of the essential rights that emanate from human nature. It is the duty of the State's organs to respect and promote those rights, guaranteed by this Constitution, as well as by international treaties which have been ratified by Chile and that are in force.

1 On the point, cf. Nash Rojas C., *Derecho internacional de los derechos humanos,* Centro de Derechos Humanos, Santiago de Chile, 2012, 15 ff. The author recalls that the 1980 Constitution, adopted during the Pinochet dictatorship, deals with international treaties under Art. 50 which sets forth that the treaty "*se someterá a los trámites de una ley*" (shall be subject to the ordinary legislative procedure). The 1980 Constitution, moreover, conferred on the President of the Republic the power to negotiate, sign and ratify treaties; and conferred on the Constitutional Court the responsibility to conduct a preventive review of constitutionality. In this initial stage, doctrine considers the treaties as a law, 16 ff. Cf. also Pérez Herrera E., *Valor jurídico y jerarquía en el derecho chileno de los Derechos Humanos contenidos en Tratados Internacionales*, 2018, 33. Available at http://repositorio.uchile.cl/bitstream/handle/2250/151648/Valor-jur%C3%ADdico-y-jerarqu%C3%ADa-en-el-derecho-chileno-de-los-derechos-humanos-contenidos-en-tratados-internacionales.pdf?sequence=1&isAllowed=y.

DOI: 10.4324/9781003229247-14

Reforms in 1989 placed the young Chilean democracy within the intellectual movement which – in the aftermath of the Second World War – used international laws on human rights as a tool to limit national sovereignty in favour of the protection of citizens' fundamental freedoms. This moment demonstrated a clear break with the historical approach, which is well evidenced by Chile's subsequent participation in the Inter-American system of human rights through the ratification in 1990 of the American Convention. An innovation leading to a meaningful debate around Chilean doctrine and magistracy and leading to discussions on the value that should be afforded to these specific treaties, specifically whether they should be distinguished from others by having a special position attached to them within the system.[2]

Before getting on to the topic of the relationship between the State of Chile and the American Convention on human rights, it is worth recalling a notable aspect of Chilean constitutionalism. The 1980 Constitution underwent several modifications,[3] and yet, despite all the modifications of the original text, the issue of constitutional reform has long remained an animated feature of political life. A unique aspect of the Chilean transition is manifested, through the fact that

> Chile is the only Country in the recent surge of democratisation inheriting a Constitution from the previous dictatorship, which, despite all the reforms adopted during democratic governments, didn't lead to a democratic Constitution, or it didn't experience a "constitutional moment."[4]

2 Nevertheless, it is only with the successive 2005 constitutional reforms that a different concept begins to form by which International treaties have to be considered as a separate source from the law. With regard to this, cf. Nogueira Alcalá H., *Reforma constitucional del 2005 y control de constitucionalidad de tratados internacionales*, in Revista de Estudios Constitucionales, 1, 2007, 59 ff. For a reconstruction of the diverse positions of doctrine, cf. Pérez Herrera E., *Valor jurídico y jerarquía en el derecho chileno de los Derechos Humanos contenidos en Tratados Internacionales*, cited above, 15 ff. and 23 ff.

3 In the Constitutional reform law (2005) there is an attempt to reduce the so-called "*enclave autoritario*" of the Constitution, by eliminating the designated senators, reducing the political role of the armed forces and affecting the duration of the Presidential mandate which decreased from 6 to 4 years. On the reform Martínez Sierra J.M., Ferrer, C., *La reforma constitucional en Chile*, 2004. Available at www2.uned.es/dpto-derecho-politico/Comunicacion_Martinez_Ferrer.pdf.

4 Garretón R., Garretón M.A., *La democracia incompleta en Chile: La realidad tras los rankings internacionales*, in Revista de ciencia políticas, 1, 2010, 144–145. Cf. also Portales F., *La inexistencia de la democracia en Chile*, in Polis Revista Latinoamericana, 2005, 1 ff., highlights, for instance, that the Constitution establishes an "authoritative regime where majoritarian popular will is impeded by a set of anti-democratic institutions: a two-member electoral system – sole in the world – where two and only two representatives are elected in each constituency and by which the first minority is anti-democratically equalled to the majority and, together with the higher quorum necessary to reform the same Constitution and the ordinary Constitutional laws, entitles the majoritarian right parties to preserve all the powers, even when constantly losing the election for the President of the Republic."

It's not by chance that some authors have described the Chilean constitution as an "ocelot" Constitution, modified several times over the years, but still preserving its original footprint which reflects its historical resistance towards genuine popular participation.[5]

The issue of political participation has been mentioned on several occasions as one of the major problems of the Constitution. According to a recent study conducted by the *Centro de Estudios de Conflicto y Cohesión Social (COES)*, for instance, nearly 43% of those interviewed reported dissatisfaction in relation to political participation.[6] Similar dissatisfaction was reported in a *Foco Ciudadano de MIDE Sociedad* study from 2015, where citizens aged between 18 and 64 years old were interviewed.[7] So, despite being considered to be one of the soundest democracies on the Latin American continent and with the highest level of economic development,[8] the 2019 uprisings in Chile showed how historic aspects of the Constitution continue to undermine the system and lead to demands for change.[9]

5 Cfr. Ruiz Tagle P., Cristi R., *La República en Chile. Teoría y Práctica del Constitucionalismo Republicano*, LOM, Santiago, 2006, 198, quoted in Busch Venthur V., *El Concepto de Constitución y la Incomodidad Constitucional en Chile*, in Global jurist, 12, 2, 2012, 11. On authoritarian constitutionalism see Muñoz F., *Arbol genealógico* del Consejo de Estado: el constitucionalismo autoritarioen nuestra historia, in Revista Ius et Praxis, Año 16, N° 22010, p 211.212: "In a nutshell, Chilean authoritarian constitutionalism accentuates the preservation of the social order before the spread of public freedoms or of social justice; gives priority to the historical continuity in favour of institutional experimentation; considers ownership and the forms of sociality associated to it – family, business – as pillars of Chilean society."

6 Cf. https://coes.cl/elsoc-estudio-revela-niveles-de-participacion-politica-de-los-chilenos-y-valoracion-de-la-democracia/.

7 De Tezanos-Pinto P., Cortes F., Concha M., *Participación política y descontento en Chile: una tensión entre el interés en los temas políticos y la desafección generalizada* in www.researchgate.net/publication/338902087_Participacion_politica_y_descontento_en_Chile_Una_tension_entre_el_interes_en_los_temas_politicos_y_la_desafeccion_generalizada. On political participation, cf. Delamaza G., *¿Espacio público y participación ciudadana en la gestión pública en Chile: límites y posibilidades?*, in Polis, 10, 30, 2011, 45 ff.; Sánchez Lobos L., *La representación política, participación ciudadana e iniciativa popular de ley en Chile*, in Ars Boni et Aequi, 11, 2, 2015, 49 ff.

8 In the 2019 Annual Report the American Committee on Human Rights highlights "the sound democratic institutions and the protection of rights in the State of Chile, who ‚since the very beginning of uprisings on 18 October 2019, denounced the situations that were causing a violation of human rights," cf. *Informe anual 2019 Comisión americana de derechos humanos*, in www.oas.org/es/cidh/docs/anual/2019/indice.asp, point 156.

9 Along with this statement that recognises the reliability of Chilean democracy, we also find reported the issues of concern which are mainly related to the repression of the citizens' protest from November 2019, *Annual report 2019 Inter-American Commission on Human Rights*, "As a result of this exaggerated use of power the Committee was informed about 26 deaths, out of them 5 caused by the action of State agents and 2 during the arrest in a *Comisaría de Carabineros*. Based on the information of the Ministry of Health, 12,652 injured people during the demonstrations were treated […] The Committee also received information about the high number of detained people during the protests started on 18 October 2019. The Committee expressed concern for the high number of detentions," point 164–165.

Law 21200 from 24 December 2019, which introduced a change to the XV of the Constitution with a view to launching a process to draft a new fundamental Charter, aimed at responding to this criticism. This law shows in fact the importance of creating a political process which is able to give birth to a Constitution perceived as the outcome of a participatory constituent process.[10] This constitutional process should mark a watershed from the previous system and represents a response to the demands advanced through the massive demonstrations going on in the Country, with a view to obtaining a change in national politics and to improve social and economic conditions.[11]

A real break with Chile's authoritarian past is represented by the ratification of the American Convention on human rights. For 30 years, in fact, Chile has been part of a supranational system of protection of rights that has recognised, since the very beginning, the jurisdiction of the Court. Chile's participation in the Convention may be seen through the lens of the judgments concerning the Country. To date, there have been 10 judgments of the Inter-American Court concerning contentious matters, that have involved Chile, namely: *Case of Órdenes Guerra et al. v. Chile*, Judgment of November 29, 2018; *Case of Poblete Vilches et al. v. Chile*, Judgment of March 8, 2018; *Case of Maldonado Vargas et al. v. Chile*, Judgment of September 2, 2015; *Case of Norín Catrimán et al. (Leaders, Members and Activist of the Mapuche Indigenous People) v. Chile*, Judgment of May 29, 2014; *Case of García Lucero et al. v. Chile. Preliminary*, Judgment of August 28, 2013; *Case of Atala Riffo and daughters v. Chile*, Judgment of

10 Sobre el tema de la Participación Cfr. Heiss C., *Participación política y elaboración constitucional: el caso del Chile*, in Derecho y Crítica Social, 4, 1, 2018, 115 ff.

11 Portales F., *La inexistencia de la democracia en Chile*, cited above, 2, also reminds us that "Based on the laws in force, it shall be reminded that all fundamental laws ruling today the economic, social and cultural system of our Country were imposed by dictatorship. This is true for the laws limiting the role of State in economy, stiffening the system of ownership, violating the labour rights of workers, polarizing the medium and low classes, establishing health, education, social security and merchant systems etc. [...] Hence, in our Country there is an economic, social and cultural neoliberist system which was established by means of the legal system imposed during dictatorship." In the same direction also Heiss C., *Participación política y elaboración constitucional: el caso del Chile*, cited above, 125: "Despite the numerous reforms, the Constitution continues to preserve the transformative project of dictatorship, thus making the central areas of that project immune to the democratic process. This was possible mainly with the introduction of several rules like the high quorum and the mechanisms of super majority preventing any major change of the key areas to occur without the agreement of the political heirs of dictatorship [...]. A system of super majorities including 18 organic constitutional laws that rule about central domains of political life, the two-member electoral system – reformed in 2015 – and the review of the constitutionality of laws by the Constitutional Court, all made a "neutralisation" of the transformative potential of democratic politics and the preservation of the status quo possible [...]." It is also worth recalling that with the successive law 21221 from 26 March 27, some aspects of the plebiscite required for the drafting of the new Constitution were amended by postponing the date of the elections (scheduled for 26 April 2020 and postponed to October of the same year) due to the pandemics.

February 24, 2012; *Case of Almonacid Arellano et al. v. Chile*, Judgment of September 26, 2006; *Case of Claude Reyes et al. v. Chile*, Judgment of September 19, 2006; *Case of Palamara Iribarne v. Chile*, Judgment of November 22, 2005; *Case of "The Last Temptation of Christ" (Olmedo Bustos et al.) v. Chile*, Judgment of February 5, 2001.

These judgments, all quite recent (the first is from 2001), can be broken down into two categories: the first concerns violations of human rights dating back to the period of dictatorship; the second includes a variety of issues ranging from the right to health, to the right to freedom of expression and the right to non-discrimination. Let's take the example of the last two judgments of the American Court on Chile, both from 2018: *Órdenes Guerra v. Chile*, judgment of November 29, 2018; *Poblete Vilches v. Chile* of March 8, 2018.

In *Órdenes Guerra* the Inter-American Court declared Chile responsible for the violation of the right to a fair trial and to judicial protection. The case fell under the category of violations of human rights perpetrated during the dictatorship, which were confirmed by the National Commission for truth and reconciliation founded in 1991. The plaintiffs couldn't have the personal injury they suffered due to the kidnapping, detention or execution of their family members by the state agents between 1973 and 1974 under the military dictatorship recognised, because the case was time-barred. In *Poblete Vilches*, however, the Inter-American Court decided on a second generation right, the right to health, particularly for elderly people, by reconstructing the obligations of Convention State parties on matters of economic and social rights.

The same double case-law line is common to earlier judgments: in *Maldonado Vargas*, from 2015, Chile was found to have been in violation of the right to judicial protection, since the criminal convictions imposed were based on evidence and confessions obtained by torture during the period of dictatorship. In this ruling the finding against the State of Chile was that there was a lack of a genuine recourse to annul criminal proceedings which had been conducted in violation of the right to a fair trial. Similarly, in *García Lucero*, from 2013, the violation of the right to a fair and to judicial protection were caused by the fact that the Chilean State did not conduct a timely investigation into the events which occurred during the dictatorship. In 1973, in fact, Mr. Lucero was arrested, tortured, and put into solitary confinement without facing any specific allegations. However, in *Atala Riffo*, from 2012, the Inter-American Court was asked to decide on a "new right" linked to the discrimination suffered by Mrs. Atala Riffo due to her sexual orientation, in a judgment concerning the custody of her two daughters.

Even further back in time, judgments show this same pattern of alternation: in *Almonacid Arellano* from 2006, the violation of Arts. 8 and 25 of the Convention in relation to fair trial and judicial protection concerned the impossibility of a fair trial being conducted in relation to the extra-legal execution of Mr. Arellano – a school teacher and activist of the Communist Party – who in 1973 was arrested and executed in front of his family. The possibility of investigating the facts was excluded by Decree Law n. 2.191 from 1978, providing an amnesty for violations of human rights perpetrated during the dictatorship.[12] In *Claude Reyes y otros*, the judgment concerned the lack of information in a trial relating to whether deforestation could be harmful to the environment and the absence of an appeal to challenge the lack of information.[13]

As is often the case in the Inter-American system, there is a co-existence of rulings on new rights and legal issues which relate to the authoritarian past. Even in still-pending cases at the merits stage before the Inter-American Court, this tendency persists: *Pavez Pavez v. Chile* and *Urrutia Laubreaux* v. *Chile*. The first, *Pavez Pavez*, presented by the Commission on 22 September 2019, concerns the international responsibility of the State for discrimination against sexual orientation. Mrs. Sandra Cecilia Pavez Pavez was disqualified from teaching religion, a job she had been exercising for more than 22 years, due to her sexual orientation. In *Urrutia Laubreaux v. Chile*, presented on 1 February 2019, the Inter-American Court was called to rule upon a disciplinary procedure against a judge who had submitted an academic paper to the *Corte Suprema de Justicia* criticising them for their work during the military regime.

No advisory opinions are, instead, available concerning the State of Chile. As for provisional measures, to date only one order was issued on 12 March 2020 within the still-pending ruling on the case *Urrutia Laubreaux*. Pursuant to Art. 63 of the Convention, in cases of extreme gravity and urgency, and when required to avoid irreparable damage to persons, the Court shall adopt such provisional measures as it deems pertinent on matters it has under consideration. In the *Urrutia Laubreaux* judgment, San José judges did not accept the request submitted by a representative of Mr. *Urrutia Laubreaux*, who was worried after death threats were directed against him and published on a web site.

If we consider the level of enforcement of these rulings, it might arguably be said that Chile has not always complied with the judgments by the Inter-American Court.[14] To date, only two cases have been closed with a total implementation

12 Cfr. Nogueira Alcalá H., *Los desafíos de la sentencia de la Corte Interamericana en el caso Almonacid Arellano*, in Ius et Praxis, 12, 2, 2006; on the issue of Amnesty, cf. BINDER C., *The Prohibition of Amnesties by the Inter-American Court of Human Rights*, German Law Journal, 12, 2011, 1203 ff.

13 Cf. on this topic. Fernández Vivas Y., *La influencia de la Sentencia de la Corte Interamericana de Derechos Humanos "Claude Reyes contra Chile" en la jurisprudencia del Tribunal Europeo de Derechos Humanos*, in Eunomía. Revista en Cultura de la Legalidad, 9, 2015–2016, 321 ff.

14 On the enforcement of Inter-American Court judgments see with a critical perspective: Schönsteiner J., Couso J., *La implementación de las decisiones de los órganos del sistema interamericano de derechos humanos en Chile: ensayo de un balance*, in Revista de derecho (Coquimbo), 22, 2, 2015, 345: "It is important to remind that the judgments of the Inter-American Court having experienced a resistance during the enforcement stage in our Country concern three main topics: the rights of indigenous people (particularly in case of enforcement of the indigenous consultation on investment projects); the law decree on amnesty; and the military justice. In these cases, the problems are mostly rooted in the legislation and concern issues perceived as 'complex.' This was even worsened by the Executive

of remedial measures achieved: *Claude Reyes v. Chile* from 19 September 2006; and the *Case of "The Last Temptation of Christ"* from 5 February 2001. In both cases, the State of Chile faced demands to ensure a legislative transformation of its legal system. To implement the *Claude Reyes* judgment, for instance, Law n. 20.285 from 2008 was adopted, "*Ley de Transparencia de la Función Pública y Acceso a la Información de la Administración del Estado*," enshrining the right of all people to request and obtain information from any governmental administrative body. Similarly, in order to enforce the decision in "*The Last Temptation of Christ*," the constitutional law on preventive censorship was amended. It is worth here recalling that it took only two years in order to close these two cases. The ruling in "*The Last Temptation of Christ*" is from 2001 and the order giving confirmation of the constitutional amendment is from 2003. The *Claudio Reyes* judgment is from 2006 and the order by the Inter-American Court to close the case is from 2008.

Nevertheless, the fact that the Inter-American System features a wide range of reparation measures which are not limited to the payment of an amount of money as a compensation, makes it tough to achieve them all. This is the reason why supervisory compliance may last several years. Therefore, it would be misleading to state that Chile is generally a non-complying State.

A number of examples can be used. In the *Atala Riffo* ruling, the Inter-American Court sentenced the State of Chile in 2012 to comply with the following reparation measures: to provide healthcare and psychological support to the victims; to publish the official summary of the judgment; to organise a public event to acknowledge the International Responsibility of the State with the participation of the victims and of national high-ranking officials; to deliver courses on human rights, sexual orientation, and LGBT community protection targeted at civil servants; and to pay an amount of money by way of material and immaterial damages compensation. According to the last Inter-American Report (from 10 February 2017) all these measures were implemented by Chile, except for the delivery of courses to civil servants, which – though being delivered – still required some improvement with a view to fully complying with the judgment.

Also, in *Maldonado Vargas* the Court ordered a number of reparation measures: publishing the judgment; organising a public event to acknowledge the international responsibility of the State; placing a stone slab with the names of the victims; making available to the victims, within one year from the service of judgment, an effective mechanism to review and annul the conviction judgments issued against them; going on to conclude the investigation of facts and settling the payments due.

power who refused to use its important co-legislative powers to push bills or constitutional modifications required to enforce the System's decisions on the said topics. On the other side, it can be foreseen that in the forthcoming years the enforcement of the rulings on the rights of indigenous people will become more relevant, because they represent the three cases declared eligible by CIDH."

As for the compliance with all these reparation measures, in the Court report following a progressive adjustment of the State (the latest order is from 30 August 2017, only two years after the adoption of the conviction judgment) it is stated that the State published the judgment, organised a public event to acknowledge its international responsibility and placed a stone slab in memory of the victims. The Supreme Court, by resolution from 3 October 2016, also accepted a review procedure of the criminal proceedings and overturned the conviction adopted by *Consejo de Guerra*. In this case the Supreme Court changed the previous case-law where similar appeals were rejected and overturned the judgment by stating that the compliance with the judgment of the Inter-American Court implies that the interpretation and fulfilment of the procedural requirements provided for the review procedure – as defined in the Code of military justice and the code of criminal procedure – shall abide by the motivations and the resolutions of the International Court.[15]

With regard to the settlement of payments as compensation, they were made to 11 out of 12 victims. The measure that didn't find meet a satisfactory implementation, according to the Court, is the investigation of the facts which resulted in the violation of victims' human rights.

In *Garcia Lucero*, the order from 7 April 2015 reports the settlement of the due compensation[16] and the publication of the judgment. However, with regard to the investigation on the illegal detention and torture suffered by Mr. Lucero – despite the reported diligence by the State in conducting the case – the Inter-American Court did not consider this part of the reparation measures to be sufficiently satisfactory.

If we go back in time with cases like *Almonacid Arellano*, the last order is dated 18 November 2010. In this order, the Court mostly deals with the part of the judgment relating to the non-application of Decree Law 2.191. The Court highlights that the State acted in accordance with the Convention when it did not apply the Decree Law on amnesty to the case concerning the death of Mr. Arellano.[17]. The Court acknowledged that Chile had "fulfilled the duties to

15 Judgment by the *Segunda Sala de la Corte Suprema de Chile* from 3 October 2016, para.36–39. Likewise the Supreme Court ruled in a judgment from 29 August 2019, overturning a ruling by the *Consejo de guerra*, to abide by the judgment of the Inter-American Court on the earlier *Maldonado Vargas* case, cf. www.diarioconstitucional.cl/noticias/asuntos-de-interes-publico/2019/09/04/cs-anula-sentencias-dictadas-por-consejos-de-guerra-de-nuble-y-concepcion/.

16 In the order on the compliance with the reparation measures, the Court deems relevant that the sum due as compensation for the damages suffered was paid to Mr. Lucero on the occasion of a ceremony organised at the Chile Embassy in London, where the damage caused was publicly admitted and a formal apology was made para. 33.

17 On this the Court emphasised that Chile is not only required to no apply the Decree Law on amnesty to the case in object, but should also find a judicial solution by which its application is prevented also in future cases. With regard to this, although Chile states that there are at least two pending bills, the Court requires it to continue being informed on the results of this parliamentary work, cf. para. 22.

rescind the resolutions and judgments issued domestically which in turn gave jurisdiction to the military courts."[18] More specifically, the order mentions that the *Fiscal del Tribunal Supremo* stated that the judgment by the Inter-American Court "necessarily implies [the need] to reopen the trial in front of the ordinary justice and the non-application of the amnesty to the defendants."[19] What still remains unfulfilled is the investigation of the facts. Although the case was ultimately left to a civil court, as requested by the Inter-American Court, at the time of the drafting of the last order, no official documents on the investigation were available. The Court, moreover, requested that Chile provide evidence that Decree Law n. 2.191 was no longer representing an obstacle to the investigation and that those responsible for the death of Mr. Arellano had been punished.

The last order by the Inter-American Court is from 2010; after this, a first instance judgment was issued on 18 August 2011, whereby the perpetrator of Mr. Arellano's murder was convicted. This judgment was subsequently also confirmed on 4 January 2013 by the *Corte de Apelaciones de Rancagua*, recalling that "the proposed issue shall be settled by the national magistracy with the application of the judgment by the Inter-American Court."[20] Indeed, the Supreme Court also confirmed the conviction.[21]

If the so-called individual measures were implemented, those related to the respect of the non-repetition guarantee still remain to be satisfied. More specifically, despite the many bills produced to prevent the Decree Law from being applied in the future, none of them has been approved yet. Nevertheless, even if the numerous bills produced were not approved, domestic case-law has followed the Inter-American Court judgment, thus not applying the law on amnesty.[22]

The subject of the limitations of military courts' jurisdiction is also the object of supervisory compliance in the *Palamara Iribarne* case. In this case the Court pointed out in the last order that ten years and nine months had gone by since Chile had been found in violation and yet still the case remained pending.[23] Out of ten measures taken, only seven had been implemented, among which were: the publication of Mr. Palamara Iribarne's book, the publication of the judgment and the payment of the amounts as compensation. The removal of the criminal history connected with the judgment issued against the victim was also fulfilled.

18 Order of the Inter-American Court of Human Rights of November 18, 2010, *Almonacid Arellano* v. *Chile*, Monitoring Compliance with Judgment, para. 14.

19 Order of Inter-American Court on the compliance with the reparation measures para. 6 a) quoted by Ivanschitz Boudeguer B., *Un estudio sobre el cumplimiento y ejecución de las sentencias de la corte interamericana de derechos humanos por el estado de chile*, in Estudios Constitucionales, 11, 1, 2013, 306.

20 *Corte de Apelaciones de Rancagua*, Rol N 103-2011, de 14 de enero de 2013, (recital 5).

21 Find the news at *Corte Suprema ratifica condena contra ex carabinero en Caso Almonacid* in www.biobiochile.cl/noticias/2013/07/31/corte-suprema-ratifica-condena-contra-ex-carabinero-en-caso-almonacid.shtml.

22 Ivanschitz Boudeguer B., *Un estudio sobre el cumplimiento y ejecución de las sentencias de la corte interamericana de derechos humanos por el estado de chile.*

23 Cf. order by the Inter-American Court from 1 September 2016.

What is still missing for the Court – as in the *Arellano* case – is the implementation of the measures to prevent a repetition of the violation.

These measures require the amendment of certain articles of the criminal code and the code of military justice concerning the crime of contempt, which represents a major limitation to the freedom of expression. Despite the reform of the criminal code, the crime of contempt still persists in the Chilean judicial system.[24] The Court has pointed out that over so many years, no bills which have been submitted to amend this offence in full compliance with the American Convention has ever been adopted. Even the changes made to the jurisdiction of military criminal courts are not fully compliant with the international standards.[25] Despite the adoption of Law n. 20.477 from 2010 which reduces the jurisdiction of the military courts, the issue is not yet satisfactorily closed. More specifically, the Court has reminded the State what standards the international legislation should comply with: military justice is only entitled to rule on active-duty military personnel; offences which, due to their own nature, constitute an attack on military legal interests; and it is not entitled to rule upon or punish violations of human rights.

So, the analysis of these cases shows how the individual measures are implemented by the State by paying the compensation, publishing the judgments and organising a public acknowledgement of its responsibility. Vice versa the legislative changes concerning non-repetition are not always satisfied by the State.

As for the measures leading to economic costs, the conclusion of the last judgment by the Court against the State of Chile, *Poblete Vilches*, concerning the violation of the right to health may be of an interest.[26] This judgment sheds light on the weaknesses of the national system of protection of vulnerable people's health and highlights the role of the state in it.[27]

24 The Inter-American Court states that "section 264 of the Criminal Code, as amended, still includes the offence of "threat" to the same authorities that constituted, before the amendment of the said Code, the passive subject of the offence of contempt. This way, the Criminal Code includes an ambiguous description and does not clearly specify the scope of the criminal conduct, thus leaving room for broad interpretation and, as a result, the conduct previously regarded as contempt may be unduly punished through the use of the criminal offence of threats," case Palamara Iribarne, judgment of November 22, 2005, para. 92.

25 On this reform, cf. Díaz Tolosa R. I., *Reforma de la Justicia Militar chilena a la luz de las consideraciones del fallo Palamara*, in Revista Chilena de Derecho, 34, 1, 2007, 139.

26 Cfr, Morales M, Clérico L. (eds.), *Interamericanización del derecho a la salud Perspectivas a la luz del caso Poblete de la Corte IDH* , México,2019; VILLARREAL P. A., *El derecho a la salud en lo individual y en lo colectivo: la calidad en lo servicio de salud a partir de Poblete Vilches vs Chile*, in https://archivos.juridicas.unam.mx/www/bjv/libros/12/5591/10.pdf.

27 In the previous case-law the Inter-American Court stated that "In this regard, the Court deems it is appropriate to recall the interdependence that exists between civil and political rights and economic, social and cultural rights, since they should be fully understood as human rights, without any rank and enforceable in all the cases before competent authorities," *Case of Acevedo Buendía et al. ("Discharged and Retired Employees of the Comptroller") v. Perú Judgment* of July 1, 2009, para. 101. In the case *Poblete Vilches* v. *Chile*, judgment

It is a highly topical subject in Chile, since social rights were at the core of the protests ongoing in 2019, which were seeking a radical change of public policy in favour of greater protection of social rights. The last order by the Inter-American Court on the reparation measures is from 2019. The order affirms that the obligation to publish the judgment was fulfilled. Compliance with the other measures, though, is still not completed. For instance, it is worth recalling the measures concerning the need to develop a general policy on the health of elderly people; to set up facilities for resuscitation in hospitals where the individuals have been hospitalised; and to improve the treatment delivered to elderly people in intensive care units. The Court is, thus, requiring Chile to take action to improve the guarantee of the right to health by introducing measures showing an actual change in its protection.[28]

The *Norín Catrimán* case and the protection of the political participation of minorities

The subject of the right to political participation has not been dealt with extensively in the rulings involving the State of Chile. The only ruling concerning Art. 23 of the Convention is the *Norín Catrimán* judgment from 29 May 2014.[29] However, in this ruling the right to political participation is not central to the Court's reasoning.

---

from 8 March 2018 it is stated "The Court also emphasizes that two types of obligations can be inferred from the content of Article 26. On the one hand, the *progressive* adoption of general measures and, on the other, the adoption of *immediate* measures. Regarding the former, to which the State referred in this case, the progressive realisation means that the States Parties have the specific and constant obligation to make the most expeditious and effective progress possible towards the full effectiveness of the ESCER; and this should not be interpreted in the sense that, while implementation is underway, these obligations are deprived of specific content; moreover, this does not mean that the States may postpone indefinitely the adoption of measures to give effect to the rights in question, especially nearly forty years after the entry into force of the Inter-American treaty. Therefore, there is also an obligation of non-retrogressivity in relation to the rights that have been realised. Regarding the obligations of an *immediate* nature, these consist in adopting effective measures in order to guarantee access, without discrimination, to the benefits recognised for each right. Such measures must be adequate, deliberate and specific in order to achieve the full realisation of such rights. Consequently, the Convention-based obligations of respect and guarantee, as well as the adoption of domestic legal provisions (Articles 1(1) and 2), are fundamental to achieve their effectiveness," para. 104.

28 On the protection of social and economic rights in Chile, cf. Nash Rojas C., *Los Derechos Económicos, Sociales y Culturales y la Justicia Constitucional Latinoamericana: tendencias jurisprudenciales*, in Estudios Constitucionales, 9, 1, 2011, particularly 99 ff..

29 On this ruling see the comments of. Becker Castellaro S., *La criminalización de la protesta: el caso Norín Catrimán y otros (Dirigentes, miembros y activista del pueblo indígena Mapuche) v. Chile*, in Anuario de Derechos Humanos, 11, 2015, 123 ff.; Contesse Singh J, *Norín Catrimán y Otros. Comentario a la sentencia de la Corte Interamericana de Derechos Humanos*, in Anuario de Derecho Público, 1, 2015, 418ff.

The case concerns the protests which originated in 2000 with some members of the Mapuche group fighting for their right to ownership over their ancestral lands. More specifically, in the South of Chile, in the region of Araucanía, there were a number of uprisings, resulting in some acts of violence, such as fires, destruction of machinery and rioting with the police forces. During this period, a major increase in the number of rulings charging executives and members of the Mapuche community was registered.

The convictions pronounced were justified by the application of the anti-terrorism Law n. 18.314. The *Norín Catrimán* case fits into this scenario, since it represents the State of Chile and the Mapuche community on opposing sides.

In this ruling the Court is mainly focused on the violation of the guarantees to a fair trial, ranging from the use of witnesses whose identity remains confidential and who cannot be cross-examined by the defence; to the holding of people in protective custody in prison without sufficient evidence; and to the absence of any appeal against the decisions of conviction in accordance with the American Convention.[30]

In such a scenario the topic of the right to political participation acquires what is effectively a secondary role. The limitation of these rights results from the fact that in such criminal convictions, a disqualification of 15 years from any public office is imposed as an ancillary punishment.[31] These charges are the effect of the application of Art. 9 of the Chilean Constitution expressly providing for disqualifications for those who were charged with terrorist offences: those found to be responsible for terrorist offences

> shall be disqualified for 15 years from discharging public duties or holding public offices, regardless of whether or not the appointment is by popular election; from being the rector or director of an educational establishment or performing teaching activities therein; from operating a social

30 In *Norín Catrimán*, the Court speculates on the structure of the anti-terrorism law. This law states that the intention of instilling fear among the population is a crucial element distinguishing terrorist conduct from ordinary offences. The intention of instilling fear is declared when a series of behaviours are perpetrated, like offences committed by means of explosives and fire. This law is considered by the Court as conflicting with the principle of legality and the presumption of innocence. It is worth also recalling that this law was subsequently amended with the elimination of such a presumption to cause the intention of instilling fear among the population.

31 The Inter-American Court also questions the violation of Art. 13 on freedom of thought, as resulting from the disqualifications deriving from the conviction: "The Court considers that this ancillary penalty entailed an undue restriction of the exercise of the right to freedom of thought and expression of Messrs. Norín Catrimán, Pichún Paillalao and Ancalaf Llaupe, not only because it was imposed based on judgments that applied a criminal law that violated the principle of legality and several procedural guarantees [...], but also because, in the circumstances of this case, it is contrary to the principle of the proportionality of the punishment. As the Court has determined, this principle signifies "that the State's response to a wrongful act of the perpetrator of an offence must be proportionate to the right affected and to the responsibility of the perpetrator, so that it should be established based on the different nature and seriousness of the acts," para. 374.

> communications media outlet or being a director or manager thereof, or performing therein functions connected with the broadcast or dissemination of opinions or information; and from being the leader of a political organisation, an organisation associated with education, or a neighbourhood, professional, business, labor, student, or trade association, during that time.[32]

Generally speaking, the American Convention introduces limitations to political rights as a result of a conviction issued by a criminal judge. Art. 23 of the American Convention, in fact, deals with the possible restrictions to political rights under its second paragraph, by stating that:

> The law may regulate the exercise of the rights and opportunities referred to in the preceding paragraph only on the basis of age, nationality, residence, language, education, civil and mental capacity, or sentencing by a competent court in criminal proceedings.

The interesting aspect of the *Norín Catrimán* judgment lies exactly in the connection between Articles 8 and 23 of the Convention. Accepting a possible limitation of the rights to political participation by means of a criminal judgment implies the respect by the same judgment of the guarantee to a fair trial, or criminal law would become a tool for repression of dissent.

What emerges in the *Norín Catrimán* judgment are the problems of the so-called criminal law of the enemy, that is the use of the criminal law tool to limit dissent. This aspect is also pointed out in the doctrine that shows how "anti-terrorism law was employed as a tool to repress groups from the political opposition by means of a vague and broad classification of offences."[33] It is also recalled by Medina Quiroga that "it shall not be forgotten that for the past the law has been mainly applied against a specific portion of the population to repress the groups of the political opposition."[34]

The Inter-American Court is committed to understanding the selective application of anti-terrorism laws to the Mapuche community. San José judges, despite the fact that the majority of proceedings conducted between 2000 and 2013 have had the Mapuche people as defendants, consider that there is no substantiated evidence to prosecute the state of Chile for the discriminatory application of the law.[35] However, the Court considers that in the individual judgments

32 Also Art. 28 of Criminal Code is here applied which establishes the penalties of "absolute and permanent disqualification from public offices or functions and political rights, as well as absolute disqualification from titled professions for the duration of the sentence."

33 Becker Castellaro S., *La criminalización de la protesta: el caso Norín Catrimán y otros (dirigentes y activistas del pueblo indígena Mapuche)* v. *Chile*, cited above, 128.

34 Medina Quiroga C., *Derechos Humanos y aplicación de la Ley 18.314, que determina las conductas terroristas y fija su penalidad*, in Doctrina procesal penal, 12, 2013, 45 ff.

35 *Norín Catrimán* Case "Nevertheless, the Court pays particular attention to the information contained in the "comments of the State of Chile on the report of the visit of the Special

issued against the victims there was a violation of Art. 24. More specifically, the Court affirmed that in order to ascertain whether this could be considered as discrimination or not, the arguments produced by the domestic judicial authorities needed to be analysed, including their actions, the language used, and the context in which those judicial decisions were taken. Starting from an analysis of individual judgments the Court deemed that the use of this reasoning, containing stereotypes and biases, to justify the judgments, was a violation of the principle of equality and non-discrimination and the right to equal protection of the law.

The Court's reasoning on the violation of the rights to political participation begins by making reference to the precedent in *Castañeda Gutman v. Mexico*, where it was stated that "the effective exercise of political rights constitutes an end in itself and, also, a fundamental means that democratic societies have to ensure the other human rights established in the Convention."[36] Based on the importance acquired by these rights, in *Norín Catrimán* the Court affirms that "in the circumstances of this case, the imposition of the said ancillary penalties," impacting

> the right to vote, direct participation in public affairs, and access to public office, of an absolute and perpetual nature or for a fixed but prolonged term (15 years), is contrary to the principle of the proportionality of the punishment and constituted a very serious impairment of the political rights (para. 383).

More specifically, the Court considered the specific position of Ancalaf Llaupe, Norín Catrimánand Pichún Paillalao, as traditional leaders of their communities. The Court states that

Rapporteur" for promotion and protection of human rights while countering terrorism, according to which, between 2000 and 2013 "the Public Prosecution Service had conducted a total of 19 proceedings under the Counter-terrorism Act, 12 of which related to land claims by Mapuche groups. Based on this information it is possible to note that, in most proceedings, this law was used against members of the Mapuche indigenous people: of the 19 proceedings in which the criminal investigation was conducted under the Counter-terrorism Act, in 12 of them, the accused were of Mapuche origin or the proceedings were related to land claims by this people. In this regard, several of the reports of the United Nations Special Rapporteurs and Committees have expressed concern owing to the application of the Counter-terrorism Act to members of the Mapuche indigenous people in relation to offences committed in the context of the social protest or have mentioned a 'disproportionate' application of the said law to the Mapuche," para. 217-2018.

36 Case of *Castañeda Gutman v. United Mexican States*, para. 143, and Case of *López Mendoza v. Venezuela*, para. 108. The Court adds that "their holders, in other words, citizens, not only enjoy rights, but also 'opportunities.' The latter term implies the obligation to guarantee with positive measures that anyone who holds formal political rights has a real opportunity to exercise them." Case of *López Mendoza v. Venezuela*, judgment of 1 September 2011, para. 108.

> owing to these penalties, they were prevented from taking part in or guiding public activities in State entities that seek to promote, coordinate and execute actions to develop and protect the indigenous communities they represented, which constituted a concrete violation of the rights protected by Article 23 of the Convention (para. 384).

The restriction of the political rights of these individuals also ends up impacting on the political rights of the whole Mapuche community, which is consequently deprived of its representatives. From this perspective, the *Norín Catrimán* judgment continues the line set by the precedent case on the rights to political participation of indigenous people which is *Yatama* v. *Nicaragua*, with regard to the connection between the restriction of the political rights of the representatives of this community and the limitation of the rights of the entire community.[37]

In *Norín Catrimán*, however, as already mentioned, the portion of the judgment concerning political rights is very succinct. The ruling, in fact, doesn't contain any mention of the execution of the test on the restrictive measures of political rights which has been developed by the Inter-American Court in its case-law and which assesses the restrictive measure, its purpose, its need in a democratic society and the proportionality. [38]

37 Case of *Yatama v. Nicaragua*, Judgment of 23 June 2005, para. 227, where it is stated that "it should be recalled that Yatama contributes to the consolidation and preservation of the cultural identity of the members of indigenous and ethnic communities of the Atlantic Coast. Its structure and purposes are related to the practices, customs and forms of organization of these communities. Consequently, the exclusion of the participation of the Yatama candidates particularly affected the members of the indigenous and ethnic communities that were represented by this organization in the municipal elections of November 2000, by placing them in a situation of inequality as regards to the options among which they could choose to vote, since those persons who, in principle, deserved their confidence because they had been chosen directly in assemblies (according to the practices and customs of these communities) to represent the interests of their members, had been excluded from participating as candidates. This exclusion resulted in a lack of representation of the needs of the members of the said communities in the regional bodies responsible for adopting policies and programs that could affect their development." Also in *Norín Catrimán*, the importance of the political participation of the victims is pointed out: "the imposition of the said penalties also had an impact on the representation of the interests of their communities in relation to other communities, as well as in relation to the rest of Chilean society" (para. 384).

38 Cf. For instance *Castañeda Gutman v. Mexico*, where the Court affirms that: "With the exception of some rights that cannot be restricted in any circumstance, such as the right not to be subjected to torture or to cruel, inhuman or degrading treatment or punishment, human rights are not absolute. As the Court has established previously, the establishment and application of requirements to exercise political rights is not, per se, an undue restriction of political rights. However, the power of the States to regulate or restrict rights is not discretional, but is limited by international law, which requires compliance with certain obligations that, if not respected, make the restriction unlawful and contrary to the American Convention," para 174. The Inter-American Court, in *Castañeda Gutman,* issued a judgment mainly on: Lawfulness of the restrictive measure; Purpose of the restrictive measure; Necessity in a democratic society and proportionality of the restrictive measure; The exist-

On other occasions, the Inter-American Court has analysed more specifically the issue of disqualifications from the exercise of political rights. In *Argüelles* et al. v. *Argentina*, for instance, the Court deals with the punishment of perpetual disqualification from public offices following a criminal conviction. In this case the Court discussed the consistency of this measure with the American Convention and the protection of political rights by making recourse to a test on the limitation of rights: the existence of a law, of a lawful purpose and the respect of the principle of proportionality. After having recalled that the same Art. 23 of the Convention allows the limitations of political rights following a criminal judgment, the Court dwells extensively on the principle of proportionality and the need to assess whether the measure "a) satisfies a social pressing necessity, or it aims at satisfying a commanding public interest; b) is the least restrictive measure available of a protected right; c) is strictly targeted to the achievement of a set goal" (para. 227).

The protection of the opposition and dissenting voices is analysed in greater detail in other judgments by the Inter-American Court. The Inter-American Court, in *Servellón-García et al. v. Honduras*, for instance, stressed how

> a massive and programmed arrest of people without legal grounds, in which the State massively arrests people that the authority considers may represent a risk or danger to the security of others, without substantiated evidence of the commission of a crime, constitutes an illegal and arbitrary arrest.[39]

In *Chitay Nech et al.* v. *Guatemala* and in *Manuel Cepeda Vargas* v. *Colombia*,[40] moreover, the right to political participation was connected to the forced disappearances or the killing of political leaders during domestic armed conflicts, highlighting the connection between political participation and the exercise of other fundamental rights.[41]

In *Chitay Nech et al.* v. *Guatemala*, the forced disappearance of a political leader of an indigenous community was the result of a doctrine of national security which pushed for members of indigenous communities to be considered as

---

ence of an essential social need – essential public interest; The exclusivity of the nomination and the least restrictive appropriate mechanisms to regulate the right to be elected; Proportionality of the interest that is justified and adaptation to the achievement of the legitimate objective para. 175 ff.

39 *Case of Servellón-García et al.* v. *Honduras* Judgment of September 21, 2006, para. 93. The Court also affirms that "Programmed and collective arrests, which are not well-founded on the individualization of punishable acts and that lack judicial control, are contrary to the presumption of innocence, they wrongfully coerce personal liberty and they transform preventive detention into a discriminatory mechanism, reason for which the State may not perform them under any circumstance," para.96.

40 On this, Cfr. Caballero Ochoa J.L, Rábago Dorbecker M., García Huerta D., *Art. 23. Derechos políticos*, in Stenier C., Fuchs M-C. (eds.), *Convención Americana sobre Derechos Humanos*, Berlin Bogota, 2019, 685.

41 Cfr. Caballero Ochoa J.L, Rábago Dorbecker M., García Huerta D., *Op cit.*, 684.

internal enemies. In this judgment the Inter-American Court analyses a "form of absolute repression of political rights."[42] In this case the limitation of the political rights of the individual also reflected on the political participation of the whole community in question:[43] "The representation of groups in situations of inequality becomes a necessary prerequisite for the self-determination and the development of the indigenous communities within a plural and democratic State." (par. 113).[44]

In *Norín Catrimán*, however, the Inter-American Court reserved a very limited section to the decision on the principle of proportionality and the guarantee of political rights. Art. 23, as already mentioned, remains in the background in this case which is mainly concentrated on the violation of other rules of the Convention.

The implementation of reparative measures provided by the Court

In *Norín Catrimán* judgment, the State of Chile was found to have violated the principle of legality, of the right to the presumption of innocence, the principle of equality and non-discrimination, the right to individual freedom, the right of defence connected to the possibility of cross-examining witnesses, the right to challenge a judgment before a higher court, the right to freedom of thought and expression, the political rights and the right to protect the family.

The Inter-American Court required Chile to introduce seven reparation measures. More specifically, the State was required to: pay compensation for the material and immaterial damages suffered by the victims and to cover the costs incurred; to deliver medical and psychological treatment; to publish and circulate the judgment; to make study grants available for the children of the victims; to

42 Cfr. Caballero Ochoa J.L, Rábago Dorbecker M., García Huerta D., *Op. Cit,*, 684.

43 *Case of Chitay Nech et al.* v. *Guatemala,* Judgment of May 25, 2010, para. 114. The Court also affirms that "In this sense, the Court has acknowledged that the State shall guarantee that 'the members of the indigenous and ethnic communities [...] are able to participate in the making of decisions regarding matters and policies that affect or may affect their rights and the development of such communities, in a manner that they can integrate themselves into the State institutions and organs and participate in a direct manner proportional to their population in the leadership of public affairs [...] and in accordance with their values, traditions, customs and forms of organization.' The contrary affects the lack of representation in the institutions charged with adopting policies and programs that could affect their development."

44 The Court underlines that "Due to the foregoing, with the harassment and later disappearance of Florencio Chitay Nech, not only was the exercise of his political right shattered during the period of his charge, but he was also prevented from fulfilling a mandate and a vocation within the process of formation of community leaders. Likewise, the community was deprived of the representation of one of its leaders in the various forums of its social structure, and principally in access to the full exercise of the direct participation of an indigenous leader in the structures of the State" para. 113.

modify the use of secret witnesses; and to adopt judicial, administrative measures or any such type of measure able to nullify the effect of the criminal convictions.

It is clear that the measures are quite diverse and imply the need for both legislative modifications and direct action to protect the victims. Among the other measures, the recognition of study grants and health treatments are those requiring an economic cost to be borne by the State, even if their amount is not estimated by the Court.

The last order by the Inter-American Court concerning the compliance with this judgment is from 2018. The order reports that the State has fully satisfied the measures requiring the payment of the compensation, of the fees and the publication and circulation of the judgment. As for the remaining measures, they were only partially implemented or are still to be fully completed.

The Court, as observed, has requested a series of measures imposing certain economic costs. More specifically, it is worth mentioning here the creation of study grants to the children of the victims, which will provide funding for the entire cost of their education up to university level. The Ministry of Education has set numerous criteria for the recognition of these study grants, in compliance with the judgment, and also addressed a broader public by including also, for instance, the grandchildren of the victims. The Court positively judges this attitude, though it has also required Chile to obtain additional information on the individuals actually benefitting from these study grants, as well as the total amount offered by the grants and the duration of this economic aid. The Court is also interested in the mode of payment and has requested that Chile not make retroactive payments, which would require initial contributions to be made by the families, which would be subsequently reimbursed by the State, since this mode would constitute further prejudice.

Another measure provided by the judgment requiring a cost is the delivery of medical and psychological treatment to the victims. The State specified that the treatment was also requested by the relatives of the victims and it will be delivered extensively to them, as well as the wider Mapuche community. 427 people will be the beneficiaries of this measure. To this end a project, entitled "Integral reparation program: Lonkos" was developed, through which in 2016 a general diagnosis of the health conditions of the community was conducted. Although the State clarified the relevance and the broad spectrum of this integral program, the Court stated that, based on the information received, there is no indication that the victims are actually receiving the necessary treatment. Indeed, based on the information available to the Court, it appeared that the victims were not receiving any medical treatment at all.

Hence, out of these measures imposing economic costs, the first, the study grants, has only partially been implemented; the second, the medical treatments, appears not to have been implemented at all.

As for the legislative modifications and the rules regarding the confidentiality of the identity of witnesses, the order from 2018 reports that numerous law bills have been presented, but none of them has been converted into law. The Inter-American Court sets out in *Norín Catrimán*, a series of standards to be satisfied by the States in making this protection of the confidentiality of the witness' identity possible: the measure ensuring the preservation of the confidentiality of the witness' identity must have been subject to judicial control and is based on the principles of necessity and proportionality. It is an exceptional measure taken upon attesting the presence of a situation of risk for the witness.

The Court in the end is requesting that the effect of the conviction, i.e. the measures limiting the freedom, the ancillary sanctions and the registration into any type of registry binding the victims to acts of terrorism shall be nullified. The State of Chile hasn't provided the Court with any information about the procedure it intends to follow to annul the effect of the criminal convictions imposed on the victims. Concerning the measures limiting their freedom, however, based on the information received, the Court deems that there was no order to detain the victims. Chile was also able to demonstrate that the ancillary sanctions limiting their political rights had been lifted. The victims in fact are "qualified to exercise their right to vote" in the national electoral lists.

Following the last order by the Inter-American Court, the Supreme Court of Chile, back in April 2019, declared that by virtue of *Norín Catrimán* judgment:

> the criminal judgments cannot remain in force when their existence implies a harmful conduct to the fundamental rights specified by the international court having jurisdiction, hence this Supreme Court will consequently state that the mentioned convictions have lost their effect.[45]

The Supreme Court has fully incorporated the arguments advanced by the Inter-American Court with its unprecedented decision demonstrating a synergy in the protection of rights.[46] This cooperation between national and supranational bodies has also resulted in the protection of the political rights of the victims which were limited by criminal convictions.

This case is the proof of a progressive convergence of the State towards the standards of protection required by the Inter-American Court and a fruitful

45 Supreme Court of Chile, Decision AD 1386-2014 (May 16, 2019) *cf. CS acogió argumentos de la Defensoría al dejar sin efecto sentencia del 'caso loncos*, in *Diario constitucional*, www.dpp.cl/resources/upload/files/documento/91da6cb37c17bb02b9c985213a3c5cce.pdf.

46 Contesse Singh J, *The Supreme Court of Chile as anIinter-American Tribunal*, in Int'l J. Const. L. Blog, 31 May 2019, highlights that "Chile's Supreme Court's ruling is unprecedented. It is the first time that the Grand Chamber explicitly endorses the view that "national judges are part of the inter-American human rights system," a position that the Inter-American Court has fervently advanced, for instance, through the creation of doctrines such as conventionality control. [...] The Chilean court's decision deserves praise because it affirms a domestic court's authority to declare itself an inter-American tribunal. In so doing, Chile's highest court has not only enhanced its own authority, but also that of the Inter-American Court's. In the current context of resistance against international institutions, the court's unprecedented decision is welcomed news."

collaboration between the national judges and the San José ones, ensuring a restoration of the protection of the right to political participation.

Conclusions

In the *Norín Catrimán* judgment the Inter-American Court endorses the link between Articles 8 and 23 of the Convention. The possibility offered by Art. 23 of the Convention to limit a person's political rights following a criminal conviction demonstrates a connection between the right to a fair trial and the protection of political rights. Chile's responsibility for the violations of a right to a fair trial suffered by some members of the Mapuche people also results in a violation of their political rights, whose restriction is a consequence of the conviction. This decision means that only a conviction which is in line with the Convention can legitimately justify the imposition of disqualification measures. The *Norín Catrimán* judgment adds another piece to the interpretation of Art. 23.

This judgment also shows a synergy existing between the national and Inter-American judges. As is clear, among the reparation measures, there is a requirement to annul the effect of the conviction. These measures were satisfied by the State of Chile in 2019 by means of an unprecedented judgment by the Supreme Court. On the other hand, the reparation measures involving the political bodies had not yet been fully satisfied. In addition, the measures requiring an economic cost, based on the last order of the Court in 2018, are still to be implemented.

So, even though the rights to political participation were protected first by the Inter-American Court by means of an acknowledgement of the international responsibility, and subsequently by means of a process to enforce the judgment, we should not forget that the implementation of numerous reparation measures, which are bound to the need for legislative modifications as well as the execution of the measures requiring certain economic costs still remain pending, preventing the closure of the case.

In conclusion, this judgment belongs to a jurisprudence current that protects the voices of dissent, deeming the presence of an opposition as a crucial element for a democracy. National minorities (political and ethnic) often enjoy a high level of protection among San José judges, given the central role attached to political rights. Although the judgment is mainly focused on the right to a fair trial, it also contains a confirmation of the importance of political participation in order to enable any such voice to join the game of democracy. Hence, criminal law, if not supported by the appropriate guarantees, cannot be used as a tool to repress dissent and to silence the minority voices.

Bibliography

Becker Castellaro S., *La criminalización de la protesta: el caso Norín Catrimán y otros (Dirigentes, miembros y activista del pueblo indígena Mapuche) vs. Chile*, in Anuario de Derechos Humanos, 11, 2015, 123–133.

BINDER C., *The Prohibition of Amnesties by the Inter-American Court of Human Rights*, German Law Journal, 12, 2011, 1203 ff.

Comisión Interamericana de Derechos Humanos, *Informe Anual 2019*, 2020. Available at http://www.oas.org/es/cidh/docs/anual/2019/indice.asp.

CONTESSE SINGH J., *Norín Catrimán y Otros. Comentario a la sentencia de la Corte Interamericana de Derechos Humanos*, in Anuario de Derecho Público, 1, 2015, 418–432.

CONTESSE SINGH J., *The Supreme Court of Chile as an inter-American Tribunal*, in Int'l J. Const. L. Blog, 31 May 2019.

DELAMAZA G., *¿Espacio público y participación ciudadana en la gestión pública en Chile: límites y posibilidades?* in Polis, 10, 30, 2011, 45–75.

DÍAZ TOLOSA R. I., *Reforma de la Justicia Militar chilena a la luz de las consideraciones del fallo Palamara*, in Revista Chilena de Derecho, 34, 1, 2007, 139–151.

FERNÁNDEZ VIVAS Y., *La influencia de la Sentencia de la Corte Interamericana de Derechos Humanos "Claude Reyes contra Chile" en la jurisprudencia del Tribunal Europeo de Derechos Humanos*, in Eunomía. Revista en Cultura de la Legalidad, 9, 2015–2016, 321 ff.

GARRETÓN R., GARRETÓN M.A., *La democracia incompleta en Chile: La realidad tras los rankings internacionales*, in Revista de ciencia políticas, 1, 2010, 115–148.

HEISS C., *Participación política y elaboración constitucional: el caso del Chile'*, in Derecho y Crítica Social, 4, 1, 2018, 115–138.

IVANSCHITZ BOUDEGUER B., *Un estudio sobre el cumplimiento y ejecución de las sentencias de la corte interamericana de derechos humanos por el estado de chile*, in Estudios Constitucionales, 11, 1, 2013, 275–332.

MARTÍNEZ SIERRA J.M., FERRER C., *La reforma constitucional en Chile*, 2004. Available at https://www2.uned.es/dpto-derecho-politico/Comunicacion_Martinez_Ferrer.pdf

MEDINA QUIROGA C., *Derechos Humanos y aplicación de la Ley 18.314, que determina las conductas terroristas y fija su penalidad*, in Doctrina Procesal Penal, 12, 2013, 7 ff.

MUÑOZ F., *Arbol genealógico* del Consejo de Estado: el constitucionalismo autoritarioen nuestra historia, in Revista Ius et Praxis, Año 16, N° 22010.

NASH ROJAS C., *Derecho internacional de los derechos humanos*, Centro de Derechos Humanos, Santiago de Chile, 2012.

NASH ROJAS C., *Los Derechos Económicos, Sociales y Culturales y la Justicia Constitucional Latinoamericana: tendencias jurisprudenciales*, in Estudios Constitucionales, 9, 1, 2011, 65–118.

NOGUEIRA ALCALÁ H., *Los desafíos de la sentencia de la Corte Interamericana en el caso Almonacid Arellano*, in Ius et Praxis, 12, 2, 2006, 363–384.

NOGUEIRA ALCALÁ H., *Reforma constitucional del 2005 y control de constitucionalidad de tratados internacionales*, in Revista de Estudios Constitucionales, 1, 2007, 59–88.

PÉREZ HERRERA E., *Valor jurídico y jerarquía en el derecho chileno de los Derechos Humanos contenidos en Tratados Internacionales*, 2018. Available at www.repositorio.uchile.cl/bitstream/handle/2250/151648/Valor-jurídico-y-jerarquía-en-el-derecho-chileno-de-los-derechos-humanos-contenidos-en-tratados-internacionales.pdf?sequence=1&isAllowed=y.

PORTALES F., *La inexistencia de la democracia en Chile*, in Polis revista latinoamericana, 10, 2005, 1–15.

Ruiz Tagle P., Cristi R., *La República en Chile. Teoría y Práctica del Constitucionalismo Republicano*, LOM, Santiago, 2006.

Sánchez Lobos L., *La representación política, participación ciudadana e iniciativa popular de ley en Chile*, in Ars Boni et Aequi, 11, 2, 2015, 49–74.

Schönsteiner J., Couso J., *La implementación de las decisiones de los órganos del sistema interamericano de derechos humanos en chile: ensayo de un balance*, in Revista de derecho (Coquimbo), 22, 2, 2015, 315–355.

Villarreal P. A., *El derecho a la salud en lo individual y en lo colectivo: la calidad en lo servicio de salud a partir de Poblete Vilches vs Chile*, in Morales, M., Clérico, L. (coords.), Interamericanización del derecho a la salud Perspectivas a la luz del caso Poblete de la Corte IDH, Instituto de Estudios Constitucionales del Estado de Querétaro, México, 2019, 279–313.

12 Threats against democracy in Colombia

Execution of political leaders*

José Antonio Estrada Marún, Luis Efrén Ríos Vega, and Lillian Sánchez Calderoni

Introduction

Colombia has had a protagonic participation in the impulse behind the creation of the Organization of American States (OAS). Indeed, the IX Inter-American Conference, in which the American Declaration of the Rights and Duties of Man was adopted and met with the OAS Charter's approval, was hosted in Bogotá (1948). This charter committed its signing parties to forming the OAS to "achieve an order of peace and justice, promote their solidarity, strengthen their collaboration, and defend their sovereignty, territorial integrity, and independence," as established in its Art. 1.[1] Furthermore, Colombia's leadership on this was also down to the country's former president Alberto Lleras Camargo (1945–1946 and 1958–1962), who had been director of the Pan American Union (1947) and was subsequently elected as the first General Secretary of the OAS.[2]

Internally, Colombia has been recognised for containing early legal and constitutional provisions on human rights:

> The forefather of human rights in Colombia, Antonio Nariño, translated the 1789 French Declaration of the Rights of Man from French to Spanish. As a result of his work, Colombia was perhaps the first nation in the Spanish-speaking New World where the subject of legal protection for human rights was discussed.[3]

* The translation of the sources that were originally in Spanish was made by the authors.

1 Herrera Robles, A., *El Estado colombiano frente al sistema interamericano de derechos humanos*, in Revista de Derecho. Universidad del Norte, I, 16, 2001, 104–141, at 107; Washington-OEA, *Colombia en la OEA*, in Misión permanente de Colombia ante la OEA, 2020. Available at: https://washington-oea.mision.gov.co/colombia-la-oea#:~:text=La%20OEA%20ha%20tenido%20un,su%20nacimiento%20formal%20en%201948 [Visited on 10 September 2020].

2 Herrera Robles, A., *El Estado colombiano frente al sistema interamericano de derechos humanos*, cited above, 105; Washington-OEA, *Colombia en la OEA*, cited above.

3 Inter-American Commission of Human Rights, *Colombia Country Report, Chapter II, Human Rights Protection in the Colombian Legal and Political System*, Washington, 1999, para. 40.

DOI: 10.4324/9781003229247-15

Nevertheless, this country has faced a particular context that has severely affected the level of human rights protection and exercise. In the Colombian regime's transition to democracy, strong struggles have developed between conservatives and liberals seeking public power, and serious problems have gained more visibility, including: general nonconformity, social injustice, socioeconomic inequity in some sectors and regions of the country, as well as claims of lower classes for justice, equality, and better living conditions (middle and lower/working class people v. ruling elites).[4] Indeed, the assassination of the popular, liberal candidate Jorge Eliécer Gaitán in 1948 triggered the well-known internal conflict that Colombian society has lived with for more than 50 years.[5]

Along with the development of "a cross-national state of 'undeclared' war, which has different levels of intensity depending on the region, city or town, and even the neighbourhood,"[6] the Colombian judicial framework has evolved in a way that has been qualified as contradictory, paradoxical,[7] even cynical: "the production of law has allowed the shell of the State and its atomized ruling members to remain stable, while there is a general sense of society falling apart."[8] Nonetheless, Colombia signed and

4 López Daza, Y. A., *Violencia política, democracia y derechos humanos*, in Derecho y Realidad, 14, 27, 2016, 145–156, at 147–148.

5 Multiple *guerrillas* started to emerge in disputes over territorial control; paramilitary and self-defence groups emerged, which were then followed by their successors. Some groups allied with the illegal drug industry. They increasingly dominated communities and regions through ongoing violence; the armed fighting context, in which the FARCs (*Fuerzas Armadas Revolucionarias de Colombia*) were constituted (Córdoba Triviño, J., *Aplicación de la jurisprudencia de la Corte Interamericana de Derechos Humanos al derecho constitucional colombiano*, in Anuario de Derecho Constitucional Latinoamericano, 2007, 667–684), eventually turned into a civil war (López Daza, Y. A., *Violencia política, democracia y derechos humanos*, cited above, 149). Non-State leaders and actors surpassed security forces (US Bureau of Democracy, Human Rights and Labor, *Colombia 2018 Human Rights Report*, in US Department of Justice, US Department of State, 2018. Available at: www.justice.gov/eoir/page/file/1148416/download [Visited on 15 September 2020]), to the point where the State became absent, neglectful, and even condescending (Eslava, L., *Constitutionalization of Rights in Colombia: Establishing a Ground for Meaningful Comparisons*, in Revista de Derecho del Estado, 22, 2009, 183–229, at 199; Amnesty International, *Colombia 2019*, in Amnesty.org, section Countries, 2019. Available at: www.amnesty.org/en/countries/americas/colombia/report-colombia/ [Visited on 20 September 2020]). The reported abuses include killings; threats; displacements; abductions; physical abuse, punishment, and torture; recruitment of children; enforced disappearances; arms and illegal substance trafficking; forced confinement (US Bureau of Democracy, Human Rights and Labor, *Colombia 2018 Human Rights Report*, cited above; Amnesty International, *Colombia 2019*, cited above). Also see Herrera Robles, A., *El Estado colombiano frente al sistema interamericano de derechos humanos*, cited above, 106; Cosoy, N., *¿Por qué empezó y qué pasó en la guerra de más de 50 años que desangró a Colombia?*, in BBC Mundo, 24 August 2016. Available at: www.bbc.com/mundo/noticias-america-latina-37181413 [Visited on 10 September 2020].

6 Eslava, L., *Constitutionalization of Rights in Colombia: Establishing a ground for meaningful comparisons*, cited above, 199.

7 Herrera Robles, A., *El Estado colombiano frente al sistema interamericano de derechos humanos*, cited above, 106.

8 Eslava, L., *Constitutionalization of Rights in Colombia: Establishing a ground for meaningful comparisons*, cited above, 192, 195.

adopted the Inter-American system's instruments.[9] The American Convention on Human Rights was ratified in 1973 and, a few years later, in 1985, the competence of the Inter-American Commission on Human Rights and of the Inter-American Court on Human Rights was accepted.

However, it was not until the 1991 Constitution (Art. 93) that the ACHR received constitutional value (in the form of the "constitutionality block") and was considered directly applicable to the national framework.

The commitment of the Colombian State and the further efforts it has made (such as the elaboration of a new constitutional text published in 1991)[10] have

9 Colombia is a Member State of the following: OAS Charter (1948); American Declaration of the Rights and Duties of Man; American Convention on Human Rights (1948); Additional Protocol to the American Convention on Human Rights in the Area of Economic, Social and Cultural Rights "Protocol of San Salvador" (1988); Protocol to the American Convention on Human Rights to Abolish the Death Penalty (1990); Inter-American Convention to Prevent and Punish Torture (1985); Inter-American Convention on Forced Disappearance of Persons (1994); Inter-American Convention on the Prevention, Punishment, and Eradication of Violence against Women "Convention of Belém do Pará" (1994).

10 In 1991, following an international (and regional) trend of transformative constitutionalism focused on the constitutionalisation of human rights (Eslava, L., *Constitutionalization of Rights in Colombia: Establishing a ground for meaningful comparisons*, cited above, 185; Herrera, J. C., *Judicial Dialogue and Transformative Constitutionalism in Latin America: The Case of Indigenous Peoples and Afro-descendants*, in Revista Derecho del Estado, 43, 2019, 191–233. Available at: www.redalyc.org/jatsRepo/3376/337660349008/html/index.html#fn2 [Visited on 22 September 2020]), Colombia introduced a new Constitution. Its core concept is the Social Rule of Law State (*Estado social de derecho*), based on the ideas of diversity, equality, and participatory democracy, with the materialisation of human rights as the benchmark of justice (Eslava, L., *Constitutionalization of Rights in Colombia: Establishing a ground for meaningful comparisons*, cited above, 185). Like most other new constitutions made on the basis of this trend, the Colombian text includes in the Constitution's title II: fundamental rights; social, economic, and cultural rights; collective and environmental rights. Moreover, it introduces improved and new protection and application mechanisms, like judicial review, a constitutional court, and the *tutela*; as well as duties and obligations (Arts. 11–95). It outlines the function of institutions like the Public Ombudsman (*Defensoría del Pueblo*), it extends constitutional jurisdiction to all judges, and dictates new procedures (to order the administrative fulfilment of legal mandates, to protect collective rights, to secure specific social groups' rights, in addition to the one for the protection of fundamental rights (*tutela*)) (Eslava, L., *Constitutionalization of Rights in Colombia: Establishing a ground for meaningful comparisons*, cited above, 202).

Art. 93 establishes that international treaties and conventions on human rights (ratified by the Congress) prevail in Colombia's domestic law and are considered an integral part of its Constitution, thus, all rights and duties enshrined in the Constitution shall be interpreted according to them. The Constitutional Court has also established that international humanitarian and human rights law treaties ratified by the legislative are constitutionally relevant and directly enforceable, in the sentences C-574/92 and C-295/93. Moreover, in its decision C-225/95, the Colombian Constitutional Court coined the concept "*bloque de constitucionalidad*," which refers to incorporating as part of the Constitution other norms that do not appear in its written content (Uprimny,

been avowed. However, in accordance with its functions,[11] the Commission has noted serious human rights violations in four study reports, which include: inefficient judicial investigations; abuse of authority, such as massive arrests and captures; irregularities in detention procedures, violations of personal integrity; insufficient government action; displacement; restrictions to movement and association because of the continued state of siege; systematic and indiscriminate violation of human rights such as those mentioned, but also the right to peace.[12] Additionally, in the short period between 2006 and 2019, the Commission has received 5,442 individual petitions.[13]

R., "La fuerza vinculante de las decisiones de los organismos internacionales de derechos humanos en Colombia: un examen de la evolución de la jurisprudencia constitucional," in Krsticevic, V. (coord.), *Implementación de las decisiones del Sistema Interamericano de Derechos Humanos. Jurisprudencia, normativa y experiencias nacionales*, Buenos Aires, 2007, 130; Escobar Martínez, L. M. *et al.*, *La influencia de los estándares interamericanos de reparación en la jurisprudencia del Consejo de Estado Colombiano*, in Estudios Constitucionales, 2, 2011, 165–190, 166–167; Uprimny, R., *El bloque de constitucionalidad en Colombia. Un análisis jurisprudencial y un ensayo de sistematización doctrinal*, in Dejusticia.org, 2017. Available at: www.dejusticia.org/wp-content/uploads/2017/04/fi_name_recurso_46.pdf [Visited on 23 September 2020], 2). It's a body of constitutional law that addresses supranational normative, values, principles, case-law, and standards in the matter of human rights, even though they're beyond the constitutional text (Córdoba Triviño, J., *Aplicación de la jurisprudencia de la Corte Interamericana de Derechos Humanos al derecho constitucional colombiano*, cited above, 672; Eslava, L., *Constitutionalization of Rights in Colombia: Establishing a ground for meaningful comparisons*, cited above, 204; Herrera, J. C., *Judicial Dialogue and Transformative Constitutionalism in Latin America: The Case of Indigenous Peoples and Afro-descendants*, cited above).

11 It promotes the observance and defence of human rights, serves as an OAS advisory body in this matter, conducts on-site visits, prepares reports on the human rights situation in the member States, and receives individual complaints regarding violations of human rights, examines them, issues recommendations, and remits cases to the Court when the requirements are met (IACtHR, *ABC de la Corte Interamericana de Derechos Humanos: El qué, cómo, cuándo, dónde y porqué de la Corte Interamericana*, San José, 2019, 3–4).

12 View reports, mainly conclusions: OEA/Ser.L/V/II.53, Doc. 22, 30 June 1981; OEA/Ser.L/V/II.84, Doc. 39 rev., 14 October 1993; OEA/Ser.L/V/II.102, Doc. 9 rev. 1, 26 February 1999; OEA/Ser.L/V/II., Doc. 49/13, 31 December 2013. Available at: www.oas.org/es/cidh/informes/pais.asp [Visited on 24 September 2020].

13 In 2019 alone, 881 petitions were received. Peru had the highest number of petitions in 2006, 2007, and 2008; while Mexico did from 2012 to 2018. To observe the total number of individual petitions received by the IACHR against Colombia and their procedural advance, go to: www.oas.org/en/iachr/multimedia/statistics/statistics.html [Visited on 27 September 2020]. To view the comparison of individual petitions received by the IACHR against the Inter-American Member States from 2006 to 2019, go to: www.oas.org/en/iachr/multimedia/statistics/statistics.html [Visited on 27 September 2020].

Nonetheless, only 23 cases have actually reached the highest level of the Inter-American Court.[14] The IACtHR[15] has declared the Colombian State responsible for all of them, mainly for violations related to the violent acts that have taken place in the context of the internal conflict. Colombia has not fully complied with the reparations ordered in any of the Court's judgments. Except for three of them, which are completely pending of national implementation, the rest of the decisions have been partially met.[16]

14 The affairs that have been forwarded to the IACtHR are the following: *Caballero Delgado and Santana v. Colombia*. Merits. Judgment of 8 December 1995. Series C No. 22; *Las Palmeras v. Colombia*. Preliminary Objections. Judgment of 4 February 2000. Series C No. 67; *19 Merchants v. Colombia*. Merits, Reparations, and Costs. Judgment of 5 July 2004. Series C No. 109; *Gutiérrez Soler v. Colombia*. Merits, Reparations, and Costs. Judgment of 12 September 2005 Series C No. 132; *Mapiripán Massacre v. Colombia*. Merits, Reparations, and Costs. Judgment of 15 September 2005. Series C No. 134; *Pueblo Bello Massacre v. Colombia*. Merits, Reparations, and Costs. Judgment of 31 January 2006. Series C No. 140; *Ituango Massacres v. Colombia*. Preliminary Objection, Merits, Reparations, and Costs. Judgment of 1 July 2006. Series C No. 148; *Rochela Massacre v. Colombia*. Merits, Reparations, and Costs. Judgment of 11 May 2007. Series C No. 163; *Escué Zapata v. Colombia*. Merits, Reparations, and Costs. Judgment of 4 July 2007. Series C No. 165; *Valle Jaramillo et al. v. Colombia*. Merits, Reparations, and Costs. Judgment of 27 November 2008. Series C No. 192; *Cepeda Vargas v. Colombia*. Preliminary Objections, Merits, Reparations, and Costs. Judgment of 26 May 2010. Series C No. 213; *Vélez Restrepo and family v. Colombia*. Preliminary Objection, Merits, Reparations, and Costs. Judgment of 3 September 2012. Series C No. 248; *Santo Domingo Massacre v. Colombia*. Preliminary Objections, Merits and Reparations. Judgment of 30 November 2012. Series No. 259; *Afro-descendant Communities displaced from the Cacarica River Basin (Operation Genesis) v. Colombia*. Preliminary Objections, Merits, Reparations, and Costs. Judgment of 20 November 2013. Series C No. 270; *Rodríguez Vera et al. (The Disappeared from the Palace of Justice) v. Colombia*. Preliminary Objections, Merits, Reparations, and Costs. Judgment of 14 November 2014. Series C No. 287; *Duque v. Colombia*. Preliminary Objections, Merits, Reparations, and Costs. Judgment of 26 February 2016. Series C No. 310; *Yarce et al. v. Colombia*. Preliminary Objection, Merits, Reparations, and Costs. Judgment of 22 November 2016. Series C No. 325; *Vereda La Esperanza v. Colombia*. Preliminary Objections, Merits, Reparations, and Costs. Judgment of 31 August 2017. Series C No. 341; *Carvajal Carvajal et al. v. Colombia*. Merits, Reparations, and Costs. Judgment of 13 March 2018. Series C No. 352; *Isaza Uribe et al. v. Colombia*. Merits, Reparations, and Costs. Judgment of 20 November 2018. Series C No. 363; *Villamizar Durán et al. v. Colombia*. Preliminary Objection, Merits, Reparations, and Costs. Judgment of 20 November 2018. Series C No. 364; *Omeara Carrascal et al. v. Colombia*. Merits, Reparations, and Costs. Judgment of 21 November 2018. Series C No. 368; and *Petro Urrego v. Colombia*. Preliminary Objections, Merits, Reparations, and Costs. Judgment of 8 July 2020. Series C No. 406. Available at: www.corteidh.or.cr/casos_sentencias.cfm?lang=en [Visited on September 24, 2020].

15 It is the autonomous judicial institution in charge of interpreting and applying the ACHR. It works as a contentious tribunal; as a judgment supervision mechanism; as advisor; and as provisional measures emissor (IACtHR, *ABC de la Corte Interamericana de Derechos Humanos: El qué, cómo, cuándo, dónde y porqué de la Corte Interamericana*, cited above, 3–4).

16 The reparations that haven't been met are mainly those related to: continuing the judicial investigations and procedures with due diligence and to determine who is responsible, to provide medical assistance, and to make payment of compensation. In contrast, the publish-

Against such a background, we can make the observation that Colombian democracy is threatened. A democratic State is based on the pillar of security, because it reflects the certainty required for free individual aspirations to be enjoyed, which are backed up by sovereign power.[17] López Aguilar[18] affirms that, without the effective exercise of human rights, there is no justice, and without efficient and effective public institutions there is no democracy; for instance, a constitutional State cannot be conceived of without justice or democracy. However, there is some consensus on the impact of the 1991 Constitution on Colombia's democracy, for the implications it has brought to the political system by proposing a representative democracy with various popular participation mechanisms.[19] Has this constitutional renovation been enough to guarantee Colombians' political rights? In the following section we analyse three judgments which the IACtHR has considered on this matter.

Analysis of cases

Manuel Cepeda Vargas v. Colombia

Manuel Cepeda Vargas was a social communicator and leader of the opposition group, the Colombian Communist Party (PCC, for *Partido Comunista Colombiano*) and the Patriotic Union (UP, for *Unión Patriótica*). Moreover, Mr. Vargas was a Senator (elected for the 1994–1998 term) when he was killed on 9 August 1994. His assassination took place within the framework of a pattern of violent acts against UP militants. These systematic[20] misconducts athwart the members of the UP and the PCC, were perpetrated by an alleged operational coordination between affiliates of the Army and paramilitary groups under the so-called "*coup de grâce plan.*" Furthermore, Mr. Vargas' execution revealed the situation of harassment and persecution faced by the UP members, as well as the

ing of the sentences and the public events to honour the victims are the actions that have been fulfilled the most. View the Inter-American Court's website section called "Monitoring Compliance with Judgment" at: www.corteidh.or.cr/casos_en_supervision_por_pais.cfm?lang=en [Visited on 26 September 2020].

17 This is Rousseau's notion of the social contract, by virtue of which people submit and surrender their respective individual rights to the sovereign, to receive from it the same rights but supported by the State's force, with guarantee and security to exercise them (Osterling Parodi, F., *El Equilibrio entre los Poderes Legislativo y Ejecutivo*, in Thémis, 26, 1993, 29–36).

18 López Aguilar, H. B., *Para comprender el fenómeno de la corrupción*, en Sistema Nacional Anticorrupción, Estudios jurídicos n. 7, Judicial Power of Mexico State-Tirant lo Blanch, Mexico City 2019, 23–24.

19 García Suárez, A. L., *El desarrollo de la democracia colombiana y sus efectos en el binomio Fuerzas Militares-ciudadanía*, in Revista Científica General José María Córdova, 17, 26, 2019, 254.

20 See note 29 below, particularly the reference to the pattern of violence across the country of Colombia.

impunity that perpetrators enjoyed,[21] in spite of the fact that wide-ranging investigations were carried out.

One of those investigations led to military disciplinary proceedings against the corresponding sergeants; however, the Court indicated that the minor punishments imposed meant that the sanctions were disproportionate. Instead of being discharged, they were subjected to a reprimand, which was considered inconsistent and inefficient.[22]

A second attempt was made under administrative law, through two independent lawsuits. They both declared the State responsible for not complying with their duty to protect the Senator's life.[23] Nonetheless, the Inter-American Court sustained that, when analysing the domestic procedures, it was required to

> verify whether the decisions taken by the jurisdiction [would] have made an effective contribution to end[ing] impunity, to ensure [the] non-repetition of the harmful acts, and to guarantee the free and full exercise of the rights protected by the Convention.[24]

The point is to determine to what extent these decisions may serve to give full reparation for any rights violated, instead of being limited to the payment of compensation. Moreover,

> the administrative law courts did not establish the institutional responsibility, by act, of State officials in the execution of Senator Cepeda Vargas, [...] even though, when arriving at their decisions, they were already aware of the partial results of the criminal proceedings and even of the disciplinary proceedings. Consequently, they did not make a substantial contribution to compliance with the obligation to investigate and clarify the facts.[25]

The third and last proceedings were attempted through the criminal route. These investigations were frustrated by demobilisation processes, extraditions of clue testifiers, and mismanagement of information related to individualisation or identification of the implicated persons. Overall, the procedures were not conducted with sufficient due diligence, being carried out neither within a reasonable time, nor in a way which took into account the alleged pattern of violence and attacks directed at political leaders and members of the UP and the PCC. In this sense, the proceedings did not constitute effective remedies, meaning that impunity prevailed.[26]

21 IACtHR, *Cepeda Vargas v. Colombia*. Preliminary Objections, Merits, Reparations, and Costs, cited above, para. 2.
22 *Ivi*, paras. 132, 137.
23 *Ivi*, para. 138.
24 *Ivi*, para. 139.
25 *Ivi*, para. 140.
26 *Ivi*, para. 167.

Reasoning under Art. 23 of the ACHR

The applicants claimed the transgression of, among others rights,[27] both Mr. Vargas' and the State population's political rights, enshrined in Art. 23 of the ACHR. Colombia accepted these accusations in part. In fact, the State sought to refute them under the same argument that had been previously used in the *Escué Zapata*'s judgment:[28]

> the only purpose of including a social dimension in the analysis would be to incorporate new victims in the proceedings, and that the loss of legal status of the UP resulted from a failure to comply with the legal and constitutional requirements.[29]

Nonetheless, on this occasion, the regional court developed its analysis to emphasise the importance of the State's obligation in assuring a propitious

27 The alleged human rights and liberties violations that were recognised by the Court were: obligation to respect other rights (Arts. 1 and 1.1); life (Arts. 4 and 4.1); personal integrity (Arts. 5 and 5.1); judicial guarantees (Arts. 8 and 8.1); honour and dignity (Arts. 11 and 11.2); thought and expression (Art. 13); association (Art. 16); circulation and residence (Art. 22.1); political rights (Art. 23); judicial protection (Art. 25); all from the ACHR.

28 There was a first claim of violation of political rights (among others) against the Colombian State that was heard before the IACtHR, which was the case of *Escué Zapata v. Colombia* (cited above). Mr. Germán Escué Zapata, was a *Cabildo* Governor (and defensor) of the Indigenous Protection of Jambaló. It was proved that a pattern of violence was crossing the country in 1988, which involved State armed forces, private militias, narco-traffickers, and other groups; and rural and indigenous areas were profoundly affected. Some communities began to resist and fight back to uphold or recover their lands. Framed within this context, one night that year, Mr. Zapata was accused of being a *guerrillero* and of having firearms at his house, from where he was then violently taken by Colombian Army agents. Moments later, he was found dead nearby with signs of physical abuse and torture. The national investigations produced no results. The applicants' representatives sustained that Mr. Zapata's assassination had infringed political rights in its "two-fold dimension": an "individual" one as the "exercise of the right to participate in the conduit of public affairs," and a "social" one: the prerogatives of Paez People "to designate who will govern and take care, in accordance with their traditions, usages and customs, of their political affairs, as well as the right to influence and participate, through their representatives, in the making of decisions that affect the collective life project." The Court did not analyse this claimed violation because it included "new victims who had not been identified by the Commission in the proper procedural time," but it recognised that "the loss of a leader for the Paez People meant a 'dismemberment and damage to the whole community; frustration in view of the great confidence people gave him to help them having a good standard of living and feelings of loss in view of the collective efforts made to, with the support of the Community, develop its mission as a special person'." Finally, the Court ordered a sum of 40,000.00 US Dlls to a fund for the indigenous community, in memory of Germán Escué Zapata, so that works or services of collective interest could be developed, in accordance with their own uses, customs, and traditions (IACtHR, *Escué Zapata v. Colombia*. Merits, Reparations, and Costs. Judgment of 4 July 2007. Series C No. 165, paras. 3, 98, 104, 113, 114, 118, 119, 120–125).

29 IACtHR, *Cepeda Vargas v. Colombia*. Preliminary Objections, Merits, Reparations, and Costs, cited above, para. 169.

environment for political, and particularly electoral, rights to be exercised with the guarantee that they would not suffer threats to their liberties, such as that of expression, association with political purposes, and life itself, because they are all fundamental elements for a successful democracy.

Indeed, the IACtHR considered the right to participate in government (Art. 23) along with the freedoms of thought, expression (Art. 13), and of association (Art. 16) because Senator Cepeda Vargas had exercised all of them

> continuously, simultaneously, and in an interrelated manner, so that the violation of these rights represented an attack on the values of the democratic system; because he was murdered to silence his voice and his political activities; and because his death prevented him from being a member of the UP and curtailed his possibility of continuing to make a contribution towards achieving the political objectives of this party.[30]

The Senator was, "at one and the same time, a leader of the UP and the PCC, a social communicator and a parliamentarian; consequently, it is unnecessary to disaggregate his activities in order to decide which of them was the origin or cause of each alleged violation."[31]

For the Court, these rights are essential for democracy since they are tools for assuring access to power, this means the right to be elected, which the State must promote with effective measures to guarantee the optimum conditions and offer a real opportunity of their full exercise. In such tenor, this exercise may be unlawfully restricted by *de facto* circumstances that directly or indirectly suggest a risk or a situation of increased vulnerability for those who have an interest in taking political and public participation.[32]

Additionally, opposition voices are essential in a democratic society, otherwise, no agreements that satisfy the different visions in societies can be reached. Hence, just as experts[33] have affirmed, for a functional democratic society to exist its State

30 *Ibídem*.

31 *Ivi*, para. 171.

32 *Ivi*, para. 172.

33 The authors have developed their doctrine of the democratic pyramid, which shows three basic components for a functional system: open government, free and fair elections, as well as civil and political rights. Free and fair, clean elections allow the peaceful replacement of rulers when the former don't satisfy the population, which fosters true political competition as the key incentive for public officials is to be responsible and to strive to serve the interests and common welfare of the people. In addition, free and fair elections must be held in conditions allowing freedom of expression, a plurality of information, freedom of political organisation, and electoral participation. In this way, a well formed and enlightened public opinion can be built, and through free association, political parties can be created, furthering civil and political rights that are an obvious pillar for democracy (Molina V., J. E. & Pereira, V., *La democracia en América Latina: ¿éxito o fracaso?*, in campus.usal.es, online, no/date. Available at: http://campus.usal.es/~dpublico/areacp/Doctorado0406/Seminario0405/Evaluaci%F3nDemocracia.PDF [Visited on 28 September 2020], 3–5; Beetham, D. & Boyle, K., *Democracia. Preguntas y respuestas*, Unesco, France, 1995, 38–40).

must safeguard the effective participation of opposition individuals, groups, and political parties by appropriate judicial means, such as regulations and practices to accomplish deliberative mechanisms on equal terms, including adequate measures that prevent and take into consideration the situation of vulnerability of the members of some social groups or sectors.[34]

The Court also found that the "agreement to prolong the truce," signed between the FARCs and the Peace Commission regarding the UP, evidenced the acknowledgement of the situation of risk that members of the UP and the PCC lived through. Furthermore, it was proved that the Senator's life was in constant danger, that he was faced with continuous harassment and threats by virtue of his political position, which eventually led to the motivation for his extrajudicial execution. Therefore, the Court concluded that there was a clear objective of restricting the Senator's political rights, which also impacted the rules and principles upon which democracy and the rule of law is based, so it directly violated the democratic system. As a matter of fact, for the Inter-American judges, the violation of Mr. Cepeda's rights also had threatening and intimidating effects for the collective of militants, party members, supporters, or anyone else who sympathised with his ideas.[35]

Measures of reparation for the violation of Art. 23

The Court ordered several reparation measures, without pointing out which of them were strictly connected to the political rights violation, instead making a general mention of the affected human rights. For pecuniary damages, the Court fixed an amount of 60,000.00 US Dlls, for non-pecuniary damages, an amount of 245,000.00 US Dlls, and for costs and expenses, 35,000.00 US Dlls were due. The total amount was 340,000.00 US Dlls.

The Court imposed upon Colombia the obligation to guarantee the victim's family members security to avoid repeated threats, harassment, and persecution and so they did not have to relocate or leave the country. The State was obliged to issue medical and psychological treatment. Furthermore, Colombia was ordered to carry out an investigation with due diligence in order to hold all those responsible for the death of Senator Cepeda Vargas, as well as to remove all material and legal obstacles that contribute to a situation of impunity, to publish the judgment, to hold a public ceremony recognising the international responsibility through the corresponding authorities, and to prepare, project, and distribute an audiovisual documentary about Senator Cepeda Vargas' political life, journalism, and his political role. Finally, the IACtHR stated that the State must create and provide on a one-off basis, a grant or scholarship associated with the victim's name to cover academic and maintenance costs, including the cost of the degree,

34 IACtHR, *Cepeda Vargas v. Colombia*. Preliminary Objections, Merits, Reparations, and Costs, cited above, para. 173.

35 *Ivi*, paras. 174, 175, 177, 178.

for a scholar to take up a professional career in communication or journalism at a public university in Colombia chosen by the beneficiary, awarded and carried out through a contest on merit. This grant's administration would be held by the Manuel Cepeda Vargas Foundation to journalists.

Petro Urrego v. Colombia

On 8 July 2020, the Inter-American Court on Human Rights issued the most recent sentence through which it declared the Colombian State responsible for a violation of Mr. Gustavo Francisco Petro Urrego's political rights, among others,[36] as a result of the sanctions proceedings he was subjected to while he was Mayor of Bogotá. Identifying himself as a left wing opposition leader, Mr. Petro was an economist and politician who initially belonged to *Movimiento Guerrillero 19 de abril*, which was subsequently incorporated into the Democratic Alliance M-19 party (AD for *Alianza Democrática M-19*). He then moved to the Progressive Movement party (MP for *Movimiento Progresista*), from which he served as Mayor in Bogotá. In addition, he had been a member of the Parliament (and indeed remained a member of the Senate), and had also put himself forward for the country's presidency twice.

During his time as the Mayor of Colombia's capital city, Mr. Petro implemented several measures including, by way of example, a boundary rearrangement plan and the reduction of public transport costs. For this reason, he was suspended.

Reasoning under Art. 23 of the ACHR

In this case, the Commission observed that the sanctions against Mr. Petro by the Attorney General's Office were not imposed by a criminal court, through a final conviction, as required by the standards of the Convention. Additionally, it considered that the Attorney General's Office was not the appropriate authority to impose severe sanctions of that nature, due to its administrative nature, and that the disciplinary offences incurred by Mr. Petro did not constitute a criminal offence.[37]

The representatives stated that the disciplinary code and the laws that regulated fiscal processes, the criminal code in relation to the protection of democratic participation mechanisms, and the interpretation of disciplinary powers carried out by the Constitutional Court, were all contrary to the ACHR and the duty to implement a *conventionality control*, in accordance with the interpretations of the Inter-American Court. Likewise, the applicants' representatives stated that

36 The alleged violations were against the duty to adapt internal law (Art. 2), judicial guarantees and protection (Arts. 8 and 25), as well as equality before the law (Art. 24), all of the ACHR.

37 IACtHR, *Petro Urrego v. Colombia*. Preliminary Objections, Merits, Reparations, and Costs, cited above, para. 79.

the sanctions that were imposed on Mr. Petro pursued a discriminatory purpose due to his political ideology, since these actions were aimed at restricting his participation in the 2018 presidential elections. In addition, they concluded that the discriminatory actions against Mr. Petro constituted an act of misuse of power, that they lacked the elements of suitability, necessity, and proportionality, and that these discriminatory acts continued to be exercised.[38]

The Court sustained, regarding the protection of political rights, that representative democracy is one of the pillars of the whole system of which the Convention forms part, and constitutes a principle reaffirmed by the American States in the OAS Charter. In this sense, the Charter is the constitutive treaty of the organisation to which Colombia has been a party since 12 July 1951, which establishes as one of its essential purposes the promotion and consolidation of representative democracy while respecting the principle of non-intervention.[39]

The tribunal also cited the Inter-American Democratic Charter, approved on 11 September 2001, to outline the relationship between human rights, representative democracy, and political rights. In particular, Arts. 1, 2, and 3 were cited[40] in order to point out that the effective exercise of political rights constitutes an objective in itself and, at the same time, a fundamental prerogative that democratic societies must guarantee. Moreover, in accordance with Art. 23 of the Convention, citizens must not only enjoy *rights*, but also *real opportunities* to exercise them, because in that way democracy and political pluralism are strengthened. Therefore, just as was said in the case of Senator Cepeda Vargas, the State must promote the conditions and mechanisms so that these rights can be exercised effectively, which includes the respect for the equality and non-discrimination principle. Political participation implies broad and diverse activities that people carry out individually or through organisations, in order that they can take part in the designation of governors or take charge of directing public affairs,

38 *Ivi*, para. 84.

39 *Ivi*, para. 90.

40 "Art. 1. The peoples of the Americas have a right to democracy and their governments have an obligation to promote and defend it. Democracy is essential for the social, political, and economic development of the peoples of the Americas."

"Art. 2. The effective exercise of representative democracy is the basis for the rule of law and of the constitutional regimes, of the member states of the Organization of American States. Representative democracy is strengthened and deepened by permanent, ethical, and responsible participation of the citizenry within a legal framework conforming to the respective constitutional order."

"Art. 3. Essential elements of representative democracy include, inter alia, respect for human rights and fundamental freedoms, access to and the exercise of power in accordance with the rule of law, the holding of periodic, free, and fair elections based on secret balloting and universal suffrage as an expression of the sovereignty of the people, the pluralistic system of political parties and organizations, and the separation of powers and independence of the branches of government."

as well as to be able to influence the formation of politics or matters of public interest, such as the defence of democracy.[41]

The highest regional organ also emphasised that, although political rights are not absolute, any limitations or restrictions cannot be interpreted in such a way that they exceed the Convention's provisions or the Inter-American standards. Art. 23.2 of the Convention is clear, it dictates that for a restriction to be valid it must be issued through a criminal sentence and by a criminal authority; the administrative route is therefore not considered a competent one. This criterion was established since the judgment of *López Mendoza v. Venezuela*, on 1 September 2011.[42]

The Colombian State, on the other hand, argued that the Mayor's political rights were not affected because he could still exercise them while the internal process was taking place. Moreover, it suggested that the Council of State had provided a final decision that favoured Mr. Petro Urrego. According to the Court, the *conventionality control* exercised by the Council was adequate and in due consideration of the Inter-American standards: it declared the domestic sanctions null and void, it also ordered the payment of salaries due during the period he was not in his public position, and urged the government to carry out reforms to achieve compatibility with the American Convention.[43]

However, due to its complementary function,[44] the Tribunal studied other remaining areas in which the State had not yet developed measures to meet the specific standards to be in compliance with the ACHR, an obligation that is enshrined in the Convention at Art. 2. Some of the incompatible Colombian regulations are: Arts. 277 and 278 of the Political Constitution; Arts. 44 and 45 of the Single Disciplinary Code (regarding the powers of dismissal and disqualification of the Attorney General's Office); Arts. 38 and 66 of the Single Disciplinary Code (regarding the possible effects of sanctions imposed by control bodies such as the Comptroller's Office or the *Personerías*); Art. 60 of Law 610 (which contemplates a public bulletin with the names of those persons –natural and legal entities – against whom, through a final judgment, fiscal responsibility, and obligations had been imposed but not complied); and Art. 4 of Law 1864 of

41 IACtHR, *Petro Urrego v. Colombia*. Preliminary Objections, Merits, Reparations, and Costs, cited above, para. 93.

42 *Ivi*, paras. 95–96.

43 *Ivi*, paras. 101 and 108.

44 The complementary nature of international jurisdiction means that the protection system established by the ACHR does not stand as a substitute for national jurisdictions, but rather complements them. In this way, the State is the main guarantor of human rights of the person, therefore, if there is an act that violates these rights, the State must resolve the matter internally and, if applicable, make reparation, before having to respond to international bodies. In this sense, recent jurisprudence has recognised that all the authorities of a State party to the Convention have the obligation to exercise convention control in such a way that the interpretation and application of national law is consistent with the State's international obligations on human rights (IACtHR, *Petro Urrego v. Colombia*. Preliminary Objections, Merits, Reparations, and Costs, cited above, para. 103).

2017 (which introduces the "illegal election of candidates" as a crime for whenever a person, previously disqualified from performing a public position by a judicial, disciplinary, or a fiscal decision, is elected; the sanction was of prison and a fine); as well as several Constitutional Court's interpretations that consider that the Attorney General's Office is empowered to restrict or limit political rights.[45]

In particular, the Court emphasised that the mentioned active rules constitute a breach of Colombia's duty to adapt its domestic law provisions in accordance with the international commitments and principles. These laws empower the Attorney General's Office and the Comptroller's Office to punish democratically elected officials by disqualification or dismissal, and have a negative impact on the exercise of political rights.[46]

Measures of reparation for the violation of Art. 23

The Court (without pointing out which of them were strictly connected with the political rights violation) indicated that the State must guarantee the effective and immediate payment of the salaries and benefits not received during the time that the applicant was removed from his position as Mayor of Bogotá, in the terms established in the Council of State decision of 15 November 2017. Additionally, for non-pecuniary damages the Court fixed the amount of 10,000.00 US Dlls; and for costs and expenses the quantity of 17,834.44 US Dlls for MINGA and 5,146.91 US Dlls for CCAJAR (the representative associations). Furthermore, Colombia was ordered to publish the judgment and to carry out the corresponding internal normative reforms in order to comply with its obligations, established in Arts. 2 and 23 of the ACHR, to which it had committed through the document's ratification. No measures of restitution and rehabilitation were determined.

Legal and economic impact

In the *Manuel Cepeda Vargas* case, the Court declared that Colombia had complied with the required monetary payment (340,000.00 US Dlls) since the State advertised in its report that the compensation for victims was to be deposited in a bank because the victims had not requested them.[47] The publication of the judgment was reported on behalf of the Court as totally complied with by Colombia by the virtue of the reports that the country presented. This also figures in the Court's resolution of 30 November 2011. In regards to the requirement of a public ceremony to recognise Colombia's international responsibility, it must be noted that there was a peculiar situation. Indeed, while an initial statement was

45 IACtHR, *Petro Urrego v. Colombia*, cited above, para. 110.

46 *Ivi*, para. 136.

47 IACtHR, *Manuel Cepeda Vargas v. Colombia*, Monitoring Compliance with Judgment, 30 November 2011, para. 35.

made by the former president Álvaro Uribe Vélez in 2010, Senator Cepeda Vargas' son, Iván Cepeda Castro, rejected the delivered message. Instead, the victim's family addressed a letter to Colombia's s executive representative, in order to let them know that the terms and the spirit in which the speech was delivered made it unacceptable. On the contrary, they considered that it even constituted a new grievance for the victims, that it ignored the conditions dictated by the regional Court, and that it denied the accusations that had been proven before national and international authorities. In this way, there was no recognition of the State responsibility for the transgressions committed by the Army in complicity with paramilitary groups members, against the Senator, a responsibility that was clearly established by the Inter-American Court. In addition, the apology didn't take place within a formal and solemn public ceremony as required.[48] In fact, another public apology was finally carried out by the Interior Minister, Germán Vargas Lleras, on 9 August 2011, meaning this measure could be included in the cited resolution of 30 November 2011.

We must point out that the financial costs related to the publishing of the judgment and the recognition of public responsibility are not clearly identified in Colombia's national budget for 2011. These obligations were paid using resources from the existing presidential budget, which was a total of 242,580,744,355.00 Colombian Pesos,[49] approximately 126,741,525.18 US Dlls[50] by that time. The judgment is available on the government's website, in the section on the Presidential Counseling for Human Rights and International Affairs (founded in 1987).[51] The compliance with the requirement to publish the judgement[52] and

48 Manuel Cepeda Foundation, *Declaración del presidente Uribe Vélez sobre sentencia de la Corte Interamericana sobre el caso Manuel Cepeda, es un nuevo agravio para las víctimas*, in Colectivo de Abogados José Alvear Restrepo, 2010. Available at: www.colectivodeabogados.org/?Declaracion-del-presidente-Uribe [Visited on 30 September 2020].

49 Ministerio de Hacienda y Crédito Público, *Decreto 4803, "por el cual se liquida el Presupuesto General de la Nación para la vigencia fiscal de 2011, se detallan las apropiaciones y se clasifican y definen los gastos,"* 29 December 2010. Available at: http://wsp.presidencia.gov.co/Normativa/Decretos/2010/Documents/Diciembre/29/dec480329122010.pdf [Visited on 19 March 2021].

50 Currency exchange consulted on 19 March 2021 at: www.dolar-colombia.com/.

51 At: www.derechoshumanos.gov.co/Prensa/Paginas/Sentencias-Convocatorias-Documentos-Destacados.aspx [Visited on 19 March 2021]. Since the Counseling was created, one of its functions is to develop activities to comply attending claims of national and international human rights organisms (Presidencia de la República, *Decreto 2111 por el cual se asignan funciones al Consejero Presidencial para la Defensa, Protección y Promoción de los Derechos Humanos y se dictan otras disposiciones,"* 8 November 1987. Available at: http://2014.derechoshumanos.gov.co/Documents/130912-Decreto%202111-1987.pdf [Visited on 19 March 2021]).

52 Departamento Administrativo de la Presidencia de la República, *Informe al Congreso*, 2011. Available at: https://dapre.presidencia.gov.co/oci/DocumentosOCI/informe-congreso-dapre-2011.pdf [Visited on 19 March 2021]. In particular, page 167.

the recognition of international responsibility[53] were included in the presidential reports of activities given to the Congress, with no details of their costs.

In 2011, the Ministry of Finance and Public Credit published a document with general guidelines on the Colombian public budget:[54] at that time the costs of all judgments (with no distinction between national and international judgments) were gathered together as "general operating expenses" of the State, classified into a sub-account designated "transfers." With that update, the presidential government was limited in its use of public resources. In other words, there was a general amount assigned to the presidency for "judgments and conciliations" (as we mentioned, with no distinction between national and international judgments), but for other variable expenses in relation to IACtHR decisions, the Ministry of Finance and Public Credit would make a monetary transfer to the presidential administrative department, conceptualised under the titles "Judicial, Quasijudicial Decisions or Friendly Settlements of International Human Rights Organs – Prior Distribution of DGPPN Concept" and "Inter-American Court of Human Rights Judgments." This process can be observed in relation to the costs of the documentary, a measure that the Court has evaluated as partially completed.[55] For its realisation, the Colombian government's Transparency Portal shows that an administrative contract was agreed with the national radio and television system. This contract included the "reproduction, production, postproduction, and transmission through the institutional channel of an audiovisual documentary on the political life, journalistic and political role of Senator Manuel Cepeda Vargas, and efforts." The costs were recorded on the budget for 2017 and with the Republic's Presidency, under the label "General Management" (*Gestión General*). Although the presidency had been assigned 543,000,000.00 Colombian Pesos[56] (approximately 179,818.00 US Dlls at that time) for general duties of "judgments and conciliations," the Ministry of Finance and Public Credit separately transferred two amounts of money in order to cover the specific expenses of the

53 Departamento Administrativo de la Presidencia de la República, *Programa Presidencial de Derechos Humanos y Derecho Internacional Humanitario, Informe de gestión. Ejes temáticos*, 2011. Available at: http://historico.derechoshumanos.gov.co/Programa/Documents/InfGestionPPDH-2011.pdf [Visited on 19 March 2021]. View page 30 of 36.

54 Ministerio de Hacienda y Crédito Público, *Aspectos Generales del Proceso Presupuestal Colombiano*, 2011. Available at: https://colaboracion.dnp.gov.co/CDT/Normograma/Lineamiento%20Ministerio%20de%20Hacienda%20y%20Credito%20P%C3%BAblico.pdf [Visited on 19 March 2021]. View pages 319, 320, 324-329, and 338.

55 IACtHR, *Manuel Cepeda Vargas v. Colombia*, Monitoring Compliance with Judgment, 12 March 2020. The video is titled: *"Documental 'Manuel Cepeda Vargas: un artista en la política'"* and is available at YouTube: www.youtube.com/watch?v=oWjkeW8igNY&t=4s&ab_channel=UIS [Visited on 30 September 2020].

56 Ministerio de Hacienda y Crédito Público, *Decreto 2170, "por el cual se liquida el Presupuesto General de la Nación para la vigencia fiscal de 2017, se detallan las apropiaciones y se clasifican y definen los gastos,"* 27 December 2016. Available at: https://dapre.presidencia.gov.co/normativa/normativa/Decreto-2170-diciembre-27-2016.pdf [Visited on 19 March 2021].

documentary, as publicised by the official Transparency Portal website[57], under the aforementioned "Judicial, Quasijudicial Decisions or Friendly Settlements of International Human Rights Organs – Prior Distribution of DGPPN Concept" (175,661,143.00 Colombian Pesos) and "Inter-American Court of Human Rights Judgements" (207,449,900.00 Colombian Pesos).

For the obligation to provide an academic grant, which the Court's cited Supervision Resolution of March 2020 refers to as totally complied with, establishing its cost has to be done differently. The Manuel Cepeda Vargas Foundation held a contest[58] for the "Scholarship for University studies in Communication Sciences 'Manuel Cepeda Vargas.'" It was offered as a stimulus for young victims of political violence who wished to pursue related undergraduate university studies in communication sciences. It was to be awarded on a one-off occasion in honour of the journalist Manuel Cepeda Vargas, emphasising that he was a man of peace and last elected Senator of the Patriotic Union, and that this was pursuant to an order of the Inter-American Court of Human Rights. The beneficiary began her studies in political science at the *Universidad del Cauca* in the first semester of 2017, but due to difficulties attributable to the State, she only began receiving the scholarship funds in February 2018.[59]

57 The concepts are codified with a letter and numbers that identify the origin of the transfer, this means, the Ministry of Finance and Public Credit budget, and the presidential public administration entries where they were applied. The concepts, in English, officially would figure as follows: *A-3-6-3-167 – Judicial, Quasijudicial Decisions or Friendly Settlements of International Human Rights Organs – Prior Distribution of DGPPN Concept – 21833*, with a value of 58,171.33.00 US Dlls; and *A-3-6-1-3 – Inter-American Court of Human Rights Judgements – 426*, with the value of 68,698.39 US Dlls (currency exchange consulted on 19 March 2021 at: www.dolar-colombia.com/). The information is available at: www.pte.gov.co/WebsitePTE/AQuienSeContrataDetalle?CodigoEntidad=02-01-01&NombreEntidad=PRESIDENCIA%20DE%20LA%20REPUBLICA%20-%20GESTION%20GENERAL&Anio=2017&Mes=7&NumeroCompromiso=60817&Beneficiario=RADIO%20TELEVISION%20NACIONAL%20DE%20COLOMBIA%20RTVC [Visited on 29 September 2020]. Since 2011, the national public budget has been published with the provision of sums for *3-6-1-3 – Inter-American Court of Human Rights Judgements*; and 2013 was the first year to provide resources for *3-6-3-167 – Judicial, Quasijudicial Decisions or Friendly Settlements of International Human Rights Organs – Prior Distribution of DGPPN Concept* (available at: http://wsp.presidencia.gov.co/Normativa/Decretos/2011/Documents/Diciembre/30/dec497030122011.pdf and http://wsp.presidencia.gov.co/Normativa/Decretos/2013/Documents/DICIEMBRE/27/DECRETO%203036%20DEL%2027%20DE%20DICIEMBRE%20DE%202013.pdf [Visited on 19 March 2021]).

58 Although the resolution mentions that the contest was carried out in 2016, several sites on the internet show the contest was launched on 2014 and, a year later, the winner was announced. This is Angie Alexandra Pino Narváez, a peasant woman originally from La Vega, department of Cauca, an area suffering from violence. The scholarship, which is awarded only once by the Colombian State, includes maintenance costs throughout the person's career. The beneficiary enables the person to undertake a career in the field of political science. This can be viewed at: www.ivancepedacastro.com/joven-campesina-gana-beca-manuel-cepeda-vargas-para-cursar-estudios-universitarios/ [Visited on 30 September 2020].

59 IACtHR, *Manuel Cepeda Vargas v. Colombia*, Monitoring Compliance with Judgment, 12 March 2020: para. 18.

In 2018, the average cost of each semester that the student was enrolled on the course in political science was 321,722.00 Colombian Pesos; by 2020 the value was 318,995.00 Colombian Pesos.[60] The total programme consisted of 8 semesters (4 years), which multiplied by the latest value per semester of enrolment gives a total of 2,551,960.00 Colombian Pesos (equivalent to 666.83 US Dlls).[61]

Concerning the obligation to provide medical and psychological assistance, the Colombian government's Ministry of Health designed a project to begin the process of providing assistance for the victims of the following cases: *19 Merchants*, *Wilson Gutiérrez Soler*, *Massacres of Mapiripan*, *Pueblo Bello*, *Ituango and La Rochela*, *Germán Escué Zapata*, *Jesús María Valle Jaramillo*, and *Manuel Cepeda Vargas*. The Ministry of Health published an initial document (dated 17 August 2018) which shows 1 October 2018 as the probable starting date, with the project due to come to an end on 15 December 2020. The estimated total value of the project is 8,984,835,581.00 Colombian Pesos, including taxes and other direct and indirect costs that may arise.[62] The funding was distributed in each of 2018, 2019, and 2020. A second document published by the Ministry of Health[63] on 13 October 2020 indicates that a total value of 6,990,660,100.00 Colombian Pesos including taxes,[64] is to be distributed during the last trimester of 2020, the whole year of 2021 and with an end date of 30 July 2022. The sum of both projects rises up to 15,975,495,681.00 Colombian Pesos (5,001,927.73 US Dlls).

Nonetheless, the most recent resolution[65] establishes that the compliance observation will continue in regards to the measures related to the security guarantees for the victim's family, the conduction of an investigation with sufficient due diligence aimed at tackling impunity, as well as the required medical and psychological treatment, since the information given by the State was not sufficient to be able to declare the State compliant with the measures.

The *Petro Urrego* case is too recent and it is therefore too early to analyse the extent of the State's compliance. The Court allowed the Colombian State one year to respond to the reparations it ordered, the exception to that being the salary payment, which was required to be paid immediately and according to the Council of State's sentence. The pecuniary compensation amount is of

60 The Political Science career semester values for 2018 and 2020 are available at: www.unicauca.edu.co/versionP/sites/default/files/files/Valor_matricula_promedio_2018.pdf and: www.unicauca.edu.co/versionP/sites/default/files/files/Valores_Matricula_Unicauca_2020OK.pdf [Visited on 30 September 2020].

61 Average currency exchange consulted at: www.dolar-colombia.com/.

62 The amount is equal to 3,043,457.91 US Dlls. Average currency exchange consulted at: www.dolar-colombia.com/.

63 Available at: www.minsalud.gov.co/sites/rid/Lists/BibliotecaDigital/RIDE/DE/PS/10-13-20-resumen-tecnico9-sentencias-2021-2022.pdf [Visited on 19 March 2021].

64 Equivalent to 1,958,469.82 US Dlls. Currency exchange consulted on 19 March 2021 at: www.dolar-colombia.com/.

65 IACtHR, *Manuel Cepeda Vargas v. Colombia*, Monitoring Compliance with Judgment, 12 March 2020.

10,000.00 US Dlls; and costs and expenses of 17,834.44 US Dlls for MINGA, and 5,146.91 US Dlls for CCAJAR (the representative associations). The total sum is 32,981.35 US Dlls.

Without restitution or rehabilitation measures ordered in this affair, Colombia only has two more measures which it needs to comply with, namely: to publish the judgment and to carry out the normative reforms. The first obligation does not represent a major challenge. However, the legal reforms may do more so, even though the legislative structure already exists. On 6 January 2021, the General Procurator, Fernando Carrillo Flórez, proposed a law project to the Camera of Representatives; however, there is no information on the status of this on the website.[66]

Overall, in the case of *Cepeda Vargas*, the total estimated sums for each ordered measure would be 627,969,800.00 Colombian Pesos (340,000.00 US Dlls) corresponding to the compensation requirement (complied with on 2011), 383,111,043.00 Colombian Pesos (129,772.25 US Dlls) for the documentary (finished by 2018), 2,551,960.00 Colombian Pesos (666.83 US Dlls) for the scholarship (finally paid on 2020), and 15,975,495,681.00 Colombian Pesos (5,001,927.73 US Dlls) for psychosocial assistance[67] (to be given between 2018 to 2022); as well as 127,932,677.77 Colombian Pesos (32,981.35 US Dlls) established as compensation (on 2020) in the *Petro Urrego* judgement.[68] These amounts add up to a total of 17,117,061,161.77 Colombian Pesos (5,505,348.16 US Dlls).

By 30 December 2020, Colombia had invested approximately 3,140,590.91 US Dlls, for complying partially with the cited obligations. In contrast, the State is still required to cover 1,866,328.30 US Dlls for psychosocial assistance during 2021 and 2022 (for *Cepeda Vargas* and the other 8 judgements we mentioned before), as well as Petro Urrego's compensation of 32,981.35 US Dlls (a total of 1,899,309.65 US Dlls).

Conclusions

Colombia certainly offers a unique context. Several authors have pointed it out and called the situation the *Colombian Paradox*. On one hand, the country has been a pioneer in the building of the regional system of human rights protection

66 The proyect is available at: www.procuraduria.gov.co/portal/media/file/Proyecto%20de%20Ley%206%20de%20Ene%20VF.pdf [Visited on 19 March 2021]. Its status can be viewed at: http://leyes.senado.gov.co/proyectos/index.php/proyectos-ley/cuatrenio-2018-2022/2020-2021?option=com_joodb&view=catalog&format=html&reset=false&ordering=&orderby=&Itemid=478&task=&search=Por+la+cual+se+adoptan+medidas+de+garant&searchfield=Titulo&limit=10 [Visited on 19 March 2021].

67 This is a project created to cover the medical and psychosocial assistance ordered in eight more Inter-American judgments, calculated to be executed during the next three years.

68 The year in parenthesis refers to the average currency exchange at the time, consulted at: www.dolar-colombia.com/.

and has developed and improved a national system for internal promotion and protection of human rights. On the other hand, this has not been enough to ensure the effective configuration of a real democratic and equal judicial structure in its territory. From 1948 to 2020, this path has coexisted with the internal civil war, which has escalated at almost the same pace that spaces and institutions have been modified and expanded in order to promote new ideals and participants for the public decisions. Although significant effort has been made to accomplish peace and an agreement was even signed in 2016, there are still serious challenges. Indeed, if there's no effective protection for citizens, voters, candidates, and politicians, democracy is unachievable.

Not only are individuals' right to participate infringed by the prevailing violence, but their citizenship rights are also being contravened. If opposition members are excluded, decisions cannot be made in an inclusive manner. If there's no propitious channel of exchange and feedback between society and government, there cannot be cohesion. Moreover, if the message that is given to the people is that public participation and political enrolment is extremely risky, the reaction may be to stop them getting involved in the public sphere, to encourage them to avoid voting, and to disguise their preferences, among other examples. Civil and political rights are fundamental for constructing a democracy, but reciprocally, the Inter-American Commission on Human Rights has established that only through the effective exercise of representative democracy can human rights be fully guaranteed. It is true when it is said that the greatest social confrontations and the most serious human rights violations have occurred or are still present in those countries where the authorities do not guarantee citizen participation.[69]

The case study in this chapter provides a very modest overview on how the democratic elements and human rights are both conditions *sine qua non* from each other, so that they have to be safeguarded integrally. As can be observed, even the Court's approach has demonstrated an evolved analysis from one decision to the other. In *Escué Zapata v. Colombia*, the leader was not recognised as the political representative of his community, but the IACtHR ordered the issuing of a fund to compensate the group for the loss of their deputy, even if political rights violations were not declared in any of the dimensions (individual–collective). Instead, the Inter-American Tribunal was less timid when solving the case of *Manuel Cepeda Vargas v. Colombia*, in which it declared the responsibility of the Colombian State for the transgression of the Senator's political rights, but also those of his supporters and the general public who had voted for him as their representative. In the third judgment, *Petro Urrego v. Colombia*, the Court maintained the second criteria, and even went through a normative revision to determine that there were contradictions between, on one hand, the international

69 Inter-American Commission of Human Rights, *Informe Anual de la Comisión Interamericana de Derechos Humanos 1985–1986*, Oea/Ser.L/V/II.68, Doc. 8 rev. 1, 26 September 1986: chap. V.

human rights and democracy law and standards, and on the other hand, the Colombian constitutional and legal provisions at stake in the case.

Nevertheless, the scope of the effectiveness of the Court's reparations does not appear to be encouraging. Colombia's responsibility has been declared in all of the regional Tribunal's decisions, and yet the country has not fully complied with any of the judgments. By way of example in the *Manuel Cepeda Vargas'* judgement, ten years later, it still has pending reparation measures to accomplish. In addition, the reparations ordered to promote the carrying out of judicial investigations with due diligence, and law enforcement, have not been successful at all, nor have they had any positive impact. The Court cannot seem to penetrate the structure's core, in any case, it is necessary to include innovative measures in order to try to counter the political deterioration that the internal conflict's events have caused.

Although three judgments may not provide a full overview of the whole Inter-American system's potential, it does not make it any less concerning that a considerable time has been taken for the sanctioned State, in this case Colombia, to take action to comply with the required reparations. In the Senator Cepeda Vargas' affair, the former president Uribe Vélez resisted and did not even act on the Court's order to give a public apology. It took a further year for another authority to hold the ceremony. The delay in awarding the scholarship, and to produce and promote the victim's documentary, as well as to develop and provide the medical/psychological assistance, gives the country the appearance that it is almost being negligent.

Certainly, the construction of democracy requires breaking through relational and organisational hermeticism, hierarchical habits, and traditions. It involves updating capacities, skills, and infrastructure.[70] In Colombia in particular, the fight for democracy requires peace and real opportunities for the involvement of citizens in political life and decision-making. Equally important is that there is a subordination of all sectors and members of the State – including public institutions and authorities – within the constitutional order and the legal framework, which also include international human rights law, standards, and principles. Otherwise, there is not even a safeguard of certainty or legal security for the citizens to know that government actions will be carried out in accordance with the legitimate and representative order of the State.

From an economic point of view, the construction of democracy also represents additional challenges and efforts in terms of finance and investment. In Colombia, as we have said, a national system has been developed and enhanced and work has been done to monitor and ensure compliance with international and regional judgments. Nevertheless, it is necessary to implement coercive mechanisms to guarantee their execution. Moreover, the changes within the use

70 MICHALSKI, W. et al., *Governance in the 21st Century: Power in the Global Knowledge Economy and Society*, in OCDE Forum 2001. Sustainable Development and the New Economy, Paris, 2001, 7–26.

of the Colombian public budget propound two points: certainly, there is better control and it is positive that (at least) resources are being set aside specifically for human rights issues; however, it also means that resources lose flexibility and may be limited. Indeed, the Inter-American Court declaring that a State holds responsibility for having violated human rights suggests obligations and actions that generate costs to the country, as has been observed through this study, and proposing solutions requires persistent, thorough, and serious analysis, endeavour, and a balancing act.

Bibliography

Amnesty International, *Colombia 2019*, in Amnesty.org, section Countries, 2019. Available at: https://www.amnesty.org/en/countries/americas/colombia/report-colombia/ [Visited on 20 September 2020].

Beetham, D., Boyle, K., *Democracia. Preguntas y respuestas*, Unesco, France, 1995.

Córdoba Triviño, J., *Aplicación de la jurisprudencia de la Corte Interamericana de Derechos Humanos al derecho constitucional colombiano*, in Anuario de Derecho Constitucional Latinoamericano, 2007, 667–684.

Cosoy, N., *¿Por qué empezó y qué pasó en la guerra de más de 50 años que desangró a Colombia?*, in BBC Mundo, 24 August 2016. Available at: https://www.bbc.com/mundo/noticias-america-latina-37181413 [Visited on 10 September 2020].

Departamento Administrativo de la Presidencia de la República, *Informe al Congreso*, 2011. Available at: https://dapre.presidencia.gov.co/oci/DocumentosOCI/informe-congreso-dapre-2011.pdf [Visited on 19 March 2021].

Departamento Administrativo de la Presidencia de la República, *Programa Presidencial de Derechos Humanos y Derecho Internacional Humanitario, Informe de gestión. Ejes temáticos*, 2011. Available at: http://historico.derechoshumanos.gov.co/Programa/Documents/InfGestionPPDH-2011.pdf [Visited on 19 March 2021].

Escobar Martínez, L. M. et al., *La influencia de los estándares interamericanos de reparación en la jurisprudencia del Consejo de Estado Colombiano*, in Estudios Constitucionales, 2, 2011, 165–190.

Eslava, L., *Constitutionalization of Rights in Colombia: Establishing a Ground for Meaningful Comparisons*, in Revista de Derecho del Estado, 22, 2009, 183–229.

García Suárez, A. L., *El desarrollo de la democracia colombiana y sus efectos en el binomio Fuerzas Militares-ciudadanía*, in Revista Científica General José María Córdova, 17, 26, 2019, 253–268.

Herrera, J. C., *Judicial Dialogue and Transformative Constitutionalism in Latin America: The Case of Indigenous Peoples and Afro-descendants*, in Revista Derecho del Estado, 43, 2019, 191–233. Available at: https://www.redalyc.org/jatsRepo/3376/337660349008/html/index.html#fn2 [Visited on 22 September 2020].

Herrera Robles, A., *El Estado colombiano frente al sistema interamericano de derechos humanos*, in Revista de Derecho. Universidad del Norte, I, 16, 2001, 104–141.

IACtHR, *ABC de la Corte Interamericana de Derechos Humanos: El qué, cómo, cuándo, dónde y porqué de la Corte Interamericana*, San José, 2019.

Inter-American Commission of Human Rights, *Colombia Country Report, Chapter II, Human Rights Protection in the Colombian Legal and Political System*, Washington, DC, 1999.

Inter-American Commission of Human Rights, *Informe Anual de la Comisión Interamericana de Derechos Humanos 1985–1986*, Oea/Ser.L/V/II.68, Doc. 8 rev. 1, 26 September 1986.

López Aguilar, H. B., *Para comprender el fenómeno de la corrupción*, en Sistema Nacional Anticorrupción, Estudios jurídicos n. 7, Judicial Power of Mexico State-Tirant lo Blanch, Mexico City 2019, 23–34.

López Daza, Y. A., *Violencia política, democracia y derechos humanos*, in Derecho y Realidad, 14, 27, 2016, 145–156.

Manuel Cepeda Foundation, *Declaración del presidente Uribe Vélez sobre sentencia de la Corte Interamericana sobre el caso Manuel Cepeda, es un nuevo agravio para las víctimas*, Colectivo de Abogados José Alvear Restrepo, 2010. Available at: https://www.colectivodeabogados.org/?Declaracion-del-presidente-Uribe [Visited on 30 September 2020].

Michalski, W. et al., *Governance in the 21st Century: Power in the Global Knowledge Economy and Society*, in OCDE Forum 2001. Sustainable Development and the New Economy, Paris, 2001, 7–26.

Ministerio de Hacienda y Crédito Público, *Aspectos Generales del Proceso Presupuestal Colombiano*, 2011. Available at: https://colaboracion.dnp.gov.co/CDT/Normograma/Lineamiento%20Ministerio%20de%20Hacienda%20y%20Credito%20P%C3%BAblico.pdf [Visited on 19 March 2021].

Ministerio de Hacienda y Crédito Público, *Decreto 4803, "por el cual se liquida el Presupuesto General de la Nación para la vigencia fiscal de 2011, se detallan las apropiaciones y se clasifican y definen los gastos"*, 29 December 2010. Available at: http://wsp.presidencia.gov.co/Normativa/Decretos/2010/Documents/Diciembre/29/dec480329122010.pdf [Visited on 19 March 2021].

Molina V. J. E., Pereira, V., *La democracia en América Latina: ¿éxito o fracaso?*, in campus.usal.es. Available at: http://campus.usal.es/~dpublico/areacp/Doctorado0406/Seminario0405/Evaluaci%F3nDemocracia.PDF [Visited on 28 September 2020].

Osterling Parodi, F., *El Equilibrio entre los Poderes Legislativo y Ejecutivo*, in Thémis, 26, 1993, 29–36.

Presidencia de la República, *Decreto 2111 por el cual se asignan funciones al Consejero Presidencial para la Defensa, Protección y Promoción de los Derechos Humanos y se dictan otras disposiciones*, 8 November 1987. Available at: http://2014.derechoshumanos.gov.co/Documents/130912-Decreto%202111-1987.pdf [Visited on 19 March 2021].

Uprimny, R., "La fuerza vinculante de las decisiones de los organismos internacionales de derechos humanos en Colombia: un examen de la evolución de la jurisprudencia constitucional," in Krsticevic, V. (coord.), *Implementación de las decisiones del Sistema Interamericano de Derechos Humanos. Jurisprudencia, normativa y experiencias nacionales*, CEJIL, Buenos Aires, 2007, 127–142.

Uprimny, R., *El bloque de constitucionalidad en Colombia. Un análisis jurisprudencial y un ensayo de sistematización doctrinal*, in Dejusticia.org, 2017. Available at: https://www.dejusticia.org/wp-content/uploads/2017/04/fi_name_recurso_46.pdf [Visited on 23 September 2020].

US Bureau of Democracy, Human Rights and Labor, *Colombia 2018 Human Rights Report*, US Department of Justice, US Department of State, 2018. Available at: https://www.justice.gov/eoir/page/file/1148416/download [Visited on 15 September 2020].

WASHINGTON-OEA, *Colombia en la OEA*, Misión permanente de Colombia ante la OEA, 2020. Available at: https://washington-oea.mision.gov.co/colombia-la-oea#:~:text=La%20OEA%20ha%20tenido%20un,su%20nacimiento%20formal%20en%201948. [Visited on 10 September 2020].

13 Political rights of human rights defenders and indigenous leaders in the Inter-American Court

A case study from Guatemala

Diana Vanessa Gutiérrez Espinoza and Magda Yadira Robles Garza

Context of human rights development in Guatemala

Throughout history, humanity has witnessed serious human rights violations which have resulted in the need to ensure the tools exist to protect and guarantee these rights. Consequently, international systems for the protection of human rights have emerged as an institutional and organic response to provide guarantees of protection and reparation for the damage caused by such violations.

Historically, the universal system for the protection of human rights, which was created after the devastating effects of the Second World War, was the first system to emerge amid the need to establish an international consensus for the protection of human rights. Almost developed in parallel to this global phenomenon were the regional systems for the protection of human rights, which emerged in response to the specific needs of each region, as is the case with the European system for the protection of human rights and the Inter-American system of human rights.

Thanks to the study and systematisation of the proceedings of the two most important organs of the Inter-American human rights system: The Inter-American Court of Human Rights (IACtHR) and the Commission (IACHR), it is possible to analyse the human rights situation in each country that is part of this system.

In the Inter-American context, the present investigation aims to analyse the resolutions that the IACtHR has issued against the State of Guatemala regarding the protection of political rights safeguarded by Art. 23 of the American Convention on Human Rights (ACHR). To achieve this purpose, the first part will develop the context and place of the Inter-American system of human rights within the constitutional structure of Guatemala, including the adoption of the ACHR, the ratification of the contentious jurisdiction of the Court, the country's presence in the IACtHR, how its case law is received and applied at the national level.

Subsequently, a breakdown of the three judgments in which the IACtHR has ruled that Guatemala holds responsibility for a violation of Art. 23 of the ACHR protecting political rights will be presented, namely the cases of: 1) *Carpio Nicolle et al.*; 2) *Chitay Nech et al.*; and 3) *Human Rights Defender et al.*

DOI: 10.4324/9781003229247-16

The analysis of these judgments will address the facts, the democratic argument established by the IACtHR, and reparations ordered in relation to the violation of Art. 23 of the ACHR. Finally, a secondary analysis will be made of the impact of the judgments in relation to legal and economic aspects.

Next, this chapter will outline the context of the development of human rights, how international law in Guatemala is received and it will establish the background of the international human rights system with a special emphasis on the Inter-American one. To begin, it is essential to present the context of human rights development from within Guatemala.

The first precedent for the recognition of rights was formulated in *Los Apuntamientos de Agricultura y Comercio de Reino de Guatemala* in 1809. Subsequently, on 22 November 1824, the Federal Republic of Central America was created by the union of Guatemala, Nicaragua, Honduras, El Salvador and Costa Rica. This union adopted its own Constitution, which provided rights such as: the right to life, the right to freedom, the right to equality before the law, and the right not to be held in servitude.[1]

On 14 December 1839 the "*Declaración Derechos y Garantías que Pertenecen a todos los Ciudadanos y Habitantes del Estado de Guatemala*" was adopted. In this Declaration, the following rights were outlined for all citizens: the right to life, the right to honour, the right to property, and the faculty to procure honest means for freedom, and the right to rebellion, as long as it is for the improvement of the common good.[2]

Likewise, this Declaration contained very important aspects that must be highlighted, such as: 1) the protection of the laws of the weak against the strong, because of the improvement of conditions for the indigenous population, this was the first instrument that ensured the protection of the rights of indigenous peoples in Guatemala; 2) the prohibition of torture, abolishing it definitively; 3) the provision according to which no one can be forced to incriminate themselves in any criminal case; and 4) the application of penalties that are indicated by law.[3]

Later, in 1871, religious freedom, the right to property and the inviolability of housing were incorporated. In 1944, in the midst of a revolutionary context in Guatemala, social rights were included for the first time, such as social security, the right to free association and unionisation, the right to culture, the right to the environment, and the right to development and peace.

Guatemala is located in Central America, has a territory of 108,889 kilometres, and more than 16,000,000 inhabitants. The 60% of its inhabitants are

1 Office of the High Commissioner United Nations Human Rights, *¿Cuál es la historia de los derechos humanos en Guatemala?* www.oacnudh.org.gt/index.php/derechos-humanos/historia.

2 Sagastume M., *¿Que son los derechos humanos? evolución histórica*, Colección de derechos humanos, Guatemala: Ministerio de Gobernación 1991.

3 Office of the High Commissioner United Nations Human Rights, *¿Cuál es la historia de los derechos humanos en Guatemala?* https://www.oacnudh.org.gt/index.php/derechos-humanos/historia.

indigenous, and it is considered a multi-ethnic, multicultural, and multilingual society.[4]

Guatemala's historical context is represented by colonialism, wars, and military dictatorships. The past and present of this country are perpendicular lines that have a meeting point which is the constant and invariable situations of poverty, racism, exclusion, violence, and impunity, framed by corruption.

Starting from the general and well-known idea that Latin America has suffered serious and massive human rights violations as a result of coups d'état, dictatorships, and internal conflicts, specifically between the 1960s and 1980s of the last century, Guatemala, like many countries in the continent, has gone through several periods of internal violence since the 1960s. The armed conflict began in 1962 and ended on 29 December 1996, with the signing of the 12 Peace Accords between the State and the *Unidad Revolucionaria Nacional Guatemalteca* (URNG).

The creation of the *Comisión para el Esclarecimiento Histórico de las Violaciones a los Derechos Humanos y los Hechos de Violencia que han causado sufrimiento a la población guatemalteca*, specifically the Oslo Agreement of 1994, sought to end the conflict between the guerrillas and the State that had been present for 30 years.

The Truth Commission for Guatemala resulted in the presentation of the final report *Memoria del Silencio* which highlighted that in Guatemala, massive and systematic human rights violations were suffered over a long period of time. This resulted in more than 42,000 victims, 23,000 murders, 6,000 disappearances, 623 villages massacred. The 93% of the attacks were carried out by the army and other state forces.

During the armed conflict between 1978 and 1983, the governments of Generals Fernando Romeo Lucas García and Efraín Ríos Montt concentrated their efforts on annihilating the guerrillas and systematically attacking social movements and the civilian population in areas with a strong presence, mainly the Mayan population.

The political options for the Mayan population were insufficient, so the *guerrillas* promoted their integration into their social and active base. Beginning in 1981, the army identified indigenous Mayans as a military objective and began a systematic campaign of repression and persecution against a civilian population which lacked the capacity to defend itself. The indigenous population was tortured and brutally murdered, women were raped, children were beaten to death, thrown alive into mass graves, or kidnapped into slavery, and numerous forced displacements also occurred.[5]

4 Organization of American States, Inter-American Comission on Human Rights, *Informe de la situación de derechos humanos en Guatemala.* www.oas.org/es/cidh/informes/pdfs/Guatemala2016.pdf.

5 Information retrieved from the final report "Memoria del silencio" de la Comisión para el Esclarecimiento Histórico de las Violaciones a los Derechos Humanos y los Hechos de Violencia que han causado sufrimiento a la población guatemalteca (1999).

The above was identified by the IACHR as acts of genocide. In addition, judges and lawyers were murdered with the aim of completely paralysing justice and any action taken to protect human rights.

In its report on the human rights situation in Guatemala, the IACHR stresses that the importance of the *Comisión para el Esclarecimiento Histórico de las Violaciones a los Derechos Humanos y los Hechos de Violencia que han causado sufrimiento a la población guatemalteca* (CEH) lies in the fact that its work dramatically evidences the exclusion and discrimination to which the indigenous peoples in Guatemala were subjected.[6]

In addition, the CEH established that Guatemala's internal conflict was the result of a series of factors, such as structural impunity, the closing of political spaces, racism, and the deepening of exclusionary and anti-democratic institutions. It concluded that the violence during the period 1960 to 1996 was directed at the poor and those who were fighting for justice and greater social equality, but above all at the Mayan population.

The result of 30 years of armed conflict in Guatemala represented great human, material, institutional, and moral loss as a consequence of massive and systematic human rights violations: massacres, extrajudicial executions, forced disappearances, rapes, forced displacements, illegal detentions, and kidnappings, among others.[7]

In spite of the adoption of the Peace Accords and their intention to implement them to end the armed conflict in Guatemala, in addition to their subsequent follow-up by successor governments, they have still not been fully implemented 20 years after their acceptance.

Currently, the primary reasons that generated the internal conflict in Guatemala persist, such as: the concentration of economic power, a weak state structure with high levels of corruption, racial discrimination, social inequality, poverty, and lack of access to justice. The above leads inevitably to a move away from the respect and guarantee of human rights. In this sense, we can establish that human rights violations are not part of Guatemala's past; rather in the present there remains a framework of illegality and disrespect for rights.[8]

With regard to the reception of international human rights law in Guatemala, this development should be analysed on the basis of three relevant political events: the first one is the promulgation of the *Constitución Política de la República de Guatemala*[9] of 1985 (later reformed in 1993). Art. 46 of the Constitution

6 Organization of American States, Inter- American Comission on Human Rights, *Informe de la situación de derechos humanos en Guatemala*. www.oas.org/es/cidh/informes/pdfs/Guatemala2016.pdf.

7 *Ibidem.*

8 Organization of American States, Inter- American Comission on Human Rights, *Informe de la situación de derechos humanos en Guatemala*. www.oas.org/es/cidh/informes/pdfs/Guatemala2016.pdf.

9 Declaración del Buen Pueblo de Virginia y la Declaración Francesa de los Derechos del Hombre y el Ciudadano had a marked influence on the constitution of the State of Guatemala.

states the principle of pre-eminence of international law over domestic law as far as human rights are concerned. This article is essential for determining the normative status of international treaties within the State. Based on their content, it is established that the international instruments accepted and ratified by Guatemala are predominant over domestic law.[10]

Therefore, the relationship between international human rights law and Guatemalan domestic law belongs to the supra-legal rank, since it has a higher value than domestic regulations but does not allow for the modification of its Constitution. This system of reception has also been embraced by other Latin American countries, such as El Salvador, Honduras, and Colombia.[11]

On the other hand, Art. 204 of the Constitution, with reference to the essential conditions for the administration of justice, states that "The courts of justice in any resolution or judgment shall necessarily observe the principle that the Constitution of the Republic takes precedence over any law or treaty." This provision sets forth the principle of the prevalence of the fundamental law that must be observed by judges. However, it should be clarified that there is an exception in the area of human rights, in accordance with the aforementioned Article 46. The picture is completed by Art. 149 on international relations, which states that

> Guatemala shall regulate its relations with other States in accordance with international principles, rules and practices in order to contribute to the maintenance of peace and freedom, respect and defence of human rights, and the strengthening of democratic processes and international institutions that guarantee mutual and equitable benefit among States.

With respect to this provision, we can note that there are precepts in both international human rights law and international humanitarian law that must be complied with by all international subjects, as they are norms agreed upon by the international community. In this way, the Constitution respects the imperative nature of universal norms that are considered fundamental prerogatives for every person.

The second fundamental political event is the functioning of the Constitutional Court. The characteristics of specialty, concentration, and independence in the performance of the jurisdictional function of the Constitutional Court resulted in the effective reception of international human rights law. This is due to the fact that the Court has been adopting decisions with the support of international instruments, making them operative in the domestic sphere.[12]

10 Maldonado A., *Guatemala: recepción del Derecho Internacional de los Derechos Humanos* en Anuario de Derecho Constitucional Latinoamericano 2001.

11 Gutiérrez Solé C., *Aplicación del Derecho Internacional de los Derechos Humanos en el ámbito del derecho interno de Guatemala* 2001.

12 Maldonado A., *Guatemala: recepción del Derecho Internacional de los Derechos Humanos* en Anuario de Derecho Constitucional Latinoamericano 2001.

Finally, the negotiation and signing of the *Acuerdo Paz Firme y Duradera*, 1996. The Peace Accords contributed to strengthening the normative value of the Constitution, since the clause that opens up international human rights law and allows for the incorporation of rights and guarantees that were not provided for in the fundamental law is derived from Art. 46.

With regard to the international system, the Universal Declaration of Human Rights (1948) is part of Guatemala's legal system. The reception of international human rights law into domestic law in Guatemala can be explained by saying that the former enters into force when there is an insufficiency of the latter to guarantee fundamental rights. According to Gutiérrez Solé de Colmenares

> International law enters as a consequence of the verification that, in practice and especially when power is exercised in an arbitrary manner, the resources of domestic law are often insufficient, if not illusory, to safeguard the victim from the abuses of such power and from the recognition that the offense to the superior values of human dignity, wherever it is committed, affects humanity as a whole.[13]

On the other hand, Guatemala has signed and/or ratified other international human rights instruments.[14]

As far as the Inter-American system of protection of human rights is concerned, Guatemala ratified the ACHR on 27 April 1978 and ratified the contentious jurisdiction of the IACtHR. Its reception is mainly reflected in Art. 46 of the Constitution, since its content establishes the pre-eminence of international human rights law, with the exception already mentioned.[15] Art. 46 of

13 Gutiérrez Solé C., *Aplicación del Derecho Internacional de los Derechos Humanos en el ámbito del derecho interno de Guatemala* 2001, 72.

14 Guatemala accessed to the Convention against Torture and other Cruel, Inhuman or Degrading Treatment or Punishment on 5 January 1990, the International Pact on Civil and Political Rights on 5 May 1992, the International Pact on Economic, Social and Cultural Rights on 19 May 1988, signed the International Convention for the Protection of all Persons from Enforced Disappearance on 6 February 2007, ratified the Protocol to the Convention against Torture and Other Cruel, Inhuman or Degrading Treatment or Punishment on 9 June 2008, the Convention on the Elimination of All Forms of Discrimination against Women on 12 August 1982, the International Convention on the Elimination of All Forms of Racial Discrimination on 18 January 1983, the International Convention on the Protection of the Rights of All Migrant Workers and Members of Their Families on 14 March 2003, the Convention on the Rights of the Child on 6 June 1990, the Protocol to the Convention on the Rights of the Child on the involvement of children in armed conflict and the Protocol to the Convention on the Rights of the Child on the sale of children, child prostitution and child pornography on 9 May 2002 and Convention on the Rights of Persons with Disabilities on 7 April 2009. Cfr. Office of the High Commissioner United Nations Human Rights, *Guatemala estado de ratificaciones.* Available at the following link: www.ohchr.org/SP/Countries/LACRegion/Pages/GTIndex.aspx.

15 The Inter-American system of protection of human rights includes various instruments, the majority of which have been ratified by Guatemala: the American Declaration of the Rights

the Constitution should include also the IACtHR case law, which constitutes an interpretation of the scope and content of the ACHR.

To date,[16] 34 cases have been decided by the IACtHR corresponding to Guatemala.[17]

With specific reference to political rights, the IACtHR declared Guatemala responsible of the violation of Art. 23 of the ACHR in three cases: *Carpio Nicolle et al.* (22 November 2004); *Chitay Nech* (25 May 2010); and *Human Rights Defender et al.* (28 August 2014), that will be analysed in the following pages.

Analysis of the selected judgments

Case of Carpio Nicolle et al. v. Guatemala

The context of the first judgment condemning Guatemala for the violation of Art. 23 of the ACHR, is the self-coup of the former President Jorge Serrano Elias. The facts of the judgment refer to the journalist and politician Jorge Carpio Nicolle, a well-known figure in the country, who founded the newspaper *El Gráfico* and the political party *Unión del Centro Nacional* (UCN).

As a precursor to what would ultimately be a tragic outcome for Mr. Carpio Nicolle, he faced censorship of a publication written by him in which he expressed a critical view of the self-coup. The UCN also pronounced itself on the self-coup, which led to its members being intimidated by the police and military forces.

Later, on 3 July 1993, while on a proselytising tour, Mr. Carpio Nicolle and his entourage were intercepted and attacked by 15 armed men wearing ski masks. The attack resulted in the death of Mr. Carpio Nicolle and two of his companions. In addition, a minor accompanying them was seriously injured, while the other companions survived.

Due to these events, the internal resources of the State were used to deal with the case, but no investigation was carried out and, as a consequence, the persons responsible were not punished. As a result, the case arrived before the IACtHR, which determined that the State's international responsibility for the violations of Arts. 4.1 (Right to Life), 5.1 (Right to Personal Integrity), 5.2 (Right to Personal Integrity), 19 (Rights of the Child), 13.1, 13.2 a), and 13.3 (Freedom

and Duties of Man (30 March 2007); the American Convention on Human Rights (27 April 1978); the Inter-American Convention to Prevent and Punish Torture (10 December 1986); the Additional Protocol to the American Convention on Human Rights in the Area of Economic, Social and Cultural Rights (30 May 2000); the Inter-American Convention on the Prevention, Punishment and Eradication of Violence against Women (4 January 1995); the Inter-American Convention on Forced Disappearance of Persons (27 July 1999); the Inter-American Convention on the Elimination of All Forms of Discrimination against Persons with Disabilities (8 August 2002); and the Inter-American Convention on the Granting of Civil Rights to Women(11 June 1970).

16 20 September 2020.

17 Organization of American States, Inter- American Comission on Human Rights, *Casos contenciosos Guatemala*. www.corteidh.or.cr/casos_sentencias.cfm.

of Thought and Expression), 8.1 (Judicial Guarantees), 25 (Judicial Protection), including Article 23.1 a), b), and c) (Political Rights).

More specifically, as far as political rights are concerned, the IACtHR stated – very briefly – that, due to his activity as a journalist and politician, Mr. Carpio Nicolle's execution was politically motivated.[18] Thus, the IACtHR ordered Guatemala to comply with several reparation measures (also) related to Art. 23 of the ACHR. First of all, among the restitutive measures, the Inter-American tribunal ordered the State to effectively investigate the facts in order to identify, judge, and punish the material and intellectual authors of the extrajudicial execution of the victims, to remove all *de facto* and *de jure* obstacles and mechanisms that maintain impunity, provide sufficient security guarantees to witnesses, judicial authorities, prosecutors, other justice operators and the victims' families, and use all measures available to them to expedite the process and to take concrete steps to strengthen its investigative capacity.

As far as the satisfaction measures are concerned, the State was ordered to carry out a public act of recognition of their responsibility and to publish within a period of six months, counted from the notification of the judgment, at least once, in the Official Gazette, in another newspaper of national circulation, and in the bulletin with the largest circulation within the Guatemalan armed forces.[19]

Finally, some compensation measures were disposed.[20]

Case of Chitay Nech et al. v. Guatemala

Mr. Chitay Nech was an indigenous Mayan, who belonged to a movement of peasants in the region he lived in, later affiliated to the political party Democracia Cristiana (DC). In 1977 Mr. Chitay Nech was nominated by DC as a council candidate for the municipality of San Martin Jilotepeque and was duly elected.

From June 1980, Mr. Chitay Nech began to receive threats and harassment. Almost a year later, he was intercepted in a store by a group of armed men who beat him and put him in a vehicle. Despite the fact that the State has the necessary resources to undertake the investigation and punishment of those responsible, it has not provided any response. The case arrived to the IACtHR, which established that States have an obligation to guarantee the enjoyment of political rights, in condition of equality and non-discrimination. Therefore, social groups that are in a situation of vulnerability must be taken into account, as is the case with indigenous populations, in order to guarantee the strengthening of democracy and political pluralism.[21]

18 Para. 77

19 The section of this judgment called Proven Facts, without the corresponding footnotes, paragraphs 77 and 78 of the section called Merits of said judgment, as well as the resolutive part of it.

20 See paras. 106 ff. of the judgements.

21 I/A Court H.R., Case of *Chitay Nech et al. v. Guatemala*. Preliminary Objections, Merits, Reparations, and Costs. Judgment of May 25, 2010. Paragraph 107 of the judgment states:

The importance of respecting and guaranteeing political rights in a democratic State is the reiteration of the principle already established in the 2005 case *Yatama et al. v. Nicaragua*[22] and in the *Opinión Consultiva* OC-18/03,[23] according to which States have an obligation with two dimensions. The first one implies that States must adopt positive measures to guarantee rights, avoiding any initiative that may restrict them; the second one provides that States must suppress any measure that leads to the violation of a fundamental right. Moreover, OC-18/03 also points out that the principle of equality and non-discrimination constitutes a *jus cogens* norm of international law, being fundamental and non-derogable under any circumstances, since it allows the safeguarding of human rights.

Therefore, the IACtHR has recognised the obligation of States to ensure that members of indigenous and ethnic communities can make decisions on matters and policies that may affect their rights and that they can be integrated into State institutions and bodies in a manner that is direct and proportional to their population, in accordance with their values, customs, and forms of organisation. This criterion is a reiteration of what was adopted in the *Yatama et al. v. Nicaragua* judgment.

In the case of Mr. Chitay Nech, a violation of Art. 23 of the ACHR was found because he was prevented by the State from participating in the democratic process as a result of his selective forced disappearance. The Court ordered Guatemala to conduct effectively, with due diligence and within a reasonable time, the investigation and, if applicable, the criminal proceedings in relation to the detention and subsequent forced disappearance of the victim, in order to determine the corresponding criminal responsibilities and effectively apply the sanctions and consequences provided for by law, and to continue to effectively search for and locate the victim. Moreover, the IACtHR ordered the State to publish some paragraph of the decision in the official journal and, in another newspaper of wide national circulation, the official summary of the Judgment on Preliminary Objections, Merits, Reparations, and Costs issued by the Court. Thirdly, Guatemala was condemned to carry out a public act of recognition of responsibility in relation to the facts of the present case and in reparation for the memory of the victim, to be carried out in Spanish and in Maya Kaqchikel, and to place in San Martin Jilotepeque, Chimaltenango, a commemorative plaque with the name of the victim, in which reference is made to his activities.

"The political rights enshrined in the American Convention, as well as in various international instruments, are conducive to the. In particular, the right to effective political participation implies that citizens have not only the right but also the possibility to participate in the conduct of public affairs. Furthermore, it has been recognized that the effective exercise of political rights constitutes both an end in itself and a fundamental means for democratic societies to guarantee the other human rights provided for in the Convention."

22 See the chapter on Nicaragua in this volume.

23 Legal Status and Rights of Undocumented Migrants.

Finally, the State must pay \$386,000 in compensation to the victims and \$10.000 for the costs of the proceedings.[24]

Case of Human Rights Defender et al. v. Guatemala

The facts that gave rise to the *Human Rights Defender et al.* decision are located in the context following the signing of the *Acuerdos de Paz* mentioned above. The long period of violence that Guatemala experienced left as a legacy numerous victims of serious human rights violations. As was the case in this particular instance, human rights defenders were exposed to situations of risk such as threats and attacks against their integrity, among others, leaving those in the media in a serious situation of vulnerability.

As in the cases analysed above, it was found that the main perpetrators were agents of the State. On 20 February 2004, "B.A.," identified as a human rights defender, reported that she was being threatened. In December of the same year, her father "A.A.," who was also a human rights defender, was found dead from gunshot wounds.

Despite making the Human Rights Ombudsman's Office and the then Mayor of Santa Lucía Cotzumalguapa aware of what had happened, threats continued to be made by people who were heavily armed near the place where they lived. Later, in 2005, "B.A." was the victim of an attack, which he reported, but which was dismissed in 2008.

In this case, the IACtHR determined that the following provisions of the ACHR had been violated: 1) Art. 1 (Obligation to respect rights), 2) Art. 22 (Right to movement and residence), 3) Art. 23 (Political rights), 4) Art. 25 (Judicial protection), 5) Art. 4 (Right to life), 6) Art. 5 (Right to personal integrity), and 7) Art. 8 (Judicial guarantees).

In our opinion, the most important point of the argument regarding the violation of Article 23 of the ACHR established by the IACtHR is to point out that this provision not only protects the right to be elected, but also involves the real opportunity to exercise the office for which one was elected. Therefore, the State has the obligation to adopt the necessary measures to guarantee the full exercise of the right.

The IACtHR takes this opportunity to reiterate the criterion it had already established in previous judgments, that the principle of equality and non-discrimination must be pursued in all measures adopted by States to guarantee political rights.

The fact that B.A. had been displaced by the threats and the attack she had suffered meant that she could not take up the position and exercise the duties of the office to which she had been elected, until February 2016. Therefore, the IACtHR considered that the State had violated Art. 23 of the ACHR, by not

24 See paras. 242 ff. of the decision issued in the case of *Chitay Nech et al. v. Guatemala*, Preliminary Objections, Merits, Reparations, and Costs, 25 May 2010.

taking the necessary measures so that B.A. could take up the position for which she was elected.

Due to the complexity of the case and the high number of the victims, the reparation measures dictated by the Court in the case of *Human Rights Defender et al. v. Guatemala* are summarised in the following Table 13.1.

Analysis of the legal and economic impact of the implementation of the judgments of the IACHR

Legal impact

Once the IACtHR exercises its jurisdictional function to determine state responsibility, it follows a strict procedure related to the implementation of reparations measures. In accordance with a long jurisprudential tradition developed by the IACtHR itself in its more than 40 years of operation, the measures refer to different actions to be undertaken by States, which can be grouped under these headings: compensation and reimbursement of costs, restitution, rehabilitation, satisfaction, and guarantees of non-repetition.

This process of monitoring compliance with the judgments is based on Arts. 33, 62(1), 62(3), 67, and 68(1) of the ACHR, as well as Arts. 24 and 30 of the Statute of the IACtHR and Arts. 31(2) and 69 of its own Rules of Procedure.

Currently, the IACtHR has a list of 208 cases in the compliance supervision stage, including those that have not yet expired within the time period set forth in the judgments themselves. This implies the supervision of 1,140 reparations measures (Official website of the IACtHR).

To date (September 20, 2020), there are 34 judgments against Guatemala, of which only 2 have been filed, that is, 2 where total compliance has been declared by the Court itself and accepted by the victims. While 32 cases remain under the compliance supervision process.

It is important to mention that the three judgments analysed in this document are under compliance supervision; that is, none of them has been fully complied with by the State.

The following is a list of the reparation measures dictated in each of the judgments that are being analysed with respect to the violation of Article 23 of the ACHR, which recognises and protects political rights.

From the above list of reparation measures issued in the Case of *Chitay Nech et al. v. Guatemala*, Case of *Carpio Nicolle et al. v. Guatemala* and Case of *Human Rights Defender et al. v. Guatemala*, we can highlight the following:

The total number of reparation measures to be carried out by Guatemala in these matters is 27. Of these, only 14 have been complied with, which represents 51.85% of the total number of measures. In other words, Guatemala has only complied with slightly more than half of the judgments involving violations of political rights. While 13 measures are awaiting compliance (48.14%). An important fact for this analysis is that Guatemala took an average of 30 months to comply with just half of the reparation's measures.

Table 13.1 Reparation measures dictated in Case of *Human Rights Defender et al. v. Guatemala*. Own elaboration from the Case of *Human Rights Defender et al. v. Guatemala*. Preliminary Objections, Merits, Reparations, and Costs. Judgment of August 28, 2014.

Category	*Action*	*Relationship to the violation of Art. 23*
Non-repetition	To carry out, with due diligence and within a reasonable period of time, the corresponding investigations and criminal proceedings in accordance with the provisions of its domestic law, in order to identify, identify, and, as the case may be, punish those materially and intellectually responsible for the facts related to the death of Mr. A.A. and the threats suffered by his family members, as well as to establish the truth about them, taking into account the criteria indicated regarding investigations in this type of case.	Yes
Non-repetition	Examine possible procedural and investigative irregularities and, if necessary, sanction the conduct of the corresponding public servants, without it being necessary for the victims of the case to file complaints to that effect.	Yes
Restitution	To guarantee adequate security conditions so that the victims can return to their places of residence, if necessary and if they wish, without this representing an additional expense for the beneficiaries of this measure.	Yes
Rehabilitation	To provide free of charge, through its specialised health institutions and in an immediate, adequate, and effective manner, the psychological and psychiatric treatment required by the victims, with prior informed consent and for the time necessary, including the provision of free medication.	Yes
Satisfaction	Publish a) the official summary of this Judgment prepared by the Court, for one time only, in the official journal; b) the official summary of this Judgment prepared by the Court, for one time only, in a journal of broad national circulation; and c) the version of this Judgment with the names of the victims reserved, in its entirety, available for a period of one year, on an official website of Guatemala.	Yes
Satisfaction	Implement a public policy for the protection of human rights defenders, taking into account the requirements of paragraph 263.	Yes

(*Continued*)

Table 13.1 (*Continued*)

Category	*Action*	*Relationship to the violation of Art. 23*
Compensation	To reimburse an amount of USD $30,000.00 for material damage in favour of each of C.A., B.A., E.A. and L.A., and an additional amount of USD $10,000.00 for those who moved out of Guatemala. Likewise, the Court presumes that the ladies E.A. and B.A. incurred additional expenses for the travel of their children with them that must be reimbursed, for which reason an additional amount of USD $5,000.00 is ordered for B.A., who travelled with a minor, and USD $10,000.00 for E.A., who travelled with two minors.	Yes
Compensation	To pay an amount in equity of USD $7,000.00 to C.A., D.A., E.A., B.A., F.A., G.A., I.A., J.A., K.A., L.A., M.A., and N.A. as a result of the impunity in which Mr. A.A.'s death is found, B.A., E.A., L.A., N.A., J.A., and K.A. as a result of their displacement, an equity payment of USD $5,000.00 is ordered to be made to each of the aforementioned persons.	Yes
Compensation	To pay Mrs. E.A. the sum of USD $2,000.00 and Mrs. B.A. the sum of USD $3,000.00, for costs incurred at the national level.	Yes
Compensation	To reimburse the victims' representatives the sum of USD $3,439.22. In addition, the State must reimburse the representatives the sum of USD $5,000.00 for costs and USD $12,000.00 for fees.	Yes

For each individual case, an analysis of compliance with the particular measures is presented, presenting the cases in chronological order. The first judgment is that of the *Carpio Nicolle* case, in this sense we present the following graph.

The graph above allows us to visualise Guatemala's behaviour in the matter in question. In this regard, we can say that when it comes to the protection of journalist and politician Carpio Nicolle, the Court determined that there had been compliance with eight measures of integral reparation for his surviving victims; however, only four are in a status of total compliance. In other words, only 50% of the reparation measures have been observed.

Now, which measures have been complied with and which have not? In an average of 43 months, Guatemala has complied with all 3 measures of compensation and 1 of satisfaction. While those that have been delayed correspond to

Table 13.2 Compliance with reparation measures regarding the violation of Article 23 of the ACHR (by case). Own elaboration based on compliance supervision resolutions updated to September 20, 2020.

Case	*Category*	*Reparation measures*	*Accomplished*	*Pending compliance*	*Average time (months)*
Case of *Carpio Nicolle et al. v. Guatemala*	Compensation	3	3	0	55
	Restitution	3	0	3	0
	Satisfaction	2	1	1	31
Total		8	4	4	43
Case of *Chitay Nech et al. v. Guatemala*	Compensation	1	1	0	18
	Restitution	2	0	2	0
	Satisfaction	4	3	1	24.6
	Rehabilitation	1	0	1	0
Total		8	4	4	21.3
Case of *Human Rights Defender et al. v. Guatemala*	Compensation	5	5	0	17
	Restitution	1	1	0	36
	Satisfaction	2	0	2	0
	Rehabilitation	1	0	1	0
	Non-repetition	2	0	2	0
Total		11	6	5	26.5
Total general		27	14	13	30.26

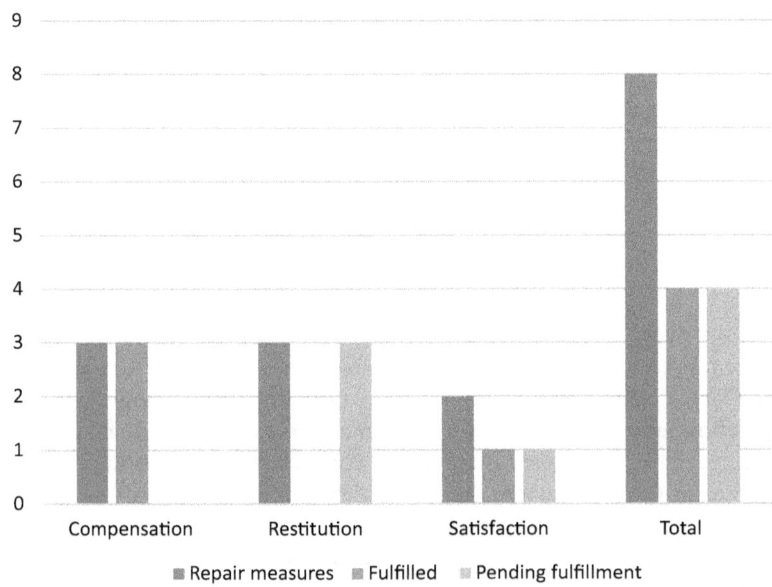

Figure 13.1 Fulfilment of the measures of reparation in case of *Carpio Nicolle et al. v. Guatemala*. Own elaboration based on compliance supervision resolutions updated to September 20, 2020.

three measures of restitution and one of satisfaction. This means that Guatemala has complied with the obligation to compensate the victims in terms of material damage, immaterial damage, and the costs and expenses of the trial; and it also complied by publishing the judgment.

Leaving the public act of recognition of responsibility pending for the victims' families, and in terms of restitution, Guatemala has not taken action to investigate the violations committed, nor has it removed obstacles to a life free of violence in the journalists' guild that would allow them to have sufficient guarantees to carry out their profession.

The second analysis corresponds to the reparation measures dictated in the judgment of the Case of *Carpio Nicolle et al. v. Guatemala*. In this case, compliance with the judgment is very similar to the previous one. Here, too, there are eight reparations measures in the judgment, and only half of them have been fulfilled. In terms of the heading, we can say that Guatemala has paid the compensation and has carried out three measures of satisfaction that are related to the publication of the judgment, the radio broadcast of the judgment, and the public act of recognition.

What does this leave unfulfilled: the two measures of restitution that relate to the investigation of the facts and the consequent disappearance of Mr. Chitay, as well as the pending search for the indigenous politician; it also failed to provide medical and psychological treatment to his family members. Probably, as the judgment seems to indicate, his wife and son left the place where they lived because of threats and risks to their own safety and lives. This can be seen in the graph below.

Finally, we have the most recent judgment in the case of *Defensor de Derechos Humanos*. From this judgment we can highlight the following findings: 1)

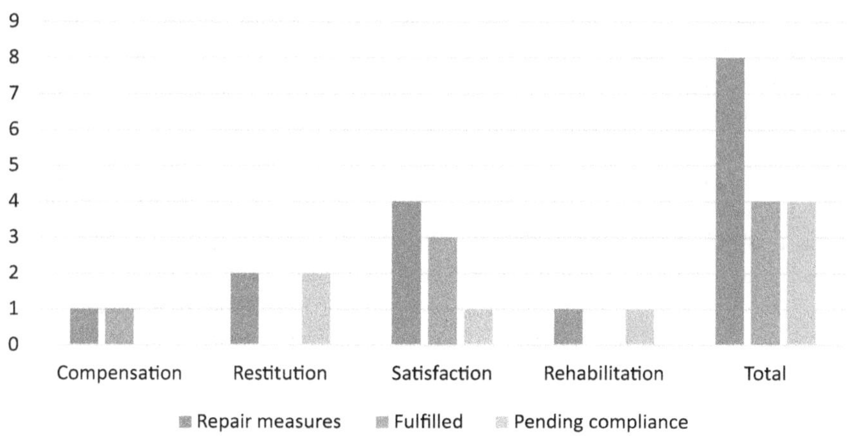

Figure 13.2 Compliance with the measures of reparation of the Case of *Chitay Nech et al. v. Guatemala*. Own elaboration based on compliance supervision resolutions updated to September 20, 2020.

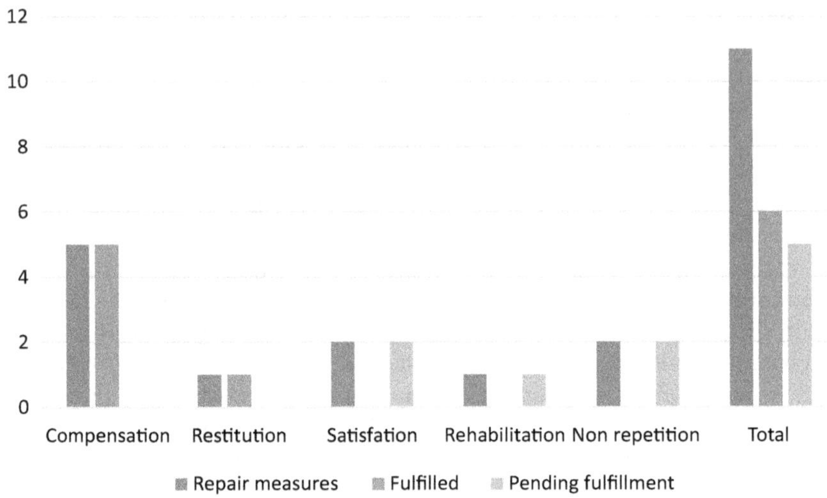

Figure 13.3 Compliance with the measures of reparation of the Case of *Human Rights Defender et al. v. Guatemala.* Own elaboration based on compliance supervision resolutions updated to September 20, 2020.

the total of the averages dictated is 11; and, as in the two previous judgments, Guatemala took an average of 26 months to pay the amounts arising from the compensation indicated in the judgment and a measure of restitution fulfilled that refers to the assurance of the safe return of the victim and his relatives. In terms of percentage, the measures complied with represent a figure of 54.54%.

A global analysis of the measures of these three judgments is now required, based on the category in which the Court classifies the reparations measures. This is relevant because it will later help us to analyse the economic impact that the judgments have had on the State.

Thus, we say again that the total number of measures in the 3 judgments analysed is 27 measures of integral reparation. According to the category, these are grouped as follows: a) fulfilled: 9 measures of compensation, 1 of restitution, 4 of satisfaction; b) pending fulfilment: 5 restitution, 4 of satisfaction, 2 of rehabilitation, and 2 in the category of non-repetition.

From this information we can highlight that only the compensation category is 100% fulfilled, which represents 33% of the total reparation measures.

In addition, an important piece of information can be seen from the above: at first glance we can see that 51.85% of the total measures have been complied with out of 48.14% of measures pending compliance. However, the detailed analysis of the measures complied with tells us that Guatemala has complied with half of its judgments in the area of political rights because it has covered the economic sanctions.

However, the measures that relate to non-repetition or satisfaction show that the State has not been able to implement the measures that refer to the

Table 13.3 Compliance with reparation measures regarding the violation of Article 23 of the ACHR (general). Own elaboration from the compliance supervision resolutions updated to September 20, 2020.

Category	*Measures of reparation*	*Fulfilled*	*Pending compliance*
Compensation	9	9	0
Restitution	6	1	5
Satisfaction	8	4	4
Rehabilitation	2	0	2
Non-repetition	2	0	2
Total	27	14	13

anticipation of similar events in the future, such as the implementation of a public policy, the management of legislative changes that guarantee the exercise of political rights, among other measures that we have already pointed out. This is reflected in the table and graph below.

Economic impact

Throughout 41 years of work, the IACtHR has established very important criteria in relation to integral reparation for the victims. In this section of the text, we will focus on reparations measures that have caused an economic impact.

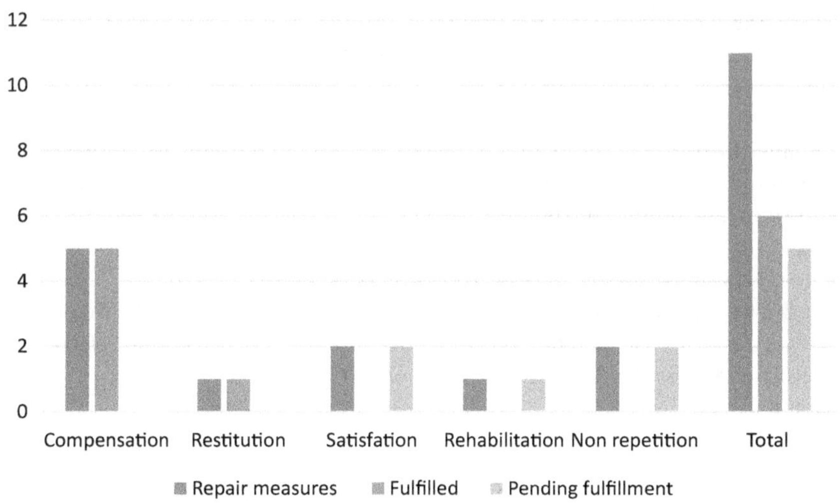

Figure 13.4 Compliance with reparation measures regarding the violation of Article 23 of the CADH (general). Own elaboration based on compliance supervision resolutions updated to September 20, 2020.

Therefore, it is important to establish what is included in the category of compensatory reparations as defined by the IACHR Court. This category is made up of several concepts, among which are:

1) Material damage: this implies the loss of or a detrimental effect on income, the expenses incurred as a result of the facts, and the consequences of a pecuniary nature that have a causal link to the facts.

Material damage includes: consequential damage, which is the reduction or detrimental effect on the assets of the victims or their families, or the expenses incurred as a result of the violation, and loss of earnings, which is the economic loss suffered as a result of the violation. It is based both on the age of the victims at the time of their death or subsequent inability to live, and on the future years of life expectancy in their country.

2) Immaterial damage: is the damage to the honour, suffering, and pain of the victims resulting from the rape. "It is the result of the humiliation to which the victim is submitted, of the lack of knowledge of their human dignity, of the suffering and pain that is caused as a consequence of a violation of human rights."[25]

3) Costs and expenses

For the economic analysis, it was necessary to break down the reparation measures with their exact amounts in order to show the total cost of the three judgments in question. From this detail we can establish the following:

1) The judgment in Case of *Carpio Nicolle et al. v. Guatemala* meant a total cost for the State of $1,835,500 US dollars. The following is the breakdown of this particular case.
2) The total cost in relation to the Case of *Carpio Nicolle et al. v. Guatemala* was $396,000 US dollars. The following is the breakdown of this particular case.
3) From the last judgment *Defensor de Derechos Humanos et al. v Guatemala* the total cost for the State was $1,670,439.22 US dollars. The following is the breakdown of this particular case.

And, finally, from the account of the costs involved in the reparations awarded in the judgments that found a violation of Art. 23 of the ACHR, which protects political rights, we highlight the following:

1) The total cost of the reparations to the State is $3,901,939.22.
2) All the measures of compensation have been complied with by the State.
3) The judgment that dictates the highest compensation is the one related to the Case of *Human Rights Defender et al. v. Guatemala.*
   Graph 13.1

25 Calderón J., *La reparación integral en la jurisprudencia de la Corte Interamericana de Derechos Humanos: estándares aplicables al nuevo paradigma mexicano*, Instituto de Investigaciones Jurídicas, Suprema Corte de Justicia de la Nación, Fundación Konrad Adenauer 2013.

Table 13.4 Distribution of compensation measures for Case of *Carpio Nicolle et al. v. Guatemala*. Own elaboration from I/A Court H.R., Case of *Carpio Nicolle et al. v. Guatemala*. Merits, Reparations and Costs. Judgment of November 22, 2004.

Concept	*Quantity (USD)*	*N°*	*Total (USD)*
Immaterial damage	$55,000	6	$330,000
Immaterial damage	$50,000	1	$50,000
Immaterial damage	$100,000	1	$100,000
Immaterial damage	$20,000	2	$40,000
Immaterial damage	$25,000	1	$25,000
Immaterial damage	$40,000	14	$560,000
Immaterial damage	$8,000	2	$16,000
Immaterial damage	$80,000	3	$240,000
Material damage	$60,000	2	$120,000
Material damage	$110,000	1	$110,000
Material damage	$50,000	1	$50,000
Material damage	$25,000	2	$50,000
Material damage	$12,500	1	$12,500
Material damage	$8,000	1	$8,000
Costs and expenses	$62,000	2	$124,000
Total			$1,835,500 USD

Table 13.5 Distribution of compensation measures for the Case of *Carpio Nicolle et al. v. Guatemala*. Prepared by the authors based on the Case of *Chitay Nech et al. v. Guatemala*. Preliminary Objections, Merits, Reparations, and Costs. Judgment of May 25, 2010.

Concept	*Quantity (USD)*	*N°*	*Total (USD)*
Material damage – emerging damage from search costs	$1,000	1	$1,000
Material damage – loss of income	$75,000	1	$75,000
Immaterial damage	$80,000	1	$80,000
Immaterial damage	$50,000	3	$150,000
Immaterial damage	$40,000	2	$80,000
Costs and expenses	$10,000	1	$10,000
Total			$396,000 USD

Table 13.6 Breakdown of the measures for compensation of the Case *Human of Rights Defender et al. v. Guatemala*. Prepared by the authors based on the Case of *Human Rights Defender et al. v. Guatemala*. Preliminary Objections, Merits, Reparations and Costs. Judgment of August 28, 2014.

Concept	*Quantity (USD)*	*N°*	*Total (USD)*
Material damage	$30,000	4	$120,000
Additional material damage due to displacement	$10,000	3	$30,000
Additional material damage due to displacement	$5,000	1	$5,000
Additional material damage due to displacement	$10,000	1	$10,000
Material damage due to impunity	$7,000	12	$84,000
Additional material damage due to displacement	$5,000	7	$35,000
Costs and expenses	$2,000	1	$2,000
Costs and expenses	$3,000	1	$3,000
Representatives' expenses and costs	$3,439.22	1	$3,439.22
Representatives' expenses and costs	$5,000	1	$5,000
Concept of representatives' fees	$12,000	1	$12,000
Immaterial damage	$55,000	6	$330,000
Immaterial damage	$100,000	1	$100,000
Immaterial damage	$40,000	14	$560,000
Immaterial damage	$8,000	2	$16,000
Immaterial damage	$80,000	3	$240,000
Immaterial damage	$20,000	2	$40,000
Immaterial damage	$25,000	1	$25,000
Immaterial damage	$50,000	1	$50,000
Total	$ 1,670,439.22 USD		

Table 13.7 Compensation for judgments condemning Guatemala for the violation of Art. 23 of the ACHR. Own elaboration.

Judgment	*Quantity (USD)*
Case of *Carpio Nicolle et al. v. Guatemala*	$1,670,439.22
Case of *Carpio Nicolle et al. v. Guatemala*	$396,000
Case of *Human Rights Defender et al. v. Guatemala*	$1,835,500
Total	$3,901,939.22

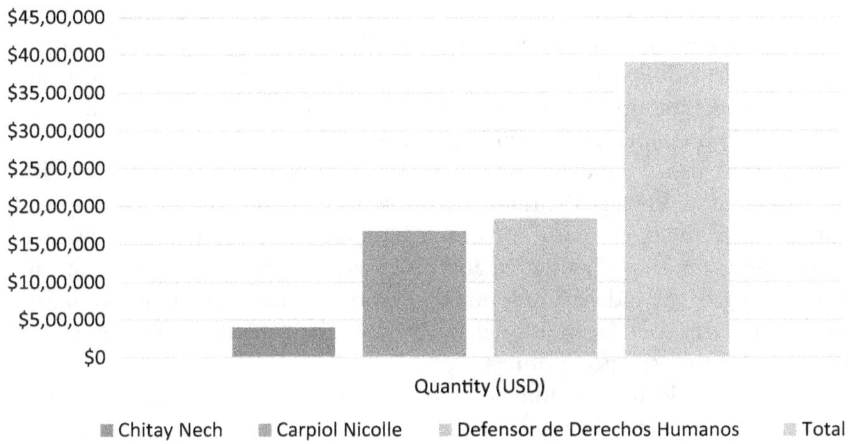

Graph 13.1 Compensation for judgments condemning Guatemala for the violation of Art. 24 of the ACHR. Own elaboration.

Conclusions

Based on the analysis of the judgments issued by the Court of San José against the State of Guatemala regarding the violation of Art. 23 of the American Convention, it is possible for us to outline some considerations that point in three directions. The first concerns the analysis of the right in question: the guarantee of the exercise of political rights.

The judgments establish that Article 23 should not only be understood in terms of the direct exercise of the right to be elected to public office, but that it requires the necessary actions for the State to guarantee the full exercise of the right; that is, to have the guarantees and assurance that its election can be fully carried out. Thus, it ruled with the cases of political leaders (Chitay Nech and Carpio Nicolle). As for the activity of human rights defenders, this guarantee of the full access to the enjoyment of the democratic life of a country was also reiterated in the duty of the State to promote the necessary measures for the performance of the defender of human rights.

The second direction aims to consider the character of the victims in the judgments. All of them: an indigenous political leader, a journalist and a politician, and a human rights defender, have in common the right to exercise a full enjoyment of a political life in a country. Not only in terms of the expression of ideas, but also in terms of participation in the political life of a nation. Here the Court calls on states to create the necessary conditions for the full exercise of this right.

And, the third aspect indicates the need to analyse in greater detail the role of the Inter-American Court in terms of the reparation measures adopted in its judgments. In the case of Guatemala, in 3 judgments that violate political rights, it has been determined that this country complies with 27 measures imposed. Of these, only half have been complied with. The measures complied with are those referring to the payment of compensation and the publicity of the Inter-American judgments. It is worth noting here the high cost of the economic sanctions imposed on Guatemala in two of the matters noted here.

On the other hand, the Court has made an effort, as shown by more than 400 judgments handed down at the time of writing, to generate a varied catalogue of measures that involve, in addition to the economic component for the victims, other measures involving legislative and executive actions, and even some calls for the training of the judiciary, adoption of protocols, implementation of public policies for the free exercise of journalistic work or the defender of human rights, and security measures, among others.

Finally, we would like to point out that these types of measures, including restitution and guarantees of non-repetition, are not enforced in Guatemala. And those of total compliance have a high economic cost for the States, but, as we have seen here, they are the ones that represent more than 50% of the measures complied with. On the one hand, the economic reparation to the victims of the cases is satisfied, but the intention of the Court – to prevent similar violations of political rights in the future – remains unfulfilled.

Bibliography

Academia Interamericana de Derechos Humanos, *Informe sobre la ejecución de sentencias de la Corte Interamericana de Derechos Humanos*, 2019.

Calderón J., *La reparación integral en la jurisprudencia de la Corte Interamericana de Derechos Humanos: estándares aplicables al nuevo paradigma mexicano*, Instituto de Investigaciones Jurídicas, Suprema Corte de Justicia de la Nación, Fundación Konrad Adenauer, 2013.

Gutiérrez Solé C., *Aplicación del Derecho Internacional de los Derechos Humanos en el ámbito del derecho interno de Guatemala*, 2001.

Maldonado A., *Guatemala: recepción del Derecho Internacional de los Derechos Humanos en Anuario de Derecho Constitucional Latinoamericano*, 2001.

Moller, C. M. P., *Introducción al Sistema Interamericano de Derechos Humanos*, Comisión Nacional de Derechos Humanos, México, 2015.

Office of the High Commissioner United Nations Human Rights, *¿Cuál es la historia de los derechos humanos en Guatemala?* https://www.oacnudh.org.gt/index.php/derechos-humanos/historia

Organización de Estados Americanos, *Comisión Interamericana de Derechos Humanos*, ¿Qué es la Cidh?. http://www.oas.org/es/cidh/desca/mandato/origen.asp

Organization of American States, Inter-American Commission on Human Rights, *Informe de la situación de derechos humanos en Guatemala*. http://www.oas.org/es/cidh/informes/pdfs/Guatemala2016.pdf

Sagastume M., *¿Que son los derechos humanos? evolución histórica*, Colección de derechos humanos, Ministerio de Gobernación, Guatemala, 1991.

14 Electoral rights in Nicaragua

The unbearable lightness of non-implementation?

*Gabriella Citroni**

Introduction and context

Nicaragua is a presidential republic, made up of 15 departments (*departamentos*) and 2 autonomous regions, namely the North and South Atlantic Autonomous Regions (*Región Autónoma del Atlántico Norte* – RAAN; and *Región Autónoma del Atlántico Sur* – RAAS). These autonomous regions, which include several municipalities, were established in 1987,[1] and the elections of the respective governments were held for the first time in 1990. They are the least developed regions in the country and are mostly inhabited by indigenous peoples and ethnic communities (*Miskitus*, *Creoles*, *Mestizos*, *Sumu-Mayagnas*, *Ramas*, and *Garífunas*) who follow customary forms of social organisation and government. The last elections for the regional councils in the RAAN and the RAAS were held in 2014.

At the national level, elections are held every five years and the president is directly elected. The constitutional reform of 2014 eliminated any term limits for

* The author wishes to express her gratitude to Dr. Elena Carpanelli and Prof. Tullio Scovazzi for their comments and invaluable suggestions on an earlier version of this contribution. The information contained in this chapter is updated at December 2020 and does not cover the latest events related to the national elections of 7 November 2021. In this connection, the situation of human rights in the country considerably worsened and several persons seen as political opponents were subjected to arbitrary arrests, enforced disappearance and ill-treatment. On 5 June 2021, the Inter-American Commission of Human Rights referred to the Inter-American Court of Human Rights the case *Fabio Gadea Mantilla v. Nicaragua*, concerning an alleged violation of, among others, Article 23 of the American Convention on Human Rights. The case is currently pending.

1 The autonomous regions were established pursuant to the Statute on the Autonomy of the Atlantic Coast (Law No. 28 of 2 September 1987, amended on 29 July 2016, integral text in Spanish available at: http://extwprlegs1.fao.org/docs/pdf/nic163854.pdf). Relevant for their composition and functioning are also the Rules to regulate the Statute on the Autonomy, adopted by decree No. 3584 of 9 July 2003 (integral text in Spanish available at: www.ilo.org/dyn/natlex/docs/ELECTRONIC/92444/107676/F-622526820/NIC92444.pdf). Articles 89-91 and 180–181 of the Constitution (as amended in 2014) regulate the "rights of the communities of the Caribbean Coast" (previously referred to as Atlantic Coast). Relevant with regard to the political and administrative organisation of the autonomous regions is Law No. 40 of 13 June 2012, known as *Ley de Municipios* (integral text in Spanish available at: www.ilo.org/dyn/natlex/docs/ELECTRONIC/7210/107670/F2130983275/NIC7210.pdf).

DOI: 10.4324/9781003229247-17

the president to stay in power and required the winner of the presidential ballot to secure a simple majority of votes.

Article 5 of the Nicaraguan Constitution provides that the State recognises the principles of "peaceful settlement of international disputes through the means offered by international law," and that it adheres to "the principles that constitute the American International Law [*sic*] as recognised and ratified pursuant to national sovereignty."[2] Article 10 clarifies that Nicaragua "recognises on its territory only those international obligations freely undertaken and in conformity with the Political Constitution of the Republic and with the rules of international law." Article 10 should be read in conjunction with Article 182 of the Constitution, which establishes that the "Political Constitution is the fundamental charter of the Republic, to which other laws are subordinated. Laws, ***treaties***, decrees, rules, orders or provisions that are ***at odds with the Constitution*** or amend its contents ***will not have any value***" (emphasis added).

The Supreme Court of Justice of Nicaragua held that "domestic tribunals must always apply the principle pursuant to which ***the Political Constitution prevails over any other law or international treaty***" (emphasis added).[3] However, Article 46 of the Constitution guarantees to each person found in the territory of the State the enjoyment of fundamental human rights as recognised, among others, in the American Convention on Human Rights (hereinafter, "ACHR") and scholars have held that this grants to international human rights treaties ratified, or acceded to, by Nicaragua in general – and to the ACHR in particular – "constitutional value".[4]

Indeed, Nicaragua ratified the ACHR on 25 September 1979 and it recognised the adjudicatory competence of the Inter-American Court of Human Rights (hereinafter, "IACtHR") on 12 February 1991. As of November 2020, the IACtHR issued provisional measures in relation to five cases concerning Nicaragua, although none of them is directly related with electoral rights.[5]

2 Integral text in Spanish available at: www.poderjudicial.gob.ni/pjupload/archivos/documentos/LA_CONSTITUCION_POLITICA_Y_SUS_REFORMAS(3).pdf.

3 Supreme Court of Justice, judgment No. 125 of 20 December 1993. In the same sense, see also judgments No. 21, 22, and 23 of 8 February 1996.

4 Dulitzky A., *La aplicación de los tratados sobre derechos humanos por los tribunales locales: un estudio de derecho comparado*, in Abramovic V., Bovino A., Courtis C. (eds.), *La aplicación de los tratados sobre derechos humanos en el ámbito local – la experiencia de una década*, Buenos Aires, 2004, at 49.

5 IACtHR, Case *Matter of Members of the Miskitu Indigenous Peoples of the North Caribbean Coast regarding Nicaragua*, orders of 1 September 2016, 23 November 2016, 30 June 2017, 22 August 2017, 23 August 2018 and 6 February 2020; Case *Matter of the Nicaraguan Center for Human Rights and the Permanent Commission of Human Rights (CENIDH-CPDH) regarding Nicaragua*, orders of 12 July 2019 and 14 October 2019; Case *Matter of 17 Persons Deprived of Liberty regarding Nicaragua*, orders of 21 May 2019 and 14 October 2019; Case *Mayagna (Sumo) Awas Tingni v. Nicaragua*, orders of 6 September 2002 and 26 November 2007, and *Matter Alemán Lacayo regarding Nicaragua*, orders of 2 February 1996 and 6 February 1997.

Moreover, it rendered judgments on six cases concerning Nicaragua,[6] including the one that will be analysed in-depth in this chapter and that has led to the adoption of a landmark ruling on electoral rights and the right to the political participation of indigenous peoples in the country.[7] At the time of writing, only one of the six aforementioned judgments rendered by the IACtHR has been fully implemented,[8] while the monitoring process on the other five remains open and the measures of reparation ordered therein have not yet been entirely enforced.[9] This seems to suggest that Nicaragua is not especially keen on enforcing the rulings of the IACtHR and the situation concerning the judgment in the *YATAMA* case to be analysed here is no exception. In fact, this case has somehow triggered Nicaragua's "rebellious" stance vis-à-vis the IACtHR's pronouncements and the corresponding procedure to monitor their implementation. Since 2013, Nicaragua has openly challenged the binding nature of the IACtHR's judgments and has refused to participate in public hearings in the context of the procedure directed at monitoring the status of implementation of the said judgments.[10] In 2019, it went as far as publicly declaring its intention not to implement one of the measures of reparation ordered by the IACtHR.[11] The latter found that the State's failure to participate in public hearings on the monitoring of judgments' compliance amounts to a

> blunt and grave disregard of the obligations stemming from the judgment issued by this Court and of the conventional commitments of the State, which prevents granting adequate reparation for the human rights violations

6 Inter-American Court of Human Rights (IACtHR), Case *Genie Lacayo v. Nicaragua*, judgment of 27 January 1995, Ser. C No. 21 (Preliminary Objections) and judgment of 29 January 1997, Ser. C No. 30 (Merits and Reparations); Case *Mayagna (Sumo) Awas Tingni v. Nicaragua*, judgment of 1 February 2000, Ser. C No. 66 (Preliminary Objections) and judgment of 31 August 2001, Ser. C No. 79 (Merits and Reparations); Case *Acosta and others v. Nicaragua*, judgment of 25 March 2003, Ser. C No. 334; Case *V.R.P., V.P.C. and others v. Nicaragua*, judgment of 8 March 2018, Ser. C No. 350; and Case *Roche Azaña and others v. Nicaragua*, judgment of 3 June 2020, Ser. C No. 403.

7 IACtHR, Case *YATAMA v. Nicaragua*, judgment of 23 June 2005, Ser. C No. 127. Hereinafter, "*YATAMA* case."

8 IACtHR, Case *Genie Lacayo v. Nicaragua*, resolution monitoring compliance with judgment of 29 August 1998.

9 IACtHR, Case *Mayagna (Sumo) Awas Tingni*, resolutions monitoring compliance with judgment respectively of 14 March 2008, 7 May 2008 and 3 April 2009; and Case *Acosta and others*, resolution monitoring compliance with judgment of 22 November 2019. At the time of writing, the IACtHR has not yet pronounced itself on the status of the implementation of its judgments in the cases *V.R.P., V.P.C. and others* and *Roche Azaña and others*. With regard to the resolutions monitoring compliance concerning the *YATAMA* case, they will be analysed below.

10 Nicaragua openly challenged for the first time the IACtHR and interrupted its cooperation in the procedure of monitoring of compliance in the YATAMA case. However, the corresponding events will be analysed in detail below.

11 IACtHR, Case *Acosta and others*, order monitoring compliance with judgment of 22 November 2019, operative §§ 6 and 7.

> found in the judgment and frustrates the useful effect (*effet utile*) of the Convention in the specific case.[12]

Accordingly, the IACtHR declared that the State's failure to appear in court is an "affront to the procedure of monitoring of judgments' compliance"[13] and it held that

> Nicaragua's position represents an act of *evident contempt of the State party vis-à-vis the mandatory nature of the judgments issued by this Court*, contrary to the international principle of abiding by conventional obligations in good faith, as well as a *serious affront to one of the most effective mechanisms developed* in the Inter-American System to advance in the compliance with the judgments.[14]

However, it took quite some time before Nicaragua's bold attitude of disregard towards its international undertakings attracted any tangible consequence within the Inter-American system, thus fostering the perception of an intrinsic "lightness" of non-implementation. The latter will be here disputed, with the argument that the analysis of the consequences of non-implementation should not be limited solely to the adoption of measures with regard to the non-abiding State, but should be extended to the implications on the sustainability of democracy.[15]

Over the past few years, Nicaragua's "resistance" vis-à-vis international human rights mechanisms and the corresponding monitoring systems has increased, and the country's human rights record is far from idyllic.[16] Arguably, non-implementation of international judgments and decisions is not the "illness," but rather a symptom of a broader problem and should be understood and tackled as such. As a matter of fact, despite its "disengagement" attempts with the Inter-American human rights system, Nicaragua remains very much "on the radar," including through the establishment of a special monitoring mechanism (*Mecanismo Especial de Seguimiento para Nicaragua* – hereinafter, "MESENI"),[17] of an interdisciplinary group of independent experts (*Grupo Interdisciplinario de Expertos Independientes* – hereinafter, "GIEI")[18] and of a Rapid and Integrated Response Coordination Unit (*Sala de Coordinación para monitorear la situación*

12 ibid., operative § 8 (translation by the author).

13 ibid., operative § 9 (translation by the author).

14 ibid., final clause No. 1 (emphasis added, translation by the author).

15 In general, on the need to re-interpret the notion of compliance and the way to "measure" it, see, Palacios Zuloaga P., *Judging Inter-American Human Rights: The Riddle of Compliance with the Inter-American Court of Human Rights*, in 42:2 Human Rights Quarterly, 2020, at 392–432.

16 This is analysed in detail below.

17 On its composition and mandate, see www.oas.org/en/iachr/media_center/PReleases/2018/135.asp.

18 On its composition and mandate, see www.oas.org/en/iachr/media_center/PReleases/2018/145.asp.

en Nicaragua – hereinafter, "SACROI").[19] Although none of these mechanisms is mandated with the monitoring of the implementation of the IACtHR's judgments, as their creation is linked with the crisis which commenced with the violent repression of social protests in April 2018, their ongoing scrutiny over the situation of human rights in Nicaragua is instrumental in the efforts to keep the State in check and ensure that it eventually abides by all its international obligations. These special mechanisms were created by the Inter-American Commission on Human Rights (hereinafter, "IACHR") which, within the Inter-American system, is the organ most involved in dealing with Nicaragua, be it in the form of precautionary measures, individual petitions, or country reports.[20]

Due to space constraints, precautionary measures and individual petitions concerning Nicaragua before the IACHR will not be analysed. However, it is noteworthy that, since 2018, there has been a spike in the number of requests for precautionary measures and individual petitions concerning Nicaragua, thus somehow supporting the point here made that the failure to implement international rulings is hardly compatible with a sustainable democracy and usually goes hand in hand with a more general worsening of the respect of human rights and fundamental freedoms. Moreover, one could argue that, in the face of the State's public contempt for the judgments issued by the IACtHR and the measures of reparation ordered therein, people have not lost faith in the Inter-American human rights organs, but rather have turned to the latter with increased frequency.[21] Most of the requests for precautionary measures lodged since 2018 concern instances of threats and intimidation, or acts of violence perpetrated against human rights defenders, journalists, and people who took part in protests against the government,[22] thus confirming the existence of a climate that seems hardly to be compatible with a healthy democracy. With regard to the petitions received

19 On its composition and mandate, see www.oas.org/en/iachr/media_center/PReleases/2018/094.asp.

20 Inter-American Commission on Human Rights (IACHR), *Report on the Situation of Human Rights in Nicaragua*, OEA/Ser.L/V/II.45 doc. 18 of 17 November 1978; *Report on the Situation of Human Rights in Nicaragua*, OEA/Ser.L/V.53 doc. 25 of 30 June 1981 (in particular Chapter VII on electoral rights); *Report on the Situation of Human Rights of a Segment of the Nicaraguan Population of Miskito Origin*, OEA/Ser.L/V.II.62 doc. 10 rev.3 of 29 November 1983; *Report on Gross Human Rights Violations in the Context of Social Protests in Nicaragua*, OEA/Ser.L/V.II. Doc. 86 of 21 June 2018; and *Persons Deprived of Liberty in Nicaragua in Connection with the Human Rights Crisis that Begun on April 18, 2018*, OEA/Ser.L/V/II.Doc.287 of 5 October 2020.

21 According to the statistics published by the IACHR (www.oas.org/en/iachr/multimedia/statistics/statistics.html), the requests for precautionary measures received with regard to Nicaragua went from an average of 4 per year between 2008 and 2017, to 383 in 2018 and 54 in 2019; and the individual petitions received went from an average of 10 per year between 2006 and 2017, to 294 in 2018, and 59 in 2019.

22 See, among others, IACHR, Resolution No. 27/20 of 17 June 2020, Precautionary measures 399–20 (*Eduardo Walter Montenegro Chavarría et al. v. Nicaragua*); and Resolution No. 61/19 of 24 December 2019, Precautionary Measures 1045–19 (*Bayron José Correa Estrada and his family v. Nicaragua*).

by the IACHR since the IACtHR issued its judgment on the *YATAMA* case, the majority of those declared admissible contain allegations of a violation of, among others, Article 23 (right to participate in government) of the ACHR,[23] thus confirming that problems concerning the respect and guarantee of electoral rights are far from solved. In the annual report for 2020 on the status of democracy published by Freedom House, Nicaragua scores 31/100, therefore qualifying as "not free."[24] The record, which has steadily worsened since 2017 (when it was 47/100 and the country was considered as "partly free"), is especially poor when it comes to political rights, where Nicaragua scores 10/40.

After several failed attempts to overcome the above-described impasse, the Organization of American States (hereinafter, "OAS") is ultimately considering the possibility of suspending Nicaragua's membership, after having formally detected an alteration of the country's constitutional order that seriously affects its democracy. It is unclear whether, beyond having a strong symbolic value, the suspension of the country would be the most effective tool to re-establish the respect for fundamental human rights and democracy, or whether it would only exacerbate the situation, thus making the permanence of the State in the organisation preferable to maintain some leverage and to foster dialogue.

But, how did Nicaragua reach this point? In hindsight, the facts that led to the IACtHR's judgment on the *YATAMA* case and the ensuing non-implementation saga can be regarded as a turning point and a powerful alarm bell that remains unheard.

Analysis of the judgment on the case *YATAMA v. Nicaragua*

The judgment issued by the IACtHR on 23 January 2005 in the case *YATAMA v. Nicaragua* is considered a landmark,[25] not only for its implications at the national

23 See, among others, IACHR, Case *Movimiento renovador Sandinista et al. v. Nicaragua* (Petition No. 1261–08), Admissibility Report No. 18/19 of 24 February 2019; Case *Fabio Gadea Mantilla v. Nicaragua* (Petition No. 1360–11), Admissibility Report No. 179/18 of 26 December 2018; Case *Ana Margarita Vijil Gurdián v. Nicaragua* (Petition No. 1720–11), Admissibility Report No. 102/18 of 16 September 2018; Case *Azucena Ferry Echaverry et al. v. Nicaragua* (Petition No. 11.878), Admissibility Report No. 1/07 of 27 February 2007; and Case *Alejandro Fiallos Navarro v. Nicaragua* (Petition No. 799–04), Admissibility Report No. 59/06 of 20 July 2006.

24 Freedom House, *Annual Report 2020*, available at: https://freedomhouse.org/country/nicaragua/freedom-world/2020.

25 See, among others, González Volio L., *Los pueblos indígenas y el ejercicio de los derechos políticos de acuerdo a la Convención Americana: el Caso Yatama contra Nicaragua*, in 41 Revista del Instituto Interamericano de Derechos Humanos, 2005, 317 ff.; Campbell M. S., *The Right of Indigenous Peoples to Political Participation and the Case of* YATAMA *v.* Nicaragua, in 24:2 Arizona Journal of International & Comparative Law, 2007, at 499 ff.; and Thompson Jiménez J., *Las obligaciones internacionales en materia electoral. Un enfoque a partir del Sistema interamericano de derechos humanos*, in 20 Derecho electoral, 2015, at 111 ff.

level, but also, more generally, for the interpretation given by the IACtHR to Article 23 (right to participate in government) of the ACHR and the corresponding States' obligations, in particular, where indigenous peoples are concerned.

The case originated in a petition lodged before the IACHR on 26 April 2001 by two NGOs (*Centro Nicaragüense de Derechos Humanos* and Center for Justice and International Law) and the main indigenous regional political organisation, known as YATAMA (*Yapti Tasba Masraka Nanih Asla Takanka*, which can be roughly translated as "Organisation of the Peoples of the Mother Earth").[26]

YATAMA was founded on the Atlantic Coast of Nicaragua in 1986, although it had been active under a different name since 1978. Its membership is mostly *Miskitu* and it promotes indigenous self-government and the protection of ancestral lands. The structure of YATAMA reflects the traditions and customs of the indigenous peoples of the Atlantic Coast and is based on the notion of "communitarian democracy." To become representatives of YATAMA, candidates must pass through communal, territorial, and regional approval. Hence, YATAMA candidates have the backing of all the communities of the area to conduct their electoral campaigns. Indigenous communities, especially in the RAAN, consider YATAMA to be their protector and they turn to its representatives before resorting to any other authority. Notably, "political parties" are a form of social organisation that is alien to the indigenous peoples of the Atlantic Coast of Nicaragua.[27]

The existence of YATAMA must be seen against the backdrop of a traditionally bipartisan system, where the main political parties are the *Partido Liberal Constitucionalista* (hereinafter, "PLC") and the *Frente Sandinista de Liberación Nacional* (hereinafter, "FSLN").

On 24 January 2000, a new electoral law ("the Electoral Act No. 331 of 2000") was enacted, allowing only organisations formally registered and recognised as political parties to participate in the electoral process and specifically not recognising the category of "public subscription association," to which YATAMA belonged.[28] Article 77(1) of the Electoral Act No. 331 of 2000 required that in the case of organisations wishing to participate in the elections other than for national authorities (e.g. municipal elections), they must have obtained their legal status at least six months before the date of the elections, and submitted to such end a written request to the Supreme Electoral Council (hereinafter, "SEC").

Since elections were scheduled for 5 November 2000, this left YATAMA with barely nine months in which to meet the new requirements introduced by Electoral Act No. 331 to participate. In March 2000, YATAMA notarised the

26 The IACHR declared the case admissible (Report No. 125/01 of 3 December 2001) and issued its report on the merits on 4 March 2003 (Report No. 24/03). Eventually, it lodged the petition against Nicaragua before the IACtHR on 17 June 2003.

27 IACtHR, Case YATAMA, cit., § 124.20.

28 As a "public subscription association," YATAMA took part in the regional elections of 1990 and 1994; in the municipal elections in 1996; and in the elections for councillors in the regional parliament in 1998.

statute of the organisation, with the aim of being recognised as a "regional political party." The SEC granted such status to YATAMA through a resolution on 4 May 2000, i.e. one day before the deadline to obtain such status pursuant to the new electoral law. YATAMA had the numbers to run autonomously in the RAAN, while, to meet the requirements for the RAAS, it formed an electoral alliance with the Coastal People Party (hereinafter, "PCC") and the Indigenous Multi-ethnic Party (hereinafter, "PIM"). A few days later, the SEC notified the PCC that it had not obtained the required signatures to be considered a political party and cancelled its juridical personality, rendering it ineligible to participate in the elections. YATAMA was never notified of this decision. Between 31 July and 11 August 2000, YATAMA repeatedly requested to be authorised to also participate in the RAAS using only its name and list of candidates. The SEC did not respond to these requests and, on 15 August 2000, it issued a resolution excluding YATAMA from elections in both the RAAN and the RAAS. The decision was based on the failure of the PCC to meet the requirements under the new electoral law. The SEC did not give YATAMA the opportunity to correct the alleged defects or to substitute its candidates. This caused manifestations and protests, especially in the autonomous regions. On 18 August 2000, YATAMA lodged an appeal for a review of the decision of the SEC, but it never received a response. On 30 August 2000, YATAMA filed writs of *amparo* in regional appellate courts. In October 2000, the Court of Appeals of the RAAN suspended the effects of the SEC resolution, but this decision was reversed 14 days later by the Supreme Court of Justice, which found the *amparo* unconstitutional pursuant to Article 173 of the Nicaraguan Constitution which does not provide jurisdiction to regular courts to hear electoral claims.

YATAMA was thus prevented from taking part in the November 2000 elections and was arguably left without any effective remedy to challenge the decision of the SEC. Around 80% of eligible voters in the Atlantic Coast region boycotted the elections due to the lack of indigenous candidates. It is noteworthy that, on 8 November 2002, in judgment No. 103, the Supreme Court of Justice of Nicaragua declared the unconstitutionality of certain provisions of the Electoral Act No. 331 of 2000, on the grounds that they violated Nicaraguans' political guarantees and interfered with their individual rights. In particular, the requirement to identify and produce the signatures of 3% of those voters supporting a particular candidate was considered an "undue and abhorrent interference in the political activity of the voters, typical of totalitarian countries."[29]

When the case reached the IACtHR, the latter was requested to establish whether Nicaragua had violated Articles 8 (right to a fair trial), 23, 24 (right to equal protection), and 25 (judicial protection), read in conjunction with Articles 1 (obligation to respect rights), and 2 (domestic legal effects) of the ACHR, because of the exclusion of the candidates presented by YATAMA from the

29 IACtHR, Case YATAMA, cit., § 124.75.

municipal elections of November 2000.[30] In particular, the IACHR alleged that the new electoral law was at odds with international standards due to the lack of norms that would facilitate the political participation of the indigenous organisations in the electoral process of the RAAN and the RAAS, in accordance with customary law, values, practices, and traditions of indigenous peoples residing there.

With regard to the alleged violation of Article 23 of the ACHR in particular, in view of the specifics of the case and the involvement of indigenous peoples, the IACtHR decided to consider it in conjunction with Article 24, reading both provisions in relation to Articles 1(1) and (2) of the ACHR, which impose positive obligations on the States parties. The IACtHR first recalled that the principle of non-discrimination enshrined in Article 24 of the ACHR is a norm of *jus cogens* and therefore States are under an obligation not to introduce discriminatory regulations into their legislation, to eliminate provisions and to combat practices of a discriminatory nature, and to enact laws and undertake measures to recognise and ensure the effective equality before the law of each individual.[31] Moreover, with regard to political rights as recognised in Article 23 of the ACHR, the IACtHR recalled that they are included among non-derogable rights pursuant to Article 27 of the ACHR, which prohibits their suspension, as well as that of the judicial guarantees essential to ensure their protection. Furthermore, the IACtHR referred to its previous findings in the sense that

> in a democratic society, the rights and freedoms inherent in the human person, the guarantee applicable to them and the rule of law form a triad in which each component defines itself, complements and depends on the others for its meaning. [...] representative democracy is the determining factor throughout the system of which the Convention is a part [...] The political rights protected in the American Convention, as well as in many international instruments, promote the strengthening of democracy and political pluralism.[32]

The IACtHR referred to the Inter-American Democratic Charter adopted on 11 September 2001 by the Ministers of Foreign Affairs of the member States of the OAS,[33] which spells out the essential elements of representative democracy, including respect for human rights and fundamental freedoms, and the holding of periodic, free, and fair elections based on secret balloting and universal suffrage as an expression of the sovereignty of the people, and the pluralistic system of

30 The determination of the alleged victims was especially complicated and, during the proceedings, Nicaragua failed to cooperate with the IACtHR, by not responding to its requests for information in a timely manner. IACtHR, Case YATAMA, cit., § 136. The list of alleged victims eventually approved by the IACtHR can be found at §§ 140–141.

31 IACtHR, Case YATAMA, cit., §§ 184–185.

32 ibid., §§ 191–192.

33 The consequences that the application of the Inter-American Democratic Charter may trigger in the case of Nicaragua are analysed below.

political parties and organisations. Article 23 of the ACHR is pivotal in ensuring the enjoyment of the latter. In this regard, the IACtHR requires States parties to "generate the optimum conditions and mechanisms to ensure that these political rights can be exercised effectively, respecting the principles of equality and non-discrimination."[34]

The IACtHR held that

> political participation may include broad-ranging and varied activities that can be executed individually or in an organized manner, in order to intervene in the designation of those who will govern a State or who will be responsible for managing public affairs, as well as influencing the elaboration of State policy through direct participation mechanisms. The exercise of the rights to be elected and to vote, which are closely related to each other, is the expression of the individual and social dimension of political participation.[35]

The IACtHR recalled that the right to vote is an essential element for the existence of democracy and one of the ways in which citizens exercise the right to political participation, implying that the citizens may freely elect those who will represent them, in conditions of equality. The IACtHR thus affirmed that, pursuant to Articles 23, 24(1), and (2) of the ACHR,

> the State has the obligation to guarantee the enjoyment of political rights, which implies that the regulation of the exercise of such rights and its application shall be in keeping with the principle of equality and non-discrimination, and it should adopt the necessary measures to ensure their full exercise. *This obligation to guarantee is not fulfilled merely by issuing laws and regulations that formally recognize these rights, but requires the State to adopt the necessary measures to guarantee their full exercise considering the weakness or helplessness of the members of certain social groups or sectors.*[36]

The application of the above-mentioned principles in the *YATAMA* case requires special attention to be paid to the fact that the alleged victims in the case were members of indigenous and ethnic communities of the Atlantic Coast, who, in the words of the IACtHR, "differ from most of the population, inter alia, owing to their languages, customs and forms of organization, and they face serious difficulties that place them in a situation of vulnerability and marginalization."[37]

The IACtHR interpreted Articles 23 and 24 of the ACHR pursuant to the criteria set forth in Article 29 thereof, in the sense that

34 IACtHR, Case YATAMA, cit., § 195.
35 ibid., §§ 196–197.
36 ibid., § 201 (emphasis added).
37 ibid., § 202.

> the full scope of political rights cannot be restricted in such a way that their regulation or the decisions adopted in application of this regulation prevent people from participating effectively in the governance of the State or cause this participation to become illusory, depriving such rights of their essential content.[38]

Bearing in mind the special vulnerability and marginalisation of the indigenous communities of the Nicaraguan Atlantic Coast, the IACtHR reaffirmed the existence of positive obligations on the State, also through the adoption of special measures, to ensure their effective participation in the electoral process. The IACtHR analysed whether, conversely, a State can introduce specific requirements for the exercise of political rights and held that this, *per se*, does not amount to an undue restriction of political rights, as such rights are not absolute. The IACtHR affirmed that regulation of political rights must

> *respect the principles of legality, necessity and proportionality in a democratic society*. Observance of the principle of legality requires the State to define precisely, by law, the requirements for voters to be able to take part in the elections, and to stipulate clearly the electoral procedures prior to the elections. According to Article 23(2) of the Convention, the law may regulate the exercise of the rights and opportunities referred to in the first paragraph of this Article, only for the reasons established in this second paragraph. *The restriction should be established by law, non-discriminatory, based on reasonable criteria, respond to a useful and opportune purpose that makes it necessary to satisfy an urgent public interest, and be proportionate to this purpose. When there are several options to achieve this end, the one that is less restrictive of the protected right and more proportionate to the purpose sought should be chosen.*[39]

The IACtHR explained that

> States may establish minimum standards to regulate political participation, provided they are reasonable and in keeping with the principles of representative democracy. These standards should guarantee, among other matters, the holding of periodic free and fair elections based on universal, equal and secret suffrage, as an expression of the will of the voters, reflecting the sovereignty of the people, and bearing in mind, as established in Article 6 of the Inter-American Democratic Charter, that "[p]romoting and fostering diverse forms of participation strengthens democracy"; to this end, "*States may design norms to facilitate the participation of specific sectors of society, such as members of indigenous and ethnic communities.*"[40]

38 ibid., § 203.
39 ibid., § 206 (emphasis added).
40 ibid., § 207 (emphasis added).

In the *YATAMA* case, the IACtHR found that the requirements introduced by Electoral Act No. 331 of 2000 did not respect the principles here recalled, being unduly restrictive and ambiguous, especially because they did not clearly establish the consequences of non-compliance with certain requirements and they did not regulate in a precise manner which fundamental decisions the SEC must adopt. The IACtHR found that the law concerned did not

> allow the voter or the electoral bodies to have a clear understanding of the process and encourages its arbitrary and discretional application through extensive and contradictory interpretations that unduly restrict the participation of voters; a restriction that is particularly undesirable when it severely affects fundamental rights, such as recognized political rights.[41]

With regard to the fact that Electoral Act No. 331 of 2000 only allowed political parties to participate in the electoral process, the IACtHR clarified that

> *there is no provision in the American Convention that allows it to be established that citizens can only exercise the right to stand as candidates to elected office through a political party.* The importance of political parties as essential forms of association for the development and strengthening of democracy are not discounted, but it is recognized that *there are other ways in which candidates can be proposed for elected office in order to achieve the same goal, when this is pertinent and even necessary to encourage or ensure the political participation of specific groups of society, taking into account their special traditions and administrative systems*, whose legitimacy has been recognized and is even subject to the explicit protection of the State.[42]

The finding of the IACtHR is seminal in its reading of political rights in a culturally sensitive manner. Indeed, diversity and the preservation of cultural identity are as essential for a sustainable democracy as regular and free elections.

In the case of YATAMA, the requirement to participate in the electoral process as a political party (a form of organisation alien to the practices, customs, and traditions of the indigenous peoples concerned) did not obey a useful and opportune purpose, which made it necessary so as to satisfy an urgent public interest. To the contrary, this restriction imposed an impediment on the full exercise of the right of the members of the indigenous and ethnic communities that formed YATAMA to be elected. The IACtHR thus found the restriction concerned an undue limitation of the exercise of a political right, imposing an unnecessary restriction on the right to be elected, explicitly bearing in mind the special circumstances of the case "which are not necessarily comparable to the circumstances of all political groups that may be present in other national societies

41 ibid., § 212.
42 ibid., § 215 (emphasis added).

or sectors of a national society."[43] Aware of the need to develop its reasoning with regard to organisations different from political parties and the applicable requirements for political participation, the IACtHR indicated that any such condition originally designed for political parties

> which cannot be fulfilled by groups with a different form of organization, is also contrary to Articles 23 and 24 of the American Convention, to the extent that it limits the full range of political rights more than strictly necessary, and becomes an impediment for citizens to participate effectively in the conduct of public affairs.[44]

Analysing the requirements introduced by the Electoral Act No. 331 of 2000, the IACtHR found them to be a disproportionate restriction that unduly limited the political participation of the candidates proposed by YATAMA for the municipal elections of November 2000.

Furthermore, the IACtHR held that Nicaragua had failed to fulfil its positive obligations, in that it did not adopt the necessary measures to guarantee the enjoyment of the right to be elected of the candidates proposed by YATAMA, who were members of the indigenous and ethnic communities of the Atlantic Coast, because they were affected by legal and actual discrimination, which prevented them from participating, under equal conditions, in the municipal elections of November 2000. The IACtHR added that

> the State should adopt all necessary measures to ensure that the members of the indigenous and ethnic communities of the Atlantic Coast of Nicaragua can participate, in equal conditions, in decision-making on matters and policies that affect or could affect their rights and the development of these communities, so that they can incorporate State institutions and bodies and participate directly and proportionately to their population in the conduct of public affairs, and also do this from within their own institutions and according to their values, practices, customs and forms of organization, provided these are compatible with the human rights embodied in the Convention.[45]

The IACtHR found the violation of the rights of the candidates proposed by YATAMA particularly serious because it eventually affected a much broader group, i.e. the voters, who were deprived of an option to freely express their preference. The IACtHR saw it as a direct limitation to the exercise of the vote, which affected negatively the broadest and freest expression of the will of the electorate, with grave consequences for democracy. This harm to the electors constituted

43 ibid., § 219.
44 ibid., § 220.
45 ibid., § 225.

non-compliance by the State with the general obligation to guarantee the exercise of the right to vote embodied in Article 1(1) of the ACHR.

This "broader" or "collective" scope of the damage is especially grave, bearing in mind that YATAMA

> contributes to the consolidation and preservation of the cultural identity of the members of the indigenous and ethnic communities of the Atlantic Coast. Its structure and purposes are related to the practices, customs and forms of organization of these communities. Consequently, the exclusion of the participation of the YATAMA candidates particularly affected the members of the indigenous and ethnic communities that were represented by this organization in the municipal elections of November 2000, by placing them in a situation of inequality as regards the options among which they could choose to vote, since those persons who, in principle, deserved their confidence because they had been chosen directly in assemblies (according to the practices and customs of these communities) to represent the interests of their members, had been excluded from participating as candidates. This exclusion resulted in a lack of representation of the needs of the members of the said communities in the regional bodies responsible for adopting policies and programs that could affect their development.[46]

In light of all the above, the IACtHR found that Nicaragua violated Articles 23 and 24 of the ACHR, in relation to Article 1(1) to the detriment of the candidates proposed by YATAMA to participate in the municipal elections of November 2000, because it established and applied provisions of Electoral Act No. 331 of 2000, which created an undue restriction on the exercise of the right to be elected and regulated these provisions in a discriminatory manner. The IACtHR further declared a violation of Article 23(1) of the ACHR, in relation to Article 1(1) to the detriment of YATAMA candidates, because the decisions that excluded them from exercising this right were adopted in violation of the guarantees embodied in Article 8 of the ACHR and could not be contested by means of a judicial recourse. In fact, the IACtHR found – by seven votes to one – that the decisions of the SEC amounted to a violation of Article 8(1) in conjunction with Articles 1(1) and 2 of the ACHR; it further declared a violation of Article 25 (1) of the ACHR, to the detriment of the candidates proposed by YATAMA, in relation to Articles 1(1) and 2 of the ACHR. In particular, it held that

> irrespective of the regulations that each State establishes for its supreme electoral body, the latter must be subject to some form of jurisdictional control that allows it to be determined whether its acts have been adopted respecting the minimum guarantees and rights established in the American Convention, and those established in its own laws; this is not incompatible with regard

46 ibid., § 227.

> for the functions inherent in this body concerning electoral matters. This control is essential when the supreme electoral bodies such as the Supreme Electoral Council in Nicaragua, have broad powers, which exceed administrative faculties and which could be used, without an adequate control, to favor determined partisan objectives. In this sphere, this recourse must be simple and prompt, taking into account the characteristics of the electoral process.[47]

With regard to the measures of reparation, the IACtHR first pointed out that it would consider "injured parties" entitled to redress to be "the candidates for the positions of mayors, deputy mayors and municipal councillors proposed by YATAMA for the 2000 municipal elections in the RAAN and the RAAS."[48] When quantifying the pecuniary compensation to be awarded, the IACtHR affirmed that the injured parties and also YATAMA as an organisation had incurred various expenses during the electoral campaign prior to the SEC decision not to register these candidates. Moreover, the members of the communities of the Atlantic Coast who selected the candidates in assemblies had made material contributions to support their participation. The recognition of the collective scope of the damage inflicted led the IACtHR to draw some relevant consequences. This is also reflected in the following considerations put forward by the IACtHR:

> with regard to the non-pecuniary damage caused to the candidates, the Court must bear in mind that being proposed as a candidate to participate in an electoral process has particular importance and is a great honour among the members of the indigenous and ethnic communities of the Atlantic Coast. Those who accept a candidacy must demonstrate capacity, honesty, and commitment to the defence of the needs of the communities, and assume the significant responsibility of representing their interests. [...] The Court considers these special circumstances when assessing the frustration that the candidates felt at finding themselves unduly excluded from participating in the elections and representing their communities. This feeling was accentuated by the fact that the Supreme Electoral Council did not provide any justification to explain why the candidates proposed by YATAMA could not be registered. This meant that the *communities did not understand the reasons for the exclusion of their candidates. The latter felt powerless to give an explanation to their communities and considered that the exclusion was the result of their condition as members of indigenous communities.*[49]

47 ibid., § 175.
48 ibid., § 237.
49 ibid., §§ 246–247 (emphasis added).

The IACtHR ordered Nicaragua to pay YATAMA US$80,000 as compensation for pecuniary and non-pecuniary damage. YATAMA would then distribute the amount among the beneficiaries, as appropriate.

Furthermore, the IACtHR ordered Nicaragua, within a year from the date of the notification of its decision, to publish in the Official Gazette and in another newspaper with widespread national circulation selected excerpts of the judgment and the full version of the latter on the State's official website. Bearing in mind that indigenous communities use community radio as a means of information, the IACtHR ordered Nicaragua to broadcast (on four occasions, with a break of two weeks between each broadcast) the same excerpts of the judgment on a radio station with broad coverage on the Atlantic Coast, reading them in Spanish, Miskito, Sumo, Rama, and English. [50]

With regard to legislative and structural changes, the IACtHR ordered Nicaragua to adopt, within a reasonable time, the necessary legislative measures to establish a simple, prompt, and effective judicial recourse that would allow the decisions of the SEC, which affect human rights, such as political rights, to be appealed, respecting the corresponding treaty-based and legal guarantees, and derogating the norms that prevent the filing of this recourse.[51] In this regard, the IACtHR recalled that the remedy established should enable the delivery of a decision within the electoral calendar.

The IACtHR also ordered Nicaragua to reform Electoral Act No. 331 of 2000, ensuring that it clearly regulated the consequences of non-compliance with the requirements for electoral participation, the procedures that the SEC should observe when determining such non-compliance, and the reasoned decisions that the SEC should adopt in this regard, as well as the rights of those whose participation is affected by a decision of the State.[52] The IACtHR added that Nicaragua must

> reform the regulation of the requirements established in Electoral Act No. 331 of 2000 that, it has been declared, violate the Convention and adopt, within a reasonable time, the necessary measures to ensure that the members of the indigenous and ethnic communities may participate in the electoral processes effectively and taking into account their traditions, practices and customs, within the framework of a democratic society. The requirements established should permit and encourage the members of these communities to have adequate representation that allows them to intervene in decision-making processes on national issues that concern society as a whole, and on specific matters that pertain to these communities; therefore, these requirements should not constitute barriers for such political participation.[53]

50 ibid., §§ 252–253.
51 ibid., §§ 254.
52 ibid., § 258.
53 ibid., § 259 (emphasis added).

These structural measures ordered by the IACtHR should be implemented by Nicaragua within "a reasonable time."

Finally, the IACtHR ordered the payment of US$15,000 to YATAMA to cover the costs and expenses incurred in relation to the litigation.

Analysis of the consequences at the national level

The non-implementation saga begins

The IACtHR requested that Nicaragua inform it of the status of the implementation of the measures ordered in its judgment within one year of the notification of the ruling. In its resolution of 29 November 2006 monitoring the compliance with the judgment,[54] the IACtHR found that Nicaragua had complied with two of the measures ordered, namely the publication of excerpts of the judgment in the Official Gazette and of the integral version of the judgment on the website of the Ministry of Foreign Affairs. With regard to the broadcasting of excerpts of the judgment in indigenous languages on radio channels of the Atlantic Coast, the State complied only partially. With regard to the payment of the compensation and the legal expenses, the State indicated that it had tried to include them in the 2006 budget, but had not succeeded in doing so, due to "urgent social demands."[55] With regard to the amendment of the electoral law and corresponding regulations requested by the IACtHR, the latter noted that the State referred to an ongoing process of adoption of a draft, but this was not considered enough to comply. Indeed, Nicaragua also tried to put the blame on YATAMA for the failure to advance the adoption of the said reform, because allegedly YATAMA had been due to present a draft law by a given deadline but had failed to do so. YATAMA countered that, while it was true it had agreed to present a draft, it had specified that it needed legal advice from the State to do so and never received it. Nevertheless, the responsibility of complying with the IACtHR's judgment lays with the State and the failure to implement could not be attributed to YATAMA.

The IACtHR requested that Nicaragua submit new information on the status of implementation by 5 March 2007. In the subsequent resolution of 4 August 2008 on monitoring compliance with the judgment, despite the information submitted by the State, the IACtHR considered that the situation had not evolved and the measures concerned remained unimplemented. Accordingly, it requested the State to provide updated information by 8 December 2008 and informed Nicaragua of its intention to consider the possibility of organising a hearing to discuss the progress of implementation.[56]

54 IACtHR, Case YATAMA, resolution monitoring compliance with judgment of 29 November 2006.

55 ibid., § 4(e).

56 IACtHR, Case YATAMA, resolution monitoring compliance with judgment of 4 August 2008, final clause, § 5.

In September 2008 (i.e. following more than 2 years of delay), the State eventually paid the compensation and the legal expenses: instead of the US$95,000 ordered by the IACtHR, it paid US$111,425 to include the accumulated interest on the arrears. However, it turned out that the latter had not been covered in their totality (approximately nine months had been unduly left out).[57] The measures concerning the amendment of the electoral legislation remained unimplemented, and the State either submitted very vague and generic information on the steps undertaken to comply or failed to submit any information at all, thus concretely hindering the ability of the IACtHR to assess the progress (or lack thereof) of the enforcement of the judgment.[58] The IACtHR thus decided to convene the parties in a private hearing on the subject matter on 26 May 2010. The hearing indeed took place and Nicaragua actively participated. With regard to the broadcasting of relevant excerpts of the judgment on the radio in Spanish, English and indigenous languages, Nicaragua admitted to being unable to provide precise information on when this would have happened. Accordingly, the IACtHR requested that the State re-broadcast the relevant excerpts of the judgment at its earliest convenience, including in *Rama* (which the State admitted it had not done) and to provide copies of the broadcasts to the IACtHR.

With regard to the reform of the electoral law, the State acknowledged that the measures ordered by the IACtHR had not been implemented, allegedly due to "a situation of legal conditions [*sic*] and lack of consensus among political parties in the National Congress."[59] Allegedly, the reform of the electoral law would have first required a constitutional amendment, and this implied an especially complex process. However, during the private hearing, the State's representatives reaffirmed Nicaragua's will to comply with the IACtHR's orders and undertook to submit within three months a detailed "plan of action and timetable" to ensure the integral implementation of the judgment. The IACtHR accepted this proposal and additionally requested that the State submit progress reports every four months thereafter.[60]

This was the last occasion on which the State demonstrated a collaborative attitude and showed any willingness to abide by its international undertakings and to cooperate in good faith with the IACtHR. Despite two reminders sent by the IACtHR, Nicaragua never submitted the promised "implementation plan and timetable." The IACtHR issued a resolution criticising the lack of cooperation and the failure to comply, fixing a new deadline for the said submission by the State (i.e. 4 October 2011).[61]

57 IACtHR, Case YATAMA, resolution monitoring compliance with judgment of 21 April 2010, § 15.
58 ibid., §§ 20–25.
59 IACtHR, Case YATAMA, resolution monitoring compliance with judgment of 28 May 2010, § 13 (translation by the author).
60 ibid., final clauses §§ 2–3.
61 IACtHR, Case YATAMA, resolution monitoring compliance with judgment of 30 June 2011, § 8 and final clause, § 2.

At this stage, things went from bad to worse; degenerating from an initial "passive" stance of the State to an openly "rebellious" one. The IACtHR repeatedly contacted Nicaragua, soliciting it to submit the information due. The State did not respond, leading the IACtHR to convene a new private hearing on 28 May 2013. As referred to above, Nicaragua chose not to participate in the hearing.[62] In the face of this open "challenge," the IACtHR declared that Nicaragua's conduct was in breach of the State's obligation to inform it about its progress in the implementation of the judgment and twice requested that Nicaragua submit its observations in writing. The State also ignored these requests.[63] Vis-à-vis Nicaragua's obstinate silence, the IACHR, instead of taking a "proactive" or critical position, decided to follow the same path and, although its representatives participated in the private hearing of 28 May 2013, it did not submit any written observation to the IACtHR either.[64]

YATAMA's representatives were the ones who informed the IACtHR of the State's adoption of Law No. 790, called "Law to Reform Electoral Act No. 331," published on the Official Gazette on 23 May 2012.[65] However, none of the amendments within this reform concerned the provisions relevant for the measures ordered by the IACtHR, thus leaving the judgment unimplemented (also with regard to the new broadcasting on the radio of the translated excerpts of the judgments and the payment of the remaining interest of arrears).

The IACtHR emphasised the positive role that hearings can play in facilitating the implementation of its judgments, recalling concrete examples (including one from Nicaragua)[66] and regretting the lost opportunity in the *YATAMA* case.

Nicaragua then stopped interacting with the IACtHR and the latter considered this

> a frontal disregard for the obligations stemming from the judgment issued by the Court and the conventional commitments of the State party, which prevents the human rights violations declared in the judgment from being repaired and deprives the Convention of its *effet utile* in the specific case.[67]

62 IACtHR, Case YATAMA, resolution monitoring compliance with judgment of 22 August 2013, §§ 5–6.

63 ibid., § 8.

64 ibid., § 8 of the IACtHR's considerations.

65 The integral text (in Spanish) is available at: http://legislacion.asamblea.gob.ni/Normaweb.nsf/b92aaea87dac762406257265005d21f7/3a4008061c4902f706257a100074cc9f?OpenDocument.

66 IACtHR, Case *YATAMA*, resolution monitoring compliance with judgment of 22 August 2013, § 13 of the IACtHR's considerations. The reference is to the case *Comunidad Mayagna (Sumo) Awas Tingni*.

67 IACtHR, Case *YATAMA*, resolution monitoring compliance with judgment of 22 August 2013, § 15 of the IACtHR's considerations (translation by the author).

Despite the seriousness of the IACtHR's findings, they did not trigger any immediate "action" vis-à-vis the non-compliant State. Instead, the process entered a vicious circle: where, on the one hand, the IACtHR harshly criticised the State, while on the other, it simply reiterated its need for the information submitted by Nicaragua, fixing a new deadline for such purpose (i.e. 25 November 2013) and announcing its intention to summon the parties to a public hearing on the subject matter, to be heard within a year.[68] So despite being on the receiving end of much chastising, paradoxically, the non-compliant State in fact seemingly paid a very light "price" (if any) for failing to comply with its international obligations and for openly ignoring the IACtHR's requests.

Against such a *crescendo* in the State's impudence, one would have expected some escalation in the IACtHR's response. In fact, the latter went as far as its mandate allows, albeit at a remarkably slow pace. The last resolution on monitoring Nicaragua's compliance with the judgment on the *YATAMA* case was issued on 20 November 2015.[69] It came after several reminders had been sent by the IACtHR to Nicaragua with a view to obtaining information on the implementation of the judgment, all met by the State's deafening silence. The IACtHR affirmed that a State's passiveness vis-à-vis an international human rights mechanism is "contrary to the object, purpose and spirit of the ACHR."[70] However, while remaining passive and silent before the IACtHR, the State took a turn for the worst at the domestic level, allegedly harassing YATAMA's representatives at precisely the same time they were required to collect information on the status of implementation of the judgment.[71]

In its resolution, the IACtHR denounced these events and attached special blame on the State's failure to implement the measures ordered in its judgment to amend the electoral legislation, considering that this continued to hamper the political rights of indigenous peoples and their participation in the electoral process, contrary to what should happen in a democratic society.[72]

The IACtHR thus played its "heaviest card," announcing that it would inform the General Assembly of the OAS of Nicaragua's failure to comply with the judgment and to cooperate with the IACtHR itself, calling on the

> system of collective guarantees where all the States parties must undertake all the efforts to avoid the evident abandonment by the States of their obligation to comply and abide by the judgments of the Court. [...] This notion of collective guarantee is closely related to the *effet utile* of the judgments of the Court, since the ACHR establishes a system that constitutes a true regional public order, the maintenance of which is in the interest of each and every one of the States parties. The interest of the contracting States

68 ibid., final clauses, §§ 4 and 6.

69 IACtHR, Case *YATAMA*, resolution monitoring compliance with judgment of 20 November 2015.

70 ibid., § 6.

71 ibid., § 9.

72 ibid., § 10.

is the maintenance of the system of protection of human rights that they themselves have created, and if a State violates its obligation to comply with what is adjudicated by the only judicial body competent on the matter, it is breaking the commitment assumed towards the other States to comply with the Court's judgments. Therefore, the task of the General Assembly of the OAS when confronted with a manifest breach by one of the States of a judgment issued by the IACtHR, is precisely that of protecting the *effet utile* of the ACHR and of preventing Inter-American justice from becoming illusory by being left to the discretion of the internal decisions of a State.[73]

The IACtHR decided that, in the given circumstances, it did not make sense to call for a new public hearing, but instead, pursuant to Article 65 of the ACHR,[74] it proceeded to include the information on Nicaragua's failure to comply in its annual report to the General Assembly of the OAS.[75]

The process of monitoring the implementation of the judgment on the *YATAMA* case remains formally open before the IACtHR, but the "match" is now being played on the OAS' field.

Overall, it may seem that Nicaragua got off the hook relatively easily and that the non-implementation of the IACtHR's judgment would have an inherent lightness to it. But, is that really so? Arguably, it very much depends on how the weight is measured. Both in terms of where Nicaragua stands today vis-à-vis the Inter-American system (and other international human rights mechanisms), and of the overall human rights situation at the domestic level, it can be argued that the consequences have been anything but light.

Advocating for implementation outside the Inter-American system

In the case of Nicaragua, the use of domestic litigation to propel the implementation of international decisions – a strategy that had proved effective in some other contexts[76] – was out of the question due to the flawed legal framework and the lack of an independent judiciary.[77] Hence, when the monitoring process within

73 ibid., §§ 12–13 (translation by the author).

74 Article 65 of the ACHR provides that "to each regular session of the General Assembly of the Organization of the American States the Court shall submit, for the Assembly's consideration, a report on its work during the previous year. *It shall specify, in particular, the cases in which a State has not complied with its judgments, making any pertinent recommendations*" (emphasis added).

75 IACtHR, Case YATAMA, resolution monitoring compliance with judgment of 20 November 2015, §§ 14–15 and final clause, § 5.

76 See, among others, Kunz R., *Judging International Judgments Anew? The Human Rights Courts before Domestic Courts,* in 30:4 *European Journal of International Law*, 2020, 1129–1163; Baluarte, D.C., *Strategizing For Compliance: The Evolution of a Compliance Phase of Inter-American Court Litigation and the Strategic Imperative for Victims' Representatives*, in 27:2 American University International Law Review, 2012, at 263–321.

77 This aspect is further analysed below.

the Inter-American system entered the lengthy impasse described in the previous section, the concern for Nicaragua's failure to implement the judgment of the IACtHR in the *YATAMA* case and its implications with regard to the sustainability of the country's democracy were brought before other international human rights mechanisms, including the United Nations Human Rights Committee. In the latter's concluding observations on Nicaragua's periodic report pursuant to the International Covenant on Civil and Political Rights, there is a specific reference to the flawed enforcement of the judgment at stake and the Committee expressed its regret that Nicaragua "has not undertaken the necessary legislative reform to introduce a simple legal remedy ensuring that indigenous and ethnic communities in the autonomous regions can take effective part in elections with due regard for their traditions, conventions and customs."[78] In the Committee's view, the described situation raised issues pursuant to Articles 25 (electoral rights) and 27 (prohibition of discrimination) of the International Covenant on Civil and Political Rights. Hence, the Committee recommended for Nicaragua to

> meet the targets laid down in the Inter-American Court's ruling and, in particular, take steps to bring about the necessary reforms in the Elections Act as recommended [*sic*] by the Court and introduce a simple legal remedy against decisions by the Supreme Electoral Board.[79]

The Committee's concluding observations, which were issued in 2008, referred also to the lack of implementation of another judgment of the IACtHR, whose non-enforcement is notorious and has been the subject of international analysis.[80] This seems to confirm the systemic nature of the non-implementation of international decisions by Nicaragua and, more generally, a certain resistance towards indications (be they orders or recommendations) coming from international human rights mechanisms. Nicaragua's subsequent periodic report to the Committee, which was due by 29 October 2012, was submitted only on 13 May 2019. The examination of the State's report was scheduled for the Committee's session in November 2020 and the Committee included a specific question on the status of implementation of the IACtHR's judgments in its list of issues prior to the examination. Namely, the Committee requested for Nicaragua to provide information on the steps that have been taken to increase the representation of indigenous persons in decision-making positions and on the measures taken to comply with the judgment of the IACtHR in the *YATAMA* case.[81]

78 Human Rights Committee, *Concluding Observations on Nicaragua*, UN Doc. CPPR/C/NIC/CO/3 of 29 October 2008, § 20.

79 ibid.

80 ibid., § 21. The reference is to the IACtHR's judgment on the case *Mayagna (Awas Tingni)*. On the lack of implementation of the latter see, among others, Gómez Isa F., *The Decision by the Inter-American Court of Human Rights on the Awas Tingni* v. *Nicaragua Case (2001): The Implementation Gap,* in 8 The Age of Human Rights Journal, 2017, at 67–91.

81 Human Rights Committee, *List of Issues in relation to the fourth periodic report of Nicaragua,*

Besides providing an interesting example of cross-fertilisation among international human rights mechanisms, the "indirect monitoring" exercised by the Human Rights Committee on the status of implementation of judgments issued by the IACtHR shows how a non-compliant State can be kept under pressure before different fora in the attempt to make it abide by its obligations, including with regard to electoral rights. In the same sense, although without an explicit reference to the *YATAMA* case, Nicaragua received recommendations in the context of the latest Universal Periodic Review it underwent concerning the need to reform the electoral system without delay, and to organise fairer, free, transparent, and inclusive elections, that truly allow the participation of all political parties and movements.[82]

However, Nicaragua has not proven responsive to any of these recommendations and, although not reaching the levels of tension currently existing with the OAS, the State's attitude vis-à-vis any openly critical institution is hostile, refusing any form of dialogue. By way of token example, upon the publication on 29 August 2018 of a report by the UN Office of the High Commissioner for Human Rights (hereinafter, "OHCHR") on the human rights situation in the country,[83] on 30 August 2018, the Minister of Foreign Affairs of Nicaragua rescinded its invitation to the OHCHR and the team of human rights experts deployed to Managua was withdrawn. This "refusal" of international scrutiny and of any interlocution with critical counterparts, *per se* indicative of a rather weak democracy, reached its apex with the IACHR and, more in general, with the OAS.

Non-implementation paves the way to a serious impairment of the democratic order: Nicaragua (and the Inter-American system) at a crossroads

Based on the concerns raised by the IACtHR in its annual reports to the General Assembly of the OAS, the latter has also been closely monitoring the situation in Nicaragua, which goes beyond the mere problem of non-implementation of the IACtHR's judgments and which is witnessing a progressive deterioration of the

UN Doc. CCPR/C/NIC/Q/4 of 29 November 2019, § 27. In the same document, § 29 includes a question on the measures undertaken by Nicaragua to adequately guarantee participation in public affairs: "comment on reports that the Government has control over the electoral authority and provide information on the measures that have been taken to ensure free and transparent elections. Please include information on the bodies responsible for overseeing the electoral process and ensuring that elections are fair and impartial, as well as information on the measures taken to investigate the fraudulent practices reported in past elections."

82 Report of the Working Group on the Universal Periodic Review on Nicaragua, UN Doc. A/HRC/42/16 of 5 July 2019, §§ 125.39, 125.112 and 125.114.

83 Office of the High Commissioner for Human Rights, *Report on Human rights violations and abuses in the context of protests in Nicaragua, 18 April-18 August 2018*, available at www.ohchr.org/Documents/Countries/NI/HumanRightsViolationsNicaraguaApr_Aug2018_EN.pdf.

condition of human rights in the country, culminating with the violent repression of protests in April 2018.

Indeed, the overall situation of human rights and democracy in the country had spiralled downwards since the beginning of 2007, when the leader of the FSLN Daniel Ortega Saavedra was elected president and launched a campaign to consolidate the control of all institutions by his party. He was re-elected in November 2011 and 2016 respectively, although through severely flawed elections,[84] after having altered the constitutional requirements to remain in power and, in 2016, not allowing independent observers to monitor the process. The defective electoral law was an enabler, as well as the lack of any independent monitoring authority at the domestic level, because in the meantime only persons loyal to the FSLN were appointed as members of the SEC, as well as in the Supreme Court of Justice.

At the regional level, the latest elections were held in 2014 and, despite YATAMA's protests and reports of irregularities, the FSLN obtained the largest share of the vote in the RAAN and the RAAS. In November 2017, municipal elections were held and the FSLN allegedly put its preferred candidates in power, triggering clashes between opposition and government supporters. From 18 April 2018 onwards, a mass anti-government movement engaged in protests, which were violently put down by the government, with hundreds of arbitrary detentions, enforced disappearances, torture, extra-judicial killings, and more than 1,000 wounded protesters.

In response to this violence, in May 2018, the IACHR requested to visit the country and established a Coordination Unit mandated to monitor the events and provide rapid response (i.e. the SACROI).[85] Between 17 and 21 May 2018, the IACHR was allowed to conduct a preparatory mission to Nicaragua, which resulted in the release of preliminary observations[86] and, later on, the publication of a full report. It is noteworthy that therefore, in this phase, Nicaragua was still willing to cooperate in some way with the IACHR and accepted the presence of its representatives on site.

The IACHR's preliminary observations, and subsequent full report, noted a serious human rights crisis, characterised by the excessive use of force by the security forces and para-military groups, and resulted in hundreds of persons being killed and wounded, arbitrary detentions, torture, censorship and attacks on the press, and other threats aimed at dissolving the protests and inhibiting citizen

84 See, among others, OAS, *Informe de la misión de acompañamiento electoral – Elecciones generales del 6 de noviembre de 2011*, available at: https://reformaspoliticas.org/wp-content/uploads/2015/03/nicaraguainformemoe2011.pdf; European Union, *Final Report on the Electoral Monitoring Mission*, 2011, available at: http://aceproject.org/ero-en/regions/americas/NI/nicaragua-eo-reports/nicaragua-final-report-general-elections-eu/view; and Centro Nicaragüense de Derechos Humanos, *Informe final elecciones nacionales de noviembre de 2016*, available at: www.cenidh.org/noticias/959/.

85 *Supra* footnote 19.

86 Integral version available at: www.oas.org/en/iachr/media_center/PReleases/2018/113.asp.

participation. On its part, the State asserted that the events at stake could not be regarded as social protests, but rather as "an attempt at constitutional and institutional rupture in order to remove the legitimately elected authorities and oust the government."[87] The link between the repression of manifestations and the impairment of the democratic order in the country was emphasised by the IACHR:

> 'public protest is one of the usual ways of exercising the right of assembly and the right to freedom of expression, as well as a mechanism of political participation of defence of human rights, which has an essential social interest.'

In guaranteeing the proper functioning of the democratic system and the defence of human rights. In this regard, it has held that public demonstrations and other forms of protest against government plans or policies, far from being a provocation of violence, are common to any pluralistic democracy and deserve maximum protection. Likewise, the Inter-American Court has held that the relationship between the rights of assembly, freedom of expression and political participation, taken as a whole, make the democratic process possible and

> 'it is even clearer, especially when they are all exercised at the same time in order to protest against actions by the public authorities that are contrary to the constitutional order, and to reclaim the return to democracy.' [...] As regards the right to demonstrate, it is a core part of the right to participate in any democratic body or system. [...] political and social participation through the exercise of freedom of assembly is critical to the consolidation of democratic life in societies and thus contains a keen social interest.[88]

In short, as aptly noted by the IACHR, "repression and violence cannot be the response of a democratic State to the demands of its people."[89]

In the immediate aftermath of the protests of 18 April 2018 and the ensuing violent repression, a "national dialogue" was undertaken, with the Catholic Church as a mediator. This process foresaw the creation of an "electoral table," made up of six members – three from the government and three from the Civil Alliance for Justice and Democracy (i.e. a coalition regrouping individuals and civil society organisations, including from the autonomous regions) – and an agenda, containing a road map to operationalise the design and reform of the electoral system.[90] The work of the electoral table has encountered several obstacles and the reform has not yet seen the light of the day.

On 27 April 2018, the government established a Truth, Justice, and Reconciliation Commission mandated to clarify the events concerning the

87 IACHR, *Report Gross Human Rights Violations in the Context of Social Protests in Nicaragua*, cit., § 53.
88 ibid., §§ 54–55 and 82–83.
89 ibid., § 67.
90 ibid., § 75.

protests of 18 April and the events which occurred afterwards.[91] However, the mandate and overall independence of the Truth Commission have been questioned since its inception,[92] and this can be regarded as the moment when the Nicaraguan government and the IACHR commenced slowly parting ways.

On its part, following one of the recommendations which emerged during its visit, the IACHR established the GIEI,[93] with the objective of investigating, within a mandate of six months (renewable by agreement of the parties), the violent acts perpetrated in Nicaragua since 18 April. The five independent experts of the GIEI, appointed by the Secretary-General of the OAS, travelled to Managua on 1 July 2018. A few days before (i.e. on 24 June 2018), the IACHR had also established the MESENI,[94] with the mandate to follow-up on the recommendations that the GIEI would eventually provide, as well as on those contained in the IACHR report on its mission to Nicaragua.

The IACHR had therefore put in place a sophisticated strategy and mechanisms to support Nicaragua to overcome the human rights and democratic crisis. At the beginning, it counted on the support and acceptance of the State. However, this was not meant to last. In its report, the GIEI indicated that, since the beginning of its work, it had had to carry out its activities without the cooperation of the government of Nicaragua, which systematically denied the requested information in the context of State violence and repression that continued after the GIEI was instituted.[95]

In its report, the GIEI explicitly recalled the violations found by the IACtHR in its judgment on the *YATAMA* case and the State's failure to implement the measures ordered therein. The GIEI also pointed out how the non-implementation directly reflected on the subsequent degeneration of the democratic order in the country, emphasising that in 2008 the SEC committed the same violations perpetrated against YATAMA with respect to another political movement, with the consequence of excluding it from the electoral process.[96] Among its recommendations, the GIEI highlighted the importance of a thorough institutional and legislative reform, in the sense already indicated by the IACtHR in its judgment in the *YATAMA* case.[97] The GIEI also stressed the need for impartial,

91 The Truth, Justice, and Reconciliation Commission was established through resolution No. 03-2018 of 27 April 2018. More information, documents, and reports, available at: www.cvjp.org.ni/.

92 IACHR, *Report Gross Human Rights Violations in the Context of Social Protests in Nicaragua*, cit., § 249.

93 *Supra* footnote 18.

94 *Supra* footnote 17.

95 Interdisciplinary Group of Independent Experts (GIEI), *Report*, 21 December 2019, available at: www.oas.org/es/cidh/actividades/giei-nicaragua/GIEI_INFORME.pdf (integral version in Spanish), chapter III and at 358.

96 ibid., at 44.

97 ibid., recommendations No. 3, 5, 13, and 14.

independent, thorough, and effective investigations and for the prosecution and sanction of those responsible for the abuses committed after April 2018.[98]

Ostensibly, certain recommendations – or orders, for that matter – do not sit well with Nicaragua's government. As had already happened a few months before with the OHCHR,[99] on 19 December 2018, alongside the release of the GIEI's report, the government announced that it would not agree to any extension of its mandate. It expelled GIEI's members from the country and, for "good measure," also those of the MESENI. The Secretary-General of the OAS stated that such action further placed Nicaragua "into the terrain of authoritarianism."[100] From there, things only deteriorated, to a point where the suspension of Nicaragua's membership from the OAS has become a tangible option.

Besides the establishment of the MESENI, GIEI, and SACROI by the IACHR, the OAS, also with the aim of answering IACtHR's concerns vis-à-vis the non-implementation of its judgments, including on the *YATAMA* case, has been proactively engaging with Nicaragua with a view to strengthening institutions and promoting democracy, including through the reform of the existing electoral legislation. In this realm, on 15 October 2016, the OAS and the government of Nicaragua signed an agreement to foster constructive dialogue on issues concerning electoral matters,[101] and on 28 February 2017, they signed a memorandum of understanding so that the OAS could assist Nicaragua in drafting and implementing the electoral reform, including by enforcing the measures ordered by the IACtHR in its judgment on the *YATAMA* case. However, the terms of the memorandum were not complied with and the situation further escalated.

On 28 June 2019, the General Assembly of the OAS found that the situation in Nicaragua was heading towards "an alteration of the constitutional regime that seriously impairs the democratic order."[102] Through a resolution adopted on 28 August 2019 by the Permanent Council,[103] an OAS High-Level Commission on Nicaragua was set up and mandated to carry out diplomatic efforts to seek a peaceful and effective solution to the political and social crisis in Nicaragua. The government refused to meet with the High-Level Commission and prohibited its members from entering the country, while Nicaraguan diplomats rejected any kind of dialogue. Nevertheless, the High-Level Commission managed to meet with representatives of NGOs and civil society organisations, collecting testimo-

98 Notably, also this recommendation was openly disregarded by Nicaragua's government, which, on 8 June 2019, adopted Law No. 996 (integral text in Spanish: www.refworld.org.es/pdfid/5d2cb2eb4.pdf), a sweeping amnesty law for crimes committed in the context of the 2018 protests.

99 This aspect was analysed in more detail above.

100 See the press release issued by the Secretary-General of the OAS on 19 December 2018: www.oas.org/en/media_center/press_release.asp?sCodigo=E-082/18.

101 Available (in Spanish) at: www.oas.org/es/sla/ddi/docs/acuerdos_bilaterales_28-2017.PDF.

102 General Assembly of the OAS, Resolution AG/RES.2943 (XLIX-O/19) of 28 June 2019.

103 Permanent Council of the OAS, Resolution CP/RES.1135 (2244/19) of 28 August 2019.

nies and documentation, with an emphasis on the situation of indigenous and Afro-descendent communities in the RAAS and the RAAN.

On 19 November 2019, the High-Level Commission issued a report[104] finding the existence of "an alteration of the constitutional regime that seriously impairs the democratic order" in Nicaragua, as outlined in Article 20 of the 2001 Inter-American Democratic Charter.[105]

The High-Level Commission, referring, among others, to the reports of the OHCHR, the IACHR and the GIEI, declared that

> Nicaragua has shown an ongoing pattern of efforts designed to curtail the rights of its citizens, including: ongoing harassment and intimidation, *restrictions of political rights*, freedom of the press, freedom of expression, the right to personal liberty and human treatment.[106]

Besides a serious pattern of harassment and intimidation of any form of opposition to the government, the High-Level Commission found that Nicaragua has enacted several measures restricting the political rights of its citizens, including by revoking the legal permits of several local NGOs in response to their criticism of the government. Moreover, the High-Level Commission identified

> a pattern of wide reaching executive control of State institutions, which is used to consolidate executive power and influence State institutions. [...] the impartiality and independence of the judicial system has been widely questioned. [...] *There are also numerous reports on actions by the Government*

104 The integral version of the report is available at: http://scm.oas.org/pdfs/2019/CP41661EREPORTCOMMISSIONONNICARAGUA.pdf. Hereinafter "High-Level Commission Report."

105 Article 20 of the Inter-American Democratic Charter establishes: "In the event of an unconstitutional alteration of the constitutional regime that seriously impairs the democratic order in a member State, any member State or the Secretary General may request the immediate convocation of the Permanent Council to undertake a collective assessment of the situation and to take such decisions as it deems appropriate. The Permanent Council, depending on the situation, may undertake the necessary diplomatic initiatives, including good offices, to foster the restoration of democracy. If such diplomatic initiatives prove unsuccessful, or if the urgency of the situation so warrants, the Permanent Council shall immediately convene a special session of the General Assembly. The General Assembly will adopt the decisions it deems appropriate, including the undertaking of diplomatic initiatives, in accordance with the Charter of the Organization, international law, and the provisions of this Democratic Charter. The necessary diplomatic initiatives, including good offices, to foster the restoration of democracy, will continue during the process." On the Inter-American Charter and the activation of the measures it envisages in case of impairment of the democratic order, see Levitt B.S., *A Desultory Defense of Democracy: OAS Resolution 1080 and the Inter-American Democratic Charter*, in 48:3 Latin American Politics and Society, 2006, at 93–123.

106 High-Level Commission Report, *Findings of the Commission*, at 4 (emphasis added).

> *of Nicaragua to dismantle political opposition and to manipulate electoral processes to ensure the Executive power control over the electoral system.*[107]

Hence, the High-Level Commission concluded

> that the *control and subordination mechanisms that the Government of Nicaragua has been developing* with respect to other branches of government, including the judiciary, the legislature, *the Supreme Electoral Council, and others, make the democratic functioning of the country impossible, thus making it a co-opted state that is incompatible with the rule of law.* To re-establish the democratic system in the country, *institutional reforms are indispensable and urgent, starting with a comprehensive reform of the electoral system* to allow the holding of fair, free, and transparent elections in the country, in accordance with Inter-American standards.[108]

By questioning the independence of the SEC and emphasising the need for a comprehensive reform of the electoral system, the High-Level Commission *de facto* reproduced the findings of the IACtHR in the *YATAMA* case, somehow confirming that, had the judgment been implemented by the State in due course, the country would most likely not find itself where it is now and its democratic order would arguably be healthier.

Based on its conclusions, the High-Level Commission recommended that the Permanent Council of the OAS endorse its findings and convene a special session of the General Assembly to review the matter. Pursuant to Article 21 of the Inter-American Democratic Charter, if convened in a special session, by two-thirds of the member States, the General Assembly of the OAS can take the decision to suspend a member State from the OAS where there has been an alteration of the constitutional regime that seriously impairs the democratic order.[109]

Seemingly, Nicaragua (and the Inter-American system) is standing at a crossroads, or on the edge of the precipice. Indeed, the suspension of a State from the organisation is a measure of "last resort," which has only happened twice before in the history of the OAS.[110] The decision to be made at this stage is at the crux of

107 ibid., *Subordination of the State by the executive*, at 8 (emphasis added).

108 ibid., *Conclusions*, §§ 2–3 (emphasis added).

109 Article 21 of the Inter-American Democratic Charter adds that "The suspended member State shall continue to fulfil its obligations to the Organization, in particular its human rights obligations. Notwithstanding the suspension of the member State, the Organization will maintain diplomatic initiatives to restore democracy in that State." Moreover, Article 22 of the Charter establishes that "once the situation that led to suspension has been resolved, any member State or the Secretary General may propose to the General Assembly that suspension be lifted. This decision shall require the vote of two thirds of the member States in accordance with the OAS Charter."

110 Honduras was suspended from the OAS in 2009, after the coup, and previously Cuba in 1959, in the context of the Cold War.

a dilemma that is very much related to the issue of non-implementation.[111] What is the most effective manner to ensure that democratic order is restored in a country and, *en passant*, that the State concerned eventually abides by its international human rights obligations, including by enforcing the judgments of international courts, as it is bound to do? If the "softer" attitude maintained for several years by the Inter-American organs, including the IACtHR, did not pay, will a "tougher" one drive Nicaragua closer to the desired outcome or rather push it farther away?

Whatever the answer, it is clear that the toll paid by Nicaraguans in terms of the degeneration of the human rights situation and of democracy is an especially high one, and much could arguably have been avoided had the judgment of the IACtHR on the *YATAMA* case been implemented and the electoral legislation and system been duly reformed without delay.

Conclusions

The situation illustrated is that of a country which, in a little more than a decade, has sunk into a grave human rights crisis and whose democratic order has been disrupted, while the government is increasingly isolated. On the one hand, because of the growing criticism of international organisations, and on the other, because those organisations and a number of countries – seeing that all attempts at dialogue have failed – are now considering measures such as the suspension of Nicaragua's membership or have imposed financial and travel sanctions on certain State officials. [112]

On 21 December 2020, Nicaragua legislation was indeed amended through the adoption of the Law of Defence of Peoples' Right to Independence, Sovereignty and Self-determination for Peace. However, the new law further restricts electoral

111 Dzehtsiarou K., Coffey D. K., *Suspension and Expulsion of Members of the Council of Europe: Difficult Decisions in Troubled Times*, in 68:2 International and Comparative Law Quarterly, 2019, at 443–476.

112 Although they will not be analysed in this chapter due to space limitations, it is noteworthy that there have been other initiatives to chastise and sanction Nicaragua vis-à-vis the human rights crisis and the deterioration of the democratic order, including the approval in 2018 in United States of America of an act known as "the Nica Act" (www.treasury.gov/resource-center/sanctions/Programs/Documents/nica_2018.pdf) to oppose loans at international financial institutions for Nicaragua unless it takes effective steps to hold free, fair, and transparent elections. Sanctions have also been imposed on Nicaragua by the European Union and Switzerland respectively. On 14 October 2019, the EU Council adopted a framework – Council Implementing Regulation (EU) 2019/1716 and Council Decision (CFSP) 2019/1720 – to impose sanctions, enabling the targeted restrictive measures, including travel bans and asset freezes, against persons, entities or bodies responsible for serious human rights violations and for undermining democracy – on 4 May 2020, six Nicaraguan government officials were included in the list of those subjected to restrictive measures – Council Implementing Regulation (EU) 2020/606 and Council Decision (CFSP) 2020/607. On 24 June 2020, the Swiss Federal Council adopted an ordinance, imposing financial and travel sanctions against six officials with ties to the Nicaraguan president.

participation, generating yet new concerns with regard to the respect of Article 23 of the ACHR.[113] Article 1 of the new law prohibits the participation in popular elections to those Nicaraguans who, in the opinion of the authorities, "led or financed a coup," "promote terrorist acts," "favour foreign interference in internal affairs," "organise themselves with foreign funds to carry out terrorist acts and destabilization," or "applaud sanctions imposed against the State of Nicaragua and its citizens." The new legislation seems to be taking non-implementation to a new level. Not only orders or recommendations issued by international human rights mechanisms are blatantly disregarded, but those who advocate for their implementation (activity which could be interpreted to fall under the overly broad notion of "applauding sanctions imposed against the State"), could be declared unfit for election, thus restricting even more the enjoyment of electoral rights, with all the consequences that this will have on democracy.

Perhaps this grim scenario could have been foreseen. In an "official statement to the heroic people of Nicaragua and friendly peoples of the world on the electoral process in the Sandinista Popular Revolution," issued by the National Directorate of the FSLN on 23 August 1980, it was affirmed that

> for the Sandinista Front, *democracy is not measured only in political terms, nor is it confined merely to participation in elections.* It is more, much more. For a revolutionary, for a Sandinista, it means PARTICIPATION by the people in political, economic, social and cultural affairs. The more the people take part in these things, the more it will be democratic. And it must be said once and for all, *democracy does not begin and end with elections. It is a myth to what to reduce democracy to that.*[114]

The Directorate of the FSLN then considered that Nicaraguans were not "mature" enough to vote and announced that elections would be held only five years later (i.e. in 1985), in the meantime prohibiting any nomination or designation of candidates for positions in the general elections, as well as the corresponding public campaigning. [115]

Forty years later, it seems that the misconception about the crucial importance of free, transparent, and participative elections for a genuine and healthy democracy is still very much present. The judgment rendered in 2005 by the IACtHR in the *YATAMA* case clearly pinpointed many of the underlying problems and

113 In its press release No. 03/21 of 8 January 2021, available at www.oas.org/es/cidh/prensa/comunicados/2021/003.asp, the IACHR expressed serious concerns at the new law, already identifying loopholes and potential breaches of Article 23 of the ACHR.

114 Statement reproduced in IACHR, *Report on the Situation of Human Rights in Nicaragua of 1981*, cit., chapter VIII, C § 2. Capitalisation of the word "participation" is in the original, Italics are added.

115 See, among others, Barnes W.A., *Incomplete Democracy in Central America: Polarization and Voter Turnout in Nicaragua and El Salvador*, 40:3 Journal of Inter-American Studies and World Affairs, 1998, at 63–101.

provided indications as to the measures to be adopted to overcome the impasse and lay the foundations for a sustainable democracy. Arguably, Nicaragua's failure to enforce those measures paved the way to the degeneration that followed, thus showing that there is no lightness at all in the non-implementation of international judgments.

Whatever happens with regard to the suspension of Nicaragua from the OAS, until the electoral and institutional reforms (duly reflecting the multicultural nature of the State and the needs, rights, and cosmo-vision of indigenous peoples and ethnic groups in the RAAN and the RAAS) – as requested by the IACtHR already in 2005 – are implemented, there does not seem to be any chance for a sustainable democracy in the country. And this is certainly unbearable.

Bibliography

Baluarte D.C., *Strategizing For Compliance: The Evolution of a Compliance Phase of Inter-American Court Litigation and the Strategic Imperative for Victims' Representatives*, in 27 American University International Law Review, 2012, 263 ff.

Barnes W.A., *Incomplete Democracy in Central America: Polarization and Voter Turnout in Nicaragua and El Salvador*, in 40 Journal of Interamerican Studies and World Affairs, 1998, 63 ff.

Campbell M.S., *The Right of Indigenous Peoples to Political Participation and the Case of YATAMA v. Nicaragua*, in 4:2 Arizona Journal of International & Comparative Law, 2007, 499 ff.

Courtney R., *Access to Electoral Rights – Nicaragua*, in EUDO Citizenship Observatory, March 2015.

Dulitzky A., *La aplicación de los tratados sobre derechos humanos por los tribunales locales: un estudio de derecho comparado*, in Abramovic V., Bovino A., Courtis C. (eds.), La aplicación de los tratados sobre derechos humanos en el ámbito local – la experiencia de una década, Buenos Aires, 2004, 33 ff.

Dzehtsiarou K., Coffey D.K., *Suspension and Expulsion of Members of the Council of Europe: Difficult Decisions in Troubled Times*, in 68:2 International and Comparative Law Quarterly, 2019, 443 ff.

Gómez isa F., *The Decision by the Inter-American Court of Human Rights on the Awas Tingni vs. Nicaragua Case (2001): The Implementation Gap*, in 8 The Age of Human Rights Journal, 2017, 67 ff.

González-salzberg D., *The Effectiveness of the Inter-American Human Rights System: A Study of the American States' Compliance with the Judgments of the Inter-American Court of Human Rights*, in 16 Revista colombiana de derecho internacional, 2010, 155 ff.

González volio L., *Los pueblos indígenas y el ejercicio de los derechos políticos de acuerdo a la Convención Americana: el Caso Yatama contra Nicaragua*, in 41 Revista Instituto Interamericano de Derechos Humanos, 2005, 317 ff.

Hitters J.C., *¿Son vinculantes los pronunciamientos de la Comisión y de la Corte Interamericana de Derechos Humanos? (control de constitucionalidad y convencionalidad)*, in 10 Revista Iberoamericana de Derecho Procesal Constitucional, 2008, 131 ff.

Jonas S., Stein N., *The Sandinista Legacy: The Construction of Democracy*, in 17:3 Latin American Perspectives, 1990, 10 ff.

Kunz R., *Judging International Judgments Anew? The Human Rights Courts before Domestic Courts*, in 30:4 European Journal of International Law, 2020, 1129 ff.

Levitt B.S., *A Desultory Defense of Democracy: OAS Resolution 1080 and the Inter-American Democratic Charter*, in 48:3 Latin American Politics and Society, 2006, 93 ff.

Palacios zuloaga P., *Judging Inter-American Human Rights: The Riddle of Compliance with the Inter-American Court of Human Rights*, in 42:2 Human Rights Quarterly, 2020, 392 ff.

Thomson jiménez J., *Las obligaciones internacionales en materia electoral. Un enfoque a partir del sistema interamericano de derechos humanos*, in 20 Revista Derecho electoral, 2015, 111 ff.

15 Political rights in Venezuela

An outstanding issue

Yessica Esquivel Alonso and Fernando Gustavo Ruz Dueñas

Introduction and context

The constitutional structure of Venezuela and the Inter-American System of Human Rights

On August 9, 1977, the Bolivarian Republic of Venezuela ratified the American Convention on Human Rights, being the third State of the Organization of American States (OAS) to do so. Later, on June 24, 1982, it accepted the jurisdiction of the Inter-American Court of Human Rights.[1] However, the relationship between the Inter-American System of Human Rights and Venezuela can best be characterised as intermittent, the most tangible proof being that none of the 22 judgments issued against Venezuela to date have been brought to a close as a result of Venezuela's compliance.[2] Venezuela's legal context is complex. Thus, it seems appropriate to begin by noting that Article 23 of the Constitution of the Bolivarian Republic of Venezuela establishes that treaties, pacts, and conventions on human rights, signed and ratified by the State, have a constitutional hierarchy. This provision indicates that international instruments must be immediately and directly applied by the State's courts and all other public organs. It establishes constitutionally that international treaties are hierarchically on a par with the Constitution.

This constitutional hierarchy was legitimised in the consultative referendum of April 25, 1999, which concerned the preparation of a new constitution. In this referendum, voters approved, by a majority of 81.74%, a measure to convene a National Constituent Assembly, among other things. Later, on December 15 of that same year, a new constitutional text was approved through another referendum.[3] According to this legal framework, all State's subjects and organs

1 Inter-American Commission on Human Rights, *Recognition of the jurisdiction of the Court.* Available at: "www.acnur.org/fileadmin/Documentos/BDL/2002/4534.pdf"

2 See more about the extent of compliance with sentences at: "www.corteidh.or.cr/canes_en_supervision_por_pais.cfm?lang=es"

3 Carao A., *Unconstitutionality of the denunciation of the American Convention on Human Rights by Venezuela*, in Yearbook of Latin American Constitutional Law, year XIX, Bogotá, 2013, 43–79. Available at: "www.corteidh.or.cr/tablas/r32197.pdf"

DOI: 10.4324/9781003229247-18

must guarantee and respect human rights enshrined in those international instruments that contain the most favourable provisions for their enjoyment and exercise. Accordingly, the Supreme Court of Justice of Venezuela has recognised this constitutional block and has invoked different human rights treaties on several occasions. For example, in its judgment, no. 1860/2001 – *case of the Barinas State Legislative Council* – of October 5, 2001, the Court amplified its powers of constitutional review and the direct application of international treaties and conventions.[4]

The relationship since the ratification of the American Convention on Human Rights and the acceptance of the contentious jurisdiction of the Inter-American Court of Human Rights

However, despite the clarity of the constitutional mandate on the application of international instruments and the ratification of the American Convention, on December 18, 2008,[5] the Supreme Court of Justice declared the judgment of *Apitz* v. *Venezuela* non-enforceable and requested that the National Executive strike down the IDH Convention, based on Article 78 of the Convention.[6]

Subsequently, on September 10, 2012, President Hugo Chávez Frías, the Minister of Popular Power for Foreign Relations of the Bolivarian Republic of Venezuela – by then Nicolás Maduro Moros – withdrew from the American Convention on Human Rights. Hence, since then, the Inter-American Court no longer has jurisdiction over any violation of human rights in Venezuela. The notice of withdrawal from the Convention expressly states that

> as of the term in it established, its international effects cease to exist, as far as it is concerned, as well as the jurisdiction of its organs over our country, both the Inter-American Commission on Human Rights and the Inter-American Court of Human Rights.[7]

4 This criterion is reaffirmed in the judgment *Analya Belisario et al. v. National Electoral Council*, July 13, 2001; and in the Esteban Gersabi judgment, June 15, 2004, n. 1173. See more in Carao, A., 2013.

5 "Article 78. 1. The States Parties may denounce this Convention after the expiration of five years from the date of its entry into force and by giving a one-year notice, notified to the Secretary General of the Organization, who should inform the other parties; 2. Said denunciation shall not have the effect of displaying to the interested State Party the obligations contained in this Convention concerning any fact that, while it may constitute a violation of those obligations, has been fulfilled by it before the date on which the complaint produces effect. American Convention on Human Rights."

6 Vittorio C., *Implementation of the judgments and resolutions of the Inter-American Court of Human Rights: a necessary debate*, in IIDH Magazine, 49, 2009, 13–28. Available at: "www.corteidh.or.cr/tablas/r24576.pdf"

7 Inter-American Commission on Human Rights, *Denunciation and departure of Venezuela from the Inter-American Court of Human Rights*, 2013. Available at: "www.minci.gob.ve/wp-content/uploads/downloads/2013/09/DISCURSO-CIDH-20-9-13-web.pdf"

The State based its withdrawal of the Convention on seven arguments. Among them, it is worth noting its view that Chapter IV of the Annual Report on the Situation of Human Rights in the region lacked a methodological basis, given that it did not provide criteria that allowed an objective and universal analysis of the situation. Likewise, it pointed out that the Inter-American Commission on Human Rights did not provide an express and equitable basis for the precautionary measures that it granted. Also, the Government of Venezuela pointed out that just a few hours after the *coup d'état* of April 11, 2002, it had requested precautionary measures to be granted in favour of President Hugo Chávez, who had been kidnapped. Nevertheless, in its view, the Inter-American Commission did not grant such a measure, nor did it present any excuses for its "lack of due action in relation to a coup attempt."[8]

On the same date of the notice of withdrawal, the OAS General Secretariat issued press release C-307/12, in which it stated that it regretted Venezuela's decision and expressed hope that the Venezuelan State would reconsider its decision.[9] Venezuela´s withdrawal from the Inter-American System was formalised on April 27, 2017, when the President of the Republic, Nicolás Maduro, sent a letter to the Secretary General of the OAS, notifying them of the decision to withdraw from the OAS Charter.[10] This decision was a consequence of the government's discontent with resolution CP/RES. 1078 (2108/17) of the OAS Permanent Council, which expressed deep concern regarding the "unconstitutional alteration of the democratic order of the Bolivarian Republic of Venezuela"[11] and the suspension of the powers of the National Assembly. Upon the notice of withdrawal presented by President Maduro, on May 2, 2017, the National Assembly passed an agreement ratifying Venezuela´s accession to the OAS and declaring Maduro's withdrawal unconstitutional and null.[12]

Subsequently, on January 22, 2019, the National Assembly passed the "Agreement of Ratification of Venezuela's accession to the OAS Charter," which, taking into account its previous agreement – aforementioned – declared that the Venezuelan State would remain a member of the OAS as if no withdrawal had ever been filed.[13] On that same date, Gustavo Tarre Briceño was

8 *Ibidem.*

9 The complaint became effective as of September 10, 2013. See press release at: "www.oas.org/es/centro_noticias/comunicado_prensa.asp?sCodigo=C-307/12"

10 The letter signed by the President of Venezuela is available at: "www.oas.org/es/sla/ddi/docs/a41_nota_venezuela_04-28-2017.pdf"

11 See press release at: "www.oas.org/es/centro_noticias/comunicado_prensa.asp?sCodigo=C-022/17"

12 Agreement to ratify the Bolivarian Republic of Venezuela's accession to the letter of the Organization of American States of May 2, 2017. Available at: "www.asambleanacional.gob.ve/actos/_acuerdo-de-ratificacion- from-the-adhesion-of-the-Bolivarian-republic-of-venezuela-to-the-charter-of-the-organization-of-american-states-oas"

13 Agreement of Ratification of the accession of Venezuela to the OAS Charter on January 22, 2019. Available at: "www.asambleanacional.gob.ve/actos/detalle/acuerdo-de-ratificacion-de-la-Adhesion-of-the-Bolivarian-Repu blic-of-Venezuela-to-the-Charter-of-the-Organization-of-American-States-OEA-336"

appointed the Permanent Representative of Venezuela. Later, on February 8, 2019, the President of the National Assembly, Juan Guaidó, submitted an official letter to the General Secretariat of the OAS, ratifying the will of the Venezuelan State to be a State Party, based on the Agreements of May 2, 2017, and January 22, 2019, issued by the authority that he represented. Consequently, on April 9, 2019, the OAS Permanent Council issued resolution 1124 (2217/19), whereby it accepted the appointment of Tarre Briceño.[14] However, the polarisation of opinions on whether or not to join the OAS has not proven to be a peaceful issue among the different Venezuelan political actors. Therefore, various authorities have announced that they will withdraw from the American Convention on Human Rights or the OAS Charter on more than one occasion. [15]

Venezuela's actual situation within the Inter-American System of Human Rights

Between 1995 and 2019, the Inter-American Court of Human Rights has ruled on 24 occasions on Venezuela cases. On 22 of those occasions, the Venezuelan State has been condemned for the violation of some of the rights contained in the American Convention on Human Rights.[16] Of the remainder, on one occasion, the case was dismissed because a preliminary objection was filed by the State on the basis that there had been a failure to exhaust domestic remedies;[17] and on another occasion, the international responsibility of the State for any violation of the content of the Convention was not established.[18]

14 Statement available at: "www.oas.org/es/centro_noticias/comunicado_prensa.asp?sCodigo=C-019/19"

15 See more in: Civilis, "Withdrawal of Venezuela from the inter-American human rights system (SIDH)." Available at: "www.civilisac.org/civilis/wp-content/uploads/retiro-de-venezuela-del-sidh-1-1-1.pdf"

16 In chronological order: *El Amparo* v. *Venezuela*, January 18, 1995; *Case of the Caracazo* v. *Venezuela*, November 11, 1999; *Blanco Romero et al.* v. *Venezuela*, November 28, 2005; *Montero Aranguren et al. (Detention Center of Catia)* v. *Venezuela*, July 5, 2006; *Apitz Barbera et al. ("First Court of Administrative Disputes")* v. *Venezuela*, August 5, 2008; *Ríos et al.* v. *Venezuela*, January 28, 2009; *Perozo et al.* v. *Venezuela*, January 28, 2009; *Reverón Trujillo* v. *Venezuela*, June 30, 2009; *Barreto Leiva* v. *Venezuela*, November 17, 2009; *Usón Ramírez* v. *Venezuela*; November 20, 2009; *Chocrón Chocrón* v. *Venezuela*, July 1, 2011; *López Mendoza* v. *Venezuela*, September 1, 2011; *Barrios family* v. *Venezuela*, November 24, 2011; *Díaz Peña* v. *Venezuela*, June 26, 2012; *Uzcátegui et al.* v. *Venezuela*, September 3, 2012; *Landaeta Mejías Brothers et al.* v. *Venezuela*, August 27, 2014; *Granier et al. (Radio Caracas Television)* v. *Venezuela*, June 22, 2015; *Ortiz Hernández et al.* v. *Venezuela*, August 22, 2017; *San Miguel Sosa et al.* v. *Venezuela*, February 8, 2018; *López Soto et al.* v. *Venezuela*, September 26, 2018; *Álvarez Ramos* v. *Venezuela*, August 30, 2019; and *Díaz Loreto et al.* v. *Venezuela*, November 19, 2019.

17 This decision sets an important precedent over the Court's doctrine regarding the exhaustion of domestic remedies: *Brewer Carías* v. *Venezuela*, May 26, 2014.

18 *Castillo González et al.* v. *Venezuela*, November 27, 2012.

One of the consequences of the deterioration of Venezuela's relationship with the organs of the Inter-American Human Rights System is the constant institutional reluctance to abide by the decisions of the Inter-American Court. In the international sphere, it is possible to measure the State's disobedience through the supervisory mechanism of the Inter-American Court itself, specifically through its assessment of the State's compliance with sentences; in the national sphere, silence predominates. According to the oversight mechanism, between 2012 and 2018, the Court has applied Article 65 of the American Convention in 12 of the judgments condemning Venezuela.[19] Only three other countries have had some of their sentences, those relating to non-compliance granted under Article 65: Haiti, Nicaragua, and Trinidad and Tobago. Even taken together, the instances involving these three countries do not add up to even half of the sentences that Venezuela contributes to this list.

The recurrent application of Article 65 to the judgments against Venezuela is due, in the words of the Court, to Venezuela´s prolonged failure to "report on the execution of the judgment and to implement the reparations ordered."[20] This State silence coincides, chronologically, with the Venezuelan State's withdrawal from the American Convention on Human Rights in September 2012.[21] The failure to comply is, in this case, a deliberate act by the State that has broken its commitments to the values contained in the American Convention.

Now, a similar situation is evident at the national level and it is possible to argue that impunity persists in many cases. Unfortunately, the Court's judgments have not served, as they have in other States, as a catalyst for the advancement of domestic processes in the interests of justice. Take, for example, the case of El Amparo. Twenty-five years after the Inter-American Court's ruling, no sentence has yet been handed down in the domestic courts condemning any of those responsible for the murder of fourteen fishermen by the Venezuelan army. Although in 2016, the Constitutional Chamber of the Venezuelan Supreme Court of Justice annulled the sentence that acquitted those involved in the massacre in the first instance, the case continues under military jurisdiction.[22] This situation contradicts the already consolidated jurisprudence of the Inter-American Court on military jurisdiction and human rights violations.

19 Article 65 of the Convention empowers the Court to indicate, in the annual report it submits to the General Assembly of the Organization of American States, the cases in which a State has failed to comply with its resolutions. Once the Court determines this article's application, it will continue to include the failure to comply each year, unless the State proves that it has adopted the necessary measures to comply with the Inter-American tribunal's reparations.

20 Monitoring of Compliance with Judgment in the Cases of *Díaz Peña and Uzcátegui et al.* v. *Venezuela*, November 22, 2019: par. 22. These two judgments were the last to be considered under the terms of Article 65 of the Convention.

21 In this sense, the first case that was considered to be unfulfilled in terms of Article 65 was *Apitz Barbera et al. ("First Court of Administrative Disputes")* v. *Venezuela*; included in the 2012 Annual Report.

22 See PSUV, *28 años de la masacre de El Amparo*, on psuv.org, 29 October, 2016. Available at: "www.psuv.org.ve/temas/noticias/28-anos-masacre-amparo/#.X10L1pNKi3K"

General references of the democratic situation in Venezuela

It is no secret that the democratic institutions in Venezuela have deteriorated in recent years. The Inter-American Commission on Human Rights has documented, through various reports, how interference by the executive branch has weakened the independence of the legislative and judicial branches. One of the most serious consequences of institutional weakness is the existence of a generalised context of impunity, which has impacted on the exercise of fundamental human rights for a democratic regime, such as political rights.[23]

For more than a decade, the Inter-American Commission and Venezuelan human rights organisations have criticised a pattern of serious human rights violations against political dissidents by the executive branch, undertaken with the consent of the legislative and judicial branches.[24] The Venezuelan opposition has protested against it being the victim of persecution through the media, as well as of acts of harassment, political disqualification, irregular searches, criminalisation acts, arbitrary detention, and violations of the right to life and personal integrity.[25]

The Inter-American Court has ruled on violations of political rights contained in Article 23 of the American Convention in cases against Venezuela on several occasions, namely: *Apitz Barbera and others*, *Reverón Trujillo*, *Chocrón Chocrón*, *López Mendoza*, *San Miguel Sosa et al.*, and recently in *Álvarez Ramos* v. *Venezuela*. These rulings represent a series of essential precedents for understanding the content and scope of political rights in the context of the instability and deterioration of democratic institutions. This text will focus the analysis on two of these cases: *Reverón Trujillo* and *López Mendoza*. Knowing the current state of compliance with the reparation measures ordered by the Court in the cases mentioned above can help provide a general vision of how Inter-American regional justice has helped (or conversely has failed to help), to deal with human rights violations in an adverse political climate for supranational institutions. The political crisis in Venezuela is far from over, but the Court's precedents, together with the Inter-American standards established to date, may help discern a way out

23 Venezuela had formed part of Chapter IV of the Annual Report of the Inter-American Commission on Human Rights since 2002, where it had remained until 2019 (except for 2004 when incorporated in Chapter V on follow-up to the recommendations of the country report published the previous year).

24 For example: on September 2, 2020, the Commission adopted three resolutions by which it granted precautionary measures in favour of two persons deprived of their liberty and one person whose official whereabouts were unknown following his detention in Venezuela. The Commission considered that such persons face a severe and urgent risk of irreparable damage to their rights.

25 These testimonies have been documented in the country chapters of the annual report and special reports prepared by the Commission on Human Rights, compiling official information from the State and Venezuelan civil society. See: Inter-American Commission on Human Rights, *Institucionalidad democrática, Estado de derecho y derechos humanos en Venezuela. Informe de país (OEA/Ser.L/V/II/Doc.209)*, December 31, 2017: par. 11 and 12.

which is consistent with the regional consensus on the rights that should govern a democratic society.

Case analysis

Reverón Trujillo v. Venezuela

Case summary

The case of *Reverón Trujillo* v. *Venezuela* (June 30, 2009) was started by a complaint from Judge María Cristina Reverón Trujillo against the Venezuelan State for the violation of Articles 25.1, judicial protection; and 23.1, political rights; as well as Articles 8.1, judicial guarantees; and 5.1, right to humane treatment of the American Convention. The facts of the case indicate that Reverón Trujillo was dismissed as a Criminal Judge of First Instance. She had held the judicial position from July 21, 1999, until February 6, 2002, when the Commission for the Functioning and Restructuring of the Judicial System established that she was to face disciplinary offences for exceeding her authority and failing to act with due attention and diligence in her functions as the director of the process.

Subsequently, the Political-Administrative Chamber of the Supreme Court of Justice heard the challenge against the alleged wrongful acts and declared the dismissal sanctions to be null and void. However, it did not order the restitution or payment of lost wages. Therefore, in the victim's opinion, the Supreme Court's decisions failed to provide an effective judicial remedy, which is a vital part of remedying the violation of her human rights. It is worth noting that the victim's appointment as a judge was "provisional". Put another way, the status of her appointment was exceptional, as she did not obtain the role through an open contest based on merit, unlike those holding a permanent position.

According to Venezuelan regulations, provisional judges are freely appointed and can be removed by the competent authority without the need to ground its respective decision on any particular justification. In this sense, while the guarantees available for permanent judges generally apply equally to provisional judges, they do not provide the same protection for the latter since they are selected differently, and their tenure in office is not unlimited. Hence, in relation to provisional judges, litigation focuses primarily on the analysis of the appointment process's appropriateness and the existence of a guarantee not to be arbitrarily removed from their position, as well as other guarantees against external pressure, in light of the interpretation adopted in the United Nations Basic Principles on judicial independence and its guarantees. Failure to comply with any of these guarantees implies a lack of protection of judicial independence.

Regarding the adequate process in the appointment of judges, according to the established jurisprudence of the Inter-American Court, it must be carried out with "integrity, suitability, and training or appropriate legal qualifications," which implies that, whenever these criteria are not met, objectivity and reasonableness do not meet the minimum procedural requirements. Regarding the guarantee not to be arbitrarily removed from their position, it has been established that judges can only be suspended or separated from their positions: a) due to incapacity, or b) due to behaviour that disqualifies them from continuing to perform their functions. This guarantee includes permanence in the position and a fair promotion process, and the absence of unjustified dismissals. Consequently, the State is obliged to offer such guarantees to both regular and provisional judges alike.

In the opinion of the Inter-American Court, the guarantee of not to be arbitrarily removed from their position, requires that those individuals who have been removed arbitrarily be reinstated to the position. Otherwise, States would be able to intervene in the judicial functions. In turn, this could raise fear among other judges of being removed without the possibility of being reinstated, even in cases of arbitrary removal from office, which would affect judicial independence by incentivising judges to follow instructions from others. Therefore, the nullification of a dismissal necessarily involves the reinstatement. Finally, the guarantee against external pressure provides that there must be no undue or unjustified interference in the judicial process. Both guarantees are closely linked, since whenever "provisional judges do not have security of permanence during a certain period, they will be vulnerable to pressure from different sectors, mainly from those who have the power to decide on dismissal or promotion in the Judiciary."[26]

Reasoning developed of the regional court with a specific focus on Article 23 of the American Convention on Human Rights

Based on the reasons above, the Inter-American Court established that the provisional nature of a public position is not a relevant factor for any decision not to reinstate the victims to their office. Moreover, the Court emphasised that in its judgment of the case of the *Constitutional Court* v. *Peru* (2011), it determined that, if arbitrary dismissals occur, the "State must compensate said magistrates for the salaries and benefits they lost."[27] Consequently, the Inter-American Court concluded that Article 25.1 of the Convention had been violated because the remedy that was available for Reverón Trujillo did not provide her with adequate reparation. Also, the State authorities failed to justify the failure to reinstate the victim to her judicial position, as well as the non-payment of the wages lost. Therefore, the domestic remedy was not effective.[28]

In relation to political rights, which are protected by Article 23.1 of the American Convention, in the opinion of the Inter-American Court, individuals have the right "to have access to public functions under general conditions of equality; [which] protects access to a direct form of participation in the design, implementation, development, and execution of state directives through public

26 *Reverón Trujillo* v. *Venezuela*, June 30, 2009, par. 117.
27 *Ivi*: par. 126.
28 *Ivi*: par. 127.

functions."[29] In this regard, it should be noted that, according to the jurisprudence of the Inter-American Court, political-electoral rights must be analysed using three concepts: 1) a broad interpretation of the idea of opportunity,[30] 2) access to and maintenance of the position, and 3) restrictions.[31] For our present analysis, we will be focusing on the concept of access to and maintenance of the position.

In the judgment of *Apitz Barbera and others* v. *Venezuela* (2008), it was established that Article 23.1.c should not be interpreted merely as a guarantee of access to public office and the requirement that it should be exercised under general conditions of equality.[32] In other words, such a right includes both access to and membership of a position, as well as suspension and dismissal processes, under similar conditions. Therefore, the Court concluded that simply providing equal access to the office is an insufficient guarantee, since it should also include an effective protection of permanence once in office. From this perspective, in the opinion of the Inter-American Court, the State was giving different treatment to permanent judges and provisional judges, since it only provides a guarantee of protection to the former. For this reason, Reverón Trujillo "suffered arbitrary unequal treatment with respect to the right to stay, under conditions of equality." Notwithstanding that, according to the jurisprudence of the local courts, provisional judges are freely appointed, and the "right to stability" is reserved for career judges (Reverón Trujillo: 101 and 102). According to each type of judge, this difference of treatment is precisely what constitutes a violation of Article 23.1.c of the ADH Convention in connection with the obligations established in Article 1.1 thereof.

In sum, for the right to access public functions to be duly guaranteed, the State must create those conditions and mechanisms that are optimal for access to the public functions to be provided and for the individual to remain in them under "general conditions of equality" and without suffering discrimination. Regarding the alleged violation of Article 8.1, the Court established that two obligations arise from the right to a hearing. The first obligation is borne by judges, who must be independent, whereas the second one is borne by the State, which must respect and guarantee the individuals' right to be tried by an independent judge. The duty of respect consists of the obligation that public authorities have to refrain from undue interference with the Judicial Power or any of its members. In this context, the Court concluded that the right to be heard by an independent court, protected in Article 8.1 of the Convention, was not violated.[33] Lastly, from

29 *Ivi*: par. 139.

30 See more in: *López Mendoza* v. *Venezuela*, September 1, 2011.

31 See more in: *Yatama* v. *Nicaragua*, June 23, 2005; *Castañeda Gutman* v. *Mexico*, August 6, 2008; and *Argüelles et al. others* v. *Argentina*, November 20, 2014.

32 See more on this issue in: *Case of the Constitutional Court* v. *Peru*, January 31, 2001; *Chocrón Chocrón* v. *Venezuela*, July 1, 2011; *Constitutional Court (Camba Campos and others)* v. *Ecuador*, August 28, 2013; and *López Lone and others* v. *Honduras*, October 5, 2015.

33 *Reverón Trujillo* v. *Venezuela*, June 30, 2009, par. 148.

the various allegations presented by the parties, the Inter-American Court did not find a violation of the right to personal integrity, protected in Article 5.1 of the Convention, since no corresponding facts about the dismissal of Reverón Trujillo were specifically outlined in the complaint.

Measures of reparation

In light of all of the above, the Inter-American Court ordered the reinstatement of Reverón Trujillo to a position similar to the one she had held initially, as well as the payment of lost wages, as well as any social benefits that she had not received in the seven years that had elapsed since her dismissal.[34] The Court also ordered that any mention of her dismissal in the victim's file be immediately eliminated. The Court also established that, if the State failed to reinstate the victim to a judicial position within the next six months, compensation should be paid. Concerning the reparation measures for violating the victim's political rights and judicial protection, the Court determined that they should be included as part of non-pecuniary damages.[35] This is since the suffering that people experience due to the violation of such rights is not necessarily repaired economically.

Regarding the estimation of damages, the Inter-American Court has established a set of fundamental principles for its regulation. Damages are classified as either pecuniary or non-pecuniary. Pecuniary damages address the consequences of an economic nature and are directly related to the wrongful act. In contrast, non-pecuniary damages include "the suffering and afflictions caused to the victims, the impairment of very significant values for the people, as well as the alterations, of a non-pecuniary nature, in the living conditions of the victims."[36] These types of damages include moral, psychological, physical, and collective. In the present case, the Court ordered the State to pay the amount of US$30,000, or its equivalent in national currency, as compensation for non-pecuniary damages. As a guarantee of non-repetition, the Court also established that the State should, within a reasonable time, make the necessary adjustments to its domestic legislation, concerning its norms and practices with the removal of provisional judges. Also, it requested the publication of the judgment as a satisfaction measure and the payment of costs and expenses.

López Mendoza v. Venezuela

Case summary

Leopoldo López Mendoza has served, in recent years, as one of the leaders of the opposition against the regime of Nicolás Maduro. The case under analysis, called *López Mendoza* v. *Venezuela*, resolved by the Inter-American Court on

34 *Reverón Trujillo* v. *Venezuela*, June 30, 2009, par. 173.

35 See more in: *Cantoral Huamaní and García Santa Cruz* v. *Peru*, July 10, 2007.

36 *Ibidem.*

September 1, 2011, declares the international responsibility of the State for the violation of Articles 8.1, 23.1.b, and 23.2, in relation to Articles 1.1 and 2 of the American Convention on Human Rights. The above finding was based on the violation of Mr. López Mendoza´s right to be elected as a result of two sanctions of disqualification imposed on him by the Comptroller General of the Republic, based on Article 105 of the Organic Law of the Comptroller General of the Republic and the National System of Fiscal Control, in 2005, which impacted on his ability to exercise public functions. This constitutional article contemplated different sanctions for those who had been found to have breached administrative rules, meaning that they incurred responsibility, in addition to the payment of a fine, namely: suspension, dismissal, or disqualification.

In 2005, Leopoldo López was disqualified from holding public office as a result of two administrative proceedings. The first was for acts committed in 1998 while working as an analyst in the company Petróleos de Venezuela; and the second, for events that occurred in 2002, when Mr. López was mayor of the municipality of Chacao. While working in the Office of the Chief Economist of Petróleos de Venezuela, two donations were made to the civil association Primero Justicia, of which Mr. López was a founding member. These facts led to an administrative process to determine his responsibility for an alleged "conflict of interest." In October 2002, as mayor of the municipality of Chacao, Mr. López declared a partial shortage in some of the budget appropriations that he was due to transfer to the Metropolitan District of Caracas. As a result, an administrative process was also initiated against him because Mr. López had granted a different purpose to the respective budgetary funds than the one established by law.

Both administrative proceedings concluded with the imposition of a fine on Mr. López due to the declaration of administrative responsibility. Mr. López filed appeals for reconsideration to challenge these decisions, which were subsequently declared to be "without merit" by the Office of the Comptroller's Director of Accountability. Subsequently, between August and September 2005, the Comptroller issued resolutions which imposed the previous sanction of disqualification, for three and six years, based on the article mentioned above. Mr. López filed the respective appeals for reconsideration to challenge the resolutions; however, they were declared "without place" by the Republic's Comptroller General. The victim again challenged this refusal before the Political-Administrative Chamber of the Supreme Court of Justice, which ruled in the same vein as the previous authorities. Mr. López Mendoza also challenged the constitutionality of Article 105 of the Organic Law of the Comptroller's Office. The Constitutional Chamber that heard the case declared the appeal "without merit" when it analysed the compatibility of Articles 42 and 65 of the Venezuelan Constitution with the aforementioned impugned precept.

Finally, Leopoldo López Mendoza aspired, in 2008, to be mayor of the Metropolitan District of Caracas; however, the National Electoral Council, upon approving the norms regulating the nomination of candidates for the general election that year, determined that those who were subject to disqualification were not eligible for these positions. Mr. López could not register his candidacy that year, through the web platform that the National Electoral Council had created to record the nominations, as his name was found to have been placed in the database of politically disqualified persons.

Reasoning developed by the regional court with a specific focus on Article 23 of the American Convention on Human Rights

The reasoning used by the Court to determine the international responsibility of the State for the violation of Article 23 of the American Convention has a direct bearing on the nature of the authority that imposed the sanction of disqualification on Mr. López Mendoza. The Court understood that its duty in the case was to analyse whether or not the sanctions imposed by an administrative body, which resulted in the impossibility of registering his candidacy, were compatible with the American Convention.

Article 23 of the American Convention contains in its first paragraph the essential core of political rights;[37] and in its second paragraph, the applicable grounds and requirements for "restricting" these rights.[38] As Mr. López's disqualification derives from a "sanction" by the State, it should be a "conviction, by a competent judge, in criminal proceedings," in terms of the second paragraph of Article 23 of the Convention. The sanction imposed on the victim did not meet any of these three requirements: the organ that imposed the sanction was not a "competent judge," there was no "conviction," and the sanctions were not applied as a result of "criminal proceedings."[39] This was sufficient to consider that the State had violated Articles 23.1.b and 23.2 in relation to Article 1.1 of the Convention.

Regardless of the preceding, the Court reviewed the compatibility of the actions taken during the administrative sanction proceedings against Mr. López Mendoza and the guarantees of due process contained in Article 8 of the Convention. From this analysis, the Court concluded that: there had been no violation of Mr. López Mendoza's right to defence and right to appeal the sanctioning decision; his presumption of innocence had not been violated; and that the proceedings had been conducted within a reasonable time. However, the Court did determine that the rulings' lack of reasoning for imposing the respective sanctions was evident. In the Court's terms, "the Comptroller had to develop

37 The first part of Article 23 states: "All citizens shall enjoy the following rights and opportunities: (a) to take part in the conduct of public affairs, directly or through freely chosen representatives; (b) to vote and to be elected at genuine periodic elections which shall be by universal and equal suffrage and shall be held by secret ballot, guaranteeing the free expression of the will of the electors; and (c) to have access, on general terms of equality, to public service in their country."

38 Article 23.2: "The law may regulate the exercise of the rights and opportunities referred to in the previous paragraph, exclusively on the grounds of age, nationality."

39 As mentioned in the summary of the case, the sanction was imposed administratively by the Comptroller General of the Republic and reviewed by the Political Administrative Chamber of the Supreme Court of Justice.

specific reasons and grounds for the gravity and entity of the offense allegedly committed by Mr. López Mendoza and for the proportionality of the sanction adopted."[40] The lack of reasoning turned the sanction of disqualification from running for office into an almost automatic formulation, "through a procedural incident that ends up being a mere formality." Therefore, the State was declared responsible for the violation of the content of Article 8.1 in relation to 1.1 of the Convention.

Finally, regarding the duty to adopt domestic law provisions contained in Article 2 of the Convention,

> by not complying with the requirement of predictability and, furthermore, taking into account the fact that Article 105 of the [Organic Law on the Office of the Comptroller General of the Republic and the National System of Fiscal Control] allows for the restriction of the right to be elected by an authority that is not a criminal judge,

the Court concluded that in the instant case Articles 8.1, 23.1.b, and 23.2, in relation to Articles 1.1 and 2 of the American Convention were violated.

Measures of reparation

For the human rights violations described in the previous section, the Court ordered a series of specific reparation measures. As a restitution measure, the Court ordered that the State, through its competent organs, ensure that the sanctions of disqualification imposed on Mr. Leopoldo López constituting an impediment to his candidacy to register as a candidate in electoral processes be suspended following the issuance of the judgment. It also ordered that the State was to leave without effect, the resolutions issued by the Comptroller General of the Republic, by which the disqualification of Mr. López Mendoza had been declared.

As a measure of satisfaction, the Court ordered the State to publish, within six months of the notification of the judgment, the official summary of the judgment prepared by the Court in the Official Gazette and in a newspaper of wide national circulation. In addition, it was to publish the complete judgment, for a period of one year, on an official website. As a guarantee of non-repetition, the Court ordered the State to adapt the content of Article 105 of the Organic Law of the Office of the Comptroller General of the Republic and the National System of Fiscal Control within a reasonable time, as determined in the judgment; however, the Court held that "based on the control of conventionality, it is necessary that judicial and administrative interpretations and judicial guarantees be applied, in accordance with the principles established in the jurisprudence of this Court that

40 *López Mendoza* v. *Venezuela*, September 1, 2011: par. 147.

have been reiterated in the instant case."[41] Finally, the Court ordered that taking into account the arguments and observations of the parties, as well as the evidence provided, the State should deliver the amount of US$12,000 to the victim, by way of costs and expenses.

Analysis of the legal and economic impact of the implementation of the judgments of the Inter-American Court at the national level

Reverón Trujillo v. Venezuela

Article 63.1 of the American Convention establishes that, whenever it is determined that a right or freedom contained in it has been violated, the Inter-American Court has the power to request the reparation of damages and the payment of fair compensation in favour of the victim, as a guarantee of the enjoyment of the violated right or freedom. The jurisprudence indicates that the reparation of damages must be adequately fulfilled by a State whenever an illicit act is attributable to it, in virtue of the international responsibility that arises from the violation of an international norm, and the obligation of the responsible State to repair and cease such violation.[42] In general terms, reparation measures are classified as satisfaction and compensation. In addition, three factors must be taken into account when determining them, which can be either individually or jointly: "justice, non-repetition of the facts and public recognition of responsibility or satisfaction."[43]

Pecuniary compensation by the responsible State is especially relevant in the present case. Its main purpose is to remedy the damage caused to the injured parties. This concept includes the payment of expenses and costs incurred by the victim or her next of kin, which derive from her legal representation throughout the different domestic and international proceedings.[44] Upon addressing the application of remedies in the present case, the Court obliged the State to reinstate the victim to her position. Nevertheless, it also established that, if the victim could not be reinstated into the Judiciary within 6 months from the date that the sentence was notified, the State would have to pay compensation of US$60,000, or its equivalent in the national currency, within a maximum period of 18 months. Regarding lost wages, the Court ordered the payment of US$150,000, payable within a maximum of one year. Concerning non-pecuniary damages, the Court assessed an estimated penalty of US$30,000 and a further US$30,000 for the payment of costs and expenses.

41 *Ivi*: par 228.

42 Ventura Robles M., *Impact of the reparations ordered by the Inter-American Court of Human Rights and contributions to the justiciability of economic, social and cultural rights*, in IIDH Magazine, vol. 56, 2012, 139–156. Available at: "www.corteidh.or.cr/tablas/r30350.pdf"

43 *Ibidem*.

44 *Ivi*: 141.

Accordingly, remedies in the present case involve either a primary set of measures for compliance with the judgment or a unique set of measures in the event of an external impediment to compliance with it. In the first case – of primary measures – reparation of damages and a total compensation of US$210,000, payable within a maximum period of 1 year, of the handing down of the judgment. Thus, considering that the ruling was issued on June 30, 2009, the amount would have to be paid before July 1, 2010. In the second case – of exceptional measures – applicable if the victim was not reinstated in her judicial position, reparation would total US$270,000, to be paid in a maximum period of 18 months, starting from the notification of the judgment. Thus, the deadline for payment would be January 1, 2011.

However, according to the Inter-American Court, as of today, the Venezuelan State has not complied with the reparation measures imposed upon it. The representatives of the victim have expressed that the only measure that the State has complied with so far is the approval of the Code of Ethics for the Venezuelan Judges, which, in their opinion, did not comply materially with the requirements of the particular judgment, since it did not meet the minimum requirements that the Court demanded as necessary for an independent judicial system. Moreover, the Court concluded that, given Venezuela's failure so far to comply with its obligation to report on the adopted measures, it lacks the necessary information in order to confirm whether the State has repaired the damage as instructed.

In this context, it is essential to assess the economic impact that the judgment would have on the responsible State from a quantitative perspective. To that end, it is worth making a couple of clarifications. First, the price of the official US dollar on the last day of the second semester of 2010 (date of the judgment) was 4.281155 bolivares. Therefore, in the primary measures, it would be equivalent to (210 × 4.281155) = $900,753 bolivares. In contrast, by applying the exceptional measures – specified above – it would be equivalent to (270 × 4.281155) = $1,158,111 bolivares. Second, an update of the economic impact, without considering the accumulated inflation, would elevate the amount of the damages, as of today, to a total equivalent to $25,174,632,949.57, in the case of primary measures, and $32,367,385,220.88, in the case of exceptional measures.

The economic impact of the judgment is visible when compared with the budget assigned for 2010.[45] Had Venezuela complied with the penalty that same year, the judgment would represent 0.000726516% of its budget.[46] In contrast, to this day, it would equal 0.012843283% of its budget.[47] These figures can be compared in the following tables:

45 The budget for 2010 is available at: "https://transparencia.org.ve/wp-content/uploads/2016/07/02.1.-Ley-de-Presupuesto-2010-T%C3%ADtulo-I-II .pdf"

46 In accordance with the 2010 Budget Law, issued by the National Assembly, the budget for expenditure and Financial Applications of the Republic was estimated at $159,406,061,762 bolivares. That is, $37,163,654,153.82 dollars.

47 The budget is unofficial, as the Budget Law for fiscal year 2020 has yet to be published. Neither has the Official Gazette No. 6,495. It is estimated that the budget is 252,018 billion

Table 15.1 Penalty equivalent to $210,000 US dollars

Year	*Value of the dollar*	*Equivalent in national currency*	*Annual budget*	*US Dollar*	*Equivalent to the budget*
			National currency		
2010	$4.289300	$900,753.00	$159,406,061,762.00	$37,163,654,154	0.000565068%
2020	$119,879.20	$25,174,632,949.58	$252,018,000,000,000.00	$2,102,266,202.09	0.00998922%

Table 15.2 Penalty equivalent to $270,000 US dollars

Year	*Value of the dollar*	*Equivalent in national currency*	*Annual budget*	*Equivalent to the budget*	
			National currency	*US dollar*	
2010	$4.289300	$1,158,111.00	$159,406,061,762.00	$37,163,654,154	0.00072652%
2020	$119,879.20	$32,367,385,220.88	$252,018,000,000,000.00	$2,102,266,202.09	0.01284328%

Table 15.3 Penalty talking inflation into account Information available at: "www.inflation.eu/es/tasas-de-inflacion/estados-unidos/inflacion-historica/ipc-infl acion-estados-unidos.aspx"

210,000.00	Penalty 2010	1	
270,000.00	Penalty 2010	2	
	Inflation	Penalty 1	Penalty 2
IPC United States 2019	2.29%	246,211.86	316,558.11
IPC United States 2018	1.91%	240,699.83	309,471.21
IPC United States 2017	2.11%	236,188.63	303,671.10
IPC United States 2016	2.07%	231,308.03	297,396.04
IPC United States 2015	0.73%	226,617.06	291,364.79
IPC United States 2014	0.76%	224,974.74	289,253.24
IPC United States 2013	1.50%	223,277.83	287,071.50
IPC United States 2012	1.74%	219,978.16	282,829.06
IPC United States 2011	2.96%	216,216.00	277,992.00

Table 15.4 Penalty until 2019

2019	*Budget*	*$167,322,158,870,000.00*	
	US dollar	*National currency 46620.83 bolivar per US dollar*	*Equivalent to the annual budget*
Penalty 1	246,211.86	11,478,601,269.04	0.00686018%
Penalty 2	316,558.11	14,758,201,831.43	0.00882023%

In the best of cases, if we take into account the accumulated inflation of the past few years, the updated figure that we have is as follows:

In sum, it is evident that the economic quantification of the present judgment does not represent a significant expenditure in relation to the annual budget of a State such as the Bolivarian State of Venezuela. Therefore, we can make a preliminary conclusion that Venezuela's non-compliance with the judgment is due to a lack of political will.

López Mendoza v. Venezuela

To date, the Inter-American Court of Human Rights has issued an order on the Monitoring of Compliance with Judgment in *López Mendoza* v. *Venezuela's* case. In it, the Court takes note of a resolution of the Constitutional Chamber of the Venezuelan Supreme Court of Justice. It held that the judgment issued in the López Mendoza case was "unenforceable." The Constitutional Chamber argued that: a) the Venezuelan Constitution does not grant international treaties

bolivars or 2,102,266,202.09 dollars "https://transparencia.org.ve/wp-content/uploads/2020/04/Bolet%C3%ADn-Finanzas-PRepúblicas-—-Transparencia -Venezuela-1.pdf"

"supra constitutional" status, so the Venezuelan Judiciary is empowered to decide on the contradictions that may arise between any international treaty and the Constitution itself; b) there are other international treaties ratified by Venezuela, such as the Inter-American Convention against Corruption and the United Nations Convention against Corruption, from whose interpretation different conclusions may be inferred from those issued in the *López Mendoza* v. *Venezuela* judgment.

The Chamber also argued that the ruling was unenforceable because the Inter-American Court usurped functions as "if it were a colonial power and pretended to impose on a sovereign and independent country political and ideological criteria incompatible with the national system."[48] It is not the first time that Venezuela has brought before the Court such considerations in response to a failure to comply with a sentence in which it has been condemned; in the case of *Apitz Barbera et al.*, the State used the same arguments. Hence, the Court brought up the resolution of November 23, 2012, in which it indicated that the State "could not justify non-compliance with the Judgment in a decision of a domestic court that disregards the orders of the Judgment, even if it is the highest court in the national legal system."[49] The Court stated that the mere existence of a ruling in a domestic jurisdiction that considers a judgment of the Inter-American Court as "unenforceable" ignores the basic principles of international law on which the implementation of the American Convention is based. [50]

The Court considered that such a resolution: a) evidences an action contrary to the international principle of good faith in fulfilling the obligations that inspire the Inter-American Human Rights System; b) prevents the useful effect of the Convention and its application in the specific case; and c) ignores the principle of international res judicata and makes illusory the right to access Inter-American justice of the victims of human rights violations, which generates impunity. Therefore, the Court considered that the State was not complying with the provisions of Article 68 of the Convention; and applied, in a reasoned manner, Article 65 of the Convention in order to submit to the General Assembly of the Organization of American States the clear breach of the judgment.[51] The logic of submission to the General Assembly when a manifest breach occurs is to avoid rendering the useful effect of the American Convention illusory by leaving it to the domestic decisions of each State. [52]

48 Order on the Monitoring of Compliance with Judgment in *López Mendoza* v. *Venezuela's* case, November 20, 2015: par. 6.

49 *Ivi*: par. 8.

50 *Ibídem*.

51 Submission to the General Assembly, in the Court's terms, functions as a "collective guarantee" in which all States Parties must make every effort to ensure that there is no evident abandonment by States of their obligation to comply with and abide by the Court's judgments.

52 The State completed none of the five measures of reparation ordered by the Court; among them, the only one that required a direct monetary outlay was the one that ordered payment of the amount established in the judgment for the items and expenses of the proceeding.

The case of Leopoldo López fits a pattern in which the State uses, apparently legal figures and mechanisms, to attack political opponents. Following the sentence under analysis, the situation did not improve. Proof of this is the very history of Leopoldo López. In 2014, he was accused by the Maduro government of inciting violence during the public protests that took place that year. Because of these events, Leopoldo was held in the Ramo Verde military prison until August 2017, when he was granted house arrest until his release in 2019. The imprisonment of Mr. López Mendoza was condemned by many organisations, national and international, that defend human rights since he and other opponents of the regime were considered political prisoners.

Within the institutional uncertainty that Venezuela is experiencing, it is essential to mention that Juan Guaidó, who appears as "President in Charge of the Republic of Venezuela," deposited before the Organization of American States a new ratification of the American Convention on Human Rights on July 31, 2019. The effects of this ratification are uncertain since although the update corresponding to this legal act appears on the OAS website, the position of the regime that, de facto, controls the institutions in Venezuela has not changed. The ratification document in question also recognises the contentious jurisdiction of the Inter-American Court of Human Rights. In the same sense, Juan Guadió ratified Venezuela's will to remain as part of the OAS. [53]

Even though the above might seem to be transcendental news, the Inter-American Commission barely dedicates a paragraph to it in its 2019 Annual Report, without offering any press releases or other resolutions where it states the legal implications of this ratification, in view of the "duplicity" of authorities. Regardless of this, the Inter-American Commission continues to monitor the human rights situation in Venezuela. So far in 2020 alone, the Commission has granted 10 "precautionary measures" for situations of extreme gravity and urgency denounced before this body.[54] Also, in early 2020 the Commission attempted to make an on-site visit to Venezuela.[55] This visit could not be in fact be made in Venezuelan territory due to the State's refusal; however, the

53 On January 25, 2019, it issued Resolution 1/2019 by which it granted precautionary measures in favour of Juan Gerardo Guaidó Márquez and his family, since he was "the most visible figure of opposition in a context of great political agitation and profound social convulsion, which has led to the mobilization of thousands of people in the streets of Venezuela, where acts of violence have taken place."

54 For example: on February 5, 2020, through resolution 5/2020, the Commission granted precautionary measures in favour of Williams Alberto Aguado Sequera and other persons, both military and civilian, who are deprived of their liberty in the National Center for Military Processors, known as "Ramo Verde." The Commission alleged that the beneficiaries are at risk due to the state of health and lack of access to adequate medical treatment. Furthermore, some of the persons deprived of their liberty have also suffered injuries as a result of the treatment they received at the time of detention and which were not attended to afterward.

55 The Commission's last on-site visit to Venezuela was in 2002. Since that date, the Commission has attempted on multiple occasions, without success, to monitor the human rights situation in the country.

Commission visited the city of Cúcuta, Colombia, on the border with Venezuela. During its stay at this border, the Commission noted the severe effects of the humanitarian crisis as a factor in the displacement of millions of Venezuelans. [56]

The "official" position from Venezuela on the role played by the organs of the Inter-American Human Rights System, and even the OAS, continues to be one of repudiation. However, it is important to mention that, within the compliance supervision resolutions, it is possible to account for the fact that, in December 2017, the Venezuelan State made a payment to the Secretariat of the Inter-American Court for "reimbursement to the victims legal assistance fund" in the cases of *Uzcátegui et al., Hermanos Landaeta Mejías et al.* and *Familia Barrios.* The amount amounted to US$12,116.78. With the above, the State complied with the measures ordered in these judgments on the payment of the costs of the substantive stage of the procedure.[57] Within the section on compliance supervision, this is the last contribution made by Venezuela as part of its obligations before the Court.

Conclusions

The judgment in the case of *Reverón Trujillo* v. *Venezuela* reaffirms the view adopted by the Inter-American Court in the case of *Apitz Barbera et al.* v. *Venezuela*, in the sense that the scope of Article 23.1 guarantees access to public office under general conditions of equality, and that such a safeguard extends to the criteria and procedure for appointments, promotion, suspension, and dismissal. In other words, the Court emphasised that reasonable and objective causes must be met in each of the indicated stages, while ensuring as well that people are not discriminated against. In the present case, as observed, the judge was not reinstated into office because her appointment was "provisional." Here, a difference in treatment was noted between permanent judges, who enjoy a full tenure guarantee, and provisional judges, who lack any protection in relation to their permanence. In the opinion of the High Court, these circumstances do not follow reasonable or objective criteria. Thus, the Inter-American Court established that Reverón Trujillo suffered unequal and arbitrary treatment concerning the right to remain in the exercise of public functions under conditions of equality, which constitutes a violation of Article 23.1 of the American Convention.

56 According to the Commission: "On February 6 and 7, from the city of Cúcuta, the IACHR held numerous meetings with congressmen and journalists in exile, victims' groups living in Colombia, and others who came from Venezuela, particularly from the states of Táchira and Zulia. The Commission also held working meetings with international organizations such as the United Nations Agency for Refugees, the International Organization for Migration, and the United Nations Office on Drugs and Crime. Additionally, the IACHR held virtual meetings with civil society organizations and victims' groups connected from different cities within and outside Venezuela."

57 In the same resolution, the Court recognised that in the case of the Barrios Family, a balance of US$559.15 is pending. Order of the Inter-American Court of Human Rights of November 21, 2018. Reimbursement of Victims' Legal Assistance Fund in the Cases of *Barrios family, Uzcátegui et al.*, and *Landaeta Mejías Brothers et al. v. Venezuela.*

Ten years after the judgment was delivered, the Venezuelan State authorities have not expressed any willingness to comply with the judgment issued by the Inter-American Court. As observed, this non-compliance is, to a large extent, due to a lack of political will, given that the economic penalty (reparation of damages, lost wages, and compensation) represents only a micro percentage of the total budget of Venezuela. Therefore, it is possible to affirm that the economic impact of the judgment is not nearly the problem, rather it is instead down to the State's stance of ignoring the Inter-American authorities and questioning the binding effect of their resolutions. Finally, despite the worrying human rights crisis in Venezuela, the State continues to be reluctant to comply with the Inter-American Court's judgments. It has openly spoken out against the Inter-American Court on several occasions. However, it remains subject to the quasi-jurisdiction of the Inter-American Commission on Human Rights and the political and economic sanctions of the Organization of American States.

In this context, it is no surprise that the Supreme Court of Justice of Venezuela has disregarded the various judgments against the Venezuelan State,[58] considering that since 1999 it has not issued a single ruling that opposes pro-government interests.[59] In addition, President Nicolás Maduro has claimed, on more than one occasion, that he has been prey to an alleged smear campaign by the States under the jurisdiction of the Inter-American Court. In sum, the leading cause of non-compliance with a resolution of the Inter-American Court of Human Rights is the lack of political will and the national government's resistance to respect for the human rights of the people and their full restoration in the event of their violation. The international community is particularly concerned about the evident disdain and contempt for the respect of the human rights of all Venezuelans.[60]

The institutional crisis that Venezuela is going through has meant a deterioration in terms of respect for and guarantee of political rights. The Executive Power, interfering with the other powers of the State, has led and orchestrated

58 The Supreme Court declared the *Apitz Barbera et al.* sentence unconstitutional "for usurping powers of the internal Venezuelan authorities." For instance, in a case dealing with the allegedly wrongful removal of a judge, the CPAM held that "[The] legal judgment [of the removed judge] was reasonable and based on a decision adopted in the legitimate exercise of her functions, that is, [...] at no point did it constitute the serious infraction of which she was accused by the [CORJS], for the purposes of applying the highest sanction, that is, removal from her position. Accordingly, the aforementioned Commission usurped the powers of the jurisdictional sphere and, in so doing, robbed her of the constitutional guarantee of autonomy and independence that the sanctioned judge possessed at the time of the aforesaid decision." CPAM, *Judgment num. 01771*, October 14, 2004. Available at: "www.corteidh .or.cr/do cs/casos/articulos/seriec_182_ing.pdf"

59 Bandeira Galindo, George Rodrigo (2013): "The value of the jurisprudence of the Inter-American Court of Human Rights," in *Multilevel Protection of Human Rights*, 255–273. Available at: "www.upf.edu/dhes-alfa/materiales /res/pmdh_pdf/PMDH_Manual.255-274.pdf"

60 See "Report of the United Nations Office for Human Rights on Venezuela urges the immediate adoption of measures to stop and remedy serious violations of rights." Available at: "www.ohchr.org/SP/NewsE"

a persecution against its opponents; in the first instance, by using judicial and "apparently legal" mechanisms; and, secondly, through various acts of repression such as the deprivation of liberty or censorship.[61] The story of Leopoldo López, who was a victim of political rights violations in terms of the Inter-American Court, is proof of this. After being disqualified from participating in the elections, Mr. López was considered a "political prisoner" of the regime in the world´s eyes. Leopoldo López's sentence was filed under the terms of Article 65 of the Convention for non-compliance like many others in which Venezuela has been condemned.

Finally, the situation in Venezuela, rather than improving, has worsened in recent years. Attempts by the opposition to take power, with the international community's support, have not been strong enough to weaken Nicolás Maduro´s regime. Venezuela's return to the Inter-American Human Rights System, through the ratification of the Convention by opposition leader Juan Guaidó, has not represented progress in the enforcement of existing judgments of the Inter-American Court. The situation in Venezuela, and the evolution of the crisis, should be taken by the other States of the region as an example of the weakening of the rule of law and the violation of the principles that govern a democratic society. Not recognising the above in this sense puts the democratic advances of the Latin American region at risk.

Bibliography

Bandeira Galindo G., *The value of the jurisprudence of the Inter-American Court of Human Rights*, in Multilevel Protection of Human Rights, 2013.

Carao A., *Unconstitutionality of the denunciation of the American Convention on Human Rights by Venezuela*, in Yearbook of Latin American Constitutional Law, year XIX, Bogotá, 2013.

Inter-American Commission on Human Rights, *Denunciation and departure of Venezuela from the Inter-American Court of Human Rights*, 2013.

Inter-American Commission on Human Rights, Recognition of the jurisdiction of the Court.

PSUV, *28 años de la masacre de El Amparo*, on psuv.org, 29 October, 2016.

Ventura Robles M., *Impact of the reparations ordered by the Inter-American Court of Human Rights and contributions to the justiciability of economic, social and cultural rights*, in IIDH Magazine, vol. 56, 2012, 139–156.

Vittorio C., *Implementation of the judgments and resolutions of the Inter-American Court of Human Rights: a necessary debate*, in IIDH Magazine, vol. 49, 2009.

61 For example: In the *Alvarez Ramos* case, issued on 2019, the Court declared Venezuela internationally responsible for the violation of Mr. Tulio Alvarez Ramos' rights to freedom of expression, political participation, circulation, judicial guarantees, and judicial protection, due to criminal proceedings filed against him and the consequent condemnation which followed the publication of an opinion article on alleged irregularities in the management of the Venezuelan National Assembly's Savings Bank.

Part III

An empirical assessment based on political economy

16 The Relationship between the Courts of Human Rights decisions and voter turnout

An empirical analysis on Europe and Latin America

Simone Pellegrino and Gilberto Turati *

Introduction

Voter participation is vital for democracy. This might explain why, during the last two decades, increasing effort has been devoted towards research on voter turnout. Given the significant variability observed in the data, research has been carried out at both the national and sub-national levels and across many different countries around the world. According to the available literature, several institutional and socio-economic variables help to explain voter participation. These include country characteristics at the macro-level (such as population size, the level of economic inequality, the level of economic development), proxies for voters' preferences (like the age composition of the population, indicators for altruism or for corruption), as well as political variables (like the level of campaign expenditure and competition among candidates, the type of electoral system, the level of political fragmentation in the jurisdiction). However, voter turnout can also depend on how citizens perceive the rules defining voting rights in each country. And these perceptions may be influenced by the decisions of Courts, such as the European Court of Human Rights (hereafter, ECHR) and the Inter-American Court of Human Rights (hereafter, IACHR), when decisions are being made about violations of voting rights.

Unlike the other chapters in this book, our aim here is to provide a quantitative analysis of the correlation between the judgments of both the ECHR and the IACHR and voter turnout. We do so first by building an extensive and original dataset containing all the decisions made by the two Courts to date and the type of judgments they have made. The dataset also includes information on voter turnout for different types of elections in all the countries under the jurisdiction of the two Courts (46 countries for Europe and 25 for Latin America), as well as information on the countries' political and economic characteristics. By controlling a number of important variables which the literature deems to be important in explaining voter turnout, we then estimate a multivariate regression model which allows us to assess the relationship between turnout and the

* We would like to thank Irene Valotti for valuable research assistance in building the dataset. The usual disclaimers apply.

DOI: 10.4324/9781003229247-20

decisions made by the Courts in both Europe and Latin America. Our findings suggest very different patterns of correlation in Europe as compared to Latin America, and a large heterogeneity across different countries within them. In both cases, whether the country has experienced limitations in the functioning of the democratic process is important in determining the signs of correlation. As for European countries, for which results are much stronger given the higher number of judgments in comparison with Latin America, we find that judgments have a positive correlation on voters' participation, but this correlation turns negative for countries belonging to the former Yugoslavia and the former Warsaw Pact. For Latin American countries, the small number of judgments suggest caution in making an interpretation: we do find that judgments reduce participation, but the correlation turns positive in relation to military dictatorships.

The remainder of the chapter is structured as follows. We first discuss the main findings of the literature examining voter turnout. We then present our empirical analysis, starting from the description of the data and the modelling strategy, and finally the results. We draw some conclusions in the last section.

What do we know about voter turnout?

The issue of voter turnout has attracted growing interest from many researchers across different disciplines over the last two decades (e.g., Cancela and Geys, 2016). Scholars from disciplines like political science, economics, law, sociology, psychology (Harder and Krosnick, 2008), and also biology (Fowler et al., 2008; Fowler and Schreiber, 2008) have discussed and analysed the topic. Research has mainly been devoted to understanding the motivations behind the observed changes in voting participation across time and space, and, in particular, to explaining the decline in voter participation observed in many countries during the previous decades.

In this section we primarily focus our attention on the literature in respect of economics, seeking to highlight the main findings. Researchers have followed different approaches, including theoretical (i.e., Downs, 1957; Matsusaka, 1995; Coate and Conlin, 2004; Geys, 2006b; Degan and Merlo, 2011; Smith et al., 2017), experimental (Bowler et al., 2001; Sondheimer and Green, 2010; Gerber et al., 2020) as well as empirical papers, on which we will now focus.

There are numerous empirical investigations, each of them evaluating several dimensions, according to the availability of data, but with a focus in particular on specific variables. In explaining people's propensity to vote, the most discussed covariates can be split into macro variables (characterising the environment in which voters cast their votes) and micro variables (characterising the voters). A potential classification includes the following groups:

(i) variables reflecting the political and institutional characteristics of the country: the political systems (Francia and Herrnson, 2004; De Paola and Scoppa, 2014; Wilford, 2017; Bornschier, 2019), the characteristics of the electoral systems (Blais and Aarts, 2006), the different levels of government involved (Andersen et al. 2014; Cancela and Geys, 2016; Sørensen, 2019);

(ii) variables reflecting political supply: the number of parties and political competition (Francia and Herrnson, 2004; De Paola and Scoppa, 2014; Wilford, 2017; Bornschier, 2019), the variety of platforms offered by parties to their electorates (Hobolt and Hoerner, 2019), the role of campaign spending (Matsusaka and Palda, 1999);

(iii) variables reflecting the economic characteristics of the country: socio-economic differences (Lahtinen et al, 2019), GDP per capita and GDP growth rate, the distribution of income within a society and class conflicts (Winders, 1999), the level of taxation and public spending (Percival et al, 2007) and public debt (Roubini and Sachs, 1989);

(iv) variables reflecting voters' characteristics: demographic variables, such as age and education (Nagler, 1991; Grasso, 2013), race (Filer, 1991), gender (De Paola et al., 2014), nationality (Tuckel and Maisel, 2008), family structure (Wolfinger and Wolfinger, 2008), residential mobility (Squire et al, 1987), disability (Schur, 2002), the level of satisfaction with democracy (Ezrow and Xezonakis, 2016);

(v) variables characterising possible external influence on voters: the role of television (Gentzkow, 2006; Sørensen, 2019) and mass media (Banning, 2006; Larcinese, 2007); the role of military influence on government (Beck et al., 2001).

All these variables affect the probability of voting, as will be discussed in greater detail below.

For what concerns the geographical dimension, several papers have dealt with cross-country empirical investigations. For example, Kostadinova (2003) and Pacek et al. (2009) focus their attention on post-Communist European countries, whilst Jackman (1987), Jackman and Miller (1995), Gray and Caul (2000) and Bischoff (2012) focus on industrial democracies; Fornos et al. (2004) focuses on Latin America, Kuenzi and Lambright (2007) focus on Africa; and Dettrey and Schwindt-Bayer (2009) focus on presidential democracies. There are also papers focusing on single countries: for instance, De Paola et al. (2014), De Paola and Scoppa (2014) and De Benedetto and De Paola (2019) focus on Italy, Lehoucq and Wall (2004) focus on Guatemala, Larcinese (2007) focuses on the UK, and many others focus on the United States (i.e., Nagler, 1991; Winders, 1999; Bowler et al., 2001; McDonald, 2002; Francia and Herrnson, 2004). Very few of the papers base their analysis on very large datasets: for example, Beck et al. (2001) consider 177 countries and 113 variables over the period 1975–1995; their main goal is to create an exhaustive and comprehensive dataset useful both for cross-country investigations and for single-country studies over time. Very few are also single-country studies considering a significant time span: for instance, Winders (1999) studies voter turnout in the US over the period 1840–1996, identifying four phases in which voter turnout changed significantly and explaining these findings in light of class conflicts and mass mobilisation.

Another important difference that characterised the literature on voter turnout is the focus on aggregate data or individual-level data. Geys (2006a) considered and classified papers on this topic by employing aggregate data published between 1968–2004, whilst Smets and van Ham (2013) discuss 90 papers employing individual data published between 2000–2010. Finally, Cancela and Geys (2016) extended the dataset employed by Geys (2006a) up to 185 papers and provided updated results.

A separate discussion is to be deserved for papers based on natural or quasi-natural experiments. This recent strand of study tries to establish a causal link between certain specific variables and voter turnout, exploiting exogenous changes in the institutional rules characterising a country. For example, Sondheimer and Green (2010) use a natural experiment to study a very important issue: the link between voter turnout and education. It is undoubtedly the case that there is a correlation between the two variables at least at the individual level, voter participation being less likely for less educated people. On the contrary, there is no clear view in the literature on the causal link between education and participation. By employing two randomised experiments and one quasi-experiment, the authors argue "*that exogenously induced changes in high school graduation rates have powerful effects on voter turnout rates. These results imply that the correlation between education and turnout is indeed causal.*" Other papers, like Gerber et al. (2020), employ a mixed empirical strategy, using both lab experiments and real data, trying to understand whether voters' beliefs about election closeness matter in explaining turnout.

Turning to the strand of literature which considers cross-country aggregate empirical works and employs multivariate regression analyses, we have focused on those based on data similar to that which we have used here. This literature focuses primarily on socio-economic and institutional characteristics in order to study their effect on turnout rates. As Cancela and Geys (2016) pointed out, all the papers they consider include at least one of the 14 most relevant covariates, such as: *economic variables (i.e. population size, population concentration, population stability, income homogeneity, ethnic homogeneity, proportion of minorities, and past turnout), political variables (i.e. electoral closeness, campaign expenditures, and political fragmentation), and institutional variables (i.e. electoral system, compulsory voting, concurrent elections and registration requirements).*

Most of this literature, which is based on several different factors, including the geographical area under study, provides mixed evidence. In this respect, every world macro-zone or group of countries is characterised by a specific institutional historical evolution. For instance, in post-Communist countries, the democratisation process experienced during the 90s (with the introduction of rules for universal suffrage) enlarged the political choice, and one of the main consequences was the increase of mass participation; this effect has lost its influence over time, because of both the level of corruption and the economic situation which has discouraged political participation (Kostadinova, 2003). With respect to these countries, Kostadinova (2003) emphasises that the empirical evidence is also mixed in relation to the impact of the number of parties and the levels of participation. Another example is Latin America: as we argue below, military dictatorships may help in explaining a different effect of voter turnout with respect to developed democracies. Fornos et al. (2004) identified that turnout in Latin American countries is mostly affected by institutional and political variables, whereas socio-economic variables do not play a crucial role.

Other groups of variables lead to results that are more robust; for example, the role of institutions on voter turnout seems to be confirmed in this literature. Focusing on the 14 most important and discussed covariates, Cancela and Geys (2016) summarised the expected effects of each variable (a discussion on the direction of the a priori expected effects for each variable is discussed in Geys (2006a)) and evaluated statistics on the results of all the papers on this topic. In particular, Geys (2006a) categorises a "success" when the coefficient is significant in the predicted direction, a "failure" when it is not significant, and an "anomaly" when it is significant in the wrong direction. They then evaluated an index of the success of each covariate (also proposing an index using the ratio, at the numerator, of the difference between the number of successful cases and the number of anomalous cases, and, at the denominator, the total number of tests). According to these rules: population size is expected to negatively affect voter turnout and this is verified in 57% of tests; population concentration is also expected to negatively affect participation and this is verified only in 33% of cases; and so on for all of the most important covariates: population stability (positive effect, 78%); income homogeneity (positive effect, 11%); ethnic homogeneity (positive, 50%); proportion of minorities (negative, 66%); past turnout (positive, 86%); closeness of election (positive, 69%); campaign expenditures (positive, 83%); fragmentation (positive, 19%); electoral system (positive effect for proportional system, 53%); compulsory vote (positive, 86%), concurrent election (positive, 63%); registration requirements (negative, 91%).

For what concerns elections at differing levels of governments, voter turnout can be affected by different covariates depending on the type of election. In this respect, Cancela and Geys (2016) found that "*campaign expenditures, election closeness and registration requirements have more explanatory power in national elections, whereas population size and composition, concurrent elections, and the electoral system play a more important role for explaining turnout in subnational elections.*"

Empirical analysis

Data

The aim of our empirical analysis is to understand if and how decisions by the ECHR and the IACHR are related to voter participation in countries under their jurisdiction. As is clear from the previous section, the existing literature has not yet focused any attention on this issue, so our aim is to make the first step towards filling this gap. To this end, we have created an original dataset including all the 47 European countries under the jurisdiction of the ECHR and the 25 countries of Southern and Central America under the jurisdiction of the IACHR (including the 5 countries that have ratified the Inter-American Convention). The dataset includes data on voter turnout, as well as on a number of variables that the literature discussed in the previous section deems to be important in understanding voting behaviour. This data is collected from the Voter Turnout Database provided by the International Institute for Democracy and Electoral Assistance (International IDEA). In particular, we consider the following variables: type of electoral system (presidential or parliamentary); election type (parliamentary or presidential); year of election; voter turnout (%); number of parties/candidates; competition (%, a variable measuring the percentage distance between the vote shares registered for the first two parties/candidates in each election; if the difference is small, competition for votes is expected to be high); GDP per capita (in USD); share of urban population (%). More importantly, we also collected first hand data on the date and the type of judgments by the two Courts. We then merged these two datasets.

As for countries, we have dropped from the final sample all the observations (15 in total) regarding Bosnia and Herzegovina, since one of the variables used as a covariate in the multivariate regression exercise was available only at the sub-national level. As a consequence, the final sample includes the following European countries (listed in alphabetical order): Albania, Andorra, Armenia, Austria, Azerbaijan, Belgium, Bulgaria, Croatia, Cyprus, Czech Republic, Denmark, Estonia, Finland, France, Georgia, Germany, Greece, Hungary, Iceland, Ireland, Italy, Latvia, Liechtenstein, Lithuania, Luxemburg, Malta, Republic of Moldova, Monaco, Montenegro, Netherlands, North Macedonia, Norway, Poland, Portugal, Romania, Russian Federation, San Marino, Serbia, Slovak Republic, Slovenia, Spain, Sweden, Switzerland, Turkey, Ukraine, United Kingdom; and the following Central and Latin American countries: Argentina, Barbados, Bolivia, Brazil, Chile, Colombia, Costa Rica, Dominica, Dominican Republic, Ecuador, El Salvador, Grenada, Guatemala, Haiti, Honduras, Jamaica, Mexico, Nicaragua, Panama, Paraguay, Peru, Suriname, Trinidad and Tobago, Uruguay, Venezuela. The time span covers the period 1995–2019 for European countries (from the year that Protocol 11 ECHR started up to now), whilst it covers the period 1979–2019 for Latin American countries, since that is the period that the IACHR has had jurisdiction. The final dataset we use in our empirical analysis includes 825 observations: 413 refer to the 46 European countries and 412 to the 25 Central and Latin American countries. Tables 16.1 and 16.2 report the summary statistics for all the quantitative variables employed in our empirical investigations.

The dependent variable in all our empirical models is the voter turnout defined as the share of people who actually voted in an election out of all the people having the right to vote. This variable presents with a high heterogeneity across countries: the mean is similar in the two groups, 67% in Europe and 67.9% in Latin America, whilst the standard deviation is higher in Latin American

Table 16.1 Summary statistics for European countries

Variables	*Mean*	*St. dev.*	*Min*	*Max*
Voter turnout (%)	67.0	13.2	37.8	97.2
Dummy proportional	0.5	0.5	0.0	1.0
Dummy parliamentary	0.6	0.5	0.0	1.0
Competition	15.2	16.1	0.1	94.1
No. of parties/candidates	17.4	14.0	2.0	97.0
GDP per capita (USD)	24,276.4	28,126.0	397.0	185,722.0
Urban population (%)	68.1	15.1	14.3	100.0
No. of judgments	0.7	2.1	0.0	21.0
No. Judgments within 0 years	0.1	0.3	0.0	3.0
No. Judgments within 1 years	0.1	0.4	0.0	5.0
No. Judgments within 2 years	0.1	0.5	0.0	9.0
No. Judgments within 3 years	0.1	0.4	0.0	6.0
No. of countries	46	–	–	–
No. of observations	413	–	–	–

Source: Own elaborations.

Table 16.2 Summary statistics for Latin American countries

Variables	*Mean*	*St. dev.*	*Min*	*Max*
Voter turnout (%)	67.9	16.3	2.7	94.7
Dummy proportional	0.3	0.5	0.0	1.0
Dummy parliamentary	0.1	0.3	0.0	1.0
Competition	16.3	16.6	0.1	89.7
No. of parties/candidates	11.3	8.4	2.0	67.0
GDP per capita (USD)	4,448.4	4,005.3	242.0	18,332.0
Urban population (%)	63.6	17.5	20.5	94.9
No. of judgments	0.1	0.4	0.0	2.0
No. Judgments within 0 years	0.0	0.0	0.0	1.0
No. Judgments within 1 years	0.0	0.1	0.0	1.0
No. Judgments within 2 years	0.0	0.1	0.0	1.0
No. Judgments within 3 years	0.0	0.1	0.0	1.0
No. of countries	25	–	–	–
No. of observations	412	–	–	–

Source: Own elaborations.

countries, 16.3 against 13.2. In relation to Europe, the lowest value is 37.8%, registered in Romania during the election in 2016, whilst the highest value is 97.2%, registered in Malta during the election in 1996. For Latin American countries the lowest value is 2.7%, registered in Jamaica during the election in 1983 (when the main opposition party boycotted the election in protest against the refusal of the ruling party to update the electoral roll) and the maximum value is 94.7% registered in Chile during the election in 1989 (it was 94.5% in Bolivia during the 2009 election).

Before turning to the other variables, Tables 16.3 and 16.4 report a more detailed description of voter turnout and the number of elections for all European and Latin American countries, respectively. In particular, the number of elections (both presidential and parliamentary) registered in the period 1995–2019 varies from 5 (Monaco and Luxembourg) to 13 (in Croatia, Georgia and Portugal) in Europe; and from 7 (Suriname) to 27 (Argentina) in Latin America.

The explanatory variables we consider in our multivariate empirical models characterise the electoral system and the competitiveness of elections in each

Table 16.3 Average voter turnout and number of election in Europe

Country	*Voter turnout*	*No. of elections*	*Country*	*Voter turnout*	*No. of elections*
Albania	59.5	7	Lithuania	53.7	12
Andorra	75.3	7	Luxemburg	90.0	5
Armenia	59.6	12	Malta	94.4	6
Austria	75.9	12	Republic of Moldova	62.1	9
Azerbaijan	67.1	10	Monaco	73.4	5
Belgium	90.2	7	Montenegro	65.9	8
Bulgaria	54.3	12	Netherlands	77.8	7
Croatia	58.5	13	North Macedonia	60.3	12
Cyprus	84.7	10	Norway	77.3	6
Czech Republic	64.1	9	Poland	53.4	12
Denmark	85.9	7	Portugal	57.7	13
Estonia	62.6	7	Romania	56.6	12
Finland	68.6	11	Russian Federation	63.2	12
France	68.5	10	San Marino	66.9	7
Georgia	62.1	13	Serbia	56.3	9
Germany	76.2	6	Slovak Republic	59.7	11
Greece	69.7	8	Slovenia	59.6	12
Hungary	65.2	6	Spain	72.7	8
Iceland	80.2	11	Sweden	83.5	6
Ireland	59.7	8	Switzerland	46.0	7
Italy	79.4	6	Turkey	83.9	9
Latvia	64.2	8	Ukraine	64.4	12
Liechtenstein	84.1	6	United Kingdom	65.8	7

Source: Own elaborations.

Table 16.4 Average voter turnout and number of election in Latin America

Country	*Voter turnout*	*No. of elections*
Argentina	79.5	27
Barbados	64.6	9
Bolivia	81.2	22
Brazil	80.9	18
Chile	78.0	15
Colombia	45.3	21
Costa Rica	72.1	20
Dominica	63.4	9
Dominican Republic	64.3	17
Ecuador	72.8	24
El Salvador	53.0	19
Grenada	71.5	8
Guatemala	52.6	22
Haiti	35.6	14
Honduras	66.5	21
Jamaica	58.0	9
Mexico	59.6	21
Nicaragua	73.5	14
Panama	72.9	15
Paraguay	71.4	18
Peru	80.2	19
Suriname	68.3	7
Trinidad and Tobago	65.2	10
Uruguay	89.3	16
Venezuela	66.7	17

Source: Own elaborations.

country, as well as socio-economic characteristics of the country. As for the system of government, in Europe most of the observations within the dataset (about two-thirds) refer to countries characterised by a parliamentary system, whilst observations referring to countries characterised by a presidential system are about one quarter; in the remaining observations, an assembly-elected president is in place. In Latin American countries, the great majority (87.1%) of observations refer to countries characterised by a presidential system, whilst most of the remaining observations (11.9%) refer to those with a parliamentary system; only four observations refer to an assembly-elected president system. In our empirical exercises, we include the dummy variable "parliamentary," in order to test for differences with regard to this dimension; this dummy variable indicates a mean value equal to 0.6 in Europe and 0.1 in Latin America, as reported in Tables 16.1 and 16.2, respectively.

For what concerns the type of electoral system, in Europe more than a half of the observations refer to countries characterised by a proportional system, whilst about one quarter refer to a two-rounds system and about 16% a mixed one; the remaining observations refer to countries characterised by other types of electoral systems, such as a first-past-the-post system. In Latin American countries this picture is different: about 30% of observations refer to countries characterised by a proportional system, about 21% to countries where a two-round system is registered, but other kinds of electoral systems are also present: about 10% of observations refer to a plurality/majority system, about 8% a first-past-the-post system and 5% a mixed one; in addition to other kinds of systems, for this variable we also get some cases for which the information is not available. In our empirical exercises, we include the dummy variable "proportional," which shows a mean value equal to 0.5 in Europe and 0.3 in Latin America, as reported in Tables 16.1 and 16.2.

Finally, in relation to the type of elections, in Europe 72.4% of observations refer to parliamentary elections, whilst 27.6% refer to presidential elections. A close but different picture is shown for Latin American countries: 59% of observations refer to parliamentary elections, whilst the remaining 41% refer to presidential ones. We included this variable in our original empirical models. However, as it turned out to be insignificant in all of our specifications, we decided not to include this control variable in the final specifications (as well as in Tables 16.1 and 16.22).

As for the number of parties or candidates registered in each election, Tables 16.1 and 16.2 register the statistics considering both the number of parties and the number of candidates: the mean value is 17.4 in Europe and 11.3 in Latin America. This variable also indicates a very high heterogeneity. By splitting this variable by election type (presidential or parliamentary), a more representative picture can be outlined, since the lowest value of this variable is affected by the election type. In particular, in relation to presidential elections, the lowest value for Europe, only two candidates, is observed in Austria (2004) and Montenegro (2013), whilst the highest number, 39 candidates, is observed for Ukraine in 2019. Focusing on Latin American countries, the lowest value, only 2 candidates, is observed in El Salvador (2009), whilst the highest number, 56 candidates, is observed for Haiti in 2015. Considering parliamentary elections, we observed that the lowest value for Europe was 3 parties, in Liechtenstein (1997, 2001, 2005, and 2009), Malta (1996, 1998, and 2003), and Monaco (1998, 2008, 2013 and 2018). The highest number, 97 parties, is observed for Spain in 2000. Focusing on Latin American countries, the lowest value, only 2 parties, is observed in Barbados (1981, 1999, 2003), Dominica (2014, 2019), Jamaica (1980, 1989, and 1993), and Venezuela (2015), whilst the highest number, 67 parties, is observed in Venezuela in 1988.

Turning to the variable "Competition," its mean value is 15.2% in Europe and 16.3% in Latin America. In other words, the difference between the first and the second candidate/party was quite significant on average. Also, the variable "Competition" indicates a huge range of variation: the lowest value is 0.1% for both the geographical areas (in Europe this value is registered for Italy in 2006 and Switzerland in 1999; for Latin America it was registered in Bolivia in both the presidential and parliamentary election occurring in 1979), whilst the highest value is 94.1% in Europe (for Georgia in 2004) and 89.7% in Latin America (for Haiti in 2000).

We also consider other variables characterising each country. Urban population also indicates significant differences among countries. The average value is 68.1% in Europe and 63.6 in Latin America. The lowest value is registered in Liechtenstein (about 14%) and Honduras in the 1980s; the highest value is 100% for both Monaco and Uruguay in the last decade. Another economic variable we considered is the nominal GDP per capita. As expected, this variable is very different among countries, for two basic reasons: socio-economic characteristics are different among countries and the inflation dynamics over a long time span show different patterns as well. Given these observations, the overall nominal mean value is about 24.3 thousand dollars in Europe and 4.4 thousand dollars in Latin America. The highest value in European countries is registered for Monaco, whilst the lowest is registered for Azerbaijan. In relation to Latin American countries, the highest values were observed in Trinidad and Tobago, whilst the lowest values were in Nicaragua.

The covariates we are mostly interested in refer to judgments by the two Courts. In particular, we collected information on those for which the ECHR found violations of Article No. 3 of Protocol 1 to the Convention for the Protection of Human Rights and Fundamental freedoms and on those for which the IACHR found violations of Article No. 23 of the American convention on human rights, that is violations of electoral rights. Starting from this information, we defined two variables. First, we defined a variable called "No. of Judgments" counting the overall number of judgments taking place before each election in each country. It should be noted that very few judgments (only ten on aggregate) were registered in Latin America: only three countries received two judgments, whilst four received one judgment, whilst no judgment was registered for the remaining countries. A very different picture is observed for Europe, where 92 judgments are registered: 23 of these being registered in Azerbaijan, 14 in Italy, 9 in Turkey, 7 in Romania, 6 in United Kingdom and Russian Federation, 4 in Bulgaria, 3 in Hungary, 2 in Greece, Latvia, Ukraine, and Georgia, and only 1 in Belgium, Lithuania, Cyprus, Serbia, Armenia, Austria, Moldova; 27 countries had no judgments: Denmark, Ireland, Luxemburg, Iceland, Malta, Portugal, Liechtenstein, San Marino, Monaco, Andorra, Estonia, France, North Macedonia, Poland, Spain, Albania, Netherlands, Croatia, Germany, Finland, Czech Republic, Montenegro, Switzerland, Slovenia, Norway, Slovak Republic, and Sweden.

Second, we define a set of variables called "No. of judgments within t years" (with t varying from 0 to 3) capturing the number of judgments within t years from an election (with $t = 0$ identifying the number of judgments in the same year of the election that were issued before the election, $t = 1$ identifying the number of judgments occurring in the same year as the election or in the year previous, and similarly for $t = 2$ and for $t = 3$). The descriptive statistics of these variables are also included in Tables 16.1 and 16.2.

Modelling strategy

The aim of our empirical analysis is to understand if and how decisions by the ECHR and the IACHR correlate with voter participation in countries under their jurisdiction. In order to test this correlation, our empirical strategy is based on multivariate regression models considering voter turnout as the dependent variable and the whole set of institutional and socio-economic factors as covariates, along our main variable of interest, i.e., a dummy picking up whether the two Courts have identified a violation of voting rights before an election takes place. In particular, we test different specifications of the following general empirical model:

$$VOTER\ TURNOUT_{it} = \alpha + \varphi\, JUDGE_{it} + \sum \beta X_{it} + \sum \delta D_t + \varepsilon_{it} \qquad (1)$$

where the dependent variable is voter turnout, *JUDGE* represents the judgments referring to country *i* at time *t* ("No. of Judgments"), *X* is the vector of covariates, *D* are temporal dummies identifying the decade in which the election takes place, ε is the error term, whilst α, ϕ, β, δ are the unknown coefficients to be estimated. Our main interest is in the parameter ϕ: a positive (negative) sign will imply a positive (negative) correlation between Courts' judgments and voter participation. We estimate all the models using OLS, considering robust standard errors.

We also replicate this exercise using a second set of models defined by replacing the variable *JUDGE* with the variable *JUDGE WITHIN T* ("No. of judgments within *t* years"):

$$\begin{aligned} VOTER\ TURNOUT_{it} = {} & \alpha + \varphi\, JUDGE\_WITHIN\_T_{it} \\ & + \sum \beta X_{it} + \sum \delta D_t + \varepsilon_{it} \end{aligned} \qquad (2)$$

Also, these models are estimated using OLS, considering robust standard errors.

Results

We separately studied the dataset concerning Europe and the one concerning Latin American countries. Table 16.5 presents the estimates of Eq. (1) for Europe considering the number of judgments. Model I includes, as variables, the dummy proportional, the dummy parliamentary, competition, number of parties/candidates, GDP per capita, urban population and the number of judgments; Models II and III augment this specification by including the interactions between the number of judgments and dummies identifying Eastern European countries. The coefficient for the variable "number of judgments" is positive and statistically significant in all three models, in particular in Models II and III. This suggests that there is a positive correlation between the number of judgments by the ECHR and voter participation. However, this result does not hold for the whole of Europe. In Model II we interacted this variable with a dummy which picked Eastern European countries. We found that the interaction between the

Table 16.5 Role of ECHR judgments – total number before an election

Model	*I*	*II*	*III*
Dummy Proportional	5.454***	5.405***	5.257***
	(1.105)	(1.098)	(1.090)
Dummy Parliamentary	1.986	1.681	2.369*
	(1.257)	(1.260)	(1.285)
Competition	0.010	0.029	0.024
	(0.044)	(0.045)	(0.045)
No. of parties/candidates	– 0.074**	– 0.067**	– 0.061*
	(0.030)	(0.030)	(0.031)
GDP per capita (USD)	0.000***	0.000***	0.000***
	(0.000)	(0.000)	(0.000)
Urban population (%)	0.241***	0.237***	0.233***
	(0.043)	(0.044)	(0.044)
Election between 2000 and 2009	– 6.196***	– 6.287***	– 6.203***
	(1.638)	(1.635)	(1.633)
Election between 2010 and 2019	– 12.518***	– 12.329***	– 12.002***
	(1.625)	(1.637)	(1.635)
No. of judgments	1.004***	1.521***	1.470***
	(0.215)	(0.350)	(0.343)
No. of judgments x Dummy East		– 1.181**	
		(0.526)	
No. of judgments x Dummy USSR			– 0.727*
			(0.431)
No. of judgments x Dummy Yugoslavia			– 1.033
			(1.511)
No. of judgments x Dummy Warsaw			– 3.252***
			(0.852)
Constant	51.888***	52.028***	51.943***
	(3.297)	(3.319)	(3.331)
No. of countries	46	46	46
Observations	413	413	413
R-squared	0.342	0.351	0.362

Note: Robust standard errors in parentheses; *** p<0.01, ** p<0.05, *p<0.1.

number of judgments and the dummy East (Model II) has a negative coefficient, statistically significant, with a magnitude greater than the coefficient for the number of judgments; this implies a negative correlation between judgments and voter turnout in this area. More precisely, Model III shows that this negative effect is driven by countries belonging to the former USSR and those countries formerly part of the Warsaw Pact.

Turning to the other covariates, the dummy "proportional" is positive and highly statistically significant in all these models, implying that voter turnout is higher when a proportional electoral system is in place with respect to alternative systems. The dummy variable "parliamentary" is also positive, but statistically significant in Model I and III: we then observe a higher voter turnout on average for parliamentary elections with respect to presidential elections. The variable "competition" does not show any statistically significant effect on voter turnout, whilst the variable "number of parties/candidates" is statistically significant in all models; the sign of this coefficient is negative, but very close to zero: the higher the number of alternatives, the lower the voter turnout. We also find a very small correlation in size for the GDP per capita, albeit the coefficient is positive and statistically significant in all the specifications. The variable "urban population" is also positive and statistically significant. In richer countries, where the share of people living in cities is higher, voter participation is also higher. As for time dummies, results clearly highlight a decline in voter participation over time.

Table 16.6 reports the estimates for the second set of models referring to Eq. (2) above, including the number of judgments occurring within the same year as the elections and the interaction between this variable and Eastern European countries dummies. Previous results are substantially confirmed for all covariates. Model I shows that the coefficient for the number of judgments occurring in the same year as elections is positive albeit not statistically significant, but it turns significant when accounting for the differences in former USSR countries and countries formerly belonging to the Warsaw Pact. Finally, Appendix Table A.1 shows that these results are largely replicated when considering the number of judgments within 1 to 3 years of elections.

Overall, our findings suggest different correlations between judgments by the ECHR and voter participation between Western and Eastern European countries. A possible interpretation is that a higher number of judgments in Eastern European countries is a sign of substantial violations of voting rights, which has the effect of depressing voters' participation. On the contrary, in most of the Western European countries, more judgments are a sign of vital participation by citizens in the democratic process.

Tables 16.7 and 16.8 (and Appendix Table A.2) replicate the same exercises symmetrically for Latin American countries. The pattern of results is very different from estimates involving European countries. In particular, the sign of the coefficient related to the number of judgments is now mainly negative and statistically significant in most of the specifications. However, in this case the effect is also different depending on whether a country was characterised by a restriction of voting rights. In the case of Latin America, we generate a dummy variable in order to identify former military dictatorships before 1970. Countries which have been free of dictatorship since 1970 are characterised by a higher turnout on average, and judgments are positively correlated with turnout. Most of the other variables are statistically insignificant, but for the number of parties/candidates and urban population. Coefficients for these two variables largely replicate results for Europe: the higher the number of alternatives, the lower the participation by voters; the higher the share of people living in urban areas, the higher the participation by voters. Also dummy variables on time are in line with findings for Europe, and clearly emphasise a decline in voter turnout in Latin American countries.

Table 16.6 Role of ECHR judgments – total number before the election in the same year

Model	*I*	*II*	*III*
Dummy Proportional	5.374***	5.230***	4.998***
	(1.129)	(1.119)	(1.121)
Dummy Parliamentary	2.321*	2.071	2.428*
	(1.286)	(1.289)	(1.303)
Competition	0.031	0.035	0.034
	(0.045)	(0.045)	(0.044)
No. of parties/candidates	– 0.074**	– 0.069**	– 0.068**
	(0.031)	(0.031)	(0.030)
GDP per capita (USD)	0.000***	0.000***	0.000***
	(0.000)	(0.000)	(0.000)
Urban population (%)	0.244***	0.240***	0.240***
	(0.044)	(0.044)	(0.044)
Election between 2000 and 2009	– 6.089***	– 6.126***	– 6.018***
	(1.637)	(1.637)	(1.635)
Election between 2010 and 2019	– 11.290***	– 11.196***	– 11.123***
	(1.613)	(1.611)	(1.612)
No. of judgments within 0 years	1.796	5.026***	4.955***
	(1.253)	(1.074)	(1.073)
No. of judgments within 0 years × Dummy East		– 6.557***	
		(1.924)	
No. of judgments within 0 years × Dummy USSR			– 4.696***
			(1.724)
No. of judgments within 0 years × Dummy Yugoslavia			–
No. of judgments within 0 years × Dummy Warsaw			– 16.078***
			(3.788)
Constant	51.394***	51.744***	51.670***
	(3.345)	(3.343)	(3.351)
No. of countries	46	46	46
Observations	413	413	413
R-squared	0.323	0.330	0.336

Note: Robust standard errors in parentheses; *** $p<0.01$, ** $p<0.05$, * $p<0.1$.

Concluding remarks

The empirical exercise conducted in this chapter is the first attempt towards an understanding of the relationship between the rulings of the Courts of Human Rights and voter turnout. Participation of voters is essential for democracy, and the judgments of the Courts of Human Rights, both in Europe and Latin America, guarantee a legal framework for free and democratic elections.

Table A.1 Role of ECHR judgments – total number before the election within 1 to 3 years

Model	*t = 1*			*t = 2*			*t = 3*		
	I	*II*	*III*	*I*	*II*	*III*	*I*	*II*	*III*
Dummy Proportional	5.399*** (1.129)	5.476*** (1.120)	5.576*** (1.111)	5.309*** (1.125)	5.309*** (1.126)	5.156*** (1.117)	5.397*** (1.123)	5.460*** (1.120)	5.460*** (1.120)
Dummy Parliamentary	2.333* (1.285)	2.117 (1.288)	2.571** (1.291)	2.258* (1.281)	2.258* (1.284)	2.731** (1.294)	2.436* (1.282)	2.220* (1.275)	2.220* (1.275)
Competition	0.025 (0.045)	0.034 (0.045)	0.018 (0.046)	0.031 (0.043)	0.031 (0.044)	0.025 (0.044)	0.020 (0.044)	0.024 (0.044)	0.024 (0.044)
No. of parties/ candidates	−0.074** (0.031)	−0.077** (0.031)	−0.073** (0.030)	−0.069** (0.030)	−0.069** (0.030)	−0.070** (0.030)	−0.074** (0.031)	−0.076** (0.031)	−0.076** (0.031)
GDP per capita (USD)	0.000*** (0.000)	0.000*** (0.000)	0.000*** (0.000)	0.000*** (0.000)	0.000*** (0.000)	0.000*** (0.000)	0.000*** (0.000)	0.000*** (0.000)	0.000*** (0.000)
Urban population (%)	0.243*** (0.044)	0.240*** (0.044)	0.237*** (0.044)	0.243*** (0.044)	0.243*** (0.044)	0.241*** (0.044)	0.244*** (0.044)	0.241*** (0.044)	0.241*** (0.044)
Election between 2000 and 2009	−5.992*** (1.637)	−6.163*** (1.638)	−6.061*** (1.641)	−6.072*** (1.634)	−6.073*** (1.636)	−6.024*** (1.635)	−5.927*** (1.635)	−5.991*** (1.638)	−5.991*** (1.638)
Election between 2010 and 2019	−11.375*** (1.614)	−11.451*** (1.614)	−11.256*** (1.615)	−11.333*** (1.604)	−11.333*** (1.614)	−11.002*** (1.614)	−11.416*** (1.608)	−11.586*** (1.608)	−11.586*** (1.608)
No. Judgments within t year	1.781 (1.765)	8.184*** (2.368)	7.868*** (2.385)	1.866* (0.999)	1.868* (1.129)	1.847* (1.113)	2.515** (1.027)	10.121*** (3.907)	10.121*** (3.907)
No. Judgments within t year × Dummy East		−7.538** (3.161)			- 0.012 (2.504)			−8.274** (4.029)	

No. Judgments within t year x Dummy USSR			- 4.293 (2.606)			2.996** (1.450)			–8.274** (4.029)
No. Judgments within t year × Dummy Yugoslavia			–7.843*** (2.781)			–			–
No. Judgments within t year × Dummy Warsaw			–15.425*** (2.435)			–10.374*** (3.615)			–
Constant	51.466*** (3.348)	51.706*** (3.352)	51.831*** (3.343)	51.403*** (3.341)	51.402*** (3.348)	51.527*** (3.355)	51.430*** (3.333)	51.702*** (3.330)	51.702*** (3.330)
No. of countries	46	46	46	46	46	46	46	46	46
Observations	413	413	413	413	413	413	413	413	413
R-squared	0.323	0.329	0.345	0.326	0.326	0.337	0.327	0.332	0.332

Robust standard errors in parentheses; *** p<0.01, **: p<0.05, * p<0.1.

Table 16.7 Role of IACHR judgments – total number before an election

Model	*I*	*II*	*III*
Dummy Proportional	1.760	– 0.311	1.621
	(1.726)	(1.733)	(1.723)
Dummy Parliamentary	– 3.934	1.137	– 4.004
	(2.590)	(2.646)	(2.609)
Competition	– 0.116*	– 0.105*	– 0.110*
	(0.066)	(0.063)	(0.066)
No. of parties/candidates	– 0.368***	– 0.329***	– 0.391***
	(0.106)	(0.105)	(0.108)
GDP per capita (USD)	0.001**	0.001**	0.001**
	(0.000)	(0.000)	(0.000)
Urban population (%)	0.252***	0.302***	0.265***
	(0.052)	(0.049)	(0.053)
Election between 1990 and 1999	– 8.983***	– 8.534***	– 8.928***
	(2.164)	(2.146)	(2.168)
Election between 2000 and 2009	– 11.649***	– 11.626***	– 11.643***
	(2.353)	(2.243)	(2.358)
Election between 2010 and 2019	– 14.631***	– 15.483***	– 14.726***
	(3.294)	(3.264)	(3.315)
No. of judgments	– 1.029	0.955	– 4.785*
	(2.209)	(2.013)	(2.848)
Dummy no dictatorship after 1970		9.632***	
		(1.612)	
No. of judgments × Dummy no dictatorship after 1970			7.196**
			(3.552)
Constant	64.060***	53.879***	63.411***
	(3.807)	(4.016)	(3.836)
No. of countries	25	25	25
Observations	412	412	412
R-squared	0.190	0.257	0.197

Note: Robust standard errors in parentheses; *** p<0.01, ** p<0.05, * p<0.1.

Our empirical analysis, based on an original dataset including information on voter turnout for all countries under the jurisdiction of the ECHR and the IACHR and all the judgments of the two Courts, provides evidence of a positive correlation between judgments and turnout for European countries, albeit

Table 16.8 Role of IACHR judgments – total number before the election in the same year

Model	*I*
Dummy Proportional	1.665 (1.724)
Dummy Parliamentary	- 3.815 (2.599)
Competition	- 0.111* (0.066)
No. of parties/candidates	- 0.367*** (0.106)
GDP per capita (USD)	0.001** (0.000)
Urban population (%)	0.256*** (0.052)
Election between 1990 and 1999	- 8.943*** (2.162)
Election between 2000 and 2009	- 11.639*** (2.335)
Election between 2010 and 2019	- 14.758*** (2.982)
No. of judgments within 0 years	- 20.792*** (2.664)
Constant	63.716*** (3.801)
No. of countries	25
Observations	412
R-squared	0.193

Note: Robust standard errors in parentheses;
*** p<0.01, ** p<0.05, * p<0.1.

it turns negative when considering countries which were formerly part of USSR and countries belonging to the former Warsaw Pact. The general conclusion is that decisions might be a sign of substantial violations of voting rights in these countries, which in turn reduces the incentive to participate for voters. On the contrary, for most Western countries, ECHR decisions might be a sign of a strong interest by voters in participation. The Latin American experience appear to be different, military dictatorships seem to matter; but the small number of judgments suggest caution when interpreting correlation results. Future research should address these issues further in order to understand what mechanisms drive the correlations we have just begun to uncover.

Table A.2 Role of IACHR judgments – total number before the election within 1 to 3 years

Model	*t = 1*		*t = 2*		*t = 3*	
	I	*II*	*I*	*II*	*I*	*II*
Dummy Proportional	1.736	1.681	1.749	1.790	1.657	1.761
	(1.721)	(1.721)	(1.723)	(1.730)	(1.712)	(1.712)
Dummy Parliamentary	– 3.752	– 3.813	– 3.838	– 3.811	– 4.215	– 4.223
	(2.606)	(2.613)	(2.592)	(2.599)	(2.582)	(2.584)
Competition	– 0.115*	– 0.115*	– 0.116*	– 0.116*	– 0.116*	– 0.115*
	(0.066)	(0.066)	(0.066)	(0.066)	(0.066)	(0.066)
No. of parties/candidates	–0.361***	–0.368***	–0.365***	–0.366***	–0.362***	–0.354***
	(0.106)	(0.106)	(0.106)	(0.106)	(0.105)	(0.105)
GDP per capita (USD)	0.001**	0.001**	0.001**	0.001**	0.001***	0.001***
	(0.000)	(0.000)	(0.000)	(0.000)	(0.000)	(0.000)
Urban population (%)	0.254***	0.257***	0.252***	0.252***	0.252***	0.249***
	(0.052)	(0.053)	(0.052)	(0.052)	(0.052)	(0.052)
Election between 1990 and 1999	–9.016***	–9.024***	–9.002***	–8.998***	–9.068***	–9.119***
	(2.161)	(2.163)	(2.161)	(2.164)	(2.157)	(2.159)
Election between 2000 and 2009	–11.766***	–11.739***	–11.698***	–11.675***	–11.891***	–11.947***
	(2.351)	(2.354)	(2.338)	(2.341)	(2.334)	(2.338)
Election between 2010 and 2019	–15.252***	–15.508***	–14.982***	–14.909***	–15.123***	–15.266***
	(3.056)	(3.084)	(3.039)	(3.056)	(2.973)	(2.977)
No. of judgments within t year	2.052	– 2.804	– 2.276	2.496	–18.350**	2.900
	(3.078)	(3.475)	(2.829)	(2.231)	(9.079)	(1.995)
No. of judgments within t year × Dummy no dictatorship after 1970		9.913**		– 7.200**		–31.974***
		(4.668)		(2.973)		(2.251)

Constant	63.836***	63.686***	64.001***	64.043***	63.872***	63.885***
	(3.821)	(3.833)	(3.796)	(3.804)	(3.786)	(3.792)
No. of countries	25	25	25	25	25	25
Observations	412	412	412	412	412	412
R-squared	0.190	0.192	0.190	0.190	0.198	0.205

Note: Robust standard errors in parentheses; *** p<0.01, ** p<0.05, * p<0.1

Bibliography

ANDERSEN J. J., FIVA J. H., NATVIK G. J., *Voting When the Stakes are High*, Journal of Public Economics, 110, 2014, 157–166.

BANNING, S., *Third-Person Effects on Political Participation*, Journalism & Mass Communication Quarterly, 83, 2006, 785–800.

BECK, T., CLARKE G., GROFF A., KEEFER P., WALSH P., *New Tools in Comparative Political Economy: The Database of Political Institutions*, The World Bank Economic Review, 15, 2001, 165–176.

BISCHOFF C. S., *Electorally Unstable by Supply or Demand? - An Examination of the Causes of Electoral Volatility in Advanced Industrial Democracies*, Public Choice, 156, 2012, 537–561.

BLAIS, A., AARTS K., *Electoral Systems and Turnout*, Acta Politica, 41, 2006, 180–196.

BORNSCHIER, S., *Historical Polarization and Representation in South American Party Systems, 1900–1990*, British Journal of Political Science, 49, 2019, 153–179.

BOWLER S., BROCKINGTON D., DONOVAN T., *Election Systems and Voter Turnout: Experiments in the United States*, The Journal of Politics, 63, 2001, 902–915.

CANCELA, J., GEYS B., *Explaining Voter Turnout: A Meta-Analysis of National and Subnational Elections*, Electoral Studies, 42, 2016, 264–275.

COATE, S., CONLIN M., *A Group Rule: Utilitarian Approach to Voter Turnout: Theory and Evidence*, The American Economic Review, 94, 2004, 1476–1504.

DE BENEDETTO, M. A., DE PAOLA M., *Term Limit Extension and Electoral Participation. Evidence from a Diff-in-discontinuities Design at the Local Level in Italy*, European Journal of Political Economy, 59, 2019, 196–211.

DE PAOLA M., SCOPPA V., DE BENEDETTO M., *The Impact of Gender Quotas on Electoral Participation: Evidence from Italian Municipalities*, European Journal of Political Economy, 35, 2014, 141–157.

DE PAOLA, M. SCOPPA V., *The Impact of Closeness on Electoral Participation Exploiting the Italian Double Ballot System*, *Public Choice*, 160, 2014, 467–479.

DEGAN, A., MERLO A., *A Structural Model of Turnout and Voting in Multiple Elections*, Journal of the European Economic Association, 9, 2011, 209–245.

DETTREY B. J., SCHWINDT-BAYER L. A., *Voter Turnout in Presidential Democracies*, *Comparative Political Studies*, 42, 2009, 1317–1338.

DOWNS A., *An Economic Theory of Political Action in a Democracy*, *Journal of Political Economy*, 65, 1957, 135–150.

EZROW L., XEZONAKIS G., *Satisfaction with Democracy and Voter Turnout: A Temporal Perspective*, Party Politics, 22, 2016, 3–14.

FILER J. E., KENNY L. W., MORTON R. B., *Voting Laws, Educational Policies, and Minority Turnout*, The Journal of Law and Economics, 34, 1991, 371–393.

FOWLER, J., SCHREIBER D., *Biology, Politics, and the Emerging Science of Human Nature*, Science, 322, 2008, 912–914.

FOWLER J., BAKER L., DAWES C., *Genetic Variation in Political Participation*, The American Political Science Review, 102, 2008, 233–248.

FORNOS C. A., POWER T. J., GARAND J. C., *Explaining Voter Turnout in Latin America, 1980 to 2000*, Comparative Political Studies, 37, 2004, 909–940.

FRANCIA P., HERRNSON P., *The Synergistic Effect of Campaign Effort and Election Reform on Voter Turnout in State Legislative Elections*, State Politics and Policy Quarterly, 4, 2004, 74–93.

GENTZKOW M., *Television and Voter Turnout*, The Quarterly Journal of Economics, 121(3), 2006, 931–972.

GERBER A., HOFFMAN M., MORGAN J., RAYMOND C., *One in a Million: Field Experiments on Perceived Closeness of the Election and Voter Turnout*, American Economic Journal: Applied Economics, 12, 2020, 287–325.

GEYS B., *Explaining Voter Turnout: A Review of Aggregate-Level Research*, Electoral Studies, 25, 2006, 637–663.

GEYS B., *Rational Theories of Voter Turnout: A Review*, Political Studies Review, 4, 2006, 16–35.

GRASSO M., *The Differential Impact of Education on Young People's Political Activism: Comparing Italy and the United Kingdom*, Comparative Sociology, 12, 2013, 1–30.

GRAY M., CAUL M., *Declining Voter Turnout in Advanced Industrial Democracies, 1950 to 1997*, Comparative Political Studies, 33, 2000, 1091–1122.

HARDER J., KROSNICK J. A., *Why Do People Vote? A Psychological Analysis of the Causes of Voter Turnout*, Journal of Social Issues, 64, 2008, 525–549.

HOBOLT S., HOERNER J., *The Mobilising Effect of Political Choice*, European Journal of Political Research, 59, 2019, 229–247.

JACKMAN R. W., MILLER R. A., *Voter Turnout in the Industrial Democracies during the 1980s*, Comparative Political Studies, 27, 1995, 467–492.

JACKMAN R. W., *Political Institutions and Voter Turnout in the Industrial Democracies*, American Political Science Review, 81, 1987, 405–423.

KOSTADINOVA T., *Voter Turnout Dynamics in Post-Communist Europe*, European Journal of Political Research, 42, 2003, 741–759.

KUENZI M., LAMBRIGHT G. M. S., *Voter Turnout in Africa's Multiparty Regimes, Comparative Political Studies*, 40, 2007, 665–690.

LAHTINEN, H., MARTIKAINEN P., MATTILA M., WASS H., RAPELI L., *Do Surveys Overestimate or Underestimate Socioeconomic Differences in Voter Turnout? Evidence from Administrative Registers*, Public Opinion Quarterly, 83, 2019, 363–385.

LARCINESE V., *Does Political Knowledge Increase Turnout? Evidence from the 1997 British General Election*, Public Choice, 131, 2007, 387–411.

LEHOUCQ F., WALL D. L., *Explaining Voter Turnout Rates in New Democracies: Guatemala*, Electoral Studies, 23, 2004, 485–500.

MATSUSAKA J. G., PALDA F., *Voter Turnout: How Much Can We Explain?*, Public Choice, 98, 1999, 431–446.

MATSUSAKA J. G., *Explaining Voter Turnout Patterns: An Information Theory*, Public Choice, 84, 1995, 91–117.

MCDONALD M. P., *The Turnout Rate among Eligible Voters in the States, 1980–2000*, State Politics and Policy Quarterly, 2, 2002, 199–212.

NAGLER J., *Where Is the Schema? Going Beyond the "S" Word in Political Psychology*, American Political Science Review, 85, 1991, 1393–1405.

PACEK A. C., POP-ELECHES G., TUCKER J. A., *Disenchanted or Discerning: Voter Turnout in Post-Communist Countries*, The Journal of Politics, 71, 2009, 473–491.

PERCIVAL G. L., CURRIN-PERCIVAL M., BOWLER S., VAN DER KOLK H., *Taxing, Spending, and Voting: Voter Turnout Rates in Statewide Elections in Comparative Perspective*, State and Local Government Review, 39, 2007, 131–143.

ROUBINI N., SACHS J. D., *Political and economic determinants of budget deficits in the industrial democracies*, European Economic Review, 33, 1989, 903–933.

Schur L., Shields T., Kruse D., Schriner K., *Enabling Democracy: Disability and Voter Turnout*, Political Research Quarterly, 55, 2002, 167.

Smets K., van Ham C., *The Embarrassment of Riches? A Meta-Analysis of Individual-Level Research on Voter Turnout*, Electoral Studies, 32, 2013, 344–359.

Smith A., de Mesquita B., LaGatta T., *Group Incentives and Rational Voting*, Journal of Theoretical Politics, 29, 2017, 299–326.

Sondheimer R. M., Green D. P., *Using Experiments to Estimate the Effects of Education on Voter Turnout*, American Journal of Political Science, 54, 2010, 174–189.

Sørensen R., *The Impact of State Television on Voter Turnout*, British Journal of Political Science, 49, 2019, 257–278.

Squire, P., Wolfinger R. E., Glass D. P., *Residential Mobility and Voter Turnout*, American Political Science Review, 81, 1987, 45–65.

Tuckel, P., Maisel R., *Nativity Status and Voter Turnout in the Early Twentieth-Century Urban United States*, Historical Methods: A Journal of Quantitative and Interdisciplinary History, 41, 2008, 99–108.

Wilford A. M., *Polarization, Number of Parties, and Voter Turnout: Explaining Turnout in 26 OECD Countries*, Social Science Quarterly, 98, 2017, 1391–1405.

Winders B., *The Roller Coaster of Class Conflict: Class Segments, Mass Mobilization, and Voter Turnout in the U.S., 1840–1996*, Social Forces, 77, 1999, 833.

Wolfinger N. H., Wolfinger R. E., *Family Structure and Voter Turnout*, Social Forces, 86, 2008, 1513–1528.

Conclusions

Are contemporary democracies sustainable? Some concluding remarks

Gabriella Citroni, Irene Spigno, and Palmina Tanzarella

Measuring sustainability

The central idea of this work is to "measure" the sustainability of contemporary democracies within the European and Inter-American systems of human rights protection. The methodology used for the research is based on an assessment of the extent to which judgments issued by the ECtHR and the IACtHR in which the violation of Art. 3 of Protocol No. 1 to the ECHR and Art. 23 of the ACHR respectively has been declared are implemented.

The choice to centre the analysis on the violation of these provisions lies in the fact that the two regional systems refer to a comparable concept of democracy, that is extremely similar in many respects, but at the same time very much distinct from each other (especially with regard to the two Courts' case law). The concept of "democracy" which has been taken into account corresponds to that of "electoral democracy," whose core is represented by the right to free elections and political rights.

As far as the concept of sustainability is concerned, in this work we consider it to possess the characteristics of a process or State that can be maintained at a certain level indefinitely.

At the same time, it is necessary to specify the methodology chosen to "measure" the sustainability of democracy as defined above. The analysis of the results of the research carried out in the various national chapters takes as a starting point a quantitative datum which consists of the number of judgments per State concerning the violation of the provisions concerned, as well as the impact that such judgments have produced at the national level, both in economic terms (as regards the payment of compensation) and in regulatory or public policy terms (as regards general measures and requests for changes in legislation, for example).

This data offers only a partial and perhaps superficial picture of a reality, which to be fully understood inevitably requires a more in-depth analysis of a contextual, juridical, and comparative nature which explains the common characteristics, as well as the differences highlighted in the research results.

Common features

First of all, from a comparative point of view, we can see that both in the European and the Inter-American systems, the number of States that have been

DOI: 10.4324/9781003229247-21

declared internationally responsible for the violation of the provisions on electoral democracy is relatively low and the cases correspond to 31% of the Council of Europe members (15 States out of 47).[1] This percentage drops further in the Inter-American system, reaching 25% of the countries that have accepted the contentious jurisdiction of the Inter-American Court (5 States out of 20, namely Chile, Colombia, Guatemala, Nicaragua, and Venezuela).

Furthermore, another interesting quantitative figure can be seen in the relatively low number of judgments where breaches of Art. 3 of Protocol No. 1 to the ECHR and Art. 23 of the ACHR respectively have been found. This record is even more evident with reference to those States with serious problems of democracy, understood in a broad sense, also including human rights issues: as a consequence, the violation of provisions on electoral democracy does not represent a major problem.

Turkey, for example, is the State with the highest number of judgments and pending applications in Strasbourg (with a total number of 3,645 judgments as of 2019) and is ranked 110 out of 167 in the Democracy Index of 2019.[2] However, there are only 11 judgments where it has been held internationally responsible for violating Art. 3 of Protocol No. 1 to the ECHR.[3] The same can be seen with Russia, the second most challenged State before the ECtHR, which has been found responsible for violating Art. 3 of Protocol No. 1 to the ECHR only six times.[4]

Notably, in the European context, the State that has most frequently been held responsible for violations of the right to vote is Azerbaijan, with 25 judgments out of a total of 169 (representing almost 15% of the total amount of judgments, nonetheless this quantity may not stand out if read in conjunction with the total violations registered with reference to other fundamental rights).[5]

We can see a similar scenario in the Inter-American context: Chile has been declared internationally responsible for violating at least 1 provision of the ACHR in 11 cases, but only in 1 was this due to a violation of Art. 23 of the ACHR; in Colombia, out of 29 judgments, only 2 concern Art. 23 of the ACHR; in Venezuela, out of 25 judgments where the international responsibility of the State was found, 3 entail a violation of Art. 23 of the ACHR; in Guatemala, 3 out of a total of 34 judgments concern political rights; while in Nicaragua it is 1 out of 6.

1 In addition to the 11 States analysed in this volume, Belgium, Georgia, Greece, and the Republic of Moldova have also been declared responsible for violating Art. 3 of the Protocol No. 1 to the ECHR. Their exclusion is justified due to the low relevance, on a statistical level, of the judgments to be analysed.

2 See The Economist, *Democracy Index 2019. A Year of Democratic Setbacks and Popular Protest*, 2020, available at www.eiu.com/public/topical_report.aspx?campaignid=democracyindex2019.

3 Turkey is the State that has received the highest number of judgments for violations of Art. 3 of Protocol No. 1 to the ECHR after Azerbaijan. See the chapter on Turkey in this Volume.

4 See also the chapter on Italy in this Volume.

5 See the chapter on Azerbaijan in this Volume.

Therefore, in both contexts there are relatively few judgments in which the international responsibility of the State is declared for the violation of the provisions on "electoral democracy." Nonetheless, beyond a merely quantitative assessment, these are serious violations, which can affect the democratic system as a whole and consequently human rights in general. In the words of the ECtHR itself: "the right to free elections is 'crucial to establishing and maintaining the foundations of an effective and meaningful democracy governed by the rule of law.'"[6] In fact, the Court of Strasbourg recognised the indispensability of the protection of these rights in the affirmation and preservation of a fully democratic order.[7] Furthermore, the adhesion to the ECHR of many ex-communist countries accentuates the centrality of these rights with respect to the processes of democratic transition. The analysis of these cases is fundamental to understanding the effective guarantee of the rule of law.

The differences: The types of violations

Despite these initial shared characteristics, it is possible to identify profound differences between the two systems analysed. The first difference concerns the nature of the violations at stake. In the European system, it is possible to group the violations of Art. 3 of Protocol No. 1 to the ECHR into three strands. The first one refers to the rights to run for elections, which includes those cases concerning registration on the electoral roll (as in Azerbaijan, as far as the verification of signatures is concerned,[8] and for ethnic minorities in Cyprus),[9] the invalidation of electoral results (as in Azerbaijan); the illegitimate exclusion of a political party from an election (Russia), and the dissolution of a political party (Turkey).

The second strand refers to the right to vote and it includes cases on the automatic and indiscriminate disfranchisement, usually as a consequence of incarceration (as in Romania, the United Kingdom, Russia, and Turkey) or the application of public security measures (in Italy), but also in the case of people placed under total or partial guardianship as a consequence of mental disability (as in Hungary), or in cases of moral unworthiness (as in Italy, with reference to people declared bankrupt). Within this second strand, we can also include cases on the right to vote of ethnic minorities (as in Bosnia and Herzegovina and Romania) and on political parties' control over the mandate of elected MPs (as in Serbia). Finally, the third strand concerns the right to a democratic and fair electoral process (as in the Russian context).

In the Inter-American system, the violation of Art. 23 of the ACHR was found with reference to the enforced disappearance (as in the case of *Chitay Nech v. Guatemala*) or murder of a political leader (as in the case of *Manuel Cepeda*

6 *Orlovskaya Iskra v. Russia*, 21 February 2017, para. 110.

7 *United Communist Party of Turkey et al. v. Turkey*, 30 January 1998, para. 45.

8 See the chapter on Azerbaijan in this Volume.

9 Also in Bulgaria. See the chapter on Bulgaria in this Volume.

Vargas v. Colombia), in matters concerning the right to vote and to political participation in conditions of equality and non-discrimination for indigenous organisations other than political parties (as in the case of *YATAMA v. Nicaragua*) and arbitrary dismissal (as in Venezuela with the arbitrary dismissal of the Judge María Cristina Reverón Trujillo and in Colombia with the dismissal of the former mayor of Bogotá). The IACtHR also issued some judgments on disfranchisement arising from criminal reasons (as in the case of *López Mendoza v. Venezuela*, where there was no firm conviction made by a competent criminal judge and in the case *Norín Catrimán v. Chile*, in which the applicant received a disqualification of 15 years from any public office as an accessory penalty to their conviction).

The distinction between the types of cases in which the violation of the provision on free elections is declared can be explained through contextual lenses. Electoral issues in Europe are mainly related to the idea of discrimination against specific categories of voters, which are considered to be unworthy to play a part in the democratic arena (as in the United Kingdom, Italy, and Hungary). Moreover, there are some cases related to the integration and inclusion of ethnic and national minorities (as in Bosnia and Herzegovina and Cyprus). Finally, we can identify some specific cases of "militant democracies" (Turkey).

On the contrary, in the Inter-American system there is a clear problem of electoral violence, mainly related to the general context of violence many States in the country have experienced or are still experiencing. Also, in the Inter-American system, the judgments issued by the IACtHR are related to the debate on the right to participate in governmental issues directly or indirectly.

The use of the democratic argument

These important contextual differences are also reflected in the construction of the reasoning put forward by the two Courts. Although to different degrees, both the ECtHR and the IACtHR are confronted with the need to contextualise their judgments in order to adopt "reasonable" and "proportionate" solutions in relation to the contemporary political-constitutional reality of each State.

Within the European system, the ECtHR clearly established that the right to vote is not a privilege. Rather, it is an individual right of which citizens can be deprived only under very exceptional circumstances and always following the decision of a judicial authority. The ECtHR also holds that electoral rights are not absolute: they are subjected to implicit limits that allow States to condition their exercise[10] and are necessary for the stability of the democratic system. According to the ECtHR, democracy must be "capable of defending itself" and, therefore, interference with the exercise of political rights must be assessed very

10 This is a consistent approach; see *ex plurimis Mathieu-Mohin and Clerfayt v. Belgium*, 2 March 1987, para. 52; *Yumak and Sadak v. Turkey*, 8 July 2008, para. 60; *Hirst v. United Kingdom*, 6 October 2005, para. 61.

carefully, in relation to the purpose it intends to pursue.[11] States must establish conditions and limits to the exercise of the rights recognised in Art. 3 of Protocol No. 1 to the ECHR, whose compatibility with the convention must be assessed pursuant to the principles of legality, necessity, non-discrimination, and proportionality.[12] Furthermore, limitations must not affect the essential contents of the right, their purpose must be legitimate and, finally, they must be proportionate.[13] However, States have a wide margin of appreciation, wider than that applicable to other rights recognised as convention rights.[14] On the one hand, over time, the margin of appreciation has gradually undergone some downsizing, but only with regard to the surrounding electoral legislation and limitations relating to the right to vote. On the other hand, the margin of appreciation remains very wide in relation to electoral systems with regard to which the ECtHR takes a completely exceptional intervention only in the event of a "democratic emergency."[15] This means that, with regard to electoral systems, according to the ECtHR, Art. 3 of Protocol No. 1 to the ECHR does not impose any specific electoral system nor does it allow any inference of a preference for certain technical elements of the electoral system. These are options that remain within the exclusive competence of each State. In this sense, the ECtHR gives particular importance to the variety and diversity of electoral systems which are an expression of the plurality of political and cultural traditions that characterise the European system.[16] The same limitation or condition, considered unacceptable in a given political and constitutional context, may be admissible with respect to another.[17]

Within the Inter-American system, unlike the general IACtHR attitude characterised by a certain form of "universalism",[18] judgments concerning electoral

11 *Zdanoka v. Letvia*, 16 March 2006, para. 100.

12 *Mathieu-Mohin and Clerfayt v. Belgium*, cit., paras. 52–54; *Hirst v. Regno Unito*, cit., para. 62. See also *Aziz v. Cyprus*, 22 June 2004, paras. 28–30.

13 *Yumak and Sadak v. Turkey*, cit., para. 65.

14 *Zdanoka v. Latvia*, cit., para. 115. See also DICKMANN R., *Rappresentanza vs governabilità. Rileggendo la sent. Corte EDU, Saccomanno vs Italia, del 13 marzo 2012, alla luce della sent. Corte cost. 1/2014*, in www.forumcostituzionale.it, 2014. This is due to the "hybrid" nature of the rights recognised in Art. 3, Protocol No. 1. In this sense, see STARITA M., *Il 'diritto al voto' secondo la Corte comunitaria e secondo la Corte europea dei diritti umani*, 3 Diritti umani e diritto internazionale 2007, 525–526, 544. See also DE SANTIS V., *Articolo 23 – Diritti di partecipazione politica*, in CAPPUCCIO L., TANZARELLA P. (eds.), *Commentario alla prima parte della Convenzione americana dei diritto dell'uomo*, Editoriale Scientifica, 2017, 587 ff.

15 See TRUCCO L., *Sistema di elezione e di giustizia elettorale (italiani): anche per Strasburgo, tutte le strade portano al legislatore (italiano)*, in www.forumcostituzionale.it, 2013.

16 See *Mathieu-Mohin and Clerfayt v. Belgium*, cit., para. 54 and *Py v. France*, 11 January 2005, para. 46.

17 *Py v. France*, cit., para. 46 and *Paksas v. Lithuania*, 6 January 2011, para. 96.

18 See CAPPUCCIO L., *La Corte interamericana e la protezione dei diritti fondamentali: una bussola per gli Stati*, in L. CAPPUCCIO, A. LOLLINI, P. TANZARELLA (eds.), *Le Corti regionali tra Stati e Diritti. I sistemi di protezione dei diritti fondamentali europeo, americano e africano a confronto*, Editoriale Scientifica, 2012, 196 ss. and DE SANTIS V., *Articolo 23 – Diritti di partecipazione politica*, cit., 599.

systems and political rights adopt a more nuanced approach. In these cases, the IACtHR takes into consideration the national framework, especially focusing on the constitutional and historical reality of the country in which it is applied.[19] Nonetheless, the IACtHR has recognised that States must, in addition to taking measures to ensure the exercise of convention rights,[20] create a climate in which a political debate can allow voters to make a real choice.[21]

Furthermore, the IACtHR has established that States have an obligation to strengthen not only political parties, but also other political organisations, including groups with traditions and cultures different from those of the "traditional political parties," as a priority for the democracy and for the Inter-American system.[22] Consequently, according to the Inter-American case law on political rights, State-imposed limits on political participation must be rational; the protection and primacy given to the "traditional political parties" appears unnecessary and aggravates the condition of vulnerability in which the indigenous communities find themselves and which have the right to give themselves a different political organisation.[23] Although the IACtHR also makes extensive reference to the need to enhance the political evolution of each State and constitutional traditions, it does not apply the European doctrine of the margin of appreciation.[24]

Probably, we can conclude that it is the very nature of political rights that forces both Courts to value the historical and social contexts in which the provisions are intended to be applied. Indeed, the ECtHR considers the diversity of national disciplines as a "value," an expression of the pluralism of the European legal system, and is, at least generally, very cautious in developing an interpretation of electoral rights independent from that enshrined at the constitutional level of the various States, ultimately refraining from setting common, useful principles to raise the level of protection. The IACtHR also takes into account the historical-constitutional context, to be considered as the effective degree of "democracy" of each national system and, in so doing, it resizes the tendency

19 See *Castañeda Gutman v. México*, 6 August 2008.

20 *Chitay Nech v. Guatemala*, 25 May 2010, para. 107.

21 As in *Manuel Cepeda Vargas v. Colombia*, 26 May 2010, the IACtHR found Colombia internationally responsible for not having created the conditions for Senator Cepeda to perform the functions for which he had been democratically elected and did not protect him, despite being – as a member of an opposition group – in a condition of objective vulnerability. According to the Court, it is clear that the execution of a political opponent not only violates the most elementary human rights, but also undermines the democratic system in its complexity, because it creates a climate of intimidation for members of opposition groups and parties (paras. 177–178).

22 As in *YATAMA v. Nicaragua*, 23 June 2005, paras. 202–206. See also DE SANTIS V., *Articolo 23 – Diritti di partecipazione politica*, cit., 598.

23 *Ibidem.*

24 DE SANTIS V., *Articolo 23 – Diritti di partecipazione politica*, cit., 610 underlines that normally the IACtHR concedes very little to the "regional consent"; however, in the matter of political rights it is forced to take into consideration the specificities of the constitutional realities and traditions of the States.

towards the so-called "universalism"[25] which, instead, usually characterises Inter-American case law on the protection of fundamental rights.

Furthermore, this – albeit subtle – difference in the approach undertaken by the two Courts towards electoral democracy is related to the relationship between "elections" and "justice." The European constitutional tradition conceives of electoral matters as a "grey area" for judicial oversight, since electoral disputes are generally removed from judicial control.[26] On the contrary, within the Inter-American system, electoral disputes are generally entrusted to the judiciary.[27]

Finally, a third reason to explain the differences between the European and Inter-American systems as far as electoral democracy and political rights are concerned can be found in a textual element enshrined in the wording of the relevant provisions – Art. 3 of Protocol No. 1 to the ECHR and Art. 23 of the ACHR, and the distinct configuration of the various rights provided for therein.

In fact, if on the one hand Art. 23 of the ACHR is clear in establishing political rights,[28] the wording of Art. 3 of Protocol No. 1 to the ECHR reflects a somewhat difficult gestation.

In the European system of human rights protection, the right to political participation was not included in the text of the ECHR due to the opposition of some States, in particular the United Kingdom.[29] The reasons behind these difficulties reside in the existence of different notions of the idea of the universal suffrage, given the diversity of State legislation and the consideration that it was a right reserved to States.[30] It was therefore decided, on the proposal of the Danish government, to include a reference in the preamble of the ECHR to consider the right to free elections as a political precondition for membership to the Council of Europe.[31]

This gap was addressed in 1952, with the adoption of Protocol No. 1 to the ECHR, whose Art. 3 establishes only the commitment of the Parties to organise "free elections at reasonable intervals by secret ballot, under conditions which will ensure the free expression of the opinion of the people in the choice of the legislature." This provision, unlike Art. 23 of the ACHR is directed at the "High

25 BENAVIDES CASALS M.A., *El consenso y el margen de apreciación en la protección de los derechos humanos*, 1 Ius et Praxis, 2009, 308.

26 MILANI G., SPIGNO I., *Reflexiones sobre la declaratoria de inconstitucionalidd de la Ley Electoral: ¿Qué consecuencias tiene para el sistema democrático italiano?*, in PENAGOS LÓPEZ P.E., *Seguridad jurídica en el sistema democrático*, Tirant lo Blanch, 2014, 225.

27 OROZCO HENRÍQUEZ J.J., *Justicia electoral comparada de América Latina*, UNAM, 2019.

28 See CABALLERO OCHOA J.L., RÁBAGO DORBECKER M., GARCÍA HUERTA D., *Artículo 23. Derechos políticos*, in STEINER C., FUCHS M.-C. (eds.), *Convención Americana sobre Derechos Humanos. Comentario*, Konrad Adenauer Stiftung, 2019, 671 ff.

29 See RUIZ ROBLEDO A., *The construction of the right to free elections by the European Court of Human Rights*, 7 Cambridge International Law Journal 2018, 225–240, 226.

30 See DE SANTIS V., *Articolo 23 – Diritti di partecipazione politica*, cit., 591.

31 See RUIZ ROBLEDO A., *The construction of the right to free elections by the European Court of Human Rights*, cit.

Contracting Parties." It is only in 1994 that Protocol No. 11 to the ECHR included the provision on the "right to free elections."[32] Both the European Commission of Human Rights and the ECtHR developed significant case law granting protection to the fundamental rights to vote and to be elected.[33]

On the contrary, in the Inter-American system of human rights, the right of political participation was already present in the draft version of the ACHR, approved by the Council of the Organization of American States with the Resolution of 2 October 1968. In its original formulation, the provision recognised that all citizens have the rights to political participation with the exceptions provided for by the respective national laws to be adopted in compliance with the principle of non-discrimination. From the final formulation of the rule, a rather broad definition of participation rights emerges, understood as participation in government functions, as the right to vote and to be voted for, as well as the right to have equal access to government offices. However, there is no reference to the freedom to join a political parties and the freedom to form political parties, nor are there any references to the internal "democracy" of political parties.

This absence is probably linked to the fact that Latin American States, at the end of the 1960s, were largely young democracies neither accomplished nor mature and consequently were probably not yet able to express a common position regarding the key role of political parties in the democratic process.[34]

Measures of reparation and their implementation

In the majority of the cases analysed in the national chapters, the violation of Art. 3 of Protocol No. 1 to the ECHR and Art. 23 of the ACHR respectively is the consequence of, or is accompanied by, the violation of another provision. This makes it more complicated, in many cases, to identify which measures of reparation each regional court has ordered for infringements of the relevant provisions and, consequently, to assess the level of implementation and the fulfilment of these measures.

Within the European system, in the vast majority of cases the ECtHR orders compensation as a measure of reparation (the just satisfaction, non-pecuniary damages and costs and expenses).

32 See TRUCCO L., *La democrazia elettorale tra margine di apprezzamento degli stati e tutela dei diritti individuali*, in CARTABIA M. (ed.), Dieci casi sui diritti in Europa, Bologna, 2011, 239–240.

33 On this point see GARCÍA ROCA J., *Del compromise internacional de los Estados de organizer elecciones libres al derecho de sufragio de los ciudadanos (art. 3 P1)*, in GARCÍA ROCA J., SANTOLAYA P. (eds.), *la Europa de los Derechos. El Convenio Europeo de Derechos Humanos*, Centro de Estudios Políticos y Constitucionales, 2014, 713 ff.

34 DE SANTIS V., *Articolo 23 – Diritti di partecipazione politica*, cit., 587–588. See also CABALLERO OCHOA J.L., RÁBAGO DORBECKER M., GARCÍA HUERTA D., *Artículo 23. Derechos políticos*, 678 ff.

At other times, the ECtHR orders general or structural measures. Sometimes, general measures have an implicit character that can be inferred from the Court's argumentation rather than from a specific order. Among all the judgments analysed in the national chapters of this Volume, it is only in the case of the United Kingdom, that the ECtHR dictated a "pilot judgment" to "force" the respondent State to amend its legislation.[35]

Sometimes the ECtHR only "encourages" States to consider structural reforms (as in *Gahramanli and Others* case,[36] where it encouraged Azerbaijan to consider a reform of the structural composition of the electoral commission, with the aim of improving the effectiveness of the examination of individual election-related complaints).[37] Sometimes, the ECtHR orders a State to enforce all the measures needed to fulfil its obligation to secure a specific right.[38] Finally, in some cases, States have realised a sort of "anticipated execution" where specific legislation challenged in front of the ECtHR has been amended before the judgment's release.[39]

In general, in both the European and the Inter-American systems, the fulfilment of pecuniary measures does not represent a problem: States usually comply, maybe also because the amounts are usually quite modest. However, in both systems, States encounter more difficulties and show a greater resistance in complying with general and structural measures. Azerbaijan has shown that it has been very reluctant to comply: none of the 25 judgments issued by the ECtHR has yet been fully implemented. In the majority of the cases, only the just satisfaction awarded by the Court was fully paid (and in 4 of them, the payment was partial).[40]

35 See the chapter on the United Kingdom in this Volume.

36 *Gahramanli and Others v. Azerbaijan*, 8 October 2015.

37 As Palmina Tanzarella underlines in the chapter on Azerbaijan, after the ECtHR's judgment in the *Namat Aliyev* case (*Namat Aliyev v. Azerbaijan*, 8 April 2010), the Committee of Ministers specified the need for the State to adopt general measures to implement a new electoral law to ensure independence, transparency and legal quality of the procedure before the electoral commission. See also the Russian experience. As Simone Penasa points out in the chapter on Russia, we are facing an example of "spontaneous" adaptation to the ECtHR's judgments, which have "occurred through the declaration of the unconstitutionality of provisions which were the reason for [the] ECHR's violation and the subsequent adaptation of national laws in line with the ruling of the Court."

38 As in the case of Cyprus, with specific reference to the right of Turkish Cypriots living in the government-controlled areas to vote. See also Hungary, where the Fundamental Law was amended and Section 6 provides that "those disenfranchised by a court for a criminal offence or limited mental capacity shall not have the right to vote and to be voted for. Citizens of another Member State of the European Union with domicile in Hungary shall not have the right to be voted for if they have been excluded from the exercise of this right in their country pursuant to the law, a court decision or an authority decision of their State of citizenship." Therefore, as Simone Gianello points out in the chapter on Hungary "by virtue of the Fundamental Law, the disenfranchisement of people with mental illness is no longer automatic as provided for by art. 70 Section 5 of the old post-communist Constitution but must be adjudicated upon by a court ruling based on an individualized assessment."

39 As in Italy. See the chapter on Italy in this Volume.

40 See the chapter on Azerbaijan in this Volume.

The experience of Bosnia and Herzegovina is also emblematic. For example, in the *Zornić* and *Šlaku* cases, the Court explicitly referred to the imperative need to introduce legislative and constitutional amendments in order to put an end to the violation of the ECHR. However, the Court's orders remain unimplemented.[41]

Conversely, the Romanian cases offer a good example of the implementation of legislative reforms to comply with the ECtHR's judgments. With specific reference to the execution of *Grosaru* and *Ofensiva Tinerilor* cases, legislative reform was adopted in 2015[42] and the Constitutional Court issued an important decision moving towards the recognition of the right to an effective remedy before national courts.[43]

The same situation concerns the level of implementation of the IACtHR's judgments. Within the Inter-American system, in many cases it is difficult to identify which of the measures of reparation are aimed at repairing the violation of Art. 23 of the ACHR, as its breach is normally part of a set of other violations and the reparations dictated by the IACtHR have an integral character, often encompassing all the rights and freedoms violated. Nevertheless, it can be deduced that the Inter-American's States are also more likely to implement economic measures or satisfaction measures (such as the publication of the sentence, the awarding of a scholarship, public apologies), while they show a greater resistance to the implementation of general and structural measures. Emblematic is

41 See the chapter on Bosnia and Herzegovina and Serbia in this Volume.

42 Law No. 68/1992 (which was the law in force at the material time) was repealed by Law No. 208/2015, with reference to the election of the Senate and the Deputies Chamber of Deputies and the functioning of the Permanent Electoral Authority. Furthermore, Law No. 208/2015 clarifies that the mandate of deputy will be allocated to the ethnic minority organisation which secures the greatest number of votes at the national level. See the chapter on Romania in this Volume.

43 As Francesca Mussi underlines in the chapter on Romania in this Volume, the action report on the *Grosaru* and *Ofensiva Tinerilor* cases notes a binding decision issued by the Constitutional Court on 14 September 2004, which declared that the rulings delivered by the Central Electoral Bureau are defined as jurisdictional administrative acts and thus can be challenged before the ordinary administrative courts. Furthermore, the document highlights that, according to Law n. 208/2015, the decisions by the electoral bureaux are made in the context specific to electoral activities and can be contested in court by the interested parties pursuant to the administrative legislation. See also the chapter on Turkey in this Volume, in which Valentina Rita Scotti points out that Turkey respected the judgments and implemented them within the due time, not only as far as economic measures are concerned, but also with reference to other measures: as for example the 2011 amendment to Art. 69 of the Constitution or the decision taken by the Supreme Board of Elections to allow some categories of people to vote (among others, prisoners convicted of negligence offences, those released on probation, or on conditional release, or subject to suspended sentences). This approach by the Supreme Board of Elections was followed by a judgment issued by the Constitutional Court partially annulling Art. 53 of the Criminal Code, holding that by extending the ban on voting beyond the period actually served in prison it had exceeded the restriction defined in the Constitution. The effect of this decision is that only persons convicted of intentional offences and currently serving their sentence in prison are denied the right to vote.

the case of Nicaragua, which has not adopted the reforms necessary to allow the effective political participation of groups that find themselves in a position of vulnerability and marginalisation.[44] Also in Venezuela, the measures ordered in the *López Mendoza* case, concerning the order to ensure that the sanctions of disqualification by administrative authorities do not constitute an impediment to the nomination of the victim as a candidate in the subsequent electoral process has not been fulfilled yet. Nor has the measure to annul the administrative resolutions where the sanctions of disqualification were imposed on the victim been fulfilled yet.[45] Also in the *Reverón Trujillo* case, the Court ordered the elimination of the victim's personal record, in addition to the modification of the norms and practices according to which provisional judges can be freely removed from their position. These measures had not yet been fulfilled.

In the vast majority of the IACtHR judgments, including those where a violation of Art. 23 of the ACHR is found, the Court dictates, among the measures of reparation, the obligation for the State to carry out investigations with due diligence to determine who is criminally responsible. Probably in line with the existing high level of impunity in the region, this measure is almost never carried out.[46] In this case, it does not seem that States embrace as a priority the reform of the judicial system, even when this is required to implement the measures of reparation ordered by the IACtHR.

The reasons for the resistance

This pattern of resistance to the implementation of general and structural measures of reparation can be explained by several factors. A first one revolves around the role and position that the ECHR and the ECtHR's case law have within the respective national legal orders.

In the majority of the European States, the ECHR has an explicit or implicit constitutional position[47] and in a few cases, a sub-constitutional one (Russia and Bulgaria). Some of them adopt a dualistic approach (as in Hungary) and the ECtHR case law has no direct impact on the national system, but rather only produces declaratory effects. Some others have a monist approach: this is the case of Romania, where the ECHR is automatically incorporated into the national legal system and has a complementary role to the Constitution, enjoying supremacy over national law. In Romania, the ECHR has a self-executing character and rights and freedoms recognised therein are directly enforceable by

44 See the chapter on Nicaragua in this Volume.

45 See the chapter on Venezuela in this Volume.

46 See the chapter on Colombia in this Volume.

47 See Art. 151 of the Constitution of Azerbaijan according to which in case of contradictions between the normative acts of the country's legislative system – with the exception of the Constitution – and the acts adopted by a referendum and international documents to which Azerbaijan is party, the international document shall prevail. See the chapter on Azerbaijan in this Volume.

Romanian courts.[48] Some States have a harmonious and fruitful relationship with the ECtHR,[49] others a more complicated one.[50]

In the Inter-American system, generally the ACHR has constitutional value through the "constitutionality block," which recognises that treaties and instruments on human rights have the same constitutional position, at least from a formal point of view.[51] The influence of the judgments of the IACtHR on domestic systems is generally quite significant and almost all States have also adapted their Constitutions, albeit in different ways, affirming the primacy of convention law, the complementarity between domestic and international law on human rights, the criterion of compliant interpretation, or, in the event of a conflict, the need to apply the discipline that protects human rights more widely, according to the principle of "greater favour."[52]

The ACHR has shown a remarkable ability to catalyse the processes of affirming and consolidating human rights, generating, as far as judicial power is concerned, a dialogue between jurisdictions: in this sense, national judges tend to comply with the IACtHR judgments, while the degree of concrete fulfilment at the national level remains quite variable.[53]

There may be other contextual reasons behind the resistance in enforcing general and structural measures of reparation. In Europe, the ECHR has played a pivotal role in shaping democratic transitions (as in the case of Cyprus, Hungary, Bosnia and Herzegovina and Serbia). However, in some experiences there are still difficulties related to the not yet completed consolidation of the democratic transition process.

48 The self-executing character refers to both the ECHR and the ECtHR case law. See Art. 11.2 of the 1991 Romanian Constitution according to which "[t]reaties lawfully ratified by Parliament shall form an integral part of the domestic legal order."

49 This is the case of Cyprus, where Part II of the Constitution (Fundamental Rights and Liberties) is inspired by Section I of the ECHR and provides an extensive charter of human rights. Judicial power in Cyprus has been extremely active in ensuring the full protection of the rights and liberties enshrined in the Constitution and developed in connection with the ECHR system. On the critical issues on this Law, see the chapter on Azerbaijan in this Volume.

50 See the chapter on the United Kingdom in this Volume.

51 This is also the case of Venezuela, where the ACHR has constitutional value as provided in Article 19 of the Constitution. In the same sense, Art. 23 of the Constitution establishes that "the treaties, pacts and conventions related to human rights, signed and ratified by Venezuela, have constitutional hierarchy and prevail in the internal order, insofar as they contain norms on their enjoyment and exercise more favourable to those established in this Constitution and in the laws of the Republic, and are of immediate and direct application by the courts and other organs of the Public Power." Thus, Venezuela is a monistic system because the application of the ACHR and the IACtHR case law should be automatic. However, in practice, Venezuela has not even applied international human rights law through the Constitutional Chamber of the Supreme Court of Justice whose rulings, on many occasions, have inconsistently interpreted the *corpus jure* of human rights.

52 See HERNÁNDEZ VALLE R., *L'utilizzazione della giurisprudenza della Corte interamericana dei diritti dell'uomo da parte dei supremi Tribunali e dei Tribunali costituzionali dell'America Latina*, in ROLLA G. (ed.), *Il sistema europeo di protezione dei diritti fondamentali e i rapporti tra le giurisdizioni*, Giuffré, 2010, 73 ff.

53 With the exception of Nicaragua. See the chapter on Nicaragua in this Volume.

In the case of Bosnia Herzegovina, for example, the key obstacle in the adoption of general and structural measures is due to the "inability and unwillingness of the relevant actors to confront the high degree of penetration of ethnic agendas within the domestic institutional system."[54]

In Azerbaijan, the resistance relates more to the refusal of the political majority to take steps that concretely convert the system towards a democratic perspective. And this attitude is also supported by judicial powers.[55] In the case of the United Kingdom, the weak execution of the *Hirst* saga is clearly related to political reasons and the underlying debate on British parliamentary sovereignty.[56]

In the case of Nicaragua, non-compliance goes hand in hand with the situation of human rights in the country and a general tension with the Inter-American human rights system. In Venezuela, the non-implementation is due to the fact that the State claimed Venezuelan judicial independence and assumed a critical position regarding how international human rights law was received. In this case, the apparent refusal to comply is due to the political position of the State in ignoring the competence of the IACtHR and the binding nature of its judgments.

Are European and Inter-American democracies really sustainable?

As a result of this research, we can deduce that the democratic systems within the two regional systems of human rights protection tend to be sustainable since the violation of the respective regional provisions does not represent a serious violation of human rights. We can reach the same optimistic conclusion regarding voter turnout. According to the analysis conducted in the chapter on "The Relationship Between the Courts of Human Rights Decisions and Voter Turnout. An Empirical Analysis on Europe and Latin America," judgments issued by the ECtHR and the IACtHR guarantee a legal framework for free and democratic elections, and there is a positive correlation between judgments and turnout for European countries (albeit with a few exceptions, as in the case of the States of the former Yugoslavia). According to this research, for most Western countries, the ECtHR's judgments might be the sign of a strong interest by voters in participation, while the experience of States of the Inter-American system is slightly different due to the strong influence by military dictatorships.

However, both in Europe and the Americas, democracies need to be strengthened, especially as far as the implementation process of regional court judgments is concerned. This will make Inter-American and European democracies truly sustainable in the long term and enhance the rule of law, the situation of human rights in general, and, ultimately, the trust vis-à-vis both national and international institutions.

54 See the chapter on the former Yugoslavia in this Volume.
55 See the chapter on Azerbaijan in this Volume.
56 See the chapter on the United Kingdom in this Volume.

Index

Note: Page numbers in *italics* indicate figures, bold indicate tables and page numbers with "n" indicates the end notes in the text.

For Product Safety Concerns and Information please contact our EU representative GPSR@taylorandfrancis.com
Taylor & Francis Verlag GmbH, Kaufingerstraße 24, 80331 München, Germany

www.ingramcontent.com/pod-product-compliance
Lightning Source LLC
LaVergne TN
LVHW011105300926
849160LV00008B/283
* 9 7 8 1 0 3 2 1 3 4 4 7 5 *